THE APOSTOLATE'S FAMILY CATECHISM™

Abridged One-Volume Edition

The Catholic Faith
Instruction and Prayer
by
Father Lawrence G. Lovasik, S.V.D.

The Family Apostolate™— Bloomingdale, Ohio U.S.A.

The Apostolate's
Family Catechism™
by Father Lawrence G. Lovasik, S.V.D.

Nihil Obstat:
Rev. John A. Hardon, S.J.
Censor Deputatus

† Imprimatur:
Rev. Msgr. John F. Donoghue,
Vicar General for the Archdiocese of Washington, D.C.
I October MCMLXXXIV

Thought Provoker Section
by Burns K. Seeley, Ph.D.

Nihil Obstat:
Rev. Msgr. Joseph P. Malara
Censor Librorum

† Imprimatur:
Most Rev. Albert Ottenweller
Bishop of Steubenville
XXIII September MCMXCI

Library of Congress Card Number: 93-07 2655
ISBN: 0-932406-12-2
Family Apostolate Book Number: 380-18

Printed in the United States of America

Canonical Global Center — Archdiocese of New York

The Apostolate's Family Catechism™ is dedicated to the Mother of God

IMMACULATE CONCEPTION
PRAY FOR US

The mission of the Apostolate for Family Consecration is to renew parish and family life through consecration to Jesus, through Mary, in union with St. Joseph in the joyful and family-centered spirit of Pope John Paul II.

The Apostolate's
Family Catechism™
by Father Lawrence G. Lovasik, S.V.D.

Edited by
Burns K. Seeley, Ph.D.

Initiated and Structured by
Jerome F. Coniker

Illustrated by Charles Jaskiewicz

Published by
Apostolate for Family Consecration
John Paul II Holy Family Center
Seminary Road, Rt. 2, Box 750, Bloomindale, OH 43910
Telephone (614) 765-4301 — Fax (614) 765-4941

Contents

Section One — The Creed-I
God, the Holy Trinity, Creation, and the Fall

Part One - God and His Perfections

Part Two - The Revelation of God: the Holy Trinity

Part Three - Creation: Material and Spiritual

Part Four - The Creation of Man

Part Five - The Sins of Man: Original Sin and Personal Sin

Section Two — The Creed-II
Jesus Christ, Son Of God, Savior

Part One - The Incarnation

Section Three — The Creed-III
The Holy Spirit

Section Four — The Creed-IV
The Church, the Communion of Saints, and the Forgiveness of Sins

Part One - The Church

ix

Part Two - The Individual Sacraments: Baptism, Confirmation, Penance

Part Three - The Individual Sacraments: Holy Orders, Anointing of the Sick, Matrimony

Section Six — The Sacraments-II
The Holy Eucharist and Prayer

Section Seven
The Ten Commandments
The Creed V - Final Reunion with God

Part One - The Ten Commandments

Part Two - Final Reunion with God

Peace of Heart Forums™

Peace of Heart Forums consist of programs to build family and parish community life and are grounded in the truths of our Faith. Forum participants use books for reflection on Forum themes for their specified daily readings, and view thematic video programs at weekly gatherings.

We recommend that you:

1. Gather a group of people who want to grow in the Faith;

2. Encourage the group participants to make a commitment to invest one half-hour a day in quiet reflective reading of a particular book.

3. Have the participants come together weekly for a 1-1/2 or 2-hour Peace of Heart Forum gathering, during which they watch a half-hour video tape to review the past week's readings; then they discuss their spiritual insights, pray, and sing. The meeting closes with another half-hour video that previews the next week's readings.

Peace of Heart Forum video tapes are available for this catechism (see page 846) and other formation programs (see pages 866 to 881 for partial listings).

Write us about our other catechetical series for children and adults. Also, see the Apostolate's Family Catechism *audio tapes (featured on page 845).*

**Logo
of the
Papally Blessed
Marian Era
of Evangelization
Campaign in
Preparation for
the Year 2000.**

Logo Symbols
- The Holy Spirit
- The Priesthood
- The Holy Eucharist
- Mary
- The Papacy
- The Rosary
- Mother Teresa -
  a sign of Fidelity

This *Family Catechism* is an integral part of the Apostolate for Family Consecration's papally blessed "Marian Era of Evangelization Campaign" in preparation for the year 2000, as described in Cardinal Bevilacqua's letter to Cardinal Laghi, and in the Pope's apostolic blessing found on pages 832 to 834.

This illustration depicts three great papal theologians who have made valuable contributions to the Church. The first was St. Dominic, founder of the Dominican order. St. Thomas Aquinas, the Angelic Doctor, was the fourth papal theologian. Mario Luigi Cardinal Ciappi, O.P. (foreground), the eighty-fourth successor to St. Dominic as papal theologian, has been the primary theological advisor for the Apostolate for Family Consecration since 1979. He is one of the greatest theologians and mariologists of our time.

On the following page, you will find a letter from Cardinal Ciappi to the Apostolate's founder, Jerome F. Coniker, endorsing this catechism.

Forward

Il Teologo Emerito
della Casa Pontificia

Rome, 9 September 1993

Jerome F. Coniker
President
President Apostolate for Family Consecration
John Paul II Holy Family Center
Seminary Road, Route 2, Box 700
Bloomingdale, OH 43910

Subject: The Apostolate's Family Catechism

Dear Mr. Coniker:

I want to thank you for recently sending me the complete text of *The Apostolate's Family Catechism* by Fr. Lawrence G. Lovasik, S.V.D. for my final review before publication of the first edition.

It is indeed providential that you are publishing your family catechism at this time so that it can serve the new *Catechism of the Catholic Church*, promulgated by Pope John Paul II. Your methodical cross-references from the *Catechism of the Catholic Church* into *The Apostolate's Family Catechism* are a major service to the Church and to family life. This is because your family catechism will make it extremely easy for parents and teachers to confidently teach their children and students the Faith, and have easy access to the new *Catechism of the Catholic Church* which is a vital resource for every Catholic family and school. I am also extremely pleased to learn that the Apostolate for Family Consecration is a co-publisher of the English edition of the new *Catechism of the Catholic Church*.

Francis Cardinal Arinze's audio and video taped reviews and commentaries on *The Apostolate's Family Catechism* adds a priceless dimension to your entire catechetical program, since the Holy Father has so clearly stated that we are living in a "media culture" and that audio and video cassettes should be used to evangelize this generation.

I understand that your staff theologian, Burns K. Seeley, Ph.D., has thoroughly reviewed and edited the manuscript since my last review and approval while I was the Pro Theologian of the Supreme Pontiff.

I am happy to approve the edited and cross-referenced version of *The Apostolate's Family Catechism* and highly recommend it to families and schools as a sure source for authentic Catholic doctrine.

May God continue to bless you, your family, and your apostolate.

Yours in the Hearts of Jesus and Mary,

Mario Luigi Card. Ciappi, O.T.

Mario Luigi Cardinal Ciappi
Pro Theologian Emeritus for Pope Pius XII,
Pope John XXIII, Pope Paul VI,
Pope John Paul I, and Pope John Paul II

Pope John Paul II blesses the Coniker family, and the entire work of the Apostolate for Family Consecration, as Jerry, Gwen, and Joe Coniker present *The Apostolate's Family Catechism* to His Holiness.

Mother Teresa of Calcutta embraces Gwen Coniker, Family Apostolate's co-Founder and mother of 13 children.

Mother Teresa later wrote:

"*The Apostolate's Family Catechism* will now enable parents to fulfill their primary obligation in teaching their children. I pray that every parent will join the Apostolate for Family Consecration and use the Apostolate's catechetical program in their neighborhood." Mother Teresa joined The Family Apostolate's Advisory Council on May 1, 1976.

About the Author
Father Lawrence Lovasik, S.V.D.

Father Lawrence Lovasik (now deceased) is the author of *The Apostolate's Family Catechism.* A Divine Word missionary, Father was born on June 22, 1913 and ordained a priest on August 14, 1938. For over forty years he preached at parish missions and conducted retreats thoroughout the world.

He also wrote more than thirty books and over 100 articles; these include catechisms, Bible stories for children, lives of the saints, prayer books, and homilies for priests. His works have passed the test of time, since he had a rare gift of being able to write for children and adults alike.

In 1954, Father Lovasik founded the Congregation of the Sisters of the Divine Spirit, and in 1967, he founded the Family Service Corps, a secular institute devoted to charitable work for the needy, the sick and the elderly.

Father was a close friend of the Apostolate for Family Consecration, serving on its Advisory Council and writing several books for it, the largest being this seven-section family catechism.

A dedicated priest, he had an immense love for the Holy Eucharist, often spending hours at a time in Its Presence. Providentially, he died as he lived, in the Eucharistic Presence of our Lord on June 9, 1986.

May his catechetical teachings go on into the Third Millenium and prepare the People of God for the Second Coming. *"Christ has died, Christ has risen, Christ will come again!"*

Preface

There is no better way of absorbing the truths of our Catholic Faith and living them than by studying them prayerfully. The use of this handbook of catechetical meditations will strengthen your faith by encouraging you to make at least a brief daily meditation consisting of instruction and prayer.

The instruction will provide you with basic information on the teaching of the Catholic Church, while the prayers, centered on the doctrine explained, will be the best means of obtaining God's grace not only to understand your Faith, but also to practice it. The meditations are arranged according to seven periods of twenty-one days. Faithfulness to the practice of daily meditation will surely have a lasting impact on your spiritual life.

The catechetical material is according to the "Basic Teachings for Catholic Education" contained in the National Catechetical Directory for Catholics of the United States approved by the Sacred Congregation for the Clergy, October 30, 1978, Vatican II documents, and Holy Scripture. (*Editor's note: All of the questions are cross-referenced with the new* Catechism of the Catholic Church *issued by Pope John Paul II. See page xxx.*)

The sixteen documents of Vatican II constitute the most remarkable message that God has sent, through His Church, to modern man. Echoing the preaching of the Prophets, the Apostles, the Fathers and Doctors of the East and West, the Council has proclaimed to the whole world the faith of the entire Church. It is the solemn proclamation of the Gospel, which is handed down in history as God's supreme command. Pope Paul VI wrote: "We must give thanks to God and have confidence in the future of the Church when we think of the Council: it will be the great catechism of our times."

Passages from the sixteen documents of Vatican II have been chosen to explain the meaning of the revealed truths taught by the Church. It is very important that the thought of the Council be consulted on the essential question which man asks of the Church of Christ today.

Prayer is a very important part of this catechism because it is a means by which we communicate with God. It is also a means of grace, as God is the source of all grace. Without prayer, it is impossible to lead a Christian life. Jesus said, "Without Me you can do nothing" (John 15:5). The prayers used in this catechism have their source in the Liturgy of the Church. By using them devoutly we can obtain the actual grace we need to make the use of this catechism fruitful: we shall receive the light we need to understand God's truth, and the strength to keep His commandments and lead a holy life.

I entrust this work to the loving care of the Blessed Virgin Mary, the Mother of God and the Mother of the Church.

Father Lawrence G. Lovasik, S.V.D.
Divine Word Missionary

Acknowledgments

The publisher is deeply grateful to Father Lawrence Lovasik for his timeless work in writing this catechism and to all who have given their generous assistance to make *The Apostolate's Family Catechism* a reality. Dr. Burns K. Seeley spent thousands of hours gathering cross-references from the new *Catechism of the Catholic Church*, and from other major catechetical and theological books and papal documents. He was also responsible for the final theological editing of the project. We thank Mario Luigi Cardinal Ciappi, O.P., Papal Theologian for Pope Pius XII, Pope John XXIII, Pope Paul VI, Pope John Paul I, and Pope John Paul II, for his thorough review and endorsement of the catechism. Edouard Cardinal Gagnon, while President of the Pontifical Council for the Family, took the time to review and approve our catechism. We thank Silvio Cardinal Oddi, who, while Prefect of the Sacred Congregation for the Clergy (which has direct authority in the universal Church for catechesis), reviewed and approved this family catechism for use by the universal Church. We thank Rev. John Hardon, S.J. for his reading and approval of the catechism for the imprimatur issued by the Archdiocese of Washington, D.C.

This project has been a labor of love for family life. There are so many people who have contributed to this work that we cannot list them all. We do, however, want to thank the Family Apostolate's Catholic Corps members who were responsible for the typesetting, layout, and production—Diane Boston, Amy Gardner, Hilda A. Gomez, Margie Menendez and Tricia Hauber. We especially wish to acknowledge Diane, whose faith and sacrifices enabled the typesetting of this project to get underway and become viable. Montserrat Friedrich was tireless in her efforts to develop the design plans for thousands of pictures which will be an important part of the unabridged seven-volume set of *The Apostolate's Family Catechism*. We also thank Gwen Coniker and Kay Kocisko for adding their motherly touch to this family classic. Artist Charles Jaskiewicz drew the line art illustrations for the catechism, which makes the unabridged seven-volume edition a teaching classic for the family. Tim Boudreaux of the Apostolate's Catholic Corps invested years in drawing the charcoal renderings that Fr. Lovasik designed. We want to sincerely thank Andrew Seeley for assisting his father, Dr. Burns K. Seeley, in the methodical review of this work. We are grateful to Michele Herbst for her assistance in gathering cross-references from various papal documents. We are thankful to David Moss for coordinating the production of the Catechism project and to Fr. Kevin Barrett and Mother Immaculata, H.M.S., for the final readings. We thank Jerry Coniker for the overall structuring and formatting of the catechism, and for developing the idea of the cross-referencing.

We are sincerely grateful to Cardinal Francis Arinze for the many hours that he spent in reviewing and producing the 44 audio and video tape commentaries for the Family Catechism, which has made it come to life for families and students alike. We also want to thank the Family Apostolate's television staff, headed by Peter Mergen, with Josel Pingol and Jim Kocisko, for their competent assistance in making *The Apostolate's Family Catechism* on tape a reality. We thank Cardinal William Baum, Cardinal Anthony Bevilacqua, and Mother Teresa of Calcutta for their endorsements of this catechism. We thank Cardinal John O'Connor for his ecclesiastical approval of the Apostolate for Family Consecration and its work in the universal Church. Finally, we thank Monsignor John Woolsey, Cardinal O'Connor's liaison with the Family Apostolate and a tireless worker in the defense of life and family values, for his invaluable assistance over the years.

Introduction

by Jerome and Gwen Coniker

The Apostolate's Family Catechism can be used in a number of ways by the entire family and by teachers. It opens the door:

• for systematically using the new papally promulgated *Catechism of the Catholic Church*, which is meticulously cross-referenced with *The Apostolate's Family Catechism*.

• for using Roman Curia Cardinal Francis Arinze's catechism video and audio tape series (see pages 843-846). The series includes 304 questions and answers on the Faith, taken from *The Apostolate's Family Catechism*, plus stimulating dialogue, which supplements the questions and answers in this book.

This Catechism has been a labor of love. We are parents of 13 children (one with the Lord), and we have often been faced with the dilemma of how to teach our children the catechism in an organized way. The biggest problem was finding a catechism that would suit the whole family — most catechisms are written only for particular age brackets.

We asked Fr. Lawrence Lovasik to write a catechism that every family could use. We asked him to make it simple enough for the children to understand, yet with a spiritual depth to challenge the parents.

Initially, we developed a seven-volume catechism set that includes thousands of pictures and cross-references with other orthodox catechisms, theology books, and papal documents. Because of a lack of funds, we were temporarily unable to publish the illustrated seven-volume set. Providentially, however, during the interim period, the Holy Father formally issued the new *Catechism of the Catholic Church*, which is so needed today. We have been able to include comprehensive cross-references to it in our *Apostolate's Family Catechism*, thus putting our catechism at the service of the new *Catechism of the Catholic Church*, making the latter completely accessible to average families, Catholic schools and CCD groups. (see pages 27 to 31.

The seven-volume (unabridged) version of *The Apostolate's Family Catechism* contains thousands of vibrant pictures and many additional features which will enable parents and teachers to teach their children the Faith in depth. These include comprehensive thought provokers and discussion cues.

In order to immediately serve the new *Catechism of the Catholic Church*, and to raise the funds to publish the unabridged version, we have consolidated the seven volumes into one abridged volume. However, the first chapter of this edition remains unabridged, to give you a sample of how the complete seven-volume set looks. As you go through chapter one, which is in full color, you will see its benefits, which are listed on page XXXII.

Recommendations for family use of this unique Family Catechism at home

1. Do not rush through the questions and answers. Take your time and discuss them with your children at dinner time, while driving in the car, or at other opportune times that you may have throughout the week.

2. If you are attending the "Be Not Afraid Family Hours" on video at your church or in someone's home, try to cover the same questions that Cardinal Arinze will be talking about on the Family Hours. (See page 849-865 for more details about these Be Not Afraid Family Hours on video.)

3. Obtain a copy of the new papally promulgated *Catechism of the Catholic Church* from the Family Apostolate (see page 839-842). Look up the cross-references which apply to each question and answer in *The Apostolate's Family Catechism*. Our Family Catechism will make the Holy Father's *Catechism of the Catholic Church* come alive for your family. It will help you to delve more deeply into this very valuable reference book, which every family should have in its library.

4. Listen to Cardinal Arinze on *The Apostolate's Family Catechism* tapes (audio or video - see pages 843 to 846). The tape series covers the same subject matter as this book, but has more information than the book version because of the stimulating discussions with Cardinal Arinze. All you have to do to find more information on a particular question being reviewed is to look at the cross-reference box in this *Apostolate's*

Family Catechism, which will give you the references in the Holy Father's *Catechism of the Catholic Church*. (See page xxx.)

5. The Holy Father has said that we are a "media culture," and that we must evangelize this culture with video and audio tapes. Audio tapes are normally used in a different setting than video tapes. Audio tapes can be used very easily at dinner time, while in the car or while engaged in other activities. The video tapes are designed for a more formal teaching environment.

6. The "truth will make you free..." (cf. John 8:32). If we use the multi-media resources that are now available to help us learn the Faith and share it with others, we will see our families grow in that joy and unity which we all long for. But we must put our trust, first, in the Lord, and not in ourselves or the world. See pages 837 to 887 for some resources.

7. Again, do not rush through this book. Use it as a guide to bring you and your family to a deeper knowledge of the Faith. It may take you an entire day to exhaust one question before going on to the next one. Do not worry about getting through each of the questions in a prescribed period of time. It is amazing that when you start to talk about the truth with your family, you will begin to communicate in an entirely new way. You will discover the art of conversation focused on the truth.

8. We never intended that this catechism be used as a rote type of formation program where you just memorize the answer and then go on; our intention is that it may inspire you to really grow in your Faith and to live and share it with zeal and joy. Altogether, we now have, for your use, four distinct catechetical tools with which to learn and share the Faith:

• This *Apostolate's Family Catechism* text

• the Pope's new *Catechism of the Catholic Church* text

• the audio and video tape series which covers the 304 questions and answers of *The Apostolate's Family Catechism*, with Cardinal Arinze's extensive, lively and candid commentaries.

9. Families can use these multi-media tools as a method of

evangelization and as a method for transforming their neighborhoods into God-centered communities and, thereby, renewing their parishes. We have found that even 11-year old youths are evangelizing their friends by bringing them to their homes for these programs.

10. The 54 "Be Not Afraid Family Hours" on videotape (see pages 849 to 865 for more details) are an excellent means to present the catechism in the home or church on a weekly basis. The "Be Not Afraid Family Hours," featuring the Pope, Mother Teresa and other teachers, highlight Cardinal Arinze's teachings from *The Apostolate's Family Catechism*. He reminds us that we should be studying our catechism and the Pope's *Catechism of the Catholic Church* everyday at home with our families.

Please see the complete list of multi-media catechetical tools that are now available on pages 835 to 887.

In the School

The Apostolate's Family Catechism can be an excellent program for a school environment. The teacher should encourage the family to also obtain a copy of the Holy Father's new *Catechism of the Catholic Church*, and *The Apostolate's Family Catechism* on audio or video tape with Francis Cardinal Arinze (see pages 839 to 846). These four catechetical resources will become a powerhouse of formation to spiritually activate families and make them instruments of evangelization to transform their neighborhoods into God-centered communities and renew their parishes.

Simply show a segment of Cardinal Arinze's videotape in the classroom which reviews the questions to be covered for that session. Refer the students to the cross-references in *The Apostolate's Family Catechism* from the *Catechism of the Catholic Church* and discuss them in greater detail.

Encourage the students and their parents to play the audiotapes at home, so that they can review the subject material which was presented on videotape in the classroom. Cardinal Arinze's discussions far surpass anything we could ever put in book form! He has such wisdom and candor — the tapes will really bring the Faith alive for the entire family. Keep in mind, however, that Cardinal Arinze is a member of the Pope's "Roman Curia" and Canon 360 of the new *Code of Canon Law* states:

> **"The Supreme Pontiff usually conducts the business of the universal Church through the Roman Curia, which acts in his name and with his authority for the good and for the service of the Churches**. *The Curia is composed of the Secretariat of State or Papal Secretariat, the Council for the public affairs of the Church, the Congregations, the Tribunals and other Institutes. The constitution and competence of all these is defined by special law."*

Because of our society's addiction to television today, it is sad to say that printed materials are not as powerful as video and audio tape. What the Holy Father said is so true — we are a media culture (see page xviii); therefore, we must use the media — audiotape and videotape — to evangelize our families today. So let's use the audio and video tapes, along with the printed word, to drive home the Faith to students and families alike.

CCD Applications

We strongly suggest that when parents bring their children for formation at their parish every week, they be invited to stay for a half-hour. All of the children, with the parents that stay, may be brought into one room together to view a portion of Cardinal Arinze's videotapes on the subject matter selected for that day for all classes regardless of age levels.

As stated above, Cardinal Arinze is a member of the Roman Curia, which is the Pope's direct staff. He teaches with authority but is also one of the best communicators living in the Church today; he explains the Faith in such a way that it is understandable for all ages.

Pads of paper should be provided so that teachers, parents, and students can take notes from Cardinal Arinze's discussions. These points can then be the subject matter to be discussed in the individual classrooms.

At the end of the video portion, we suggest that each of the CCD teachers take their students into the separate classrooms to go over the same points which Cardinal Arinze covered, but at the student's own age level. If the parents want to stay while their children are in class, another video tape of

Cardinal Arinze on Vatican II or papal documents, pertinent to the laity can be shown. (For a partial list of these video tapes, see page 846, 867-871)

This program makes it possible for the parents to know exactly what was being discussed and to continue the discussion with their children on the way home from CCD.

Giving everyone a pad of paper and a pen so that they can write down the questions and the question numbers, in the Apostolate's Family Catechism, they want to discuss from Cardinal Arinze's presentation, will enable teachers and students to indicate which areas need more review. This will help the teachers to know what to look up in the Pope's *Catechism of the Catholic Church* for current and future class discussions.

We recommend that all of the families acquire the *Apostolate's Family Catechism* printed edition and audiotape edition with Cardinal Arinze. Cardinal Arinze's audio tapes (see page 845), in the car and at home, will keep your family spellbound, because of his interesting style and his unique way of dialoging with a parent on the Faith that will enable you to remember the truths that were presented.

Our Blessed Mother taught at Fatima that consecration would save the world and would bring an "era of peace." Our Lord describes consecration in John 17:17, "Consecrate them in truth. Your word is truth." By using the formation offered by the *Catechism of the Catholic Church*, as promulgated by the Holy Father, we will be immersed in that truth which will make us free (cf. Jn 8:32). (See page 839 to 842 for more details about the papally promulgated *Catechism of the Catholic Church.)*

The Apostolate's Family Catechism

Chapter Six
The Mystery of the Holy Trinity

Q. 25. What is the mystery of the Holy Trinity?

The mystery of the Holy Trinity is the mystery of the one true God in three Persons; the Father, the Son, and the Holy Spirit.

There is in the one God only one divine substance, but there are three divine Persons. This is called a mystery, since we will never be able to understand the Trinity fully.

Jesus Christ has revealed to us the secrets of the Kingdom of Heaven. The greatest of His teachings is the secret of God Himself. He told us of the life of God. Jesus taught us that in the one God there are three Persons, each equal to the other. He told us the names of these three Divine Persons: Father, Son, and Holy Spirit.

Vatican Council II

"By divine revelation God wished to manifest and communicate both himself and the eternal decrees of his will concerning the salvation of mankind. He wished, in other words, 'to share with us divine benefits which entirely surpass the power of the human mind to understand." *Divine Revelation, 6*

"The highest exemplar and source of this mystery [that is, the unity of the Church] is the unity, in the Trinity of Persons, of one God, the Father and the Son in the Holy Spirit." *Decree on Ecumenism, 2*

Q. 26. Why do we believe in the mystery of the Holy Trinity?

We believe in the mystery of the Holy Trinity because God revealed it, and He is all-wise and all-truthful.

The Holy Trinity is a mystery. To better discover how it can be so, we must await God's unveiling of Himself in Heaven.

See Papally Promulgated
Catechism of the Catholic Church
Q. 25. See paragraphs: 238-267
Q. 26. See paragraphs: 238, 240, 243-245

Sacred Scripture

"But when the Paraclete comes Whom I will send you from the Father, the Spirit of truth, Who proceeds from the Father, He shall give testimony of Me." *John 15:26*

Vatican Council II

"Before the whole world let all Christians confess their faith in God, one and three, in the incarnate Son of God, our Redeemer and Lord. United in their efforts, and with mutual respect, let them bear witness to our common hope which does not play us false." *Ecumenism, 12*

Q. 27. How was the mystery of the Trinity expressed in the New Testament?

The mystery of the Trinity was expressed in the Person, words and actions of Jesus Christ.

God the Father has revealed this mystery to us through His Son, Who taught us that in the one God there are three Persons, each equal to each other. He taught us the names of these Divine Persons: Father, Son and Holy Spirit.

Vatican Council II

"After God had spoken many times and in various ways through the prophets, 'in these last days he has spoken to us by a Son' (Heb. 1:1-2). For he sent his Son, the eternal Word who enlightens all men, to dwell among men and to tell them about the inner life of God. Hence, Jesus Christ, sent as 'a man among men,' 'speaks the words of God' (Jn. 3:34), and accomplishes the saving work which the Father gave him to do (cf. Jn. 5:36; 17:4). As a result, he himself — to see whom is to see the Father (cf. Jn. 14:9) — completed and perfected Revelation and confirmed it with divine guarantees. He did this by the total fact of his presence and self-manifestation — by words and works, signs and miracles — but above all by his death and glorious resurrection from the dead, and finally by sending the Spirit of truth. He revealed that God was with us, to deliver us from the darkness of sin and death, and to raise us up to eternal life." *Divine Revelation, 4*

See Papally Promulgated
Catechism of the Catholic Church

Q. 25. See paragraphs: 238-267
Q. 26. See paragraphs: 238, 240, 243-245

Each of the 304 questions and answers has a concise statement in a format similar to that of the Baltimore Catechism.

Accompanying the questions and answers are:

- *Scriptural passages*
- *Vatican II quotes*
- *A prayer to summarize each chapter*
- *Chapter cross-references to the papally promulgated new **Catechism of the Catholic Church***
- *The Appendix includes key papal documents.*

The Apostolate's Family Catechism *can be used with the video tape version featuring Francis Cardinal Arinze.*

Vatican Council II
Document Abbreviations

The Second Vatican Council (1962-1965) was the twenty-first ecumenical, or general, council of the Catholic Church. The first ecumenical council (Nicea) was held in 325 A.D. Ecumenical councils are the most solemn assemblies of Bishops and other Church dignitaries within the Catholic Church. Their purpose is to deal primarily with matters of doctrine and discipline affecting the universal Church. They are presided over by the Pope or his delegate. Their teaching, once confirmed by the Pope, is binding on all Catholics.

The Second Vatican Council was convoked by Pope John XXIII to address the pressing needs of the Church in our age. As is true of every ecumenical council, its teaching, contained in sixteen documents, is in total accord with, and faithfully reflects, the substantially unchangeable teaching of the Catholic Church. Whatever is new in the Vatican II documents either consists of new insights into the Faith or expresses new ways of adapting the Faith to contemporary situations and needs. The many excerpts of Vatican II documents contained in *The Apostolate's Family Catechism* confirm and, in many instances, further develop the teaching contained in the catechism proper.

Abbreviations for the Vatican Council II documents used.

Christian Education ...	*Declaration on Christian Education*
Divine Revelation	*Dogmatic Constitution on Divine Revelation*
Eastern Churches	*Decree on the Catholic Eastern Churches*
Ecumenism	*Decree on Ecumenism*
Lay People	*Decree on the Apostolate of Lay People*
Liberty	*Declaration on Religious Liberty*
Missionary Activity	*Decree on the Church's Missionary Activity*
Modern World	*Pastoral Constitution on the Church in the Modern World*
Non-Christian Religions	*Declaration on the Relation of the Church to Non-Christian Religions*
Office of Bishops	*Decree on the Pastoral Office of Bishops in the Church*
Priests	*Decree on the Ministry and Life of Priests*
Religious Life	*Decree on the Up-to-date Renewal of Religious Life*
Sacred Liturgy	*The Constitution on the Sacred Liturgy*
Social Communication	*Decree on the Means of Social Communication*
The Church	*Dogmatic Constitution on the Church*

About the full color seven-volume unabridged
Apostolate's Family Catechism

The following 32 page full-color chapter 1 of this 147 chapter catechism provides you with a sample of what the seven-volume unabridged set of *The Apostolate's Family Catechism* is like.

The added features of the seven-volume unabridged set include:

1. Full-color pictures and text on high quality paper stock and binding.

2. Thousands of inspiring pictures and illustrations which make each concept presented in the catechism come to life. Also presents a variety of art from icons of the Easter Church and classical art to charcoal renderings and illustrations.

3. Dr. Seeley's "Thought Provokers," which stimulate discussion on the questions and answers following each chapter.

4. Additional cross-references from the new *Catechism of the Catholic Church* after each of the "Thought Provokers," for more information.

5. An extensive cross-reference guide that lists other books and page numbers which contain detailed information on the Faith. See pages 25 to 32 for a sample of one of the 147 cross-referenced chapters. This guide alone would justify your investment since it opens up an entire universe of knowledge on the Faith for the family and teacher.

6. More complete texts of papal documents that are pertinent to families, youth and the laity at large.

If you want more information on the complete unabridged seven-volume set of *The Apostolate's Family Catechism,* write to:

Apostolate for Family Consecration
Seminary Road, Route 2, Box 700
Bloomingdale, OH 43910-9606   U.S.A.

or call (614) 765-4301   or fax (614) 765-4941

The Creed - I

—

God, the Holy Trinity, Creation, and the Fall

"We believe in one God, the Father, the Almighty, Creator of Heaven and earth, of all that is seen and unseen..."

God and His Perfections

The Perfections of God

The triangle signifies that there are three Persons in one God; just as there are three sides in a triangle, yet there is only one triangle.

God is an infinitely perfect Spirit, possessing infinite goodness. All His perfections, all of His attributes, are without limit.

God is omnipotent. He is all-powerful and can do all good and non-contradictory things. God is all-knowing. He knows all things: past, present, and future. God is eternal. He has no beginning or end, just as a circle has no beginning or end.

Chapter One

God is the Supreme Being

Q. 1. Who is God?

God is the Supreme Being. The word supreme means above all others. God is the source of all being. He is above all that exists.

Q. 2. Who made God?

No one made God. He always was, and He always will be.

Vatican Council II

"Throughout history even to the present day, there is found among different peoples a certain awareness of a hidden power, which lies behind the course of nature and the events of human life. At times there is present even a recognition of a Supreme Being, or still more of a Father. This awareness and recognition results in a way of life that is imbued with a deep religious sense." *Non-Christian Religions, 2*

See Papally Promulgated
Catechism of the Catholic Church

Q. 1. See paragraphs: 1, 14, 27-28, 30, 32, 34-35, 37, 41-43, 46-48, 64, 200, 203-279
Q. 2. See paragraphs: 45, 213

Q. 3. Can there be more than one God?

There cannot be more than one God because there cannot be two supreme beings. To say otherwise would be a contradiction.

Sacred Scripture

"Hear, O Israel, the Lord our God is one Lord." *Deuteronomy 6:4*

"Remember the former age, for I am God, and there is no God beside Me, neither is there the like to Me." *Isaiah 46:9*

Q. 4. Why must there be a God?

There must be a God because nothing happens in the universe unless someone intelligent ultimately makes it happen. When scientists study how the world developed, they come to a point where they have to ask, "Who started it all?"

See Papally Promulgated
Catechism of the Catholic Church

Q. 3. See paragraphs: 27-28, 46, 200, 222-231, 268, 2096
Q. 4. See paragraphs: 32, 37, 282-289

There must be someone who was not made by anyone else, someone who never had a beginning. That someone is God.

> **Prayer:** *Most loving Father, we worship You as our first beginning. We long for You as our last end, we praise You as our constant helper, and call on You as our loving protector, through our Lord Jesus Christ in unity with the Holy Spirit. Amen.*

God the Infinitely Perfect Spirit

Q. 5. Why is God an infinitely perfect being?

God is an infinitely perfect being because in Him there is no limitation of any kind. God is an infinitely perfect spiritual being, without beginning or end. He knows and loves without limit.

Angels and men are also spiritual beings, but being creatures they are limited or finite. Consequently, their perfections are limited.

Angels are pure spirits, meaning that they have no bodies. Men are both spiritual and material. They have material bodies and spiritual souls. Being spiritual, angels and men have minds and wills. They can know and love, but only to a limited degree. — God alone is the infinitely perfect being. He is the infinitely perfect Spirit.

See Papally Promulgated
Catechism of the Catholic Church

Q. 5. See paragraphs: 1, 41-43, 48, 206, 251, 385, 393, 1064, 2086, 2096

Thought Provokers

by Burns K. Seeley, Ph.D.

Q. 1. Who is God?

God is the Supreme Being. The word supreme means above all others. God is the source of all being, above all that exists.

Thought Provokers:

1. Where in the Bible is it taught that God is the supreme Being?

See, for example, Psalm 95:3 — "For the Lord is a great God, and a great King above all gods"; Psalm 135:6 — "For I have known that the Lord is great; and our God is above all gods;" and Revelation 21:6 — "And He said to me, 'It is done. I am the Alpha and Omega; the Beginning and the End...' ".

2. By the use of reason alone, how can we conclude that God is the Supreme Being in the universe?

See Papally Promulgated
Catechism of the Catholic Church

Q. 1. See paragraphs: 31-39, 46-50, 269, 286

One of the most convincing reasons for concluding that God is the Supreme Being in the universe is as follows: Everything in the universe, whether in the outer reaches of space, or visible to the naked eye on earth, or visible only

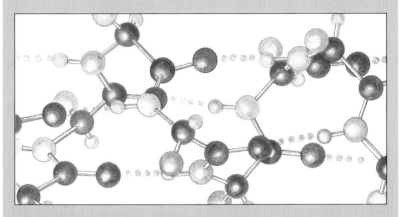

through the lens of an electron microscope, makes up an orderly whole. This amazing unity among such diversity can only be reasonably explained by the existence of a Supreme Intelligent Being, Whom we call God. This argument for the existence of a Supreme Being has been given by individuals of great intelligence since ancient times.

Q. 2. Who made God?

No one made God. He always was, and He always will be.

Thought Provokers:

1. Where in Sacred Scriptures can we learn that God is uncreated?

See, for example, Psalm 90:2 — "Before the mountains were made, or the world and the earth were formed; from

See Papally Promulgated
Catechism of the Catholic Church

Q. 2. See paragraphs: 31-36, cf. 34, 46-50

eternity to eternity, You were God."

2. How can reason alone demonstrate that God is uncreated?

We can note that everything in the universe comes from something else. We can argue in this manner, from effect

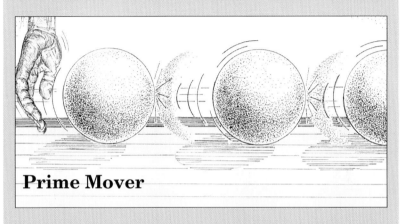

Prime Mover

to cause, until we come to the very first particles of matter and energy that came into existence. But where did these changing and changeable first things come from? Of necessity, they came from something uncreated and outside the chain of effect and cause [and cause and effect] found in the created universe. This Something we call God. To maintain that the most primitive particles in the universe had no beginning is not a scientific conclusion; rather, it is an arbitrary one without scientific support. The fact that these particles are changing and changeable indicates that they are derived from something else. Only something unchanging and unchangeable can be said to have always existed. To argue that all changing and changeable matter and energy have been eternally coming into existence in an unending chain of cause and effect, especially an intelligent and orderly chain of cause and effect, is unreasonable. And it is most certainly an unscientific conclusion.

Q. 3. Can there be more than one God?

There cannot be more than one God because there cannot be two supreme beings. To say otherwise would be a contradiction.

Russian Icon of The Holy Trinity

Thought Provokers:

1. Where in the Bible does it say that there is only one God?

See Deuteronomy 4:39 — "Know therefore this day, and think in your heart that the Lord He is God in Heaven above, and in the earth beneath, and there is no other."

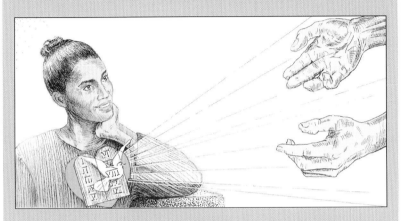

2. Is it reasonable to say that there is only one God?

Yes. As was shown above, the universe indicates that there is an ultimate First Cause to explain its existence and unity. Experience shows that where disunity does exist (in the moral order, for example), it is due not to the existence of another Supreme Being (which is a contradiction in terms), but to the abuse of created, not uncreated, freedom.

Where apparent disunity exists in the physical order (earthquakes, for instance), we can reasonably conclude that they are not disruptive of the unity in the universe as a whole. Moreover, the forces that cause such apparent

See Papally Promulgated
Catechism of the Catholic Church

Q. 3. See paragraphs: 31-34, 200-202

disunity, while they may be sometimes demonic in origin, are quite often (and perhaps most often) derived from the ultimate unifying force of the universe, namely God. Consequently, in these latter instances, what is perceived as disunity by us is not so in the eyes of the Creator.

On a purely human level, a snow storm, for example, is viewed differently by a trucker and by a skier. And prolonged hot, dry weather is viewed differently by a farmer and by a seaside resorter. In other words, what appears to

be an "evil" to one person, on the purely physical plane, is not necessarily viewed as such by another. And in some instances, (for example, soil erosion, and certain illnesses), the improper use of created human freedom is directly to blame. — It can be seen that the above examples support the reasonableness of the existence of only one God.

Q. 4. Why must there be a God?

There must be a God because nothing happens unless someone intelligent ultimately makes it happen. When scientists study how the world developed, they come to a point where they have to ask, "Who started it all?"

See Papally Promulgated
Catechism of the Catholic Church

Q. 4. See paragraph: 32

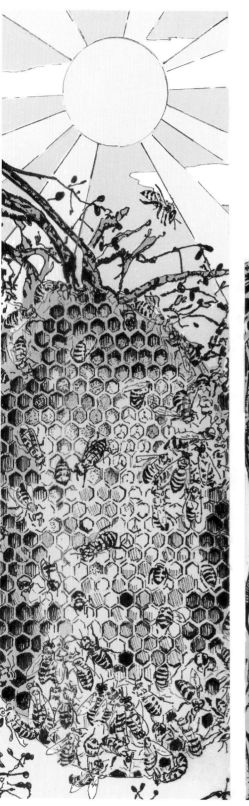
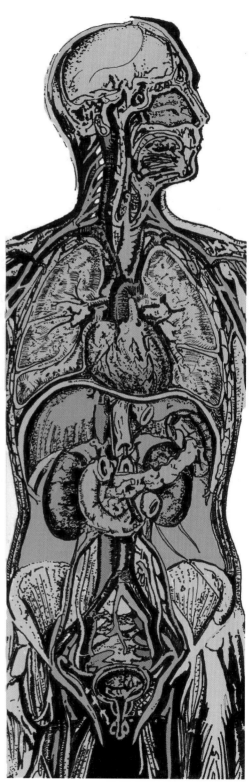

Thought Provoker:

If you had never heard of computers before, and someone showed you one (and explained how it worked, demonstrated some of the many intricate problems it could solve) and then showed you a detailed diagram of its inner work-

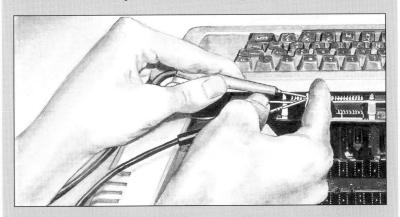

ings, would you conclude that no one had designed it and made it, or that it just happened to come together by chance? If so, you would be very unreasonable in your conclusions.

By the same token, what sort of conclusion might you reach about the origin of the human body, if someone pointed out to you its vast complexity and at the same time demonstrated the harmonious working of its parts? Could you reasonably conclude that nothing intelligent had designed and created it?

Now for the sake of argument, what if you insisted that God did not exist; how would you then explain the vast complexity and harmonious workings of the human being?

Q. 5. Why is God an infinitely perfect being?

See Papally Promulgated
Catechism of the Catholic Church

Q. 5. See paragraph: 42

God is an infinitely perfect Being because in God there is no limitation of any kind. God is an infinitely perfect spiritual being, without beginning or end.

Thought Provoker:

A spirit means something which has no body. It cannot be seen because it is made up of no parts. There is nothing that can ever be broken up. There is nothing subject to corruption or decay. A spirit is immortal by nature.

Prayer

My God, we believe that You are the infinitely perfect Spirit. You can know and love. Your knowledge and love have no limit.

Lord, we believe in You; increase our faith. We trust in You; strengthen our trust. We love You; may we love You more and more.

Almighty God, increase our strength of will for doing good that Christ may find an eager welcome in our hearts and call us to His side in the Kingdom of Heaven. We ask this through the same Christ our Lord. Amen.

Cross-Reference Guide

Additional Reliable Resources Which Are Faithful to the Magisterium of the Church

referenced by page number

A Quick Reference Guide for Busy Parents and Teachers

When questions arise — you could ask your children to look up cross-references and to report back to the family the next day.

Please Note: A complete Cross-Reference Guide (like the following) will appear at the end of each chapter of *The Apostolate's Family Catechism* unabridged 7-volume set.

Also Note: The cross-references for the new papally promulgated *Catechism of the Catholic Church* will be found both in the body of the basic text and in the Thought Provoker sections included at the end of each of the 147 chapters in the unabridged 7-volume set.

"Finally, in order to draw closer to men and give them a more convincing proof of His love, Eternal Wisdom [the Son of God] went so far as to become man, even to become a little child, to embrace poverty and to die upon a cross for them." *St. Louis de Montfort, Eternal Wisdom*, 70

"Madonna of the Goldfinch" by Giovanni Battista Tiepolo, Samuel H. Kress Collection, © 1992 National Gallery of Art, Washington

Cross-Reference Guide (for Chapter One) of *The Apostolate's Family Catechism*™

The Cross-Reference Guide opens up an entire world of literature for the family and school.

Listed below are references to further information regarding the catechetical questions and answers contained in the unabridged seven volume catechism. The list of books / works referred to in the Cross-Reference Guide are as follows:

Catechisms / Theology Books

The Teaching of Christ by Lawler, Wuerl and Lawler [First Edition]
The Teaching of Christ by Lawler, Wuerl and Lawler [Second Edition]
The Catholic Catechism by Father John A. Hardon, S.J.
Fundamentals of Catholicism [Three volumes] by Father Kenneth Baker, S.J.
Basics of the Faith: A Catholic Catechism by Alan Schreck, Ph.D.
The Church's Confession of Faith published by the German Bishops' Conference
Faith for Today by Father Richard M. Hogan and Father John M. LeVoir
Modern Catholic Dictionary by Father John A. Hardon, S.J.
Pocket Catholic Dictionary by Father John A. Hardon, S.J.
Fundamentals of Catholic Dogma by Doctor Ludwig Ott

Philosophy Books

Transformation in Christ by Dietrich von Hildebrand, Ph.D

Papal Documents

On Evangelization in the Modern World by Paul VI
On Human Life (Humanae Vitae) by Paul VI

Catechesis in Our Time by John Paul II
Familiaris Consortio by John Paul II
Guardian of the Redeemer by John Paul II
Mother of the Redeemer by John Paul II
On Human Work by John Paul II
On Reconciliation and Penance by John Paul II
On the Christian Meaning of Human Suffering by John
    Paul II
On the Dignity and Vocation of Women by John Paul II
On the Holy Spirit in the Life of the Church and the World
    by John Paul II
On the Hundredth Anniversary of Rerum Novarum by
    John Paul II
On the Mystery and Worship of the Eucharist by
    John Paul II
Redeemer of Man by John Paul II
Reflections on Humanae Vitae by John Paul II
Rich in Mercy by John Paul II
To the Youth of the World by John Paul II

Q. 1. Who is God?

Catechisms / Theology Books

The Teaching of Christ [First Edition], Lawler, Wuerl and Lawler, pp. 48-54;

The Teaching of Christ [Second Edition], Lawler, Wuerl and Lawler, pp. 36-42;

The Catholic Catechism, Hardon, pp. 68-69;

Fundamentals of Catholicism, Baker, Vol. 1, pp. 27-34, Vol. 2, pp. 41-59;

Basics of the Faith: A Catholic Catechism, Schreck, pp. 3-14;

The Church's Confession of Faith, German Bishops' Conference, pp. 52-54, 63-66;

Faith for Today, Hogan and LeVoir, pp. 4-10;

Modern Catholic Dictionary, Hardon, see "God";

Pocket Catholic Dictionary, Hardon, see "God ";

Fundamentals of Catholic Dogma, Ott, pp. 24.

Papal Documents

On Evangelization in the Modern World, Paul VI, sect. 26;

Familiaris Consortio, John Paul II, sect. 11;

On Reconciliation and Penance, John Paul II, sect. 10;

On the Dignity and Vocation of Women, John Paul II, sect. 7;

On the Holy Spirit in the Life of the Church and the World, John Paul II, sect. 8-12;

Redeemer of Man, John Paul II, sect. 9;

Rich in Mercy, John Paul II, sect. 1-2.

Q. 2. Who made God?

Catechisms / Theology Books

The Teaching of Christ [First Edition], Lawler, Wuerl and Lawler, pp. 44-45; 48-49;

The Teaching of Christ [Second Edition], Lawler, Wuerl and Lawler, pp. 32-33; 36-37;

The Catholic Catechism, Hardon, p. 56;

Fundamentals of Catholicism, Baker, Vol. 1, p. 35;

The Church's Confession of Faith, German Bishops' Conference, pp. 36f, 62, 79;

Faith for Today, Hogan and LeVoir, pp. 4-10;

Modern Catholic Dictionary, Hardon, see "God";

Pocket Catholic Dictionary, Hardon, see "God ";

Fundamentals of Catholic Dogma, Ott, p. 36f.

Q. 3. Can there be more than one God?

Catechisms / Theology Books

The Teaching of Christ [First Edition], Lawler, Wuerl and Lawler, p. 54;

The Teaching of Christ [Second Edition], Lawler, Wuerl and Lawler, p. 42;

The Catholic Catechism, Hardon, p. 55;

Fundamentals of Catholicism, Baker, Vol. 1, pp. 27-29;

Basics of the Faith: A Catholic Catechism, Schreck, pp. 11-13;

The Church's Confession of Faith, German Bishops' Conference, pp. 59-61;

Faith for Today, Hogan and LeVoir, pp. 4-6;

Modern Catholic Dictionary, Hardon, see "God";

Pocket Catholic Dictionary, Hardon, see "God";

Fundamentals of Catholic Dogma, Ott, p. 32f.

Papal Documents

On the Dignity and Vocation of Women, John Paul II, sect. 7.

Q. 4. Why must there be a God?

Catechisms / Theology Books

The Teaching of Christ [First Edition], Lawler, Wuerl and Lawler, pp. 44-45;

The Teaching of Christ [Second Edition], Lawler, Wuerl and Lawler, pp. 32-33;

The Catholic Catechism, Hardon, pp. 232-233;

Fundamentals of Catholicism, Baker, Vol. 1, pp. 34-36;

The Church's Confession of Faith, German Bishops' Conference, pp. 28-31;

Faith for Today, Hogan and LeVoir, pp. 2-3;

Modern Catholic Dictionary, Hardon, see "God ";

Pocket Catholic Dictionary, Hardon, see " God";

Fundamentals of Catholic Dogma, Ott, p. 14f.

Papal Documents

On the Hundredth Anniversary of Rerum Novarum, John
Paul II, sect. 13, 24.

Q. 5. Why is God an infinitely perfect Being?

Catechisms / Theology Books

The Teaching of Christ [First Edition], Lawler, Wuerl and
Lawler, p. 49;

The Teaching of Christ [Second Edition], Lawler, Wuerl and
Lawler, p. 37;

The Catholic Catechism, Hardon, pp. 56-57;

Fundamentals of Catholicism, Baker, Vol. 2, pp. 38-41;

The Church's Confession of Faith, German Bishops'
Conference, p. 33;

Faith for Today, Hogan and LeVoir, pp. 4-9;

Modern Catholic Dictionary, Hardon, see "God";

Pocket Catholic Dictionary, Hardon, see "God";

Fundamentals of Catholic Dogma, Ott, pp. 30-31.

Papal Documents

On the Holy Spirit in the Life of the Church and the World,
John Paul II, sect. 34.

"I will put enmity between you and the woman, and your seed and her seed. She* shall crush your head, and you shall lie in wait for her heel." Genesis 3:15

---

* [See Section 55 of *The Dogmatic Constitution of the Church* of the Second Vatican Council on pages 668-677 of *The Apostolate's Family Catechism* and Paragraph 411 of the *Catechism of the Catholic Church.*]

[For key Scriptures about Our Blessed Mother, see page 667 of *The Apostolate's Family Catechism* and pages 668-677 for the complete text of Chapter 8 about Mary as found in *The Dogmatic Constitution of the Church* of the Second Vatican Council.]

Chapter Two

God's Perfections

Q. 6. What are God's perfections?

The attributes of God are His perfections; that is, such things as His love, goodness, truthfulness, and justice.

Q. 7. Is God infinitely good?

God is infinitely good. His goodness is limitless, as are all of His perfections.

Sacred Scripture

"None is good but God alone." *Luke 18:19*

"God is faithful and without any iniquity." *Deuteronomy 32:4*

Vatican Council II

"God in his great and merciful kindness freely creates us and moreover, graciously calls us to share in his life and glory. He generously pours out, and never ceases to pour out, his divine goodness." *Missionary Activity, 2*

Prayer: *My God, we believe that You are infinitely perfect and infinitely good. Gifts without measure flow from Your goodness to bring us Your peace.*

Our lives are Your gift. Guide them on their journeys, for only Your love makes us whole. Keep us strong in Your love.

From Your goodness we have received all that is good. Direct our steps in our everyday efforts. May the changing moods of the human heart and the limits which our failings impose on hope never blind us to You, source of every good, forever and ever. Amen.

See Papally Promulgated
Catechism of the Catholic Church

Q. 6. See paragraphs: 1, 30, 42, 47, 212-221, 268-276, 1429, 2086
Q. 7. See paragraphs: 1, 214, 310, 339, 384

Q. 8. Is God eternal?

God is eternal. This is true because He always was, is now, and always will be.

Sacred Scripture

"Before the mountains were made, or the earth and the world were formed; from eternity to eternity You are God."

Psalm 90:2

Q. 9. Why is God all-knowing?

God is all-knowing because He knows all things in the past, present, and future, as well as all potential things. God knows all things that are or ever could be. Everything is like one thought in the mind of God. Therefore, we say God is all-knowing.

Sacred Scripture

"O Lord, You have knowledge of all things." *Esther 14:14*

Prayer: *My God, we believe that You are eternal, because You always were, are now, and always will be.*

We believe that You are all-knowing, because You know the past, present, and all that ever will or can be. Teach us to realize that this world is passing, that our true future is the happiness of Heaven, that life on earth is short, and that the life to come is eternal. Help us to follow Christ with love to gain eternal life with You. Amen.

Q. 10. Is God present everywhere?

God is present everywhere, all the time. There is no place where God is not.

Sacred Scripture

"For if heaven and the heaven of heavens cannot contain You, how much less the house which I have built." *1 Kings 8:27*

See Papally Promulgated
Catechism of the Catholic Church

Q. 8. See paragraphs: 34, 101, 108, 220, 240, 243, 257, 262, 276
Q. 9. See paragraphs: 37, 207-209, 217, 291, 302-303, 310-312, 599-600
Q. 10. See paragraphs: 207, 300-301, 2671

Q. 11. Is God almighty?

God is almighty because He can do and make anything which is good and non-contradictory. Thus, God cannot commit sin because He cannot contradict His infinite goodness. Nor can He violate the principle of non-contradiction which states that a thing cannot both be and not be at the same time.

Sacred Scripture

"With God all things are possible." *Matthew 19:26*

Prayer: *Eternal Father, You are almighty, reaching from end to end of the universe, and ordering all things with Your mighty arm. For You, time is the unfolding of truth that already is and the unveiling of beauty that is yet to be.*

Guide us by Your wisdom, correct us with Your justice, comfort us with Your mercy, and protect us with Your power, through our Lord Jesus Christ. Amen.

See Papally Promulgated
Catechism of the Catholic Church

Q. 11. See paragraphs: 269-278

Prayer

*F*ather of everlasting goodness, our origin and guide, be close to us and hear our prayers which we offer to praise You. Our Faith gives us the promise of peace and makes known the demands of love. Remove our selfishness which blurs the vision of the virtue of faith.

*L*et our spiritual sacrifice, offered with Your Son in the Mass, make us an everlasting gift to You. Give us the strength of new life by the gift of the Eucharist. Protect us with Your love and prepare us for eternal life. Grant us in this life the good things that lead to the everlasting life You have prepared for us.

*M*erciful Father, fill our hearts with Your love and keep us faithful to the Gospel of Christ. Give us the grace to rise above our human weaknesses. Fill our hearts with the light of Your Gospel, that our thoughts may please You and our love may be sincere. We ask this through Jesus Christ our Lord. Amen.

Chapter Three

More of God's Perfections

Q. 12. Is God all-wise?

Yes, God alone, the Creator of all things, is all-wise. He knows what is best for all His creatures.

Sacred Scripture

"His wisdom is without measure." *Psalm 147:5*

> **Prayer:** *O my God, we believe that You are all-wise, for You know best the things which You have created. We abandon ourselves to Your loving care, and we cheerfully accept all that You send us. All glory and praise be to the Father, the Son and the Holy Spirit. Amen.*

Q. 13. Why is God all-holy?

God is all-holy because He is infinitely full of all that is good and lovable.

Sacred Scripture

"Holy, holy, holy, the Lord God of hosts, all the earth is full of His glory." *Isaiah 6:3*

> **Prayer:** *O God, we believe You are all-holy. All creation rightly gives You praise; for all life and all holiness comes from You.*
>
> *In the plan of Your wisdom, she who bore the Christ in her womb was raised in glory to be with Him in Heaven. May we follow her example in reflecting Your holiness and join in her hymn of endless love and praise, through the same Christ our Lord. Amen.*

See Papally Promulgated
Catechism of the Catholic Church

Q. 12. See paragraphs: 30, 310, 339, 2500
Q. 13. See paragraphs: 208, 826, 2809-2810

Q. 14. Why is God all-merciful?

God is all-merciful because there is no end to His mercy. As often as we are sorry for our sins and confess them, so often will God forgive us.

Sacred Scripture

"All the ways of the Lord are mercy and truth to them that seek after His covenant and His testimonies." *Psalm 25:10*

Vatican Council II

"We know neither the moment of the consummation of the earth and of man nor the way the universe will be transformed. The form of this world, distorted by sin, is passing away and we are taught that God is preparing a new dwelling and a new earth in which righteousness dwells, whose happiness will fill and surpass all the desires of peace arising in the hearts of men." *Modern World, 39*

Q. 15. Why is God all-just?

God is all-just because He is completely honest and fair with everybody.

He promises to reward us for our good deeds and to punish us for our evil deeds. Yet, He is always merciful to those who turn to Him. (See Q. 14 above.)

Sacred Scripture

"He has prepared His throne in judgment and He shall judge the world in equity. He shall judge the world in justice."
Psalm 9:8-9

See Papally Promulgated
Catechism of the Catholic Church

Q. 14. *See paragraphs: 211, 270, 393, 1261, 1429, 1489, 1608*

Q. 15. *See paragraphs: 54, 271, 1040, 1991-1994, 2006-2007, 2009, 2020, 2091*

Prayer

Source of all holiness, the work of Your hands is reflected in Your saints. The beauty of Your truth is reflected in the faith they had on earth. May we who aspire to have a part in their joy be filled with the Spirit that blessed their lives, so that having shared their faith* on earth, we may also know their peace in Your Kingdom.

We believe You are all-just and all-merciful. In You, justice and mercy meet. With unparalleled love, You have saved us from death and have drawn us into the circle of Your life. Open our eyes to the wonders this life sets before us, so that we may serve You free from fear and address You as God, our merciful Father.

Oh God, make us steadfast in faith, joyful in hope, and untiring in love all the days of our lives. We ask this through Jesus Christ our Lord, to Whom, with You and the Holy Spirit, be all honor and glory. Amen.

---

*[Editorial note - In Heaven, there is no need for the theological virtue of faith since the blessed have knowledge given directly by God (infused knowledge). They also have self-evident knowledge of God and divine matters.]

Chapter Four

Worship of God

Q. 16. How has God shown His love for us?

God has shown His love for us by: (1) *making firm promises to men;* (2) *by freeing and saving us;* and (3) *by loving each of us with the love of a father and always caring for us.*

1. *God made firm promises to men.*

After our first parents, Adam and Eve, sinned, God made a promise to redeem all men. He kept His promise by choosing Abraham's descendants (the people of Israel) to be His own special people. He then established the Mosaic Covenant with His people, within which were contained the Ten Commandments.

Though Israel did not always live up to the Covenant, God did not forsake His people. At last, He came among His people in the Person of His Son, Jesus, Who made a New Covenant in His Blood by His death on the Cross.

2. *God freed us and saved us.*

Through Jesus Christ, God freed us (both Jews and Gentiles) from the power of eternal death and the domination of sin. Through the suffering, death, and Resurrection of Jesus, we have received grace and God's own life, and a sharing in His nature. Through Him, we have the hope of complete freedom from sin and the hope of eternal life with God in Heaven.

3. *God truly loves each of us and takes care of us as a loving father.*

He has made us His children through Baptism and has prepared His heavenly Kingdom to be our eternal home.

See Papally Promulgated
Catechism of the Catholic Church

Q. 16. See paragraphs: 55-56, 61-62, 64-67, 69, 72-75, 122, 128, 211-212, 215, 422, 426, 497, 609, 638, 652, 822

Sacred Scripture

"For God so loved the world, so as to give His only-begotten Son; that whosoever believes in Him may not perish, but may have everlasting life." *John 3:16*

Vatican Council II

"It pleased God, in his goodness and wisdom, to reveal himself and to make known the mystery of his will (cf. Eph. 1:9). His will was that men should have access to the Father, through Christ, the Word made flesh, in the Holy Spirit, and thus become sharers in the divine nature (cf. Eph. 2:18; 2 Pet. 1:4). By this revelation, then, the invisible God (cf. Col. 1:15; 1 Tim. 1:17), from the fullness of his love, addresses men as his friends (cf. Ex. 33:11; Jn. 15:14-15), and moves among (Bar. 3:38) them in order to invite and receive them into his own company." *Divine Revelation, 2*

> **Prayer:** *Almighty God, Father of the world to come, Your goodness is beyond what our spirit can touch. Your strength is more than the mind can bear.*
>
> *You draw people to Yourself by making firm promises to free and save us. You love each of us with the love of a father who always cares for us, through Jesus Christ our Lord. Amen.*

Q. 17. What should the thought of God's goodness do for us?

The thought of God's goodness should (1) *make us find joy in the God Who gives us eternal hope* and (2) *prompt us to worship and serve Him.*

1. *We should find joy in God.*

We belong to God Who loves us and wants us to love Him so that we may be with Him forever in Heaven. Through fervent

See Papally Promulgated
Catechism of the Catholic Church

Q. 17. See paragraphs: 30, 301, 346-347, 425, 736, 901, 1070, 1089, 1121, 1172, 1697

prayer and the proper reception of the sacraments, God gives us the grace to love Him and find our joy in Him.

2. We should worship and serve God.

We worship God by our love and adoration. We show our loving service to Him by obedience to His will.

Sacred Scripture

"Blessed be the God and Father of our Lord Jesus Christ, who according to His great mercy has regenerated us unto a lively hope, by the Resurrection of Jesus Christ from the dead, unto an inheritance incorruptible, and undefiled, and that cannot fade, reserved in Heaven for you." *1 Peter 1:3-4*

Vatican Council II

"The spiritual life, however, is not limited solely to participation in the liturgy. The Christian is indeed called to pray with others, but he must also enter into his bedroom to pray to his Father in secret; furthermore, according to the teaching of the apostle, he must pray without ceasing."

Sacred Liturgy, 12

> **Prayer:** *Almighty God and Father, may the thought of Your goodness make us find joy in You and prompt us to worship You. We worship You by offering ourselves to You through Jesus Christ Your Son. We are determined to do Your will in all our actions, and to use well the talents You have given us. From Your goodness we hope to receive the grace to live a life of love for You, and to be able to love and help the people around us, through Jesus Christ Your Son. Amen.*

Q. 18. How do we worship God?

We worship God in the sacred liturgy; especially when we adore Him in the Holy Sacrifice of the Mass and offer our-

See Papally Promulgated
Catechism of the Catholic Church

Q. 18. See paragraphs: 901, 1173, 1378, 1388, 1478, 1813, 2006-2011, 2041-2042, 2080, 2192, 2558-2865

selves to Him together with the offering of Jesus. We worship God also when we pray to Him by ourselves or with others.

We worship God when we do His will by keeping His Commandments as obedient children.

We worship God by using well the talents He has given us. We are in this world to know God, to love and to serve Him, and to use our talents in His service.

Vatican Council II

"Through the ministry of priests the spiritual sacrifice of the faithful is completed in union with the sacrifice of Christ the only mediator, which in the Eucharist is offered through the priests' hands in the name of the whole Church in an unbloody and sacramental manner until the Lord himself come [sic] (cf. 1 Cor. 11:26)." *Priests, 2*

> **Prayer:** *Lord, may the sacrifice of Your Son in the Mass, and our sacrifice of praise, purify us in mind and heart and make us always eager to serve You. You give us the Body and Blood of Your Son to renew Your life within us. In Your mercy, assure our redemption and bring us to the eternal life we celebrate in the Eucharist through Christ our Lord. Amen.*

Q. 19. What should we hope for from the goodness of God?

From the goodness of God we hope to receive the grace we need to live a life of love for Him and for our neighbor.

We trust that God will help us to live a life of love for Him and our fellow men. We do this when we devote ourselves to our Creator. God will give us His help to love Him as He wants us to love Him. Our life can be very happy, if we open our hearts to Him and use the graces He offers us each day to love Him and to help the people around us.

See Papally Promulgated
Catechism of the Catholic Church

Q. 19. See paragraphs: 274, 301, 304-305, 313, 2086, 2728, 2828, 2836-2837

Sacred Scripture

"But doing the truth in charity, we may in all things grow up in Him Who is the head, even Christ." *Ephesians 4:15*

Vatican Council II

"For if man exists it is because God has created him through love, and through love continues to hold him in existence. He cannot live fully according to truth unless he freely acknowledges that love and entrusts himself to his creator." *Modern World, 1*

Q. 20. Why do so many people today pay little attention to God?

So many people today pay little attention to God because they have decided that modern life consists chiefly in the affairs of men rather than those of God.

God continues to be good to us, and yet there are very many people in the world who hardly ever think of Him; many even deliberately break His Commandments. They are too interested in their own pleasures and in the things the world offers them.

There are many people who are not ready to believe in God. We must accept God's word with deep faith, and trust in His love for us, for He is faithful to His promises.

Vatican Council II

"Man therefore is divided in himself. As a result, the whole life of men, both individual and social, shows itself to be a struggle, and a dramatic one, between good and evil, between light and darkness. Man finds that he is unable of himself to overcome the assaults of evil successfully, so that everyone feels as though bound by chains." *Modern World, 13*

Sacred Scripture

"For I do not do that good which I will. But the evil which I hate, that I do. ... Now it is no more I who do it, but sin that

See Papally Promulgated
Catechism of the Catholic Church

Q. 20. See paragraphs: 2113, 2123-2125, 2127-2128, 2514-2516

dwells in me. For I know that there does not dwell in me, that is, in my flesh, that which is good. For to will is present with me, but to accomplish that which is good, that I do not find. For the good which I will, I do not, but the evil which I do not will, that I do. Now if I do that which I do not will, it is no more I that do it, but sin that dwells in me. I find then, a law, that when I have a will to do good, evil is present with me. For I am delighted with the law of God, according to the inward man. But I see another law in my members, fighting against the law of my mind and captivating me in the law of sin that is in my members. Unhappy man that I am. Who shall deliver me from the body of this death? The grace of God, by Jesus Christ our Lord. Therefore, I myself, with the mind serve the law of God, but with the flesh, the law of sin." *Romans 7:15-25*

Q. 21. Does every man have some desire for God?

No matter how hidden, some desire for God is in the heart of every man.

God has made us for Himself and we cannot find true happiness unless we look for it in Him. Even when we do not want to think so, there is a secret desire in our hearts for God. To the degree that God has helped us to know Him more than many others do, He expects us to love Him more, and serve Him better. Our life will be blessed if we do so, and we can look forward to being with God forever in Heaven.

Vatican Council II

"The dignity of man rests above all on the fact that he is called to communion with God. The invitation to converse with God is addressed to man as soon as he comes into being."

Modern World, 19

See Papally Promulgated
Catechism of the Catholic Church

Q. 21. See paragraphs: 27-30

Prayer

Lord, may we both know and cherish the heavenly gifts You have given us. Your love never fails. The hand of Your loving kindness powerfully, yet gently, guides all the moments of our day. In You we live and move and have our being. Each day You show us a father's love. Your Holy Spirit, dwelling within us, gives us on earth the hope of unending joy. Your gift of the Spirit is the foretaste and promise of the paschal feast of Heaven. With thankful praise, in company with the angels, we glorify the wonders of Your power.

Father in Heaven, be with us in our pilgrimage of life, anticipate our needs, and prevent our falling. Send Your Spirit to unite us in faith, that sharing in Your service, we may rejoice in Your presence. Increase our faith in You and bring our trust to its promised fulfillment in the joy of Your Kingdom.

God of the universe, we worship You as Lord. We rejoice to call You Father. In the midst of this world's uncertainty we look to Your Covenant. Keep us in Your peace and secure in Your love. Grant us an unfailing respect for Your Name, and keep us always in Your love, through Jesus Christ our Savior. Amen.

The Revelation of God: the Holy Trinity

Chapter Five

God Reveals Himself

Q. 22. What is the history of salvation?

The history of salvation is the story of God's dealings with men.

The history of salvation tells us how God saved us. In it, is the plan by which God the Father, God the Son, and God the Holy Spirit revealed Themselves to mankind, made peace between Themselves and man by Christ's death on the Cross, and united with Themselves those who turned away from sin.

Vatican Council II

"The eternal Father, in accordance with the utterly gratuitous and mysterious design of his wisdom and goodness, created the whole universe, and chose to raise up men to share in his own divine life; and when they had fallen in Adam, he did not abandon them, but at all times held out to them the means of salvation, bestowed in consideration of Christ, the Redeemer, 'who is the image of the invisible God, the firstborn of every creature' all the elect the Father foreknew and predestined before time began 'to become conformed to the image of his Son, that he should be the firstborn among many brethren' (Romans 8:29). He determined to call together in a holy Church those who should believe in Christ." *The Church, 2*

"By divine Revelation God wished to manifest and communicate both himself and the eternal decrees of his will concerning the salvation of mankind. He wished, in other words, 'to share with us divine benefits which entirely surpass the powers of the human mind to understand' (First Vatican Council, Dogm. Const. on Cath. Faith, 2)." *Divine Revelation, 6*

"This economy of Revelation is realized by deeds and words, which are intrinsically bound up with each other. As a result, the works performed by God in the history of salvation

See Papally Promulgated
Catechism of the Catholic Church

Q. 22. See paragraphs: 431-432, 586, 758-769, 1040, 1066, 1080, 1095, 1217, 2591, 2606, 2738

show forth and bear out the doctrine and realities signified by the words; the words, for their part, proclaim the works, and bring to light the mystery they contain." *Divine Revelation, 2*

Prayer: *Almighty God, the history of salvation tells us how You saved us; You revealed Yourself to men, and made peace by Christ's death on the Cross. You united with Yourself those who turned away from sin.*

You revealed Yourself as an all-powerful Being existing above and beyond man and his world. You became real for us when You willed to let us know You personally through divine revelation. We thank You for giving Yourself to us and showing us Your will for the salvation of mankind, through Christ our Lord. Amen.

Q. 23. How did God deal with man?

God revealed Himself to man and saved him from sin.

God made Himself known to man. Revelation means that God showed us something of Himself. He made Himself known to us so that He might save us. The Bible tells us about this revelation. The Bible is the written record of God's actions in the world. It is true because it is God's own Word, which He made known to the writers of the Bible.

God saved man from sin. Sin made us lose God's life within us and made us slaves of death. God sent His Son to save us from sin and death, and to give us God's life of grace. Because of His Son, God now forgives our sins, if we are truly sorry, and if we want to be His friends.

Vatican Council II

"After the era of the patriarchs, he taught this nation [Israel] by Moses and the prophets, to recognize him as the only living and true God, as a provident Father and just judge. He

See Papally Promulgated
Catechism of the Catholic Church

Q. 23. See paragraphs: 35, 50-73, 74-141, 161, 169, 183, 289

taught them, too, to look for the promised Saviour. And so, throughout the ages, he prepared the way for the Gospel."

Divine Revelation, 3

Sacred Scripture

"He was in the world, and the world was made by Him, and the world knew Him not. He came unto His own, and His own received Him not. But as many as received Him, He gave them power to be made sons of God, to them that believe on His Name." *John 1:10-12*

"For God so loved the world, as to give His only begotten Son, that whosoever believes in Him may not perish but have everlasting life." *John 3:16*

> **Prayer:** *Most loving Father, through the death and Resurrection of Your Son Jesus Christ, You, in fact, redeemed man. But we must now successfully complete our pilgrimage in the wilderness of this life in order to gain eternal happiness in Heaven.*
>
> *Grant us Living Water from the Rock and Bread from Heaven, that we may survive our desert pilgrimage and thank You eternally for Your kindness, through Your only begotten Son, Jesus Christ. Amen.*

Q. 24. How did God reveal Himself in the Old Testament?

God revealed Himself in the Old Testament as the one, true, personal God, and prepared to reveal the Trinity later on. Thus we read, for example: "For You, O Lord, are loving and kind, and full of mercy to all who call upon You" (Psalm 86:5) and "Just as a father has pity on his children, so the Lord pities those who fear Him" (Psalm 103:10).

God is the one, all-powerful being, existing above and beyond man and his world. The true God is real. He becomes

See Papally Promulgated
Catechism of the Catholic Church

Q. 24. See paragraphs: 54-64, 77-78, 121-123, 128, 200-201, 204, 238-239, 286-288

real for us when we come to know Him. To know God personally, we have to be very attentive to whatever He shows us of Himself. This is called divine revelation. By making Himself known to us through revelation, God gave Himself to us and showed us His will for the salvation of all men.

God shows Himself in all of creation and history. But the Catholic Church is interested in the personal way in which God showed and continues to show Himself to men. This revelation is found in the Bible and in Sacred Tradition, and from it we learn what our life really is and how we must live it.

Vatican Council II

"And furthermore, wishing to open up the way to heavenly salvation, he [God] manifested himself to our first parents from the very beginning. After the fall, he buoyed them up with the hope of salvation, by promising redemption (cf. Gen. 3:15); and he has never ceased to take care of the human race. For he wishes to give eternal life to all those who seek salvation by patience in well-doing (cf. Rom. 2:6-7). In his own time God called Abraham, and made him into a great nation (cf. Gen. 12:2)." *Divine Revelation, 3*

In the Old Testament we read about God showing Himself to us as the one true personal God. People learned that God was real, that He was faithful to His promises, and that people could be His friends, if they put their trust in Him.

Prayer: *Heavenly Father, You revealed Yourself in the Old Testament as the one true personal God. Abraham, Joseph and Moses prefigured Your plan, Father, to redeem mankind from slavery and to lead them into the land of promise. Through the death and Resurrection of Your Son, You, in fact, redeemed man. But we must now successfully complete our pilgrimage in the wilderness of this life in order to gain eternal happiness in Heaven. Grant us Living Water from the Rock and Bread from heaven, that we may survive our desert pilgrimage and thank You eternally for Your kindness, through Jesus Christ our Redeemer and Lord. Amen.*

Prayer

Lord, You established peace within the borders of Jerusalem. Give the fullness of peace to Your faithful people. May peace rule us in this life and possess us in eternal life. You fill us with the best of wheat, the Bread of Life, in the Eucharist. Grant that what we see dimly now as in a mirror, we may come to perceive clearly in the brightness of Your truth.

Almighty God, every good thing comes from You. Fill our hearts with love for You. Increase our faith, and by Your constant care, protect the good You have given us. May the Holy Sacrifice of the Mass bring us Your blessing and accomplish within us its promise of salvation.

Father of our Lord Jesus Christ, faith in Your Word is the way to wisdom, and to ponder Your divine plan is to grow in the truth. Open our eyes that we may do Your will, and our ears to hear the sound of Your call, so that our every action may increase our sharing in the life you have offered us, through Christ our Lord. Amen.

Chapter Six

The Mystery of the Holy Trinity

Q. 25. What is the mystery of the Holy Trinity?

The mystery of the Holy Trinity is the mystery of the one true God in three Persons: the Father, the Son, and the Holy Spirit.

There is in the one God only one divine substance, but there are three divine Persons. This is called a mystery, since we will never be able to understand the Trinity fully.

Jesus Christ has revealed to us the secrets of the Kingdom of Heaven. The greatest of His teachings is the secret of God Himself. He has told us of the life of God. Jesus taught us that in the one God there are three Persons, each equal to the other. He told us the names of these three Divine Persons: Father, Son, and Holy Spirit.

Vatican Council II

"By divine revelation God wished to manifest and communicate both himself and the eternal decrees of his will concerning the salvation of mankind. He wished, in other words, to share with us divine benefits which entirely surpass the power of the human mind to understand." *Divine Revelation, 6*

"The highest exemplar and source of this mystery [that is, the unity of the Church] is the unity, in the Trinity of Persons, of one God, the Father and the Son in the Holy Spirit."

Ecumenism, 2

Q. 26. Why do we believe in the mystery of the Holy Trinity?

We believe in the mystery of the Holy Trinity because God revealed it, and He is all-wise and all-truthful.

See Papally Promulgated
Catechism of the Catholic Church

Q. 25. See paragraphs: 238-267
Q. 26. See paragraphs: 238, 240, 243-245

The Holy Trinity is a mystery. To better understand, as best we can, how it can be so, we must await God's unveiling of Himself in Heaven.

Sacred Scripture

"But when the Paraclete comes Whom I will send you from the Father, the Spirit of truth, Who proceeds from the Father, He shall give testimony of Me." *John 15:26*

Vatican Council II

"Before the whole world let all Christians confess their faith in God, one and three, in the incarnate Son of God, our Redeemer and Lord. United in their efforts, and with mutual respect, let them bear witness to our common hope which does not play us false." *Ecumenism, 12*

Q. 27. How was the mystery of the Trinity expressed in the New Testament?

The mystery of the Trinity was expressed in the Person, words and actions of Jesus Christ.

Vatican Council II

"After God had spoken many times and in various ways through the prophets, 'in these last days he has spoken to us by a Son' (Heb. 1:1-2). For he sent his Son, the eternal Word who enlightens all men, to dwell among men and to tell them about the inner life of God. Hence, Jesus Christ, sent as 'a man among men,' 'speaks the words of God' (Jn. 3:34), and accomplishes the saving work which the Father gave him to do (cf. Jn. 5:36; 17:4). As a result, he himself — to see whom is to see the Father (cf. Jn. 14:9) — completed and perfected Revelation and confirmed it with divine guarantees. He did this by the total fact of his presence and self-manifestation — by words and works, signs and miracles — but above all by his death and glorious resurrection from the dead, and finally by sending the Spirit of truth. He revealed that God was with us, to

See Papally Promulgated
Catechism of the Catholic Church

Q. 27. See paragraphs: 238, 240

deliver us from the darkness of sin and death, and to raise us up to eternal life." *Divine Revelation, 4*

Sacred Scripture

"God, Who, at various times and in various ways, spoke in times past to the fathers by the prophets, last of all, in these days has spoken to us by His Son, Whom He appointed heir of all things, by Whom also He made the world." *Hebrews 1:1-2*

"And I will ask the Father, and He shall give you another Paraclete, that He may abide with you forever; the Spirit of truth, Whom the world cannot receive because it does not see Him or know Him. But you shall know Him, because He shall abide with you and shall be in you." *John 14:16-17*

Jesus Reveals Himself

Q. 28. What principally did Jesus reveal about Himself?

Jesus principally revealed Himself as the eternal and divine Son of God.

Sacred Scripture

"I and the Father are one." *John 10:30*

"All things the Father has are Mine." *John 16:15*

"He that sees Me sees the Father also." *John 14:9*

"And now glorify Me, Father with Yourself, with the glory which I had with You before the world was." *John 17:5*

"For God so loved the world, as to give His only begotten Son; that whoever believes in Him, may not perish, but may have life everlasting." *John 3:16*

Vatican Council II

"Christ established on earth the kingdom of God, revealed

See Papally Promulgated
Catechism of the Catholic Church

Q. 28. See paragraphs: 443, 445

his Father and himself by deeds and words; and by his death, resurrection and glorious ascension, as well as by sending the Holy Spirit, completed his work." *Divine Revelation, 17*

Jesus Reveals the Father

Q. 29. How did Jesus reveal the Father?

Jesus revealed the Father by calling Him by that name.

When Jesus drove the money changers from the temple, He said, "Do not make My Father's house a trading place" (John 2:16).

He said to His disciples, "In this is My Father glorified; that you bring forth much fruit, and become My disciples. As the Father has loved Me, I also have loved you. Abide in My love" (John 15:8-9).

Jesus taught us to love our heavenly Father because He loves us and wants to help us in all the needs of our body and soul. He wants to bring His children to His heavenly home.

Jesus Reveals the Holy Spirit

Q. 30. What did Jesus reveal about the Holy Spirit?

Jesus revealed the Holy Spirit as the third Divine Person of the Holy Trinity Whom the Father and He, as the Risen Lord, would send to teach, guide and strengthen His Church, the Mystical Body of Christ.

Jesus taught that God the Holy Spirit was the equal of Himself and the Father. At the Last Supper Jesus told the Apostles:

"But the Paraclete, the Holy Spirit Whom the Father will send in My Name, He will teach you all things, and bring all things to your mind, whatsoever I shall have said to you."

John 14:26

See Papally Promulgated
Catechism of the Catholic Church

Q. 29. See paragraphs: 238-242
Q. 30. See paragraphs: 243, 687

"But when the Paraclete comes Whom I will send you from the Father, the Spirit of truth, Who proceeds from the Father, He shall give testimony of Me." *John 15:26*

Prayer

*F*ather, all-powerful and ever-living God, when Your children sinned and wandered from Your friendship, You reunited them with Yourself through the Blood of Your Son and the power of the Holy Spirit. You gather them into Your Church to be one as You, Father, are one with Your Son and the Holy Spirit. You call them to be Your people, to praise Your wisdom in all Your works. You make them the Body of Christ and the dwelling-place of the Holy Spirit.

*F*ather, all-powerful and ever-living God, we joyfully proclaim our faith in the mystery of Your Godhead. You have revealed Your glory as the glory also of Your Son and of the Holy Spirit: three Persons equal in majesty, undivided in splendor, yet one Lord, one God, ever to be adored in Your everlasting glory. With all the choirs of angels in Heaven we proclaim Your glory, through Jesus Christ our Savior to Whom with You and the Holy Spirit be all honor and glory. Amen.

Chapter Seven

The Holy Trinity: Father, Son and Holy Spirit

Q. 31. What did Jesus, the Divine Teacher, teach His disciples about God: God the Father, God the Son and God the Holy Spirit?

Jesus, the Divine Teacher, taught His disciples about the true God, and that He, His Son, is the way to Him, i.e., to the Father. By getting to know Jesus, they would get to know the Father also. They would also be able to see the love of the Father in the actions of Jesus, because Jesus said that He and His Father were one.

Jesus also taught His disciples about becoming sons of God through the gift of the Spirit. Jesus calls us as well to become sons (or children) of God. We do this through a new life which He gives us. This new life is God's own life, given to us by the Holy Spirit. This is called "grace" or "sanctifying grace" or "habitual grace." Because Jesus is the Son of God, He is able to give us a share of God's life and to make us children of God.*

Sacred Scripture

"Philip said to Him, 'Lord, show us the Father, and it is enough for us.' Jesus said to him, 'Have I been with you such a long time and you have not known Me? Philip, he that sees Me sees the Father also. Why do you say, 'Show us the Father'? Do you not believe that I am in the Father, and the Father in Me? The words that I speak to you, I speak not of

---

[Editorial Note: Quite often, when the word "God," by itself, is used in Scripture or in the Church's liturgy, it refers solely to God the Father.]

See Papally Promulgated
Catechism of the Catholic Church

Q. 31. See paragraphs: 240, 243, 423, 443

Myself. But the Father who abides in Me does the works. Do you not believe that I am in the Father and the Father in Me? Otherwise believe for the very works' sake. Amen, amen, I say to you, he that believes in Me, the works that I do, he also shall do, and greater than these he shall do. Because I go to the Father, and whatsoever you ask the Father in My Name, that I will do, that the Father may be glorified in the Son. If you shall ask anything in My Name that I will do.

"If you love Me, keep my commandments. And I will ask the Father, and He will give you another Paraclete, that He may abide with you forever, the Spirit of truth, Whom the world cannot receive because it does not see Him, nor know Him. But you shall know Him, because He will abide with you and be in you." *John 14:8-17*

"But as many as received Him, He gave them power to be made the sons of God." *John 1:12*

"For you have not received the spirit of bondage again in fear; but you have received the spirit of adoption of sons, whereby we cry, 'Abba [Father].' " *Romans 8:15*

Vatican Council II

"After God had spoken many times and in various ways through the prophets, 'in these last days he has spoken to us by a Son' (Heb. 1:1-2). For he sent his Son, the eternal Word who enlightens all men, to dwell among men and to tell them about the inner life of God. Hence, Jesus Christ, sent as 'a man among men,' 'speaks the words of God' (Jn. 3:34), and accomplishes the saving work which the Father gave him to do (cf. Jn. 5:36; 17:4). As a result, he himself – to see whom is to see the Father (cf. Jn. 14:9) – completed and perfected Revelation and confirmed it with divine guarantes. He did this by the total fact of his presence and self-manifestation – by words and works, signs and miracles – but above all by his death and glorious resurrection from the dead, and finally by sending the Spirit of truth. He revealed that God was with us, to deliver us from the darkness of sin and death, and to raise us up to eternal life." *Divine Revelation, 4*

"When the work which the Father gave the Son to do on earth (cf. Jn. 17:4) was accomplished, the Holy Spirit was sent on the day of Pentecost in order that he might continually sanctify the Church, and that, consequently, those who believe might have access through Christ in one Spirit to the

Father (cf. Eph. 2:18). He is the Spirit of life, the fountain of water springing up to eternal life." *The Church, 4*

Q. 32. Who is God the Father?

God the Father is the First Person of the Holy Trinity Who eternally begets or generates God the Son.

This begetting is similar to a person who begets an idea or work in his mind.

Vatican Council II

"This plan flows from 'fountain-like love,' the love of God the Father. As the principle without principle from whom the Son is generated and from whom the Holy Spirit proceeds through the Son, God in his great and merciful kindness freely creates us and moreover, graciously calls us to share in his life and glory." *Missionary Activity, 2*

Q. 33. Who is God the Son?

God the Son is the Second Person of the Holy Trinity, because from all eternity He is begotten in the mind of the Father.

He is called the Divine Word because He is the mental word in which God the Father expresses the thought of Himself; this thought or Word being the perfect and eternal Image of the Father.

Q. 34. Who is God the Holy Spirit?

God the Holy Spirit is the Third Person of the Holy Trinity.

He is infinitely perfect, living Love which flows or proceeds eternally from the Father and the Son as love personified. He is the love of the Trinity.

See Papally Promulgated
Catechism of the Catholic Church

Q. 32. See paragraphs: 238-248, 279
Q. 33. See paragraphs: 422-483
Q. 34. See paragraphs: 243-248, 687-701, 737-741

Prayer

Most Merciful Father, in loving gratitude for all that You have accomplished for our salvation through Jesus Christ our Lord, we pray for the fullness of the gifts of the Holy Spirit, that we may praise You as we ought, as we await the full outcome of Your divine purposes; for You indeed are our God together with God the Son and God the Holy Spirit. To You, Tirune God, be all honor and glory, now and forever. Amen.

Chapter Eight

How We Honor the Holy Trinity

Q. 35. How do we honor the Holy Trinity?

We honor the Holy Trinity by trying to remember the presence of God the Father, God the Son, and God the Holy Spirit in our souls.

We honor the Holy Trinity by trying to understand, as much as we can by faith, that by Baptism we are called to a close union of love with the three Divine Persons. God, the Holy Trinity, Who is closer to us than we are to ourselves, lives in our soul by grace. God the Father is our Father and Author of Life; God the Son is our Lord and Savior; and God the Holy Spirit is our Teacher and Guide.

Jesus said, "If any one loves Me, he will keep My word, and My Father will love him, and We will come to him, and will make Our home with him" (John 14:23).

"And I will ask the Father and He shall give you another Paraclete, that He may abide with you for ever" (John 14:16).

We show our love for the Holy Trinity when we pray. We may pray simply as the Church does most often — to the Father, through the Son, in union with the Holy Spirit.

Sacred Scripture

"For no man can lay another foundation than that which is laid; which is Christ Jesus." *1 Corinthians 3:11*

Vatican Council II

"Thus by Baptism men are grafted into the paschal mystery of Christ; they die with him, are buried with him, and rise with him. They receive the spirit of adoption as sons 'in which we cry, Abba, Father' (Rom. 8:15) and thus become true adorers such as the Father seeks." *Sacred Liturgy, 6*

See Papally Promulgated
Catechism of the Catholic Church

Q. 35. See paragraphs: 1239, 2655, 2662-2672, 2705-2708, 2789

Prayer: *Most Holy Trinity, one true God in three Divine Persons, help us to honor You by trying to remember Your presence in our souls. Help us to show our love for You, Father, Son, and Holy Spirit, by frequent prayer. Help us to show our love for You by trying to understand, as much as we can through faith, that through Baptism we are called to a close union of love with You, for You live in our souls by grace. God, You are our Father. Jesus Christ, You are our Lord and Savior. Holy Spirit, You are our Teacher and Guide.*

Father, Son and Holy Spirit, Holy Trinity, merciful Friend of mankind, grant that we may stand before You in purity and holiness and reverently serve You as our God, to Whom worship is due from all, now and forever. Amen.

Prayer

Father, You revealed Your Son to the nations by the guidance of a star. Lead us to Your glory in Heaven by the light of faith.

Father of light, unchanging God, You revealed to men of faith the resplendent fact of the Word made flesh. Your light is strong, Your love is near; draw us beyond the limits which this world imposes to the life where Your Spirit makes all life complete.

Almighty Father, eternal God, when the Spirit descended upon Jesus at His baptism in the Jordan River, You revealed Him as Your own beloved Son. Keep us, Your children born of water and the Spirit, faithful to our calling. May all who share in the sonship of Christ follow in His path of service to man, and reflect the glory of His Kingdom even to the ends of the earth.

Accept the prayers of Your servants, Lord, and prepare our hearts to praise Your Holy Name. Come to our aid in times of trouble, and make us worthy to praise Your Holy Name.

Father, You sent Your Word to bring us truth and Your Spirit to make us holy. Through Them we come to know the mystery of Your life. Help us to worship You, one God in three Persons, by proclaiming and living our faith in You.

God, we praise You: Father all-powerful; Christ, Lord and Savior; and Spirit of love. You reveal Yourself in the depths of our being, drawing us to share in Your life and Your love. One God, three Persons, be near to the people formed in Your image, close to the world Your love brings to life.

We worship You, O Trinity of Persons, one eternal God. May our faith and the Sacrament of the Eucharist we receive bring us health of mind and body, now and forever. Amen.

The Creation
of Man

Chapter Nine

The Creation

Q. 36. What is creation?

Creation means that God brought all things into existence, and He keeps them in existence. We owe all that we have to God. Creation means that God made the whole universe out of nothing. Only God, Whose power is without limit, can do that.

In the beginning God said, "Let there be light," and there was light. "Let there be a firmament made amid the waters, and let it divide the waters from the waters," and so it happened (cf. Genesis 1:3, 6).

Sacred Scripture

"My son, look upon heaven and earth and all that is in them. And consider that God made them out of nothing, and mankind also." *2 Maccabees 7:28*

Vatican Council II

"The eternal Father, in accordance with the utterly gratuitous and mysterious design of his wisdom and goodness, created the whole universe, and chose to raise up men to share in his own divine life." *The Church, 2*

Prayer: *Heavenly Father, creation is the way You gave both life and the world to man. All that we see about us and all that we have are from You. You are the Lord of life and of the universe.*

Not only do You bring all things into existence, but You keep them in existence. If You should withdraw from any of Your creatures, they would fall back into the nothingness from which they came. For our

See Papally Promulgated
Catechism of the Catholic Church

Q. 36. See paragraphs: 279-301

Q. 37. Can man come to know God through created things?

Yes (among other ways), God makes Himself known to us through the things He has made.

Sacred Scripture says that man can come to know God through created things.

The Church teaches that from thinking about created things, man can come to know God as the beginning and end of all that is.

The Church also teaches that created things around us help us to see that the One who made them is God and that He can do all things. If we really love God, we will try to learn as much as we can about Him, including learning about Him from the things He made.

Sacred Scripture

"The heavens show forth the glory of God, and the firmament declares the work of His hands. Day to day utters speech, and night to night displays knowledge." *Psalm 19:2-3*

"For from the creation of the world, the invisible things of Him are clearly perceived; His external power also, and divinity being understood by the things that are made."

Romans 1:20

"But all men are vain, in whom there is no knowledge of God. And who by the good things that are seen could not understand Him that is. Neither by considering the works have acknowledged Who was the Workman, but have imagined ei-

See Papally Promulgated
Catechism of the Catholic Church

Q. 37. See paragraphs: 31-35

ther the fire or the wind, or the swift air, or the circle of the stars, or the great water, or the sun and moon, to be the gods that rule the world.

"With whose beauty, if they, being delighted, took them to be gods, let them know how much the Lord of them is more beautiful than they are. For the first Author of beauty made all those things.

"Or if they admired their power and their effects, let them understand by them, that He that made them is mightier than they are. For by the greatness of the beauty and of the creature, the Creator of them may be seen, so as to be known thereby.

"But yet as to these they are less to be blamed, for they perhaps err, seeking God and desirous to find Him. For being conversant among His works, they search, and they are persuaded that the things are good which are seen.

"But then again they are not to be pardoned. For if they were able to know so much as to make a judgment of the world, how did they not more easily find out its Lord?"

Wisdom 13: 1-9

Vatican Council II

"The sacred Synod professes that 'God, the first principle and last end of all things, can be known with certainty from the created world, by the natural light of human reason' (cf. Rom. 1:20). It teaches that it is to His Revelation that we must attribute the fact 'that those things, which in themselves are not beyond the grasp of human reason, can, in the present condition of the human race, be known by all men with ease, with firm certainty, and without the contamination of error' (First Vatican Council, Dogm. Const. on Cath. Faith, 2)." *Divine Revelation, 6*

Prayer: *Almighty God and Father, we believe that from thinking about the things You have created we can come to know You as the beginning and end of all that exists. You love us by making Yourself known to us in creation. Created things around us help us to see that You are God and that You can do all things. We love You, our Creator, and we want to try to learn as much as we can about You, even from the things You made. Enrich us all from the fullness of Your eternal wisdom and power, through Jesus Christ our Lord. Amen.*

Prayer

Father, all powerful and ever-living God, all things are of Your making. All times and seasons obey Your laws. You know the number of the stars and call each of them by name. We believe that You made the whole universe out of nothing, for Your power is without limit. You created all things in wonderful beauty and order.

You have placed all the powers of nature under the control of man and his work. May we reflect you in all our efforts and work with our brothers and sisters at our common tasks, establishing Your love and guiding Your creation to perfect fulfillment.

By the human labor we offer You, join us to the saving work of Christ, Who is Lord forever. Guide and govern us by Your help in this life as You have renewed us by the mystery of eternal life, through the same Christ our Lord. Amen.

Chapter Ten

Angelic Creation and the Fall of the Bad Angels

Q. 38. What is the beginning of the mystery of salvation?

The creation of angels and of the world is the beginning of the mystery of salvation.

We fallen creatures quite often think of salvation only in terms of being saved from sin and hell. But more importantly, we are saved for something, namely God, and to share in His happiness for all eternity. This is the end for which mankind and the angels were first created. God's plan for our salvation was at work in the universe from the first moment of its creation. Creation itself, for instance, points to God its Maker. This fact, known by God from all eternity, would later help many fallen humans recognize the One to Whom they owe their primary allegiance (Cf. Romans 1:18-20).

Q. 39. Who are the angels?

Angels are pure spirits, that is, beings with minds and wills, but without bodies. Angels are complete persons without bodies or the need for bodies, far superior to human beings.

Long before God created man, He made the angels. They had brilliant minds to understand God's goodness and beauty; they had free wills to love and praise Him.

God created the angels with free wills so that they might be able to make acts of love for God, freely choosing to serve Him. Only after they had done so would they see God face to face, and enter into that everlasting union with God which we call Heaven.

See Papally Promulgated
Catechism of the Catholic Church

Q. 38. See paragraphs: 27, 198, 289, 332, 342
Q. 39. See paragraphs: 328-336

The Bible tells us that the number of angels is very great. It says, "Thousands of thousands ministered to Him, and ten thousand times a hundred thousand stood before Him" (Daniel 7:10).

Sacred Scripture

"And I beheld, and I heard the voice of many angels round about the throne, and the living creatures, and the ancients; and the number of them was thousands of thousands, saying with a loud voice, 'The Lamb that was slain is worthy to receive power, divinity, wisdom, strength, honor, glory, and benediction.' "*Revelation 5:11-12*

The Bible mentions four important angels by name: (1) Gabriel, who announced to Mary that she was to be the Mother of God; (2) Raphael, who accompanied Tobias on his journey to Media and brought him home safely with a new bride; (3) Michael, who drove (4) satan* into hell when he and other angels rebelled against God. St. Michael is the special protector of the Catholic Church.

Q. 40. Who are the devils?

The devils are fallen angels, enemies of mankind. Their efforts are directed toward leading people into their own rebellion against God.

God has not made known to us the test to which the angels were put prior to the fall of the devils. Some Church Fathers and theologians have speculated that God the Father gave the angels a preview of Jesus Christ, the Redeemer of the human race, and commanded that they adore Him. They, perhaps, could not bring themselves to make an act of adoration of Jesus Christ and rebelled against the Father's plan of salvation.

---

* *[Editorial note - Satan is the name of the principal fallen angel.]*

See Papally Promulgated
Catechism of the Catholic Church

Q. 40. See paragraphs: 391-393

Led by one of the most gifted of all the angels, satan [or Lucifer, that is, Lightbearer], many of the angels turned away from God. Satan cried out, "I will not serve!" Then the Archangel Michael took up the battle cry: "Who is like God?". Michael and the good angels cast the rebellious angels out from heaven. "And there was a great battle in heaven. Michael and his angels fought with the dragon, and the dragon fought, and his angels. And they did not prevail, neither was there found a place any more in heaven. And that great dragon was cast out, that old serpent, who is called the devil and satan, who seduces the whole world. And he was cast onto the earth, and his angels were thrown down with him" (Revelation 12:7-9).

There was no second chance for the sinning angels. By their willful rejection of God, their wills were fixed against Him forever. They did not and do not want to turn back. There burns in them an everlasting hatred for God and all His works.

The devils tempt us to commit sin, but they can never force us to do so. They cannot get inside the human soul and use it to suit themselves. They cannot destroy our freedom of choice, but they are enemies to be feared. They still have great intelligence and power.

Sacred Scripture

"Be sober and watch, because your adversary the devil, as a roaring lion, goes about seeking whom he may devour. You must resist, strong in faith: knowing that the same affliction befalls your brethren who are in the world." *I Peter 5:8-9*

"How you have fallen from heaven, O Lucifer, who did rise in the morning. How fallen to the earth, you who wounded the nations. And you said in your heart, 'I will ascend into heaven, I will exalt my throne above the stars of God, I will sit in the mountain of the Covenant, in the sides of the north. I will ascend above the height of the clouds, I will be like the Most High.' "* *Isaiah 14:12-14*

Vatican Council II

"Although set by God in a state of rectitude, man, enticed by the evil one, abused his freedom at the very start of history." *Modern World, 13*

---

* [Editorial note - The literal sense of the text refers to a heavenly light, quite likely to the planet Venus. Traditionally, however, Church writers have treated it allegorically as referring to satan.]

Q. 41. Where are the angels who remained faithful to God?

The angels who remained faithful to God are now with Him in Heaven, engaged in the eternal love and adoration of God which one day will be our joy. Their will always conforms to God's will. The angels pray for us, and use their power to aid those who want and will accept their help.

"See that you despise not one of these little ones. For I say to you that their angels in Heaven always see the face of My Father Who is in Heaven." *Matthew 18:10*

Many of our temptations come from the devil who tries to lead us into eternal damnation. God's good angels help us to overcome these temptations, especially by aiding us to secure God's grace through regular Confession and frequent Holy Communion, prayer, and good works.

We believe that each of us has an individual guardian angel. We should often ask for his help. As we honor God by our devotion to His friends, the saints, we should also honor and invoke the angels, His first masterpieces. We need the help of the angels to reach the heavenly kingdom. They are gifts of God for us.

See Papally Promulgated
Catechism of the Catholic Church

Q. 41. See paragraphs: 326, 329, 331, 1024

Prayer

God our Father, in a wonderful way, You guide and govern the work of angels and men. May those who serve You constantly in Heaven keep our lives safe and sure on earth. With the care of the angels, especially our guardian angels, may we make progress in the way of salvation.

In praising Your faithful angels and archangels, we also praise Your glory, for in honoring them, we honor You, their Creator. Their splendor shows us Your greatness, which surpasses in goodness the whole of creation.

Through Christ our Lord, the great army of angels rejoices in Your glory. In adoration and joy, we make their hymn of praise our own. "Holy, holy, holy, Lord, God of power and might. Heaven and earth are full of Your glory. Hosanna in the highest!" Amen.

Creation:
Material and
Spiritual

Chapter Eleven

The Creation of Man

Q. 42. How was man created?

After creating the universe, God formed man's body out of the dust of the earth. Then He breathed into him a soul that would never die.*

The story of the creation of the world and man is told in the Book of Genesis. Scripture says that on the sixth day God made all the animals. Then God said, "Let us make man in Our image and likeness. And let him have dominion over the fish of the sea, and the birds of the air, and the beasts, and the whole earth, and every creeping creature that moves upon the earth" (Genesis 1:26).

God gave man a body and a soul. Like the animals, man has a body. And like the spiritual angels, man has a spiritual mind to know his Creator, and a spiritual will to love Him.

Sacred Scripture

"You have crowned him with glory and honor, and have set him over the works of Your hands..." *Psalm 8:6-7*

Prayer: *Lord our God, we believe that after creating the universe You formed man out of the dust of the earth, and then breathed into him a soul that would never die. The spirit that gives us life is an image of You, the infinitely perfect Spirit. Help us to use our minds to know You and our free wills to love You, through our Lord Jesus Christ, to Whom with You and the Holy Spirit be all honor and glory. Amen.*

---

*[Editorial Note: This was not written as a scientific statement, but as a theological truth. Nevertheless, man's body consists of the material elements of the earth. "Dust thou art and to dust thou shalt return."—Genesis 3:19]

See Papally Promulgated
Catechism of the Catholic Church

Q. 42. See paragraphs: 359-362

Q. 43. In what way was man created in the image and likeness of God?

Man is created in the image and likeness of God because he has an immortal soul, which, like God, has a mind and a free will. Moreover, our bodies remind us of the power and wisdom and greatness of God in the perfection of their intricate organization and unity.

Vatican Council II

"Man, though made of body and soul, is a unity. Through his very bodily condition he sums up in himself the elements of the material world. Through him they are thus brought to their highest perfection and can raise their voice in praise freely given to the creator. For this reason man may not despise his bodily life. Rather he is obliged to regard his body as good and to hold it in honor since God has created it and will raise it up on the last day. Nevertheless man has been wounded by sin. He finds by experience that his body is in revolt. His very dignity therefore requires that he should glorify God in his body, and not allow it to serve the evil inclinations of his heart.

"When he is drawn to think about his real self he turns to those deep recesses of his being where God who probes the heart awaits him, and where he himself decides his own destiny in the sight of God. So when he recognizes in himself a spiritual and immortal soul, he is not being led astray by false imaginings that are due to merely physical or social causes. On the contrary, he grasps what is profoundly true in this matter." *Modern World, 14*

Prayer: *Father of everlasting goodness, You have made us into Your own image and likeness. Our bodies remind us of Your power and wisdom and greatness; our souls especially are portraits of You, our*

See Papally Promulgated
Catechism of the Catholic Church

Q. 43. See paragraphs: 355-357, 364

Maker. May we praise You forever, through Jesus Christ our Lord. Amen.

Q. 44. Is the soul directly created by God?

Yes, God personally and directly creates each soul and infuses it into the body.

We must believe that the human race is descended from Adam and Eve, our First Parents, and that Adam's and Eve's souls were directly created by God.

Husbands and wives cooperate with God in the formation of the human body. But the soul, which makes that body a human being, is directly created by God, and given to the tiny body within the mother's womb.

Sacred Scripture

"The potter also, tempering soft earth, with labor fashions every vessel for our service, and of the same clay he makes both vessels that are for clean uses, and likewise such as serve to the contrary: but what the use of these vessels is, the potter is the judge.

"And of the same clay by a vain labor he makes a god: he who a little before was made of earth himself, and a little after returns to the same out of which he was taken, when his life which was lent to him shall be called for again.

"But his care is, not that he shall labor, nor that his life be short, but he strives with the goldsmiths and silversmiths: and he endeavors to do like the workers in brass, and counts it a glory to make vain things.

"For his heart is ashes, and his hope vain earth, and his life more base than clay:

"Forasmuch as he did not know his Maker and Him that inspired into him the soul that works, and breathed into him a living spirit." *Wisdom 15:7-11*

See Papally Promulgated
Catechism of the Catholic Church

Q. 44. See paragraph: 366

Vatican Council II

"For Sacred Scripture teaches that man was created 'to the image of God,' as able to know and love his creator, and as set by him over all earthly creatures [cf. Gen. 1:26; Wis. 2:23] that he might rule them, and make use of them, while glorifying God. 'What is man that thou art mindful of him, and the son of man that thou dost care for him? Yet thou hast made him little less than God, and dost crown him with glory and honor. Thou hast given him dominion over the works of thy hands; thou hast put all things under his feet' (Ps. 8:5-7).

"But God did not create man a solitary being. From the beginning 'male and female he created them' (Genesis 1:27). This partnership of man and woman constitutes the first form of communion between persons. For by his innermost nature man is a social being; and if he does not enter into relations with others he can neither live nor develop his gifts.

"So God, as we read again in the Bible, saw 'all the things that he had made, and they were very good' (Gen. 1:31)."

Modern World, 12

Prayer: *Lord of Heaven and earth, in Your love You created man. Through Your beloved Son You created our human family. Through Him You restore us to Your likeness. Therefore it is Your right to receive the obedience of all creation, the praise of the Church on earth, and the thanksgiving of Your saints in Heaven, through the same Christ our Lord. Amen.*

Prayer

Creator and ruler of Heaven and earth, You made man in Your likeness to subdue the earth and master it, and to recognize the work of Your hands in created beauty. Grant that Your children, thus surrounded on all sides by signs of Your presence, may live continually in Christ, praising You through Him and with Him.

God, devoted to us as a Father, You created us as a sign of Your power and elected us, Your people, to show Your goodness. Accept the thanks Your children offer, that all men may enter Your courts, praising You in song.

We thank You for Your blessings in the past and for all that, with Your help, we must yet achieve through Christ our Lord. Amen.

Chapter Twelve

Our First Parents: Adam and Eve

Q. 45. What special gifts did Adam and Eve receive?

The special gifts received from God by Adam and Eve were wisdom or a clear knowledge of God, strength of will and control of the senses and the emotions, as well as freedom from suffering and death.

God's plan was that when their years of life in paradise were ended, Adam and Eve would then enter into eternal life, body and soul, without having to die. Most of all, they received a new kind of life because of their union with God. God let His love flow into their souls. This supernatural life is called sanctifying, or habitual, grace. With this grace they would know God as He is, face to face, after their life on earth had ended.

Vatican Council II

"While the mind is at a loss before the mystery of death, the Church, taught by divine Revelation, declares that God has created man in view of a blessed destiny that lies beyond the limits of his sad state on earth. Moreover, the Christian faith teaches that bodily death, from which man would have been immune had he not sinned, will be overcome when that wholeness which he lost through his own fault will be given once again to him by the almighty and merciful Saviour."

Modern World, 18

> **Prayer:** *Father of everlasting goodness, our origin and guide, You created Adam and Eve as a sign of Your power and to show Your goodness. We thank You for the special gifts You bestowed upon our First Parents: for wisdom, strength of will, freedom from suffering and death, and sanctifying grace. It was Your will that all of their*

See Papally Promulgated
Catechism of the Catholic Church

Q. 45. See paragraphs: 356-361, 369-370, 374-383, 402-403

children should enjoy these blessings. You made all human beings that they might give glory to You by their love for You. But Adam failed to give his love to You. He failed the test of obedience and committed the first sin. Thankfully, however, You, Father, have redeemed us through Your Incarnate Son, Who is the New Adam, in cooperation with Mary, the New Eve. May all glory, honor and praise be to You, to Jesus, and the Holy Spirit, now and forever. Amen.

Q. 46. What commandment did Adam and Eve receive?

God gave Adam and Eve a commandment. They were not to eat the fruit that grew on a certain tree.

In this life, love for God can prove itself by doing God's will, by being obedient to Him. But Adam and Eve failed the test. They committed the first sin — the original sin.

Sacred Scripture

"For God did not make death." *Wisdom 1:13*

"By one man sin entered into the world and by sin death. And so death passed upon all men." *Romans 5:12*

See Papally Promulgated
Catechism of the Catholic Church

Q. 46. See paragraphs: 396-409

Prayer

Heavenly Father, teach us that in this life we must prove our love for You by doing Your will and being obedient to Your commandments.

Moreover, You have taught us that faith in Your word is the way to wisdom, and to ponder Your divine plan is to grow in the truth. Open our eyes to Your deeds, and our hearts to the sound of Your call, so that our every act may increase our sharing in the life You have offered us. Heal hearts that are broken; gather together those who have been scattered, and enrich us all from the fullness of Your wisdom. It is Your right to receive the obedience of all creation, the praise of all those You have made in Your own image and likeness.

You made man in Your own image and set him over all creation. We praise You as the God of creation, as the Father of Jesus, the Savior of mankind, in Whose image we seek to live. We thank You for the blessings You have bestowed on mankind, through the same Jesus our Lord. Amen.

Chapter Thirteen

The Creation of Man: God's First Gift Leading to Christ

Q. 47. What is the first gift of God leading us to Christ?

The creation of man is the first gift of God leading us to Christ.

If God had not created our First Parents, there would have been no need for God to become man in order to save us. Why not?...because there would have been no humans to be saved from sin and eternal death, and there would have been no humans to whom God could reveal the fullness of divine love.

Jesus Christ is the One Whom God the Father sent to lead people to Him. It is only through Jesus that we can be saved. That is why we can say that the creation of man is the first gift of God leading us to Christ.

Sacred Scripture

"We glory in God, through our Lord Jesus Christ, by whom we have now received reconciliation. Wherefore as by one man, sin entered into this world, and by sin death. And so death passed upon all men, since all have sinned." *Romans 5:11-12*

Vatican Council II

"For sacred Scripture teaches that man was created 'to the image of God,' as able to know and love his creator, and as set by him over all earthly creatures that he might rule them, and make use of them, while glorifying God. 'What is man that thou are mindful of him, and the son of man that thou dost care for him? Yet thou hast made him little less than God, and dost crown him with glory and honor. Thou hast given him dominion over the works of thy hands; thou hast put all things under his feet' (Ps. 8:5-8).

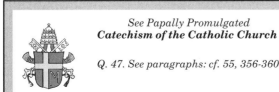

See Papally Promulgated
Catechism of the Catholic Church

Q. 47. See paragraphs: cf. 55, 356-360

"Although sent by God in a state of rectitude, man, enticed by the evil one, abused his freedom at the very start of history. He lifted himself up against God, and sought to attain his goal apart from him. Although they had known God, they did not glorify him as God, but their senseless hearts were darkened, and they served the creature rather that the creator. What Revelation makes known to us is confirmed by our own experience. For when man looks into his own heart he finds that he is drawn towards what is wrong and sunk in many evils which cannot come from his good creator. Often refusing to acknowledge God as his source, man has also upset the relationship which should link him to his last end; and at the same time he has broken the right order that should reign within himself as well as between himself and other men and all creatures.

"Man therefore is divided in himself. As a result, the whole life of men, both individual and social, shows itself to be a struggle, and a dramatic one, between good and evil, between light and darkness. Man finds that he is unable of himself to overcome the assaults of evil successfully, so that everyone feels as though bound by chains. But the Lord himself came to free and strengthen man, renewing him inwardly and casting out the 'prince of this world' (Jn. 12:31), who held him in bondage of sin. For sin brought man to a lower state, forcing him away from the completeness that is his to attain.

"Both the high calling and the deep misery which men experience find their final explanation in the light of this Revelation." *Modern World, 13*

"While the mind is at a loss before the mystery of death, the Church, taught by divine Revelation, declares that God has created man in view of a blessed destiny that lies beyond the limits of his sad state on earth. Moreover, the Christian faith teaches that bodily death, from which man would have been immune had he not sinned, will be overcome when that wholeness which he has lost through his own fault will be given once again to him by the almighty and merciful Saviour. For God has called man, and still calls him, to cleave with all his being to him in sharing forever a life that is divine and free from all decay. Christ won this victory when he rose to life, for by his death he freed man from death. Faith, therefore, with its solidly based teaching, provides every thoughtful man with an answer to his anxious queries about his future lot. At the same time it makes him able to be united in

Christ with his loved ones who have already died, and gives hope that they have found true life with God." *Modern World, 18*

Prayer

*L*ord God, we praise You for creating us human beings, and still more for restoring us in Christ. Through Your Catholic Church, You always work to save us, and now we rejoice in the great love You give us, Your chosen people. Protect all who have become Your children, and continue to bless those who are baptized.

*I*n the Sacrament of Baptism, You restore us to life. Forgive our sins, and fulfill our hopes and desires. We thank You for calling us to share in Your divine life.

*F*ather in Heaven, You prepared the Virgin Mary to be the worthy mother of Your Son. You let her share beforehand in the salvation Christ would bring by His death, and kept her sinless from the first moment of her conception. Help us by her prayers to live in Your presence without sin. Father, help us to be like Christ, Your Son, Who loved the world, and died for our salvation. Inspire us by His love and guide us by His example. The love of Your Son led Him to accept the suffering of the Cross so that His brothers might glory in new life. All glory be to the Father, to the Son, and to the Holy Spirit. Amen.

Chapter Fourteen

God's Presence in Created History

Q. 48. What did the action of God in the Old Testament show and prove?

The action of God in the Old Testament showed His divine power or omnipotence, and proved that He is always with His people.

In the Old Testament, God's people learned the truth of God's almighty power in creation.

This reminded the people that God always remains with His people to protect and help them. His wonderful deeds of power and victory show that He kept His promises, and that He loved His people.

After speaking through the Old Testament prophets, God the Father sent our Savior, Jesus Christ, Who is God the Son made man. Being both God and man, Jesus gave us the "Good News" of salvation. This message is found in the New Testament. By His words and actions, Jesus made known the deepest truths about God. The Blessed Trinity of the Father, Son and Holy Spirit is the deepest of all these truths.

Sacred Scripture

"Why do you say, O Jacob, and exclaim, O Israel, 'My way is hid from the Lord, and my judgment is passed over from my God?' Do you not know or have you not heard? The Lord is the everlasting God, Who created the ends of the earth. He shall not faint, nor labor, neither is there any searching out of His wisdom. It is He that gives strength to the weary, and increases force and might to those that are not." *Isaiah 40:27-29*

"I, I myself will comfort you. Who are you, that you should be afraid of a mortal man, and of the son of man, who shall wither away like grass? And have you forgotten the Lord,

See Papally Promulgated
Catechism of the Catholic Church

Q. 48. See paragraphs: 56-64, 761-762

your Maker, who stretched out the heavens, and founded the earth?" *Isaiah 51:12-13*

Vatican Council II

"In his fatherly care for all of us, God desired that all men should form one family and deal with each other in a spirit of brotherhood. All, in fact, are destined to the very same end, namely God himself, since they have been created in the likeness of God who 'made from one every nation of men who live on all the face of the earth (Acts 17:26)." *Modern World, 24*

"God, who creates and conserves all things by his Word, (cf. Jn. 1:3), provides men with constant evidence of himself in created realities (cf. Rom. 1:19-20). And furthermore, wishing to open up the way to heavenly salvation, he manifested himself to our first parents from the very beginning. After the fall, he buoyed them up with the hope of salvation, by promising redemption (cf. Gen. 3:15); and he has never ceased to take care of the human race. For he wishes to give eternal life to all those who seek salvation by patience in well-doing (cf. Rom. 2:6-7). In his own time God called Abraham, and made him into a great nation (cf. Gen. 12-2). After the era of the patriarchs, he taught this nation, by Moses and the prophets, to recognize him as the only living and true God, as a provident Father and just judge. He taught them, too, to look for the promised Saviour. And so, throughout the ages, he prepared the way for the Gospel." *Divine Revelation, 3*

> **Prayer:** *Almighty Father, Your power in creation reminds Your people that You remain always with them to protect and help them. Your wonderful deeds of power showed that You kept Your promises and that You loved Your people.*
>
> *But Your all-powerful action for our salvation is especially seen in the coming of Your Son, Jesus Christ, Who told us about our hope of salvation. He made known the deepest truths about You, especially about the Blessed Trinity. May all glory and honor be given to you, Father, Son, and Holy Spirit, now and forever. Amen.*

Q. 49. Where is the all-powerful action of God for our salvation seen especially?

The all-powerful action of God for our salvation is seen especially in Christ's Resurrection from the dead.

Though man was made by God in a state of holiness, he turned against God, of his own free will, being led to do so by the evil spirit. God sent His Son to free man from the slavery of sin and to make him holy again. He did this through the sufferings and death of Jesus and through His glorious Resurrection. In this way God showed His all-powerful action for our salvation.

Vatican Council II

"The wonderful works of God among the people of the Old Testament were but a prelude to the work of Christ our Lord in redeeming mankind and giving perfect glory to God. He achieved his task principally by the paschal mystery of his blessed passion, resurrection from the dead, and glorious ascension, whereby by 'dying, he destroyed our death, and rising, restored our life.' " *Sacred Liturgy, 5*

Q. 50. How should we look upon creation?

We should look upon creation as God's continuing action, from the beginning of time till the end, as He works out the salvation and destiny of man.

When we think of the creation of the angels, the world, and man, we should see it as part of God's all-powerful work in the salvation of mankind. His great love for man led Him to create and save him. The whole work of salvation receives its meaning from Jesus Christ, the Incarnate Word. That work, beginning with the creation of the world, showed itself especially in Christ's coming, His life on earth, His death and Resurrection, and will show itself especially at His second glorious coming, which will complete the work of God.

Vatican Council II

"God, who creates and conserves all things by his Word, (cf. Jn. 1:3), provides men with constant evidence of himself in created realities (cf. Rom. 1:19-20)." *Divine Revelation, 3*

"The Church, taught by divine Revelation, declares that

See Papally Promulgated
Catechism of the Catholic Church

Q. 49. See paragraphs: 638-658
Q. 50. See paragraphs: 302-324

God has created man in view of a blessed destiny that lies beyond the limits of his sad state on earth." *Modern World, 18*

Q. 51. How was God specially present in human history?

God was specially present in the history of Israel: God worked powerfully in the life, death, and Resurrection of His Incarnate Son.

When we think about creation, we not only should think of God's act of making the world, but we should turn our mind to all that He did to save the people in this world. His deeds of salvation can be seen in the history of man and of the world, especially in the history of Israel. They lead to the most important events of Our Lord's life, His death and Resurrection.

Vatican Council II

"The Word of God, through whom all things were made, became man and dwelt among men: a perfect man, he entered world history, taking that history into himself and recapitulating it. He reveals to us that 'God is love' (1 Jn. 4:8) and at the same time teaches that the fundamental law of human perfection, and consequently of the transformation of the world, is the new commandment of love." *Modern World, 38*

Q. 52. How is God present among us today?

God is present among us today using His limitless power to help us. He will finish His saving work only at the end of the world.

The life, death, and Resurrection of Jesus are the most important events of all time, through which God shows Himself and His love for man. He also shows Himself in other events which are found in the Bible and in the life of the Church. God will continue to be present among us, showing His power and His love.

Vatican Council II

"Therefore, the world which the Council has in mind is the

See Papally Promulgated
Catechism of the Catholic Church

Q. 51. See paragraphs: 62-64, 218-219, 518
Q. 52. See paragraphs: 763-776, 830-838

whole human family..., the world, which in the Christian vision has been created and is sustained by the love of its maker, which has been freed from the slavery of sin by Christ, who was crucified and rose again in order to break the stranglehold of the evil one, so that it might be fashioned anew according to God's design and brought to its fulfillment."

Modern World, 2

"The Church holds that to acknowledge God is in no way to oppose the dignity of man, since such dignity is grounded and brought to perfection in God. Man has in fact been placed in society by God, who created him as an intelligent and free being; but over and above this he is called as a son to intimacy with God and to share in his happiness." *Modern World, 21*

Prayer

God and Father of all who believe in You, You promised Abraham that he would become the father of many nations, and through the death and Resurrection of Christ, You fulfill that promise. Everywhere throughout the world You increase Your Chosen People. May we respond to Your call by joyfully accepting Your invitation to the new life of grace.

Jesus freed us from the slavery of sin and made it possible for us to be holy again through His sufferings and death, and through His glorious Resurrection. We see creation as Your continuing action as You work out the salvation of mankind.

You are now present in human history using Your limitless power to help us. Save us from our sins. Protect us from all dangers and lead us to salvation. Teach us to live by Your wisdom and to love the things of Heaven by our sharing in the mystery of the Eucharist. We ask this through Jesus Christ our Lord. Amen.

The Sins of Man: Original Sin and Personal Sin

The Sacraments and sacramentals will give us the strength to avoid sin.

Chapter Fifteen

The Fall of Man and Original Sin

Q. 53. How was original sin committed?

Adam, the first man, abused his liberty by disobeying and rejecting God's care. He wanted to search for happiness in his own way. This, coupled with the sin of Eve, constituted the "original sin."

God made man in a state of holiness, but man abused his liberty. He set himself against God and looked for happiness apart from God.

Man was the crown of God's creation; of all God's creatures on earth, he alone could give back to God the love which God first gave him. God wanted men to live as His family, united to each other and to Himself in love. Nothing was to harm this family: sickness, death, ignorance or weakness.

Sacred Scripture

"And to Adam He said, 'Because you have listened to the voice of your wife, and have eaten of the tree, which I commanded you not to eat, cursed will be the earth in your work; with labor and toil you shall eat from it all the days of your life. In the sweat from your face you shall eat bread till you return to the earth, out of which you were taken. For dust you are, and into dust you shall return.'" *Genesis 3:17,19*

"Wherefore as by one man, in whom all have sinned, sin entered into this world, and by sin death; and so death passed upon all men." *Romans 5:12*

Vatican Council II

"Although set by God in a state of rectitude, man, enticed by the evil one, abused his freedom at the very start of history. He lifted himself up against God, and sought to attain his

See Papally Promulgated
Catechism of the Catholic Church

Q. 53. See paragraphs: 397-401

goal apart from him. Although they had known God, they did not glorify him as God, but their senseless hearts were darkened, and they served the creature rather than the creator."

Modern World, 13

Prayer: *Loving Creator, in Your infinite goodness You made man in a state of holiness. Man was the crown of Your visible creation, for he alone could give back to You the love which You first gave him. For this we give You thanks through Christ our Lord. Amen.*

Q. 54. Why are all men conceived and born in original sin?

When Adam sinned, he cut himself off from God. This action resulted in his being stripped of the grace God had given him. Furthermore, his human nature was harmed in its natural powers. Sickness and death entered his life. Adam's descendants were to suffer in the same way.

People are born into this world separated from their loving Father, and subject to death.

The main sign of sin in the world is man rejecting God. Other signs are war, poverty, starvation, hatred of people, violence and other injustices.

Vatican Council II

"In the course of history the use of temporal things has been tarnished by serious defects. Under the influence of original sin men have often fallen into very many errors about the true God, human nature and the principles of morality. As a consequence human conduct and institutions became corrupted, the human person itself held in contempt."

Lay People, 7

"What Revelation makes known to us is confirmed by our own experience. [For] when man looks into his own heart he

See Papally Promulgated
Catechism of the Catholic Church

Q. 54. See paragraphs: 402-406

finds that he is drawn towards what is wrong and sunk in many evils which cannot come from his good creator. Often refusing to acknowledge God as his source, man has also upset the relationship which should link him to his last end; and at the same time he has broken the right order that should reign within himself as well as between himself and other men and all creatures." *Modern world, 13*

Q. 55. What happens in Baptism?

In Baptism, God unites our soul to Himself. God's Love, the Holy Spirit, is poured into our soul. Our soul is lifted to a new kind of life which is a sharing in God's own life.

Although Baptism gives us the supernatural gift of sanctifying grace, it does not bring us some special gifts which Adam and Eve alone received, such as freedom from suffering and death. But God has restored to us the really important gift of the supernatural life of grace. This gift was given to us through the sufferings and death of His Son.

Q. 56. Was anyone exempt from original sin?

The Blessed Virgin Mary was to be the Mother of the Son of God, and thus she was preserved, from the very first moment of her existence, from the spiritual darkness of original sin.

She was always united with God; her soul was flooded with His love. We call this privilege her Immaculate Conception.

See Papally Promulgated
Catechism of the Catholic Church

Q. 55. See paragraphs: 1226-1228, 1262-1284
Q. 56. See paragraphs: 490-493

Prayer

Loving Creator, in Your infinite goodness You made man in a state of holiness. Man was the crown of Your visible creation, for he alone could give back to You the love which You first gave him. It was Your will that people should live as Your family, united to each other and to You in love.

But Adam sinned. He cut himself off from You, the source of all that is good. He was stripped of the grace You had given him. His human nature was harmed in its natural powers. Sickness and death entered his life as well. Thus, we are born into this world separated from You, and subject to death.

Jesus, you came among us as a man, to lead mankind from darkness into the light of faith. Through Adam's fall we were born as slaves of sin, but now through Baptism in You we are reborn as Your adopted children.

Lord God, we praise You for creating man, and still more for restoring him in Christ. Your Son shared our weakness; may we share His glory now and forever. Amen.

Chapter Sixteen

Personal Sin

Q. 57. What is personal sin?

Personal or actual sin, as opposed to original sin, is the willful disobedience of God's will.

This disobedience may be an action, a thought, a desire, or an intention. A sin must be a conscious and deliberate violation of the moral law. Thus, a sin is actually saying "no" to God. We sin when we refuse God's love, and turn down His invitation to give of ourselves to God and our fellow men. Furthermore, we sin through personal acts of selfishness that cause harm to others or ourselves.

Q. 58. What happens when someone commits a personal sin?

Someone who commits a personal sin: (1) fails in loving God; (2) turns away from his lifetime goal of doing God's will; and (3) by a serious offense (mortal sin) breaks his relationship with the Father, Son, and Holy Spirit.

Sin is refusing to let God have His way in our life. We turn away from God because we want to live without regard for His will. When we sin, we choose whatever we think will make us happy, even though it does not fit into God's plan for our eternal happiness. We fail to trust God completely when we sin. Serious sin makes us unhappy and sometimes even enslaves us to sin. Jesus said, "I tell you most solemnly, everyone who commits sin is a slave" (John 8:34).

Prayer: *God our Father, make us deeply conscious of the evil of personal sin, which we commit when we, acting knowingly and willingly, break Your moral law. When we sin we refuse Your love and*

See Papally Promulgated
Catechism of the Catholic Church

Q. 57. See paragraphs: 404, 1849-1876
Q. 58. See paragraphs: 311, 1440, 1849-1855

turn down Your invitation to give of ourselves to You and our fellow men. Such personal acts of selfishness cause harm to us and to others. For these, we beg Your forgiveness and help, through Jesus Christ our Lord. Amen.

Sacred Scripture

"Do you not know that the unjust will not inherit the Kingdom of God?" *1 Corinthians 6:9*

"Then He shall say to them also that shall be on His left hand, 'Depart from Me, you cursed, into everlasting fire which was prepared for the devil and his angels.'" *Matthew 25:41*

Papal Documents

"Throughout history Christians have always believed that sin is not only a breaking of God's law but that it shows contempt for or disregard of the friendship between God and man. The latter is not always directly evident. Further, they have believed that sin is a real offense against God, the effect of which cannot be estimated. Again, it is a display of ingratitude, a rejection of the love God has shown us through Jesus Christ." *Paul VI, Revision of Indulgences, 2*

"The very fact that punishment for sin exists and that it is so severe make it possible for us to understand how foolish and malicious sin is and how harmful its consequences are."
Paul VI, Revision of Indulgences, 3

"To speak of *social sin* means in the first place to recognize that, by virtue of a human solidarity which is as mysterious and intangible as it is real and concrete, each individual's sin in some way affects others. This is the other aspect of that solidarity which on the religious level is developed in the profound and magnificent mystery of the *Communion of Saints*, thanks to which it has been possible to say that 'every soul that rises above itself, raises up the world.' To this *law of ascent* there unfortunately corresponds the *law of descent*. Consequently one can speak of a *communion of sin*, whereby a soul that lowers itself through sin drags down with itself the Church and, in some way, the whole world. In other words, there is no sin, not even the most intimate and secret one, the most strictly individual one, that exclusively concerns the person committing it. With greater or lesser violence, with greater or lesser harm, every sin has repercussions on the en-

104

tire ecclesial body and the whole human family. According to this first meaning of the term, every sin can undoubtedly be considered as *social* sin."

Pope John Paul II, Apostolic Letter, Reconciliation and Penance, 16

"By the hidden and kindly mystery of God's will a supernatural solidarity reigns among men. A consequence of this is that the sin of one person harms other people just as one person's holiness helps others." *Paul VI, Revision of Indulgences, 4*

Prayer

God Our Father, help us to realize that when we sin we fail in loving You. In fact, we turn away from You by refusing to do Your will. A serious or grave sin breaks our relationship with You.

Lord, God of power, You rescued Your Son from the grasp of evil men. Deliver us from evil and confirm our trust in You, so that with our rising we may sing of Your power, and exult in Your mercy.

Make our lives blameless, Lord. Help us to do what is right, and to speak what is true, that we may dwell in Your presence and find rest in Your heavenly home, through Christ our Lord. Amen.

Chapter Seventeen

Mortal and Venial Sin - I

Q. 59. What is mortal sin?

Mortal sin is a serious or grave violation of the law of God. It is the fully deliberate choice of a person who knows what he chooses is gravely forbidden by God. The result of committing a mortal sin is the destruction of the life of God in the soul.

By committing a mortal sin we lose God's life regained for us by our Redeemer, Jesus Christ.

Sacred Scripture

"For the wages of sin is death. But the grace of God, life everlasting, in Christ Jesus our Lord." *Romans 6:23*

> **Prayer:** *Our Heavenly Father, preserve us from mortal sin, which is the loss of Your life in our souls. It destroys the life that You share with us, Your creatures. Keep us from all sin, but especially from a serious violation of Your law, so that we may never be separated from You. Keep us even from venial sin, which weakens our love for You and harms us and other people. We ask this through Jesus Christ our Lord to Whom, with You and the Holy Spirit, be all honor and glory. Amen.*

Q. 60. What are the effects of mortal sin?

As explained before, the effects of mortal sin are separation from God and damage to ourselves and others.

If we do not wish to change, and always refuse to do what God wants us to do, the separation from God is permanent. The permanent separation from God after death takes place in hell.

See Papally Promulgated
Catechism of the Catholic Church

Q. 59. See paragraphs: 1855-1861
Q. 60. See paragraphs: 1446, 1855-1856

"But your iniquities have divided you from yourselves and your God, and your sins have hid His face from you, that He should not hear." *Isaiah 59:2*

"The way of sinners is made plain with stones, and in their end is hell, and darkness, and pains." *Ecclesiasticus 21:11*

Q. 61. What is a venial sin?

Venial sin is a minor violation of the law of God. It does not take away God's life from the soul or break God's friendship, but it weakens our love for God. It also harms us and other people.

Sacred Scripture

"He that despises small things, shall fall by little and little." *Ecclesiasticus 19:1*

"He that is faithful in that which is least, is faithful also in that which is greater. And he that is unjust in that which is little, is unjust also in that which is greater." *Luke 16:10*

Vatican Council II

"Often refusing to acknowledge God as his source, man has also upset the relationship which should link him to his last end [God]; and at the same time he has broken the right order that should reign within himself as well as between himself and other men and all creatures.

"Man therefore is divided in himself." *Modern World, 13*

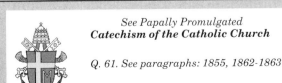

See Papally Promulgated
Catechism of the Catholic Church

Q. 61. See paragraphs: 1855, 1862-1863

Prayer

God of wisdom and love, source of all goodness, send Your Spirit to teach us the truth about sin, and guide our actions in Your way of peace. May Your healing love turn us from every sin and keep us on the way that leads to You. Help us always to overcome evil with good, that we may rejoice in Your triumph forever.

God our Savior, bring us back to You, and fill our minds with Your wisdom concerning the evil of sin. May we be enriched by the sacraments of the Eucharist and Reconciliation, and by earnest prayer, so that the offering of our love may be acceptable to You.

May Your grace transform our lives and bring us Your mercy. May we rejoice in Your healing power and experience Your saving love in mind and body. Make us grow in our desire for You that we may be protected from the sins that would separate us from You. We ask this through Jesus Christ our only Savior. Amen.

Chapter Eighteen

Mortal and Venial Sin - II

Q. 62. Under what conditions does a Christian commit a mortal sin?

To commit a mortal sin the Christian must: (1) *have committed a grave sin;* (2) *have known its gravity;* and (3) *have been free to avoid offending God.*

1. *The offense in itself must be serious or grave,* that is, something that has been forbidden by God under pain of losing His friendship.

2. *The person who commits the sin must know what he is doing,* and that what he is doing is a serious offense against God. (If, on the other hand, he does not know this, but deliberately kept himself in ignorance about the matter, his ignorance is not excusable.)

3. *There must be full consent of the will.* A person who acts under any circumstance which would deprive him of the full exercise of his will would not be guilty of mortal sin.

Sacred Scripture

"He that knows his brother to sin a sin which is not to death, let him pray, and life shall be given to him, who sins not to death. There is a sin unto death. For that I say that not any man pray. All iniquity is sin. And there is a sin unto death." *1 John 5:16-17*

Roman Curia Document

"Nor should one fail to mention the doctrine of the nature and effects of personal sin, by which a person knowingly and deliberately transgresses the moral law and offends God gravely in a grave manner." *General Catechetical Directory, 62 [1971]*

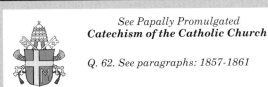

See Papally Promulgated
__Catechism of the Catholic Church__

Q. 62. See paragraphs: 1857-1861

Q. 63. When is an act right or wrong?

An act is right if it is something that God wants us to do. It is wrong if it is something that God does not want us to do.

We may sin not only by doing what God has forbidden, but also by failing to do what God has commanded.

Papal Document

"During the Synod Assembly some Fathers proposed a threefold distinction of sins, classifying them as *venial, grave* and *mortal*. This threefold distinction might illustrate the fact that there is a scale of seriousness among grave sins. But it still remains true that the essential and decisive distinction is between sin which destroys charity, and sin which does not kill the supernatural life: there is no middle way between life and death.

"Likewise, care will have to be taken not to reduce mortal sin to an act of *'fundamental option'* — as is commonly said today — against God, intending thereby an explicit and formal contempt for God or neighbour. For mortal sin exists also when a person knowingly and willingly, for whatever reason, chooses something gravely disordered. In fact, such a choice already includes contempt for the divine law, a rejection of God's love for humanity and the whole of creation: the person turns away from God and loses charity. Thus the fundamen-

See Papally Promulgated
Catechism of the Catholic Church

Q. 63. See paragraphs: 1749-1761

tal orientation can be radically changed by individual acts. Clearly there can occur situations which are very complex and obscure from a psychological viewpoint, and which have an influence on the sinner's subjective culpability. But from a consideration of the psychological sphere one cannot proceed to the construction of a theological category, which is what the 'fundamental option' precisely is, understanding it in such a way that it objectively changes or casts doubt upon the traditional concept of mortal sin.

"While every sincere and prudent attempt to clarify the psychological and theological mystery of sin is to be valued, the Church nevertheless has a duty to remind all scholars in this field of the need to be faithful to the word of God that teaches us also about sin. She likewise has to remind them of the risk of contributing to a further weakening of the sense of sin in the modern world."

Pope John Paul II, Apostolic Letter, Reconciliation and Penance, 17

Prayer

Father, without You we can do nothing to please You. By Your Spirit, help us to know what is right, and to be eager to do Your will.

Guide us in Your gentle mercy; for left to ourselves, we cannot do Your will. Make our hearts obedient to Your will. May the power of Your holy sacraments free us from sin, and help us to please You in our daily life.

Father of love, hear our prayer. Help us to know Your will and to do it with courage and faith. Make us grow in holiness. Through the Mass, may our whole life be a sacrifice pleasing to You. We ask this through Your Son, and our Lord and Savior, Jesus Christ. Amen.

111

Chapter Nineteen

Knowing God's Will and His Merciful Forgiveness

Q. 64. How do we know God's will?

We know God's will through our reason, through the Bible through Sacred Tradition, and through the teaching office or magisterium of the Church, which is God's living voice.

Prayer: *Almighty God, we thank You for Your infinite mercy and love. We proclaim Your mighty works, for You have called us out of darkness into your own wonderful light.*

Heavenly Father, teach us to know Your will. Give us a better understanding of the Bible, of Sacred Tradition, and of the teaching office of Your Church — Your living voice on earth. Especially give us a better understanding of the Ten Commandments and of the Precepts of the Church. We ask this through Jesus Christ our Lord. Amen.

Q. 65. What must we believe concerning God's forgiveness?

We must believe that God is merciful and will pardon the sinner who is truly sorry, and that by the power of His grace He will draw him to salvation.

God forgives our sins. He chose His Son to be the One to suffer and to die for our sins. Jesus is called our Savior because He saved us from sin. He is called our Redeemer because He paid the price for us; He bought us back from slavery to sin and death.

God will pardon us if we are truly sorry for our sins and

See Papally Promulgated
Catechism of the Catholic Church

Q. 64. See paragraphs: 1951, 1954, 1961-1962, 1965, 2032-2037, 2057

Q. 65. See paragraphs: 208, 210, 218, 270, 393, 545, 1428, 1448, 1450

want to change our sinful ways. We can always look to God for merciful forgiveness.

Q. 66. How does God draw the sinner to salvation?

The power of God's grace draws the sinner to salvation.

In the Sacrament of Penance or Reconciliation, through the priest, Christ meets the sinner, forgives his sins, and gives him again the peace which belongs to God's children. He also gives the sinner the added power of grace to overcome sin in the future, and the strength to be faithful to God's law of love. Furthermore, He gives the sinner grace to love God with all his heart, and his neighbor as himself for the love of God. Jesus also gives the sinner the help he needs to forgive his brothers and sisters even as He has forgiven him, to purge grudges out of his life, and to work in harmony with others in God's family.

As the Good Shepherd, Christ knows His sheep. When one strays, He goes out in search of it. Finding it, He places it on His shoulders and returns rejoicing to the fold. This shows the joy which Christ feels when a sinner has a change of heart.

In the Sacrament of Reconciliation, Christ, through His Church, and through the ministry of His priest, comes to us with pardon and peace. In the Name of Christ, and by the power given to him at ordination, the priest absolves the sinner saying, "I absolve you in the Name of the Father, and of the Son and of the Holy Spirit."

Christ and the Holy Spirit require us to be sorry for our sins and to have a change of heart. When we encounter Christ

See Papally Promulgated
Catechism of the Catholic Church

Q. 66. See paragraphs: 504, 545, 588-589, 605, 827, 1424, 1444, 1446

in this sacrament, we pledge to reverse our sinful ways. Furthermore, we promise to make genuine moral improvements in our lives. A continual conversion to Christ and His Church is required of us. We must continue to fight our sinful desires and refrain from whatever caused us to hurt God and His family.

Sacred Scripture

"Receive the Holy Spirit. Whose sins you will forgive, they are forgiven, and whose sins you shall retain, they are retained." *John 20:22-23*

Vatican Council II

"No one is freed from sin by himself or by his own efforts, no one is raised above himself or completely delivered from his own weakness, solitude or slavery; all have need of Christ who is the model, master, liberator, saviour, and giver of life."

Missionary Activity, 8

> **Prayer:** *Heavenly Father, we believe that You love us so much that, when we have sinned, You are ready to draw us to salvation by the power of Your grace. We thank You for giving us the Sacrament of Reconciliation (Penance), where Your loving Son meets the sinner, forgives his sins, and gives him again the peace which belongs to Your children. He also gives the sinner the power of grace to overcome sin in the future. He is the Good Shepherd who goes out in search of the sheep that has strayed. We thank You for this merciful love, through Jesus Christ our Lord. Amen.*

Q. 67. How are venial sins forgiven?

Venial sins are forgiven by God even without the Sacrament of Reconciliation. A sincere act of contrition and the will to amend our lives is enough to obtain forgiveness. Nonetheless, the Church encourages us to confess frequently even our

See Papally Promulgated
Catechism of the Catholic Church

Q. 67. See paragraphs: 1394, 1416, 1447, 1452, 1875

venial sins in the Sacrament of Reconciliation, since it is of such great benefit to the soul, especially with respect to the grace received.

Prayer

Father of our Lord Jesus Christ, in Your unbounded mercy You have revealed the beauty of Your power through Your constant forgiveness of our sins. May the power of this love be in our hearts, so we may bring Your pardon and Your Kingdom to all we meet.

Your love for us surpasses all our hopes and desires. Forgive our failings, keep us in Your peace and lead us in the way of salvation. May our obedient service bring us to the fullness of Your redemption.

Father, we see Your infinite power in Your loving plan of salvation. You came to our rescue by Your power as God, but You wanted us to be saved by one like us. Man refused Your friendship, but it was restored by the sacrificial death of the God-man, Jesus Christ, Your Son.

Loving Father, our hope and our strength, without You we falter. Help us to follow Christ and to live according to your will.

Help us remember the sufferings and death on the Cross which Your loving Son endured to destroy the effects of sin. Help us also to recall the power of grace which is greater than sin. We hope in the super-abundant love of Your heart which restores the penitent and draws him toward salvation.

Father, You show Your almighty power in Your mercy and forgiveness. Continue to fill us with Your gifts of love. Help us to hurry toward the eternal life You promise, and to share in the joys of Your Kingdom, where You live forever and ever with Your Divine Son and Holy Spirit. Amen.

Chapter Twenty

Capital Sins

Q. 68. What is a capital sin?

Every personal sin can be traced to one of seven human weaknesses. These are called capital sins.

"Capital sins" do not necessarily refer to grave sins, but rather to those sins which are the source of all others.

Q. 69. What are the capital sins?

The capital sins are: pride, avarice, lust, anger, gluttony, envy, and sloth.

Pride is seeking after one's own honor. Self-seeking and vanity are examples of pride.

Avarice is seeking after wealth by stealing, fraud, injustice, and stinginess.

Lust refers to impurity or sexual sins.

Anger, as a capital sin, refers to a loss of temper. It is often reflected in fits of rage, quarrelling, gossip, profanity, and property damage.

Gluttony is an excessive consumption of food or drink, which can lead to a lack of self-control.

Envy is a certain sadness of the mind. It leads to hatred and resentment of others. We are envious when we resent the fact that another is better off than ourselves.

Sloth is laziness in doing one's duty to God and to others. It leads to missing Mass and prayer, and neglect of work.

Sacred Scripture

"Pride goes before destruction. And the spirit is puffed up before a fall." *Proverbs 16:18*

See Papally Promulgated
Catechism of the Catholic Church

Q. 68. See paragraph: 1866
Q. 69. See paragraph: 1866

Vatican Council II

"The whole of man's history has been the story of our combat with the powers of evil, stretching, so our Lord tells us, from the very dawn of history until the last day. Finding himself in the midst of the battlefield man has to struggle to do what is right, and it is at great cost to himself, and aided by God's grace, that he succeeds in achieving his own inner integrity. Hence the Church of Christ, trusting in the design of the creator and admitting that progress can contribute to man's true happiness, still feels called upon to echo the words of the apostle: 'Do not be conformed to this world' (Rom. 12:2). 'World' here means a spirit of vanity and malice whereby human activity from being ordered to the service of God and man is distorted to an instrument of sin.

"To the question of how this unhappy situation can be overcome, Christians reply that all these human activities, which are daily endangered by pride and inordinate self-love, must be purified and perfected by the cross and resurrection of Christ." *Modern World, 37*

Prayer

Lord, You are the source of unfailing light. Give us true knowledge of Your mercy, that we may renounce our pride, and any of the other capital sins of which we are guilty, and that we may be filled with the riches of Your grace. Help us to remember that the capital sins are the source of all other sins.

Teach us goodness, discipline and wisdom. These gifts will keep us from becoming hardened by evil, weakened by laziness, or ignorant because of our foolishness.

God, our Creator, how wonderfully You made man. You transformed dust into Your own image, and gave it a share in Your own nature. Yet You are more wonderful in pardoning the man who has rebelled against You. Grant that where sin abounds, grace may abound even more, so that we can become holier through Your merciful forgiveness, and be more grateful to you, through Jesus Christ our Lord. Amen.

117

Chapter Twenty-One

Temptation

Q. 70. What is temptation?

Temptation is an invitation to sin that comes either from within us or from the outside.

Sin occurs only when we consent to the temptation. Temptations are not sins. With God's help we can resist them.

Sacred Scripture

"Let no temptation take hold on you, but such as is human. And God is faithful, Who will not allow you to be tempted above that which you are able to bear. But with the temptation, will make a way out, that you may be able to bear it."

1 Corinthians 10:13

> **Prayer:** *God, our help and deliverer, do not abandon us among the many temptations of life, but deliver us from evil, and turn our tears and struggles into joy. We ask this through Jesus Christ our Lord and Savior. Amen.*

Q. 71. Where do temptations come from?

Not all temptations come from the devil. Many temptations come from the world around us and from the forces within us called passions. These are inclinations towards rebellion against God's will.

We can conquer temptation, if we want to do so. We gain merit before God by conquering temptation, and we grow in holiness. We must, however, have God's help to make our weak wills strong. His grace, that is, His help, will be given to us if we ask for it, if we receive Holy Communion often, and if

See Papally Promulgated
Catechism of the Catholic Church

Q. 70. See paragraphs: 2846-2849
Q. 71. See paragraphs: 409, 1520, 1707, 2514-2516, 2846-2849

we go to Confession regularly. Furthermore, we must avoid unnecessary danger; people, places and things that might lead us to sin. We should also remember the indwelling Holy Spirit Who will give us the grace we need to overcome evil. With His help we can remain true to God and refuse the invitation to commit sin.

Sacred Scripture

"For the flesh lusts against the spirit, and the spirit against the flesh; for these are contrary one to another; so that you do not do the things that you would." *Galatians 5:17*

"And the Lord said, 'Simon, Simon, behold Satan desires to have you, that he may sift you as wheat, but I have prayed for you, that your faith may not fail. And upon being converted, strengthen your brethren.'" *Luke 22:31-32*

"Seek not to be like evil men, neither desire to be with them." *Proverbs 24:1*

Vatican Council II

"For when man looks into his own heart he finds that he is drawn towards what is wrong and sunk in many evils which cannot come from his good creator." *Church in the Modern World, 13*

"Man therefore is divided in himself. As a result, the whole life of men, both individual and social, shows itself to be a struggle, and a dramatic one, between good and evil, between light and darkness. Man finds that he is unable of himself, to overcome the assaults of evil successfully, so that everyone feels as though bound by chains. But the Lord himself came to free and strengthen man, renewing him inwardly and casting out the 'prince of this world' (Jn. 12:13), who held him in the bondage of sin." *Modern World, 13*

Prayer: *Lord, Jesus Christ, remember Your pilgrim Church. Do not let us be drawn into the current of the passing world, but free us from every evil and raise our thoughts to the heavenly Jerusalem. We ask this in Your most holy Name. Amen.*

Prayer

Lord God, the creation of man was a wonderful work, but his redemption was still more wonderful. May we persevere in right reason against all that entices us to sin, and so attain to everlasting joy.

God our Father, by the waters of Baptism You give new life to the faithful. May we not succumb to the influence of evil but remain true to Your gift of life. May we who are redeemed by the suffering and death of Jesus, Your Son, always rejoice in His Resurrection, for He is Lord forever.

Lord, send Your mercy and Your truth to rescue us from the snares of the devil, and to make us happy to be known as companions of Your Son.

God of strength, You gave Your Son victory over death. Direct Your Church's fight against evil in the world. Clothe us with the weapons of light and unite us under the one banner of love, that we may receive our eternal reward after the battle of earthly life.

Heavenly Father, Who by the death of Your Son and His glorious rising again, have redeemed us, grant us to die daily to sin that we may live forever in the joy of His Resurrection.

Lord Jesus Christ, in Your suffering You cried out to Your Father and He delivered You out of death. By the power of Your Holy Cross, rescue us from the abyss of sin, renew this world of Yours, and flood our minds with the the light of Your Resurrection, Savior of the world, living and reigning forever and ever. Amen.

The Creed - II

Jesus Christ, Son of God, Savior

"...We believe in one Lord, Jesus Christ, the only Son of God, eternally begotten of the Father, God from God, Light from Light, true God from true God, begotten, not made, one in Being with the Father. Through Him all things were made. For us men He came down from Heaven: by the power of the Holy Spirit He was born of the Virgin Mary, and became man.

For our sake He was crucified under Pontius Pilate; He suffered, died, and was buried. On the third day He rose again in fulfillment of the Scriptures; He ascended into Heaven and is seated at the right hand of the Father. He will come again in glory to judge the living and the dead, and His kingdom will have no end."

The Incarnation

The Annunciation

" 'Hail, full of grace, the Lord is with thee: blessed art thou among women.' " *Luke 1:28*

The Incarnation

" 'Behold the handmaid of the Lord; be it done unto me according to Thy word.' " *Luke 1:38*

And the Word was made flesh and dwelt amongst us.

The Angelus Prayer

The angel of the Lord declared unto Mary.
And she conceived by the Holy Spirit. ...*Hail Mary...*

Behold the handmaid of the Lord.
May it be done unto me according to Thy word. ...*Hail Mary...*

And the Word was made flesh.
And dwelt amongst us. ...*Hail Mary...*

Pour forth we beseech You, O Lord, Your grace into our hearts, that we to whom the Incarnation of Christ your Son was made known by the message of an angel, may by His Passion and Cross be brought to the glory of His Resurrection, through the same Christ our Lord. Amen.

Chapter Twenty-Two

The Incarnation - I

Q. 72. What is the greatest of God's works?

The greatest of God's works is the taking on of human flesh [i.e., human nature] by His Son, Jesus Christ. This is called the Incarnation.

Sacred Scripture

"But when the fullness of the time was come, God sent His Son, made of a woman, made under the law, that He might redeem them who were under the law, that we might receive the adoption of sons." *Galatians 4:4-5*

Vatican Council II

"This plan flows from 'fountain-like love,' the love of God the Father. As the principle without principle from whom the Son is generated and from whom the Holy Spirit proceeds through the Son." *Missionary Activity, 2*

"For when the time had fully come (cf. Gal. 4:4), the Word became flesh and dwelt among us full of grace and truth (cf. John 1:14)." *Divine Revelation, 17*

> **Prayer:** *Jesus, the divine Word of God, we believe that God's greatest work was Your taking on our human nature when You became man and came to live among us. At Mary's consent to Your Father's request, You became man in her immaculate womb by means of the Holy Spirit. To You be all honor and glory, now and forever. Amen.*

Q. 73. What does the Incarnation mean?

The Incarnation means that the Second Person of the Blessed Trinity, the Son of God, (the Divine Word), became man and came to live among us.

See Papally Promulgated
Catechism of the Catholic Church

Q. 72. See paragraphs: 456-483.
Q. 73. See paragraphs: 461-464.

"And Mary said, 'Behold the handmaid of the Lord. Be it done to me according to your word' " (Luke 1:38). [At that very moment Jesus Christ, God's own Son, became man in the Blessed Virgin Mary.]

The Son is begotten from the Father, and the Holy Spirit proceeds from the Father and the Son. By an act of His almighty power, God the Son united His own divine nature to a true human nature, to a body and soul like ours. The two natures were united in one divine Person. Mary is the Mother of God because she is the Mother of God the Son, Who became man in her womb.

Mary gave her free consent to become the Mother of Jesus. At that moment, by the operation of the Holy Spirit, she conceived Jesus within her womb. The result was one divine Person with one divine and one human nature.

Sacred Scripture

"The angel said to her: 'Hail, full of grace, the Lord is with you; blessed are you among women.' " *Luke 1:28*

"And Mary said to the angel, 'How shall this be done, because I know not man?' And the angel answering, said to her, 'The Holy Ghost shall come upon you and the power of the Most High shall overshadow you. And therefore also the Holy One which shall be born of you shall be called the Son of God.' " *Luke 1:34-35*

Vatican Council II

"In reality it is only in the mystery of the Word made flesh that the mystery of man truly becomes clear. For Adam, the first man, was a type of Him Who was to come. Christ the Lord, Christ the new Adam, in the very revelation of the mystery of the Father and of his love, fully reveals man to himself and brings to light his most high calling." *Modern World, 22*

"The sacred writings of the Old and New Testaments, as well as venerable tradition, show the role of the Mother of the Saviour in the plan of salvation in an ever clearer light and call our attention to it." *The Church, 55*

"The Father of mercies willed that the Incarnation should be preceded by assent on the part of the predestined mother, so that just as a woman had a share in bringing about death, so also a woman should contribute to life." *The Church, 56*

Prayer

Eternal Word of God, in the Incarnation You have brought to our eyes of faith a new and radiant vision of Your glory. In You we see God made visible.

We recognize in You the revelation of God's love. Before all ages, You were predestined to be born in time. You have come to lift up all things to Yourself, to restore unity to creation, and to lead mankind from exile into Your heavenly Kingdom.

We welcome You as Lord, the true light of the world. Bring us to eternal joy in the Kingdom of Heaven where You live and reign forever and ever. Amen.

Chapter Twenty-Three

The Incarnation - II

Q. 74. Why did the Son of God come to earth?

The Son of God came to earth: (1) to bring the world His own divine life; (2) to save us from sin, and; in this way; (3) to make the world new again.

1. The Son of God came to earth to bring the world His own divine life.

Born of the Virgin Mary, the Son of God has truly been made one of us, like us in all things except sin. The human race lost God's life of grace through sin, the sin of our First Parents. Because of His love for us, Jesus brought grace back to us by His Life, Passion, Death, and Resurrection. He showed us what it means to be a child of God.

2. The Son of God came to earth to save us from sin.

By offering His life on the Cross for us, Jesus gave the highest of gifts to His Father. In this way He redeemed the world. The Passion and Death of Our Lord teaches us the great evil of sin. It was sin that caused Him to suffer so much and to die, but He took away our sins and made us free to serve God and to reach Heaven with the help of divine grace.

3. The Son of God came to earth to make the world new again.

Through the Catholic Church, with its truths and sacraments, we are able to keep a life of grace in our souls. With sanctifying grace we are united with God in this world and in Heaven. Through this grace, Jesus is for us the source of eternal life and salvation; in this way He renews the world.

Sacred Scripture

"For God so loved the world, as to give His only begotten

See Papally Promulgated
Catechism of the Catholic Church

Q. 74. See paragraphs: 456-460.

Son, that whoever believes in Him should not perish, but have eternal life." *John 3:16*

Vatican Council II

"So the Son of God entered the world by means of a true incarnation that he might make men sharers in the divine nature; though rich, he was made poor for our sake, that by his poverty we might become rich (2 Cor. 8:9). The Son of man did not come to be served, but to serve and to give his life as a ransom for many, that is for all (cf. Mk. 10:45)." *Missionary Activity, 3*

Prayer

Jesus, Divine Savior, we believe that You came to earth to bring to the world Your divine life, to save us from sin, and to make the world new again. We thank You for Your mercy and generosity.

When You came to us as man, You, the Son of God, scattered the darkness of this world, and filled it with Your glory. God of infinite goodness, scatter the darkness of sin and brighten our hearts with holiness. When You, the Divine Word, became man, earth was joined to Heaven. Give us Your peace and good will. Give us a foretaste of the joy that You will grant us when the fullness of Your glory has filled the earth.

Jesus, born of a Virgin, in coming to us, You show the world the splendor of Your glory. Give us true faith and love to celebrate You properly Who are God made man. All glory be to You, to the Father, and to the Holy Spirit. Amen.

Chapter Twenty-Four

Jesus is God - I

Q. 75. Why is Jesus true God?

Jesus is true God because He is a divine Person having a full divine nature.

Jesus Christ is the divine Word of God made man. But He is only one Person, and that Person is divine, the Second Person of the Blessed Trinity.

Sacred Scripture

"Behold a virgin shall be with child and bring forth a Son: and they shall call His name Emmanuel, which being interpreted is God with us." *Matthew 1:23*

"Therefore the Lord Himself shall give you a sign. Behold a virgin shall conceive and bear a Son, and His name shall be called Emmanuel." *Isaiah 7:14*

"Behold your God will bring the revenge of recompense. God Himself will come and will save you." *Isaiah 35:4*

Vatican Council II

"Jesus Christ was sent into the world as the true Mediator between God and men. Since he is God, all the fullness of the divine nature dwells in him bodily (Col. 2:9). *Missionary Activity, 3*

> **Prayer:** *Lord Jesus Christ, we believe that You are the true God because You are God's only begotten Son. In You there is the fullness of divinity. You are the divine Word of God made man. In You there is only one Person, the Second Person of the Blessed Trinity. May we give You glory now and forever. Amen.*

See Papally Promulgated
Catechism of the Catholic Church

Q. 75. See paragraphs: 461-469.

Q. 76. How does the Nicene Creed express our faith in the divinity of Christ?

Speaking of the divinity of Christ, the Nicene Creed states that:

"God from God, Light from Light, true God from true God, begotten not made, of one substance with the Father."

The chief teaching of the Catholic Church about Jesus Christ is that He is God made man. It is Jesus Christ the God-man Who we hear speaking to us in the Gospels and Whom we receive in the Eucharist. It is to Jesus with the Father and the Holy Spirit that we pray:

"Glory be to the Father, and to the Son, and to the Holy Spirit."

Sacred Scripture

"In the beginning was the Word: and the Word was with God, and the Word was God. The same was in the beginning with God. All things were made by Him, and without Him was made nothing that was made. In Him was life, and the life was the light of men." *John 1:1-4*

Vatican Council II

"This plan flows from 'fountain-like love,' the love of God the Father. As the principle without principle from whom the Son is generated and from whom the Holy Spirit proceeds through the Son." *Missionary Activity, 2*

See Papally Promulgated
Catechism of the Catholic Church

Q. 76. See paragraphs: 184-185.

Prayer

Jesus, You are the way to God. By getting to know You, we meet God in human form and really see His love for us in action. Finding You, we reach the very presence of our heavenly Father.

You brought to us a whole new life. This new life, which is sanctifying grace, is a participation in God's own life and is communicated to us by the Holy Spirit. Because You are the Son of God, You are able to give us a share in divine life and make us adopted children of God through the gift of the Holy Spirit Whom You give us.

To enlighten the world, You, the Divine Word, came to us as the Sun of Truth and Justice shining upon mankind. Illumine our eyes that we may discern Your glory in the many works of Your hand. May Your presence bring lasting light to the People of God that we may pray to You with deep faith:

"God from God, Light from Light, true God from true God, begotten not made, of one substance with the Father," may we love You forever. Amen.

Chapter Twenty-Five

Jesus is God - II

Q. 77. Did Jesus say He was God?

Yes, Jesus said He was God. For instance, He said to the Jews: "I and the Father are one" (John 10:30).

"If God were your Father, you would indeed love Me. For from God I proceeded and came. For I came not of Myself, but He sent Me... And you have not known Him, but I know Him. And if I shall say that I know Him not, I shall be like to you, a liar. But I do know Him and do keep His word... Amen, amen I say to you, before Abraham was made, I Am" [i.e.; Pure Existence having neither beginning nor ending, existing only in the eternal present] (John 8:42, 55, 58).

Men come to believe in God because He shows something of Himself to them. Catholics believe in what the Catholic Church teaches about Christ because they have the supernatural gift of faith. Thus, God the Son revealed Himself in what He said and did, how He lived with others, and by what He revealed of His thoughts and feelings. He revealed more of Himself than we can fully understand. Nevertheless, through faith and the virtue of love, we can understand a great deal about Him.

Jesus is the center of our Catholic Faith. Everything that He said and did is important, because in Him we find God our Father and come to believe in Him. Jesus is our Way, our Truth, and our Life (cf. John 14:6).

Sacred Scripture

"And the Word was made flesh and dwelt among us."

John 1:14

Vatican Council II

"The eternal Father, in accordance with the utterly gratu-

See Papally Promulgated
Catechism of the Catholic Church

Q. 77. See paragraphs: 589-590.

itous and mysterious design of his wisdom and goodness, created the whole universe, and chose to raise up men to share in his own divine life; and when they had fallen in Adam, he did not abandon them, but at all times held out to them the means of salvation, bestowed in consideration of Christ, the Redeemer, 'who is the image of the invisible God, the firstborn of every creature.' [All] the elect the Father foreknew and predestined before time began 'to become conformed to the image of his Son, that he should be the firstborn among many brethren' (Rom. 8:29)." *The Church, 2*

Prayer: *Jesus, we firmly believe, by the gift of faith, that You are the Son of God. Your words and Your deeds also attest to Your divine nature. You revealed Your glory to the disciples to strengthen them for the scandal of the Cross. Your glory shone from a body like our own, to show that the Church, which is Your Mystical Body, would one day share Your glory. All glory be to You, to the Father, and to the Holy Spirit, now and forever. Amen.*

Prayer

Jesus, our Savior, on the holy mountain of Tabor, You revealed Your glorified body in Your wondrous Transfiguration in the presence of Your disciples. You had already prepared them for Your approaching death. On Mount Tabor You wanted to teach them, through the Law and the Prophets, that the long-awaited Christ had first to suffer before coming to the glory of the Resurrection.

Jesus, in You, the Father has renewed all things and has given us all a share in Your riches. Though Your nature was divine, You stripped Yourself of all glory, and by shedding Your Blood on the Cross, You brought Your peace to the world. Therefore, You are exalted above all creation and have become the source of eternal life to all who serve You. With all the choirs of angels in Heaven, we proclaim Your glory and profess our faith in You as Peter did when he said: "You are Christ, the Son of the living God!" (Matthew 16:16). All glory and honor be to You, to the Father, and to the Holy Spirit. Amen.

Chapter Twenty-Six

Jesus is God - III

Q. 78. Did Jesus say He was God during His Passion?

Yes, the night before He died, at the Last Supper, Jesus spoke as being equal to His Father when He said He had power to give eternal life.

Sacred Scripture

Jesus prayed, "Father, the hour is come, glorify Your Son, that Your Son may glorify You. As You have given Him power over all flesh, that He may give eternal life to all whom You have given Him." *John 17:1-2*

Vatican Council II

"What had revealed the love of God among us is that the only-begotten Son of God has been sent by the Father into the world, so that, being made man, he might by his redemption of the entire human race give new life to it and unify it. Before offering himself up as a spotless victim upon the altar of the cross, he prayed to his Father for those who believe: 'that all may be one, as you, Father, are in me, and I in you; I pray that they may be one in us, that the world may believe that you sent me' (Jn. 17:21). In his Church he instituted the wonderful sacrament of the Eucharist by which the unity of the Church is both signified and brought about. He gave his followers a new commandment to love one another, and promised the Spirit, their Advocate, who, as Lord and life-giver, should remain with them forever." *Ecumenism, 2*

Prayer

Jesus, in the high-priestly prayer which You uttered at the Last Supper, You spoke to Your Father as Your equal. You prayed that He might glorify You. You prayed for Your disciples and for those

See Papally Promulgated
Catechism of the Catholic Church

Q. 78. See paragraph: 591.

who, through the teachings of these disciples, would believe in You, that they all might be one even as You and the Father are one.

Jesus, we believe that You are the Word through Whom God the Father made the universe. You are also the Savior He sent to redeem us. By the power of the Holy Spirit, You took on flesh and were born of the Virgin Mary. For our sake You opened Your arms on the Cross; You put an end to death and revealed the Resurrection. In this way, You fulfilled Your Father's will and won for Him a holy people.

Divine Redeemer, we believe that You are the Son of God and that we will see You "seated at the right hand of the Father and coming on the clouds of Heaven" (Matthew 26:64). You have ascended into Heaven and have taken Your seat in majesty at the right hand of the Father. When You appear as Judge, may we be pleasing forever in Your sight. Amen.

Chapter Twenty-Seven

Jesus is God - IV

Q. 79. Does the Catholic Church teach Jesus is truly God?

Yes, the Catholic Church has always taught, and will always teach, that Jesus is truly God, existing from all eternity together with the Father and the Holy Spirit. It is He Who, upholding the universe with His almighty power, came and "lived among us" (John 1:14) as the Word made flesh.

St. John said, "For the life was manifested; and we have seen and bear witness to it, and declare unto you the eternal life which was with the Father and has appeared to us" (1 John 1:2).

"But these are written, that you may believe that Jesus is the Christ, the Son of God, and that believing, you may have life in His Name" (John 20:31).

In the Prologue to St. John's Gospel, Jesus, the Word of God, is referred to as a divine Person, existing in the beginning with God the Father. Thus St. John said: "In the beginning was the Word, and the Word was with God, and the Word was God... All things were made by Him, and without Him nothing was made that was made" (John 1:1, 3).

"And the Word was made flesh, and dwelt among us, (and we saw His glory, the glory as it were of the only begotten of the Father), full of grace and truth" (John 1:14).

Jesus the man, then, is also the eternal Word of God.

Vatican Council II

"Jesus Christ was sent into the world as the true Mediator between God and men. Since he is God, all the fullness of the divine nature dwells in him bodily (Col. 2:9)." *Missionary Activity, 3*

See Papally Promulgated
Catechism of the Catholic Church

Q. 79. See paragraph: 464.

Prayer: *Heavenly Father, give us the light of faith that we may always acknowledge Jesus as our God and our Redeemer. May we become more like Him and share in His life completely by living as He taught. We ask this through His most powerful and holy Name. Amen.*

Prayer

Our Father in Heaven, You sent us Your only begotten Son, Your Word, when He took flesh from the Virgin Mary and became man. Open our hearts to receive His life, and increase our faith in Him. May the light of that faith shine in our words and actions.

With gratitude we adore His humanity, containing the human life He shared with us. May the power of His divinity help us answer His call to receive forgiveness and life. May we welcome Christ as our Redeemer, and meet Him with confidence when He comes to be our Judge.

May we share in the glory of His Incarnation, see Him in His heavenly Kingdom, and enjoy His presence forever.

You have shown men the splendor of Jesus Christ, our Light. We love Him as Lord, the true Light of the world.

May we come to live more fully the life we profess, and come to the glory of His Kingdom where He lives and reigns forever and ever. Amen.

Chapter Twenty-Eight

Jesus is God - V

Q. 80. Is there any further evidence in the New Testament pointing to Jesus as God?

There are several passages, apart from those already cited in which Jesus' divinity is taught:

1. Expressing his faith in the Resurrection, St. Thomas cried out: "My Lord and my God!" (John 20:28).

2. God the Father, speaking to Christ addresses Him as God in the following words: "To the Son He says, 'Your throne, O God, is forever and ever!' " (Hebrews 1:8).

3. "Whose [i.e., belonging to the Israelites] are the fathers, and of whom is Christ, according to the flesh, Who is over all things, God blessed forever. Amen" (Romans 9:5).

4. "For let this mind be in you, which was also in Christ Jesus: Who being in the form of God thought it not robbery to be equal with God" (Philippians 2:5-6).

5. Christian life is lived in eager anticipation, "looking for the blessed hope and coming of the glory of the great God and our Savior Jesus Christ" (Titus 2:13; see also Peter 1:1; Romans 9:5).

6. Most frequently the title "Lord" is given to Jesus. He is called this because His divinity is acknowledged. "That in the Name of Jesus every knee should bow, of those that are in Heaven, on earth, and under the earth: and that every tongue should confess that Jesus Christ is Lord..." (Philippians 2:10-11).

7. Jesus also applies terms to Himself which are proper to God, such as "I am," already noted in Chapter 25. This refers to God's eternal existence and being. "Before Abraham was made, I am..." (John 8:58; cf. Exodus 3:14).

See Papally Promulgated
Catechism of the Catholic Church

Q. 80. See paragraphs: 448-449, 461, 590, 635, 1130

Q. 81. How does the New Testament portray Jesus?

Throughout the New Testament, Jesus is portrayed as divine. For instance, He is described as the "Word made flesh;" that is, God Who assumed human nature. He is also spoken of as Creator. St. John said: "All things were made by Him" (John 1:3).

St. Paul wrote, "For in Him were all things created in Heaven and on earth, visible and invisible... all things were created by Him and in Him. And He is before all, and by Him all things hold together" (Colossians 1:16-17).

Salvation and forgiveness are found only in God. Thus Jesus is called the Savior of all, Who personally forgives sins by His own authority (cf. e.g. Luke 5:10-25).

Vatican Council II

"It pleased God, in his goodness and wisdom, to reveal himself and to make known the mystery of his will (cf. Eph. 1:9). His will was that men should have access to the Father, through Christ, the Word made flesh, in the Holy Spirit, and thus become sharers in the divine nature (cf. Eph. 2:18; 2 Pet. 1:4). By this revelation, then, the invisible God (cf. Col. 1:15; 1 Tim. 1:17), from the fullness of his love, addresses men as his friends (cf. Ex. 33:11; Jn. 15:14-15), and moves among them (cf. Bar. 3:38), in order to invite and receive them into his own company."

Divine Revelation, 2

See Papally Promulgated
Catechism of the Catholic Church

Q. 81. See paragraphs: 151, 291.

followers of this Light. Make us faithful to Your Word. We ask this in His most powerful and holy Name. Amen.

Prayer

Heavenly Father, keep before us the wisdom and love You have revealed in Your Son. Help us to be like Him in our thoughts, words, and deeds. Open our eyes to His deeds, and our ears to the sound of His words in the Gospel, so that all the acts of our lives may increase our sharing in the life He has offered us.

Form us in the likeness of Your Son and deepen His life within us. Help us to live His example of love.

Help us to be like Christ, Your Son, Who loved the world and died for our salvation. Inspire us by His love, and guide us by His example. Change our selfishness into self-giving, that we may imitate His sacrifice of love.

May we always remain one with Jesus. Give us the grace to follow Him more faithfully so that we may come to the joy of His Kingdom forever and ever. Amen.

Jesus is True Man and Our Redeemer

Chapter Twenty-Nine

Jesus is True Man - I

Q. 82. Is Jesus Christ true Man?

Jesus, the Son of God, became a real man, having real flesh, a human body and soul.

Jesus is a man just as we are, with the exception of sin. Jesus felt the joys and sorrows, pleasures and pains that we feel as human beings. As a man Jesus had a human mind, a human will, and a physical, mortal body.

Jesus Christ is also true God, Who became man and dwelt among us. St. John says, "And the Word was made flesh, [i.e.; the Incarnation] and dwelt among us" (John 1:14).

The ancient Fathers of the Church proclaimed that what Christ took up was our entire human nature, though without our sin. He was directly conceived by the Holy Spirit in the womb of Mary and was born in the normal course of events. Because of this extraordinary action of God, Mary is called the Blessed Virgin. Christ had no human father. Joseph was Mary's husband, and acted as foster father to Jesus during His childhood.

The greatest proof of God's goodness and love toward us is His gift of His only beloved Son. All love tends to become like that which it loves. Jesus, the Son of God, loved man, therefore He became man. Infinite love and mercy caused Him to leave the Kingdom of eternal bliss; to descend from the throne of His majesty, power and glory; to become a helpless child; to suffer and to die for us, that we might live forever in Heaven. In the crib we see the love of God, as He humbles Himself, so low as to beg the love of our hearts. When He was only forty days old, Mary brought Him to the Temple to offer Him to God as the Victim for our Redemption.

See Papally Promulgated
Catechism of the Catholic Church

Q. 82. See paragraphs: 464-470

Sacred Scripture

"The Holy One, which shall be born of you shall be called the Son of God." *Luke 1:35*

"But the free gift is not like the offense. For if by the offense of one, many died: much more the grace of God and the gift by the grace of one man. Jesus Christ, has abounded unto many." *Romans 5:15*

"And the light shines in darkness, and the darkness did not comprehend it. There was a man sent from God whose name was John. This man came for a witness, to give testimony of the light, that all men might believe through Him. He was not the light, but was to give testimony to the light. That was the true light, which enlightens every man that comes into this world. He was in the world, and the world was made by Him, and the world knew Him not. He came unto His own, and His own received Him not. But as many as received Him, He gave them power to be made the sons of God, to them that believe in His Name, who are born, not of blood, nor of the will of the flesh, nor of the will of man, but of God. And the Word was made flesh, and dwelt among us, (and we saw His glory, the glory as it were of the only begotten of the Father), full of grace and truth. John bears witness of Him, and cries out, saying, 'This was He of Whom I spoke. He that shall come after me, is preferred before me: because He was before me. And of His fullness we all have received, and grace for grace. For the law was given by Moses; grace and truth came by Jesus Christ. No man has seen God at any time: the only begotten Son Who is in the bosom of the Father, He has declared Him." *John 1:5-18*

Prayer: *Jesus, we believe that You are true man. You, the Son of God, became a real man, having real flesh, a human body and soul. You felt the joys and sorrows that we feel as human beings. You took our entire human nature, though without sin, and lived among us. Infinite love and mercy caused You to come to us as a helpless child, and to suffer and to die for us, that we might have eternal life. To You be all honor and glory. Amen.*

Vatican Council II

"For, by his incarnation, he, the Son of God, has in a certain way united himself with each man. He worked with human

146

hands, He thought with a human mind. He acted with a human will, and with a human heart he loved. Born of the Virgin Mary, he has truly been made one of us, like to us in all things except sin." *Modern World, 22*

Prayer: *Incarnate Word, in Your coming among us, a new light has dawned upon the world. God has become one with man, and man has become one again with God. You have taken upon Yourself our human limitations, and have given our mortal nature immortal value. So marvelous is this oneness between God and man, You restore to man the gift of eternal life. To You be endless power, honor and glory. Amen.*

Prayer

Jesus, we thank You for Your conception and birth. With gratitude we recall Your humanity, the life You share with the sons of men. May we, who celebrate Your coming as man, share more fully in Your divine life. May the power of Your divinity help us answer Your call to receive forgiveness and to life.

Divine Word become man, born of the Virgin Mary, Who humbled Yourself to share our human nature, may we come to share increasingly Your divinity.

Fill our hearts with Your love. Lead us through Your suffering and death to the glory of Your Resurrection. When You come again in glory, reward us with eternal life. May we meet You with confidence when You come to be our Judge. In your coming You gave us a new vision of Your glory. You were born of the Virgin Mary and came to share our life. May we come to share Your eternal life in the glory of Your Kingdom. Amen.

Chapter Thirty

Jesus is True Man - II

Q. 83. How did Jesus show His concern for men?

Jesus showed His divine concern for men by means of His human nature.

In His humanity we see God's love for man. We cannot see God, but since God sent His divine Son to live among us and to save us by His death on the Cross, we can see how much God really loves us. During His public ministry, He worked many miracles to help people.

Jesus loved everyone and spent His life trying to help them in their need, even those who opposed Him. He traveled all over Israel, teaching the people about His Father, His heavenly Kingdom, and the need for repentance. He also taught about the necessity of loving God with one's whole heart, soul, and mind, and of loving one's neighbor as one's self. He loved especially the poor, the sick, and the troubled. Jesus loved sinners and forgave their sins. He offered His life to save all mankind.

Prayer: *Lord Jesus, in Your concern for people during Your public life on earth, we see both the divine and human love for man. We see this love especially in Your Passion and death. In the Gospels we read of Your tender acts of compassion for people. You loved the poor, the sick, the sinners, and children. That is why You could say "Come to me, all you that labor, and are burdened, and I will refresh you. Take up My yoke upon you, and learn of Me, because I am meek, and humble of heart, and you shall find rest for your souls" (Matthew 11:28-29). Please, Jesus, help us in our needs. Amen.*

Sacred Scripture

"Because in Him it has well pleased the Father that all

See Papally Promulgated
Catechism of the Catholic Church

Q. 83. See paragraphs: 478, 595-617

fullness should dwell, and through Him to reconcile all things unto Himself, making peace through the blood of His Cross, both as to things that are on earth, and the things that are in Heaven. And you, whereas you were sometime alienated and enemies in mind in evil works: Yet now He has reconciled in the body of His flesh through death, to present you holy and unspotted and blameless before Him." *Colossians 1:19-22*

Vatican Council II

"God sent his Son, whom he appointed heir of all things (cf. Heb. 1:2), that he might be teacher, king and priest of all, the head of the new and universal People of God's sons."

The Church, 13

"In assuming human nature he [Christ] has united to himself all humanity in a supernatural solidarity which makes of it one single family. He has made charity the distinguishing mark of his disciples, in the words: 'By this will all men know you for my disciples, by the love you bear one another' (Jn. 13:35)." *Lay People, 8*

Prayer: *Good Shepherd of souls, attune our minds to the sound of Your voice. Lead our steps in the path You have shown, that we may know the strength of Your outstretched arm and enjoy the light of Your presence forever. Though we walk in the valley of darkness, no evil should we fear, for we follow in faith Your call; for You were sent by the Father to be our hope and our strength. Give us Your grace and lead us to join the saints in Heaven where You live and reign with the Father and the Holy Spirit forever and ever. Amen.*

Prayer

Savior of mankind, You loved the children of the lands You walked, and You enriched them with the witness of justice and truth. You lived and died that we might be reborn in the Spirit and be filled with love of all men. You came to earth to relieve the pain of our exile; You took our natural limitations as Your own. Uphold us when our hearts grow faint. May we receive forgiveness and mercy through Your coming.

Lord Jesus, our Savior and our God, give us always the water of life to drink, the free gift of the Spirit flowing from Your Sacred Heart, for You are all good and You love mankind. We glorify You, and Your eternal Father, and Your life-giving Spirit.

Lord Jesus Christ, in virtue of Your saving passover from death to life, pour Your Holy Spirit into our hearts and fill us with awe and reverence for You, and love and compassion for our neighbor, for Yours is the power and the glory forever and ever. Amen.

Chapter Thirty-One

Jesus Our Savior

Q. 84. Why did Jesus Christ become man?

Jesus Christ became man in order to be our Savior and Redeemer.

God the Father sent His Son to free men from the power of satan and to make peace between God and men. To do this Jesus became man, to preach His truth about the Kingdom of His Father.

Jesus continued preaching even though the religious leaders of the Jewish people were trying to harm Him. They finally arranged to have Him put to death by the Romans because He claimed to be God. By His freely offered sacrificial death on the Cross, Jesus became our Savior.

Sacred Scripture

" 'The Spirit of the Lord is upon Me. Wherefore He has anointed Me to preach the gospel to the poor: He has sent Me to heal the contrite of heart.'

" 'To preach deliverance to the captives and sight to the blind, to set at liberty them that are bruised, to preach the acceptable year of the Lord and the day of reward.'

"And when He had folded the book, He restored it to the minister and sat down. And the eyes of all in the synagogue were fixed on Him.

"And He began to say to them, 'This day is fulfilled this scripture in your ears.'

"And all gave testimony to Him. And they wondered at the words of grace that proceeded from His mouth. And they said, 'Is not this the son of Joseph?' " *Luke 4:18-22*

See Papally Promulgated
Catechism of the Catholic Church

Q. 84. See paragraphs: 456-460

"He was in the world, and the world was made by Him, and the world knew Him not.

"He came unto his own, and His own received him not.

"But as many as received Him, He gave them power to be made the sons of God, to them that believe in His Name.

"Who are born, not of blood, nor of the will of flesh, nor the will of man, but of God." *John 1:10-13*

"For I, through the law, am dead to the law, that I may live to God: with Christ I am nailed to the Cross.

"And I live, now not I; but Christ Who lives in me. And that I live now in the flesh, I live in the faith of the Son of God, Who loved me, and delivered Himself for me." *Galatians 2:19-20*

"For unto this you are called, because Christ also suffered for us, leaving you an example that you should follow in His footsteps." *1 Peter 2:21*

Vatican Council II

"After God had spoken many times and in various ways through the prophets, 'in these last days he has spoken to us by a Son' (Hebrews 1:1-2). For he sent his Son, the eternal Word who enlightens all men, to dwell among men and to tell them about the inner life of God." *Divine Revelation, 4*

> **Prayer:** *Jesus, we acknowledge You as our Savior and Redeemer, because, as God made man, You preached the Gospel of the Kingdom of God and gave Yourself up to death out of love for Your Father and for us. You freed all creatures from the slavery of sin, and You made peace between God and men. We thank You for Your love for all mankind, and for each and every one of us in particular. We, too, wish to give our lives to You in faithful service. All glory and honor be to the Father, to the Son, and to the Holy Spirit forever and ever. Amen.*

Q. 85. What does it mean to say that Jesus Christ is our Savior?

Jesus Christ is our Savior because through Him all mankind can be saved from the slavery of sin and be saved for everlasting life with God.

St. Paul speaks of sin as a slavery. Jesus is our Savior because He saved us from sin. He said; "You have not received the spirit of bondage again in fear, but you have received the spirit of adoption of sons, whereby we cry, 'Abba' ['Father']" (Romans 8:15). "Stand firm, and do not be held again under the yoke of bondage" (Galatians 5:1) .

Sacred Scripture

"For the expectation of the creature waits for the revelation of the sons of God. For the creature was made subject to vanity, not willingly, but by reason of Him that made it subject, in hope. Because the creature also itself shall be delivered from the servitude of corruption, into the liberty of the glory of the children of God." *Romans 8:19-21*

"Neither is there salvation in any other. For there is no other Name under Heaven given to men, whereby we must be saved." *Acts 4:12*

Vatican Council II

"However, in order to establish a relationship of peace and communion with himself, and in order to bring about brotherly union among men, and they [sic] sinners, God decided to enter into the history of mankind in a new and definitive manner, by sending his own Son in human flesh, so that through him he might snatch men from the power of darkness and of Satan (cf. Col. 1:13; Acts 10:38)." *Missionary Activity, 3*

"Through preaching and the celebration of the sacraments, of which the holy Eucharist is the center and summit, missionary activity makes Christ present, he who is the author of salvation." *Missionary Activity, 9*

Prayer: *Praise to You, our Savior. By Your death You have opened for us the way of salvation. Guide Your people to walk in Your ways. Teach them to see Your Passion in their sufferings, and to show to others Your power to save. To You be all honor and glory now and forever. Amen.*

See Papally Promulgated
Catechism of the Catholic Church

Q. 85. See paragraphs: 421, 549, 601, 605-617, 714

Q. 86. Is there any other Savior?

There is no salvation in anyone but Jesus Christ, nor has there ever been, nor will there ever be.

By his own power no one is freed from the slavery of sin. Scripture says, "There is no salvation in anyone else but Christ Jesus" (Acts 4:12). Until Jesus died upon the Cross and paid the price for man's sin, no human soul could enter Heaven.

St. Paul says, "For God was indeed in Christ, reconciling the world to Himself, not imputing to them their sins; and He has placed in us the word of reconciliation" (2 Corinthians 5:19).

The mystery of Christ appears in the history of men and of the world — a history subject to sin — not only as the mystery of the Incarnation but also as the mystery of salvation and redemption. God the Father so loved sinners that He gave His Son, reconciling the world to Himself. Christ, in His boundless love, freely underwent His Passion and death because of the sins of all men, so that all might attain salvation.

Our Lord's life shows God's own love for us because all that He said and did, His whole life and death, was for the sake of others. He spent His life teaching men the truth about His Father and about themselves; He shared their lives and suffering and He healed their illnesses. He did all this out of love for them and for His Father, Who called Him to this service. The life of Jesus shows us in a human way that God's life is a life of love. Father, Son, and Holy Spirit are forever giving Themselves to each other. Having received from Jesus a perfect human life of love, the Father now gives His own life to people who turn to Him in faith.

Sacred Scripture

"For God indeed was in Christ, reconciling the world to Himself, not imputing to them their sins; and He has placed in us the word of reconciliation." *2 Corinthians 5:19*

See Papally Promulgated
Catechism of the Catholic Church

Q. 86. See paragraphs: 432, 452

"For as by the disobedience of one man, many were made sinners; so also by the obedience of one, many shall be made just." *Romans 5:19*

Vatican Council II

"Christ, whom the Father sanctified or consecrated and sent into the world, 'gave himself for us to redeem us from all iniquity and to purify for himself a people of his own who are zealous for good deeds' (Tit. 2:14), and in this way through his passion entered into his glory." *Priests, 12*

Prayer: *Jesus, we believe that there is no salvation in anyone but You. You are the Word through Whom God made the universe; You are the Savior He sent to redeem us. By the power of the Holy Spirit, You took flesh and were born of the Virgin Mary. For our sake You opened Your arms on the Cross; You put an end to death and revealed the Resurrection. In this You fulfilled Your Father's will and won for Him a holy people. To You be all honor and glory, now and forever. Amen.*

Prayer

Savior of mankind, You destroyed death, and by rising again, restored life. Sanctify Your people, redeemed by Your blood. Give us a greater share in Your Passion through a deeper spirit of repentance, so that we may share the glory of Your Resurrection.

As You offered Your body on the Cross, Your perfect sacrifice fulfilled all others. As You gave Yourself into the hands of Your heavenly Father for our salvation, You showed Yourself to be the Priest and the Lamb of Sacrifice. Sustain us by Your love, for You offered Yourself as a perfect sacrifice on the Cross, and You are Lord forever.

By Your blood You have set all men free and saved us from death. Continue Your work of love within us. By constantly celebrating the mystery of our salvation, which is re-enacted in the Holy Sacrifice of the Mass, may we reach the eternal life it promises. All glory and honor be unto You now and forever. Amen.

Chapter Thirty-Two

Jesus Our Redeemer

Q. 87. How did Christ redeem mankind?

By His death and Resurrection, Christ redeemed mankind from slavery to sin and the devil.

We were slaves of the devil because of original sin and because of our personal sins. But Jesus made us free, giving us the freedom of the children of God, for, by His Resurrection, He destroyed death and gave us the life of grace.

In obedience to His Father's will, Jesus gave Himself for us in His Passion and arose from the dead, that He might redeem us from sin and make us a people pleasing to the Father. He is the Messiah, God's own Son. He often said that what He was doing was done so that the Scriptures, which reveal the Father's will, might be fulfilled.

To "redeem" means to buy back something that has been lost, sold, or given away. Through sin, man had lost his birthright of eternal union with God — eternal happiness in Heaven. The Son of God made man gave that birthright back to us, by offering Himself to His heavenly Father as a victim for our redemption. The Old Testament sacrifices were only symbols of the new sacrifice of the Lamb — the Lamb of God Who was sacrificed to give worthy honor and reparation to His Father. That is why He is called the Redeemer; why His work is called the work of redemption.

He offered His life for love of us and for the glory of His Father. He did His Father's will to honor Him and to make people happy forever in God's Kingdom. The Father now gives His own divine life of grace to people who turn to Him in faith.

By sinning, man failed to love God, but Christ's work of redemption was an act of infinitely perfect love and obedience,

See Papally Promulgated
Catechism of the Catholic Church

Q. 87. See paragraphs: 517, 561, 613, 616-617, 1933

which made up His whole life on earth. His infancy spent in Egypt, and his thirty years at home in Nazareth were as much a part of our redemption as were the three years of His active life and His death. His death on the Cross was the climax of His earthly lifetime of obedience to the will of the Father.

Whatever God does is of infinite value. Because Christ is God, the very least of His works or sufferings is enough to make up for man's sins. But in the plan of the Father, His Son would carry His act of perfect obedience to the point of giving Himself up to death on Calvary.

Sacred Scripture

"For there is one God, and one mediator of God and men, the man Christ Jesus, Who gave Himself a redemption for all, a testimony in due times." *1 Timothy 2:5-6*

Vatican Council II

"The Lord himself came to free and strengthen man, renewing him inwardly and casting out the 'prince of this world' (Jn. 12:31), who held him in the bondage of sin. For sin brought man to a lower state, forcing him away from the completeness that is his to attain." *Modern World, 13*

Prayer: *Jesus, we believe that by Your death and Resurrection You redeemed mankind from slavery to sin and the devil. There is no salvation in anyone but You.*

Your Father loved the world so much that He gave You, His only Son, to free us from the ancient power of sin and from death. Help us who wait for Your coming, and lead us to true liberty. In Your Father's plan of salvation, You accepted the Cross and freed us from the power of the enemy. Your Father decreed that man should be saved through the wood of the Cross. The tree of man's defeat was replaced by the wood of the Cross, a tree of victory; where life was lost, there life has been restored through You. May we come to share in the glory of Your Resurrection. We ask this in Your most powerful and holy Name. Amen.

Prayer

Jesus, Mediator of the New Covenant, in the Sacrifice of the Mass may we come to You, find salvation in the sprinkling of Your Blood, and draw closer to the Kingdom where You are Lord forever.

You renew us with the food and drink of salvation in Holy Communion. May Your Blood be for us a fountain of water springing up to eternal life. Through this sacrament defend us from those who threaten us with evil, for You have set us free and saved us from death by Your Precious Blood. Hear us during times of trouble and protect us by the power of Your Name, that we who share Your struggle on earth, may merit a share in Your victory.

Lord, Jesus, Redeemer of all and Author of our salvation, by Your sacrificial death, You conquered death. Hear the prayers of Your family and lift us from our slavery to evil, that we may be redeemed by You and see Your Father's glory. Teach us to seek for imperishable goods and to have confidence in Your Blood, poured out as the price of our redemption.

Lord Jesus, You have revealed Your justice to all nations. We stood condemned, but You came to be judged in our place. Send Your saving power to us, and, when You come in glory, bring Your mercy to those for whom You were condemned. To You be all power, honor and glory. Amen.

Chapter Thirty-Three

The Passion of Our Lord - I
The Agony on Mount Olivet

"Then Jesus came with them into a country place which is called Gethsemani; and He said to His disciples, 'Sit here, till I go over there and pray.' And taking with Him Peter and the two sons of Zebedee, He began to grow sorrowful and to be sad. Then He said to them, 'My soul is sorrowful even unto death. Stay here, and watch with Me.'

"And going a little further, He fell upon His face, praying, and saying, 'My Father, if it be possible, let this chalice pass from Me. Nevertheless, not as I will, but as You will.'

"And He came to His disciples, and found them asleep. And He said to Peter, 'What? Could you not watch one hour with Me? Watch and pray that you enter not into temptation. The spirit indeed is willing, but the flesh is weak.'

"Again the second time, He went and prayed, saying, 'My Father, if this chalice may not pass away, unless I drink it, Your will be done.' And He came again, and found them sleeping: for their eyes were heavy. And leaving them, He went again, and He prayed the third time, saying the very same thing.

"Then He came to His disciples, and said to them, 'Sleep and take your rest; behold the hour is at hand, and the Son of Man shall be betrayed into the hands of sinners. Rise, let us go. Behold he is at hand that will betray Me.' " *Matthew 26:36-46*

Q. 88. What did the agony and prayer in the garden express?

The agony and prayer of Jesus in the Garden of the Mount of Olives expressed His desire to do His Father's will at all costs. "Nevertheless, not My will but Yours be done" (Mark 14:36).

See Papally Promulgated
Catechism of the Catholic Church

Q. 88. See paragraphs: 539, 555, 607, 612

It also expressed all the spiritual torment Jesus experienced for our sake, as He placed Himself fully in the Father's hands. The torment He experienced, due to mankind's rejection of Him, caused Him unimaginable pain.

Sacred Scripture

"He was in the world, and the world was made by Him, and the world knew Him not. He came unto His own, and His own received Him not." *John 1: 10-11*

Q. 89. Why were the sufferings Christ bore for us so severe?

The sufferings Christ bore for us were extremely severe, in large measure, because of our rejection of His infinite love for us.

Vatican Council II

"The Church always held and continues to hold that Christ out of infinite love freely underwent suffering and death because of the sins of all men, so that all might attain salvation. It is the duty of the Church, therefore, in her preaching to proclaim the cross of Christ as the sign of God's universal love and the source of all grace." *Non-Christian Religions, 4*

See Papally Promulgated
Catechism of the Catholic Church

Q. 89. See paragraphs: 312, 572, 766, 1851

Prayer

Jesus, Your Passion begins. Yours is the suffering of the soul. Fear takes hold of You; fear caused by the certainty and nearness of Your death and by the sufferings which will bring it about. You experience disgust at the thought of the sins for which You are to suffer so much. How terrible are the sins of all men and nations and ages, in all their vileness and malice, as compared with God's supreme authority, infinite goodness, justice, and beauty!

Sadness fills the very depths of Your soul — sadness caused by Your knowledge of those who will ultimately reject what You will gain by all Your sacrifices. You foresee that men will neglect Your Church, or misuse it, to their own ruin. All these dreadful pictures rise before You and cut You to Your very heart. You are sorrowful unto death. We humbly beg you to forgive us for our part in this agony of Your soul by committing our many sins.

Humble obedience to Your Father and tender love for us made You willing to suffer even the greatest torments. Help us to show that we are grateful for Your generosity by granting us true contrition for our sins and a burning love for You, our best Friend and our God, now and forever. Amen.

Chapter Thirty-Four

The Passion of Our Lord - II
Jesus before Pilate

"Then he released to them Barabbas, and having scourged Jesus, delivered Him unto them to be crucified. Then the soldiers of the governor taking Jesus into the hall, gathered together unto Him the whole band; and stripping Him, they put a scarlet cloak about Him. And platting a crown of thorns, they put it upon His head, and a reed in His right hand. And bowing the knee before Him, they mocked Him, saying Hail, King of the Jews. And spitting upon Him, they took the reed, and struck His head." *Matthew 27:26-30*

"Pilate therefore went forth again and said to them, 'Behold, I bring Him forth unto you, that you may know that I find no cause in Him.' (Jesus therefore came forth, bearing the crown of thorns and the purple garment.) And he said to them, 'Behold the Man.'

"When the chief priests, therefore, and the servants, had seen Him, they cried out, saying, 'Crucify Him, crucify Him.' Pilate said to them, 'Take Him, and crucify Him: for I find no cause in Him.' The Jews answered him, 'We have a law; and according to the law He ought to die, because He made Himself the Son of God.' When Pilate therefore had heard this saying, he feared the more.

"And he entered into the hall again, and he said to Jesus, 'Where do You come from?' But Jesus gave him no answer. Pilate therefore said to Him, 'Do You not speak to me? Do You not know that I have power to crucify You, and I have the power to release You?' Jesus answered, 'You would not have any power against Me, unless it were given You from above. Therefore, he that has delivered Me to you has the greater sin.' And from henceforth Pilate sought to release Him.

"But the Jews cried out, saying, 'If you release this man, you are not Caesar's friend. For whoever makes himself a king, speaks against Caesar.' Now when Pilate had heard these words, he brought Jesus forth, and sat down in the judgment seat, in the place that is called Lithostrotos, and in Hebrew Gabbatha. And it was the parasceve of the pasch, about the sixth hour, and he said to the Jews, 'Behold your king.' But they cried out, 'Away with Him; away with Him; crucify Him.' Pilate said to them, 'Shall I crucify your king?'"

The chief priests answered, 'We have no king but Caesar.' Then therefore he delivered Him to them to be crucified."

John 19:4-16

Q. 90. Before His death what trials did Jesus undergo?

Before He was crucified, Jesus was falsely accused, and then was tried and cruelly treated by: (1) the chief priests and elders; (2) the Tetrarch Herod; and by (3) Pontius Pilate, the Roman governor. It was Pontius Pilate who condemned Him to die on the Cross as a common criminal.

"Then Jesus took unto Him the Twelve, and said to them, 'Behold, we go up to Jerusalem, and all things shall be accomplished which were written by the prophets concerning the Son of Man. For He shall be delivered to the Gentiles, and shall be mocked, and scourged, and spit upon. And after they shall have scourged Him, they will put Him to death, and the third day He shall rise again' " (Luke 18:31-33). But His disciples could not begin to understand this mystery of redemption (cf. Luke 18:34) until it had been accomplished (cf. Luke 24:25). Jesus, Whose very name means "Savior," had the Cross always "before His eyes."

Sacred Scripture

"And it came to pass, when the time was come that He should be received up, that he steadfastly set his face to go to Jerusalem. And he sent messengers before his face." *Luke 9:51-52*

There He was to undergo the bitter and saving baptism of the Cross: "I am come to cast fire on the earth: and what will I, but that it be kindled? And I have a baptism wherewith I am to be baptized. And how am I straitened until it be accomplished?" *Luke 12:49-50*

Jesus longed for the Cross, for by it, only, would the fire of His love be enkindled on earth (cf. Luke 12:49); by it He would "gather together in one the children of God that were dispersed." *John 11:52*

See Papally Promulgated
Catechism of the Catholic Church

Q. 90. See paragraphs: 571-597

Q. 91. What was Christ's mission on earth?

Christ's mission on earth, given to Him by His Father, was to save us from the horrors of hell, and to bring us to the joys of eternal life in the Kingdom of Heaven. He did this through His suffering and dying on the Cross.

We can also say that the Son of God became man to save us from satan, sin, and death. In the Nicene Creed we say: "For us men and for our salvation He came down from Heaven...For our sake he was crucified under Pontius Pilate; he suffered, died, and was buried."

Q. 92. In what sense do we speak of the necessity of the Passion and death of Jesus?

We speak of the necessity of the Passion and Death of Jesus in the sense that it was God's will that man's redemption be achieved in this particular manner. The Passion of our Lord was not something which absolutely had to be. Our redemption could have been obtained in a variety of other ways had God so desired it.

Q. 93. Did Jesus Himself declare that He had to suffer?

Yes, Jesus stated that it was necessary for Him to suffer in order to bring us eternal life. Thus, He said, "And as Moses lifted up the serpent in the desert, so must the Son of Man be

See Papally Promulgated
Catechism of the Catholic Church

Q. 91. See paragraphs: 456-460
Q. 92. See paragraphs: 572, 599
Q. 93. See paragraphs: 572, 606

lifted up. So that whoever believes in Him, may not perish; but may have life everlasting" (John 3:14-15).

After His Resurrection, Jesus said, "Should not Christ have suffered these things, and then to enter into His glory?" (Luke 24:26).

Centuries before Christ's Passion and Death, the Old Testament prophets prophesied them. The Suffering Servant passages of Isaiah are particularly noteworthy (cf. Isaiah 53). Speaking of the fulfillment of these ancient prophecies, Jesus said, "All things must be fulfilled, which are written in the law of Moses, and in the prophets, and in the Psalms, concerning Me" (Luke 24:44).

Speaking of His heavenly Father's will for Him, Jesus exclaimed, "Therefore the Father loves Me, because I lay down my life, that I may take it again" (John 10:17). Jesus, with perfect freedom, lovingly accepted this heavy burden placed upon Him so that we might be saved. "No man takes it away from Me, but I lay it down of Myself, and I have power to lay it down. And I have power to take it up again" (John 10:18).

Sacred Scripture

"But that the world may know that I love the Father, and as the Father has commanded I do it." *John 14:31*

"In this we have known the charity of God, because He has laid down His life for us. And we ought to lay down our lives for the brethren." *1 John 3:16*

Vatican Council II

"No one is freed from sin by himself or by his own efforts, no one is raised above himself or completely delivered from his own weakness, solitude or slavery; all have need of Christ who is the model, master, liberator, Saviour, and giver of life."

Missionary Activity, 8

165

Prayer

Jesus, You reject the crown of gold and kingly robes to accept instead a crown of thorns and the purple rags of mockery and scorn. You consent to be a mock king, when, in fact, You are the true King of our souls.

We subject ourselves entirely to Your divine kingship of love. We would rather be fools in the eyes of men for Your sake and have You reign over us than be rulers of the world and slaves of the prince of darkness. We pledge unending loyalty to You, our King, and we beg You to reign supremely in our hearts, in our lives, and in the hearts of all men.

Jesus, help us to be devoted subjects of Your kingship, ennobled by the divine powers of Your grace to do good and avoid evil; to love God with our whole heart, our whole soul, all our strength, and to love our neighbor as ourselves; to wield mastery over the evil promptings of the world, the flesh, and the devil. As children of the royal family of God through grace, we claim a loving right to be admitted to Your intimate friendship, with the privilege of feeling the sacred influence of Your holy love which has transformed us into God-like beings, making our innermost thoughts and affections like Your own. To You be all glory and praise forever and ever. Amen.

Chapter Thirty-Five

The Passion of Our Lord- III
The Crucifixion of Jesus

"And bearing His own cross, He went forth to that place which is called Calvary, but in Hebrew Golgotha. Where they crucified Him, and with Him two others, one on each side, and Jesus in the midst. And Pilate wrote a title also, and he put it upon the cross, and the writing was: JESUS OF NAZA-RETH, THE KING OF THE JEWS.

"This title therefore many of the Jews did read, because the place where Jesus was crucified was near to the city: And it was written in Hebrew, in Greek, and in Latin. Then the chief priests of the Jews said to Pilate, 'Write not, The King of the Jews; but that He said, 'I am the King of the Jews.' Pilate answered, 'What I have written, I have written.'

"The soldiers therefore, when they had crucified Him, took His garments, (and they made four parts, to every soldier a part), and also His coat. Now the coat was without seam, woven from the top throughout. They said then one to another, 'Let us not cut it, but let us cast lots for it, whose it shall be,' that the Scripture might be fulfilled saying, 'They have parted My garments among them, and upon My vesture they have cast lots.' And the soldiers indeed did these things.

"Now there stood by the Cross of Jesus, His Mother, and His Mother's sister, Mary of Cleophas, and Mary Magdalen. When Jesus therefore had seen His Mother and the disciple standing whom He loved, He said to His Mother, 'Woman, behold your son.' After that He said to the disciple 'Behold your Mother.' And from that hour, the disciple took her to his own home.

"Afterwards, Jesus knowing that all things were now accomplished, that the scripture might be fulfilled, said, 'I thirst.' Now there was a vessel set there full of vinegar. And they putting a sponge full of vinegar and put it on hyssop, put it to His mouth. Jesus therefore, when He had taken the vinegar, said 'It is consummated.' And bowing His head, He gave up the spirit." *John 19:17-30*

Q. 94. What did Jesus suffer upon the Cross?

Jesus suffered inexpressible physical and spiritual agony upon the Cross.

Crucifixion was such a horrible instrument of death that the Roman authorities would not use it on their own citizens. Added to this torment was that indescribable pain of rejected love. He was rejected not only by those in Palestine, but also by all those who prefer sinful life-styles to the will of God.

Upon the Cross, Jesus suffered not only extreme physical pain, but also loneliness and desolation, and the anguish of seeing inexpressible sorrow in the one He loved most deeply, His Mother Mary. Even in the terrible torment of those hours, Jesus, the Son of God and High Priest of our salvation, retained patience and greatness of soul.

> **Prayer:** *Jesus, You were not alone in offering Your sacrifice. To have followed You to Calvary was the most certain proof of love. That is the reason why Mary, Your loving Mother, stood beneath Your Cross, nailed to it in spirit, as a co-victim with You. No one ever loved You as Your Blessed Mother did; therefore, no one ever suffered for You as she did. May we always enjoy her maternal love and protection. Amen.*

Q. 95. What are the "seven last words" of Jesus as recorded in the Gospels?

Sacred Scripture

The "seven last words" of Jesus as recorded in the Gospels are:

1. "Father, forgive them, for they know not what they do."
Luke 23:34

2. (To a thief who had been crucified with Him and who asked for mercy, He said), "Amen I say to you, this day you shall be with Me in paradise." *Luke 23:43*

3. (To His Mother He said,) "Woman, behold your son." (And to St. John, Jesus exclaimed,) "Behold your mother."
John 19:26-27

See Papally Promulgated
Catechism of the Catholic Church

Q. 94. See paragraphs: 478, 599, 603, 766
Q. 95. See paragraphs: 603, 607, 2605

---

4. (To His Father in the prayerful words drawn from a prophetic Psalm, He said,) "My God, my God, why have You forsaken Me?" *Matthew 27:46*

5. "I thirst." *John 19:28*

6. "It is consummated." *John 19:30*

7. "Father, into Your hands I commend My spirit."
Luke 23:46; cf. Psalm 31:5

> **Prayer:** *Jesus, You are our Redeemer, Advocate, and Victim for sinners. You begin Your last words amid the deafening yell of triumphant hate, amidst the hissing curses and grim delight of Your enemies. You asked not for justice for them, but for mercy when You pleaded as a Son with Your Father, "Father, forgive them for they know not what they do" (Luke 23:34). Lord, we sinners also plead for Your mercy and the grace to live lives worthy of Your heavenly Kingdom now and forever. Amen.*

Q. 96. How did Jesus die?

Jesus died by crucifixion.

Having been nailed to the Cross for about three hours, He bowed His head and gave up His spirit (cf. John 19:30). Thus, the Son of God died for us sinners.

St. Paul wrote, "Scarcely for a just man will one die; yet perhaps for a good man some one would dare to die. But God commends His charity towards us, because when as yet we were sinners, Christ died for us" (Romans 5:7-9).

> **Prayer:** *Jesus, have pity on our souls, for which You bore all this pain, and for which You died in bloody agony. Forgive us, for we did not know what we were doing. Amen.*

See Papally Promulgated
Catechism of the Catholic Church

Q. 96. See paragraphs: 607, 609-610, 616-618, 623, 2605

Q. 97. What effects did the Passion of Jesus have?

The Passion of Jesus has eternal effects. His suffering saved us from sin and all its consequences, and we have received every grace and gift leading to eternal life.

This liberation won for us by Jesus in His Passion has effects even in this world. Redemption is not only in the soul's inner life of love and grace. Men freed from sin can, with God's grace, transform this world also into a kingdom of greater freedom, justice, and peace — into God's Kingdom.

Vatican Council II

"Since Jesus, the Son of God, showed his love by laying down his life for us, no man then has greater love than he who lays down his life for him and for his brothers (cf. 1 Jn. 3:16; Jn. 15:13)." *The Church, 42*

See Papally Promulgated
Catechism of the Catholic Church

Q. 97. See paragraphs: 601, 1020-1029, 1987-1996

Prayer

Jesus, You offered Yourself to God as a Victim for the sins of the world, and for our sins. Your bleeding wounds are proof of a love unto death. We see Your head bent down to reach us in our sinfulness; Your arms extended to embrace us, though it was we who nailed them here; Your body hanging to redeem us, though we sometimes hardly seem to care. We do not belong to ourselves, but to You, Who have purchased us at such a price.

We are Your parting gift of love to Your Mother. Your Mother is Your parting gift of love to us. She is the dearest and loveliest of mothers, who You have created for Yourself according to Your own divine desires. She has been created in every way immensely superior to all other mothers, the outstanding blessed one among women. We thank You for giving us so good and amiable a Mother. May we love her as much as she deserves to be loved, according to the way You love her. May we, like John, take her to be our very own, that in life she may make us Your very own, and in Heaven, God's very own for all eternity.

Into Your hands we commend unreservedly and forever our spirits, our souls with all their powers, our bodies with all their senses, our whole beings, to be owned and ruled by Your Holy Spirit in all things during life. Teach us to do Your will in all things and to recognize Your Divine Providence in all that may befall us. May we be ever united with You in love and confidence till our last breath, so that, mindful of Your own death for us upon the Cross, we may bow our heads in humble submission to God's will, and reverently commend our souls into Your Father's hands forever and ever. Amen.

The Resurrection and the Ascension

Chapter Thirty-Six

The Resurrection

Q. 98. How did Jesus Christ show the power He has as the Son of God?

Through His Resurrection, Jesus' power as the Son of God was made known to us.

Until the Resurrection, He remained humbly obedient even unto death, and by gloriously raising Himself from the dead He was exalted as Lord of all. He raised Himself from the dead on the third day as He had promised He would. His Resurrection gave the final proof that He was God's Son, as He had claimed to be. By conquering bodily death, through His own power, as evidenced by His Resurrection, Jesus has shown Himself master of life and death. Therefore He is true God and true man, our Savior.

In the many centuries from Adam until Jesus, there were great numbers of men and women throughout the world, who believed in God and obeyed His laws. Since such souls were not deserving of eternal punishment, they lived after death in a state of happiness but without any vision of God. This state is called the Limbo of the Fathers.

Jesus appeared with His human soul to these souls while His body lay in the tomb, to announce to them the glad tidings of the redemption, and to bring them to God the Father. During this time, His divine Person remained united both to His body and to His soul. In the Apostles' Creed we say: "He descended into hell."

Jesus rose from the dead in a glorified body, a body glorified even as the bodies of the just will be after their resurrection at the end of the world. It was a body that could no longer suffer or die; a body that showed forth the brightness and beauty of a soul united with God; a body that could pass from

See Papally Promulgated
Catechism of the Catholic Church

Q. 98. See paragraphs: 428, 444-445, 649, 651

place to place with the speed of thought; a body that could pass through a solid wall; a body that needed neither food, nor drink, nor sleep. It is in and through His risen and glorified body that Jesus makes Himself available to mankind through His Church. His divine power is at work especially in the sacraments, providing the grace we need for salvation and sanctification.

Sacred Scripture

"This Jesus has God raised again, whereof all we are witnesses." *Acts: 2:32*

"And what is the exceeding greatness of His power towards us, who believes according to the operation of the might of His power, which He wrought in Christ, raising Him up from the dead, and setting Him on His right hand in the heavenly places." *Ephesians 1:19-20*

Vatican Council II

"The wonderful works of God among the people of the Old Testament were but a prelude to the work of Christ Our Lord in redeeming mankind and giving perfect glory to God. He achieved his task principally by the paschal mystery of his blessed passion, resurrection from the dead, and glorious ascension, whereby 'dying, he destroyed our death, and rising, restored our life.' " *Sacred Liturgy, 5*

Prayer: *Jesus, we believe that in Your Resurrection Your body was glorified by being united again to Your glorified soul. You rose triumphantly by Your own power. Your body took on spiritual qualities: immortality, beauty, glory, freedom and the power to move about with speed and without hindrance. Divinity shines forth from Your glorified body, and floods of joy pour into Your soul and Your Sacred Heart. At Your Second Coming, grant that we also, through Your great mercy, may have glorified bodies, which with our souls will share forever in Your love, joy and peace. Amen.*

Prayer

*J*esus, we believe that by Your divine power You rose, as You had promised, as a glorious Victor. The earth quaked as You came forth from the tomb, and the guards trembled with fear. Your body now shines like the sun. The wounds of Your hands and feet sparkle like precious jewels. Death is conquered, its victory broken, its sting destroyed. You triumph not for Yourself alone, but that we too may triumph over the grave.

*T*his mystery strengthens our hope in another and better life after death, in the resurrection of our bodies on the last day, and in an eternity of happiness. We firmly hope that we may die in the state of grace so that You can raise us up glorified. Through Your glorious Resurrection, we hope that You will make our bodies like Your own in glory, and permit us to dwell with You in Heaven for all eternity.

*W*e adore Your sacred humanity which receives this eternal kingdom of honor, power, joy, and glory. We rejoice with You, our Master; immortal, all-glorious, and all-powerful. Amen.

Chapter Thirty-Seven

The Risen Life of Jesus - I
The Holy Women at the Tomb

"And in the end of the sabbath, when it began to dawn towards the first day of the week, came Mary Magdalen and the other Mary to see the sepulchre.

"And behold there was a great earthquake. For an angel of the Lord descended from Heaven, and coming, rolled back the stone, and sat upon it. And his countenance was as lightning, and his raiment as snow. And for fear of him, the guards were struck with terror, and became as dead men.

"And the angel answering, said to the women, 'Fear not, for I know that you seek Jesus Who was crucified. He is not here, for He is risen, as He said. Come, and see the place where the Lord was laid. And going quickly, tell His disciples that He is risen and behold He will go before you into Galilee; there you shall see Him. Lo, I have foretold it to you.'

"And they went out quickly from the sepulchre with fear and great joy, running to tell His disciples.

"And behold Jesus met them saying, 'All hail.' But they came up and took hold of His feet, and adored Him. Then Jesus said to them, 'Fear not. Go, tell My brethren to go into Galilee. There they shall see Me.' "(Matthew 28:1-10).

Q. 99. Why is the Resurrection of our Lord so important?

The Resurrection of our Lord is very important because it not only confirms the Church's Faith, but is the central mystery through which God calls us to life everlasting.

The Church celebrates the Resurrection of Jesus with great joy. Not only on Easter, but every Sunday of the year is a

See Papally Promulgated
Catechism of the Catholic Church

Q. 99. See paragraphs: 638, 651-658

celebration of our Lord's Resurrection. This is the day when Jesus Christ broke the chains of death and rose triumphant from the grave. Faith in the Resurrection is the basis for hope in "an inheritance incorruptible, and undefiled, and that cannot fade, reserved in Heaven for you" (1 Peter 1:4).

Sacred Scripture

"Faith is the substance of things hoped for, the evidence of things not seen." *Hebrews 11:1*

> **Prayer:** *Jesus, what great love You showed to the pious women! They followed You to Calvary, and wished to be with You even when they believed You were in the grave. In reward for this love and fidelity, You appeared to them soon after Your Resurrection. Through Your graces, may we share in their love and fidelity, and be with You forever in Heaven. Amen.*

Q. 100. Why does the Resurrection of Jesus play a central part in the life of faith?

The Resurrection plays a central part in the life of faith, because it is the key event underlying the The Church's Faith in Jesus as Savior and Redeemer.

The historical, bodily, and perpetual resurrection of Jesus from the dead is evidence that Jesus has conquered mankind's enemies of sin and death. The Resurrection also confirms that all Jesus taught about His divinity and messianic mission is true. Moreover, the Resurrection points to the triumph over sin and death which belongs to those who fully accept Jesus as their Savior.

The Apostles and disciples considered the Resurrection so important that they risked imprisonment, torture and death in proclaiming the historical reality of the Resurrection.

See Papally Promulgated
Catechism of the Catholic Church

Q. 100. See paragraphs: 651-655

Q. 101. What was the Easter proclamation?

The Easter proclamation was the words of the angel to the holy women, "He is not here, but is risen" (Luke 24:6).

Sacred Scripture

St. Paul wrote: "Now I make known to you, brethren, the Gospel which I preached to you, which also you have received, and wherein you stand. By which also you are saved, if you hold fast after what manner I preached unto you unless you have believed in vain. For I delivered unto you first of all, which I also received, how Christ died for our sins, according to the scriptures. And that He was buried, and that He rose again the third day, according to the scriptures. And that He was seen by Cephas, and after that by the Eleven."

1 Corinthians 15:1-5

"And in the end of the sabbath, when it began to draw towards the first day of the week, came Mary Magdalen and the other Mary, to see the sepulchre. And behold there was a great earthquake. For an angel of the Lord descended from heaven, and coming, rolled back the stone, and sat upon it. And his countenance was as lightning, and his raiment as snow. And for fear of him, the guards were struck with terror, and became as dead men. And the angel answering, said to the women: 'Fear not ; for I know that you seek Jesus Who was crucified. He is not here, for He is risen, as He said. Come, and see the place where the Lord was laid. And going quickly, tell His disciples that He is risen: and behold, He will go before you into Galilee; there you shall see Him. Lo, I have foretold it to you.' And they went out quickly from the sepulchre with fear and great joy, running to tell His disciples. And behold Jesus met them, saying: 'All hail.' But they came up and took hold of His feet, and adored Him." *Matthew 28:1-9*

"This Jesus God has raised again, whereof all we are witnesses." *Acts 2:32*

See Papally Promulgated
Catechism of the Catholic Church

Q. 101. See paragraph: 640

180

Vatican Council II

"After God had spoken many times and in various ways through the prophets, 'in these last days he has spoken to us by a Son' (Heb. 1:1-2). For he sent his Son, the eternal Word who enlightens all men, to dwell among men and to tell them about the inner life of God. Hence, Jesus Christ, sent as 'a man among men,' 'speaks the words of God' (Jn. 3:34), and accomplishes the saving work which the Father gave him to do (cf. Jn. 5:36; 17:4). As a result, he himself — to see whom is to see the Father (cf. Jn. 14:9) — completed and perfected Revelation and confirmed it with divine guarantees. He did this by the total fact of his presence and self-manifestation — by words and works, signs and miracles, but above all by his death and glorious resurrection from the dead, and finally by sending the Spirit of truth. He revealed that God was with us, to deliver us from the darkness of sin and death, and to raise us up to eternal life." *Divine Revelation, 4*

Prayer

Jesus, You are infinitely good to all, and never fail to reward those who wish to please You. Your goodness will be made manifest also in us, if we remain faithful in all sufferings and temptations. How often have we been unfaithful to You; how often, in times of sorrow and trial, have we forsaken You. We promise to be more faithful to You in the future. Give us a true love for You; an ardent, self-sacrificing love, that seeks to please You perfectly and to become like You in suffering.

Jesus, it was but a matter of course that You would appear to Your holy Mother, for she is Your nearest and dearest in the order of nature and of grace. You received from her the life that is now so glorious. She has the most intimate share in Your mysteries, of which this glory of Your Resurrection is the exceedingly great reward. She shared more than anyone else in the sorrow and bitterness of Your Passion, and so she shares more than all others in the glory of Your triumph. It is, therefore, fitting that she should now have a special share in Your glory.

Lord Jesus, early in the morning of Your Resurrection, You made Your love known and brought the first light of dawn to those who dwelt in darkness. Your death has opened a path for us. Do not enter into judgment with Your servants; let Your Holy Spirit guide us into the land of justice and heavenly bliss. This we ask in Your most holy and powerful Name. Amen.

Chapter Thirty-Eight

The Risen Life of Jesus - II
Jesus Appears to the Apostles

"Now when it was late that same day, the first of the week, and the doors were shut, where the disciples were gathered together, for fear of the Jews, Jesus came and stood in the midst, and said to them, 'Peace be to you.' And when He had said this, He showed them His hands and His side. The disciples therefore were glad, when they saw the Lord.

"He said therefore to them again, 'Peace be to you. As the Father has sent Me, I also send you.' When He had said this, He breathed on them; and He said to them, 'Receive the Holy Spirit. Whose sins you shall forgive, they are forgiven them; and whose sins you shall retain, they are retained.'

"Now Thomas, one of the twelve, who is called Didymus, was not with them when Jesus came. The other disciples therefore said to him, 'We have seen the Lord.' But he said to them, 'Except I shall see in His hands the print of the nails, and put my finger into the place of the nails, and put my hand into His side, I will not believe.'

"And after eight days again His disciples were within, and Thomas with them. Jesus came, the doors being shut, and stood in the midst, and said, 'Peace be to you,' then He said to Thomas, 'Put your finger in here, and see My hands; and My side; and be not faithless, but believing.'

"Thomas answered, and said to Him, 'My Lord, and my God.' Jesus said to him, 'Because you have seen me, Thomas, you have believed. Blessed are they that have not seen, and have believed' " (John 20:20-29).

Prayer: *Most gentle Prince of Peace, Who gave peace to Your Apostles, we beg You, from the fullness of Your Sacred Heart, give us that peace which the world cannot give, that we may faithfully keep Your commandments and serve You without fear of our enemies.*

Jesus, before Your death, You informed Peter and the other Apostles that in Your Church they would be given power to bind and loose with respect to sins. When appearing to Your Apostles You actually gave them the power to forgive sins and the authority to judge. This power was given not only to them, but also to their lawful successors.

Q. 102. How did Jesus lead His Apostles to faith in His Resurrection?

Jesus led His Apostles to believe in His Resurrection by His being present among His followers for forty days in His resurrected and glorified body, by eating with them, by speaking to them, and by allowing Himself to be touched and felt. Clearly, He Whom they saw, touched, and heard was neither a disembodied spirit nor an illusion.

Sacred Scripture

"To whom He showed Himself alive after His Passion, by many proofs, for forty days, by appearing to them and speaking of the Kingdom of God." *Acts 1:3*

Q. 103. How did the Holy Spirit lead the Apostles towards faith in the Resurrection of Jesus?

The Holy Spirit, by the means of the inner gift of faith, confirmed the Apostles in their outward acceptance of Jesus' Resurrection, as evidenced by St. Thomas and all the Apostles during the early days and years of the Church.

Sacred Scripture

"And with great power did the Apostles give testimony of

See Papally Promulgated
Catechism of the Catholic Church

Q. 102. See paragraphs: 641-645
Q. 103. See paragraph: 644

the Resurrection of Jesus Christ our Lord: and great grace was in them all." *Acts 4:33*

"And we are witnesses of these things and the Holy Spirit, Whom God has given to all that obey Him." *Acts 5:32*

Vatican Council II

"Holy Mother Church believes that it is for her to celebrate the saving work of her divine Spouse in a sacred commemoration on certain days throughout the course of the year. Once each week, on the day which she has called the Lord's Day, she keeps the memory of the Lord's resurrection. She also celebrates it once every year, together with his blessed passion, at Easter, that most solemn of all feasts.

"In the course of the year, moreover, she unfolds the whole mystery of Christ from the incarnation and nativity to the ascension, to Pentecost and the expectation of the blessed hope of the coming of the Lord.

"Thus recalling the mysteries of the redemption, she opens up to the faithful the riches of her Lord's powers and merits, so that these are in some way made present for all time; the faithful lay hold of them and are filled with saving grace."

Sacred Liturgy, 102

Prayer

Jesus, You instructed the Apostles that it was necessary that You should suffer, and, on the third day, rise from the dead. If it was necessary that You should suffer in order to enter into the glory of Heaven, there certainly is no other way for us. We have been redeemed by the Cross, and by this sign we must work out our own salvation and the salvation of others. Without the Cross there is no salvation.

Strengthen us with Your grace that, after following Your example and that of Your words in Scripture, and for the love of You, we may patiently bear the trials and sufferings that our work may bring us. In the same measure in which we share Your suffering, shall we share in Your glory in the life after death. Grant us the grace of sharing Your glory in the everlasting bliss of Heaven.

We thank You for the inestimable benefit of the institution of the Sacrament of Penance. Through frequent Confession, You give us an increase of sanctifying grace, a firm confidence in God, peace of conscience, the strength to resist temptation, ease to perform good works, and a lasting joy.

In this sacrament we receive the price of Your Precious Blood and Your five sacred wounds. We thank You for all the graces we have ever received in this sacrament, by which You have rendered spiritual resurrection possible for us. Help us to make use of this great means of grace with confidence, joy, and zeal.

How kind and patient You are in bearing with our faults and in bringing good out of them. When we reflect upon how You have sought us, wandering faithless disciples, and upon how You have visited us with Your grace, we, in admiration of Your loving kindness, exclaim, "My Lord and my God!" Amen.

Chapter Thirty-Nine

The Risen Life of Jesus - III
The Primacy Given to Peter

"When therefore they had dined, Jesus said to Simon Peter, 'Simon, son of John do you love Me more than these?' He said to Him, 'Yes, Lord, You know that I love You.' He said to him, 'Feed my lambs.'

"He said to him again, 'Simon, son of John, do you love Me?' He said to Him: 'Yes, Lord, you know that I love You.' He said to him: 'Feed My lambs.'

"He said to him the third time: 'Simon, son of John, do you love Me?' Peter was grieved, because He had said to him the third time, 'Do you love Me?' and he said to Him, 'Lord, You know all things, You know that I love You.' He said to him, 'Feed my sheep. Amen, Amen I say to you, when you were younger, you girded yourself. And walked where you would. But when you are old, you shall stretch forth your hands, and another shall gird you, and lead you where you will not want to go.' And this He said, signifying by what death he should glorify God. And when He had said this, He said to him, 'Follow me' " (John 21:15-19).

Prayer: *Jesus, in Your questions to Peter before bestowing on him the primacy of authority over Your Church, we sense three great yearnings of Your Sacred Heart: the yearning to prove to us Your love, the yearning for our love in return, and the yearning for us to be able to find You and love You in souls.*

Christian love is self-giving, Christian love is sacrificial, and Christian love is expressed in deeds rather than in words. Your Heart loves souls with an everlasting love, a love greater than that of any human being, a love that is both divine and human, a love that is symbolized by Your Sacred Heart. May Your great love flood our souls and bring us to the rewards of eternal life. Amen.

Q. 104. What does the Church teach about the Resurrection?

The Catholic Church teaches that Jesus was raised bodily from the dead by the power of the Father and by His own power.

Sacred Scripture

"Therefore the Father loves Me, because I lay down My life, that I may take it again. No man takes it away from Me, but I lay it down of Myself, and I have power to lay it down, and I have power to take it up again. This commandment have I received of My Father." *John 10:17-18*

"This Jesus God has raised again, whereof we all are witnesses." *Acts 2:32*

Q. 105. What does it mean to believe in the bodily Resurrection of Jesus from the dead?

To believe in the bodily Resurrection of Jesus from the dead is to believe that God, Who became man, has conquered sin and death. We must also believe that this victory is made available to us through His Church.

Vatican Council II

"After God had spoken many times and in various ways through the prophets, 'in these last days he has spoken to us by a Son' (Heb. 1:1-2). For he sent his Son, the eternal Word who enlightens all men, to dwell among men and to tell them about the inner life of God. Hence, Jesus Christ, sent as 'a man among men,' 'speaks the words of God' (Jn. 3:34), and accomplishes the saving work which the Father gave him to do (cf. Jn. 5:36; 17:4). As a result, he himself — to see whom is to see the Father (cf. Jn. 14:9) — completed and perfected Revelation and confirmed it with divine guarantees. He did this by the the total fact of his presence and self-manifestation — by words and works, signs and miracles, but above all by his death and glorious resurrection from the dead, and finally by sending the Spirit of truth. He revealed that God was with us, to deliver us from the darkness of sin and death, and to raise us up to eternal life." *Divine Revelation 4*

"When Jesus, having died on the cross for men, rose again from the dead, he was seen to be constituted as Lord, the

See Papally Promulgated
Catechism of the Catholic Church

Q. 104. See paragraphs: 648-649
Q. 105. See paragraphs: 651-655, 658

Christ, and as Priest for ever (cf. Acts 2:36; Heb. 5:6; 7:17-21), and he poured out on his disciples the Spirit promised by the Father (cf. Acts 2:23). Henceforward the Church, endowed with the gifts of her founder and faithfully observing his precepts of charity, humility and self-denial, receives the mission of proclaiming and establishing among all peoples the kingdom of Christ and of God, and she is, on earth, the seed and the beginning of that kingdom." *The Church, 5*

Prayer

Jesus, hitherto Peter had only received the promise of the primacy, [cf. Matthew 16:15-19] but after that morning meal, You finally conferred it upon him in all its fullness and majesty, in the presence of the other Apostles. We firmly believe that this primacy is a divinely bestowed office, divine in its origin and nature, for it represents You; divine in its extent, for it embraces the whole Church, the learning [lay faithful] as well as the teaching body [hierarchical]. It also includes the entire and supreme power, divine in its operation and significance, since the whole Church — its being, attributes, stability, life, growth, and work — stands or falls with the primacy.

Jesus, after having conferred upon Peter the highest dignity in Your Church, You predicted to him that he would be taken prisoner in his old age, bound, and led to the martyrdom of the cross. All this is a proof of his love for You and for his flock, as the good shepherd he was.

We thank You for the graces and privileges You have bestowed upon us as Catholics. Help us to use these graces well and to be grateful for each token of Your tender love. Give us a generous love like Peter's for You. Help us to love You when we have to suffer, as well as when we are able to rejoice. We ask this in Your most holy and powerful Name. Amen.

Chapter Forty

The Risen Life of Jesus - IV
The Benefits of the Resurrection

Q. 106. What has Jesus Christ done for us through His Resurrection?

When Christ passed from death to life, He made possible our passing from the death of sin to life in Him.

Being the firstborn of the dead, Jesus Christ offers eternal life to all. In Him we are made spiritually renewed persons.

We receive the new life of grace in Baptism where we become God's children. St. Peter says, "Blessed be the God and Father of our Lord Jesus Christ, Who according to His great mercy has regenerated us unto a lively hope, by the Resurrection of Jesus Christ from the dead, unto an inheritance incorruptible, and undefiled, and that cannot fade, reserved in Heaven for you" (1 Peter 1:3-4).

Sacred Scripture

"And whereas indeed He was the Son of God, He learned obedience by the things which He suffered, and being consummated, He became, to all that obey Him, the cause of eternal salvation." *Hebrews 5:8-9*

"For whom He foreknew, He also predestined to be made conformable to the image of His Son; that He might be the firstborn among many brethren." *Romans 8:29*

Vatican Council II

"In the human nature united to himself, the son of God, by overcoming death through his own death and resurrection, redeemed man and changed him into a new creation (cf. Gal. 6:15; 2 Cor. 5:17)." *The Church, 7*

See Papally Promulgated
Catechism of the Catholic Church

Q. 106. See paragraphs: 638, 651, 653-655, 989, 994-995, 1003-1004

Q. 107. How does the risen Lord now help us?

Truly risen, the Lord: (1) *gives us the supernatural life of grace* and (2) *pours out His Holy Spirit upon us.*

1. *The Lord gives us the supernatural life of grace.*

By dying Jesus destroyed our spiritual death in sin and by rising He gave back our spiritual life. He now shares with us His own divine life through the gift of grace. Jesus gives us the supernatural life of grace especially through the sacraments, beginning with Baptism.

2. *Jesus gives us His Holy Spirit to make us holy and pleasing to God.*

We must live the life of God as Jesus did. The Father gives His own life to people who turn to Him in faith and love. The Father, Son, and Holy Spirit come and share Their love with those who give themselves to Jesus. In particular, Jesus, sends us God the Holy Spirit to guide and strengthen us; to make us holy. "And I will ask the Father; and He will give you another Paraclete, that He may abide with you forever" (John 14:16).

See Papally Promulgated
Catechism of the Catholic Church

Q. 107. See paragraphs: 989, 1262-1270, 1988-2005

Sacred Scripture

"Now this He said of the Spirit which they should receive, who believed in Him, for as yet the Spirit was not given, because Jesus was not yet glorified." *John 7:39*

"Being exalted therefore by the right hand of God, and having received of the Father the promise of the Holy Spirit, He has poured forth this which you see and hear." *Acts 2:33*

"And if the Spirit of Him that raised up Jesus from the dead dwells in you; He that raised up Jesus Christ from the dead shall also make your mortal bodies alive because of His Spirit that dwells in you." *Romans 8:11*

Vatican Council II

"This conversion is, indeed, only initial; sufficient however to make a man realize that he has been snatched from sin, and is being led into the mystery of God's love, who invites him to establish a personal relationship with him in Christ. Under the movement of divine grace the new convert sets out on a spiritual journey by means of which, while already sharing through faith in the mystery of the death and resurrection, he passes from the old man to the new man who has been made perfect in Christ (cf. Col. 3:5-10; Eph. 4:20-24)."

Missionary Activity, 13

Prayer: *Lord Jesus, by Your victory You broke the power of evil, and destroyed sin and death. Make us victorious over sin all the days of our lives. You laid death low, and bought us new life. To You be all honor and glory, now and forever. Amen.*

Prayer

Christ our Savior, in conquering death You brought us joy, in rising again You raised us up and filled us with the abundance of Your gifts. Stir up our hearts and sanctify us through the gifts of Your Holy Spirit.

You have restored us to life by Your triumphant Death and Resurrection. Continue this healing work within us. May we who participate in the mystery of the Eucharistic Sacrifice never cease to serve You. Send down Your abundant blessings upon Your people who devoutly recall Your Death and Resurrection at Holy Mass in the sure hope of the resurrection in the world to come.

Lord Jesus Christ, risen Savior, You chose to suffer and be overwhelmed by death in order to open the gates of eternal life in triumph. Stay with us to help us on our pilgrimage. Free us from all evil by the power of Your Resurrection. In the company of Your saints, and constantly remembering Your love for us, may we be worthy to praise You forever in Your Father's house. May our mortal life be crowned by the ultimate joy of rising with You. Amen.

Chapter Forty-One

The Ascension
Jesus Returns to the Father

"Then He opened their understanding, that they might understand the Scriptures. And He said to them, 'Thus it is written, and thus it behooved Christ to suffer, and to rise again from the dead, the third day, and that penance and remission of sins should be preached in His Name, unto all nations, beginning at Jerusalem. And you are witnesses of these things. And I send the promise of My Father upon you, but you stay in the city, till you be endued with power from on high.'

"And He led them out as far as Bethany; and lifting up His hands, He blessed them. And it came to pass, while He blessed them, He departed from them, and was carried up to Heaven. And they adoring went back into Jerusalem with great joy. And they were always in the Temple, praising and blessing God. Amen" (Luke 24:45-53).

Q. 108. What is the meaning of the Ascension of Christ?

The Ascension of Christ means that Jesus "...was raised up and a cloud received Him out of their sight" (Acts 1:9). He ascended into Heaven with the glorified body in which He had risen, and with His soul.

> **Prayer:** *Jesus, in Your risen Body You plainly showed Yourself to Your disciples, and then You were taken up to Heaven in their sight to claim for us a share in Your divine life. May we follow You into the new creation, for Your Ascension is our glory and our hope. All praise, glory, and honor be to You now and forever. Amen*

See Papally Promulgated
Catechism of the Catholic Church

Q. 108. See paragraphs: 659-667

Q. 109. What are the two distinctive aspects of the mystery of the Ascension?

The two distinctive aspects of the mystery of the Ascension are: (1) the fullness of the glorification of Jesus' victorious humanity in Heaven and (2) the completion of His visible ministry on earth.

Sacred Scripture

"Now that He ascended, what is it, but because He also descended first into the lower parts of the earth? He that descended is the same also that ascended above all the heavens that He might fill all things." *Ephesians 4:9-10*

"He was manifested in the flesh, justified in the Spirit, seen by angels, preached to the Gentiles, believed in the world, taken up in glory." *1 Timothy 3:16*

"For which cause God also has exalted Him and has given Him a Name which is above all names, that in the Name of Jesus every knee should bow, of those that are in Heaven, on earth and under the earth, and that every tongue should confess that the Lord Jesus Christ is in the glory of God the Father." *Philippians 2:9-11*

"And what is the exceeding greatness of His power towards us, who believe according to the operation of the might of His power, which He worked in Christ, raising Him up from the dead, and setting Him on His right hand in the heavenly places." *Ephesians 1:19-20*

Prayer: *Jesus, You ascended into Heaven to enter into Your glory. While on earth You always enjoyed the vision of God, but the glory of Your sacred humanity showed forth only at Your Transfiguration and in the Resurrection. When You ascended into Heaven, You took Your place as triumphant beside Your heavenly Father and are exalted above all other creatures. We rejoice at the glory into which You*

See Papally Promulgated
Catechism of the Catholic Church

Q. 109. See paragraphs: Cf. 659-660, 2749

Q. 110. What has Christ done for us through His Ascension?

Through His Ascension, Christ has claimed for us a participation in His divine life.

He has ascended into Heaven to prepare a place for us. However, He has not abandoned us here on earth.

Sacred Scripture

"Let not your heart be troubled. You believe in God; believe also in Me. In My Father's house are many mansions. If not, I would have told you, because I go to prepare a place for you."

John 14:1-2

"And I will ask the Father, and He will give you another Paraclete, that He may abide with you forever. The Spirit of truth, Whom the world cannot receive, because it does not see Him, nor does it know Him. But you shall know Him, because He will abide with you, and shall be with you. I will not leave you orphans. I will come to you." *John 14:16-18*

"And behold I am with you always, even till the end of the world." *Matthew 28:20*

Q. 111. How is Christ present with the Church?

Christ is present with the Church through God the Holy Spirit.

It is through the Holy Spirit that Christ is present to us in the sacraments, especially in the Holy Eucharist. He is also

See Papally Promulgated
Catechism of the Catholic Church

Q. 110. See paragraphs: 662, 668-670, 788, 2743
Q. 111. See paragraphs: 737-741

present in the lives of all who love Him, and who are striving to do His will.

Vatican Council II

"From the fact of their union with Christ the head flows the laymen's right and duty to be apostles. Inserted as they are in the Mystical Body of Christ by baptism and strengthened by the power of the Holy Spirit in confirmation, it is by the Lord himself that they are assigned to the apostolate. If they are consecrated a kingly priesthood and a holy nation (cf. 1 Pet. 2:4-10), it is in order that they may in all their actions offer spiritual sacrifices and bear witness to Christ all the world over. Charity, which is, as it were, the soul of the whole apostolate, is given to them and nourished in them by the sacraments, the Eucharist above all.

"The apostolate is lived in faith, hope and charity poured out by the Holy Spirit into the hearts of all the members of the Church. And the precept of charity, which is the Lord's greatest commandment, urges all Christians to work for the glory of God through the coming of his kingdom and for the communication of eternal life to all men, that they may know the only true God and Jesus Christ whom he has sent (cf. Jn. 17:3)." *Lay People, 3*

Prayer: *Jesus, complete the work of Your grace and raise up in our days many apostolic men and women who, imbued with a burning zeal for souls and with true wisdom, will go forth to preach the Gospel to nominal Christians, to the unchurched, and the lapsed. Increase the number of devoted missionaries and give to them Your Holy Spirit to guide and direct them. We ark this in Your most powerful and holy Name. Amen.*

Prayer

Jesus, we believe in the mystery of the most Holy Trinity, that there is one God in three Persons: the Father, the Son, and the Holy Spirit, each subsisting separately and distinctly in the one divine nature.

We believe that because of Your redemption we share, through grace, in the divine nature and have become sons of God by adoption. We are Your younger brothers and sisters, so we belong to Your family, and have God as our Father.

Since You have promised to be with Your Church until the end of the world, it is infallible in doctrinal and moral matters. Because You are with it and support it, it cannot err in its office as teacher and interpreter of Your revelation. We thank You for the glorious blessings and privileges which You have conferred upon Your Church to assure our salvation. Fill our hearts with gratitude for the benefits of our Catholic Faith. Give us respect for, and submission to the ecclesiastical hierarchy, which is invested with such glorious and truly divine power. We ask this in Your all-glorious and all-holy Name. Amen.

Chapter Forty-Two

Christ the King
Christ the King in Heaven

"Then they led Jesus from Caiphas to the governor's hall. And it was morning and they went not into the hall, that they might not be defiled, but that they might eat the pasch. Pilate therefore went out to them and said, 'What accusation bring you against this man?' They answered, and said to him, 'If He were not a malefactor, we would not have delivered Him up to you.' Pilate therefore said to them, 'Take Him, and judge Him according to your law.' The Jews therefore said to him, 'It is not lawful for us to put any man to death;' that the word of Jesus might be fulfilled, which He said, signifying what death He should die. Pilate therefore went into the hall again, and called Jesus and said to Him, 'Are You the king of the Jews?' Jesus answered, 'Do you say this thing yourself, or have others told you about Me?' Pilate answered, 'Am I a Jew? Your own nation, and the chief priests, have delivered You up to me. What have You done?' Jesus answered, 'My kingdom is not of this world. If My kingdom were of this world, My servants would certainly strive that I should not be delivered to the Jews, but now My kingdom is not like this.' Pilate therefore said to Him, 'Are You a king then?' Jesus answered, 'You say that I am a king. For this was I born, and for this came I into the world; that I should give testimony to the truth. Every one that is of the truth hears My voice.' Pilate said to Him, 'What is truth?' And when he said this, he went out again to the Jews and said to them, 'I find no cause in Him' " (John 18:28-38).

Q. 112. What is God's plan for us?

In general, God's plan for us is the carrying out of our salvation which is to culminate in forming His faithful followers to become one in mind and will with Him for all eternity.

See Papally Promulgated
Catechism of the Catholic Church

Q. 112. See paragraphs: 1372, 1442

Thus, we become permanent members of the new People of God, with Jesus as our Head — we become the "Whole Christ."

In the Creed we say, "He sits at the right hand of God, the Father Almighty." Being God, Jesus is in all things the Father's equal; as man He is above all the saints in the closeness of His union with God the Father.

Since Christ is the center of all God's works of salvation, through Him all creation can give glory to God. Jesus asks us to believe in Him and to put our hope in Him for the future, and to love Him with all our hearts. In this we humans glorify God and obtain our salvation. He said, "The Father loves the Son, and He has given all things into His hand. He that believes in the Son has life everlasting" (John 3:35-36).

Jesus Christ gave Himself for us in His Passion that He might redeem us from sin and make us a people pleasing to God. He then sent the Holy Spirit, the Spirit of adoption, to make us children of God. In this way He made in Himself a new people, filled with the grace of God. The new People of God, united with Jesus as their Head, make up "the whole Christ." He offers them to His Father and gives Him glory. This is the Father's plan for the salvation of all men.

Sacred Scripture

"And He gave some apostles, and some prophets, and some evangelists, and some pastors and doctors, for the perfecting of the saints, for the work of the ministry, for the building up of the Body of Christ, until we all meet into the unity of faith, and of the knowledge of the Son of God, unto a perfect man, unto the measure of the age of the fullness of Christ."

Ephesians 4:11-13

Vatican Council II

"That messianic people has as its head Christ, 'who was delivered up for our sins and rose again for our justification' (Rom. 4:25), and now, having acquired the name which is above all names, reigns gloriously in heaven. The state of this people is that of the dignity and freedom of the sons of God, in whose hearts the Holy Spirit dwells as in a temple. Its law is the new commandment to love as Christ loved us (cf. Jn. 13:34). Its destiny is the kingdom of God which has been begun by God himself on earth and which must be further extended until it is brought to perfection by him at the end of time when Christ our life (cf. Col. 3:34) will appear and 'creation itself also will be delivered from its slavery to corruption into the freedom of the glory of the sons of God' (Rom. 8:21). Hence that messianic people, although it does not actually include all men, and at times may appear as a small flock, is however, a most sure seed of unity, hope and salvation for the whole human race. Established by Christ as a communion of life, love and truth, it is taken up by him also as the instrument for the salvation of all; as the light of the world and the salt of the earth (cf. Mt. 5:13-16) it is sent forth into the whole world."

The Church, 9

> **Prayer:** *Jesus, as God You stand before Your creatures. You are humble and submissive as You speak of Your Kingdom. You declare that Your Kingdom is upon the earth, but not of the earth; it is a spiritual, supernatural kingdom, the Kingdom of Truth. It fights with spiritual weapons and conquers by this means the hearts that by all rights belong to it. You are witness to this truth, and You Yourself are the Truth. May we always be subjects of Your Kingdom. Amen.*

Q. 113. Why is Jesus Christ the center of all God's saving works?

Jesus Christ is the center of God's saving work, because the Father chose Him to be so in view of His Incarnation, Birth, Death, and Resurrection.

Jesus Christ became man so that, as perfect man, He might save all men and re-establish in Himself all things which were hurt by the fall of man. Thus, by the mysteries of our salvation, by His Death and Resurrection; He received all power in Heaven and on earth; and He founded His Church as the means of our salvation. So in Christ, our Redeemer, we are joined to all men. Jesus said, "The Father loves the Son, and He has given all things into His hand. He that believes in the Son has life everlasting" (John 3:35-36).

See Papally Promulgated
Catechism of the Catholic Church

Q. 113. See paragraphs: 2074, 2732

The whole work of salvation receives its meaning from Jesus Christ, the Incarnate Word. That work, beginning with the creation, showed itself in Christ's coming, in His life on earth, in His death and Resurrection, and will be completed in His glorious Second Coming. Thus, God was powerfully at work in the history of Israel, and in the life, death and Resurrection of His Incarnate Son.

Sacred Scripture

"Blessed be the God and Father of our Lord Jesus Christ, Who has blessed us with spiritual blessings in heavenly places, in Christ: as He chose us in Him before the foundation of the world, that we should be holy and without blame before Him in charity.

"Who has predestinated us unto the adoption of children through Jesus Christ unto Himself: according to the purpose of His will: unto the praise of the glory of His grace, in which He has graced us in His beloved Son.

"In Whom we have redemption through His blood, the remission of sins, according to the riches of His grace, which He has lavished on us, in all wisdom and prudence, that He might make known unto us the mystery of His will, according to His good pleasure, which He has proposed in Him, in the dispensation if the fullness of times, to re-establish all things in Christ, that are in Heaven and earth, in Him."

Ephesians 1:3-10

"And when all things shall be subdued unto Him, then the Son also Himself shall be subject unto Him that put all things under Him, that God may be all in all." *1 Corinthians 15:28*

Vatican Council II

"The Word of God, through whom all things were made, was made flesh, so that as a perfect man he could save all men and sum up all things in himself. The Lord is the goal of human history, the focal point of the desires of history and civilization, the center of mankind, the joy of all hearts, and the fulfillment of all aspirations." *Modern World, 45*

"When Jesus, having died on the cross for men, rose again from the dead, he was seen to be constituted as Lord, the Christ, and as Priest for ever (cf. Acts 2:36; Heb. 5:6; 7:17-21), and he poured out on his disciples the Spirit promised by the Father (cf. Acts 2:23). Henceforward the Church, endowed with the gifts of her founder and faithfully observing his precepts of charity, humility and self-denial, receives the mission of proclaiming and establishing among all peoples the Kingdom of Christ and of God, and she is, on earth, the seed and the beginning of that kingdom." *The Church, 5*

Prayer: *Jesus, Your Ascension is the assurance of our own bodily ascension into Heaven after the Last Judgment, if we remain faithful to You, dying in the state of grace. You entered into Your glorious Kingdom to prepare a place for us, for You promised to come again to take us to Yourself. Let us ascend into the heavens with You. Grant that we may detach ourselves from all the passing things on earth, so that we may seek only the joys that are true and lasting. To You be all honor and glory, now and forever. Amen.*

Prayer

Jesus, You are truly a king because You have come into the world to institute among men the rule of God; every man owes You a loyal and undivided allegiance.

Jesus, as Catholics, we are members of Your Kingdom, and You are our King. To You we owe loyalty, obedience, and love. Help us to carry out these most sacred duties toward You. We wish to listen to Your voice and gladly follow You in all things. We accept You as our King and submit to Your authority.

Reign supremely in our hearts and in our lives. Your reign is heavenly peace; Your law is love. Help us to pray and work that Your Kingdom may come into every soul, every family, and every nation.

Jesus, You ascended into Heaven to be our Mediator with Your Father. There, pointing to the wounds which You received for the glory of God and for the salvation of souls, You are ever pleading for us.

Jesus, King of all creation, Your Father anointed You with the oil of gladness as the Eternal Priest and Universal King. As Priest You offered Your life on the altar of the Cross and redeemed the human race by this one perfect sacrifice of peace. As King You claim dominion over all creation, that You may present to Your Father an eternal and universal Kingdom: a Kingdom of truth and life, a Kingdom of holiness and grace, and a Kingdom of justice, love and peace.

Jesus, in the hour of our own homecoming, when we appear before Your Father to give account of our lives on earth, have mercy on us. May we be able to say, as You did: "I have glorified You on the earth; I have finished the work that You gave me to do" (Jn. 17:4). Amen.

The Creed - III

—

The Holy Spirit

"...We believe in the Holy Spirit, the Lord, the giver of life, Who proceeds from the Father and the Son. With the Father and the Son, He is worshipped and glorified. He has spoken through the Prophets."

The Person of the Holy Spirit

Chapter Forty-Three

The Holy Spirit - I

Q. 114. Who is the Holy Spirit ?

The Holy Spirit, the Third Person of the Blessed Trinity, is God just as the Father and the Son are God.

He is also called the Paraclete (or Comforter), and the Advocate, Who pleads mankind's cause with God. He is also called the Spirit of Truth, the Spirit of God, and the Spirit of Love. He comes to us when we are baptized, and continues to dwell within us and sanctify us as long as we do not shut Him out by mortal sin.

Sacred Scripture

"Or do you not know that your members are the temple of the Holy Spirit Who is in you, Whom you have from God, and you are not your own? For you are bought with a great price. Glorify and bear God in your body." *1 Corinthians 6:19-20*

> **Prayer:** *God, the Holy Spirit, divine Spirit of love and light proceeding from the Father and the Son, we adore You as the Third Person of the adorable Trinity, our very God. In the same way as we adore God the Father and God the Son, we adore You in union with the angels and saints who surround Your throne on high. May You be praised and glorified now and forever. Amen.*

Q. 115. The Holy Spirit proceeds from the Father and the Son. What is meant by this?

God the Father and God the Son behold the infinite lovableness of each other. There flows between these two divine Persons a Love which is divine and personal. It is a Love so

See Papally Promulgated
Catechism of the Catholic Church

Q. 114. See paragraphs: 683-686
Q. 115. See paragraphs: 246-248

perfect that it is a living Love. This Love is God, the Holy Spirit, the Third Person of the Blessed Trinity.

The Father and the Son eternally give this personal Love (God the Holy Spirit) to one another. God's love for us has led Him to make us sharers in His own divine life. We can say that the Spirit of Love, God the Holy Spirit, is the One Who makes this possible. Since the work of making souls holy is especially a work of divine Love, we say that the Holy Spirit is the Sanctifier, the One Who makes us holy; yet what one Person does, all three do.

Sacred Scripture

"But the Paraclete, the Holy Spirit, Whom the Father will send in My Name, He will teach you all things." *John 14:26*

"But when the Paraclete comes, Whom I will send from the Father, the Spirit of truth, Who proceeds from the Father, He shall give testimony of Me." *John 15:26*

"But I tell you the truth. It is expedient for you that I go. For if I do not go, the Paraclete will not come to you, but if I go, I will send Him to you." *John 16:7*

Vatican Council II

"Now, what was once preached by the Lord, or fulfilled in him for the salvation of mankind, must be proclaimed and spread to the ends of the earth (Acts 1:8), starting from Jerusalem (cf. Jn. 10:36), so that what was accomplished for the salvation of all men may, in the course of time, achieve its universal effect.

"To do this, Christ sent the Holy Spirit from the Father to exercise inwardly his saving influence, and to promote the spread of the Church. Without doubt, the Holy Spirit was at work in the world before Christ was glorified. On the day of Pentecost, however, he came down on the disciples that he might remain with them forever (cf. Jn. 14:16); on that day the Church was openly displayed to the crowds and the spread of the Gospel among the nations, through preaching, was begun." *Missionary Activity, 3, 4*

Prayer: *Divine Love, the One Who unites the Father and the Son, Spirit of power, faithful Consoler of the afflicted, let the splendor of Your light penetrate our hearts to their very depths. Send the heavenly* rays of Your love into the sanctuary of our souls that, penetrating them, they may enkindle divine love and there consume all our weaknesses and our negligences. We ask this through Jesus our Lord to Whom with You and the Father be all honor and glory. Amen.

Prayer

God, Holy Spirit, we believe that in the divinity itself, You are the completion of the inner life of God. The Father, by contemplating Himself, begets the idea of the living, perfect and perpetual "mirror image" of Himself. This is God the Son, Who is the expression of the Father's infinite self-knowledge. The Father and the Son see each other in their divine beauty and embrace each other in infinite love. You are this Love Who proceeds from the Father and the Son. You are Their blissful surrender to one another, and Their reposing in one another. You are the bond and unity, the embrace, and kiss, the streaming joy, the jubilant happiness, and the silent blessed repose of the Trinity.

Your very name, "Spirit," signifies that You are the "Breathing Forth" of God the Father and God the Son. You are the "Holy" Spirit, because by virtue of Your origin You are the holiness of God, and God's holiness is one with His infinite love of Himself. Though You are the mutual love of the Father and the Son, still, like Them, You are God, equal to Them in all things. As God You never had a beginning; You always were. As God, You are worthy of adoration, love, and devotion.

Holy Spirit, have mercy on us. Make our souls docile and upright. Show pity toward our weaknesses with such clemency that our nothingness may find grace before Your infinite greatness, that our helplessness may find mercy before Your almighty power, and that our offenses may find forgiveness before the multitude of Your mercies, through our Lord and Savior, Jesus Christ. Amen.

Chapter Forty-Four

The Holy Spirit - II

Q. 116. What did Jesus Christ say about the Holy Spirit?

Jesus promised that He would send the Holy Spirit and that this Spirit would remain with us.

Jesus said to the Apostles the night of the Last Supper, "And I will ask the Father, and He shall give you another Paraclete, that He may abide with you forever. The Spirit of Truth, Whom the world cannot receive, because it does not see nor know Him. But you shall know Him; because He shall abide with you and shall be in you" (John 14:16-17).

Sacred Scripture

"These things have I spoken to you, abiding with you. But the Paraclete, the Holy Spirit, Whom the Father will send in My Name, He will teach you all things and bring all things to your mind, whatsoever I shall have said to you." *John 14:25-26*

"But when the Paraclete comes, Whom I will send you from the Father, the Spirit of truth, Who proceeds from the Father, He shall give testimony of Me." *John 15:26*

Vatican Council II

"Before freely laying down his life for the world, the Lord Jesus organized the apostolic ministry and promised to send the Holy Spirit, in such a way that both would be always and everywhere associated in the fulfillment of the work of salvation." *Missionary Activity, 4*

Prayer: *Most Holy Spirit of God, Jesus spoke of You as the "Paraclete" or "Advocate" as He prepared to call You from Heaven.*

See Papally Promulgated
Catechism of the Catholic Church

Q. 116. See paragraphs: 692, 728, 2615

Your mission was to act as Christ's Witness before the world, by defending His character, authority, and doctrine. To assure our eternal salvation, we entrust our minds to Your guidance and our hearts to Your inspirations. Let us be witnesses to Jesus Christ in the world, especially by our good example. We ask this through the same Christ our Lord. Amen.

Prayer

Holy Spirit of God, the Incarnation of Jesus, which is the most important of the whole work of salvation, and the deepest proof of God's love for us, was wrought by Your divine power. The Incarnation was the highest union of a human nature with God and is the source of all holiness.

Spirit of Life, Your divine breath filled the sanctuary of Mary's womb and brought into existence the union of the eternal Word of God with His human nature. You were the mysterious heartbeat of His inner life, moving it in its wonderful depths of devotion.

We believe that Jesus Christ's divine and human natures are united in one divine Person, the eternal Word of God, the second Person of the adorable Trinity. Creator Spirit, You effected this wonderful union. Your infinite power created the human soul of the Savior and conceived His sacred Body in the womb of His Most Holy Mother. The angel spoke to Mary, "The Holy Spirit shall come upon you and overshadow you. And therefore also the Holy One which shall be born of you shall be called the Son of God" (Luke 1:35).

Most infinite Spirit of love and life, we praise and thank You also for Your constant work within Jesus' soul which, with His cooperation, brought forth marvelous increases of grace, wisdom, holiness and glory. May we, as sharers in Your divine life by virtue of Baptism, also be always open to Your will and to Your grace. We ask this through Jesus Christ our Lord and Savior. Amen.

213

The Holy Spirit in the Life of the Church

Chapter Forty-Five

The Work of the Holy Spirit in the Church - I

Q. 117. When did the Holy Spirit come to the Church?

Fifty days after Easter the Holy Spirit came to the early Church in a mighty wind and tongues of fire.

He changed the Apostles from weak, fearful men to the brave men of faith through whom Christ wanted to spread His Gospel to the nations.

Sacred Scripture

"And when the days of the Pentecost were accomplished, they were all together in one place. And suddenly there came a sound from Heaven, as of a mighty wind coming, and it filled the whole house where they were sitting. And there appeared to them parted tongues, as it were of fire, and it sat upon every one of them. And they were all filled with the Holy Spirit and they began to speak in different tongues, according as the Holy Spirit gave them to speak." *Acts 2:1-4*

Vatican Council II

"When the work which the Father gave the Son to do on earth (cf. Jn. 17:4) was accomplished, the Holy Spirit was sent on the day of Pentecost in order that he might continually sanctify the Church, and that, consequently, those who believe might have access through Christ in one Spirit to the Father (cf. Eph. 2:18). He is the Spirit of life, the fountain of water springing up to eternal life. To men dead in sin, the Father gives life through him, until the day when, in Christ, He raises to life their mortal bodies (cf. Rom. 8:10-11)." *The Church, 4*

Prayer: *Most Holy Spirit, on the Feast of Pentecost, You laid the foundation of the Church of Christ by coming down upon the Apostles.*

See Papally Promulgated
Catechism of the Catholic Church

Q. 117. See paragraphs: 731-732

Q. 118. How does the Holy Spirit carry out Christ's work in the Church?

The Holy Spirit carries out Christ's work in the Church when persons are willing to answer God's invitation to love Him and one another.

As Jesus Christ is the center of the history of salvation, so the mystery of God is the center from which this history takes its origin and to which it is ordered to its last end. The crucified and risen Christ leads men to the Father by sending the Holy Spirit upon the People of God.

The Holy Spirit was already at work in the world before Jesus rose from the dead and ascended into Heaven. But to finish the work of the salvation of all men, Jesus sent the Holy Spirit from the Father. The Spirit now carries out His work of salvation in the souls of men and spreads the Church throughout the world.

Vatican Council II

"The joy and hope, the grief and anguish of the men of our time, especially of those who are poor or afflicted in any way, are the joy and hope, the grief and anguish of the followers of Christ as well. Nothing that is genuinely human fails to find an echo in their hearts. For theirs is a community composed of men who, united in Christ and guided by the Holy Spirit,

See Papally Promulgated
Catechism of the Catholic Church

Q. 118. See paragraphs: 27, 243, 257, 259, 485, 494, 1824, 2055

press onward towards the kingdom of the Father and are bearers of a message of salvation intended for all men."

Modern World, 1

Prayer

*F*ather, Your Son ascended above all the heavens, and from His throne at Your right hand, He poured into the hearts of Your adopted children the Holy Spirit of Your promise. You give Your gifts of grace for every time and season, as You guide the Church in the marvelous ways of Your providence. Give us Your Holy Spirit to help us always by His power, so that with loving trust we may turn to You in all our troubles, and give You thanks in all our joys.

*H*oly Spirit, You are one God with the Father and the Son. You are the mutual Love between Them both. You formed the sacred humanity of our Lord Jesus Christ, and enriched it with the fullness of Your gifts and graces. Under Your guidance He, an innocent Victim for the sins of the world, ascended the altar of the Cross.

*G*od our Father, by raising Christ Your Son, You conquered the power of death and opened for us the way to eternal life. Raise us up and renew our lives by the Spirit that is within us, especially through the sacrifice of the Mass.

*Y*our Spirit made us Your children, confident to call You Father. Increase Your Spirit of love within us and bring us to our promised inheritance.

*T*hrough the power of the Spirit, purify our hearts and strengthen us in Your love. Send Your Spirit to live in our hearts and make us temples of His glory. May we, by Your help, never lose the gifts and graces You have given us through Him. We ask this through Jesus Christ our Lord. Amen.

Chapter Forty-Six

The Work of the Holy Spirit in the Church - II

Q. 119. Where is the Holy Spirit especially present?

The Holy Spirit is present in a special way in the Catholic Church.

The Holy Spirit gives His divine life of grace to the Catholic Church. He is present to help the Church to continue the work of Christ in the world. By His grace people are moved to unite themselves with God and men in sincere love, and to fulfill their duties to God and man. He makes the Church pleasing to God because of the divine life of grace which He gives. By the power of the Gospel, He makes the Church grow. He renews it with His gifts, and leads it to perfect union with Jesus.

The Holy Spirit is also present outside the Catholic Church in other Christian Churches and Ecclesial Communities. Moreover, He is active in what is known as the Ecumenical Movement which promotes the union of all Christians in the fullness of truth, as revealed by Christ and His Apostles.

God the Holy Spirit is active as well among other believers. He helps them to seek and find truth and goodness. Moreover He guides the efforts of the Catholic Church in its relationship with other believers.

Sacred Scripture

"But I tell you the truth; it is expedient to you that I go. For if I go not, the Paraclete will not come to you, but if I go, I will send Him to you." *John 16:7*

Vatican Council II

"On the day of Pentecost, however, he came down on the disciples that he might remain with them forever (cf. Jn. 14:16);

See Papally Promulgated
Catechism of the Catholic Church

Q. 119. See paragraphs: 748-750, 767-768, 813, 819, 822, 839-845

on that day the Church was openly displayed to the crowds and the spread of the Gospel among the nations, through preaching, was begun. Finally, on that day was foreshadowed the union of all peoples in the catholicity of the faith by means of the Church of the New Alliance, a Church which speaks every language, understands and embraces all tongues in charity, and thus overcomes the dispersion of Babel.

"The 'acts of the apostles'; began with Pentecost, just as Christ was conceived in the Virgin Mary with the coming of the Holy Spirit and was moved to begin his ministry by the descent of the same Holy Spirit, who came down upon him while He was praying. Before freely laying down his life for the world, the Lord Jesus organized the apostolic ministry and promised to send the Holy Spirit, in such a way that both would be always and everywhere associated in the fulfillment of the work of salvation." *Missionary Activity, 4*

Prayer: *Merciful Comforter, to Your mercy we recommend the entire Catholic Church in all its undertakings for the souls entrusted to its care. We pray for the Pope, the Bishops, priests and Religious. By Your supernatural power, confirm in them the desire to spend their lives in Your holy service for the salvation of souls.*

Be merciful to other Christians, to those belonging to non-Christian religions, and to agnostics, atheists, and sinners. Grant them grace to recognize You, with the Father and the Son, as the only source of true happiness, and to love You with their whole hearts. Amen.

Prayer

Holy Spirit, Finger of God's right hand, in thousands of ways in the early days of Christianity, You showed Yourself to be the Soul and Heart of the Church. You gave it supernatural strength and beauty. Your divine influence explains its irresistible attraction, that is, its power to draw souls. You worked in the early Church, bringing forth signs of new life in strength, beauty, and fruitfulness. Praise and thanks be to You, life-giving Spirit, for the wonderful power of Your grace.

Divine Fire, enkindle in all those who share Your apostolate the flames which transformed the disciples in the Upper Room. They will then no longer be ordinary men, but men living to transfuse Your divine life to the souls of their fellow men. Enkindle in their wills an ardent desire for the inner life, since their apostolate will be successful only in the measure that they themselves live that supernatural life of which You are the sovereign principle and Jesus Christ the source.

Be merciful to all the children of the Holy Catholic Church, that they may be faithful to its teaching and thereby save their souls.

Look graciously upon the Poor Souls in Purgatory. Comfort and refresh them with the graces which flow from Your merciful love. All this we ask through Christ our Lord. Amen.

Chapter Forty-Seven

The Work of the Holy Spirit in the Church - III

Q. 120. What does the Holy Spirit do for the Church?

Through the Holy Spirit, the Church is able to carry on the work of salvation which Christ gave her at her birth.

The Holy Spirit came in order to remain with the Church forever. At the first Christian Pentecost, the Church was publicly made known to those gathered in Jerusalem. From there, the Gospel began to spread throughout the nations. Today the Holy Spirit is still the Soul of the Church's apostolate.

The Holy Spirit gives His divine life of grace to the Church.

The Holy Spirit guides the Pope, Bishops, and priests of the Church in their work of teaching Christ's doctrine, guiding souls, giving God's grace, caring for the sick, teaching children, guiding young people, comforting the sorrowful, and supporting the needy.

The Holy Spirit guides the People of God in knowing the truth. He prays in them and makes them remember that they are adopted sons of God. He brings the Church together in love and worship.

Sacred Scripture

"The Paraclete, the Holy Spirit, Whom the Father will send in My Name, He will teach you all things, and bring all things to your mind, whatsoever I shall have said to you."

John 14:26

"He [Jesus] breathed on them, and He said to them, 'Receive the Holy Spirit. Whose sins you shall forgive, they are forgiven them, and whose sins you shall retain, they are retained.' " *John 20:22-23*

See Papally Promulgated
Catechism of the Catholic Church

Q. 120. See paragraphs: 692, 976, 1996-1997

Vatican Council II

"The Spirit dwells in the Church and in the hearts of the faithful, as in a temple (cf. 1 Cor. 3:16; 6:19). In them he prays and bears witness to their adoptive sonship (cf. Gal. 4:6; Rom. 8:15-16 and 26)." *The Church, 4*

"Before freely laying down his life for the world, the Lord Jesus organized the apostolic ministry and promised to send the Holy Spirit, in such a way that both would be always and everywhere associated in the fulfillment of the work of salvation." *Missionary Activity, 4*

Prayer: *God, our Father, how wonderful are the works of the Holy Spirit, which are revealed in so many gifts!*

How marvelous is the unity the Spirit creates from Your children's diversity as He dwells in their hearts, thus filling the whole Church with His presence and guiding it with His wisdom. May we always be attentive to His inspirations and trust in His never-failing strength. We ask this through Jesus Christ our Lord. Amen.

Q. 121. Why is the Holy Spirit called the Soul of the Church?

The Holy Spirit is called the Soul of the Church because He animates it with His divine presence, giving supernatural life to all its parts.

Sacred Scripture

To the Christians at Corinth, St. Paul wrote: "Don't you know that your members are the temple of the Holy Spirit, Who is in you, Whom you have from God, and you are not your own?" *1 Corinthians 6:19*

"And I will ask the Father, and He shall give you another Paraclete, that He may abide with you forever. The Spirit of

See Papally Promulgated
Catechism of the Catholic Church

Q. 121. See paragraphs: 692, 797, 809, 813

truth, Whom the world cannot receive, because it does not see Him, nor does it know Him. But you shall know Him, because He shall abide with you and shall be in you." *John 14:16-17*

Vatican Council II

"In order that we might be unceasingly renewed in him [i.e. Jesus] (cf. Eph. 4:23), he has shared with us his Spirit who, being one and the same in head and members, gives life to, unifies and moves the whole body. Consequently, his work could be compared by the Fathers to the function that the principle of life, the soul, fulfills in the human body."

The Church,7

Prayer: *Life-giving Spirit, our Creator and Sanctifier, You have given us life and being, and have led us into the fullness of Christ's revelation, which He gave to His Catholic Church. You have adorned our souls with sanctifying grace, made them Your temples, enriched them with heavenly virtues, and sanctified them through the holy sacraments. All these benefits have come to us through the Holy Catholic Church. We thank You for having made us children of this Church which is animated and directed by You in union with the Father and the Son, now and forever. Amen.*

Prayer

Heavenly Father, through Christ, You have given the Holy Spirit to all peoples. Fill our hearts with His love. May the fire of Your Spirit, which filled the hearts of the disciples of Jesus with courage and love, make our thoughts, words and our deeds holy so that our whole life may be pleasing to You.

Send the Holy Spirit of Pentecost into our hearts to keep us always in Your love, that we may perfectly love You and fittingly praise You. May we live in holiness and be Your witnesses to the world.

Fill with the Spirit of Christ those whom You call to live in the midst of the world and its concerns. Help them by their work on earth to build up Your eternal Kingdom. May they be effective witnesses to the truth of the Gospel and make Your Church a living and vibrant presence in the midst of the world.

Through Your Holy Spirit, the Soul of the Church, increase Your spiritual gifts to the Church so that Your faithful people may continue to grow in holiness in imitation of Your beloved Son.

Holy Spirit, Creator, mercifully assist Your Catholic Church, and by Your heavenly power, strengthen and establish her against the assaults of her enemies. By Your love and grace, renew the spirit of Your servants whom You have anointed, that in You they may glorify the Father and His only-begotten Son, Jesus Christ our Lord.

Help us to be ever obedient to the Holy Father, the Pope, who teaches infallibly in matters of faith and morals. Make us faithful children of the Catholic Church, which is the pillar and ground of truth. Help us to always uphold her doctrines, seek her interests, and defend her rights. We ask this in Jesus' Name. Amen.

Chapter Forty-Eight

The Work of the Holy Spirit in the Church - IV

Q. 122. What is the work of the Holy Spirit in the Church?

The Holy Spirit (1) *maintains the Church as the Body of Christ and as His Bride so that she may be faithful to Him in holiness until the end of the world* and (2) *He always helps the Church to purify and renew herself and her members.*

1. *The Holy Spirit maintains the Church as the Body of Christ.*

The Holy Spirit, Whom Jesus sent from the Father to His Church at Pentecost, continues His work in the Church, and will do so until the end of time. He brings about a union between Christ and His members. St. Paul describes this union as "the Body of Christ." Each member of the Body is united to each other, with Christ as the Head, by a strong interior bond, which is the Holy Spirit.

2. *The Holy Spirit always helps the Church to purify and renew herself and her members.*

Every Christian receives the Holy Spirit in the Sacrament of Baptism and in the Sacrament of Confirmation. The Holy Spirit, with the Father and the Son, actually lives in the Christian. Jesus said, "If anyone loves Me, he will keep My word. And My Father will love him, and We will come to him and will make Our abode with him" (John 14:23).

Through the Holy Spirit, a Christian shares in the life of grace, which is, God's life in his soul. St. Paul reminds the Christian that he is holy because the Holy Spirit dwells in him. "Don't you know that you are the temple of God and that the Spirit of God dwells in you? But if any man violates the

See Papally Promulgated
Catechism of the Catholic Church

Q. 122. See paragraphs: 687-688, 696, 733-741, 797-801

temple of God, him shall God destroy. For the temple of God is holy, which you are" (1 Corinthians 3:16-17).

The Holy Spirit enlightens our minds to accept and believe the teaching of Jesus and gives us the strength to live according to it. An openness to God and a willing response to the guidance of His Holy Spirit is necessary for holiness. St. Paul says, "Extinguish not the Spirit" (1 Thessalonians 5:19).

Holiness is expected from the whole Church. Giving Himself to all, God makes it possible for everyone to give himself completely to Him and to his fellow man. All are called to holiness, according to the gifts and talents each possesses.

St. Paul also speaks of charisms, that is, "gifts of grace," which are blessings, freely given, of an extraordinary and transitory nature that the Holy Spirit confers directly on certain individuals for the good of others. These blessings may also benefit indirectly the one who possesses them, but their immediate purpose is the spiritual welfare of the Christian community.

"Now there are diversities of graces, but the same Spirit. And there are diversities of ministries, but the same Lord. And there are diversities of operations, but the same God, Who works all in all. And the manifestation of the Spirit is given to every man unto profit. To one indeed, by the Spirit, is given the word of wisdom; and to another the word of knowledge according to the same Spirit. To another, faith in the same Spirit; to another, the grace of healing in one Spirit. To another, the working of miracles; to another, prophecy; to another, the discerning of spirits; to another, diverse kinds of tongues; to another, interpretation of speeches. But all of these things, one and the same Spirit works dividing to every one according as He wills." *1 Corinthians 12:4-11*

So that we may live well as God's children, the Holy Spirit helps us in many ways. He gives us "actual graces" to help us to think, desire and do things pleasing to God. Without His grace it is impossible to do anything to achieve our salvation or the salvation of others. With the help of the grace of the Holy Spirit, the Church is constantly purified and renewed spiritually.

Vatican Council II

"Guiding the Church in the way of all truth (cf. Jn. 16:13) and unifying her in communion and in the works of ministry, he [the Holy Spirit] bestows upon her varied hierarchic and charismatic gifts, and in this way directs her; and he adorns her with his fruits (cf. Eph. 4:11-12; 1 Cor. 12:4; Gal. 5:22). By the power of the Gospel he permits the Church to keep the freshness of youth. Constantly he renews her and leads her to perfect union with her Spouse. For the Spirit and the Bride both say to Jesus, the Lord, 'Come!' (cf. Apoc. 22:17). Hence the universal Church is seen to be 'a people brought into unity from the unity of the Father, the Son and the Holy Spirit.' "

The Church, 4

Prayer

Come, O Creator Spirit blest! And in our souls take up Thy rest; Come with Thy grace and heavenly aid, to fill the hearts which Thou hast made.

Great Paraclete! To Thee we cry, O highest gift of God most high! O font of life! O fire of love! and sweet anointing from above.

Thou in Thy sevenfold gifts art known, the finger of God's hand we own; the promise of the Father, Thou! Who dost the tongue with power endow.

Kindle our senses from above, and make our hearts o'erflow with love; with patience firm and virtue high the weakness of our flesh supply.

Far from us drive the foe we dread, And grant us Thy true peace instead; So shall we not, with Thee for guide, turn from the path of life aside.

O may Thy grace on us bestow the Father and the Son to know, and Thee through endless times confessed of both the eternal Spirit blest.

All glory while the ages run be to the Father and the Son Who rose from death; the same to Thee; O Holy Ghost, eternally. Amen.

Chapter Forty-Nine

Devotion to the Holy Spirit

Q. 123. How should we honor the Holy Spirit?

We should love and honor the Holy Spirit as our God, just as we honor the Father and the Son.

We should also let the Holy Spirit guide our lives. By prayer, we learn to discern His inspirations in our souls. His inspirations bring peace.

We should recognize the importance of the Holy Spirit and His work in the Church and in our lives. Every Christian receives the Holy Spirit in the Sacrament of Baptism and in the Sacrament of Confirmation. By His presence men are continually moved to have communion with God and men and to fulfill their duties.

United in Christ, the followers of Jesus are led by the Holy Spirit on their journey to the Kingdom of their Father and the Son. We should often ask Him for the light and strength we need to live a holy life and to save our souls.

Sacred Scripture

"But Peter said, 'Ananias, why has satan tempted your heart, that you should lie to the Holy Spirit?...You have not lied to men, but to God.'" *Acts 5:3-4*

Vatican Council II

"When the work which the Father gave the Son to do on earth (cf. Jn. 17:14) was accomplished, the Holy Spirit was sent on the day of Pentecost in order that he might continually sanctify the Church, and that, consequently, those who believe might have access through Christ in one Spirit to the Father (cf. Eph. 2:18). He is the Spirit of life, the fountain of water springing up to eternal life (cf. Jn. 4:47; 7:38-39). To men,

See Papally Promulgated
Catechism of the Catholic Church

Q. 123. See paragraphs: 684-685, 739

dead in sin, the Father gives life through him, until the day when, in Christ, he raises to life their mortal bodies (cf. Rom. 8:10-11). The Spirit dwells in the Church and in the hearts of the faithful, as in a temple. In them he prays and bears witness to their adoptive sonship." *The Church, 4*

Prayer: *Holy Spirit, our God and Sanctifier, O that we would not always move on the surface of our souls, but would delve into the depths where You dwell! Our dearest Guest, You have allowed us to look into this sacred sanctuary where You hide Yourself. Help us to try to be aware of Your presence in our souls, and of the working of Your grace within us, that we may receive strength and consolation: strength, to do good and overcome evil; and consolation, to enable us to accept the crosses and sorrows of life patiently and cheerfully.*

Free our souls from attachment to earthly things which so often hamper us from doing Your will. Let us think of You within our souls when we are dealing with others who work and live with us so that the thought of You may help to increase and preserve the peace of our souls. Make us triumph over difficulties, confirm our confidence in You, and bless all our sacrifices and labors. We ask this through Jesus Christ our Lord. Amen.

Prayer

O *Holy Spirit, You are the living soul of God's holy Church. In You alone, dwelling in the Church as in a living tabernacle, the great mystery of the Church of Christ is made possible.*

*H*oly *Spirit of God, help us to appreciate the great and inestimable happiness of being children of Holy Mother Church. Through Confirmation, in which You give us the fullness of Yourself, give us the courage and zeal to fulfill our vocation as messengers of Christ to the world. Make us sincere apostles by helping us to be faithful to our duty of proclaiming the Gospel and making its influence felt in the lives of others.*

*S*pirit *of Truth, keep us always in a spirit of devoted love and submission to Holy Mother Church. Help us to do our part in bringing about the unity of all men under God. We ask this in the most powerful and holy Name of Jesus. Amen.*

The Holy Spirit in the Life of the Christian

Chapter Fifty

Sanctifying Grace - I

Q. 124. What happens when a man accepts the Spirit of Christ?

When a man accepts the Spirit of Christ, God leads him to a new way of life.

All three Persons of the Blessed Trinity have a part in the holy work of giving grace to people. This, however, is especially the work of God the Holy Spirit because it is a work of Love, and the Holy Spirit is the Spirit of the Love of the Father and the Son. He makes our souls holy through the gift of grace.

Sacred Scripture

"For the wages of sin is death. But the grace of God, life everlasting, in Christ Jesus our Lord." *Romans 6:23*

"If any one loves Me, he will keep My word. And My Father will love him and We will come to him and will make Our home with him." *John 14:23*

Vatican Council II

"All Christians by the example of their lives and the witness of the word, wherever they live, have an obligation to manifest the new man which they put on in baptism, and to reveal the power of the Holy Spirit by whom they were strengthened at confirmation, so that others, seeing their good works, might glorify the Father (cf. Matt. 5:16) and more perfectly perceive the true meaning of human life and the universal solidarity of mankind." *Missionary Activity, 1*

Prayer: *Divine Spirit, You are our Sanctifier. By Your holy grace You wish to make us more like Jesus, our Savior. We can be holy only in so*

See Papally Promulgated
Catechism of the Catholic Church

Q. 124. See paragraphs: 1265-1266, 1997-1999, 2002-2003

far as we become similar to Him Who is the "the Way and the Truth and the Life." God has laid no other foundation for our salvation, perfection and glory. You alone can bring us to Christ and effect the union of our souls with the Son of God. Infuse Your grace into our minds and hearts, now and forever. Amen.

Prayer

O Holy Spirit, Living Fire, we desire to offer ourselves to You with the same love with which Jesus offers Himself in all the Holy Masses that are celebrated throughout the world. We beg You, through the merits of this Holy Sacrifice, have mercy on us and make us a living, pleasing sacrifice to You. Transform our souls into the image and likeness of Jesus, and grant that we may have a share in the abundance of graces hidden in His Sacred Heart. Come and live in our hearts as You live in the Sacred Heart of Jesus, that the fullness of Your light and the power of Your grace may reign in us.

Spirit of the Father and of the Son, let the might of Your love be felt forever more in the hearts of men. Let Your light shine upon the souls of those who are wandering in darkness. Turn them to the life-giving Heart of Jesus and to the healing streams of His Most Precious Blood. Strengthen souls that love You. Perfect in them Your seven gifts and Your twelve fruits. Make them Your temples here, that You may be adored by them forever in Heaven. Amen.

Chapter Fifty-One

Sanctifying Grace - II

Q. 125. What is sanctifying grace?

Sanctifying grace is a gift of God that makes us holy and pleasing to Him.

By sanctifying or habitual grace, our souls share in the very life of God even while on this earth. This grace enables us to be holy and pleasing to God, because it helps us to live as God's obedient children.

Sacred Scripture

"But by the grace of the Lord Jesus Christ, we believe we shall be saved." *Acts 15:11*

Vatican Council II

"It pleased God, in his goodness and wisdom, to reveal himself and to make known the mystery of his will (cf. Ephesians 1:9). His will was that men should have access to the Father, through Christ, the Word made flesh, in the Holy Spirit, and thus become sharers in the divine nature (cf. Eph. 2:18; 2 Pet. 1:4)." *Divine Revelation, 2*

Prayer: *Living Spirit of God, in the order of grace You have performed even more wonderful deeds. By Your divine power, You perform the work of salvation by uniting us to God in love and holiness even as You unite the Father and the Son within the Trinity. Teach us to realize that the loving union of our souls with God through sanctifying grace is the work of Your mercy. We receive grace "because the charity of God is poured forth in our hearts by the Holy Spirit Who is given to us" (Romans 5:5).*

Dearest Holy Spirit, may we never offend or lose You through sin. All glory and praise be to You, to the Father and to the Son, One God, world without end. Amen.

See Papally Promulgated
Catechism of the Catholic Church

Q. 125. See paragraphs: 1266, 1999-2000, 2023

Prayer

Creator Spirit, in nature You changed disorder into order and beauty. You formed and fashioned the universe. You called the seas, the skies, and the earth into existence by a mere act of Your will. All created things are the work of Your creative hand. We adore and praise You!

Water of Eternal Life, help us to hold in the highest esteem the priceless gift of sanctifying grace which was infused into our souls when we were baptized. Give us Your grace, that we may keep the promises which were made then on our behalf. May we always live in a manner befitting a child of God and a member of His Catholic Church, so that we may obtain hereafter the inheritance of Heaven.

May our souls walk in You and live through You, and be led by You even as the Savior Himself was led. We ask in His most holy and adorable Name. Amen.

Chapter Fifty-Two

Sanctifying Grace - III

Q. 126. What does this new way of life do for man?

This new way of life gives man the power to share in God's own life and to be joined to the Father and to Christ in a union of love that not even death can break.

Jesus said, "If anyone loves Me, He will keep My word. And My Father will love him and We will come to him, and will make Our home with him" (John 14:23).

The Spirit brings God's life to man and all that he does so that a person is said to live in the "state of grace," or the "state of sanctifying grace." Sanctifying grace is a gift of God that allows us to live in Him. This life, the life of grace, is a sharing in God's very own life.

Faith is a free gift by which the Holy Spirit enables us to accept God's word, and to realize that God loves us and cares for us and that we can count on Him.

We have hope because, in Jesus Christ, God has promised us His love and care forever. He will never leave us; we need only to remain united with Him.

Charity is the ability to love God, and our fellow men, because they too belong to God. The presence of the Holy Spirit in us means we are able to love with a love like God's. We can even love our enemies.

Sacred Scripture

"I am the vine, you are the branches. He that abides in Me and I in him, the same bears much fruit, for without Me you can do nothing." *John 15:5*

See Papally Promulgated
Catechism of the Catholic Church

Q. 126. See paragraphs: 1997, 1999-2000, 2020-2021

Vatican Council II

"All children of the Church should ... remember that their exalted condition results, not from their own merits, but from the grace of Christ. If they fail to respond in thought, word and deed to that grace, not only shall they not be saved, but they shall be the more severely judged." *The Church, 14*

Prayer: *Jesus, we believe that through Your Holy Spirit You have given us sanctifying grace. We believe that this new way of life gives us the power to share in God's own life and to be joined to the Father and to You in a union of love which not even death can break.*

Jesus, we thank You for having made us ready for Your gift of grace. By it we share with You in the divine nature, in the life of God Himself. Help us to appreciate the dignity that is ours.

We trust in the power of Your grace and in the power of Your infinite mercy to preserve us from the misfortune of offending You and of losing Your divine life by mortal sin. May we always thank You for Your infinite love for us and daily grow in grace. Amen.

Prayer

Jesus, You are the vine and we are a branch. The vine and the branch have one and the same life. They are nourished by the same sap, that is, the sap of Your grace, which the vine transmits to the branches and which makes them bear fruit.

Sin has made us like wild growth. But You have grafted us onto Yourself, the Divine Vine, and now we have become one with You, sharing in Your divine life.

You are the Head and we are members of Your Mystical Body. As the same blood gives life to the head and to the members of a human body, the same sanctifying grace flows from You into all those who are united to You by love.

You want us to abide in You. This is also our most earnest wish. You are the Way, the Truth and the Life. Without You we can do nothing; we are like a dead branch which should be cast into the fire.

Help us ever to abide in You through sanctifying grace. Increase in our souls the virtues of faith, hope and charity. We ask this in Your most holy Name. Amen.

Chapter Fifty-Three

Sanctifying Grace - IV

Q. 127. What does grace do for us?

Through grace the Holy Spirit helps us: (1) *to die to sin and live with God;* (2) *to be closely united with the Most Holy Trinity through charity;* and (3) *to live as adopted children of God.*

1. *With the help of the grace of the Holy Spirit we are able to die to sin and live with God.*

We receive the strength we need to sacrifice ourselves by avoiding everything that would lead us into sin. With God's help we can overcome the desire to do whatever is against God's commandments.

> **Prayer:** *Holy Spirit, we thank You for the gift of sanctifying grace, which enables us to die to sin, to share in the divine life of God as His children, and to be closely united with the Most Holy Trinity by love.*
>
> *Divine Healer, beautify our souls by casting out sin. From the fullness of Your gifts and graces, pour upon us the heavenly remedy against sin.*
>
> *No one needs Your divine remedy more than we. We are often blinded by our passions, chilled by obstinate lukewarmness, and defiled by many imperfections. Come and enlighten us; kindle our fervor, and destroy in us all that is displeasing to You. The greater our miseries, the more glorious will be Your triumph over our wickedness. How marvelous and glorious You are. May You be forever praised. Amen.*

2. *By grace, the Holy Spirit helps us to be closely united with the Most Holy Trinity through charity.*

St. Paul reminds Christians that they are the temple of

See Papally Promulgated
Catechism of the Catholic Church

Q. 127. See paragraphs: 1996-2005

God. "Don't you know that you are the temple of God and that the Spirit of God dwells in you?" (1 Corinthians 3:16).

The Holy Spirit was sent in order that He might make the Church holy. Through Him the Father gives supernatural life to men who are willing to give up sin, because He is the Spirit of life. United in Jesus as His followers, we are led by the Holy Spirit in our journey to the Kingdom of our heavenly Father. He helps us to fulfill our duties. He prompts us to strive for what is good. He encourages us to pray. His grace unites us to the Most Holy Trinity by the virtue of charity.

3. *By grace we share in the divine life of the Son of God because we are adopted children of God.*

We became God's children in Baptism when for the first time we received the new life of grace.

Sacred Scripture

"Amen, amen, I say to you, unless a man is born again of water and the Holy Spirit, he cannot enter into the kingdom of God." *John 3:5*

"And we, as your co-workers, exhort you not to receive the grace of God in vain." *2 Corinthians 6:1*

Vatican Council II

"For the layman ought to be, through an intimate knowledge of the contemporary world, a member well integrated into his own society and its culture.

"But in the first place he should learn to accomplish the mission of Christ and the Church, living by faith in the divine mystery of creation and redemption, moved by the Holy Spirit who gives life to the People of God and urges all men to love God the Father, and in him to love the world of men. This education must be considered the foundation and condition of any fruitful apostolate." *Lay People, 29*

Prayer

O Holy Spirit, come and create in us new hearts which will give themselves to God and not to the world. We offer You anew the chalice of our souls in love and reverence, in order that You may fill them with Your divine life.

Delightful Guest of our soul, throughout our life, as members of the Church, You are ever present within us, inspiring us, and leading us on to that goal for which we were created: union with God. Whenever we pass from sin to grace, whenever we resist temptation; whenever we perform a good act which leads to salvation, You are at work. You are the Creator of this world of wonders and glories, as St. Paul reminds us: "But in all these things, one and the same Spirit works, dividing to every one according to His will" (1 Corinthians 12:11).

May You, the Divine Fire which filled the hearts of Jesus' disciples with courage and love, make us holy. Plant Your grace deep within us, so that we can serve You with chaste bodies and please You with pure minds forever and ever. Amen.

Chapter Fifty-Four

Actual Grace

Q. 128. What is actual grace?

Actual grace is that special help which the Holy Spirit gives us to enlighten our minds and to inspire our wills to do good and to avoid evil in particular situations.

St. John tells us that God comes to illumine every man born into this world, and quotes the words of Christ about the divine call to the mind that must precede any following of the Master. "No man can come to Me, except the Father, Who has sent Me, draws him, and I will raise him up in the last day" (John 6:44).

In the Book of Revelation, St. John speaks of actual grace operating on the will. "Behold, I stand at the gate and knock. If any man shall hear My voice and open to Me the door, I will come in to him and will dine with him, and he with Me" (Revelation 3:20).

The Corinthians are reminded of the same effect when St. Paul says, "I have planted, Apollos watered, but God gave the increase" (1 Corinthians 3:6). Paul and Apollos were only the instruments of Jesus. But because they cooperated with His actual graces, the Church in Corinth continued to grow in sanctity.

"But by the grace of God, I am what I am. And His grace in Me has not been void, but I have labored more abundantly than all of them. Yet not I, but the grace of God with me. For whether I or they, so we preach, and so you have believed" (1 Corinthians 15:10-11).

Jesus told His disciples: "Abide in Me, and I in you. As the branch cannot bear fruit of itself, unless it abides in the vine, so neither can you, unless you abide in Me. I am the vine, you

See Papally Promulgated
Catechism of the Catholic Church

Q. 128. See paragraphs: 2000, 2024

are the branches. He that abides in Me, and I in him, the same bears much fruit, for without Me, you can do nothing" (John 15:4-5).

It is the actual grace of Jesus that gives us the light to see what we must do, and the strength of will to do it. Without this help we cannot live a holy life. Therefore, actual grace is a divine help enabling us to obtain, retain, or grow in sanctifying grace and in the life of God.

Vatican Council II

"The purpose of the sacraments is to sanctify men, to build up the Body of Christ, and, finally, to give worship to God. Because they are signs they also instruct. They not only presuppose faith, but by words and objects they also nourish, strengthen, and express it. That is why they are called 'sacraments of faith.' They do, indeed, confer grace, but, in addition, the very act of celebrating them most effectively disposes the faithful to receive this grace to their profit, to worship God duly, and to practice charity." *Sacred Liturgy, 59*

Prayer

Spirit of Jesus, You are our heart and soul, our innermost life and deepest strength. You unite us to the Son of God. We realize now that we cannot come to a special union with Jesus and be His own without also possessing You. St. Paul reminds us that "if the Spirit of Him, Who raised up Jesus from the dead dwells in you, He Who raised up Jesus Christ from the dead, shall also quicken your mortal bodies, by His Spirit Who dwells in you" (Romans 8:11).

We cannot be transformed into the image of the Savior except by Your grace. Especially through frequent Holy Communion, help us to think, desire, speak, and act like Christ. In this sacred union, may His love and ours become one, for the glory of God and for the salvation of our souls.

We need the help that the actual graces You send can give us. Support us by Your power. May everything that we do begin with Your inspiration, continue with Your help, and reach perfection under Your guidance. With Your loving care, give us the graces that we need to persevere with love and sincerity. May we grow in Your love and service and become more pleasing to God. We ask this though Jesus Christ our Lord. Amen.

Chapter Fifty-Five

The Indwelling of the Holy Spirit in Man - I

Q. 129. What does the indwelling of the Holy Spirit do for a person?

The indwelling of the Holy Spirit: (1) *gives us hope and courage;* (2) *heals our weakness of soul;* (3) *helps us overcome our evil desires and selfishness and aids us in practicing virtues such as charity and patience;* and (4) *makes our prayers pleasing to God.*

1. *The indwelling of the Holy Spirit gives us hope and courage.*

The Holy Spirit's presence in our souls gives us the hope that God will grant us the help we need to save our souls and to live with God forever in Heaven. At the same time, His presence gives us the courage we need to accept the sufferings and troubles of life.

2. *The indwelling of the Holy Spirit heals our weakness of soul.*

The Holy Spirit gives us actual graces, those special helps which give light to our minds and inspirations to our wills so that we can do good and avoid evil.

3. *The indwelling of the Holy Spirit helps us overcome our evil desires and selfishness and aids us in practicing virtues such as charity and patience.*

The desires of our bodies tempt us to do things unworthy of a Christian, such as sins of impurity, laziness, gluttony, anger, envy, pride, and neglect of our neighbor's needs. Evil persons, places, and things in this world can also lead us into sin. We need the help of the Holy Spirit to lead good Christian

See Papally Promulgated
Catechism of the Catholic Church

Q. 129. See paragraphs: 683-686, 733-737, 797-801, 1266

lives. Only when we allow the Holy Spirit to guide us, and when we use the help of His grace, can we continue to share in God's divine life of sanctifying grace and live as His children.

4. *The indwelling of the Holy Spirit makes our prayers pleasing to God.*

The Holy Spirit unites us with God by charity, and helps us to keep our friendship with Him by prayer. He makes our prayers pleasing to God because through His grace our lives are pleasing to God.

Sacred Scripture

"But the fruit of the Spirit is charity, joy, peace, patience, benignity, goodness, longanimity, mildness, faith, modesty, continence, chastity. Against such there is no law."

Galatians 5:22-23

Vatican Council II

"Before this faith can be exercised, man must have the grace of God to move and assist him, he must have the interior helps of the Holy Spirit, who moves the heart and converts it to God, who opens the eyes of the mind and 'makes it easy for all to accept and believe the truth.' The same Holy Spirit constantly perfects faith by his gifts." *Divine Revelation, 5*

Prayer: *Indwelling Holy Spirit, give us hope and courage. Heal the weaknesses of our souls. Help us to overcome our evil desires and selfishness. Through Your grace aid us in the practice of virtue and make our prayers more pleasing to God.*

Fill our souls with the wisdom and knowledge of Christ's teachings; sanctify us in Your grace as You sanctified the saints. Pour into our hearts a love for those virtues which You especially require of us. Imbue us, above all, with the spirit of self-sacrifice, that we may make any sacrifice to which Your grace invites us, for Your own glorification, for the honor of the Father and the Son, and for the salvation of immortal souls. Amen.

Prayer

Loving Comforter, we beg You for the grace of a personal, constant, and daily devotion to You. We were entrusted to Your care in Baptism, and we received You in a special manner at Confirmation. Be then our Guide, our Friend, our Counselor, and our Guardian. Keep us far from sin and all its occasions.

Holy Spirit, bestow upon us a love of chastity, that with tender care we may watch over the purity of our bodies and souls. As You dispense Your graces through prayer and the sacraments, grant that we may rightly love and esteem these precious means of grace, and zealously make use of them.

Glory be to the Father, our Creator; glory be to the Son, our Redeemer; glory be to You, Holy Spirit, our Sanctifier, now and forever. Amen.

Chapter Fifty-Six

The Indwelling of the Holy Spirit in Man - II

Q. 130. What is our greatest dignity?

Our greatest dignity is that we are children of God, and that we have God's life in our souls through of the grace of Christ.

We must try to live holy lives and train ourselves to keep God's grace as our most precious treasure. We should ask the Holy Spirit to help us live according to our great dignity as children of God and as true Christians.

We believe in things unseen and hope for the reward promised to those who love God. As a result, we witness the action of a superhuman power, which is divine grace operating on our minds and wills and enabling us to see and want what the purely natural man cannot understand or desire. The gifts of nature are common to the good and bad, but supernatural grace is the proper gift of the elect. They who are adorned with it are esteemed worthy of eternal life.

The Trinitarian God is the source of supernatural grace. Indeed man's greatest dignity is that he is meant to possess supernatural life from the Father, through the Son, and in union with the Holy Spirit.

We could never earn this grace. Jesus bought supernatural grace for all men by His Suffering, Death, and Resurrection. Through supernatural grace we can gain eternal life.

We receive two lives from God. One is the natural life we receive at conception. The other is the supernatural life we receive when we are baptized as Christians. Jesus said to Nicodemus, "Amen, amen, I say to you, unless a man be born again, he cannot see the Kingdom of God" (John 3:3).

See Papally Promulgated
Catechism of the Catholic Church

Q. 130. See paragraphs: 1996-1999

Sacred Scripture

"By whom He [Jesus] has given us most great and precious promises; that by these you may be made partakers of the divine nature." *2 Peter 1:4*

Vatican Council II

"The dignity of man rests above all on the fact that he is called to communion with God. The invitation to converse with God is addressed to man as soon as he comes into being. For if man exists it is because God has created him through love, and through love continues to hold him in existence. He cannot live fully according to truth unless he freely acknowledges that love and entrusts himself to his creator."

Modern World, 19

"All children of the Church should nevertheless remember that their exalted condition results, not from their own merits, but from the grace of Christ. If they fail to respond in thought, word and deed to that grace, not only shall they not be saved, but they shall be the more severely judged."

The Church, 14

Prayer: *Holy Spirit, with all the humility and love of which we are capable, we invite You to come into our hearts. We are overwhelmed by Your divine goodness and condescension in wishing to leave the splendors of Your throne of supreme majesty and glory, in order to stoop to such miserable beings as ourselves. Our greatest dignity is that You dwell in our souls through grace.*

As we cast ourselves down in humble adoration before You, we most earnestly beg You to take complete possession of our souls, and make them Your own. We are Yours because You created us. All that we have are Your free gifts to us. Our wondrous bodies, with all their senses, are so very marvelous and perfect in their operations. Still more wondrous are our souls, spiritual and immortal, and their sublime faculties of understanding, memory, and will. All these You have given us. Our one desire is to return them entirely to You, that You may make them Your own, and take forevermore complete and unreserved possession of our entire being. Amen.

Prayer

We wish to be Yours, Divine Spirit, by the gift of sanctifying grace. You have made us Your temple, and have illumined and warmed us by Your most enlivening presence. We wish to be Yours by experiencing the infusion of Your divine grace in our souls and by living the three theological virtues of faith, hope, and charity. We wish to be Yours by sharing in Your seven gifts and twelve fruits, and by receiving the grace You give us to practice the acquired virtues.

Our indwelling God, stay with us forever. Strengthen us by Your all-powerful grace against the awful possibility, which we tremble even to think about, of ever driving You out of our souls by mortal sin. Help us to keep the temples of our souls pure and, as far as poor human frailty will permit, sinless in Your sight. Thus, may You be pleased to dwell there forever with blessed delight until we see You face to face in Your heavenly Kingdom. Amen.

The Theological Virtues, the Cardinal Virtues, and the Seven Gifts of the Holy Spirit

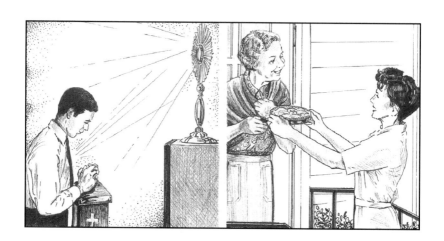

Chapter Fifty-Seven

The Theological Virtues
Faith, Hope, and Charity

Q. 131. What are the theological virtues?

The theological virtues are faith, hope, and charity.

These virtues are called theological, or divine, because they refer directly to God. They are infused into our souls, along with sanctifying grace, in the Sacrament of Baptism.

The faithful are to use faith, hope, and charity as their constant weapons in the battle against evil and their protection against the wiles of the devil. They are said to abide in the manner of enduring principles of action; and among them, charity never fails, because it continues into eternity.

Sacred Scripture

"And now there remain faith, hope and charity, these three, but the greatest of these is charity." *1 Corinthians 13:13*

"We give thanks to God always for you all; making a remembrance of you in our prayers without ceasing. Being mindful of the work of your faith, and labor and charity, and of the enduring of the hope of our Lord Jesus Christ before God and our Father." *1 Thessalonians 1:2-3*

"But let us, who are of the day, be sober, having on the breastplate of faith and charity, and for a helmet the hope of salvation." *1 Thessalonians 5:8*

Vatican Council II

"The forms and tasks of life are many but holiness is one — that sanctity which is cultivated by all who act under God's Spirit and, obeying the Father's voice and adoring God the Father in spirit and in truth, follow Christ, poor, humble and

See Papally Promulgated
Catechism of the Catholic Church

Q. 131. See paragraphs: 1812-1829

cross-bearing, that they may deserve to be partakers of his glory. Each one, however, according to his own gifts and duties must steadfastly advance along the way of a living faith, which arouses hope and works through love." *The Church, 41*

Prayer: Most *Holy Spirit, we firmly believe that You are really a Person, and that You abide in our souls through sanctifying grace. You are co-equal and co-eternal with the Father and the Son. Never let us forget that You are always living and working in our souls to make us holy by increasing in us the virtues of faith, hope, and charity. What You desire most of all is our sanctification. May Your desire evoke the same desire in our souls.*

Most Loving Friend, by Your indwelling in our souls, You make an abode with us as the Protector and Giver of all spiritual gifts and virtues. As the Spirit of adoption in a child of God, You are the cause and fountain of supernatural life and the seal of the promised full and beatific possession of God in Heaven. Your indwelling in us differs only in degree from that by which You beatify the saints in Heaven. May You dwell within us now and always. Amen.

Prayer

Loving Advocate, though Your gifts and graces are holy, they are not your greatest gift. Your greatest gift is Yourself. Jesus told us so when He made this promise to His Apostles: "I will ask the Father, and He shall give you another Paraclete, that He may abide with you forever. The Spirit of truth, Whom the world cannot receive, because it sees Him not, nor knows Him, but you shall know Him; because He shall abide with you, and shall be in you" (John 14:16-17).

Divine Author and Giver of all grace, although Your divine working in our souls is secret, hidden, and unseen, and although we do not feel Your presence there, let us never become indifferent to You. Rather, let us adore You as the dearest Guest of our souls, give You thanks for Your blessings, and listen to Your inspirations. Fill our souls with the fullness of Your gifts and virtues, especially the virtues of faith, hope, and charity. Give us peace and consolation. Direct us with Your inspirations; govern our conduct; raise us above the restlessness of this world; help us to overcome our temptations; heal our souls and inflame them with the fire of Your love; and guide us to a home of everlasting beauty in the Kingdom of God. Amen.

Chapter Fifty-Eight

The Theological Virtue of Faith

Q. 132. What is faith?

Faith, as used here, is the supernatural virtue by which we firmly believe all the truths God has revealed. Faith is possible only because God freely speaks His word to man and at the same time opens man's mind and heart to His presence and love.

Faith is applied to the body of truths that are found in the Creeds and in the teachings of the Church, which are based upon divine Revelation. Divine Revelation includes both Sacred Scripture and Sacred Tradition. Faith is essentially the power one exercises in order to believe in God's revelation of Himself and His will for us.

An act of supernatural faith is the assent of the mind to what God has revealed. Such an act requires divine grace, either actual or sanctifying or both. The act is performed under the influence of the will. If an act of faith is made in the state of grace, it is meritorious before God. A simple act of faith is, "My God, I believe in You and all that Your Church teaches, because You have said it, and Your word is true."

The virtue of faith is infused into our souls, along with sanctifying grace, when the Sacrament of Baptism is received. Even the baptized infant possesses this virtue, although he will not be able to exercise it fully until he reaches the age of reason.

The effect of faith is something called justification. This means that faith perfected by the theological virtue of charity brings man from a stage of separation from God into communion with Him and with his fellow men in God.

Sacred Scripture

"For if you confess with your mouth the Lord Jesus, and be-

See Papally Promulgated
Catechism of the Catholic Church

Q. 132. See paragraphs: 1814-1816

lieve in your heart that God has raised Him up from the dead, you shall be saved. For, with the heart, we believe unto justice, but, with the mouth, confession is made unto salvation."

Romans 10:9-10

"No man can come to Me, except the Father, Who has sent Me, draws him, and I will raise him up in the last day."

John 6:44

"For all have sinned, and need the glory of God. Being justified freely by His grace, through the redemption that is in Christ Jesus, Whom God has proposed to be a propitiation, through faith in His blood, to the showing of His justice, of the remission of former sins." *Romans 3:23-25*

"For we in spirit, by faith, wait for the hope of justice. For in Christ Jesus neither circumcision avails anything, nor uncircumcision, but faith that works by charity." *Galatians 5:5-6*

Vatican Council II

" 'The obedience of faith' (Romans 16:26; cf. Romans 1:5; 2 Corinthians 10:5-6) must be given to God as he reveals himself. By faith man freely commits his entire self to God, making the full submission of his intellect and will to God who reveals,' and willingly assenting to the Revelation given by him."

Divine Revelation, 5

"The act of faith is of its very nature a free act. Man, redeemed by Christ the Saviour and called through Jesus Christ to be an adopted son of God, cannot give his adherence to God when he reveals himself unless, drawn by the Father, he submits to God with a faith that is reasonable and free."

Liberty, 9

"Only the light of faith and meditation on the Word of God can enable us to find everywhere and always the God 'in whom we live and exist' (Acts 17:28); only thus can we seek his will in everything, see Christ in all men, acquaintance or stranger, make sound judgments on the true meaning and value of temporal realities both in themselves and in relation to man's end." *Lay People, 4*

Prayer: *Divine Spirit, pour Your heavenly light into our souls that we may, to some degree, understand the truths of the Catholic Faith and the end and object of our being in this world.*

Holy Spirit, enlighten our minds by the light of the Church's teaching, for You keep intact the deposit of Faith and guard the teaching Church from the possibility of error.

Guide our minds also by the interior light of Your divine inspirations, by the virtue of faith, by the infusion of Your gifts, and by the actual graces You impart to us. We ask this through Jesus our Lord. Amen.

Prayer

Our God, we firmly believe that You are one God in three Divine Persons: Father, Son, and Holy Spirit. We believe that God the Son became man, and died for our sins, and that He will come to judge the living and the dead. We believe these and all the truths which the Holy Catholic Church teaches, because You have revealed them, and You can neither deceive nor be deceived.

Divine Spirit, grant that everything we do may be directed by the knowledge of Your truth. May we, who have received Your gift of faith, share forever in the new life of Christ. Restore us by Your sacraments. May Your grace bring us eternal joy. In loving us, You have brought us from evil to good and from misery to happiness. Through Your blessings of grace, give the courage of perseverance to the ones You have called and justified by faith.

Holy Spirit, our God, by the coming of the Divine Word, Jesus, among us, may the light of faith shine in our words and actions. Open our hearts to receive Jesus' life and increase our vision of faith, that our life may be filled forever with Your glory and Your peace. Amen.

Chapter Fifty-Nine

The Theological Virtue of Hope

Q. 133. What is hope?

Hope is the supernatural virtue by which we firmly trust that God, Who is all-powerful and faithful to His promises, will, in His mercy, give us eternal happiness and the means to obtain it. This is given to us through the merits of the sufferings and works of Jesus Christ.

The virtue of hope is an infused theological virtue, received at Baptism together with sanctifying grace. The possession of God is its primary object.

"For we are saved by hope. But hope that is seen, is not hope. For what a man sees why does he hope for it? But if we hope for that which we do not see, we wait for it with patience" (Romans 8:24-25) .

Hope belongs to the will and makes a person desire eternal life, which is the heavenly vision of God. Hope gives one the confidence that he will receive the graces necessary to reach Heaven.

The grounds of hope are the omnipotence of God, the goodness of God and the fidelity of God to what He has promised. "But they that hope in the Lord shall renew their strength. They shall take wings as eagles. They shall run and not be weary, they shall walk and not faint" (Isaiah 40:31).

The virtue of hope is necessary for salvation. Individual acts of hope are also necessary for salvation and are commanded by God for all who have come to the age of reason. "Be sober, having on the breast plate of faith and charity and, for a helmet, the hope of salvation" (1 Thessalonians 5:8).

Acts of hope are required in times of temptation to discouragement or despair, and are implicit in every supernaturally

See Papally Promulgated
Catechism of the Catholic Church

Q. 133. See paragraphs: 1817-1821

good work. "My mercy shall not depart from you, and the covenant of My peace shall not be moved, said the Lord that has mercy on you" (Isaiah 54:10). We can make an act of hope by saying, "My God I hope in You, for grace and for glory, because of Your promises, Your mercy and Your power."

Vatican Council II

"Those with such a faith live in the hope of the revelation of the sons of God, keeping in mind the cross and resurrection of the Lord.

"On life's pilgrimage they are hidden with Christ in God, are free from the slavery of riches, are in search of the goods that last forever. Generously they exert all their energies in extending God's kingdom, in making the Christian spirit a vital energizing force in the temporal sphere. In life's trials they draw courage from hope, 'convinced that present sufferings are no measure of the future glory to be revealed in us' (Romans 8:18)." *Lay People, 4*

"Hope in a life to come does not take away from the importance of the duties of this life on earth but rather adds to it by giving new motives for fulfilling those duties. When, on the other hand, man is left without this divine support and without hope of eternal life his dignity is deeply wounded, as may so often be seen today. The problems of life and death, of guilt and of suffering, remain unsolved, so that men are not rarely cast into despair." *Modern World, 21*

Prayer: *Holy Spirit, You are the Paraclete, the mighty Comforter, the One Whom Jesus Christ, while still on earth, promised to send to His Apostles, and through them, to us. We put our hope in You. You have come to us as You came to them. Bring us comfort in our trials, joy amidst the sorrows of this life, and peace in our distress. Fill our whole being with Your consolation.*

You are the Living Spring in Whose purifying and refreshing waters our souls are cleansed, sanctified, and quickened. You are the Sweet Unction that fills all the powers of our souls and bodies with the oil of gladness, and gives to them spiritual strength and energy.

Holy Spirit, You know our weaknesses and how insistently the enemy of our salvation strives to bring about our destruction. Without Your all-powerful aid we are unable to defend ourselves against the malice, treachery, and power of such a terrible foe. With Your help, we can do all things. We have nothing to fear; we put our hope in You. All the efforts of the devil to harm us will be unavailing. Grant us assistance, we most earnestly beg You, that, under Your protection, we may journey safely on the path of life. We ask this through Jesus Christ our Lord. Amen.

Prayer

Our God, relying on Your almighty power, infinite mercy, and promises, we hope to obtain pardon of our sins, the help of Your grace, and life everlasting, through the merits of Jesus Christ, our Lord and Redeemer.

Divine Spirit, with hope we turn to You, not only for protection from our spiritual enemies, but also for that true interior peace of which You are the source. Our life on earth must necessarily be a warfare; foes within and foes without are ever seeking to destroy our peace; yet down in the depths of our souls we shall have peace, for You make Your dwelling there by giving us sanctifying grace. Our indwelling God, fill our inmost souls with peace, hope, and joy, so that nothing can disturb us. Like the little child who holds his father's hand and never thinks of fear so long as he is thus protected, help us to walk confidently upon the way to Heaven.

Holy Spirit, amidst the sorrows, trials, temptations, disappointments, and mental and physical sufferings of life, we ask for Your comfort and consolation. Console us by the sacraments, especially by the Eucharist and the Sacrament of Penance. Console us by Your actual graces. Sweeten the toils and sorrows of our lives, enlighten our understanding to know the value of suffering, and strengthen our wills to embrace that suffering with courage and joy. Console us by the thought of Heaven and of the blissful reward that awaits us. Thank you, Spirit of peace and joy, for Your indwelling in our souls. Knowing that You are with us is the source of our hope and lasting consolation. Amen.

Chapter Sixty

The Theological Virtue of Charity

Q. 134. What is charity?

Charity is the supernatural virtue by which we love God above all things for His own sake, and our neighbor as ourselves for the love of God.

"Now the end of the commandment is charity, from a pure heart, and a good conscience, and an unfeigned faith" (1 Timothy 1:5).

"You shall love the Lord your God with your whole heart, and with your whole soul, and with your whole mind. This is the greatest and the first commandment. And the second is like to this. You shall love your neighbor as yourself" (Matthew 22:37-39).

Because charity is infused into the soul at baptism, along with sanctifying grace, it is often identified with the state of grace. A person who has lost the supernatural virtue of charity has lost the state of grace, although he may still possess the virtues of hope and faith.

An act of charity is a supernatural act, based on faith, in which God is loved for Himself and not for any hope of reward. This act requires divine grace, either sanctifying or actual, or both. It is also the normal way of growing in the virtue of charity.

A simple act of charity can be made in these words, "My God, because You are so good, I love You with all my heart, and for Your sake, I love my neighbor as myself."

Supernatural love resides primarily in the will, not in the emotions. To love God means that we are willing to give up anything rather than offend God by mortal sin.

See Papally Promulgated
Catechism of the Catholic Church

Q. 134. See paragraphs: 1822-1829

We may have a genuine, supernatural love for our neighbor, even though on the natural level we feel a strong distaste for him. Thus we forgive for God's sake the wrong he has done. We pray for him and stand ready to help him if he should be in need. We then have a supernatural love for our neighbor.

Sacred Scripture

"Loving one another with the charity of brotherhood, with honor preferring one another. Not lazy in business. In spirit fervent. Serving the Lord. Rejoicing in hope. Patient in tribulation. Instant in prayer. Communicating to the necessities of the saints. Pursuing hospitality. Bless them that persecute you, bless, and curse not. Rejoice with them that rejoice; weep with them that weep." *Romans 12:10-15*

"Therefore, while we have time, let us work good to all men, but especially to those who are of the household of the faith." *Galatians 6:10*

Vatican Council II

"'God is love, and he who abides in love abides in God, and God abides in him' (1 John 4:16). God has poured out his love into our hearts through the Holy Spirit who has been given to us (cf. Romans 5:5); therefore the first and most necessary gift is charity, by which we love God above all things and our neighbor because of him. But if charity is to grow and fructify in the soul like good seed, each of the faithful must willingly hear the word of God and carry out his will with deeds, with the help of his grace; he must frequently partake of the sacraments, chiefly the Eucharist, and take part in the sacred liturgy; he must constantly apply himself to prayer, self-denial, active brotherly service and the practice of all virtues. This is because love, as the bond of perfection and fulness of the law (cf. Col. 3:14; Rom.13:10), governs, gives meaning to, and perfects all the means of sanctification. Hence the true disciple of Christ is marked by love both of God and of his neighbor."
The Church, 42

Prayer: *Holy Spirit, inflame our hearts with charity so that we may love You, our God, above and before all things, and love our neighbor as ourselves. You are the Spirit of Love. Kindle in our hearts Your ardent flame of love.*

Holy Spirit, help us to love the heavenly Father with a strong and sincere love, whereby we may realize that He is not only our Creator but also our Father. His paternal love for us is infinite, and therefore, we should love and reverence it with all the tender, filial confidence, and trust, He deserves. All this we ask through our Lord and Savior Jesus Christ. Amen.

Prayer

Our God, we love You above all things, with our whole heart and soul, because You are all-good and worthy of all love. We love our neighbor as ourselves for the love of You. We forgive all who have injured us, and ask pardon of all whom we have injured.

Enable us, Holy Spirit, to know and love Jesus Christ, the eternal Son of God, the Second Person of the ever blessed Trinity, with all the fervor and energy of our souls. He is our Savior and our Redeemer. To know Him is eternal life, for within His Sacred Heart are all the graces of Redemption that we need to save and sanctify our souls.

Grant us, Holy Spirit, a more intimate knowledge and more fervent love for You by showing us Your infinite perfections, Your wondrous attributes, and Your marvelous gifts. Grant us the grace to know You and love You daily more and more. Throughout life, give us the grace to more ardently cultivate devotion to You. Thus, through You, may we come to know and love the Father and the Son, to Whom, with You, all praise, honor, and glory belongs. Amen.

Chapter Sixty-One

The Cardinal Virtues - I

Q. 135. What are the cardinal virtues?

The cardinal virtues are *temperance, prudence, justice* and *fortitude*.

These virtues help us to lead good, moral lives by aiding us to treat persons and things in the right way, according to God's will.

"And if a man loves justice, her [Wisdom's] labors have great virtues; for she teaches temperance, and prudence, and justice, and fortitude, which are such things as men can have nothing more profitable in life" (Wisdom 8:7).

Prudence is the power to make right judgments. — "Get wisdom, because it is better than gold, and purchase prudence, for it is more precious than silver" (Proverbs 16:16).

Justice helps us to see the need to protect the rights of our fellow man. — "He that follows justice and mercy, shall find life, justice, and glory" (Proverbs 21:21).

Fortitude gives us strength to do what is good, in spite of every difficulty. — "For I consider that the sufferings of this time are not worthy to be compared with the glory to come, that shall be revealed in us" (Romans 8:18).

Temperance helps us to control our desires, especially the desires that might keep us from using correctly the things which appeal to our senses. — "My son, test your soul in your life, and if it is wicked, give it no power" (Ecclesiaticus [Sirach] 37:30).

"And take heed to yourselves, lest perhaps your hearts be overcharged with debauchery and drunkenness, and the cares of this life, and that day come upon you suddenly" (Luke 21:34).

See Papally Promulgated
Catechism of the Catholic Church

Q. 135. See paragraphs: 1805-1809

Sanctifying grace gives us a certain readiness for the practice of all of the virtues, together with a supernatural merit each time we practice them.

Vatican Council II

"Justice and equity also demand that the livelihood of individuals and their families should not become insecure and precarious through a kind of mobility which is a necessary feature of developing economies. All kinds of discrimination in wages and working conditions should be avoided in regard to workers who come from other countries or areas and contribute their work to the economic development of a people or a region." *Modern World, 66*

Prayer: *Holy Spirit, Divine Light, illumine our souls with Your brightness; fill them with love, gladness, and life; warm them and quicken them into vigorous action in God's service, through Christ Our Lord. Amen.*

Prayer

Holy Spirit, help us to practice the cardinal virtues which will enable us to lead a good life, by helping us to treat persons and things in the right way, according to God's will.

Give us the virtue of prudence, that we may be able to make right judgments; the virtue of justice, that we may be able to protect the rights of our fellow men; the virtue of fortitude, that we may have the strength to do what is good, with the willingness to make any sacrifices You require; the virtue of temperance, that we may be able to control our desires and use correctly the things which appeal to our senses.

We believe that when we are in the state of sanctifying grace, we bear Your image within our inmost being. By granting us sanctifying grace, pierce the center of our hearts and render our thoughts and actions both spiritual and supernatural. By the divine infused virtues of faith, hope, and charity, and the acquired virtues, which include humility and obedience, control our understanding and our will, and enable them to elicit supernatural acts. By bestowing Your gifts on us, set these supernatural acts in motion, guide us in them, and by Your actual graces render our performance of them easier.

Truly, You are the very source and center of our spiritual life. For this we give You our humble thanks, through Christ Our Lord. Amen.

Chapter Sixty-Two

The Cardinal Virtues - II

Q. 136. Why are prudence, justice, fortitude, and temperance called cardinal virtues?

They are called cardinal virtues, because they are the key virtues upon which all the other virtues depend.

A virtue is a habit or permanent disposition which inclines a person to do good and to avoid evil. If we acquire a virtue by our own efforts, that is, by consciously developing a certain good habit, we call that virtue a natural virtue. God, however, may directly infuse virtues into our souls without any effort on our part. Virtues of this kind, which are habits bestowed upon the soul directly by God, are called supernatural virtues.

Prudence, justice, fortitude, and temperance (which are both acquired and infused) are called cardinal virtues (Latin: "cardo" hinge) because they contain within themselves the seeds of all other virtues. The other virtues of human morality are necessarily related to them. Examples of the other virtues are obedience, patience, humility, truthfulness, and patriotism.

Sacred Scripture

"A fool laughs at the instruction of his father, but he that regards reproofs shall become prudent." *Proverbs 15:5*

"Aged men, be sober, chaste, prudent, sound in faith, in love, in patience." *Titus 2:2*

Vatican Council II

"Anyone who in obedience to Christ seeks first the kingdom of God will derive from it a stronger and purer love for

See Papally Promulgated
Catechism of the Catholic Church

Q. 136. See paragraph: 1805

helping all his brethren and for accomplishing the task of justice under the inspiration of charity." *Modern World, 72*

Prayer

O Holy Spirit, Infinite Love of the Father and the Son, through the pure hands of Mary, Your Immaculate Spouse, we place ourselves this day, and all the days of our life, upon Your chosen altar, the divine Heart of Jesus. May we be a pleasing sacrifice to You, O Consuming Fire, as we are firmly resolved, now more than ever, to hear Your voice, and to do in all things Your most holy and adorable will.

Holy Spirit, Spirit of Truth, come into our hearts. Abide in us and grant that we may ever abide in You forever, through Jesus Christ, our only Lord and Savior. Amen.

Chapter Sixty-Three

The Seven Gifts of the Holy Spirit

Q. 137. What are the seven gifts of the Holy Spirit?

The seven gifts of the Holy Spirit are *wisdom, understanding, counsel, fortitude, knowledge, piety,* and *the fear of the Lord*. They are the gifts listed in Isaiah 11 which were to characterize the Just Man — the Messiah.

These seven gifts of the Holy Spirit are the qualities given to the soul which make the soul responsive to the grace of God. They help us to practice virtue.

Just as charity (the most perfect of virtues) embraces all the other virtues, wisdom is the most perfect of gifts, since it embodies all the other gifts.

1. The gift of *wisdom* strengthens our faith, fortifies our hope, perfects our charity, and promotes our practice of virtue to the highest degree. Wisdom enlightens our minds to discern and relish things divine, so that the appreciation of earthly joys loses its savor, while the Cross of Christ yields a divine sweetness.

2. *Understanding,* as a gift of the Holy Spirit, helps us to grasp the meaning of the truths of our holy religion. By faith we know them, but by understanding we learn to appreciate and relish them. Understanding enables us to penetrate the inner meaning of revealed truths, and through them, to quicken us to the newness of life.

3. The gift of *counsel* endows our souls with supernatural prudence, enabling them to judge promptly and rightly what must be done, especially in difficult circumstances. Counsel applies the principles, furnished by knowledge and understanding, to the innumerable concrete cases which confront

See Papally Promulgated
Catechism of the Catholic Church

Q. 137. See paragraphs: 1830-1832

us in the course of our daily duty. Counsel is supernatural common sense — a priceless treasure in the quest of salvation.

4. By the gift of *fortitude*, our souls are strengthened against natural fear, and are supported in the performance of duty. Fortitude imparts to our wills an impulse and energy which moves them to undertake without hesitancy the most arduous tasks, to face dangers, to trample underfoot worldly considerations, and to endure without complaints the crosses of daily life.

5. The gift of *knowledge* enables our souls to evaluate created things for their true worth, that is, in their relationship to God. Knowledge unmasks the pretense of creatures, reveals their shallowness, and points out their only true purpose as instruments in the service of God. It shows us the loving care God has for us even in adversity, and it directs us to glorify Him in every circumstance of life. Guided by the light of knowledge, we put first things first, and prize the friendship of God beyond all else.

6. The gift of *piety* begets in our hearts a childlike affection for God as our most loving Father. It inspires us to love and respect, for His sake, persons and things consecrated to Him, as well as those who are vested with His authority, i.e., the Blessed Virgin and the saints, the Church and its visible head, the Pope, our parents and superiors, and our country with its rulers. He who is filled with the gift of piety finds the practice of his religion, not a burdensome duty, but a delightful service.

7. The gift of the *fear of the Lord* fills us with a sovereign respect for God, and makes us dread nothing so much as offending Him by sin. It is a fear that rises, not from the thought of hell, but from sentiments of reverence and childlike submission to our heavenly Father. It is the fear that is the beginning of wisdom, because it detaches us from worldly pleasures that can separate us from God.

Prayer: *O God, grant us Your Spirit of Wisdom, that He may reveal to us the enemies we ought to fear and the dangers we ought to avoid amidst the deceptive appearances of this world. May He help us to* choose, in every circumstance, what is most useful for the preservation and increase of divine life in us, and for the salvation of our souls.

O God, send us Your Spirit of Understanding, that He may help us to understand the beauty, the sweetness, and the fruitfulness of the holy truths that light our paths in this world. You, Heavenly Father, reveal these truths with much love to the humble, while You hide them from the proud.

O God, send us Your Spirit of Counsel, that in moments of action He may always incline us to the most opportune and prudent reflections; that He may make us perfectly docile to Your secret inspirations; and that He may also make us, in time of need, courageous and self-denying counselors for our neighbors.

O God, send us Your Spirit of Fortitude, that He may change our weaknesses into strengths, and make us apostles full of burning zeal.

O God, send us Your Spirit of Knowledge, that He may inspire us with a horror of lying and of error. May He inflame us with a noble and holy love of all the truths that You have taught us. May He guard these truths by placing in our hearts a constant memory of them, just as the most holy Virgin, our beloved Mother, held all Your truths in her heart.

O God, give us Your Spirit of Piety, that He may enkindle in us the fire of Your love, which makes us love Your divine will ardently, even in the smallest of our duties. That love will lend us even to heroism, and will secure for us strength, perseverance, and victory in all things by means of prayer.

O God, fill us with Your Spirit of Fear, that He may never allow us to forget the reverence which is due Your infinite majesty, Your boundless power, and Your dread judgment. Send us the Spirit of Fear, that He may keep us ever under Your gaze, Your direction, and Your sovereign dominion. Above all, form in our hearts a sublime and heavenly union of respect and love with You. May the Holy Spirit help us to see that the only real misfortune for the creature is the ingratitude which is contracted through sin. All this we ask through Christ our Lord. Amen.

Sacred Scripture

"And the spirit of the Lord shall rest upon Him; the spirit of wisdom and of understanding, the spirit of counsel and of fortitude, the spirit of knowledge and of godliness. And He shall be filled with the spirit of the fear of the Lord." *Isaiah 11:2-3*

Vatican Council II

"It is not only through the sacraments and the ministrations of the Church that the Holy Spirit makes holy the People, leads them and enriches them with his virtues. Allotting his gifts according as he wills (cf. Cor. 12:11), he also distributes special graces among the faithful of every rank. By these gifts he makes them fit and ready to undertake various tasks and offices for the renewal and building up of the Church, as it is written,' the manifestation of the Spirit is given to everyone for profit.' (1 Corinthians 12:7) Whether these charisms be very remarkable or more simple and widely diffused, they are to be received with thanksgiving and consolation since they are fitting and useful for the needs of the Church. Extraordinary gifts are not to be rashly desired, nor is it from them that the fruits of apostolic labors are to be presumptuously expected. Those who have charge over the Church should judge the genuineness and proper use of these gifts, through their office not indeed to extinguish the Spirit, but to test all things and hold fast to what is good (cf. I Thessalonians 5:12 and 19-21)."

The Church, 12

Prayer

Come, Spirit of Wisdom, and reveal to our souls the mysteries of heavenly things, and their exceeding greatness, power, and beauty. Teach us to love heavenly things above and beyond all the passing joys of earth. Help us to attain them and possess them forever.

Come, Spirit of Understanding, and enlighten our minds, that we may know and believe all the mysteries of salvation. May we merit at last to see the eternal light in Your light; and in the light of glory, may we have a clear vision of You, the Father, and the Son.

Come, Spirit of Counsel: help and guide us in all our ways, that we may always do Your holy will. Incline our hearts to that which is good and turn them away from what is evil. Direct us by the straight path of Your commandments to that goal of eternal life for which we long.

*C*ome, Blessed Spirit of Fortitude, uphold our souls in time of trouble and adversity; sustain our efforts toward holiness, and strengthen our weaknesses. Give us courage against all the assaults of our enemies, that we may never be overcome and separated from You, our God and greatest Good.

*C*ome, Blessed Spirit of Knowledge, and grant that we may perceive the will of the Father. Show us the nothingness of earthly things, that we may realize their vanity and use them only for Your glory and our own salvation. May we always look beyond them to You and Your eternal rewards.

*C*ome, Blessed Spirit of Piety, possess our hearts. Enkindle in them such a love for God that we may find satisfaction only in His service, and that, for His sake, we may lovingly submit to all legitimate authority.

*C*ome, Blessed Spirit of holy Fear, penetrate our inmost hearts, that we may set You, our Lord and God, before our face forever. Help us to shun all things which can offend You, and make us worthy to appear before the pure majesty of God. All this we ask through Jesus Christ our Lord and Savior. Amen.

The Creed - IV

The Church, the Communion of Saints, and the Forgiveness of Sins

"...We believe in One, Holy, Catholic, and Apostolic Church. We acknowledge one Baptism for the forgiveness of sins."

The Church

Chapter Sixty-Four

What is the Catholic Church?

Q. 138. What is the Catholic Church?

The Catholic Church is the community of all baptized persons united in the same true Faith, the same sacrifice, the same sacraments, under the authority of the Sovereign Pontiff, the Bishop of Rome, and the Bishops in communion with him.

The Catholic Church is the new People of God, (1) *prepared for in the Old Testament,* and (2) *given life, growth, and direction by Jesus Christ its founder and Head.*

1. *The Catholic Church is the new People of God, prepared for in the Old Testament.*

God made Israel a sacred community, dearer to Him than all other nations. They were to be the bearers of God's blessings to the world. Through them He planned to reunite a torn and divided mankind. So that they would not lose heart during their trials, He reminded them that He was caring for them as a loving Father. These were the first People of God. Even though they sinned, God remained faithful to them. He brought them out of Egypt and fed them in the desert. He said that He would always care for them because they were His special possession. He asked them to accept His love and to be His children.

After the Children of Israel had wandered in the desert for forty years, God led them into the land originally promised to Abraham. Although Israel as a whole failed in its devotion to God, a few people remained faithful. They were the remnant of the once great Israel. They depended on God alone. Through them, He would keep His promise to send the world a Savior Who would gather all men into God's family.

See Papally Promulgated
Catechism of the Catholic Church

Q. 138. See paragraphs: 781-786

2. The Catholic Church is the new People of God, given life, growth, and direction by Jesus Christ its founder and Head.

Jesus, God's own Son, born of Mary, was a descendant of the great Israelite king, David. With the scattered fragments of Israel, Jesus established a new kingdom, the Church, intended for all peoples. He brought peace to His people and freed their souls from sin and from the sadness which sin brings. He is our Savior.

To proclaim the Good News of salvation to all men everywhere, in all times, Jesus formed into one body His followers, the community of believers, the People of God. He called this body His Church, which is the Catholic Church. This was to be the new People of God.

"And He has subjected all things under His feet and has made Him head over all His Church" (Ephesians 1:22).

"Now you are the Body of Christ and members in particular" (1 Corinthians 12:27).

At the Second Vatican Council (1962-1965) this concept of the Catholic Church was qualified to include, but not fully, all who are baptized and profess their faith in Jesus Christ. These are the People of God, whom God has chosen to be His own and on whom He bestows the special graces of His providence. *[See on p. 321, "Dogmatic Constitution on the Church," 15].*

Vatican Council II

"As Israel according to the flesh which wandered in the desert was already called the Church of God (2 Esd. 13:1 cf. Num. 20:4, Deut. 23.1 ff.), so too, the new Israel which advances in this present era in search of a future and permanent city (cf. Heb. 13:14), is called also the Church of Christ (cf. Mt. 16:18). It is Christ indeed who had purchased it with his own blood (cf. Acts 20:28); he has filled it with his Spirit, he has provided means adapted to its visible and social union." *The Church, 9*

"Hence the universal Church is seen to be 'a people brought into unity from the unity of the Father, the Son and the Holy Spirit.' " *The Church, 4*

"But the society structured with hierarchical organs and the mystical body of Christ, the visible society and the spiritual community, the earthly Church and the Church endowed with heavenly riches, are not to be thought of as two realities. On the contrary, they form one complex reality which comes together from a human and a divine element." *The Church, 8*

"The Church is compared, not without significance, to the mystery of the incarnate Word. As the assumed nature, inseparably united to him, serves the Divine Word as a living organ of salvation, so, in a somewhat similar way, does the social structure of the Church serve the Spirit of Christ who vivifies it, in the building up of the body (cf. Eph. 4:15)." *The Church, 8*

"In the Old Testament the revelation of the kingdom is often made under the forms of symbols. In similar fashion the inner nature of the Church is now made known to us in various images. Taken either from the life of the shepherd or from cultivation of the land, from the art of building or from family life and marriage, these images have their preparation in the books of the prophets." *The Church, 6*

Prayer

Heavenly Father, even today we see the wonders of the miracles You worked long ago. Once You saved a single nation from slavery, and now You offer eternal salvation from slavery to sin to all through Baptism. May the peoples of the world become true sons of Abraham and prove worthy of the heritage of Israel.

Father in Heaven, from the days of Abraham and Moses until this gathering of Your Church in prayer, You have formed a people in the image of Your Son. Bless this people with the gift of Your Kingdom. May we serve You with our every desire and show love for one another even as You have loved us.

Almighty God, ever-living mystery of unity and Trinity, You gave life to the new Israel by birth from water and the Spirit, and made it a chosen race, a royal priesthood, a people set apart as Your eternal possession. May all those whom You have called to walk in the splendor of the new light render You fitting service and adoration.

Enable us to live honorably and unselfishly in this world, and so arrive at the glories of the heavenly city where, in union with all the blessed company of Heaven, we shall sing of Your majestic deeds forever and ever. Amen.

Chapter Sixty-Five

The Beginning of the Catholic Church

Q. 139. When did the Catholic Church begin?

The Catholic Church, founded by Christ, began at the time of His death and Resurrection.

Through His death and Resurrection, Jesus earned for us the privilege of belonging to God's holy family, the Church. To enter that family we need sanctifying grace, a sharing in the life of Christ, which we first receive when we are baptized.

By the power of Baptism, we become members of the Church, the Mystical Body of Christ. Thus, we become united to one another through our union with Christ, Who is the Head of the Body. Incorporated into Christ, we are freed from sin's dominion.

Sacred Scripture

Before ascending into Heaven, Jesus said to His Apostles, "All power is given to Me in Heaven and on earth. Therefore go, teach all nations; baptizing them in the Name of the Father, and of the Son, and of the Holy Spirit; teach them to observe all things whatsoever I have commanded you. And behold I am with you always, even to the end of the world."

Matthew 28:18-20

"Now you are the body of Christ, and each is a member of it." *1 Corinthians 12:27*

Vatican Council II

"The mystery of the holy Church is already brought to light in the way it was founded. For the Lord Jesus inaugurated his Church by preaching the Good News, that is, the coming of the kingdom of God, promised over the ages in the scrip-

See Papally Promulgated
Catechism of the Catholic Church

Q. 139. See paragraphs: 763-768, 787-791

tures: 'The time is fulfilled and the kingdom of God is at hand' (Mk. 1:15; Mt. 4:17). This kingdom shone out before men in the word, in the works and in the presence of Christ." *The Church, 5*

"For it was from the side of Christ as he slept the sleep of death upon the cross that there came forth the wondrous sacrament of the whole Church." *Sacred Liturgy, 5*

"Often, too, the Church is called the building of God (1 Cor. 3:9). The Lord compared himself to the stone which the builders rejected, but which was made into the cornerstone (Mt. 21:42; cf. Acts 4:11, 1 Pet. 2:7; Ps. 117:22). On this foundation the Church is built by the apostles (cf. 1 Cor. 3:11) and from it the Church receives solidity and unity. This edifice has many names to describe it: the house of God in which his family dwells; the household of God in the Spirit (Eph. 2:19, 22); the dwelling-place of God among men (Apoc. 21:3); and, especially, the holy temple. This temple, symbolized in places of worship built out of stone, is praised by the Fathers and, not without reason, is compared in the liturgy to the Holy City, the New Jerusalem. As living stones we here on earth are built into it (1 Pet. 2:5). It is this holy city that is seen by John as it comes down out of heaven from God when the world is made anew, prepared like a bride adorned for her husband (Apoc. 21:1f.)."

The Church, 6

Prayer: *Lord Jesus Christ, faithful witness and first-born from the dead, be our Life and our Resurrection. High Priest of the new and eternal covenant, intercede for Your holy Church. You Who loved us and washed away our sins in Your blood, make us holy so that we may serve our God worthily.*

When You rose from the dead, Lord Jesus, You formed the Church into Your Mystical Body and made of it the new Jerusalem, united in Your Spirit. Give us peace in our day. Guide all nations into Your Church so that they may share Your gifts in fellowship, and render You thanks without end, and come to Your eternal city. We ask this in Your most powerful and holy Name. Amen.

Prayer

Lord Jesus, our Savior, build up the faith of Your pilgrim Church on earth, that it may bear witness to Your Resurrection before the whole world. Fill our minds with the light of faith. Through Your Resurrection, You opened for us the way to eternal life; sustain us with the hope of glory. You sent the Holy Spirit into the world; set our hearts on fire with spiritual love.

Lord Jesus, in You, Who have risen from the dead, God has opened for us the way to everlasting life. Through Your victory, save the people You have redeemed.

The Father has established in You the foundation of all our hope and the principle of our resurrection. We rejoice with You, King of Glory, and we thank You for the privilege of belonging to the Church which You have founded and which began at the time of Your death and Resurrection. You were crucified to set us free; be our salvation and redemption.

Be with Your Church on its pilgrimage through life. Do not let us be slow to believe, but help us, as members of Your Church, to be ready to proclaim You as Victor over sin and death forever and ever. Amen.

Chapter Sixty-Six

Gifts of God to the Catholic Church - I

Q. 140. What are some of the basic gifts of God in the Catholic Church?

Among the basic gifts of God in the Catholic Church are: (1) *the apostolic ministries of Bishops, priests, and deacons, inherited from the Apostles,* (2) *the truths of the Faith,* and (3) *the sacraments.*

1. *Among the basic gifts of God in the Catholic Church are the apostolic ministries of Bishops, priests, and deacons, inherited from the Apostles.*

With the powers given to them by Christ (the apostolic ministries, etc.), the Apostles and their successors, Bishops, priests and deacons, were to be His witnesses in the world. He said to the Apostles before ascending into Heaven, "You shall receive the power of the Holy Spirit coming upon you, and you shall be witnesses unto Me in Jerusalem, and in all Judea, and Samaria, and even to the uttermost part of the earth" (Acts 1:8).

2. *Among the basic gifts of God in the Catholic Church are the truths of the Faith.*

To carry on Christ's teaching, the Apostles were given the authority and duty to teach the truths of the Faith to the world. They were appointed by Christ to be our chief teachers, so that, through them and their successors, He could guide us to the Kingdom of Heaven with the manna of His heavenly doctrine.

Jesus said, "He that hears you, hears Me; and he that despises you, despises Me; and he that despises Me, despises Him that sent Me" (Luke 10:16). "Amen I say to you, whatsoever you shall bind upon earth, shall be bound also in Heaven;

See Papally Promulgated
Catechism of the Catholic Church

Q. 140. See paragraphs: 14, 185-197, 861-862, 873-896, 949-951, 1210-1211

and whatsoever you shall loose upon earth, shall be loosed also in Heaven" (Matthew 18:18).

3. *Among the basic gifts of God in the Catholic Church are the sacraments.*

Christ taught the Apostles that His grace was to be given to men through them, especially by means of the seven sacraments. Through the Apostles He would, for instance, forgive sins through the Sacrament of Penance or Confession: "Whose sins you shall forgive, they are forgiven them; and whose sins you shall retain, they are retained" (John 20:23).

Through the Apostles, Christ would also give His Body and Blood to the world. "And taking bread, He gave thanks and broke it; and gave it to them, saying, 'This is My Body, which is given for you. Do this for a commemoration of Me.' In like manner the chalice also, after He had supped, saying, 'This is the chalice, the new testament in My Blood, which shall be shed for you' " (Luke 22:19-20).

Through the Apostles and their successors, the Bishops, priests, and deacons, to whom the authority and power to dispense grace was given, the Church administers the seven sacraments for the salvation of God's people.

"He said therefore to them again, 'Peace be to you. As the Father, has sent me, I also send you' " (John 20:21).

Jesus continued, through the gifts of His Apostles and their successors, to be King, Priest, and Teacher to His people. Through the Apostles and their successors, believers were gathered into the Catholic Church and were united to Christ and to each other.

Vatican Council II

"The Catholic Church is by the will of Christ the teacher of truth. It is her duty to proclaim and teach with authority the truth which is Christ and, at the same time, to declare and confirm by her authority the principles of the moral order which spring from human nature itself." *Liberty, 14*

"It is through the faithful preaching of the Gospel by the Apostles and their successors — the bishops with Peter's successor at their head — through their administering the sacraments, and through their governing in love, that Jesus Christ wishes his people to increase, under the action of the Holy Spirit; and he perfects its fellowship in unity: in the confes-

290

sion of one faith, in the common celebration of divine worship, and in the fraternal harmony of the family of God." *Ecumenism, 2*

"All men are called to belong to the new People of God. This People therefore, whilst remaining one and only one, is to be spread throughout the whole world and to all ages in order that the design of God's will may be fulfilled." *The Church, 13*

"It is through Christ's Catholic Church alone, which is the universal help towards salvation, that the fullness of the means of salvation can be obtained. It was to the apostolic college alone, of which Peter is the head, that we believe that our Lord entrusted all the blessings of the New Covenant, in order to establish on earth the one Body of Christ into which all those should be fully incorporated who belong in any way to the People of God." *Ecumenism, 3*

Prayer: *God of might and majesty, the strength of those who hope in You, rescue the troubled and afflicted, set us free from our sins, and preserve us in Your truth which is given to us in Your Church. Your light of truth guides us on the way to Christ. May all who follow Him reject what is contrary to the Gospel. We ask this through Jesus Christ our only Lord and Savior, to Whom with You and the Holy Spirit be all honor and glory. Amen.*

Prayer

Lord, You are always present in Your Church. Through Your Holy Spirit, guide it into all truth.

Father, You established Your ancient covenant by signs and wonders, but You confirmed the new one in a more wonderful way through the sacrifice of Your Son. Guide Your Church in the pathways of life, that we may be led to the land of promise and celebrate Your Name with lasting praise.

You sustain us with the word and Body of Your Son. Watch over us with loving care; help the Church to grow in faith, holiness, charity, and loving service. You have set us firm within Your Church, which You built upon the rock of Peter's faith. Bless us with a faith that never falters.

We celebrate the memorial of the love of Your Son in the Eucharist. May His saving work bring salvation to all the world through the ministry of Your Church. We ask this in the Name of Jesus Christ, our Lord. Amen.

Chapter Sixty-Seven

Gifts of God to the Catholic Church - II
The Truths of the Faith

Q. 141. What are the two sources of divine truth which constitute the Truths of the Faith?

The two sources of divine truth are: (1) *Holy Scripture* and (2) *Sacred Tradition (also known as Apostolic Tradition or simply Tradition).*

1. *One source of divine truth is Holy Scripture.*

Holy Scripture (or the Bible) is the collection of books accepted as definitive by the Catholic Church. Sacred Scripture is the authentic, inspired record of the revelations made to mankind by God about Himself and about His will for men. It is divided into the Old and New Testaments in order to distinguish between the earlier and temporary Covenant between God and the Jewish nation, given to Moses on Mount Sinai, and the later permanent Covenant between God and the followers of Jesus Christ throughout the world.

In the New Testament, the Old Testament is generally spoken of as "the Scriptures" or the "sacred writings" (cf. Matthew 21:42). Gradually the word "Scripture" has become a synonym for the Bible as a whole. "Testament" has the meaning of "covenant," with reference to the two covenants which God established with His People in human history.

The Catholic Church has, more than once, taught which books are to be regarded as inspired, and which, therefore, belong to the Bible. At the Ecumenical Council of Trent, in 1546, the biblical canon was solemnly defined and the the Latin Vulgate version of the Bible, wirtten by St. Jerome (c. 342-420) was declared to be authentic. In 1943, Pope Pius XII

See Papally Promulgated
Catechism of the Catholic Church

Q. 141. See paragraphs: 74-82, 101-105

reconfirmed the biblical canon and the authenticity of the Vulgate. But he made some important declarations which encouraged totally new editions of the Bible based on Hebrew and Greek manuscripts.

2. *The second source of divine truth is Sacred Tradition (also known as Apostolic Tradition or simply Tradition).*

The term "tradition" literally means, a "handing on," referring to the passing down of God's revealed word. It has two distinct meanings.

First, tradition means all of divine revelation, from the dawn of human history to the end of the apostolic age, as it has been passed on from one generation of believers to the next, and as it is preserved under divine guidance by the Church established by Christ.

Tradition also means, within all transmitted revelation, that part of God's revealed word which is not contained in Sacred Scripture. The Second Vatican Council tells us how Sacred Tradition was handed on: "It was done by the Apostles who handed on, by the spoken word of their preaching, by the example they gave, by the institutions they established, what they themselves had received — whether from the lips of Christ, from his way of life and his works, or whether they had learned it by the prompting of the Holy Spirit" (Divine Revelation, 7).

Sacred Scripture

"All Scripture, inspired of God, is profitable to teach, to reprove, to correct, to instruct in justice." *2 Timothy 3:16*

"Therefore, brethren, stand fast and hold the traditions which you have learned, whether by word or by our letter."
2 Thessalonians 2:14

Vatican Council II

"To compose the sacred books, God chose certain men who, all the while he employed them in this task, made full use of their powers and faculties so that, though he acted in them and by them, it was as true authors that they consigned to writing whatever he wanted written, and no more."
Divine Revelation, 11

"Holy Mother Church, relying on the faith of the apostolic age, accepts as sacred and canonical the books of the Old and the New Testaments, whole and entire, with all their parts, on the grounds that, written under the inspirations of the

Holy Spirit (cf. Jn. 20:31; 2 Tim. 3:16; 2 Pet. 1:19-21; 3:15-16), they have God as their author, and have been handed on as such to the Church herself." *Divine Revelation, 11*

"Since, therefore, all that the inspired authors or sacred writers, affirm should be regarded as affirmed by the Holy Spirit, we must acknowledge that the books of Scripture, firmly, faithfully and without error, teach that truth which God, for the sake of our salvation, wished to see confided to the Sacred Scriptures." *Divine Revelation, 11*

"Sacred Tradition and sacred Scripture, then, are bound closely together, and communicate one with the other. For both of them, flowing out from the same divine well-spring, come together in some fashion to form one thing, and move towards the same goal. Sacred Scripture is the speech of God as it is put down in writing under the breath of the Holy Spirit. And Tradition transmits in its entirety the Word of God which has been entrusted to the apostles by Christ the Lord and the Holy Spirit. It transmits it to the successors of the apostles so that, enlightened by the Spirit of truth, they may faithfully preserve, expound and spread it abroad by their preaching. Thus it comes about that the Church does not draw her certainty about all revealed truths from the holy Scriptures alone. Hence, both Scripture and Tradition must be accepted and honored with equal feelings of devotion and reverence." *Divine Revelation, 9*

"The task of giving an authentic interpretation of the Word of God, whether in its written form or in the form of Tradition, has been entrusted to the living teaching office of the Church alone. Its authority in this matter is exercised in the name of Jesus Christ. Yet this Magisterium [teaching authority] is not superior to the word of God, but is its servant. It teaches only what has been handed on to it. At the divine command and with the help of the Holy Spirit, it listens to this devotedly, guards it with dedication and expounds it faithfully. All that it proposes for belief as being divinely revealed is drawn from this single deposit of faith." *Divine Revelation, 10*

"It is common knowledge that among all the inspired writings, even among those of the New Testament, the Gospels have a special place, and rightly so, because they are our principal source for the life and teaching of the Incarnate Word, our Saviour." *Divine Revelation, 18*

"The Church has always venerated the divine Scriptures as she venerated the Body of the Lord, in so far as she never ceases, particularly in the sacred liturgy, to partake of the bread of life and to offer it to the faithful from the one table of the word of God and the Body of Christ." *Divine Revelation, 21*

"So may it come that, by the reading and study of the sacred books 'the Word of God may speed on and triumph' (2 Th. 3:1) and the treasure of Revelation entrusted to the Church may more and more fill the hearts of men. Just as from constant attendance at the eucharistic mystery the life of the Church draws increase, so a new impulse of spiritual life may be expected from increased veneration of the Word of God, which 'stands forever' (Is. 40:8; cf. 1 Pet. 1:23-25)." *Divine Revelation, 26*

"The Christian economy, therefore, since it is the new and definitive covenant, will never pass away; and no new public revelation is to be expected before the glorious manifestation of our Lord, Jesus Christ (cf. 1 Tim. 6:14 and Tit. 2:13)."

Divine Revelation, 4

"Sacred Scripture is of the greatest importance in the celebration of the liturgy. For it is from it that lessons are read and explained in the homily, and psalms are sung. It is from the Scriptures that the prayers, collects and hymns draw their inspiration and their force, and that actions and signs derive their meaning." *Sacred Liturgy, 24*

Prayer

Heavenly Father, You inspired the writers of the biblical books to write what You wanted written, and You preserved them from error. You nourish our souls through Christ present in the Eucharist, and through Your word as it is presented to us in the Bible. But You have also given us Tradition as a complement to the Bible and as an equally important source of Your truth. Give us Your Holy Spirit that He may help us to draw from the Bible and Tradition a better knowledge of Christ and His teachings.

Almighty God, You Who first ordered light to shine in darkness, flood our hearts with the glorious Gospel of Christ, Your matchless image, and transform us more and more into His very likeness. Only Your Son, our Savior, is the true Teacher of Righteousness; help us to grasp the inner meaning of His Gospel and the happiness that it promises. May we hunger for Your word more than for bodily food. Fill our hearts with His light. May we always acknowledge Christ as our Savior and be more faithful to His Gospel. We ask this in His most holy Name. Amen.

Chapter Sixty-Eight

Gifts of God to the Catholic Church - III

Sacraments and Ministries

Q. 142. What are some other gifts of the Catholic Church besides the truths of the Faith?

Other gifts of the Catholic Church besides the truths of the Faith are the sacraments (cf. Q. 140).

Christ taught the Apostles that His grace was to be given to men through them. Through them He would, for example, forgive sins and give His Body and Blood to the world.

In the Person of Jesus Christ, God first laid the foundation of His Church. This was a task spread over three years, from Jesus' first public miracle at Cana until His ascent into Heaven. During this time Jesus chose His twelve Apostles, whom He had destined to be the first Bishops of His Church. He instructed them and trained them for their duties, and prepared them for the task of establishing the Kingdom of God. During that time, Jesus gave His Church the seven sacraments — the seven channels through which the graces He would gain for mankind upon the Cross would flow into men's souls.

Q. 143. Are there other gifts of the Church besides the truths of the Faith and the sacraments?

Yes, the other gifts of the Church besides the truths of the Faith and the sacraments are the ministries inherited from the Apostles (cf. Q. 140).

St. Peter was Christ's chief ambassador on earth. The whole Church was entrusted to his care. The Apostles shared their responsibility with others, called Bishops. Today the Church continues, through the Pope and its Bishops, and aid-

See Papally Promulgated
Catechism of the Catholic Church

Q. 142. See paragraphs: 1278, 1284, 1318-1320, 1411-1412, 1481, 1530-1531, 1597-1600, 1660-1662
Q. 143. See paragraphs: 880-896

ed by priests and deacons who are in union with the Holy Father in Rome, to be a community in Christ. They serve people by giving Christ's saving truth and His divine life to them through grace and the sacraments.

The Catholic Church inherited these ministries from the Apostles. With the powers which were given to them by Christ, the Apostles were His witnesses in the world. He said to them, before ascending into Heaven, "But you will receive power of the Holy Spirit coming upon you, and you will be witnesses unto Me in Jerusalem, and in all Judea, and Samaria, and even to the uttermost parts of the earth" (Acts 1:8).

Q. 144. What does the Catholic Church do for mankind through these gifts?

Through these gifts of God, the Catholic Church is able to act and grow as a community in Christ, by serving mankind and giving it His saving word and activity.

Through God's truth, sacraments, and the apostolic ministry, the Church is able to grow. This community in Christ — the Church — continues Christ's saving work in the world by serving mankind.

Sacred Scripture

"These things I write to you, hoping that I will come to you shortly. But if I tarry long, that you may know how you ought to behave in the house of God, which is the Church of the living God, the pillar and ground of the truth." *1 Timothy 3:14-15*

Vatican Council II

"In the human nature united to himself, the son of God, by overcoming death through his own death and resurrection, redeemed man and changed him into a new creation (cf. Gal. 6:15; 2 Cor. 5:17). For by communicating his Spirit, Christ mystically constitutes as his body those brothers of his who are called together from every nation.

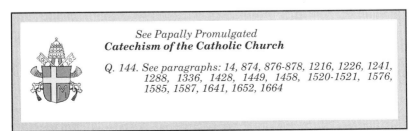

See Papally Promulgated
Catechism of the Catholic Church

Q. 144. See paragraphs: 14, 874, 876-878, 1216, 1226, 1241, 1288, 1336, 1428, 1449, 1458, 1520-1521, 1576, 1585, 1587, 1641, 1652, 1664

"In that body the life of Christ is communicated to those who believe and who, through the sacraments, are united in a hidden and real way to Christ in his passion and glorification." *The Church, 7*

Prayer

Lord, our faithful God, You permitted the great Temple in Jerusalem, the symbol of the Old Covenant, to be destroyed and Your people to be persecuted by unbelievers. Do not forget the New Covenant, sealed with the blood of Your Son. Make the Church Your spiritual house, and make us living stones built upon Christ so that a full and lasting temple may be built at last.

Heavenly Father, You anointed Your servant Jesus with holy oil and raised Him higher than all kings on earth. In this anointing You fulfilled the promise made to David's descendants and established a lasting covenant through Your first-born Son. Remember Your covenant, so that we, who are signed with the blood of Your Son, may sing Your mercies forever.

Purify and renew Your Church through Your gifts of truth and the sacraments, that it may give an ever greater witness to You. Your word of life gives us a new birth; may we receive it with open hearts, live it with joy, and express it in love. May we grow in the life of Christ through the sacraments of the Church, especially the Holy Eucharist. Keep us faithful to Your Son, Who alone has the words of eternal life and is Himself the Bread of Life, that He may lead us as the loyal sheep of His flock to the eternal joys of Your Kingdom. We ask this through Jesus our Savior. Amen.

Chapter Sixty-Nine

The Catholic Church - I
The Living Continuation of Christ on Earth

Q. 145. Why does the Catholic Church belong entirely to Christ?

The Catholic Church belongs entirely to Christ, because He is the Head of the Church, its Founder, its Spouse, and its Savior. He continues to do His saving work in and through the Church.

In the New Testament we see Christ's preparation for the Church, His promises concerning it, and the beginning of their rich fulfillment.

Christ is the Light of the world. The Church receives its being and mission from Him. The Church is not merely a society of men; it has a certain sacred dimension because of the inseparable union which Christ established between it and Himself.

Sacred Scripture

"You are Peter and on this rock I will build My Church."

Matthew 16:18

"Because the husband is the head of the wife, as Christ is the Head of the Church. He is the Savior of His body."

Ephesians 5:23

Q. 146. How does the Catholic see the Church?

The Catholic always sees the Church in its relationship to Christ. It is not the Church as such that is the primary object of Catholic faith. The Catholic believes in Christ, and in His Father, and in the Holy Spirit. In the Creed, the Catholic pro-

See Papally Promulgated
Catechism of the Catholic Church

Q. 145. See paragraphs: 763, 768, 786, 792, 796, 926, 973
Q. 146. See paragraphs: 748-749, 763-766

fesses his belief in "the Holy Catholic Church" precisely because he sees the Church as a presence of Christ and of His Spirit.

The Catholic believes what the Church teaches precisely because he recognizes Christ's authority in the Church.

The Catholic recognizes a duty to further the work of the Church precisely because he sees the mission of the Church as a continuation of Christ's work in the world.

Q. 147. Why is the Catholic Church a living continuation of Christ on earth?

The Church is a living continuation of Christ on earth because Christ spiritually and mystically lives and acts through the Church. It is a living organism, not just an organization.

Christ organized the Church to carry on His work in the world, and to bring His ministry and truth to all men and all ages.

It is Christ Who accomplishes all that is done in the Church for man's salvation. The institution which is the Church survives because it comes from Christ, and because He promises to be with it to the end of time (cf. Matthew 18:20).

The Church is a living continuation on earth of its divine Founder. Jesus is indeed the Son of God, but He is truly a man, too: the Son of Mary. Similarly, in the Church, the Mystical Body of Christ, is found the presence of Christ, its Head, and His Holy Spirit, the bearer of heavenly gifts. Yet, the Church is also very human. Its sublime mission is carried out by its baptized members. Among them are the ordained priests who perform sacred ceremonies, called the sacraments, which are entrusted to them by Christ, with ordinary realities of human life such as bread, water, wine, and oil.

The Church acts for Christ. When a priest gives us a sacrament, it is Christ Who gives us the sacrament through the priest. When the Church speaks His word to us, it is He Who

See Papally Promulgated
Catechism of the Catholic Church

Q. 147. See paragraphs: 785, 789, 792, 795, 864-865

speaks to us and calls us to faith. The teaching and ruling authority of the Church is the shepherding of Christ.

Vatican Council II

"The head of this body is Christ. He is the image of the invisible God and in him all things came into being. He is before all creatures and in him all things hold together. He is the head of the body which is the Church. He is the beginning, the firstborn from the dead, that in all things he might hold the primacy (cf. Col. 1:15-18). By the greatness of his power he rules heaven and earth, and with his all-surpassing perfection and activity he fills the whole body with the riches of his glory (cf. Eph. 1:18-23). All the members must be formed in his likeness, until Christ be formed in them (cf. Gal. 4:19)." *The Church, 7*

> **Prayer:** *Lord Jesus, eternal Shepherd, You tend Your Church in many ways and rule us with love. Help Your chosen servants, the Bishops of Your Church, as pastors for Christ, to watch over Your flock. Help them to be faithful teachers, wise administrators, and holy priests. We ask this in Your most holy Name. Amen.*

Prayer

Lord Jesus Christ, on Holy Thursday we celebrate the memory of the first Eucharist, at which time You shared with Your Apostles, and now share with Your Bishops and priests, Your offices of priestly service in Your Church. Help Bishops and priests to renew their dedication to You as priests of Your new covenant.

May their word and example inspire and guide the Church; and may they, and all those entrusted to their care, come to the joy of everlasting life. Enrich them with the gifts and virtues of true apostles for the good of Your people. You have chosen them to be shepherds of Your flock in the tradition of the Apostles. By governing with fidelity those entrusted to their care, may they guide Your Church as a sign of salvation for the world.

Give the fullness of Your blessing to the College of Bishops, and keep all those entrusted to their care faithful to the teachings of the Apostles. We ask this though the power of Your most Precious Blood. Amen.

Chapter Seventy

The Catholic Church - II
The Sacrament of Christ

Q. 148. Why is the Catholic Church called the sacrament of Christ?

The Church is called the sacrament of Christ because it is a visible reality which Christ has formed in this world as a sacred sign of His presence. It is the sign and also the means He uses to give us the unity and holiness He actually confers through it. It is a sacrament of His presence because He is really present in it.

As a family called to share in the life of the Trinity, the Church has an eternal destiny. But in its time of pilgrimage on earth, it has also visible, sacramental dimensions: it exists also as a sign. Because the Church is a sign; it leads us to what it signifies, that is, to Christ, our God. When we finally come to God in eternity the Church, as a sign, will have no further reason to exist. It will have accomplished what God put it on earth to do.

The sacrament , which is the visible Church, is now, in time, a precious indispensable gift of Christ. It is the work of Christ, and will last, as He promises, until the end of the world, when it will reach its fulfillment in glorious union in Christ. Its task on earth will not be finished until Christ brings His redemptive work to completion and God has become, as St. Paul put it, "all in all" (Colossians 3:11).

Vatican Council II

"The Church, in Christ, is in the nature of sacrament — a sign and instrument, that is, of communion with God and of unity among all men..." *The Church, 1*

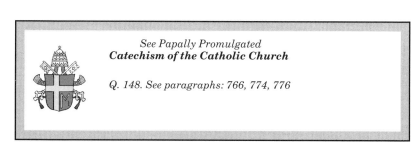

See Papally Promulgated
Catechism of the Catholic Church

Q. 148. See paragraphs: 766, 774, 776

Q. 149. What do we mean when we speak of the Church in Heaven?

When we speak of the Church in Heaven, we do not mean the Church in the condition in which it is a sign, with ministers and sacraments; these will cease; as signs and instruments, they will be absorbed into the heavenly realities which they now serve. When we speak of the Church in Heaven, we mean the union of the saints with Christ and the life they have in Him, with the Father and the Holy Spirit.

Sacred Scripture

"We shall be like Him, because we shall see Him as He is."
1 John 3:2

"We now see through a glass in a dark manner, but then face to face. Now I know in part, but then I shall know, even as I am known." *1 Corinthians 13:12*

"[God] will render to every man according to his works. To them indeed who, according to patience in good work, seek glory and honor and incorruption, eternal life." *Romans 2:6-7*

Vatican Council II

"Already the final age of the world is with us (cf. 1 Cor. 10:11) and the renewal of the world is irrevocably under way; it is even now anticipated in a certain real way, for the Church on earth is endowed already with a sanctity that is real though imperfect. However, until there be realized new heavens and a new earth in which justice dwells (cf. 2 Pet. 3:13) the pilgrim Church, in its sacraments and institutions, which belong to this present age, carries the mark of this world which will pass, and she herself takes her place among the creatures which groan and travail yet and await the revelation of the sons of God (cf. Rom. 8:19-22)." *The Church, 48*

"We must all appear 'before the judgment seat of Christ, so that each one may receive good or evil, according to what he has done in the body' (2 Cor. 5 :10)." *The Church, 48*

See Papally Promulgated
Catechism of the Catholic Church

Q. 149. See paragraphs: 1023-1029

Prayer: *Surround Your people, Lord Jesus, within the safety of Your Church, which You preserve on its rock foundation. Let us neither reach out our hands to evil deeds, nor be destroyed by the insidious snares of the enemy; instead, bring us to share the love of the saints in light. We ask this in Your most holy Name. Amen.*

Prayer

Lord God, Your only Son wept over ancient Jerusalem, which was soon to be destroyed for its lack of faith. He established the new Jerusalem firmly upon the rock and made it the Mother of the faithful. Make us rejoice in Your Church and grant that all people may be reborn in the freedom of Your Spirit. Grant us always to seek the wisdom of the Cross and the blessing of those who suffer for the sake of justice. May we always be filled with Your happiness and remain safe under the guidance and care of the shepherds to whom You have entrusted Your flock.

May the faithful respect and love the Pope, and the Bishops in union with him, and also the priests and deacons who assist them in the care of Your Church. Help all pastors to edify, both by word and example, those over whom they have charge, that they may reach everlasting life together with the flocks entrusted to them. Be their light, their strength, and their consolation.

Lord our God, King of the universe, Creator of light and darkness, origin and preserver of all that exists, remember Your Church, protect it from all evil, perfect it in Your love, gather it from the four winds, and bring it into Your Kingdom, for Yours is the power and the glory forever and ever. Amen.

Chapter Seventy-One

Members of the Catholic Church - I
The Hierarchy

Q. 150. Does the Catholic Church have leaders?

In God's plan, the Catholic Church is a society with leaders, in a hierarchy. It is a people guided by its Bishops, who are in union with the Pope, the Bishop of Rome.

Through the ordination of Bishops (the successors of the Apostles) and priests, the powers of Jesus Christ have been handed down in the Catholic Church for over nineteen hundred years. Bishops and priests, together with deacons, are those in Christ's Mystical Body who have the authority to teach for Christ, to shepherd His flock, and to dispense His grace through the sacraments. Christ lives and works in a special way through the Bishops, priests, and deacons in His Church.

Sacred Scripture

"And if he will not hear them; tell the Church. And if he will not hear the Church, let him be as the heathen and publican." *Matthew 18:17*

"Jesus Christ has loved us and washed us from our sins in His own blood, and has made us a kingdom and priests to God and His Father. To Him, then, be glory and power forever and ever. Amen." *Revelation 1:5-6*

Vatican Council II

"This sacred synod, following in the steps of the First Vatican Council, teaches and declares with it that Jesus Christ, the eternal pastor, set up the holy Church by entrusting the apostles with their mission as he himself had been sent by the father (cf. Jn. 20:21). He willed that their successors, the bish-

See Papally Promulgated
Catechism of the Catholic Church

Q. 150. See paragraphs: 876-887

ops namely, should be the shepherds in his Church until the end of the world. In order that the episcopate itself, however, might be one and undivided he put Peter at the head of the other apostles, and in him he set up a lasting and visible source and foundation of the unity both of faith and of communion." *The Church, 18*

"This Church, constituted and organized as a society in the present world, subsists in the Catholic Church, which is governed by the successor of Peter and by the bishops in communion with him. Nevertheless, many elements of sanctification and of truth are found outside its visible confines. Since these are gifts belonging to the Church of Christ, they are forces impelling towards Catholic unity." *The Church, 8*

> **Prayer:** *God, Eternal Shepherd, You tend Your Church in many ways and rule us with love. Help Your chosen servants, the Bishops of Your Church as pastors for Christ, to watch over Your flock. Help them to be faithful teachers, wise administrators, and holy priests. We ask this through Jesus Christ, our Lord, to Whom with You and the Holy Spirit be all honor and glory. Amen.*

Q. 151. Who is the Pope?

The Pope, the Bishop of Rome, is the Vicar of Christ. He is successor to the office of Peter in his care and guidance of the whole flock of Christ. As such, he has all the rights, powers, and duties pertaining to Peter's office.

The Pope is the head of the College of Bishops. Jesus solemnly told Peter he was to be supreme shepherd, the head of the Church. "And I say to you, that you are Peter; and upon this rock I will build my church, and the gates of hell shall not prevail against it" (Matthew 16:18).

See Papally Promulgated
Catechism of the Catholic Church

Q. 151. See paragraphs: 880-883

Christ gave Peter, the supreme shepherd of souls, the holy task of giving the entire People of God His teaching and His grace. After His Resurrection Jesus said to Simon Peter, 'Simon, son of John, do you love Me more than these?' He said to Him, 'Yes, Lord, You know that I love You.' He said to him, 'Feed My lambs.' He said to him again, 'Simon, son of John, do you love Me?' He said to Him, 'Lord, You know that I love You.' He said to him, 'Feed My lambs' (John 21:15-16).

The Pope, as the successor of St. Peter, holds the highest Christian teaching authority in the world; he is also the supreme ruler or shepherd of the Catholic Church.

Vatican Council II

"In this Church of Christ the Roman Pontiff, as the successor of Peter, to whom Christ entrusted the care of his sheep and his lambs, has been granted by God supreme, full, immediate and universal power in the care of souls. As pastor of all the faithful his mission is to promote the common good of the universal Church and the particular good of all the churches. He is therefore endowed with the primacy of ordinary power over all the churches." *Bishops, 2*

"In exercising his supreme, full and immediate authority over the universal Church the Roman Pontiff employs the various departments of the Roman Curia, which act in his name and by his authority for the good of the churches and in the service of the sacred pastors." *Bishops, 9*

Q. 152. Who are the Bishops of the Church?

The Pope is the successor of St. Peter; the Catholic Bishops are the successors of the Apostles. Collectively, the Bishops constitute what is known as the Episcopal College, with the Pope as its head.

Christ made the Apostles as a stable group, or college. They were jointly responsible for spreading the Gospel of Christ in the whole world. To the whole college, Christ ad-

See Papally Promulgated
Catechism of the Catholic Church

Q. 152. See paragraphs: 880-892, 1576

dressed His great missionary command, "Go therefore, teach all nations; baptizing them in the Name of the Father, and of the Son, and of the Holy Spirit. Teach them to observe all things whatever I have commanded you; and behold I am with you all days, even to the consummation of the world" (Matthew 28:19-20).

Jesus said to Peter, "But I have prayed for you that your faith may not fail, and you being once converted, strengthen your brethren" (Luke 22:32).

When the first council of the Church was held in Jerusalem in the first century, the Apostles, as a college, decided the question whether Jewish customs should be imposed on non-Jewish converts: "For it has seemed good to the Holy Spirit and to us, to lay no further burden upon you than these necessary things: That you abstain from things sacrificed to idols, and from blood, and from things strangled, and from fornication. Keeping yourselves from such things, you will do well" (Acts 15:28-29).

Vatican Council II

"By preaching everywhere the Gospel (cf. Mk. 16:20), welcomed and received under the influence of the Holy Spirit by those who hear it, the apostles gather together the universal Church, which the Lord founded upon the apostles and built upon blessed Peter their leader, the chief cornerstone being Christ Jesus Himself (cf. Apoc. 21:14; Mt. 16:18; Eph. 2:20)."

The Church, 19

"The bishop, invested with the fullness of the sacrament of Orders, 'is the steward of the grace of the supreme priesthood,' above all in the Eucharist, which he himself offers, or ensures that it is offered, from which the Church ever derives its life and on which it thrives." *The Church, 26*

"Moreover, just as the office which the Lord confided to Peter alone, as first of the apostles, destined to be transmitted to his successors, is a permanent one, so also endures the office, which the apostles received, of shepherding the Church, a charge destined to be exercised without interruption by the sacred order of bishops. The sacred synod consequently teaches that the bishops have by divine institution taken the place of the apostles as pastors of the Church, in such wise that whoever listens to them is listening to Christ and whoever despises them despises Christ and him who sent Christ (cf. Lk. 10:16)." *The Church, 21*

311

"In the person of the bishops, then, to whom the priests render assistance, the Lord Jesus Christ, supreme high priest, is present in the midst of the faithful." *The Church, 21*

Prayer

Jesus, our High Priest, on Holy Thursday we celebrate the memory of the first Eucharist, at which time You shared with Your Apostles, and now share with Your Bishops and priests, Your offices of priestly service in Your Church. Help Bishops and priests to renew their dedication to You as priests of Your New Covenant.

May their word and example inspire and guide the Church; and may they, and all those entrusted to their care, come to the joy of everlasting life. Enrich them with the gifts and virtues of true apostles for the good of Your people. You have chosen them to be shepherds of Your flock in the tradition of the Apostles. By governing with fidelity those entrusted to their care, may they guide Your Church as a sign of salvation for the world.

Give the fullness of Your blessing to the College of Bishops, and keep all those entrusted to their care faithful to the teachings of the Apostles. We ask this though the power of Your most Precious Blood. Amen.

Chapter Seventy-Two

Members of the Catholic Church - II
The Role of the Hierarchy

Q. 153. What is the role of the Pope and Bishops of the Catholic Church?

The role of the Pope and the Bishops is to teach, to make holy, and to govern the People of God. This authority and power was given them by Jesus, beginning with that received by St. Peter and the other Apostles.

After His Resurrection Jesus demanded of Peter a profession of love. "When a third time Jesus asked Peter, 'Simon, son of John, do you love Me?' Peter was grieved, because He had said to him the third time, 'Do you love Me' and he said to Him 'Lord, You know all things, You know that I love You.' He said to him 'Feed My sheep' " (John 21:17).

The Roman Pontiff, the head of the College of Bishops, is guaranteed doctrinal infallibility in virtue of his office, when, as the supreme shepherd and teacher of all the faithful, he proclaims by a definitive act some doctrine of faith and morals.

"Simon, Simon! Satan, you must know, has got his wish to sift you all like wheat; but I have prayed for you, Simon, that your faith may not fail, and once you have recovered, you in your turn must strengthen your brothers" (Luke 22:31-32).

Jesus willed that the Bishops, the successors of the Apostles, should be shepherds in His Church. He placed Peter over the other Apostles, and instituted him as a permanent source and foundation of unity, of faith, and of fellowship.

"So I now say to you: You are Peter and on this rock I will build My Church. And the gates of the underworld can never hold out against it. I will give you the keys of the Kingdom of

See Papally Promulgated
Catechism of the Catholic Church

Q. 153. See paragraphs: 888-896

Heaven: whatever you bind on earth shall be considered bound in Heaven: whatever you loose on earth shall be considered loosed in Heaven." *Matthew 16:18-19*

"At length He appeared to the Eleven as they were at table. And He upbraided them with their incredulity and hardness of heart, because they did not believe them who had seen Him after He was risen again. And He said to them, 'Go into the whole world and preach the Gospel to every creature.' "

Mark 16:14-15

"And behold, I am with you all days, even to the consummation of the world." *Matthew 28:20*

Infallibility is a gift of the Holy Spirit by which the Church's Faith is protected from error. The Holy Spirit remains in the Catholic Church to enable it to continue the work of Christ in the world. He guides the Bishops, priests, and deacons of the Church in their holy work of teaching Christ's doctrine, shepherding souls, and giving grace to the people through the sacraments.

When the Church teaches solemnly in the name of God, the teaching is infallible; that is, it cannot be mistaken in matters of faith and morals. When the Pope teaches solemnly in his official capacity as head of the Church, or when Bishops assembled with the Pope in council solemnly pronounce upon a matter of faith or morals, that doctrine is the infallible teaching of the Church. It must receive the assent of faith.

Moreover, when the Pope and the body of Bishops dispersed throughout the world teach that a certain doctrine has been revealed by God, this teaching is infallible, even though it has not been solemnly defined, for it is still Christ teaching through His universal Church. When the Pope speaks to the whole Church on a matter of faith or morals, but not "*ex cathedra*," his teaching, nevertheless, demands respect, obedience, and assent.

Vatican Council II

"Although the bishops, taken individually, do not enjoy the privilege of infallibility, they do, however, proclaim infallibly the doctrine of Christ on the following conditions: namely, when, even though dispersed throughout the world but preserving for all that amongst themselves and with Peter's successor the bond of communion, in their authoritative teaching concerning matters of faith and morals, they are in agreement that a particular teaching is to be held definitively and

314

absolutely. This is still more clearly the case when, assembled in an ecumenical council, they are, for the universal Church, teachers of and judges in matters of faith and morals, whose decisions must be adhered to with the loyal and obedient assent of faith." *The Church, 25*

"Among the more important duties of Bishops that of preaching the Gospel has pride of place. For the Bishops are heralds of the faith, who draw new disciples to Christ; they are authentic teachers, that is, teachers endowed with the authority of Christ, who preach the faith to the people assigned to them, the faith which is destined to inform their thinking and direct their conduct; and under the light of the Holy Spirit they make that faith shine forth, drawing from the storehouse of revelation new things and old (cf. Mt. 13:52); they make it bear fruit and with watchfulness they ward off whatever errors threaten their flock (cf. 2 Tim. 4:14)." *The Church, 25*

"This infallibility, however, with which the divine redeemer wished to endow His Church in defining doctrine pertaining to faith and morals, is co-extensive with the deposit of revelation, which must be religiously guarded and loyally and courageously expounded. The Roman Pontiff, head of the College of Bishops, enjoys this infallibility in virtue of his office, when, as supreme pastor and teacher of all the faithful — who confirms his brethren in the faith — he proclaims in an absolute decision a doctrine pertaining to faith or morals."
The Church, 25

> **Prayer:** *Heavenly Father, look with love on our Pope, Your appointed successor to St. Peter, on whom You built Your Church. Assist him in his position as the visible center and foundation of our unity in faith and love. May his word and example inspire and guide the Church, and may he, and all those who are entrusted to his care, come to the joy of everlasting life. We ask this in the Name of Jesus, the Lord. Amen.*

Q. 154. Who directs the work in the cause of Christ in the Catholic Church?

See Papally Promulgated
Catechism of the Catholic Church

Q. 154. See paragraphs: 879

The Pope and the Bishops direct the work in the cause of Christ in the Catholic Church, in every rite, diocese, parish, and mission.

The Pope is a visible sign of Jesus and a symbol of unity for the Church. He enjoys the primacy of jurisdiction over the Church and is the head of the College of Bishops. He is the chief teacher, and ruler over the Church.

The Bishops are visible signs of Jesus in each locality and the symbols of unity for the Church in their respective dioceses. Each diocesan Bishop, or Ordinary, is the principal teacher, priest, and governor of the Church in that locality. All the Bishops, together with the Pope, are the official witnesses to the Faith for the whole Church and are responsible for its life throughout the world.

Vatican Council II

"This sacred synod, following in the steps of the First Vatican Council, teaches and declares with it that Jesus Christ, the eternal pastor, set up the holy Church by entrusting the apostles with their mission as he himself had been sent by the Father (cf. Jn. 20:21). He willed that their successors, the bishops namely, should be the shepherds in his Church until the end of the world. In order that the episcopate itself, however, might be one and undivided he put Peter at the head of the other apostles, and in him he set up a lasting and visible source and foundation of the unity both of faith and of communion." *The Church, 18*

"Just as, in accordance with the Lord's decree, St. Peter and the rest of the apostles constitute a unique apostolic college, so in like fashion the Roman Pontiff, Peter's successor, and the bishops, the successors of the apostles, are related with and united to one another." *The Church, 22*

"The order of bishops is the successor to the college of the apostles in their role as teachers and pastors, and in it the apostolic college is perpetuated. Together with their head, the Supreme Pontiff, and never apart from him, they have supreme and full authority over the universal Church; but this power cannot be exercised without the agreement of the Roman Pontiff." *The Church, 22*

"The supreme authority over the whole Church, which this college possesses, is exercised in a solemn way in an ecumenical council." *The Church, 22*

Q. 155. What do the faithful owe the Pope and Bishops?

The faithful, the community of faith, owe the Pope and the Bishops respect, obedience, and love.

We serve God and His Church by obeying the fourth commandment of God in honoring, loving, respecting, and obeying the Pope as successor of St. Peter, our Bishop as our shepherd, and our priests as the men who are ordained to lovingly serve the faithful.

To be a Catholic means, fundamentally, to believe that Jesus Christ, the Son of God, established the Church to continue and to carry on His work of redemption. But the average Catholic cannot probe the depths of philosophical and theological arguments. He finds his security and peace in the teaching authority of the Church, to which Christ promised immunity from error, through the help of the Holy Spirit, in teaching men what they must believe and what they must do to attain salvation.

Vatican Council II

"Bishops who teach in communion with the Roman Pontiff are to be revered by all as witnesses of divine and Catholic truth; the faithful, for their part, are obliged to submit to their bishops' decision, made in the name of Christ, in matters of faith and morals, and to adhere to it with a ready and respectful allegiance of mind. This loyal submission of the will and intellect must be given, in a special way, to the authentic teaching authority of the Roman Pontiff, even when he does not speak *ex cathedra* in such wise, indeed, that his supreme teaching authority be acknowledged with respect, and that one sincerely adheres to decisions made by him, conformably with his manifest mind and intention." *The Church, 25*

See Papally Promulgated
Catechism of the Catholic Church

Q. 155. See paragraphs: 1899-1900

Prayer

Most Holy Trinity, by the power of the Eucharist, make Your Church firm in unity and love, and grant strength and salvation to Your servant, our Holy Father, the Pope, the Supreme Shepherd, together with the flock You have entrusted to his care. Give to Your shepherd a spirit of courage, right judgment, knowledge, and love. By governing with fidelity those entrusted to his care, may he, as successor to the Apostle Peter and the Vicar of Christ, guide us in building up Your Church, which is a sacrament of unity, love, and peace for all the world.

God, our Father, You guide all things by Your Word; You govern all Christian people. In Your love, protect the Pope You have chosen for us. Under his leadership, may we deepen our faith and become better Christians through Jesus our Lord. Amen.

Chapter Seventy-Three

Members of the Catholic Church - III

The Laity

Q. 156. Why does each member of the Church deserve respect?

Everyone in the Church deserves our deepest respect since, through Baptism, we are united to Christ in His Mystical Body and become His brothers and sisters.

Dedication to Christ means obedience to the Commandments, fulfillment of the duties of our state of life, offering up our sufferings in union with Christ, perseverance in doing all for the love of God, and efforts made to spread the reign of Christ. Any person with such dedication deserves respect, but the highest respect is derived from the fact that, through Baptism, we are children of God and members of Christ's Mystical Body.

Sacred Scripture

"And God created man in His own image; to the image of God He created him. Male and female He created them."
Genesis 1:27

"The Spirit Himself bears witness with our spirit, that we are the children of God. And if children, then heirs, heirs of God and joint-heirs with Christ." *Romans 8:16-17*

Vatican Council II

"Mutual esteem for all forms of the Church's apostolate, and good coordination, preserving nevertheless the character special to each, are in fact absolutely necessary for promoting that spirit of unity which will cause fraternal charity to shine out in the Church's whole apostolate, common aims to be reached and ruinous rivalries avoided." *Lay People, 23*

See Papally Promulgated
Catechism of the Catholic Church

Q. 156. See paragraphs: 782-795, 1701-1702

"This Church of Christ is really present in all legitimately organized local groups of the faithful, which, in so far as they are united to their pastors, are also quite appropriately called Churches in the New Testament." *The Church, 26*

Q. 157. Why is the Catholic Church a community?

The Catholic Church is a community because it allows its members to share with one another the life of Christ; it is a people assembled by God.

The Church is the world-wide community of those whom God has called to give witness to His Son Jesus and to the new life He has brought to man. This assembly is called the "People of God" and the "Body of Christ."

The description of the Church as the People of God and as the Body of Christ helps each of us to see himself as one with a group to whose destiny we are tied, and whose welfare we share. This is the reality of Baptism: we are joined to Christ, to the whole Christ, that is, joined to Christ and His people, the Church.

If we are thus joined in Christ, He is truly one with us in a very real and intimate sense. The Church is seen as the successor to ancient Israel, and Jesus, the Messiah and Head of the new People of God, is seen as rooted in humanity by His physical birth, life, death, and Resurrection. The infant Jesus is the Son of Mary, as well as Son of God. He is of the people of Israel, of the tribe of Judah, of the house of David.

It is through His humanity that each of us is united to Christ as our Savior. The divinity of Christ must not be slighted; still, that does not cancel out His true humanity. Each time we use the phrase the "People of God," we see Christ, greater than Moses, who shares a truly human nature with Moses and, like him, leads the People of God from slavery to freedom, from death to life. Christ is our Passover. We look to the daughter of Zion, Mary, whose Son is Jesus; think-

See Papally Promulgated
Catechism of the Catholic Church

Q. 157. See paragraphs: 782, 787

ing of Mary drills home the fact that He is one of us, truly Emmanuel, our God with us.

God has called this community to give witness to His Son Jesus, and to live the new life He has brought to men. As members of this community, we are joined to Christ through Baptism; we share in His divine life through grace, which reaches us especially in the sacraments.

Vatican Council II

"Fully incorporated into the Church are those who, possessing the Spirit of Christ, accept all the means of salvation given to the Church together with her entire organization, and who — by the bonds constituted by the profession of faith, the sacraments, ecclesiastical government, and communion — are joined in the visible structure of the Church of Christ, who rules her through the Supreme Pontiff and the bishops." *The Church, 14*

"The Church knows that she is joined in many ways to the baptized who are honored by the name of Christian, but who do not however profess the Catholic faith in its entirety or have not preserved unity or communion under the successor of Peter. For there are many who hold sacred scripture in honor as a rule of faith and of life, who have a sincere religious zeal, who lovingly believe in God the Father Almighty and in Christ, the Son of God and the Saviour, who are sealed by baptism which unites them to Christ, and who indeed recognize and receive other sacraments in their own Churches or ecclesiastical communities. Many of them possess the episcopate, celebrate the holy Eucharist and cultivate devotion of the Virgin Mother of God. There is furthermore a sharing in prayer and spiritual benefits; these Christians are indeed in some real way joined to us in the Holy Spirit. ..." *The Church, 15*

Prayer: *Lord God, eternal Shepherd, You have so tended the vineyard You planted that it now extends its branches to the farthest lands. Look down on Your Church and come to us. Help us to remain in Your Son like branches that are planted firmly on the vine of Your love, that we may testify before the whole world to Your great power working everywhere. We ask this through and in the Sacred Heart of Jesus. Amen.*

Prayer

Most Holy Trinity — Father, Son, and Holy Spirit — we beg of You, have mercy on Your Holy Catholic Church. Protect and bless the Pope, all Bishops, priests, and deacons. Fill them with wisdom, strength, and virtue, that they may live lives worthy of their sublime vocation and guide their flocks to eternal salvation. Visit all of the faithful with Your sanctifying grace, so that by leading pure and holy lives, they may persevere in Your love.

Stretch forth Your mighty arm and protect Your holy Church against all attacks of the enemy; destroy their power so that, in peace and security, we may work out our salvation and spread Your holy Faith. Exalt and glorify Your Church with the splendor of holiness so that, as the Bride of Christ, it may give praise to You forever and ever. Amen

Chapter Seventy-Four

Members of the Catholic Church - IV

Roles of the Members

Q. 158. Are all persons equal in the Church?

All the members of the Church are united as the one People of God whose Head is Christ, and are equal, but they each have different responsibilities.

In describing the Church as the "People of God," emphasis is placed on the fact that the Church is composed of people. It includes the Pope, Bishops, priests, deacons, and all the laity. That is why the Second Vatican Council said that the Church is "a people brought into unity from the unity of the Father, the Son and the Holy Spirit" (cf. St. John Chrysostom, *De Oratio Domino*, 23). In this assembly of people, there is a basic equality of all persons.

Just as God made Moses the leader of His people in the Old Testament, so Christ gave His Apostles and their successors the right to teach and to command in His Name. This authority is given to them for the service and welfare of the People of God.

The Church is also a "priestly people," but the ministerial priesthood is essentially different from "the priesthood of the laity." All, however, are equal and united as the one People of God.

By Baptism, the laity are made one body with Christ and members of the People of God. Sharing, in their own way, in the priestly, prophetic, and kingly functions of Christ, they have a part of their own in carrying out the mission of the whole Christian people in the Church and in the world. St. Peter says, "But you are a chosen generation, a kingly priest-

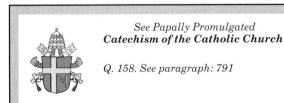

See Papally Promulgated
Catechism of the Catholic Church

Q. 158. See paragraph: 791

hood, a holy nation, a purchased people that you may declare His virtues, to sing the praises of God Who called you out of the darkness into His wonderful light" (1 Peter 2:9).

The baptized, therefore, by regeneration and the anointing of the Holy Spirit, are consecrated to be a spiritual house and a holy priesthood. Through all the works of Christian men, they may offer spiritual sacrifices to and proclaim the perfection of Him Who has called them out of darkness into His marvelous light. Thus, all the disciples of Christ, persevering in prayer and praising God, should present themselves as sacrifices, living, holy, and pleasing to God. They should everywhere on earth bear witness to Christ and give an answer to everyone who asks a reason for the hope of an eternal life which is theirs.

What distinguishes the laity is their "secular character." Although those in Holy Orders can at times be engaged in secular activities and professions, they are, by reason of their vocation, especially ordained to the sacred ministry. Living in the world, the laity are called by God to work for the sanctification of the world like a leaven, from within, by carrying out their proper tasks according to the spirit of the Gospel. They are consecrated into a royal priesthood and a holy people, in order that they may offer spiritual sacrifices through everything they do, and that they may witness to Christ in the world.

Priests should minister to the needs of one another and of the laity. The laity, in turn, should cooperate enthusiastically with their priests. All clergy, Religious, and laity are brothers and sisters in the Mystical Body of Christ. Thus, while there is a basic equity among all members of the Church, there is diversity of functions and responsibilities.

Sacred Scripture

"Christ the Lord, High Priest taken from among men, made the new people 'a kingdom of priests to God, His Father.' " *Revelation 1:6*

Vatican Council II

"Though they differ essentially and not only in degree, the common priesthood of the faithful and the ministerial or hierarchical priesthood are none the less ordered one to another; each in its own proper way shares in the one priesthood of Christ." *The Church, 10*

Q. 159. Who has a vocation of holiness in the Church?

In the Church every individual has a call from God, a vocation to holiness.

When God created man, He bestowed upon him the gifts of supernatural life, of divine sonship. Man was alive with the very life of God; but then man sinned, and, by sin, he lost the gift of divine life. Left to himself, man was incapable of winning back the divine life. But God, in His infinite mercy, conceived the wonderful plan of the Redemption. He sent His only-begotten Son into the world to save mankind.

Christ became man. He took man's sinfulness upon Himself and stood in the place of all men before His Father. He accepted death and, on Calvary, paid the penalty for all men's sins. Since He was God's Son, the bonds of death could not hold Him. He rose again to life. With Him all mankind passed from death to life, returned to the Father's sonship, and again enjoyed the intimacy of His love.

With Christ we have already died to sin and risen to newness of life. He will pour into our souls that very life of divine sonship which filled Him at His own Resurrection. This He did through the sacraments of the Church He founded. In the Church, Christ wills to continue His own life in us for the glory of the Father. This Christ-life within us is the holiness to which God has called every individual in the Church.

See Papally Promulgated
Catechism of the Catholic Church

Q. 159. See paragraphs: 825, 1714, 1720, 2012-2016

This Christ-life means that we can open our minds to Him by faith so that we may have the same outlook that He had. We open our hearts to Him so that He may live in us His own life of love and self-surrender to the Father. We pattern our conduct on His, so that in all things we become like to Him, our Model. St. Paul said, "The life I live, now not I, but Christ lives in me. I live in the faith of the Son of God , Who loved me and delivered Himself for me" (Galatians 2:20).

Sacred Scripture

"One Body and one Spirit; as you are called in one hope of your calling. One Lord, one Faith, one Baptism. One God and Father of all, Who is above all, and through all, and in us all."

Ephesians 4:4-6

Vatican Council II

"It is therefore quite clear that all Christians in any state or walk of life are called to the fullness of Christian life and to the perfection of love." *The Church, 40*

Prayer

Lord, You are the fullness of life, holiness, and joy. Fill our days and nights with the love of Your wisdom, that we, the People of God, may bear fruit in the beauty of holiness, like a tree that is watered by running streams.

Almighty God, You are our Father and we are Your people. You keep constant guard over us. Protect us from hidden snares and make us holy, that we may praise and thank You, and so live in righteousness before You.

So that Your people might walk in innocence and holiness, You gave us our Lord Jesus Christ. Help Your children to love what is truly perfect, so that we may neither speak what is evil nor do what is wrong. Let us stand in Your sight and always celebrate Your love and justice, through our Lord and Savior Jesus Christ. Amen.

Chapter Seventy-Five

The Role of the Catholic Church

Q. 160. Why is the Catholic Church missionary?

The Catholic Church is missionary because every member of the Church shares the command from Christ to carry the Good News of Christ's teaching to all mankind by word and example.

The Church, as a community of believers and brotherly love, bears Christian witness by its preaching of the Gospel and its service to others.

God has called to be witnesses all those who believe He has revealed and given Himself to men in Jesus Christ. The Church gives this witness by proclaiming in the world, by word and deed, what God has done in Jesus Christ. The Church must live the life of Jesus in His Spirit and show His love by her life of brotherhood and service to others.

Jesus said to the Apostles, "All power is given to me in Heaven and in earth. Go therefore, teach all nations; baptize them in the name of the Father, and of the Son, and of the Holy Spirit. Teach them to observe all things I commanded you: and behold I am with you always even to the end of the world" (Matthew 28:18-20).

The Church is, in reality, its members. The Christian community must act as a servant, after the example of its Founder, Jesus Christ. It must serve the larger human community by sharing with it the riches of its Faith and by doing works which concern the welfare of the whole human family. Christian witness, or missionary activity, gives testimony to the loving presence of God in the world. The Church gives Christian witness by its very existence as a community of faith and brotherly love, by the preaching of the Gospel, and especially by service to others.

See Papally Promulgated
Catechism of the Catholic Church

Q. 160. See paragraphs: 863, 905, 2044, 2472

As a community of believers, the Church must live the life of Jesus in His Spirit, and show His love by her life of brotherhood and service to others. St. Luke says of the first Christians, "And they were persevering in the doctrine of the Apostles and in the communication of the breaking of bread and in prayers" (Acts 2:42).

Vatican Council II

"Missionary activity extends the saving faith of the Church, it expands and perfects its catholic unity, it is sustained by its apostolicity, it activates the collegiate sense of its hierarchy, and bears witness to its sanctity which it both extends and promotes." *Missionary Activity, 6*

"Having been divinely sent to the nations that she might be 'the universal sacrament of salvation,' the Church, in obedience to the command of her founder (Mt. 16:15) and because it is demanded by her own essential universality, strives to preach the Gospel to all men.

"All Christians by the example of their lives and the witness of the word, wherever they live, have an obligation to manifest the new man which they put on in baptism, and to reveal the power of the Holy Spirit by whom they were strengthened at confirmation, so that others, seeing their good works, might glorify the Father (cf. Matt. 5:16) and more perfectly perceive the true meaning of human life and the universal solidarity of mankind." *Missionary Activity, 1*

"In the present state of things which gives rise to a new situation for mankind, the Church, the salt of the earth and the light of the world (cf. Mt. 5:13-14), is even more urgently called upon to save and renew every creature, so that all things might be restored in Christ, and so that in him men might form one family and one people of God." *Missionary Activity, 1*

Q. 161. What is the role of the Church in the world?

The role of the Church is to make Christ known and loved,

See Papally Promulgated
Catechism of the Catholic Church

Q. 161. See paragraphs: 756, 771, 780, 782, 785

to spread the knowledge of salvation everywhere, and to pray and suffer for the salvation of souls.

The Church is not of this world, but it speaks and listens to the world. It tries to show the world how to be faithful to the Gospel and how to journey toward Heaven; but, the Church does not accept the spirit of the world.

To His Church, Christ gave the commission to spread the message of salvation to the ends of the earth. Among all the gifts which God has given to man, the gift of the good news of the Gospel is the greatest. In the Gospel God reveals His secret plan, hidden from the eyes of ages past, to save mankind and to give each man a share in His divine life through Jesus Christ His Son. Therefore the Church both speaks and listens to the world, without being of the world or conformed to it.

Much of the effective work of bringing the Gospel of Christ to the world must be done by Catholic laymen. The layman is challenged to make holy the actual world in which he lives. He is a mediator, a go-between for the Church and the world. He discovers Christ as the Way, the Truth, and the Life, and then brings Him into the world. As a citizen of both the Church and the world, he is meant to be the bridge that connects them. The priest stands between God and man; the layman stands between the Church and the world.

Vatican Council II

"In their pilgrimage to the heavenly city Christians are to seek and relish the things that are above: this involves not a lesser, but rather a greater commitment to working with all men towards the establishment of a world that is more human." *Modern World, 57*

"Proceeding from the love of the eternal Father, the Church was founded by Christ in time and gathered into one by the Holy Spirit. It has a saving and eschatological purpose which can be fully attained only in the next life. But it is now present here on earth and is composed of men; they, the members of the earthly city, are called to form the family of the children of God even in this present history of mankind and to increase it continually until the Lord comes. Made one in view of heavenly benefits and enriched by them, this family has been 'constituted and organized as a society in the present world' by Christ and 'provided with means adapted to its visible and social union.' Thus the Church, at once 'a visible organization and a spiritual community,' travels the same journey as all mankind and shares the same earthly lot with the world; it is to be a leaven and, as it were, the soul of human society in its renewal by Christ and transformation into the family of God." *Modern World, 40*

"The presence of Christians among human groups should be one that is animated by that love with which we are loved by God, who desires that we should love each other with that self-same love (cf. 1 Jn. 4:11). Christian charity is extended to all without distinction of race, social condition, or religion, and seeks neither gain nor gratitude.

"Just as God loves us with a gratuitous love, so too the faithful, in their charity, should be concerned for mankind, loving it with that same love with which God sought man.

"As Christ went about all the towns and villages healing every sickness and infirmity, as a sign that the kingdom of God had come (cf. Mt. 9:35 ff; Acts 10:38), so the Church, through its children, joins itself with men of every condition, but especially with the poor and afflicted, and willingly spends herself for them (cf. 2 Cor. 12:15). It shares their joys and sorrows, it is familiar with the hopes and problems of life, it suffers with them in the anguish of death. It wishes to enter into fraternal dialogue with those who are working for peace, and to bring them the peace and light of the Gospel." *Missionary Activity, 12*

Prayer: *Heavenly Father, Your Son, Jesus Christ, said that He is the Light of the world. He told us, His followers, to be like lights for the whole world. May our light shine before people, so that they will see the good things we do and praise You. This is the will of Your Son. Send us Your Holy Spirit to make us holy so that the brightness of our good example, even more than our words or learning, may scatter the darkness of the spirit of the world and radiate the ideal of true happiness found in Your divine teaching. We ask this in the Name of Jesus our Lord. Amen.*

Q. 162. How does the Catholic Church minister to man's spiritual needs?

The Catholic Church ministers to man's spiritual needs by providing a community of faith, where people can find help and guidance in seeking God.

Within the community of the Church, the Holy Spirit gives and strengthens the life of God through its teaching, the sacraments, prayers, and works of service. The sacraments are special actions in the Church through which the life of God is communicated to His people. The Church is Christ still active in the world.

Vatican Council II

"Education is, in a very special way, the concern of the Church, not only because the Church must be recognized as a human society capable of imparting education, but especially it has the duty of proclaiming the way of salvation to all men, of revealing the life of Christ to those who believe, and of assisting them with unremitting care so that they may be able to attain to the fulness of that life.

"The Church as a mother is under an obligation, therefore, to provide for its children an education by virtue of which their whole lives may be inspired by the spirit of Christ. At the same time it will offer its assistance to all peoples for the promotion of a well-balanced perfection of the human personality, for the good of society in this world and for the development of a world more worthy of man." *Christian Education, 3*

Q. 163. How does the Catholic Church minister to the bodily needs of people?

The Catholic Church ministers extensively to the bodily needs of people by helping those in need, by overcoming the causes of suffering and by building up a better life for man. Its vast health care and social welfare systems are found throughout the world.

Though the Church is deeply involved in the world and its needs, it always has Heaven in view, and continues to be a light to lead people to eternal life with God.

The Church is the answer to our Lord's appeal, "Come to Me, all that labor and are burdened, and I will refresh you.

See Papally Promulgated
Catechism of the Catholic Church

Q. 162. See paragraphs: 798-799, 1113-1134, 1143, 1146, 1198
Q. 163. See paragraphs: 1928-1948, 2288-2289, 2297-2298, 2300, 2447, 2449

Take up My yoke upon you and learn of Me, because I am meek, and humble of heart. And you shall find rest for your souls. For My yoke is sweet and My burden light" (Matthew 11:28-30).

Vatican Council II

"The Church ought to be present in the community of peoples, to foster and stimulate cooperation among men; motivated by their sole desire of serving all men, it contributes both by means of its official channels and through the full and sincere collaboration of all Christians. This goal will be more effectively brought about if all the faithful are conscious of their responsibility as men and as Christians and work in their own environments to arouse generous cooperation with the international community." *Modern World, 89*

"Charitable action today can and should reach all men and all needs." *Lay People, 8*

"Indeed it is a duty for the whole people of God, under the teaching and example of the Bishops, to alleviate the hardships of our times within the limits of its means, giving generously, as was the ancient custom of the Church, not merely out of what is superfluous, but also out of what is necessary."
Modern World, 88

Q. 164. How can we help unbelievers find God?

We can help unbelievers find God by the witness of our lives of firm faith in God, personal love of Christ, and by our goodness and love towards unbelievers.

We can help people to turn to God if we give them a good example of our own deep faith in God. If people see our love for Christ in our good deeds, they will be moved to love Him also. God has willed that all men should make up one family and treat one another in a spirit of brotherhood, for all men are called to the same goal — God Himself. By our love for one another for the love of God, and by other good works, we can help those who do not believe in God to find Him.

See Papally Promulgated
Catechism of the Catholic Church

Q. 164. See paragraphs: 849-856, 863-864, 905, 2105, 2205, 2225

Vatican Council II

"Laymen have countless opportunities for exercising the apostolate of evangelization and sanctification. The very witness of a Christian life, and good works done in a supernatural spirit, are effective in drawing men to the faith and to God; and that is what the Lord has said: 'Your light must shine so brightly before men that they can see your good works and glorify your Father who is in heaven.' (Mt. 5:16).

"This witness of life, however, is not the sole element in the apostolate; the true apostle is on the lookout for occasions of announcing Christ by word, either to unbelievers to draw them towards the faith, or to the faithful to instruct them, strengthen them, incite them to a more fervent life."

Lay People, 6

Q. 165. What is our duty towards the world?

As Christians, we must help men to solve their problems as much as possible. We show our love for God by loving our neighbors — the people around us.

Love for our neighbor makes us do all we can to help those who need our help and to make the world better. Jesus said, "You are the light of the world. A city seated on a mountain cannot be hid ... So let your light shine before men that they may see your good works and glorify your Father Who is in Heaven" (Matthew 5:14, 16).

Sacred Scripture

"Anyone who says, 'I love God' and hates his brother is a liar, since a man who does not love the brother that he can see cannot love God Whom he has never seen." *1 John 4:20*

Vatican Council II

"A life like this calls for a continuous exercise of faith, hope and charity.

"Only the light of faith and meditation on the Word of God

See Papally Promulgated
Catechism of the Catholic Church

Q. 165. See paragraphs: 2419-2430

can enable us to find everywhere and always the God 'in whom we live and exist' (Acts 17:28); only thus can we seek his will in everything, see Christ in all men, acquaintance or stranger, make sound judgments on the true meaning and value of temporal reality both in themselves and in relation to man's end." *Lay People, 4*

Prayer

God, Our Father, we pray for those who do not believe in Christ, that the light of the Holy Spirit may show them the way to salvation. Enable those who do not acknowledge Christ to find the truth, as they walk before You in sincerity of heart. Help us to grow in love for one another, to grasp more fully the mystery of Your Godhead, and to become more perfect witnesses of Your love in the sight of men.

Lord God, we pray for those who do not believe in You. May they find You by sincerely following all that is right. You created mankind so that they might long to find You, and then have peace when You are found. Grant that, in spite of the worldly things that stand in their way, they may all recognize in the lives of Christians the tokens of Your love and mercy, and so gladly acknowledge You as the one true God and Father of us all. We ask this through Jesus Christ, our Lord and Savior. Amen.

Chapter Seventy-Six

Christian Unity

Q. 166. Why is Christian unity in faith and love God's will?

Christian unity in faith and love is God's will because Christ willed that all who believe in Him might be one, so that the world might know that He was sent by the Father.

The night before He died Jesus prayed for Christian unity. "And not for them only do I pray, but for them also who through their word shall believe in Me; that they all may be one, as You, Father, in Me, and I in You; that they also may be one in Us; that the world may believe that You have sent Me." (John 17:20-21).

Seeing how the early Christians loved and honored one another, the pagans came to believe that the Christian God was the true God.

Jesus said, "I am the good shepherd; I know My own and My own know Me. As the Father knows Me and I know the Father; and I lay down My life for My sheep. And there are other sheep I have that are not of this fold. They also I must bring. They will hear My voice, and there will be one flock and one shepherd" (John 10:14-16).

Jesus founded but one Church, that which is built upon Peter the Rock. Moreover, Jesus brought the same Good News to all men, and called all to the same new life. His Church subsists in the Catholic Church, which is the world-wide community of the followers of Jesus united around the Pope.

Vatican Council II

"Today, in many parts of the world, under the influence of the grace of the Holy Spirit, many efforts are being made in prayer, word and action to attain that fullness of unity which Jesus Christ desires. The sacred Council exhorts, therefore,

See Papally Promulgated
Catechism of the Catholic Church

Q. 166. See paragraphs: 1794, 1815-1816, 1826-1827

all the Catholic faithful to recognize the signs of the times and to take an active and intelligent part in the work of ecumenism." *Ecumenism, 4*

"The condition of the modern world lends greater urgency to this duty of the Church; for, while men of the present day are drawn ever more closely together by social, technical and cultural bonds, it still remains for them to achieve full unity in Christ." *The Church, 1*

Q. 167. How do Catholics promote Christian unity?

Catholics should be deeply concerned over the sad divisions between Christians. They should take the first steps in meeting with other Christians, and try to make the Church more faithful to Christ and to what it received from the Apostles.

The Church is one because there is only one Jesus, and He communicates the same life of God to all who believe in Him. At this basic level, all Christians are truly united and the Church is one. If we truly love Christ, we shall do all in our power, by prayer and work, so that Christ's will and prayer for unity may be realized: "That all may be one" (cf. John 17:20).

At the same time, the Church is not one, because historical differences and bitterness have driven the followers of Jesus apart. Consequently, much of their Christian lives is not shared with one another. Besides, men's understanding of Jesus and the meaning of His life and teaching differ and sometimes these differences prevent Christians from coming together.

There are many Churches and ecclesial communities because in the long history of Christianity there have been serious differences among our Lord's followers over the meaning of His Gospel and the way to live His life. As a result, divisions and separate groups have appeared. These groups are principally the Roman Catholic Church, the Eastern Orthodox Church, the Anglican Church, and the various Protestant

See Papally Promulgated
Catechism of the Catholic Church

Q. 167. See paragraphs: 821-822, 855

communities. This sad condition should deeply concern a zealous Catholic.

Ecumenism is the acceptance of the basic unity of the Church and the effort to make this unity present and visible in the whole life of the Church. We Catholics partake of Christ's unfathomable riches, and we should lovingly share them with others.

Vatican Council II

"Certainly, such division openly contradicts the will of Christ, scandalizes the world, and damages that most holy cause, the preaching of the Gospel to every creature." *Ecumenism, 1*

"The Church knows that she is joined in many ways to the baptized who are honored by the name of Christian, but who do not however profess the Catholic faith in its entirety or have not preserved unity or communion under the successor of Peter. For there are many who hold sacred scripture in honor as a rule of faith and of life, who have a sincere religious zeal, who lovingly believe in God the Father Almighty and in Christ, the Son of God and the Saviour, who are sealed by baptism which unites them to Christ, and who indeed recognize and receive other sacraments in their own Churches or ecclesiastical communities. Many of them possess the episcopate, celebrate the holy Eucharist and cultivate devotion of the Virgin Mother of God. There is furthermore a sharing in prayer and spiritual benefits; these Christians are indeed in some real way joined to us in the Holy Spirit for, by his gifts and graces, his sanctifying power is also active in them and he has strengthened some of them even to the shedding of their blood." *The Church, 15*

"This change of heart and holiness of life, along with public and private prayer for the unity of Christians, should be regarded as the soul of the whole ecumenical movement, and merits the name, 'spiritual ecumenism.' " *Ecumenism, 8*

"In certain circumstances, such as in prayer services 'for unity' and during ecumenical gatherings, it is allowable, indeed desirable, that Catholics should join in prayer with their separated brethren. Such prayers in common are certainly a very effective means of petitioning for the grace of unity, and they are a genuine expression of the ties which still bind Catholics to their separated brethren. 'For where two or three are gathered together in my name, there am I in the midst of them (Mt. 18:20).' " *Ecumenism, 8*

Q. 168. Why should Catholics show respect for all men of good will?

Catholics should show respect for all men of good will because the Catholic Church rejects as un-Christian any unjust discrimination or injustice because of race, national origin, ethnic origin, color, sex, class, or religion.

Man, because he has a spiritual soul, has dominion over the other earthly creatures and is a more perfect image of God than anything else on this earth. Man is made for God. He has a special dignity and value as a human being. He is free and he will live forever. This makes him deserving of our respect.

The story of the Good Samaritan teaches us that our neighbor is every man, not only those who belong to our race, our country, or our religion. Even those who hate us and injure us must be included in our love. The Divine Master gave us the example when He said, "This is my commandment: love one another, as I have loved you" (John 15:12).

Sacred Scripture

"Anyone who says, 'I love God,' and hates his brother, is a liar, since a man who does not love the brother that he can see cannot love God Whom he has never seen." *1 John 4:20*

See Papally Promulgated
Catechism of the Catholic Church

Q. 168. See paragraphs: 1930-1933

"In his fatherly care for all of us, God desired that all men should form one family and deal with each other in a spirit of brotherhood." *Modern World, 24*

"Therefore, the Church reproves, as foreign to the mind of Christ, any discrimination against people or any harassment of them on the basis of their race, color, condition in life or religion. Accordingly, following the footsteps of the holy apostles Peter and Paul, the sacred Council earnestly begs the Christian faithful to 'conduct themselves well among Gentiles' (1 Pet. 2:12) and if possible, as far as depends on them, to be at peace with all men and in that way to be true sons of the Father who is in heaven (cf. Mt. 5:45)." *Non-Christian Religions, 5*

"And so the Spirit stirs up desires and actions in all of Christ's disciples in order that all may be peaceably united, as Christ ordained, in one flock under one shepherd. Mother Church never ceases to pray, hope and work that this may be achieved." *The Church, 15*

"It is through the faithful preaching of the Gospel by the Apostles and their successors — the bishops with Peter's successor at their head — through their administering the sacraments, and through their governing in love, that Jesus Christ wishes his people to increase, under the action of the Holy Spirit; and he perfects its fellowship in unity: in the confession of one faith, in the common celebration of divine worship, and in the fraternal harmony of the family of God." *Ecumenism, 2*

Prayer

Father, You gather the nations to praise Your Name. May all who are reborn in Baptism be one in faith and love. Grant Your continuing protection to all those who have received new life in Baptism. The perfect sacrifice of Jesus Christ made us Your people. In Your love; grant peace and unity to Your Church. You are the strength of the people. Unite us as one in Your holy Church, so that we may attain the peace our hearts desire. We ask this through Christ our Lord. Amen.

Jesus, Divine Shepherd, Your life's last concern was that the Apostles, upon whom You would confer the Holy Spirit, would be able, by God's grace and their own word and example, to lead Your scattered sheep into the one true fold. You prayed to Your Father for this unity the night before You died. Help us to maintain this unity by remaining always faithful to the Holy Father, the Pope, and to all the Bishops united to him in faith and charity. We ask this in Your most powerful and holy Name. Amen.

Chapter Seventy-Seven

The Catholic Church — Means of Salvation

Q. 169. What do we believe about the Catholic Church?

We believe that Jesus made His Catholic Church the ordinary means of salvation. We should desire to share her fullness with all men.

Catholics believe that Jesus Christ entrusted the work of redemption to His Church. He said to His first disciples, "He that hears you, hears Me; and he that despises you, despises Me; and he that despises Me, despises Him that sent Me" (Luke 10:16). Not to the individual, but to the Church was the promise made by Christ: "And I will ask the Father, and He shall give you another Paraclete, that He may abide with you forever" (John 14:16).

On Pentecost, the Holy Spirit descended upon the Apostles in the form of fiery tongues, and welded those men into the strong foundation upon which Christ's Church was to be built. They who had been ignorant, weak, and timid now went bravely forward to confront the world and to save it for their Master.

Catholics believe that only through the Catholic Church can man find full security and certainty about the meaning and destiny of human life. Catholics believe that only through the Catholic Church can we know fully what God wills us to believe and do, thus attaining salvation. Without the Church, religion becomes merely a matter of opinion and conjecture, with no man having any assurance as to what is true or false.

For the Catholic Christian, life is not meaningless. Man is not at the mercy of a blind, unreasonable fate. He knows that he is walking in the sunlight of truth, under the loving care of His Father in Heaven, and with the guidance of the Church,

See Papally Promulgated
Catechism of the Catholic Church

Q. 169. See paragraphs: 1259-1260

his spiritual mother upon earth. Catholics recognize the unique fullness of the Catholic Church.

Vatican Council II

"The Church, a pilgrim now on earth, is necessary for salvation: the one Christ is mediator and the way of salvation; he is present to us in his body which is the Church. He himself explicitly asserted the necessity of faith and baptism (cf. Mk. 16:16; Jn. 3:5), and thereby affirmed at the same time the necessity of the Church which men enter through baptism as through a door. Hence they could not be saved who, knowing that the Catholic Church was founded as necessary by God through Christ, would refuse either to enter it, or to remain in it." *The Church, 14*

"All those, who in faith look toward Jesus, the author of salvation and the principle of unity and peace, God has gathered together and established as the Church, that it may be for each and everyone the visible sacrament of this saving unity." *The Church, 9*

"The Church is...a sheepfold, the sole and necessary gateway which is Christ (Jn. 10:1-10). It is also a flock, of which God foretold that he would himself be the shepherd (cf. Is. 40:11; Ex. 34:11f), and whose sheep, although watched over by human shepherds, are nevertheless at all times led and brought to pasture by Christ Himself, the Good Shepherd and prince of shepherds (cf. Jn. 10:11; 1 Pet. 5:4), who gave his life for his sheep (cf. Jn. 10:11-16)." *The Church, 6*

"It is through Christ's Catholic Church alone, which is the universal help towards salvation, that the fullness of the means of salvation can be obtained. It was to the apostolic college alone, of which Peter is the head, that we believe that our Lord entrusted all the blessings of the New Covenant, in order to establish on earth the one Body of Christ into which all those should be fully incorporated who belong in any way to the people of God." *Ecumenism, 3*

"Whether it aids the world or whether it benefits from it, the Church has but one sole purpose — that the kingdom of God may come and the salvation of the human race may be accomplished. Every benefit the people of God can confer on mankind during its earthly pilgrimage is rooted in the Church's being 'the universal sacrament of salvation,' at once manifesting and actualizing the mystery of God's love for men." *Modern World, 45*

Q. 170. How do the laity share in Christ's mission?

As Christ sent His Apostles to teach and to be witnesses to Him in the world, so too, He wants the laity to share in this mission.

The duty of proclaiming the Gospel and of making its power felt in the lives of men belongs not only to Bishops, priests, deacons, and Religious, but also to the laity in the Church.

The Catholic layman's vocation is to be Christ's witness in the world of social, economic, and political activity. In the world, he must contribute to the growth of the Kingdom of God; he must be another Christ passing among men.

In the small circle of his home and in the wide arena of public affairs, the Catholic layman has been called to help guide the world heavenward. He must work in the making of laws and in the shaping of social doctrines and practice. He must be engaged day by day in developing his country's prosperity and in bettering the lot of the poor.

It is the Catholic layman's vocation to join his work with the work of Christ by seeking to transform the kingdom of the world into the Kingdom of God. The layman's vocation is to consecrate the world for Christ. If the world is made a better place to live in, and if the many millions of those who now do not know Christ become members of His Kingdom, it will be because intelligent and zealous lay people have sincerely and successfully tried to fulfill the vocation which is theirs. In this way they can help to bring about the unity of all men under God.

See Papally Promulgated
Catechism of the Catholic Church

Q. 170. See paragraphs: 863, 905, 2044, 2472

As Christ sent His Apostles to teach and to be witnesses for Him in the world, so too, He would have the Catholic laity participate in this mission. The duty of proclaiming the Gospel, and of making its influence felt in the lives of people, belongs also to every Catholic man and woman, all of whom are called by God to be apostles, that is, messengers of Christ to the world.

The soul of the apostolate is love. We must first show Christ-like respect for all men of good will, reaching out especially to those who, with us, believe in God.

Vatican Council II

"The term 'laity' is understood to mean all the faithful except those in Holy Orders and those who belong to a religious state approved by the Church. That is, the faithful, who by Baptism are incorporated into Christ, are placed in the People of God, and, in their own way, share the priestly, prophetic, and kingly office of Christ; and to the best of their ability they carry on the mission of the whole Christian people in the Church and in the world.

"Their secular character is proper and peculiar to the laity." *The Church, 31*

"Gathered together in the People of God and established in the one Body of Christ under one head, the laity — no matter who they are — have, as living members, the vocation of applying to the building up of the Church and to its continual sanctification all the powers which they have received from the goodness of the Creator and from the grace of the Redeemer.

"The apostolate of the laity is a sharing in the salvific mission of the Church. Through Baptism and Confirmation all are appointed to this apostolate by the Lord himself. Moreover, by the sacraments, and especially by the Eucharist, that love of God and man which is the soul of the apostolate is communicated and nourished." *The Church, 33*

"The laity, however, are given this special vocation: to make the Church present and fruitful in those places and circumstances where it is only through them that she can become the salt of the earth." *The Church, 33*

"The Church can never be without the lay apostolate; it is something that derives from the layman's very vocation as a Christian." *Lay People, 1*

344

"Each individual layman must be a witness before the world to the resurrection and life of the Lord Jesus, and a sign of the living God. All together, and each one to the best of his ability, must nourish the world with spiritual fruits (cf. Gal. 5:22). They must diffuse in the world the spirit which animates those poor, meek and peace-makers whom the Lord in the Gospel proclaimed blessed (cf. Mt. 5:3-9). In a word: 'what the soul is in the body, let Christians be in the world.' "

The Church, 38

"The hierarchy entrusts the laity with certain charges more closely connected with the duties of pastors: In the teaching of Christian doctrine, for example, in certain liturgical actions, in the care of souls. In virtue of this mission the laity are fully subject to superior ecclesiastical control in regard to the exercise of these charges." *Lay People, 24*

"In the Church there is diversity of ministry but unity of mission. To the apostles and their successors Christ has entrusted the office of teaching, sanctifying and governing in His name and by his power. But the laity are made to share in the priestly, prophetical and kingly office of Christ; they have therefore, in the Church and in the world, their own assignment in the mission of the whole People of God." *Lay People, 2*

"The Church was founded to spread the kingdom of Christ over all the earth for the glory of God the Father, to make all men partakers in redemption and salvation, and through them to establish the right relationship of the entire world to Christ. Every activity of the Mystical Body with this in view goes by the name of 'apostolate;' the Church exercises it through all its members, though in various ways. In fact, the Christian vocation is, of its nature, a vocation to the apostolate as well." *Lay People, 2*

"Although by Christ's will some are established as teachers, dispensers of the mysteries and pastors for the others, there remains, nevertheless, a true equality between all with regard to the dignity and to the activity which is common to all the faithful in the building up of the Body of Christ. The distinction which the Lord has made between the sacred ministers and the rest of the People of God involves union, for the pastors and the other faithful are joined together by a close relationship: the pastors of the Church — following the example of the Lord — should minister to each other and to the rest of the faithful; the latter should eagerly collaborate with the pastors and teachers. And so amid variety all will bear witness to the wonderful unity in the Body of Christ: this very diversity of graces, of ministries and of works gathers the sons of God into one, for 'all these things are the work of the one and the same Spirit' (1 Cor. 12:11)." *The Church, 32*

"The holy People of God share in Christ's prophetic office: it spreads abroad a living witness to him, especially by a life of faith and love and by offering to God a sacrifice of praise, the fruit of lips praising his name (cf. Heb. 13:15)." *The Church, 12*

Prayer: *God our Father, inspire the hearts of all Your people to continue the saving work of Christ everywhere until the end of the world. The suffering and death of Christ Your Son won Your salvation for all the world. May the suffering and death of Your Son sanctify the Church so that it can be an instrument of salvation for the world. May the prayers and the Eucharistic sacrifice of Your Church come to You and be pleasing in Your sight. Make us holy by the Eucharist we share at Your table. Through the sacraments of Your Church, may all people receive the salvation Your Son brought us through His suffering and death on the Cross. We ask this through our Lord and Savior Jesus Christ. Amen.*

Q. 171. Why is the Church an institution of salvation?

The Church is an institution for salvation because (1) *it is a community of the People of God with Christ as its leader and Head* and (2) *it has been given the mission of bringing the message of salvation to all men.*

1. *The Church is an institution for salvation because it is a community of the People of God with Christ as its leader and Head.*

The Church is a fellowship of life, charity, and truth. Through Jesus Christ, we have been made members of the family of God, the People of God. We are joined to Christ and

See Papally Promulgated
Catechism of the Catholic Church

Q. 171. See paragraphs: 738, 774-776, 849-852

to one another in a union which is far closer than any union on earth. Our Lord compared it to the sublime union of the Blessed Trinity: "May they all be one. Father, may they be one in Us, as You are in Me and I am in You, so that the world may believe it was You who sent Me" (John 17:21).

We are one with Christ and with one another in the union of the Mystical Body of Christ here on earth. So close is this union that, Jesus said, "Amen I say to you, as long as you did it to one of these My least brethren, you did it to Me" (Matthew 25:40).

Therefore we must have special love for our fellow members in the Mystical Body of Christ, because in loving the members of His Body we are loving Christ. In practice, we must treat all men as we would treat Christ Himself since Christ died for them.

2. *The Church is an institution for salvation because it has been given the mission of bringing the message of salvation to all men.*

The Church is also a structured institution. There are two kinds of authority in the Church: the ordinary authority which every society has to organize and direct its own affairs, and the special authority given by Jesus Christ to teach and act in His name. The Church exercises her ordinary authority by enacting laws to regulate her internal affairs, to promote the good of all, and to fulfill the purposes of the Church. The Church exercises the special authority that is given by Jesus by her teaching, worship, and all service done in the name of Jesus. His person and power are present in her when she acts under this authority.

The Pope and the Bishops exercise authority for the Church. Others, clergy and laity, can share in the exercise of the Church's authority in different degrees.

The Church speaks the Good News of God's doings in the world. She does this through her teaching and preaching, through her life and worship, through her Bible and the writings of her prophets, and sometimes through the words of a single Christian expressing his hopes. The mission of the Church is to bring the message of salvation to all men.

Sacred Scripture

"And Jesus coming, spoke to them, saying: 'All power is given to Me in Heaven and in earth. Going therefore, teach all nations; baptizing them in the name of the Father, and of the Son, and of the Holy Spirit. Teaching them to observe all things whatever I have commanded you. And behold I am with you all days, even to the consummation of the world.' "

Matthew 28:18-20

Vatican Council II

"That messianic people has as its head Christ, 'who was delivered up for our sins and rose again for our justification' (Rom. 4:25), and now, having acquired the name which is above all names, reigns gloriously in heaven. The state of this people is that of the dignity and freedom of the sons of God, in whose hearts the Holy Spirit dwells as in a temple. Its law is the new commandment to love as Christ loved us (cf. Jn. 13:34). Its destiny is the kingdom of God which has been begun by God himself on earth and which must be further extended until it is brought to perfection by him at the end of time when Christ our life (cf. Col. 3:4) will appear and 'creation itself also will be delivered from its slavery to corruption into the freedom of the glory of the sons of God' (Rom. 8:21). Hence that messianic people, although it does not actually include all men, and at times may appear as a small flock, is, however, a most sure seed of unity, hope and salvation for the whole human race. Established by Christ as a communion of life, love and truth, it is taken up by him also as the instrument for the salvation of all; as the light of the world and the salt of the earth, (cf. Mt. 5:13-16), it is sent forth into the whole world."

The Church, 9

"Later, before he was assumed into heaven (cf. Acts 1:11), after he had fulfilled in himself the mysteries of our salvation and the renewal of all things by his death and resurrection, the Lord, who had received all power in heaven and on earth (cf. Mt. 28:18), founded his Church as the sacrament of salvation; and just as he had been sent by the Father (cf. Jn. 20:21), so he sent the apostles into the whole world." *Missionary Activity, 5*

Prayer

Father, You will that Your Church be the sacrament of salvation for all people. Make us feel more urgently the call to work for the salvation of all men, until You have made us all one people.

God of unchanging power and might, look with mercy and favor on Your entire Church. Bring lasting salvation to mankind, so that the world may see the fallen lifted up, the old made new, and all things brought to perfection, through Him Who is their origin, our Lord Jesus Christ.

Lord God, guide us with Your love in Your Church. Keep us faithful that we may be helped through life and brought to salvation through her teaching and sacraments.

When Jesus, Your Son, humbled Himself to come among us as man, He fulfilled the plan You had formed long ago, and so opened for us the way to salvation, especially through the Church He founded. Now we watch for the day when we hope that the salvation He promises us will be ours when He will come again in glory. Amen.

Chapter Seventy-Eight

The Marks of the Church - I
The Church is One

Q. 172. What are the marks that point out the true Church founded by Jesus?

There are four marks which point out the true Church founded by Jesus. They are four adjectives: One, Holy, Catholic and Apostolic.

Having made His Church a means of our everlasting happiness, our Lord has stamped it plainly with the mark of its divine origin. In the Nicene Creed we say: "We believe in One, Holy, Catholic, and Apostolic Church."

Vatican Council II

"A diocese is a section of the People of God entrusted to a bishop to be guided by him with the assistance of his clergy so that, loyal to its pastor and formed by him into one community in the Holy Spirit through the Gospel and the Eucharist, it constitutes one particular church in which the one, holy, catholic and apostolic Church of Christ is truly present and active." *Bishops, 11*

"We believe that this one true religion continues to exist in the Catholic and Apostolic Church to which the Lord Jesus entrusted the task of spreading it among all men when he said to the apostles: 'Go therefore and make disciples of all nations baptizing them in the Name of the Father and of the Son and of the Holy Spirit, teaching them to observe all that I have commanded you' (Matthew 18:19-20)." *Liberty, 1*

"Missionary activity extends the saving faith of the Church, it expands and perfects its catholic unity, it is sustained by its apostolicity, it activates the collegiate sense of

See Papally Promulgated
Catechism of the Catholic Church

Q. 172. See paragraphs: 811-865

its hierarchy, and bears witness to its sanctity which it both extends and promotes." *Missionary Activity, 6*

Q. 173. Why is the Catholic Church one?

The Church is one because it is unified in belief.

The truths which the members of the Catholic Church hold are the truths made known to us by Jesus Himself; they are truths which come to us directly from God. God is truth. He knows all things and cannot be mistaken. He is infinitely truthful and cannot lie. Whatever God has said is true forever and for everybody. It is not for us to pick and choose and to adjust God's revelation to our own convenience. In the Catholic Church, all are obligated to believe the same truths. Thus, every Catholic must mean exactly the same things when he recites the Apostles' and Nicene Creeds.

Vatican Council II

"All those, who in faith look towards Jesus, the author of salvation and the principle of unity and peace, God has gathered together and established as the Church, that it may be for each and everyone the visible sacrament of this saving unity." *The Church, 9*

Q. 174. How did Jesus indicate that His Church is one?

Jesus said, "And there are other sheep I have, that are not of this fold. Them also I must bring, and they shall hear My voice, and there shall be one fold and one shepherd" (John 10:16).

See Papally Promulgated
Catechism of the Catholic Church

Q. 173. See paragraphs: 813-816
Q. 174. See paragraphs: 424, 552, 816, 820

Jesus prayed to His Father: "that they all may be one, as You, Father, are in Me, and I am in You; that they also may be one in Us; that the world may believe that You have sent Me" (John 17:21).

Sacred Scripture

"And if a kingdom is divided against itself, that kingdom cannot last." *Mark 3:24*

Vatican Council II

"The Universal Church is seen to be 'a people brought into unity from the unity of the Father, the Son and the Holy Spirit.' " *The Church, 4*

Q. 175. Why are we united by a spiritual leader?

All Catholics are united under the same spiritual leadership because Jesus Christ made Peter the chief shepherd of His flock, and provided that Peter's successors, the Bishops of Rome, would be the heads of His Church and guardians of His truths until the end of time.

Loyalty to the Bishop of Rome, the Pope, will ever be the binding center of our unity and the test of our membership in Christ's Church.

Vatican Council II

"The Roman Pontiff, as the successor of Peter, is the perpetual and visible source and foundation of the unity both of the bishops and of the whole company of the faithful. The individual bishops are the visible source and foundation of unity in their own particular Churches, which are constituted after the model of the universal Church; it is in these and formed out of them that the one and unique Catholic Church exists. And for that reason precisely, each bishop represents his own Church, whereas all, together with the pope, represent the whole Church in a bond of peace, love and unity."

The Church, 23

See Papally Promulgated
Catechism of the Catholic Church

Q. 175. See paragraphs: 880-882

Q. 176. Why are we united in worship?

We are united in worship because we have but one altar, upon which Jesus Christ daily renews the offering of Himself upon the Cross. Everywhere we have the same Mass, and everywhere the same seven sacraments.

By means of the Eucharist, Christ re-offers Himself to the Father through the ministry of His priests in the Sacrifice of the Mass. At Mass, Jesus and the faithful, daily adore the Father. With Him they give glory to God and praise Him for His kindness toward mankind. With Him they ask God for His forgiveness and beg His help. We are one with Jesus in His Sacrifice.

Vatican Council II

"Liturgical services are not private functions but are celebrations of the Church which is 'the sacrament of unity,' namely, 'the holy people united and arranged under their bishops.

"Therefore, liturgical services pertain to the whole Body of the Church. They manifest it, and have effects upon it. But they also touch individual members of the Church in different ways, depending on their orders, their role in the liturgical services, and their actual participation in them."

Sacred Liturgy, 26.

See Papally Promulgated
Catechism of the Catholic Church

Q. 176. See paragraphs: 553, 641, 892

Prayer

Father, through Christ You bring us to the knowledge of Your truth, that we may be united by one Faith and one Baptism, and thus become His Body. Through Christ, You have given the Holy Spirit to all people. How wonderful are the works of the Spirit, revealed in so many gifts! How marvelous is the unity the Spirit creates from their diversity, as He dwells in the hearts of Your children, filling the whole Church with His presence and guiding it with His wisdom.

Lord, by the Sacrament of the Eucharist, You make us one family in Christ Your Son, one in the sharing of His Body and Blood, and one in the communion of His Spirit. Help us to grow in love for one another and to come to full maturity in the Body of Christ.

God of wisdom and truth, without You, neither truth nor holiness can survive. Safeguard the Church You have made one and make us glad to proclaim Your glory, through Christ our Lord. Amen.

Chapter Seventy-Nine

The Marks of the Church - II
The Church is Holy

Q. 177. Why is the Catholic Church holy?

The Catholic Church is holy because it was founded by Jesus Christ, Who is all-holy, and because it teaches holy doctrines according to the will of Christ. It provides the means of leading a holy life, thereby giving holy members to every age.

We can point to the saints as proof that the holiness of Christ is at work in the Catholic Church. But it would be an even greater proof of the holiness of the Church if all of us would live holy lives, if every Catholic were a person of outstanding Christian virtue.

Jesus prayed to His Father for His Church, "Sanctify them in truth. Your word is truth. And for them do I sanctify Myself, that they also may be sanctified in truth" (John 17:17, 19).

St. Paul reminds us that Jesus Christ "gave Himself for us, that He might redeem us from all iniquity, and might cleanse for Himself an acceptable people, jealous for good works" (Titus 2:14).

The Holy Spirit preserves the Church as the Body of Christ and His Bride, so that in spite of the sins of its members it will never fail in faithfulness to Him and will meet Him in holiness at the end of the world. The Holy Spirit also helps the Church constantly to purify and renew itself.

Vatican Council II

"Likewise the Church's holiness is fostered in a special way by the manifold counsels which the Lord proposes to his disciples in the Gospel for them to observe. Towering among these counsels is that precious gift of divine grace given to some by

See Papally Promulgated
Catechism of the Catholic Church

Q. 177. See paragraphs: 823-825

the Father (cf. Mt. 19:11; 1 Cor. 7:7) to devote themselves to God alone more easily with an undivided heart (cf. 1 Cor. 7:32-34) in virginity or celibacy." *The Church, 42*

"The state of life, then, which is constituted by the profession of the evangelical counsels, while not entering into the hierarchical structure of the Church, belongs undeniably to her life and holiness." *The Church, 44*

"The Church, whose mystery is set forth by this sacred Council, is held, as a matter of faith, to be unfailingly holy. This is because Christ, the Son of God, who with the Father and the Spirit is hailed as 'alone holy,' loved the Church as his Bride, giving himself up for her so as to sanctify her (cf. Eph. 5:25-26); he joined her to himself as his body and endowed her with the gift of the Holy Spirit for the glory of God."

The Church, 39

"Christ, 'holy, innocent and undefiled' (Heb. 7:26) knew nothing of sin (2 Cor. 5:21), but came only to expiate the sins of the people (cf. Heb. 2:17). The Church, however, clasping sinners to her bosom, at once holy and always in need of purification, follows constantly the path of penance and renewal."

The Church, 8

Prayer: *Eternal God, Your Spirit guides the Church and makes it holy. Listen to our prayers and help each of us in Your Church, in his own vocation, to do Your work more faithfully, through Christ our Lord. Amen.*

Prayer

*A*lmighty God, only hope of the world, by the preaching of the prophets, You proclaimed the mysteries we celebrate in the Sacrifice of the Mass. Help us to be Your faithful people, for it is by Your inspiration alone that we can grow in holiness.

*F*ather, the body of Your risen Son is the temple not made by human hands and the defending wall of the New Jerusalem. May this holy city, built of living stones, shine with spiritual radiance and so witness to Your greatness in the sight of all the nations.

*G*od, You are the source of all holiness. Though no one can see You and live, You give life more generously, and, in an even greater way, restore it. Sanctify Your priests through Your life-giving Word, and consecrate Your people in His blood until the day that our eyes may see Your face in heavenly bliss.

*W*ords cannot measure the boundaries of love for those who are born to a new life in Christ Jesus. Raise men beyond the limits of this world, so that we may be free to love as Christ teaches us and to find our joy in Your glory.

*C*lothe Your priests in righteousness, and make Your Chosen People joyful. Give Your people strength and holiness. Bless Your people with peace and love, through Jesus Christ our Lord. Amen.

Chapter Eighty

The Marks of the Church - III
The Church is Catholic

Q. 178. Why is the Church catholic or universal?

The Church is catholic or universal because Christ established it to proclaim all of His teaching to all men, at all times, and in all places.

Jesus said, "Go out to the whole world; proclaim the Good News to all creation" (Mark 16:15). "You will receive power when the Holy Spirit comes on you, and then you will be My witnesses not only in Jerusalem but throughout Judea and Samaria, and indeed to the ends of the earth" (Acts 1:8).

Jesus spoke of the growth of His Church when He gave us the parable of the mustard seed. "The Kingdom of Heaven is like a mustard seed which a man took and sowed in his field. It is the smallest of all the seeds, but when it has grown it is the biggest shrub of all and becomes a tree so that the birds of the air come and shelter in its branches" (Matthew 13:31).

Vatican Council II

"All men are called to belong to the new People of God. This People therefore, whilst remaining one and only one, is to be spread throughout the whole world and to all ages in order that the design of God's will may be fulfilled." *The Church, 13*

"The period, therefore, between the first and second coming of the Lord is the time of missionary activity, when, like the harvest, the Church will be gathered from the four winds into the kingdom of God. For the Gospel must be preached to all peoples before the Lord comes (cf. Mk. 13:10). Missionary activity is nothing else, and nothing less, than the manifestation of God's plan, its epiphany and realization in the world

See Papally Promulgated
Catechism of the Catholic Church

Q. 178. See paragraphs: 830-831

and in history; that by which God, through mission, clearly brings to its conclusion the history of salvation."

Missionary Activity , 9

"The special undertakings in which preachers of the Gospel, sent by the Church, and going into the whole world, carry out the work of preaching the Gospel and implanting the Church among people who do not yet believe in Christ, are generally called 'missions.' Such undertakings are accomplished by missionary activity and are, for the most part, carried out in defined territories recognized by the Holy See."

Missionary Activity , 6

Q. 179. How long has the Catholic Church been in existence?

The Church has been in existence since the the sacrificial death and resurrection of Jesus. This took place about 33 A.D.

The Catholic Church has had a continuous existence of more than nineteen hundred years, and it is the only Christian institution of which this is true.

> **Prayer:** *Heavenly Father, You will that all men be saved and come to the knowledge of Your truth. Send workers into Your great harvest, that the Gospel may be preached to every creature so that Your people may be gathered together by the Word of Life. Strengthened by the power of the sacraments, may all of mankind advance in the way of salvation and love, through Jesus Christ our Lord and Savior. Amen.*

Q. 180. Does the Catholic Church teach all the truths that Jesus Christ taught?

Yes. The Catholic Church is the only Church which teaches all the truths that Jesus Christ taught.

See Papally Promulgated
Catechism of the Catholic Church

Q. 179. See paragraphs: 767-769
Q. 180. See paragraphs: 74-79, 830-831, 838

359

Many other Christian communities have rejected the sacraments of Penance and Anointing of the Sick; the Mass and the Real Presence of Jesus in the Eucharist; the spiritual supremacy of Peter and his successors, the popes; the efficacy of grace, and man's ability to merit grace and Heaven. Some even question whether Jesus Christ is truly God. There is not a single truth that Jesus Christ revealed (whether personally or through His Apostles) which the Catholic Church does not still faithfully declare and teach.

Prayer

Lord, glorify Your Name by increasing Your Chosen People as You promised long ago. In reward for their trust, may we see, in the Church, the fulfillment of Your promise.

It is through Your Church, generously endowed with gifts of grace and fortified by the Holy Spirit, that You send out Your word to all nations. Strengthen Your Church with the best of all food, and make it dauntless in faith. Multiply its children to celebrate with one accord the mysteries of Your love at the altar on high.

God our Father, You sent Your Son into the world to be its true Light. Pour out the Spirit He promised us in order to sow truth in men's hearts and awaken in them obedience to the faith. May all men be born again to a new life in Baptism and so enter the fellowship of Your one holy people.

You command the seed to rise, Lord God, though the farmer is unaware. Grant that those who labor for You may trust not in their own work but in Your help. Remembering that the land is brought to flower not with human tears, but with those of Your Son, may the Church rely only upon Your gifts.

Strengthen the minds and hearts of missionaries with Your Spirit, and raise up a great company to help them from every nation. We ask this through Jesus Christ our only Savior. Amen.

Chapter Eighty-One

The Marks of the Church - IV
The Church is Apostolic

Q. 181. Why is the Catholic Church apostolic?

The Catholic Church is apostolic because it is able to trace its lineage in unbroken continuity back to the Apostles.

Jesus said to Peter, "You are Peter and on this rock I will build My Church. And the gates of hell shall not prevail against it" (Matthew 16:18).

Speaking to all the Apostles He said: "All authority in Heaven and on earth has been given to Me. Go, therefore, make disciples of all the nations; baptize them in the Name of the Father and of the Son and of the Holy Spirit, and teach them to observe all the commands I gave you. And know that I am with you always; yes, to the end of time" (Matthew 28:18-20).

Among the Apostles, Christ chose St. Paul to spread His Church. Speaking of him, He said, "This man is My chosen instrument to bring My Name before pagans and pagan kings and before the people of Israel; I Myself will show him how much he himself must suffer for My Name" (Acts 9:15-16). Paul became the greatest missionary of all time. He brought the Gospel of Christ to the pagan world at the cost of great sacrifices.

To the Ephesians Paul wrote: "So you are no longer aliens and foreigners; you are citizens with all the saints, and part of God's household. You are built upon the foundation of the Apostles and prophets. Christ Jesus Himself being its main cornerstone" (Ephesians 2:19-20). Paul was later beheaded in Rome and where Peter was crucified upside down.

See Papally Promulgated
Catechism of the Catholic Church

Q. 181. See paragraphs: 857-865

Since the days of the Apostles, episcopal power, that power held by the Bishops, has been passed on through the Sacrament of Holy Orders from generation to generation, from Bishop to Bishop. By the Popes, Bishops, priests, and deacons, the Gospel of Christ is preached in every part of the world, in fulfillment of the promise of Christ, "And when I am lifted up from the earth, I shall draw all men to Myself" (John 12:32). "Know that I am with you always; yes, to the end of the world" (Matthew 28:20).

Vatican Council II

"The Lord Jesus, having prayed at length to the Father, called to himself those whom he willed and appointed twelve to be with him, whom He might send to preach the kingdom of God (cf. Mk. 3:13-19; Mt. 10:1-42). These apostles (cf. Lk. 6:13) he constituted in the form of a college or permanent assembly, at the head of which he placed Peter, chosen from amongst them (cf. Jn. 21:15-17). He sent them first of all to the children of Israel and then to all peoples (cf. Rom. 1:16), so that, sharing in his power, they might make all peoples his disciples and sanctify and govern them (cf. Mt. 28:16-20; Mk. 16:15; Lk. 24:45-48; Jn. 20:21-23) and thus spread the Church and, administering it under the guidance of the Lord, shepherd it all days until the end of the world (cf. Mt. 28:20). They were fully confirmed in this mission on the day of Pentecost (cf. Acts 2:1-26) according to the promise of the Lord: 'You shall receive power when the Holy Ghost descends upon you; and you shall be my witnesses both in Jerusalem and in all Judea and Samaria, and to the remotest part of the earth' (Acts 1:8). By preaching everywhere the Gospel (cf. Mk. 16:20), welcomed and received under the influence of the Holy Spirit by those who hear it, the apostles gather together the universal Church, which the Lord founded upon the apostles and built upon blessed Peter their leader, the chief corner-stone being Christ Jesus Himself (cf. Apoc. 21:14; Mt. 16:18; Eph. 2:20)." *The Church 19*

"That divine mission, which was committed by Christ to the apostles is destined to last until the end of the world (cf. Mt. 28:20), since the Gospel, which they were charged to hand on, is, for the Church, the principle of all its life for all time. For that very reason the apostles were careful to appoint successors in this hierarchically constituted society." *The Church, 20*

"God graciously arranged that the things he had once revealed for the salvation of all peoples should remain in their entirety, throughout the ages, and be transmitted to all gen-

362

erations. Therefore, Christ the Lord, in whom the entire Revelation of the most high God is summed up (cf. 2 Cor. 1:20; 3:16-4,6) commanded the apostles to preach the Gospel, which had been promised beforehand by the prophets, and which he fulfilled in his own person and promulgated with his own lips. In preaching the Gospel they were to communicate the gifts of God to all men. This Gospel was to be the source of all saving truth and moral discipline. This was faithfully done; it was done by the apostles who handed on, by the spoken word of their preaching, by the example they gave, by the institutions they established, what they themselves had received — whether from the lips of Christ, from his way of life and his works, or whether they had learned it at the prompting of the Holy Spirit; it was done by those apostles and other men associated with the apostles who, under the inspiration of the same Holy Spirit, committed the message of salvation to writing." *Divine Revelation, 7*

"The apostolic preaching, which is expressed in a special way in the inspired books, was to be preserved in a continuous line of succession until the end of time. Hence the apostles, in handing on what they themselves had received, warn the faithful to maintain the traditions which they had learned either by word of mouth or by letter (cf. 2 Th. 2:15); and they warn them to fight hard for the faith that had been handed to them once and for all (cf. Jude 3). What was handed on by the apostles comprises everything that serves to make the People of God live their lives in holiness and increase their faith. In this way the Church, in her doctrine, life and worship, perpetuates and transmits to every generation all that she herself is, all that she believes.

"The Tradition that comes from the apostles makes progress in the Church, with the help of the Holy Spirit. There is a growth in insight into the realities and words that are being passed on. This comes about in various ways. It comes through the contemplation and study of believers who ponder these things in their hearts (cf. Lk. 2,19; and 51). It comes from the intimate sense of spiritual realities which they experience. And it comes from the preaching of those who have received, along with their right of succession in the episcopate, the sure charism of truth. Thus, as the centuries go by, the Church is always advancing towards the plenitude of divine truth, until eventually the words of God are fulfilled in her."
Divine Revelation, 8

Prayer: *Father, through the Apostles, Your Church first received the Faith; keep us true to their teaching. Through the prayers of the Apostles, may we who received this Faith through their preaching share their joy in following the Lord to the unfading inheritance which is reserved for us in Heaven. We ask this in the powerful Name of Jesus Christ our Lord. Amen.*

Prayer

Father in Heaven, You founded Your Church on the Apostles so that she might stand firm forever as the sign on earth of Your infinite holiness and as the living Gospel for all men to hear.

You are the eternal Shepherd Who never leaves His flock untended. Through the Apostles You watched over and protected the Church. You made them shepherds of the flock to share in the work of Your Son; from their place in Heaven, they guide us still.

Lord our God, encourage us through the prayers of Saints Peter and Paul. May the Apostles, who strengthened the Faith of the infant Church, help us on our way of salvation.

The light of Your revelation brought Peter and Paul the gift of faith in Jesus, Your Son. Through their prayers, may we always give thanks for Your life, which is given to us in Christ Jesus, and for the knowledge and love with which He has enriched us.

You have set us firmly within Your Church, which You built upon the rock of Peter, our first Pope. May You bless us with a faith that never falters. You have given us knowledge of the Faith through the labor and preaching of St. Paul. May his example inspire us to lead others to Christ by the manner of our lives.

May Peter, and Paul, by their undying witness and their prayers, lead us to the joy of that eternal home which Peter gained by his cross, and Paul by the sword.

Lord, our God, give Your Church the constant joy of honoring the holy Apostles. May we continue to be guided and governed by those leaders, whose teaching and example have been our inspiration.

Pour on us the Holy Spirit Who filled Your Apostles, that we may acknowledge the gifts we have received through them. Keep us faithful to the teaching of the Apostles, united in prayer and in the Breaking of Bread in the Eucharist, and in joy and simplicity of heart.

Lord God, You appointed Paul, Your Apostle, to preach the Good News of salvation. Fill the entire world with the faith he carried to so many peoples and nations, that Your Church may continue to grow. May Your Spirit fill us with the light which led Paul the Apostle to make Your glory known. May Christ be our life, and let nothing separate us from His love. Following the teachings of St. Paul, may we live in love with our brothers and sisters in Christ.

Teach us, Father, to lift up our hands and our hearts reverently in prayer and to hold to the pattern of sound teaching which You delivered to the holy Apostles. To You be glory now and all honor forever. Amen.

The Communion of Saints

Chapter Eighty-Two

The Communion of Saints - I

Q. 182. What do we mean when we say, "I believe in the Communion of Saints?"

When we say "I believe in the Communion of Saints," we mean that we believe that there is a union, a fellowship, of all souls in whom the Holy Spirit, the Spirit of Christ, dwells. This Communion is the union of the members of the Church on earth, in Heaven, and in Purgatory.

The word "communion" means "union with." The word "saint" means "holy." Every Christian soul, incorporated with Christ by Baptism, and having within himself the Holy Spirit, is holy, so long as he remains in the state of sanctifying grace. In the early Church all faithful members of the Mystical Body of Christ were called saints.

The Communion of Saints is the unity and cooperation of the members of the Church on earth with those in Heaven and those in Purgatory, who are united in the one Mystical Body of Christ.

The faithful on earth are in communion with each other by professing the same Faith, by obeying the same authority, and by assisting each other with prayers and good works. They have communion with the saints in Heaven by honoring them as glorified members of the Church, by invoking their prayers and aid, and by striving to imitate their virtues.

They are in communion with the souls in Purgatory by helping them by their prayers and good works.

The Church is not only the family of those living in faith here on earth. It is a Communion of Saints. It reaches into eternity, embracing also all who are being purified to enter the Beatific Vision and all who are already rejoicing in the be-

See Papally Promulgated
Catechism of the Catholic Church

Q. 182. See paragraphs: 946-948, 1474-1477

holding of God's glory. Our union with those we love who have gone to sleep in the peace of Christ is not in the least interrupted. Their entrance into life has not ended their union with us. Through their entrance into life we too are brought nearer to God.

Their blessedness is not yet totally fulfilled, for they await the final resurrection and the sharing of that flesh which is part of their being in the joy of eternal life. They await the Last Judgment with the gathering into total newness of life the full number of all the redeemed. But the source of their beatitude is already theirs. They have come to see and to possess their God in the Beatific Vision.

The blessed not only enjoy the blessedness of God's immediate presence, the indescribable happiness of knowing and loving God as He knows and loves Himself, but they also contribute to the building of the Kingdom by praying for their brothers and sisters in Christ who are still here on earth. Their happiness is intensified by the realization that they can influence the salvation of those whom they know and love. They look upon the goodness and share the perfect peace of Christ as they await with joyful longing the final resurrection and final judgment when all will be made perfect in God.

Vatican Council II

"When the Lord will come in glory, and all his angels with him (cf. Mt. 25:31), death will be no more and all things will be subject to him (cf. 1 Cor. 15:26-27). But at the present time some of his disciples are pilgrims on earth. Others have died and are being purified, while still others are in glory, contemplating 'in full light, God himself triune and one, exactly as he is.' All of us, however, in varying degrees and in different ways share in the same charity towards God and our neighbors, and we all sing the one hymn of glory to our God. All, indeed, who are of Christ and who have his Spirit form one Church and in Christ cleave together" (Eph. 4:16). *The Church, 49*

Prayer: *Our Father, protect those whom You have united, and look kindly on all who follow Jesus Your Son. We are consecrated to You by our Baptism; make us one in the fullness of our Faith, and keep us one in the fellowship of love through Jesus Christ our Lord. Amen.*

Q. 183. Why is the Church called the Church Militant?

The Church is called the Church Militant because it is the Church here on earth which is still fighting against sin and error. It is also called the Pilgrim Church, since its ultimate goal is Heaven, rather than earth.

If we should fall into mortal sin, we do not cease to be members of the Communion of Saints, but we are cut off from all spiritual communion with our fellow Christians as long as we continue to exclude the Holy Spirit from our souls.

Vatican Council II

"The Church...which is called 'that Jerusalem which is above' and 'our mother,' (Gal. 4:26; cf. Apoc. 12:17), is described as the spotless spouse of the spotless lamb (Apoc. 19:7; 21:2 and 9; 22:17). It is she whom Christ 'loved and for whom He delivered himself up that he might sanctify her' (Eph. 5:26). It is she whom he united to himself by an unbreakable alliance, and whom he constantly 'nourishes and cherishes' (Eph. 5:29). It is she whom, once purified, he willed to be joined to himself, subject in love and fidelity (cf. Eph. 5:24), and whom, finally, he filled with heavenly gifts for all eternity, in order that we may know that love of God and of Christ for us, a love which surpasses all understanding (cf. Eph. 3:19). While on earth she journeys in a foreign land away from the Lord (cf. 2 Cor. 5:6), the Church sees herself as an exile. She seeks and is concerned about those things which are above, where Christ is seated at the right hand of God, where the life of the Church is hidden with Christ in God until she appears in glory with her Spouse (cf. Col. 3:1-4)." *The Church, 6*

Prayer: *Lord, unite Your Church in the Holy Spirit that we may serve You with all our hearts and work together with unselfish love. Teach us to value all the good You give us in the Catholic Church. Make us strong in faith, through Jesus Christ our Lord to Whom with You and the Holy Spirit be all honor and glory. Amen.*

See Papally Promulgated
Catechism of the Catholic Church

Q. 183. See paragraphs: 821, 827, 2725-2766, 2848-2849

Q. 184. How do we help each other?

We upon earth must pray for one another so we may all be faithful to our obligations as members of the Communion of Saints. We must also perform the spiritual and corporal works of mercy.

Vatican Council II

"The Council lays stress on respect for the human person: everyone should look upon his neighbor (without any exception) as another self, bearing in mind above all his life and the means necessary for living it in a dignified way." *Modern World, 27*

Sacred Scripture

"I desire, therefore, first of all, that supplications, prayers, intercessions and thanksgivings be made for all men."
1 Timothy 2:1

"So confess your sins to one another, and pray for one another, and this will cure you; the heartfelt prayer of a good man works very powerfully." *James 5:16*

Q. 185. What is the Church Suffering?

The Church Suffering, or the Church Expectant, consists of the souls in Purgatory. This is the Church of all the faithful departed who are saved but are still being purified in purgatorial suffering. They cannot see God, but the Holy Spirit is in them. Being made ready for Heaven, they will never again sin.

Sacred Scripture

"But the most valiant Judas exhorted the people to keep themselves from sin, forasmuch as they saw before their eyes what had happened because of the sins of those that were slain. And making a gathering, he sent twelve thousand drachms of silver to Jerusalem for sacrifice to be offered for the sins of the dead, thinking well and religiously concerning

See Papally Promulgated
Catechism of the Catholic Church

Q. 184. See paragraphs: 2447, 2634-2636
Q. 185. See paragraphs: 1030-1032

the resurrection. (For if he had not hoped that they that were slain should rise again, it would have seemed superfluous and vain to pray for the dead.) And because he considered that they who had fallen asleep with godliness had great grace laid up for them. It is therefore a holy and wholesome thought to pray for the dead, that they may be loosed from sins." *2 Maccabees 12:42-46*

Vatican Council II

"In full consciousness of this communion of the whole Mystical Body of Jesus Christ, the Church in its pilgrim members, from the very earliest days of the Christian religion, had honored with great respect the memory of the dead; and, 'because it is a holy and a wholesome thought to pray for the dead that they may be loosed from their sins' (2 Mac. 12:46) she offers her suffrages for them." *The Church, 50*

Q. 186. What is our duty toward the deceased?

We must have reverence toward the bodies of those who have gone before us in death, and we must pray for the souls of our deceased relatives and friends, and all of the faithful departed. We show respect for the bodies of the deceased because they were temples of the Holy Spirit and are destined to rise gloriously.

We can help the suffering members of God's family whose souls are being purified in Purgatory by our prayers and sacrifices, especially by participation in the Holy Sacrifice of the Mass. The souls in Purgatory also benefit from indulgences that are obtained for them. They can and do pray for us, even though they cannot help themselves. Through the Communion of Saints, we are one with those loved ones and friends of ours who rest in Christ. Once they are numbered among the saints in Heaven, they will be our special intercessors with God.

Sacred Scripture

"And they sung as it were a new hymn, before the throne

See Papally Promulgated
Catechism of the Catholic Church

Q. 186. See paragraphs: 364-366, 1032

and before the four living creatures and the ancients: and no man could say the hymn, but those hundred forty-four thousand who were purchased from the earth." *Revelation 14:3*

Vatican Council II

"This sacred council accepts loyally the venerable faith of our ancestors in the living communion which exists between us and our brothers who are in the glory of heaven or who are yet being purified after their death." *The Church, 51*

Prayer: *God, our Father, may the Sacrifice of the Mass wash away our sins in the blood of Christ. You cleansed us in the waters of Baptism; in Your loving mercy, grant us pardon and peace. In the Sacrament of the Eucharist, You give us Your crucified and risen Son. Bring to the glory of the Resurrection the departed souls who have been purified by this holy mystery. We ask this in the most holy Name of Jesus our Lord. Amen.*

Prayer

Most Providential Father, keep the Church faithful to its mission: may it be a leaven in the world that renews us in Christ and transforms us into Your family. May the Church continue to grow in holiness through the sacrifice of Christ which gave it life.

Lord God, You are the glory of believers and the life of the just. Your Son redeemed us by dying and rising to life again. Since our departed brothers and sisters believed in the mystery of Your Son's Resurrection, let them share in the joys and blessings of the life to come.

God, our Creator, by Your power, Christ conquered death and returned to You in glory. May all the people who have gone before us in faith share His victory and enjoy the vision of Your glory forever. May His perfect sacrifice free them from the power of death and give them eternal life; may it bring them peace and forgiveness. Bring the new life which You gave them in Baptism to the fullness of eternal joy. We ask this through Jesus Christ our Lord and Savior. Amen.

Chapter Eighty-Three

The Communion of Saints - II

Q. 187. What is the Church Triumphant?

The Church Triumphant consists of all the souls of the blessed in Heaven. It is the Church of all those in heavenly glory who have triumphed over their evil inclinations, the seductions of the world, and the temptations of the evil spirit.

Vatican Council II

"Our communion with those in heaven, provided that it is understood in the full light of faith, in no way diminishes the worship of adoration given to God the Father, through Christ, in the Spirit; on the contrary, it greatly enriches it."

The Church, 51

Q. 188. Why does the Church honor the canonized Saints?

The Church honors the canonized Saints who are already with the Lord in Heaven because they inspire us by the good example of their lives, and because they can help us by their prayers.

We must honor the Saints not just because they can and will pray for us, but also because our love for God demands it. The Saints are masterpieces of God's grace; when we honor them we are honoring their Maker, their Sanctifier, and their Redeemer. The Saints inspire us by the heroic example of their lives. To them we pray, asking their intercession with God for us.

Jesus, having entered glory, as the eternal High Priest, continues to pray for us. Mary, ever associated with her Son, prays for us with Him. She is not alone in this; the whole community of the blessed in Heaven imitates Christ in their continual concern for us. As we pray for one another upon earth,

See Papally Promulgated
Catechism of the Catholic Church

Q. 187. See paragraphs: 1023-1029
Q. 188. See paragraphs: 956, 1173

and for the souls in Purgatory, so our brothers and sisters in Heaven intercede for us. We are united with all of them by intimate bonds of Christian love. However, Mary, our spiritual mother, has an altogether exceptional role in this union. Among those who have been redeemed by her Son, her intercessory power is by far the most extensive and effective.

To invoke the intercession of the Saints, including Mary, is really to pray that, together with them, we may grow in the love of the triune God Who wills the salvation of all; it is to express the longing that the Saints, living in personal love of God, will also embrace us in that personal God-given love, and will, by their prayers, assist us in obtaining benefits from God.

When we honor the canonized (and uncanonized) saints, we are honoring many of our own loved ones who now are with God in Heaven, because every soul in Heaven is a saint.

Sacred Scripture

"The Lamb came forward to take the scroll from the right hand of the One sitting on the throne, and when He took it, the four animals prostrated themselves before Him and with them the twenty-four elders; each one of them was holding a harp and had a golden bowl full of incense made of the prayers of the saints." *Revelation 5:8*

"From the angel's hand, the smoke of the incense went up in the presence of God and with it the prayers of the saints." *Revelation 8:4*

Vatican Council II

"The Church has always believed that the apostles and Christ's martyrs, who gave the supreme witness of faith and charity by the shedding of their blood, are closely united with us in Christ; she has always venerated them, together with the Blessed Virgin Mary and the holy angels, with a special love, and has asked piously for the help of their intercession. Soon there were added to these others who had chosen to imitate more closely the virginity and poverty of Christ, and still others whom the outstanding practice of the Christian virtues and the wonderful graces of God recommended to the pious devotion and imitation of the faithful." *The Church, 50*

"The authentic cult of the saints does not consist so much in a multiplicity of external acts, but rather in a more intense practice of our love, whereby, for our own greater good and that of the Church, we seek from the saints 'example in their way of life, fellowship in their communion, and the help of their intercession.' " *The Church, 51*

"The Church has also included in the annual cycle, memorial days of the martyrs and other saints. Raised up to perfection by the manifold grace of God and already in possession of eternal salvation, they sing God's perfect praise in heaven and pray for us. By celebrating their anniversaries, the Church proclaims achievement of the paschal mystery in the saints who have suffered and have been glorified with Christ. She proposes them to the faithful as examples who draw all men to the Father through Christ, and through their merits she begs for God's favors." *Sacred Liturgy, 104*

"To look on the life of those who have faithfully followed Christ is to be inspired with a new reason for seeking the city which is to come, while at the same time we are taught to know a most safe path by which, despite the vicissitudes of the world, and in keeping with the state of life and condition proper to each of us, we will be able to arrive at perfect union with Christ, that is, holiness. God shows to men, in a vivid way, his presence and his face in the lives of those companions of ours in the human condition who are more perfectly transformed into the image of Christ. He speaks to us in them and offers us a sign of this kingdom, to which we are powerfully attracted, so great a cloud of witnesses is there given and such a witness to the truth of the Gospel.

"It is not merely by the title of example that we cherish the memory of those in Heaven; we seek, rather, that by this devotion to the exercise of fraternal charity the union of the whole Church in the Spirit may be strengthened. Exactly as Christian communion between men on their earthly pilgrimage brings us closer to Christ, so our community with the saints joins us to Christ, from whom as from its fountain and head issues all grace and the life of the People of God itself.

"It is most fitting, therefore, that we love those friends and co-heirs of Jesus Christ who are also our brothers and outstanding benefactors, and that we give due thanks to God for them, 'humbly invoking them, and having recourse to their prayers, their aid and help in obtaining from God through his Son, Jesus Christ, our Lord, our only Redeemer and Savior, the benefits we need.' Every authentic witness of love, indeed, offered by us to those who are in heaven tends to and terminates in Christ, 'the crown of all the saints,' and through him in God who is wonderful in his saints and is glorified in them." *The Church, 50*

Prayer: *Heavenly Father, we honor the saints who consecrated their lives to Christ for the sake of the Kingdom of Heaven. What love You show us as You recall mankind to its innocence, and invite us to taste on earth the gifts of the world to come. With the saints and all the angels, we praise You forever, through Jesus Christ our Lord to Whom with You and God the Holy Spirit be all honor and glory. Amen.*

Prayer

Good Shepherd, You made us, and we belong to You; You are our first beginning and our last end. In union with all Your saints, we praise and thank You for Your enduring love.

Preserve, O God, those who take refuge in You. By the power of Christ's Resurrection from the dead, may we attain to the fullness of joy in Your presence, in union with all Your saints.

Father, we ask You to give us victory and peace. In Jesus Christ, our Lord and King, we are already seated at Your right hand. We look forward to praising You in the fellowship of all Your saints in our heavenly homeland.

Lord God, You are glorified in Your saints, for their glory is the crowning of Your gifts. In their lives on earth, You give us an example; in our communion with them, You give us their friendship; in their prayer for the Church, You give us strength and protection. The great company of witnesses spurs us on to victory, so that we may share their prize of everlasting glory.

We honor the saints who live in Your holy city, the heavenly Jerusalem, our mother. Around Your throne the saints, our brothers and sisters, sing Your praises forever. Their glory fills us with joy, and their communion with us in Your Church gives us inspiration and strength, as we hasten on our pilgrimage of faith, eager to meet them. With their great company, and all the angels, we praise Your glory, now and forever. Amen.

The Forgiveness of Sins

Chapter Eighty-Four

The Forgiveness of Sins

Q. 189. What do we mean when we say, "I believe in the forgiveness of sins?"

When we say, "I believe in the forgiveness of sins," we mean that we believe in the pardon, not only of Original Sin, but of all personal sins, mortal and venial.

Christ died for all men. By the infinite value of His sacrifice, the sin of Adam, which we inherit, is erased.

Jesus appeared to the Apostles on Easter Sunday evening and said, 'Peace be with you,' and showed them His hands and His side. "The disciples were filled with joy when they saw the Lord, and He said to them again, 'Peace be with you. As the Father sent Me, so am I sending you.' After saying this He breathed on them and said, "Receive the Holy Spirit. For those whose sins you forgive, they are forgiven; for those whose sins you retain, they are retained'" (John 20:20-23). On this occasion Jesus instituted the Sacrament of Penance.

Jesus, then, gave Peter and the other Apostles the power to forgive and retain sins. This power is given not only to the Apostles, but also to their lawful successors. When the Sacrament of Penance is administered, the very formula of absolution notes the role of the Holy Spirit in the forgiveness of sins.

Since the Apostles and their successors cannot acquire the necessary knowledge of sin unless the penitent himself gives it to them, Jesus demands a confession or an accusation of sins.

It is also true that a sinner can be restored to grace by perfect sorrow or perfect contrition. There are no sins, however serious, for which a a repentant person cannot find forgiveness from God. A merciful Father has compassion on His children who want to love and serve Him.

See Papally Promulgated
Catechism of the Catholic Church

Q. 189. See paragraphs: 976-987

" 'Come now, let us reason together,' says the Lord. 'Though your sins are like scarlet, they shall be white as snow; though they are red as crimson, they shall be like wool' " (Isaiah 1:18).

"For the mountains shall depart, and the hills shaken, but My love for you will never leave you and the covenant of My peace with you will never be removed, says the Lord Who has mercy toward you" (Isaiah 54:10).

Jesus is the Lamb of God Who takes away the sins of the world. Our sins are washed away in His blood: that blood is offered to God in the Mass.

Certainly Christ did not take away the sins of future men unconditionally, but He provided the means by which our sins can be forgiven, as long as we cooperate with grace. We receive this particular grace through the sacraments of Baptism and Penance.

Christ merited for us the benefits of His Redemption. He fully satisfied the justice of God for the infinite offense of sin; He freed mankind from its slavery; He made it possible for man to be united with God on earth by regaining for him the grace of divine life, that is, sanctifying grace. Thus man became an adopted son of God and an heir to Heaven.

The Catholic Church believes that sins forgiven are actually removed from the soul and not merely covered over by the merits of Christ. Only God can forgive sins, since He alone can restore sanctifying grace to a person who has sinned gravely and thereby lost the state of grace. God forgives the grave or mortal sins of the truly repentant sinner either immediately through an act of perfect contrition or immediately through the sacrament.

The sacraments primarily directed to the forgiveness of sins are Baptism and Penance, and secondarily, under certain conditions, the Sacrament of the Anointing of the Sick.

Vatican Council II

"Since human freedom has been weakened by sin it is only by the help of God's grace that man can give his actions their full and proper relationship to God. Before the judgment seat of God an account of his own life will be rendered to each one according as he has done either good or evil."

Modern World, 17

Prayer: *Father, we have wounded the Heart of Jesus Your Son, but He brings us forgiveness and grace. Help us to prove our grateful love and to make amends for our sins. Look on the Heart of Christ Your Son filled with love for us. Because of His love accept our contrition and forgive our sins.*

You know our hearts, Lord, but You are slow to anger and merciful in judging. Come, examine Your Church; wash her clean of sin. Forgive the sins of our youth and stupidity, and remember us with Your love. May the fire of Your word consume our sins, and its brightness illumine our hearts. Let us feel the healing calm of Your forgiveness. We ask this through Jesus Christ our Lord. Amen.

Prayer

Almighty Father, apart from You there is nothing true, nothing holy on earth. Forgive our sins, and give us strength in our weakness, so that we who believe in Your Son may rejoice in His glory.

Do not abandon us, Lord our God; You did not forget the broken body of Your Christ, nor the mockery His love received. We, Your children, are weighed down with sin; give us the fullness of Your mercy.

Almighty God, remember our lowliness and have mercy on us. Free us today from sin and give us a share in Your inheritance. We ask this in the Name of our Merciful Lord and Savior, Jesus Christ. Amen.

The Sacraments - I

——

Channels of Grace

Baptism
Confirmation
Penance
Holy Orders
Anointing of the Sick
Matrimony
the Holy Eucharist

The Sacraments
in General

Chapter Eighty-Five

Sacraments — Actions of Christ - I

Q. 190. How is the saving work of Christ continued?

The saving work of Christ is continued in the Catholic Church, especially through the seven sacraments which He instituted. The Holy Spirit gives His grace through the sacraments and sanctifies souls.

Through the gift of the Holy Spirit, the Catholic Church enjoys the presence of Christ in the sacraments and carries on His ministry and saving mission.

Jesus promised to remain with us, through the Holy Spirit. He promised this the night before He died, "But I tell you the truth. It is expedient to you that I go, for if I do not go, the Paraclete will not come to you. But if I go, I will send Him to you. And when He is come, He will convince the world of sin, and of justice, and of judgment. Of sin, because they believed not in Me. And of justice, because I go to the Father; and you shall see Me no longer. And of judgment, because the prince of this world is already judged. I have yet many things to say to you, but you cannot bear them now. But when He, the Spirit of truth, is come, He will teach you all truth. For He shall not speak of Himself; but whatever things He shall hear, He shall speak; and the things that are to come, He shall show you. He shall glorify Me; because He shall receive of Mine, and shall show it to you" (John 16: 7-14).

"A little while, and now you shall not see Me, and again a little while you shall see Me, because I go to the Father" (John 16:10).

Before ascending into Heaven, Jesus gave His Apostles a command to teach all nations and baptize them: "Teach them to observe all things whatever I have commanded you; and *behold I am with you all days, even to the consummation of the world*" (Matthew: 28:20).

See Papally Promulgated
Catechism of the Catholic Church

Q. 190. See paragraphs: 687-690, 1076, 1091-1112

Vatican Council II

"By his power he [Christ] is present in the sacraments so that when anybody baptizes it is really Christ himself who baptizes. He is present in his word since it is he himself who speaks when the holy scriptures are read in the Church. Lastly, he is present when the Church prays and sings, for he has promised 'Where two or three are gathered together in my name, there am I in the midst of them' (Matthew 18:20)."

Sacred Liturgy, 7

Prayer: *Jesus, You speak of the Holy Spirit as the "Paraclete" because You send Him from Heaven as a witness, advisor, strengthener and consoler.*

The mission of the Paraclete is to act as Your Witness before the world. He does so by defending Your character and authority. He also defends the integrity of the doctrine of the disciples who are Your representatives in the work of saving souls.

He will convince of sin and wrong-doing those who have rejected You and Your disciples. He will convince men of Your supreme justice and holiness, for it is through You alone that the Father has revealed His own infinite holiness. Finally, He will act as Heaven's official Witness in the judgment of the world.

Divine Spirit, enlighten us and give us strength so that we may continue on the path of virtue. No man who has surrendered to You the guidance of his soul has ever failed to reach the port of salvation. We ask this in the Name of Jesus. Amen.

Prayer

Holy Spirit of Truth, enkindle in our hearts the desire for invisible, supernatural riches, and never allow us to be guided by the deceitful spirit of the world, the spirit of the carnal man, or the spirit of self-love. May we never take a single step in matters concerning our salvation, without having previously implored Your divine help, through Christ our Lord. Amen.

Chapter Eighty-Six

Sacraments — Actions of Christ - II

Q. 191. What means does the Church have for carrying on Christ's work?

The Church has been given the sacraments, which Christ instituted, as the special means of carrying on Christ's work.

The sacraments are special actions of the Church through which the life of God is given to His people.

Sacred Scripture

"And Jesus coming, spoke to them, saying, 'All power is given to Me in Heaven and in earth. Go therefore, teach all nations, baptizing them in the Name of the Father and of the Son and of the Holy Spirit.' " *Matthew 28:18-19*

"He breathed on them, and He said to them, 'Receive the Holy Spirit. Whose sins you shall forgive, they are forgiven them, and whose sins you shall retain, they are retained.' "
John 20:22-23

Vatican Council II

"Accordingly, just as Christ was sent by the Father so also he sent the apostles, filled with the Holy Spirit. This he did so that they might preach the Gospel to every creature and proclaim that the Son of God by his death and resurrection had freed us from the power of Satan and from death, and brought us into the Kingdom of his Father. But he also willed that the work of salvation which they preached should be set in train through the sacrifice and sacraments, around which the entire liturgical life revolves." *Sacred Liturgy, 6*

Prayer: *God our Father, by Your gifts to us on earth we already share in Your life. In all we do, guide us to the light of Your Kingdom. May*

See Papally Promulgated
Catechism of the Catholic Church

Q. 191. See paragraphs: 1076, 1210-1211

the grace of the sacraments, especially Penance and the Eucharist, help us to reject all that is harmful; bless us with Your spiritual gifts and give us the Spirit of Love Who allows us to share in Your life.

By Your grace, allow us to come to the sacraments with renewed life. Especially through the Eucharist, may we give You worthy praise. May the holy gifts we receive help us to worship You in truth, and to receive Your sacraments with faith. We ask this through Jesus Christ our Lord to Whom with You and the Holy Spirit be all honor and glory. Amen.

Q. 192. What are the sacraments?

The Church teaches that sacraments are sensible signs, instituted by Jesus Christ, through which invisible grace and inward sanctification are communicated to the soul.

The sacraments then are outward signs of both God's grace coming to men and of men's faith. By words and signs they nourish, strengthen, and express faith. Moreover, they impart grace which helps us to worship God and practice charity.

As visible signs, they tell us that God's grace is given to the souls of the persons who receive them. We perceive the signs with our eyes, but it is only through faith that we can know that God's grace is given to us. We believe this on the word of Christ Himself, Who gave us the sacraments that we might share God's own life through grace. This grace helps us to worship God and to love Him and our neighbor.

In the sacraments, the words together with the action make up the sign. Water, since it is so necessary for life, can be used as a sign of life, and, as a sign of divine life in Baptism. Baptism not only signifies life; it really produces it. Oil is used to strengthen and heal the body. It is used in Confirmation and in the Anointing of the Sick to show the strength

See Papally Promulgated
Catechism of the Catholic Church

Q. 192. See paragraphs: 1091-1092, 1097-1098, 1122-1126, 1210-1211

which we receive from this sacrament and also to give that strength to us. Confirmation not only signifies strength, but gives it. Anointing of the Sick is not only a sign of health, but gives it.

Vatican Council II

"The purpose of the sacraments is to sanctify men, to build up the Body of Christ, and finally, to give worship to God. Because they are signs, they also instruct. They not only presuppose faith, but by words and objects they also nourish, strengthen, and express it. That is why they are called 'sacraments of faith.' They do, indeed, confer grace, but, in addition, the very act of celebrating them most effectively disposes the faithful to receive this grace to their profit, to worship God duly, and to practice charity." *Sacred Liturgy, 59*

"In the Christian community itself on the other hand, especially for those who seem to have little understanding or belief underlying their practice, the preaching of the Word is required for the sacramental ministry itself, since the sacraments are sacraments of faith, drawing their origin and nourishment from the Word." *Priests, 4*

Prayer

Father, Creator, You give the world new life by Your sacraments. May we, Your Church, grow in Your life of grace and continue to receive Your help on earth. Through the sacraments, may we receive the grace to cast off our old ways of life and to redirect our course toward the life of Heaven. May Your holy sacraments bring us life and holiness, cleanse and renew us, bring us Your help, and lead us to salvation.

Lord, may the mysteries we receive, especially in the Eucharist, heal us, remove sin from our hearts, and make us stronger under Your constant protection. You have given us these gifts to honor Your Name; let them become a source of health and strength for us.

As a man like us, Jesus wept for Lazarus, His friend; as the eternal God, He raised Lazarus from the dead. In His love for us all, Christ gives us the sacraments to bring us to everlasting life.

Father, may Christ's presence in the sacraments bring lasting light to Your people and lead us to eternal life. Amen.

Chapter Eighty-Seven

Sacraments — Actions of Christ - III

Q. 193. What do the sacraments show?

The sacraments show that (1) *God wants to make man holy* and that (2) *man wants to receive this holiness.* In this way the sacraments bring us God's grace.

1. *The sacraments show that God wants to make man holy.*

The sacraments are the signs that Christ instituted. They signify the gift of grace and produce it. Their very institution shows God's intention to make men holy, since through the sacraments He gives men His grace. By grace we share in the very life of God Himself. We are God's temples and God lives in us. We are truly children of God through grace, as St. John says: "Behold what manner of charity the Father has bestowed upon us, that we should be called, and should be the sons of God. Therefore the world knows not us, because it knew not Him" (1 John 3:1).

2. *The sacraments show that man wants to receive this holiness.*

We show our willingness to receive Christ's grace if we frequently and earnestly receive the sacraments for our sanctification. We cannot afford to neglect the means God has given us to help us grow holy and pleasing to Him by sharing His divine life.

Sacred Scripture

"For I have received of the Lord that which I also delivered to you, that the Lord Jesus, the same night in which He was betrayed, took bread. And giving thanks, broke and said, 'Take and eat. This is My Body, which shall be delivered for you. Do this as a commemoration of Me.' In like manner also the chalice, after He had supped, saying, 'This chalice is the

See Papally Promulgated
Catechism of the Catholic Church

Q. 193. See paragraphs: 2002-2003, 2013, 2014

New Testament in My Blood. Do this as often as you shall drink of it in commemoration of Me.' " *1 Corinthians 11:23-25*

Vatican Council II

"The liturgy, then, is rightly seen as an exercise of the priestly office of Jesus Christ. It involves the presentation of man's sanctification under the guise of signs perceptible by the senses and its accomplishment in ways appropriate to each of these signs. In it full public worship is performed by the Mystical Body of Jesus Christ, that is, by the Head and his members." *Sacred Liturgy, 7*

"The apostolate of the laity is a sharing in the salvific mission of the Church. Through Baptism and Confirmation all are appointed to this apostolate by the Lord himself. Moreover, by the sacraments, and especially by the Eucharist, that love of God and man which is the soul of the apostolate is communicated and nourished." *The Church, 33*

"The purpose of the sacraments is to sanctify men, to build up the Body of Christ, and, finally, to give worship to God. Because they are signs they also instruct. They not only presuppose faith, but by words and objects they also nourish, strengthen, and express it. That is why they are called 'sacraments of faith.' They do, indeed, confer grace, but, in addition, the very act of celebrating them most effectively disposes the faithful to receive this grace to their profit, to worship God daily, and to practice charity.

"It is, therefore, of the greatest importance that the faithful should easily understand the sacramental signs, and should eagerly frequent those sacraments which were instituted to nourish the Christian life." *Sacred Liturgy, 59*

Roman Curial Documents

"The Church always enjoys Christ's presence and ministers to him, the mystery of Christ continues in the Church, specifically through those signs instituted by Christ which signify and produce the gift of grace and which are known as sacraments...

"The sacraments are the primary and fundamental actions by which Jesus Christ constantly bestows his Spirit on the faithful, making them a holy people who, in him and with him, offer themselves as an acceptable offering to the Father. The sacraments are surely to be regarded as being of inestimable value to the Church, to which belongs the power to administer them. They must always however be referred to Christ, from whom their effectiveness derives. In fact, it is Christ who baptizes. It is not so much a man who celebrates the Eucharist, as Christ himself; he offers himself by the ministry of priests in the sacrifice of the Mass. The sacramental action is, first and foremost, Christ's action and the Church's ministers are, as it were, his instruments."

The General Catechetical Directory, 55
[issued by the Sacred Congregation for the Clergy, 1971]

Prayer: *All-powerful and ever-living God, fill Your Church with Your love and give Your help to all who call on You in faith. May the power of Your word and sacraments bring strength to the people who gather to worship You. May Your truth grow in our hearts. May we worship You always in Your holy temple, and come one day to rejoice with all the saints in Your presence, through Christ our Lord. Amen.*

Prayer

God, our Father, from living stones, Your Chosen People, You built an eternal temple to Your glory. Increase the spiritual gifts of grace You have given to Your Church through the sacraments, so that Your faithful people may continue to grow into the new and eternal Jerusalem.

Lord, God of the living, You give us lasting youth through the waters of rebirth, and happiness through the Bread of Life. Do not desert us when we are in need of Your help, but give us the grace to follow You in both good times and bad, so that we may forever praise Your faithfulness.

Heavenly Father, You call Your people to be Your Church. As we gather together in Your Name, may we love, honor, and follow You to eternal life in the Kingdom You promise. May we who share the sacraments of Your Church experience the life and power they promise and hear the answers to our prayers. You make Your Church on earth a sign of the new and eternal Jerusalem. By sharing in the sacraments, especially in the Eucharist, may we become the temple of Your presence and the home of Your glory. We ask this in the Name of Jesus Christ our Lord and Savior. Amen.

Chapter Eighty-Eight

Sacraments — Actions of Christ - IV

Q. 194. Why are the sacraments called actions of Christ?

Sacraments are called actions of Christ because (1) *through them He gives His Spirit to Christians and makes them a holy people*, and (2) *from Christ they get their power to make men holy.*

1. *Sacraments are called actions of Christ because through them He gives His Spirit to Christians and makes them a holy people.*

Sacraments are the principal and fundamental actions whereby Jesus Christ unceasingly bestows His Spirit on the faithful, thus making them the holy people who offer themselves, in Him and with Him, as an offering acceptable to the Father.

In the sacraments Christ gives us His grace, which He bought for us on the Cross, to help us become more like Him. In every sacrament, it is Christ our High Priest Who brings His grace to us. The priests who administer the sacraments are His ordained representatives.

2. *Sacraments are called actions of Christ because from Christ they get their power to make us holy.*

To the Church belongs the power of administering the sacraments; and yet they are always to be referred to Christ, Who acts in and through them. It is from Christ that they receive their power. It is Christ Who baptizes. It is not so much a man who celebrates the Eucharist as Christ Himself; for He it is Who offers Himself in the Sacrifice of the Mass by the ministry of the priests. Priests offer the Holy Sacrifice of the Mass in the Person of Christ. The sacramental action is, in

See Papally Promulgated
Catechism of the Catholic Church

Q. 194. See paragraphs: 1084, 1118

the first place, the action of Christ, and the priests of the Church are His instruments.

Sacred Scripture

"Now when the Apostles, who were in Jerusalem, had heard that Samaria had received the word of God, they sent unto them Peter and John, who, when they arrived, prayed for them that they might receive the Holy Spirit. For He was not as yet come upon any of them. But they were only baptized in the Name of the Lord Jesus. Then they laid their hands upon them, and they received the Holy Spirit."

Acts 8:14-17

Vatican Council II

"By his power he is present in the sacraments so that when anybody baptizes it is really Christ himself Who baptizes."

Sacred Liturgy, 7

"For it is the liturgy through which, especially in the divine sacrifice of the Eucharist, 'the work of our redemption is accomplished,' and it is through the liturgy, especially, that the faithful are enabled to express in their lives and manifest to others the mystery of Christ and the real nature of the true Church. The Church is essentially both human and divine, visible but endowed with invisible realities, zealous in action and dedicated to contemplation, present in the world, but as a pilgrim, so constituted that in her the human is directed toward and subordinated to the divine, the visible to the invisible, action to contemplation, and this present world to that city yet to come, the object of our quest." *Sacred Liturgy, 2*

Prayer: *Jesus, we believe that true life is found only in God, and that He, in His infinite love, has found a way to share His life with us. Since You, the Eternal Word, are truly divine, You possess true life in all its fullness, even as the Father possesses it. You lovingly and generously give that divine life to us through the sacraments and prayer.*

As adults, before we are able to receive Your divine life, we must believe in You and give You a love so deep and strong that it doesn't rest until, in a sense, we have become one with You as the vine is one with the branches. You said, "I am the vine; you the branches. He that abides in Me, and I in him, the same bears much fruit: for without Me you can do nothing" (John 15:5). Lord, through Your sacraments, increase our love for You. Amen.

Prayer

Lord Jesus, through the sacraments You live on in us, and we, in You. As the Vine, You give us Your grace, and with the help of this grace we can bear fruit and live virtuous lives. You compare grace to the vital sap circulating through the vine. The stem and the branches are one and the same, nourished and acting together, producing the same fruits because they are fed by the same sap. You teach us that, in the same way, You and the faithful are united in one body.

Severed from the head, the life-giving center, a bodily member must necessarily die. Preserve us from such a spiritual death. Help us to continue to share in Your pure life through prayer and the sacraments, especially the Holy Eucharist. Increase our love, for only then can we really possess You by grace in this world, and see You and possess You eternally in the next. Amen.

Chapter Eighty-Nine

The Purpose of the Sacraments - I

Q. 195. What is the purpose of the sacraments?

The purpose of the sacraments is (1) *to make men holy;* (2) *to build up the Body of Christ, the Church;* (3) *to give worship to God;* and, because they are signs, (4) *to instruct.*

1. *The purpose of the sacraments is to make men holy.*

The sacraments are the ordinary channels of God's grace and are necessary to keep and nourish the life of grace in our souls. St. John reminds us that Jesus gives us His grace in order to sanctify us: "And of His fullness we all have received, and grace for grace. For the law was given by Moses; grace and truth came by Jesus Christ" (John 1: 16-17).

2. *The purpose of the sacraments is to build up the Body of Christ, the Church.*

Each of the sacraments plays an indispensable part in the life of the Church, that is, the Mystical Body of Christ. Among them, Baptism, Confirmation, Marriage, and Holy Orders confer a distinct office.

Baptism makes us members of the Body of Christ and gives us a share in the priesthood of Christ. Confirmation makes us mature and responsible Christians and increases our participation in Christ's priesthood. Holy Orders confers the actual power of the ministerial priesthood and provides for the continuation of the Church. Marriage makes a man and woman one; it provides for the growth of the Body of Christ by conferring the vocation of parenthood and by guaranteeing the graces which enable parents to guide the new members of Christ. The Anointing of the Sick prepares us for entrance into the ranks of the Church Triumphant in

See Papally Promulgated
Catechism of the Catholic Church

Q. 195. See paragraphs: 1123, 1128

Heaven. The Sacrament of Penance grants us pardon for our sins and the strength we need to resist temptation. The Sacrament of the Eucharist nourishes our souls, and gives us an increase of the power to love God and our neighbor.

Prayer: *Lord God, Heavenly Father, Your only Son revealed Himself to us by becoming man. May we who share His humanity come to share His divinity through the grace of Your sacraments. May we hear Your Son's words with faith and become Your children in name and in fact.*

Grant Your people Your protection and grace through Your sacraments. Give them health of mind and body, perfect love for one another, and the strength to remain always faithful to You. Free us from our sins and make us worthy of Your healing. Look upon our weakness and reach out to help us with Your loving power, that we may give You loving service, through Jesus, our Savior. Amen.

3. *The purpose of the sacraments* is *to give worship to God.*

By means of the Eucharist, for example, Christ continually re-offers Himself to the Father through the ministry of His priests in the Sacrifice of the Mass. This is the greatest act of worship that can be given to God, because it is offered by the God-man in the spirit in which He offered Himself on the Cross for our redemption. All of us, members of Christ's Mystical Body, can participate in this oblation, or offering, and thereby give worthy adoration, thanksgiving, and atonement to God.

4. *The purpose of the sacraments is to instruct.*

Signs are actions which convey an idea. Words are signs which convey an idea. In the sacraments the words, together with the action, make up the sacred sign.

Sacred Scripture

"Is any man sick among you? Let him bring in the priests of the Church, and let them pray over him, anointing him with oil in the name of the Lord. And the prayer of faith shall save the sick man. And the Lord shall raise him up. And if he has committed sins, they shall be forgiven him." *James 5:14-15*

"The purpose of the sacraments is to sanctify men, to build up the Body of Christ, and, finally, to give worship to God. Because they are signs they also instruct. They not only presuppose faith, but by words and objects they also strengthen and express it. That is why they are called 'sacraments of faith.' They do, indeed, confer grace, but, in addition, the very act of celebrating them most effectively disposes the faithful to receive this grace to their profit, to worship God duly, and to practice charity." *Sacred Liturgy, 59*

Prayer

Father, our source of life, You know our weakness. May we reach out with joy to grasp Your hand and walk more readily in Your ways. May the healing power of Your grace, received through the sacraments and prayer, free us from sin and help us to approach You with pure hearts. Keep us from our old and sinful ways and help us to continue in the new life of grace.

Lord God, we thank You for Your Church in which You bless Your family as we come to You in pilgrimage. In Your Church, You reveal Your presence by sacramental signs and make us one with You through the invisible bond of grace. You bring the Church to its full stature as the Body of Christ throughout the world so that it may reach its perfection at last in the heavenly city of Jerusalem, which is the vision of Your peace. In communion with all the angels and saints, we praise Your greatness forever and ever. Amen.

Chapter Ninety

The Purpose of the Sacraments - II

Q. 196. Why does the Church urge Catholics to receive the sacraments?

The Church urges Catholics to receive the sacraments often and with great faith and eagerness, because the sacraments were instituted to nourish Christian life.

Christ Himself determined the signs to be used in the sacraments. He made them the instruments He uses to produce grace in us. This is what we mean when we say that Christ instituted the sacraments. There are references in the Bible to Christ's institution of Baptism, Penance, the Eucharist, and Holy Orders. (Cf. Matthew 9:2, Matthew 28:19-20, John 3:5, John 6:52, John 20:21-23, Acts 8:14-20, Romans 6:3-4, 1 Corinthians 10:17, 1 John 1:9.) The Church infallibly teaches that He also instituted the other sacraments.

Three of the sacraments: Baptism, Confirmation, and Holy Orders, produce in the soul a mark which can never be lost. This mark or character is a kind of badge of our membership in Christ, a participation in His eternal priesthood, by which we are dedicated to sacred worship. Baptism and Confirmation can be received only once. Holy Orders confers the grace of the diaconate, the priesthood, and the episcopate only once.

The more faith and love we have when we receive a sacrament, the more grace it will give us. We must not neglect the means God has given us to grow holy and pleasing to Him by sharing His divine life.

Sacred Scripture

"These [the seven candidates for the diaconate] they set before the Apostles. And they praying, imposed hands on them."

Acts 6:6

See Papally Promulgated
Catechism of the Catholic Church

Q. 196. See paragraphs: 1122-1134

"And when they had ordained to them priests in every church and had prayed with fasting, they commended them to the Lord." *Acts 14:22*

Vatican Council II

"It is therefore, of the greatest importance that the faithful should easily understand the sacramental signs, and should eagerly frequent those sacraments which were instituted to nourish the Christian life." *Sacred Liturgy, 59*

Prayer: *Heavenly Father, may the frequent use of Your sacraments make us Your obedient people. May the love within us be seen in what we do, and lead us to the joy of Heaven. Look upon our weakness, and through the power of the sacraments, bring us purity and strength. May the sacraments we receive cleanse us of our sins and free us from guilt. May our sins bring us sorrow and Your promise of salvation bring us joy. To You be all honor and glory. Amen.*

Prayer

Father, our source of life, You know our weakness. May we reach out with joy to grasp Your hand and walk more readily in Your ways. May Your grace, received through the frequent use of Your sacraments, make our souls more pleasing to You.

Lord God, in Your great mercy, enrich Your people with Your grace, especially through the sacraments, and strengthen them by Your blessing so that they may praise You always. We come, reborn in the Spirit, to celebrate our sonship in the Lord Jesus Christ. Touch our hearts, and help them grow toward the life You have promised. Touch our lives, and make them signs of Your love for all men.

Let Your Word, Father, be a lamp for our feet and a light to our path, above all through frequent reception of Your sacraments and through prayer, so that we may understand what You wish to teach us and follow the path that Your light marks out for us. Help us, and we shall be saved, Lord God; leave us, and we are doomed. May You remain with us always so that the fullness of life may be ours, through Christ, our Lord. Amen.

Chapter Ninety-One

The Purpose of the Sacraments and the Sacramentals

Q. 197. What are the purposes of the sacraments?

The sacraments are: (1) *sources of grace for individuals and communities* and are (2) *remedies for sin and the effects of sin.* As mentioned in Chapter Eighty-Five, the sacraments are also signs of faith.

1. *The sacraments are sources of grace for individuals and communities.*

All the sacraments produce sanctifying grace. In addition, each sacrament gives its own particular actual graces and a right to future actual graces. A sacrament is a sacred sign instituted by Christ to give grace. The graces are given for the benefit of the person who receives the sacrament, and also for the benefit of the entire community of faith. The sacraments are instruments of divine life for the family of God.

2. *The sacraments are remedies for sin and the effects of sin.*

Mortal sin is the greatest evil in the world because it drives the supernatural life of sanctifying grace out of our souls and turns us away from God, the source of all life, peace, and joy. Our Lord protects our souls from serious sin by giving us more sanctifying grace in the sacraments, especially in the Holy Eucharist.

The actual graces we receive through the sacraments give us the light we need to see what is evil and the strength we need to fight against it. In this way our souls are strengthened against temptation.

This is especially true of the Holy Eucharist, for Jesus said, "This is the bread which comes down from Heaven; that if any

See Papally Promulgated
Catechism of the Catholic Church

Q. 197. See paragraphs: 1262, 1301, 1365-1383, 1391-1405, 1467-1468, 1496, 1519-1520, 1532, 1581-1584, 1638-1642

410

man eat of it, he may not die" (John 6:50). Just as bodily food repairs what we lose by daily wear and tear, so likewise this divine food is a remedy for the spiritual infirmities of each day. The sacramental grace we receive in the Sacrament of Penance is a remedy for our spiritual sicknesses and for all the effects of sin.

Vatican Council II

"The purpose of the sacraments is to sanctify men, to build up the Body of Christ, and, finally, to give worship to God. Because they are signs they also instruct. They not only presuppose faith, but by words and objects they also nourish, strengthen, and express it. That is why they are called 'sacraments of faith.' They do, indeed, confer grace, but, in addition, the very act of celebrating them most effectively disposes the faithful to receive this grace to their profit, to worship God duly, and to practice charity. " *Sacred Liturgy, 59*

> **Prayer:** *Lord God, Maker of Heaven and earth and of all created things, You make Your just ones holy through Your sacraments. In You is fullness of life for Your faithful people; in You all hope resides. Lead us to everlasting happiness through the sacramental blessings given us in Your holy Church. Through the power of the sacraments deliver us from evil and from slavery to the senses, which blind us to goodness. Free us from all negligence and sloth, and give us joy in Your gifts of grace, through our Savior Jesus Christ. Amen.*

Q. 198. What are sacramentals?

Sacramentals are blessings, ceremonies, or religious articles instituted by the Church for our use, in order to increase our devotion and to aid in our salvation.

The difference between sacraments and sacramentals is that the sacraments were instituted by Jesus Christ; they give grace to our souls by their own power. The sacramentals

See Papally Promulgated
Catechism of the Catholic Church

Q. 198. See paragraphs: 1667-1670

were instituted by the Church, and are helps to us in receiving God's graces, chiefly through the intercession of the Church.

Sacred Scripture

"And God wrought by the hand of Paul more than common miracles. So that even there were brought from his body to the sick, handkerchiefs and aprons. And the diseases departed from them and the wicked spirits went out of them."

Acts 19:11-12

Q. 199. What is the effect of the sacramentals?

By the proper use of sacramentals, men are disposed to receive the chief effect of the sacraments, and various occasions in life are rendered holy.

Q. 200. What are some of the sacramentals?

Some of the sacramentals are: (a) The consecration and dedication of churches; (b) the blessing pronounced on men and women who enter a Religious brotherhood or sisterhood; (c) the blessing given in the Nuptial Mass to the bride, and, the blessing given to a mother after childbirth; (d) the sign of the Cross; (e) various blessed articles, like Rosaries, scapulars, medals, candles, palms, ashes, holy water, holy oil, and incense.

See Papally Promulgated
Catechism of the Catholic Church

Q. 199. See paragraphs: 1668-1670
Q. 200. See paragraphs: 1671-1673

Prayer

Almighty Father, strong is Your justice and great is Your mercy. Protect us in the burdens and challenges of life, especially through the grace of the sacraments that were given to us by Your beloved Son. Shield our minds from the distortion of pride and fill our hearts with desire for the beauty of Your truth. Help us to become more aware of Your loving design so that we may more willingly give our lives in service to You, and to our neighbor for Your sake. You promised to remain forever with those who do what is just and right. Help us to live in Your presence and to find joy in the blessings of Your grace.

God of peace, Who brought back from the dead the great Shepherd of the flock, our Lord Jesus Christ, by the blood of the new and everlasting covenant, equip us thoroughly to do Your will by the sacraments of the Church, so that we may please You in all our actions; through the same Christ our Lord, to Whom be honor and glory forever.

Gracious Father, accept our worship of praise and supplication in the Holy Sacrifice of the Mass. Give us unshakable faith, firm hope, and sincere love. Bless our comings and our goings, our deeds and our desires, our work and our prayer.

Blessed and praised be Your precious Name and Your mighty power. Amen.

The Individual Sacraments: Baptism Confirmation Penance

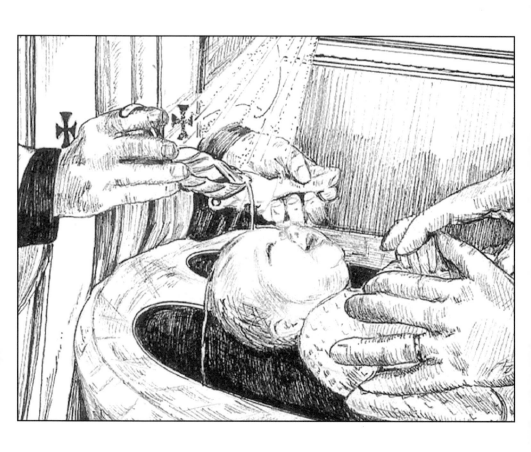

Chapter Ninety-Two

The Sacrament of Baptism - I

Q. 201. What is Baptism?

Baptism is the sacrament (1) *of our rebirth as children of God,* (2) *of our unity with Jesus in His death and Resurrection,* (3) *of our being cleansed of Original Sin and personal sins,* and (4) *of our being welcomed into the community of the Church, the Mystical Body of Christ.*

1. *Baptism is the sacrament of our rebirth as children of God.*

Baptism is directed toward our participation in the fullness of Christ's divine life. By this sacrament a man becomes truly incorporated into Christ and is reborn to a sharing in the divine life. Baptism is our new birth as children of God, a beginning of a new life in us, God's own life of grace brought to us by Jesus Christ.

It is Christ Himself Who baptizes and makes us holy with the gifts of the Holy Spirit and impresses on the soul a character or mark that cannot be taken away.

2. *Baptism is the sacrament of our unity with Jesus in His death and Resurrection.*

Baptism unites the new Christian so closely with Jesus that he shares in Christ's death and Resurrection. Through this sacrament he dies to his old self and rises to new life. St. Paul says, "Know you not that all we, who are baptized in Christ Jesus, are baptized in His death? For we are buried together with Him by Baptism into death; that as Christ is risen from the dead by the glory of the Father, so we also may walk in newness of life" (Romans 6:3-4).

3. *Baptism cleanses the soul from Original Sin and from all personal sins.*

See Papally Promulgated
Catechism of the Catholic Church

Q. 201. See paragraph: 1213

417

The result of Baptism is that a person is reconciled with God. His sins are forgiven, he receives a sharing in the life of God, and becomes part of God's people. Jesus said, "For God so loved the world as to give His only begotten Son; so that whoever believes in Him may not perish, but may have life everlasting. For God did not send His Son into the world to judge the world, but that the world may be saved by Him" (John 3:16-17).

Water is a sign of life-giving and of cleansing. The words signify that the life the person enters is that of God the Father, God the Son, and God the Holy Spirit. The Holy Spirit unites us to Jesus, so that we may share with Him the life of God He brought into the world.

4. *A person enters the Church by a new birth in Baptism.*

The Church has always held that Baptism is necessary to become a member. For the believing Christian, the Catholic Church is the only place where he can live out his faith to the fullest. He needs to hear the Gospel again and again and to be a part of the continuing work of Jesus in the world. He needs the company of his fellow Christians as he grows in faith.

Sacred Scripture

"They, therefore, that received his [Peter's] word were baptized. And there were added that day about three thousand souls." Acts 2:41

"He that believes and is baptized, shall be saved: but he that believes not, shall be condemned." Mark 16:16

St. John says, "And as many as received Him, He gave them power to be made the sons of God, to them that believe in His name" (John 1:12). Jesus said to Nicodemus, "Amen, amen I say to you, unless a man is born again, he cannot see the Kingdom of God" (John 3:3).

Vatican Council II

"From the marriage of Christians there comes the family in which new citizens of human society are born and, by the grace of the Holy Spirit in Baptism, those are made children of God so that the People of God may be perpetuated throughout the centuries." The Church, 11

"By the sacrament of Baptism, whenever it is properly conferred in the way the Lord determined and received with the

418

proper dispositions of soul, man becomes truly incorporated into the crucified and glorified Christ and is reborn to a sharing of the divine life, as the Apostle says: 'For you were buried together with Him in baptism, and in Him also rose again through faith in the working of God who raised Him from the dead' (Romans 6:4)." *Ecumenism, 22*

"By Baptism men are grafted into the paschal mystery of Christ; they die with Him, are buried with Him, and rise with Him; they receive the spirit of adoption as sons 'in which we cry, Abba, Father' (Rom. 8:15), and thus become true adorers such as the Father seeks." *Sacred Liturgy, 6*

Prayer: *Lord God, in Baptism we die with Christ to rise again in Him. Strengthen us by Your Spirit to walk in the newness of life as Your adopted children. You have renewed us in Baptism in the likeness of Christ Your Son and have united us to Your priestly people.*

Accept us through the sacrifice of Your Son offered by Your Church. Keep us one in Christ Jesus the Lord, and may our names be written in the Book of Life, for we are born to new life by water and the Holy Spirit, through Jesus Christ our Lord. Amen.

Prayer

Father in *Heaven*, *You* gave us the *Easter* mystery as our covenant of reconciliation. *May* the new birth we celebrate in *Baptism* show its effects in the way we live. *Bring* to perfection the spirit of life we receive from *Your* heavenly gifts. *Free* us from our attachment to the passing things of life and help us to set our hearts on the *Kingdom* of *Heaven*.

You are present in the *Sacrament* of our *Baptism*. *Renew Your Spirit* of adoption in us who were born again in this sacrament. *May* the work of our humble service be brought to perfection by *Your* mighty power. *Quicken* the spirit of sonship in *Your Church*, and renew us in mind and body to give *You* whole-hearted service. *May* all of us, who were buried with *Christ* in the death of *Baptism*, also rise with *Him* to newness of life.

Heavenly Father, we have been buried with *Christ* in *Baptism*, so that we may rise with *Him* to a new life. *We* now renew the promises we made in *Baptism* when we rejected satan and his works, and promised to serve *You* faithfully in *Your* holy *Catholic Church*.

We reject satan, and all his works, and all his empty promises. *We* reject sin, so as to live in the freedom of *God's* children. *We* reject the glamor of evil, and refuse to be mastered by sin. *We* reject satan, father of sin and the prince of darkness. *We* believe in *You*, *God* the *Father Almighty*, *Creator* of *Heaven* and earth. *We* believe in *Jesus Christ*, *Your* only *Son*, our *Lord*, *Who* was born of the *Virgin Mary*, was crucified, died, and was buried, rose from the dead, and is now seated at *Your* right hand.

We believe in the *Holy Spirit*, the holy *Catholic Church*, the communion of saints, the forgiveness of sins, the resurrection of the body, and life everlasting.

Father, make us mindful of the dignity *You* gave us in *Baptism*, and may we live for *You* in every moment of our lives. *We* ask this in the *Name* of our *Lord* and *Savior*, *Jesus Christ. Amen.*

Chapter Ninety-Three

The Sacrament of Baptism - II

Q. 202. What relationship with God and Christ is begun at Baptism?

Baptism (1) *permanently relates man to God as a child of God* and (2) *joins him to the priestly, prophetic, and kingly works of Christ.*

1. *Baptism permanently relates man to God as a child of God.*

This relationship or bond can never be erased. Baptism is directed toward acquiring the fullness of life in Christ, that is, toward a complete profession of faith, a complete incorporation into the system of salvation, and a integration into Eucharistic Communion. For those who have reached the age of reason, both faith in Jesus Christ and the desire to follow Him with His Church are necessary for Baptism.

2. *Baptism joins man to the priestly, prophetic, and kingly works of Christ.*

The People of God share in the kingly and priestly office of Christ because, by regeneration in Baptism and the anointing of the Holy Spirit, they are consecrated into a spiritual house and a holy priesthood. Through good works, they can offer spiritual sacrifices.

The People of God share in Christ's prophetic office by being living witnesses to Him, by means of a life of faith and charity, and by offering to God a sacrifice of praise. As Christians we should act, by the example of our lives, as the transformed persons we became at Baptism. We are children of God and followers of Jesus Christ.

Sacred Scripture

"Know you not that all we who are baptized in Christ Jesus

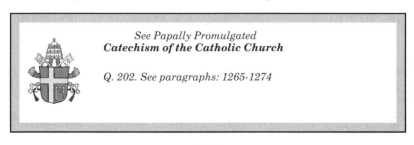

See Papally Promulgated
Catechism of the Catholic Church

Q. 202. See paragraphs: 1265-1274

are baptized in His death? For we are buried together with Him by Baptism into death that as Christ is risen from the dead by the glory of the Father, so we also may walk in newness of life." *Romans 6:3-4*

Vatican Council II

"Baptism, of itself, is only a beginning , a point of departure, for it is wholly directed toward the acquiring of fullness of life in Christ. Baptism is thus ordained toward a complete profession of faith, a complete incorporation into the system of salvation such as Christ himself willed it to be, and finally, toward a complete integration into eucharistic communion."

Ecumenism, 22

Prayer: *Lord, our God, grant that, as we have been baptized into the death of Your beloved Son, our Savior Jesus Christ; we may be buried with Him and die to our corrupt affections. Through the grave and gate of death, may we pass to our joyful resurrection; through His merits, Who died, was buried, and rose again for us, the same Christ our Lord. Amen.*

Prayer

Jesus, our Lord, by the Easter mystery, You touch our lives with the healing power of Your love. You have given us the freedom of the sons of God. May we who celebrate this gift find joy in it forever in Heaven. May we hold fast to the life You have given us and come to the eternal gifts You promise. Lord, prepare for eternal joy the people You have renewed in Baptism.

Son of God, You were raised from the dead to lead us into life. Bless and sanctify all the children of Your Father, that we may share in Your kingly and priestly and prophetic office through the Sacrament of Baptism and live our lives accordingly.

Christ our Life, through Baptism we were buried with You and rose to life with You; may we walk in the newness of life.

With joy in our hearts, we call upon You, Christ the Lord, Who died, rose again, gave us new life through Baptism, and live always to intercede for us. You are still our Priest, the Advocate Who always pleads our cause. You are the Victim Who dies no more, the Lamb, once slain, Who lives forever. Victorious King, hear our prayer. Amen.

Chapter Ninety-Four

The Sacrament of Confirmation

Q. 203. What is Confirmation?

Confirmation is a sacrament that confirms or strengthens the life of the Spirit which a person received at Baptism. In virtue of this sacrament, the faithful are obliged to spread and defend the Faith as true witnesses of Christ.

The principal sign of Confirmation is made by the Bishop, or priest, when he lays his hand upon the forehead of the candidate, anointing him with chrism [consecrated olive oil and balsam], and prays, "Be sealed with the gift of the Holy Spirit."

This sacrament, which seals a candidate with the Spirit, is linked with the other sacraments of Christian initiation — Baptism and the Eucharist.

After Baptism, through the Sacrament of Confirmation, Jesus sends the Holy Spirit again to Christian souls with the new grace and new strength that are needed in Christian lives. In the third century, St. Cyprian wrote: "They who are baptized...are presented to the Bishops...and by our prayers and the imposition of hands they receive the Holy Spirit and are perfected with the seal of the Lord" (Epistle 73).

Candidates renew their baptismal promises before Confirmation because of the intimate connection that there is between Confirmation and Baptism.

Sacred Scripture

"Now when the Apostles, who were in Jerusalem, had heard that Samaria had received the word of God, they sent unto them Peter and John. Who, when they were come, prayed for them, that they might receive the Holy Spirit. For He was not as yet come upon any of them; but they were only

See Papally Promulgated
Catechism of the Catholic Church

Q. 203. See paragraph: 1285

baptized in the Name of the Lord Jesus. Then they laid their hands upon them, and they received the Holy Spirit."

Acts 8:14-17

Vatican Council II

"By the sacrament of Confirmation they are more perfectly bound to the Church and are endowed with the special strength of the Holy Spirit. Hence they are, as true witnesses of Christ, more strictly obliged to spread the faith by word and deed." *The Church, 11*

Q. 204. What does the seal of the Spirit do for us?

The seal of the Spirit prepares us (1) *to be witnesses of Christ by living a mature Christian life* and (2) *to spread and defend the Faith while living in the world.*

1. *The seal of the Spirit prepares us to be witnesses of Christ by living a mature Christian life.*

Confirmation binds the Christian more perfectly to the Church and enriches him with a special strength of the Holy Spirit, that he may live in the world as a witness of Christ and serve his fellow men.

When the Bishop, or priest, administering this sacrament, anoints a person with chrism he says, "Be sealed with the gift of the Holy Spirit." Thus, by Confirmation, a baptized Christian becomes permanently marked as a witness and is obliged to communicate the Faith, with the price of his blood, if necessary.

Sacred Scripture

"Now He that confirms us with you in Christ, and that has anointed us, is God: Who also has sealed us, and given the pledge of the Spirit in our hearts." *2 Corinthians 1:21-22*

2. *The seal of the Spirit prepares us to spread and defend the Faith while living in the world.*

See Papally Promulgated
Catechism of the Catholic Church

Q. 204. See paragraphs: 698, 1295-1296, 1302-1305

Incorporated into Christ's Mystical Body through Baptism, and strengthened by the Holy Spirit through Confirmation, the laity are assigned to the apostolate, or the general mission of the Church, by the Lord Himself. We should remember the duty that was placed upon us when we were confirmed: we have the task of bringing Jesus Christ, His example, His way of life, and His Church to others. The strength which the grace of the Holy Spirit gives us will help us each day to fulfill our apostolate, if we are generous enough to show some effort and to ask for His help in prayer.

Vatican Council II

"The term 'laity' is understood to mean all the faithful except those in Holy Orders and those who belong to a religious state approved by the Church. That is, the faithful, who by Baptism are incorporated into Christ, are placed in the People of God, and in their own way they share the priestly, prophetic and kingly office of Christ. To the best of their ability, they carry on the mission of the whole Christian people in the Church and in the world.

"Their secular character is proper and peculiar to the laity." *The Church, 31*

"From the fact of their union with Christ the head flows the laymen's right and duty to be apostles. Inserted as they are in the Mystical Body of Christ by baptism and strengthened by the power of the Holy Spirit in confirmation, it is by the Lord himself that they are assigned to the apostolate." *Lay People, 3*

"The apostolate, through which the laity build up the Church, sanctify the world and get it to live in Christ, can take on many forms.

"A special form of the individual apostolate is the witness of a whole lay life issuing from faith, hope and charity; it is a sign very much in keeping with our times, and a manifestation of Christ living in his faithful. Then, by the apostolate of the word, which in certain circumstances is absolutely necessary, the laity proclaim Christ, explain and spread his teachings, each one according to his condition and competence, and profess those teachings with fidelity." *Lay People, 16*

"The faithful who have already been consecrated in Baptism and Confirmation are fully incorporated in the Body of Christ by the reception of the Eucharist." *Priests, 5*

"As members of the living Christ, incorporated into Him and made like Him by baptism, confirmation and the Eucharist, all the faithful have an obligation to collaborate in the expansion and spread of His body, so that they might bring it to fullness as soon as possible (cf. Eph. 4:13).

"So all the children of the Church should have a lively consciousness of their own responsibility for the world, they should foster within themselves a truly Catholic spirit, they should spend themselves in the work of the Gospel. However, let everyone be aware that the primary and most important contribution he can make to the spread of the faith is to lead a profound Christian life." *Missionary Activity, 36*

Prayer

Almighty Father, in the death and Resurrection of Your own Son, You brought us through the waters of Baptism to the shores of new life. By those waters and by the fire of the Holy Spirit, You have given each of us consolation. In union with the sacrifice of Your beloved Son in the Mass, may our lives be a total offering to You, and may we deserve to enter Your heavenly home to praise Your unfailing power there with Christ.

Lord, send us Your Holy Spirit to help us walk in unity of faith and grow in the strength of His love to the full stature of Christ. You have signed us with the Cross of Your Son and have anointed us with the oil of salvation.

As we offer ourselves with Christ in His Eucharistic Sacrifice, continue to fill our hearts with Your Spirit. You give Your Son as food to those You anoint with Your Spirit. Help us to fulfill Your law by living in freedom as Your children. May we live in holiness and be Your witnesses to the world aided by the grace of the Holy Spirit.

Lord, fulfill the promise given by Your Son by sending the Holy Spirit to enlighten our minds and to lead us to all truth. Help us to receive the gift of Your Spirit, so that He may remain in our hearts and bring us to the rewards of eternal life.

God our Father, You have made us children by water and the Holy Spirit; bless us and watch over us with Your fatherly love.

Jesus Christ, Son of God, You promised that the Spirit of truth would be with Your Church for ever; bless us and give us courage to profess the true Faith.

Holy Spirit, You came down upon the disciples and set their hearts on fire with love; bless us, keep us one in faith and love, and bring us to the joy of God's Kingdom. We ask this through Jesus Christ, our Lord. Amen.

Chapter Ninety-Five

The Sacrament of Penance - I

Q. 205. What is the Sacrament of Penance?

Penance is the sacrament which brings to the Christian God's merciful forgiveness for any sins committed after Baptism, and to bring the sinner consolation and peace. St. John writes: "If we confess our sins, He is faithful and just, to forgive us our sins, and to cleanse us from all iniquity" (1 John 1:9).

As God's Son, Jesus had the power of forgiving sins. One day, He said to a paralyzed man, "Whose faith when He saw, said: 'Man, your sins are forgiven.' And the scribes and Pharisees began to think, saying: 'Who is this Who speaks blasphemies? Who can forgive sins, but God alone?' And when Jesus knew their thoughts, answering, He said to them: 'What is it you think in your hearts? Which is easier to say, "Your sins are forgiven you;" or to say, "Arise and walk?" But that you may know that the Son of man has power on earth to forgive sins, [He said to the sick of the palsy,] I say to you, arise, take up your bed, and go into your house.' And immediately rising up before them, he took up the bed on which he lay; and he went away to his own house, glorifying God." (Luke 5:20-25)

Jesus gave the power of forgiving sins to His Apostles when He appeared to them on the evening of the day of His Resurrection, saying: " 'Peace be to you.' And when He had said this, He showed them His hands and His side. The disciples therefore were glad when they saw the Lord. He said therefore to them again: 'Peace be to you. As the Father has sent Me, I also send you.' When He had said this, He breathed on them; and He said to them: 'Receive the Holy Spirit. Whose sins you shall forgive, they are forgiven them; and whose sins you shall retain, they are retained' " (John 20: 19-23).

See Papally Promulgated
Catechism of the Catholic Church

Q. 205. See paragraphs: 1422-1424

This power to forgive sins has been handed down through the years to the priests of the Church of our day.

Vatican Council II

"Those who approach the sacrament of Penance obtain pardon from God's mercy for the offense committed against him, and are, at the same time, reconciled with the Church which they have wounded by their sins and which by charity, by example and by prayer labors for their conversion."

The Church, 11

"The apostles were endowed by Christ with a special outpouring of the Holy Spirit coming upon them (cf. Acts 1:8; John 20:22-23), and they passed on the gift of the Spirit to their auxiliaries by the imposition of hands (cf. 1 Timothy 4:14; 2 Timothy 1:6-7), which is handed on down to our day through episcopal consecration."* *The Church, 2*

Roman Curial Document

"The Church is 'continually engaged in repentance and renewal' (*Lumen Gentium,* n. 8) and religious, because of their special union with the Church, should value highly the sacrament of Penance. The sacrament of Penance restores and strengthens in members of the Church who have sinned the fundamental gift of 'metanoia', of conversion to the kingdom of Christ, which is first received in Baptism (cf. *Ap. Const. Paenitemini A.A.S.,* 58 (1966). Those who approach this sacrament receive from God's mercy the pardon of their offenses and at the same time they are reconciled to the Church which they have wounded by their sins. (cf. *Const. Lumen Gentium,* n.11)."

Decree on Confession for Religious, 1 [1970]

---

* *[Editorial Note - Episcopal consecration is the consecration or ordination of Bishops by means of the fullness of the Sacrament of Orders.]*

Prayer

Jesus, we believe that You have the power to forgive sins because You are not only God's appointed representative, but God Himself. The power to forgive resides in You, in all its fullness; through Your generous love, You designated that it remain on earth in the person of Peter, his fellow Apostles, and their successors until the end of time. You gave this power to them after Your Resurrection, when You said to them, "Receive the Holy Spirit. For those whose sins you shall forgive, they are forgiven them; and whose sins you shall retain, they are retained" (John 20:23). The priests of Your Church continue to exercise forgiveness in Your Name.

We thank You for giving such power to priests, and for confirming their power in advance by the cure of the paralytic. The power thus conferred is truly divine — divine in its operation, inasmuch as it was to remit many sins, save many souls, allay despair, and impart much comfort, peace, and joy.

Jesus, We thank You for the inestimable benefit of the Sacrament of Penance. Through its frequent use, You give us our spiritual life, firm confidence in God, peace of conscience, strength to resist temptation, ease to perform good works, and lasting joy.

In this sacrament, we receive the price of Your Precious Blood and of Your five sacred wounds. We thank You for all the graces we have ever received in the Sacrament of Reconciliation, by which You have rendered spiritual resurrection possible for us. Help us to make use of this sacrament with confidence, joy, and peace. Amen.

Chapter Ninety-Six

The Sacrament of Penance - II

Q. 206. What are the effects of Penance?

Penance has the following effects: (1) *We obtain pardon from God after we have made a sincere confession, shown true sorrow, and are resolved not to sin again.* (2) *It brings about our peace with the Church, which is wounded by our sins;* and (3) *it helps us to work for holiness of life and to overcome habits of sin.*

1. *Penance is our means of obtaining pardon from God after we have made a sincere confession, shown true sorrow, and are resolved not to sin again.*

In the Creed we say: "We believe in the forgiveness of sins." The Sacrament of Penance is the means God gave us to obtain His forgiveness for our mortal sins. We must be truly sorry for them, confess them to a priest, and receive absolution from the priest. Absolution means the words of forgiveness spoken by the priest in Confession. These words are a sign of assurance of God's forgiveness. After absolution, we are to perform a penance by saying the prayers or doing the good deeds which are assigned by the priest in Confession. The Church also encourages us to use the Sacrament of Confession frequently for obtaining the forgiveness of our venial sins.

Sacred Scripture

"He who knows that his brother commits a sin which is not to death, let him ask, and life shall be given to him, who sins not to death. There is a sin unto death: for that, I say no one should pray for it. All iniquity is sin. And there is a sin unto death." *1 John 5:16-17*

"Behold the eyes of the Lord are on them that fear Him; and on them that hope in His mercy. To deliver their souls from death; and feed them in famine." *Psalm 33: 18-19*

See Papally Promulgated
Catechism of the Catholic Church

Q. 206. See paragraphs: 1468-1470, 1496

2. It brings about our peace with the Church, which is wounded by our sins.

When we approach the Sacrament of Penance, we not only obtain from God pardon for sins we have committed against Him, but we are also reconciled to the Church, which we have wounded by our sins. By doing penance, we show our repentance in action and make our relationship with God and our fellow men more firm, since we have damaged these unions by sin.

3. It helps us to work for holiness of life and to overcome habits of sin.

Through each sacrament, the Holy Spirit makes our souls more pleasing to God because of the graces He gives us. The Sacrament of Penance brings to each individual special helps toward spiritual growth. Through the sacrament, Jesus, the Good Shepherd, forgives us our sins and sends His Holy Spirit once more to our souls with new grace and new strength to help us lead the Christian life and grow spiritually.

The purpose of the Sacrament of Penance is to make visible and present God's mercy and forgiveness.

The Sacrament of Penance also reminds us of the great love God has for us. His love should inspire us to a greater love for Him. We should grow in the love of God each time we receive this sacrament.

This sacrament also increases our hope. We realize that, even though we are sinners, we can obtain from God the help we need to reach Heaven. Moreover, faith is strengthened in the sacrament because, like any other sacrament, Penance demands the exercise of faith.

Vatican Council II

"Those who approach the sacrament of Penance obtain pardon from God's mercy for the offense committed against him, and are, at the same time, reconciled with the Church which they have wounded by their sins and which by charity, by example and by prayer labors for their conversion."

The Church, 11

"Parish priests must bear it constantly in mind how much the sacrament of penance contributes to the development of the Christian life and should therefore be readily available for the hearing of the confessions of the faithful." *Bishops, 30*

Prayer: *Father, teach us to live good lives, encourage us with Your support, and bring us to eternal life. Through the Sacrament of Penance, free us from the sins that enslave us. May our acts of penance bring us Your forgiveness. Open our hearts to Your love, and prepare us for Your coming after death.*

Lord, You reward virtue and forgive the repentant sinner. Grant us Your forgiveness as we come before You confessing our guilt in the Sacrament of Penance. May the power of this sacrament wash away our sins, renew our lives and bring us to salvation. May we never misuse Your healing gifts, especially by neglect, but always find in them a source of life and salvation. In the Sacrament of Reconciliation, forgive our sins and guide our wayward hearts. Make us worthy to attain the gift of Heaven, after having been faithful in Your service. Help us to remain faithful to a holy way of life, and guide us to the inheritance You have promised. Help us to grow in holiness and to advance the salvation of the world. We ask this through Christ, our Lord, to Whom with You and the Holy Spirit be all honor and glory. Amen.

Prayer

Lord, You desired to keep from us Your indignation and so did not spare Jesus Christ, Who was wounded for our sins. We are Your prodigal children, but by confessing our sins in the Sacrament of Penance, we come back to You. Embrace us, that we may rejoice in Your mercy, together with Christ Your beloved Son. Grant that we may do penance, find forgiveness, and so share in the fruits of Christ's redeeming death. You love Your people even when they stray. Grant us a complete change of heart, so that we may follow You with greater fidelity.

Lord Jesus Christ, set Your Passion, Your Cross, and Your death between Your judgment and our souls, now and at the hour of our death. In Your goodness, grant mercy and grace to the living and forgiveness to sinners.

By Your Cross, O Christ, You have trodden upon and overthrown the ancient enemy of the human race; grant full pardon and bring fresh salvation to those who are numbered among Your faithful people, especially through the Sacrament of Penance. To You we give all honor and glory. Amen.

Chapter Ninety-Seven

The Sacrament of Penance - III

Q. 207. Is Confession necessary if one has fallen into serious sin?

If one has fallen into serious or mortal sin, sacramental confession is the ordinary way established in the Church to bring about peace between the sinner, Christ, and His Church.

Confession is, for the Catholic, the sacramental way of obtaining pardon for sin and of submitting his offenses to the mercy and forgiving grace of God.

In this sacrament Jesus forgives our sins, no matter how terrible they are, as long as we repent and are sorry for them and are resolved, even though we are weak, not to commit the sins again. We trust in the help of God's grace to do so.

Repentance is a change of heart which leads the sinner to turn back to God and accept His loving forgiveness. God never refuses forgiveness if the sinner is sincerely sorry and is willing to give up his evil ways. The sinner can repent with the grace of God. God continues to speak to man even though he keeps on refusing Him.

The life of Christians on earth is a spiritual warfare. Therefore, it is subject to temptations and sins. But for Catholic Christians, the Sacrament of Penance is open to them, so that they might obtain pardon from the merciful God and reconcile themselves to the Church.

The sinner's manifestation of sorrow by word or gesture, the sins confessed, the sinner's willingness to make satisfaction (penance), and the words of the priest, "I absolve you from your sins in the Name of the Father, and of the Son, and of the Holy Spirit," constitute the sign of the Sacrament of Penance.

See Papally Promulgated
Catechism of the Catholic Church

Q. 207. See paragraphs: 1446, 1455-1458, 1855-1856

Sacred Scripture

"Except you repent, you shall all likewise perish." *Luke 13:5*

"Be converted, and do penance for all your iniquities: and iniquity shall not be your ruin. Cast away from you all your sins, by which you have transgressed, and make to yourselves a new heart, and a new spirit: and why will you die, O House of Israel?....Say to them: 'As I live, says the Lord God, I desire not the death of the wicked, but that the wicked turn from his way, and live. Turn, turn from your evil ways: and why will you die, O House of Israel?'" *Ezekiel 18:30-31; 33:11*

Vatican Council II

"By Baptism priests introduce men into the People of God; by the sacrament of Penance they reconcile sinners with God and the Church." *Priests, 5*

Prayer: *Father in Heaven, the light of Your truth bestows sight to the darkness of sinful eyes. May repentance bring us the blessing of Your forgiveness and the gift of Your light. Direct our hearts to better things; turn to us with mercy for we have sinned against You. Grant this through Jesus Christ our Lord. Amen.*

Prayer

Our Father in Heaven, touch our hearts so that we will seek Your friendship more often, and will make amends for our sins against Your wisdom and goodness. Guide all those who are estranged from You by sin, that they may come back to You, and remain always in Your love. Lead back to Your friendship and truth all who have gone astray; teach us how to help them.

Heavenly Father, through the grace of the Sacrament of Penance, help us to strip off our sinful selves and be clothed with Christ, Your Son, the new Adam. Help us to leave sin behind and to rejoice in professing Your Name.

God of mercy and compassion, cleanse our hearts of all faults, fill our minds with wisdom, and open our lips that we may always sing Your praises. We ask this through Jesus Christ our Lord. Amen.

Chapter Ninety-Eight

The Sacrament of Penance - IV

Q. 208. What is the effect of perfect sorrow for sin?

A person who has committed mortal sin can be restored to grace without the immediate benefit of the Sacrament of Penance, if he has perfect sorrow or contrition for the sin by which he has offended God.

We have perfect sorrow or contrition for our sins when we are sorry for them because they have offended God, our Father, and when we do not want to commit them again. Our primary motivation is contrition for having offended God and not merely fear of divine punishment. Our sorrow is sincere when it comes from the heart.

The real meaning of the virtue of perfect contrition is hatred for sin because it offends God. The virtue of perfect contrition is based on a sense of the holiness of God and the realization of God's goodness. This realization should grow each time we say an act of contrition or go to Confession.

Mortal sin is the greatest of all evils: it offends God seriously, keeps us out of Heaven, and condemns us forever to hell. By perfect contrition we can be restored to grace, but the obligation to confess mortal sins to a priest remains.

The remedy for sin is Jesus Christ Who came into the world to save His people from their sins. By sharing in His death and Resurrection, through the sacraments and by faithfully performing the duties of his state in life, man can triumph over sin and death. St. Paul says, "Christ died for us; much more therefore, being now justified by His blood, shall we be saved from wrath through Him" (Romans 5:9).

Vatican Council II

"Catechesis, as well as pointing out the social consequences of sin, must impress on the minds of the faithful the dis-

See Papally Promulgated
Catechism of the Catholic Church

Q. 208. See paragraph: 1452

tinctive character of penance as a detestation of sin because it is an offense against God." *Sacred Liturgy, 109*

Papal Document

"The full taking away and, as it is called, reparation of sins requires two things. Firstly, friendship with God must be restored. Amends must be made for offending his wisdom and goodness. This is done by a sincere conversion of mind. Secondly, all the personal and social values, as well as those that are universal, which sin has lessened or destroyed must be fully made good. This is done in two ways. The first is by freely making reparation, which involves punishment. The second is by accepting the punishments God's just and most holy wisdom had appointed. From this the holiness and splendor of his glory shine out through the world. The very fact that punishment for sin exists and that it is so severe make it possible for us to understand how foolish and malicious sin is and how harmful its consequences are."

Apostolic Constitution on Indulgences, 3 [Pope Paul VI]

> **Prayer:** *Father, He Who knew no sin was made sin for us, to save us and to restore us to Your friendship. Look upon our contrite hearts and afflicted spirits and heal our troubled consciences, so that, in the joy and strength of the Holy Spirit, we may proclaim Your praise and glory before all the nations.*
>
> *We confess, Lord, that we have sinned. Wash us clean by Your gift of salvation. Blot out our sins by the power of the Cross, and keep our lives from the assaults of the devil by the grace of Your Holy Spirit. We ask this through Jesus Christ, our only Lord and Savior. Amen.*

Q. 209. What is the wish of the Church concerning Confession?

The Church desires that every Catholic, from the "the age of discretion" (about seven years old), should be instructed on

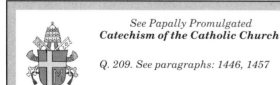

See Papally Promulgated
Catechism of the Catholic Church

Q. 209. See paragraphs: 1446, 1457

how to receive and best profit from the regular use of this sacrament.

The Church urges the faithful to confess their sins to a priest with a contrite heart in the Sacrament of Penance. She makes it very clear that she wishes the faithful to frequently use those sacraments which foster the Christian life; the Sacrament of Penance is one of them. After the Eucharist, it can be received the most frequently.

Vatican Council II

"In the spirit of Christ the pastor, they [priests] instruct them [the faithful] to submit their sins to the Church with a contrite heart in the sacrament of Penance, so that they may be daily more and more converted to the Lord, remembering his words: 'Repent, for the kingdom of heaven is at hand' (Mt. 4:17)." *Priests, 5*

"And on behalf of the faithful who are moved to sorrow or are stricken with sickness they [priests] exercise in an eminent degree a ministry of reconciliation and comfort, whilst they carry the needs and supplications of the faithful to God the Father (cf. Heb. 5:1-4)." *The Church, 28*

"Parish priests must bear it constantly in mind how much the sacrament of penance contributes to the development of the Christian life and should therefore be readily available for the hearing of the confessions of the faithful." *Bishops, 30*

Q. 210. Why is Confession useful even when only venial sins are in question?

We should keep in mind the usefulness of Confession, which retains its efficacy even when only venial sins are in question, and which gives an increase of grace and charity, allows for better dispositions in receiving the Eucharist, and also helps to perfect the Christian life.

The abundance of the fruit gained from Holy Communion is measured by the degree of our love, since the special fruit of

See Papally Promulgated
Catechism of the Catholic Church

Q. 210. See paragraph: 1458

Holy Communion is an increase of sanctifying grace and of the virtue of charity. A person who is habitually guilty of deliberate venial sin, or who receives Christ carelessly or thoughtlessly, receives the same benefits which the sacrament gives to all those who receive, but he does not allow these graces to blossom and grow in his soul, because he is poorly disposed.

Christ does not find in such souls the willingness to permit Him to act freely in them. Their vanity, self-love, sensuality, and lack of charity prevent the union between them and Christ from being made perfect. The secret of spiritual success through Holy Communion lies in the absence of obstacles to God's grace. The grace of the Sacrament of Penance helps us to overcome such obstacles.

Though we are a community of believers, we are also a sinful people. God has called us to greatness; but, conscious of the forces of sin within us, we look for understanding and mercy. We make our humble appeals for mercy in the Sacrament of Penance, and for the graces we need to live the Christian life according to God's will. Christ gives us whatever we need to love others sincerely and to promote peace and common respect among God's people.

Q. 211. Must we still suffer for our sins in other ways even after they are forgiven?

We must atone for our sins even after they are forgiven, either in Purgatory in the next life, or by acts of penance in this life.

Q. 212. What is an indulgence?

An indulgence is the Church's special intercession with God for the remission of temporal punishment due to sin which has already been forgiven.*

---

* [Editorial Note - Temporal punishment, as opposed to eternal punishment, is that restricted to life on earth and to Purgatory.]

See Papally Promulgated
Catechism of the Catholic Church

Q. 211. See paragraphs: 1472-1473
Q. 212. See paragraph: 1471

Q. 213. How does the Church have the power to grant indulgences?

The Church, making use of her power to minister the redemption of Christ, intervenes to dispense the treasure of the superabundant merits of Christ, and of the saints, to the faithful who are rightly disposed, for the remission of temporal punishment due their sins.

Q. 214. What are the conditions for gaining an indulgence?

The conditions for gaining an indulgence are:

(a) We must be in the state of grace, that is, any mortal sins we may have committed must be forgiven.

(b) We must say the prayer or do the work to which the indulgence is attached.

(c) We must have the intention of gaining the indulgence.

Q. 215. May we gain an indulgence for the benefit of the departed?

All indulgences, without exception, may be offered by way of intercession for the departed.

Q. 216. What is the difference between a plenary and a partial indulgence?

A plenary indulgence satisfies completely all the temporal punishment due to sin at the time the indulgence is gained; a partial indulgence satisfies only part of it.

Q. 217. What are some examples of partial indulgences?

The following are examples of partial indulgences:

(a) If one of the faithful, doing his duty and bearing the burdens of life, lifts his heart to God with humble trust, adding, if only mentally, a pious invocation; (b) if he, with a spirit

See Papally Promulgated
Catechism of the Catholic Church
Q. 213. See paragraph: 1478
Q. 214. See paragraph: 1471
Q. 215. See paragraph: 1479
Q. 216. See paragraphs: 1471, 1473

of faith and a merciful heart, puts himself and his goods at the service of his brethren in need; (c) if he, in a spirit of penitence, spontaneously, and with sacrifice, deprives himself of some lawful goods.

Sacred Scripture

"Ask, and it will be given to you. Seek and you will find. Knock, and it will be opened to you. For every one who asks, receives, and he that seeks, finds. And to him that knocks, it will be opened." *Matthew 7:7-8*

"For I was hungry and you fed Me. I was thirsty and you gave Me something to drink. I was a stranger and you took Me in; naked and you clothed Me; sick and you visited Me. I was in prison and you visited Me. . . .Amen, I say to you, as long as you did it to one of these, the least of My brethren, you did it to Me." *Matthew 25:35-36, 40*

"If any man would come after Me, let him deny himself, and take up his cross daily, and follow Me." *Luke 9:23*

Papal Documents

"The Church, making use of her power of ministering the redemption of Christ our Lord...authoritatively intervenes to dispense to the faithful who are rightly disposed the treasure of satisfactions of Christ and of the saints, for the remission of temporal punishment.

"The purpose that the ecclesiastical authority proposes in bestowing an indulgence is not just to help the faithful to expiate the penalties of sin, but also to urge them to carry out works of piety, penance, and charity...

"All indulgences, without exception, may now be offered 'by way of suffrage' for the departed." *Enchiridion Indulgentiarum, 8*

"A plenary indulgence may be gained only once each day; partial indulgences may be gained many times each day unless the contrary is explicitly stated." *Enchiridion Indulgentiarum, 24, 28*

Prayer

Lord Jesus Christ, move our hearts to faith, hope, love, and real sorrow for our sins; move our wills to a firm resolve to mend our ways, especially by the frequent use of the sacraments of Penance and the Eucharist. The sight of Your five wounds fills us with compassion. By Your Cross and Passion bring us to the victory of Your glorious Resurrection, O Savior of the world.

Lord Jesus Christ, Son of Righteousness, open our eyes and turn us from darkness to light, and from the dominion of satan to God, that we may receive the forgiveness of our sins and a place among those made holy by faith in Your Cross, Savior of the world, living and reigning forever.

By Your Cross, Lord Jesus Christ, the Church is redeemed, sanctified, and raised on high. Protect us, Lord, Who take refuge in Your Sacred Heart. In the Sacrament of Penance, bathe us in Your Precious Blood and in the water of life which gushed from Your wounded side. We ask this in Your most powerful and holy Name. Amen.

The Individual Sacraments:

Holy Orders
Anointing of the Sick
Matrimony

Chapter Ninety-Nine

The Sacrament of Holy Orders - I

Q. 218. What is the Sacrament of Holy Orders?

Holy Orders (1) *makes certain members of the People of God particularly like Christ the Mediator,* (2) *puts them in positions of special service in the Church,* and (3) *gives them sacred power to carry out this service.*

1. *Holy Orders makes certain members of the People of God particularly like Christ the Mediator.*

Holy Orders is the act by which certain men, called by God, are enabled to mediate, in a special way, Christ's high priestly ministry. These men, Bishops, priests and deacons, are set apart and given grace for their vocation in the Sacrament of Holy Orders.

2. *Holy Orders puts Bishops and priests in positions of special service in the Church.*

Through the Sacrament of Holy Orders, Jesus Christ makes Himself present, through Bishops and priests, to offer sacrifice, to baptize, to give the Sacrament of Confirmation, to give His Body and Blood in Holy Communion, to forgive sins in the Sacrament of Penance, to anoint the sick and to bless and sanctify marriages. Assisting the Bishops and priests in this ministry of service, and sharing with them the Sacrament of Orders, are the deacons.

3. *Holy Orders gives Bishops and priests sacred power to carry out this service.*

By His own authority Jesus appointed the Apostles to be His priests to carry on His work in the world. At the Last Supper He gave the Apostles the power to change bread and wine into His Body and Blood. "And taking bread, He gave thanks, and broke it; and gave it to them, saying: 'This is My Body,

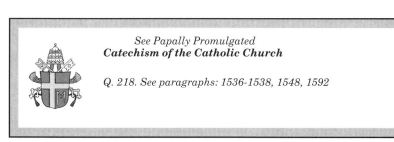

See Papally Promulgated
Catechism of the Catholic Church

Q. 218. See paragraphs: 1536-1538, 1548, 1592

which will be given for you; Do this for a commemoration of Me' " (Luke 22:19). After His Resurrection He gave them the power to forgive men's sins when He said: "Receive the Holy Spirit. Whose sins you shall forgive, they are forgiven them; and whose sins you shall retain, they are retained" (John 20:22-23).

Sacred Scripture

"And He [God] gave some Apostles, and some prophets, and other some evangelists, and other some pastors and doctors, for the perfecting of the saints, for the work of the ministry, for the edifying of the Body of Christ." *Ephesians 4:11-12*

Vatican Council II

" 'Christ, whom the Father hallowed and sent into the world' (John 10:36), has, through his apostles, made their successors, the bishops namely, sharers in his consecration and mission; and these, in their turn, duly entrusted in varying degrees various members of the Church with the office of their ministry. Thus the divinely instituted ecclesiastical ministry is exercised in different degrees by those who even from ancient times have been called bishops, priests and deacons." *The Church, 28*

Prayer: *Heavenly Father, by the power of the Holy Spirit, You anointed Your only Son as Messiah and Lord of creation. Through the Sacrament of Holy Orders, You have given to some a share in His consecration to priestly service in Your Church . Help Your priests to be faithful witnesses in the world of the salvation which Christ won for all mankind. We ask this in His most holy Name. Amen.*

Q. 219. What does episcopal consecration or ordination confer?

Episcopal consecration (or ordination) confers the fullness of the Sacrament of Orders. Episcopal consecration is called

See Papally Promulgated
Catechism of the Catholic Church

Q. 219. See paragraphs: 1555-1561

the high priesthood, because it confers, together with the office (duty, function) of sanctifying, the duties also of teaching and ruling in communion with the head and members of the College of Bishops.

Q. 220. What special grace does Christ give in the Sacrament of Holy Orders?

Through this sacrament, Christ bestows a permanent charism or grace of the Holy Spirit on the ordained man (1) *to guide and take care of those who believe,* (2) *to proclaim and explain the Gospel,* and (3) *to guide and sanctify God's people.*

1. *Through this sacrament, Christ bestows a permanent charism or grace of the Holy Spirit on the ordained man to guide and take care of those who believe.*

Before Jesus ascended into Heaven, He gave special instructions to the Apostles. He wanted to be certain that there would be helpers to carry on the work of shepherding His flock (cf. Matthew 28:18-20).

2. *Through this sacrament, Christ bestows a permanent charism or grace of the Holy Spirit to proclaim and explain the Gospel.*

Jesus sent His Apostles to preach the Gospel of the New Covenant to every nation, because He intended His Kingdom, the Church, for all people. St. Paul says, "And He gave some Apostles, and some prophets, and other some evangelists, and other some pastors and doctors, for the perfecting of the saints, for the work of the ministry, for the building up of the body of Christ" (Ephesians 4:11-12).

3. *Through this sacrament, Christ bestows a permanent charism or grace of the Holy Spirit to guide and sanctify God's people.*

The Apostles, and their successors, continued Christ's priestly work of being mediators between God and man. They

See Papally Promulgated
Catechism of the Catholic Church

Q. 220. See paragraphs: 1581-1584, 1585-1589

brought God's mercy and grace to the people of the New Covenant and, in return, offered man's praise to God. When they performed priestly functions, Christ the High Priest was present, acting through them.

Prayer

Heavenly Father, at their ordination, priests accept the responsibilities of the priesthood out of love for the Lord Jesus and His Church. May they be resolved to unite themselves more closely to Christ and to try to become more like Him by joyfully sacrificing their own pleasure and ambition in order to bring His peace and love to their brothers and sisters.

Help them to be faithful ministers of the mysteries of God, especially in celebrating the Eucharist and the other liturgical services with sincere devotion. Give them the grace to imitate Jesus Christ, the Head and Shepherd of the Church, by teaching the Catholic Faith for the well-being of the people they were sent to serve.

Bless Your priests and deacons with the fullness of Your love. Help them to be faithful ministers of Christ the High Priest, so that they will be able to lead people to Him, the fountain of their salvation.

We pray for the Bishops, that, despite their own unworthiness, they may faithfully fulfill the office of Apostles which Jesus Christ has entrusted to them. We pray that they may become more like our High Priest and Good Shepherd, the Teacher and Servant of all, and thus be a genuine sign of Christ's presence among us.

Lord, in Your love, keep Your Bishops, priests, and deacons close to You always, and may they bring all of us to eternal life, through Jesus Christ, our Lord. Amen.

The Sacrament of Holy Orders - II

Q. 221. What can priests do as Christ's representatives?

Representing Christ, priests (1) *offer the Sacrifice of the Mass*, and (2) *administer the Sacrament of Penance for the forgiveness of sins* and (3) *the Sacrament of the Anointing of the Sick.*

1. *Representing Christ, priests offer the Sacrifice of the Mass.*

Knowing that Christ's priesthood and Church were to continue to the end of time, the Apostles, by ordaining Bishops and priests, passed on their priestly power to others. In order to become a priest, a deacon is ordained by a Bishop and thereby receives the grace that is necessary to make the sacrifices required of a life so much like Christ's. He becomes a special representative of Christ, having been given his priestly powers.

The most important work of the priest is offering the Holy Sacrifice of the Mass. He acts in the Person of Christ, i.e., in union with Him, as He renews the sacrifice of the Cross in an unbloody manner for the glory of God and the salvation of mankind.

2. *Representing Christ, priests administer the Sacrament of Penance for the forgiveness of sins.*

Through His priests Christ forgives sins and becomes for all of us a merciful and faithful High Priest. As St. Paul says, "Therefore it behooved Him in all things to be made like unto His brethren, that He might become a merciful and faithful high priest before God, that He might be a propitiation for the sins of the people" (Hebrews 2:17).

See Papally Promulgated
Catechism of the Catholic Church

Q. 221. See paragraphs: 1562-1568

3. *Representing Christ, priests administer the Sacrament of the Anointing of the Sick.*

Through His priests, Christ gives comfort to those suffering serious illnesses and prepares them for their final union with God in the Sacrament of the Anointing of the Sick.

Sacred Scripture

"Is any man sick among you? Let him bring in the priests of the Church and let them pray over him, anointing him with oil in the Name of the Lord. And the prayer of faith shall save the sick man. And the Lord shall raise him up. And if he has any sins, they shall be forgiven him." *James 5: 14-15*

Vatican Council II

"Because it is joined with the episcopal order the office of priests shares in the authority by which Christ himself builds up and sanctifies and rules his Body. Hence the priesthood of priests, while presupposing the sacraments of initiation, is nevertheless conferred by its own particular sacrament. Through that sacrament priests, by the anointing of the Holy Spirit, are signed with a special character and so are configured to Christ the priest in such a way that they are able to act in the person of Christ the head." *Priests, 2*

"Whilst not having the supreme degree of the pontifical office, and notwithstanding the fact that they depend on the bishops in the exercise of their own proper power, the priests are for all that associated with them by reason of their sacerdotal dignity; and in virtue of the sacrament of Orders, after the image of Christ, the supreme and eternal priest (Heb. 5:1-10; 7:24; 9:11-28), they are consecrated in order to preach the Gospel and shepherd the faithful as well as to celebrate divine worship as true priests of the New Testament."
The Church, 28

"Priests exercise the function of Christ as Pastor and Head in proportion to their share of authority. In the name of the bishop they gather the family of God as a brotherhood endowed with the spirit of unity and lead it in Christ through the Spirit of God the Father. For the exercise of this ministry, as for the rest of the priest's functions, a spiritual power is given them, a power whose purpose is to build up." *Priests, 6*

"All priests, whether diocesan or religious, share and exercise with the bishop the one priesthood of Christ. They are thus constituted providential cooperators of this episcopal order." *Office of Bishops, 28*

"The spiritual gift which priests have received in ordination does not prepare them merely for a limited and circumscribed mission, but for the fullest, in fact the universal mission of salvation 'to the end of the earth' (Acts 1:8). The reason is that every priestly ministry shares in the fullness of the mission entrusted by Christ to the apostles." *Priests, 10*

"The People of God is formed into one in the first place by the Word of the living God, which is quite rightly sought from the mouth of priests. For since nobody can be saved who has not first believed, it is the first task of priests as co-workers of the bishops to preach the Gospel of God to all men. In this way they carry out the Lord's command: 'Go into all the world and preach the Gospel to every creature' (Mk. 16:15) and thus set up and increase the People of God." *Priests, 4*

"The Lord also appointed certain men as ministers, in order that they might be united in one body in which 'all the members have not the same function' (Rom. 12:4). These men were to hold in the community of the faithful the sacred power of Order, that of offering sacrifice and forgiving sins, and were to exercise the priestly office publicly on behalf of men in the name of Christ." *Priests, 2*

Papal Document

"For the nurturing and constant growth of the people of God, Christ the Lord instituted in the Church a variety of ministries, which work for the good of the whole body.

"From the apostolic age the diaconate has had a clearly outstanding position among these ministries, and it has always been held in great honor by the Church. Explicit testimony of this is given by the Apostle Paul both in his letter to the Philippians, in which he sends his greetings not only to the bishops but also to the deacons, and in a letter to Timothy, in which he illustrates the qualities and virtues that deacons must have in order to be worthy of their ministry."

Paul VI, Apostolic Letter Containing Norms For the Order of Diaconate

Prayer: *Heavenly Father, by Your Holy Spirit, You anointed Your only Son High Priest of the new and eternal covenant. With wisdom and love, You have planned that this one priesthood should continue in the Church.*

Christ gives the dignity of a royal priesthood to the people He has made His own. From His people, with a brother's love, He chooses men to

455

share His ministry, by having His Bishops lay hands on them. He appoints them to renew, in His Name, the sacrifice of our redemption, as they set before Your family His paschal meal. He calls them to lead Your holy people in love, nourish them by Your word, and strengthen them through the sacraments.

Father, may they give their lives in Your service and for the salvation of Your people, as they strive to grow in the likeness of Christ and to honor You by a courageous witness of faith and love. We ask Your help for those You have chosen to be deacons, priests, and Bishops. Protect the gifts You have given them, and let them yield a harvest worthy of You, through Christ our Lord. Amen.

Prayer

Jesus, Divine and Eternal High Priest, the boundless love of Your Heart moved You to establish the sacred ministry of Bishops, priests and deacons. I beg of You, let the life-giving waters of Your eternal love flow unceasingly into their hearts. Be the center of their lives and transform them into living images of You. By Your grace make them pure apostles of divine love and dispensers of the heavenly mysteries.

Act in them and through them, and grant that they may daily increase in virtue and holiness, and thus faithfully follow in Your sacred footsteps. Fill them with Your Holy Spirit, that they may do, in Your Name, those works of grace which You did in earth for the salvation of the world.

Divine Redeemer of souls, behold the vast number of souls walking in darkness, unbelief, or on the verge of eternal damnation. Look with mercy on the poor, the needy, the weak, and the innocent. Return to us through Your sacred ministers. Live in them; save souls through them; accompany them through life, teaching all of us and dispensing mercy and consolation everywhere. Unite the hearts of men to the Heart of God in that bond of love whereby You are united with the Father. To You, together with the Father and the Holy Spirit, be all honor and glory. Amen.

Chapter One Hundred One

The Sacrament of the Anointing of the Sick

Q. 222. What is the Anointing of the Sick?

The Anointing of the Sick is the sacrament for the seriously ill and those in danger of death due to old age.

Jesus showed a great love for people. He gave special care to the sick and cured them. "And when the sun was down, all they that had any sick with different types of diseases, brought them to Him. But He laying His hands on every one of them, healed them" (Luke, 4:40). Jesus continues to come to the ill in the Sacrament of the Anointing of the Sick.

The priest takes oil and anoints the sick person on the forehead and the hands, saying once: "Through this holy anointing, may the Lord in His love and mercy help you with the grace of the Holy Spirit. Amen. May the Lord Who frees you from sin save you and raise you up. Amen."

Vatican Council II

"And on behalf of the faithful who are moved to sorrow or are stricken with sickness, they [priests] exercise in an eminent degree a ministry of reconciliation and comfort, whilst they carry the needs and supplications of the faithful to God the Father (cf. Heb. 5:1-4)." *The Church, 28*

> **Prayer:** *Almighty and All-Loving Father, You are the source of eternal health for those who believe in You. May our brothers and sisters who are anointed in the Sacrament of the Anointing of the Sick, be refreshed with divine comfort from Heaven, and safely reach Your Kingdom of light and life, through our Lord and Savior Jesus Christ. Amen.*

See Papally Promulgated
Catechism of the Catholic Church

Q. 222. See paragraphs: 1511-1513

Q. 223. When is the Sacrament of the Anointing of the Sick best received?

This sacrament is best received as soon as possible when there is danger of death from sickness or old age.

This sacrament is for all who are seriously sick and not only for those whose death appears imminent. Moreover, the sacrament can be repeated for persons who get well and become seriously ill again. The priest should be called early to a sick person's side so that he can help the person to sincere sorrow for sins.

Vatican Council II

"'Extreme Unction,' which may also and more fittingly be called 'Anointing of the Sick,' is not a sacrament for those only who are at the point of death. Hence, as soon as anyone of the faithful begins to be in danger of death from sickness or old age, the fitting time for him to receive this sacrament has certainly already arrived." *Sacred Liturgy, 73*

Q. 224. What does the Church ask the Lord for by this anointing?

By this anointing and prayers, the Church, through her priests, asks the Lord (1) *to lighten the sufferings of the sick,* (2) *forgive their sins,* and (3) *bring them to eternal salvation.*

1. *By this anointing and prayers, the Church, through her priests, asks the Lord to lighten the sufferings of the sick.*

Christ comes to the ill in the Sacrament of the Anointing of the Sick. The sacrament may restore the person to health, as St. James says: "And the prayer of faith shall save the sick man: and the Lord shall raise him up; and if he be in sins, they shall be forgiven him" (James 5:15).

In this sacrament Christ gives us graces which enable us to bear the pain and distress of our illnesses with patience.

See Papally Promulgated
Catechism of the Catholic Church

Q. 223. See paragraph: 1514
Q. 224. See paragraphs: 1511, 1520-1523

Christ comes with consolation for the soul which is often experiencing pain, and sometimes fear and temptation.

2. *By this anointing and prayers, the Church, through her priests, asks the Lord to forgive the sins of the seriously sick.*

In this sacrament, Christ gives them graces enabling them to have a deep sorrow for their sins. This sorrow or contrition is required to have sins forgiven. In this regard, it is good to call a priest as soon as possible so he may help the sick person develop a sincere sorrow for sins and to otherwise help him prepare for a fruitful reception of the sacrament.

3. *By this sacrament, the Church, through her priests, asks the Lord to bring the seriously ill to eternal salvation.*

By the fruitful reception of the Sacrament of Anointing of the Sick, the seriously ill are prepared for a holy death. Besides forgiving their sins, Jesus helps the sick to offer themselves, their lives and the pains of their illness to Him with sincere Christian resignation, and with deep sorrow for their sins.

Vatican Council II

"By the sacred anointing of the sick and the prayer of the priests, the whole Church commends those who are ill to the suffering and glorified Lord that he may raise them up and save them (cf. Jas. 5:14-16)." *The Church, 11*

> **Prayer:** *God our Father, Your Son accepted His sufferings to teach us the virtue of patience in human illness. Hear the prayers that we offer for our sick brothers and sisters. May all who suffer pain, illness, or disease realize they are chosen to be saints, and know that they are joined to Christ in His suffering for the salvation of the world. We ask this in His Name. Amen.*

Q. 225. What does the Church encourage the sick to do?

The Church encourages the sick to help the People of God

See Papally Promulgated
Catechism of the Catholic Church

Q. 225. See paragraphs: 1505-1506, 1508

by offering their sufferings with the sufferings and death of Jesus.

The Anointing of the Sick prepares us for eternal life, if it is our time to die. It promotes the restoration to health, if it is God's will that we serve Him still longer here on earth. Since Christ increases the divine life in souls through this sacrament, He enables us to offer our sufferings in union with His own on the Cross, that we might share in the work of redemption. Thus we can contribute to the welfare of the Church, not only by atoning for sin, but also by meriting grace for the sanctification of the Church. If we share in the sufferings of Christ, we can expect to share also in His glory.

Before the Sacrament of the Anointing of the Sick, the priest usually offers the sick person the Sacrament of Penance, and, after the anointing, he gives him the Body and Blood of Christ. The Last Blessing, which may bring with it a plenary indulgence, is given at this time, too. This is what St. James had in mind when he said: "Confess therefore your sins one to another and pray for one another, that you may be saved. For the continual prayer of the just man obtains much" (James 5:16). The loving Christ pours His love and consolation upon a sick Christian through this sacrament.

Vatican Council II

"And indeed She [the Church] exhorts them to contribute to the good of the People of God by freely uniting themselves to the passion and death of Christ (cf. Rom. 8:17; Col. 1:24: Tim. 2:11-12; 1 Pet. 4:13)." *The Church, 11*

Prayer

Heavenly Father, Your Son, Jesus Christ, is our Way, our Truth, and our Life. May those who are anointed in the Sacrament of the Anointing of the Sick, entrust themselves to You with full confidence in all Your promises. Hear us as we ask Your loving help for the sick; restore their health, that they may again offer joyful thanks in Your Church. Show them the power of Your loving care. In Your kindness, make them well, if it is Your will. We ask this through Jesus Christ our Lord. Amen.

The Sacrament of Matrimony - I

Q. 226. Who instituted Marriage?

Marriage was instituted by the Creator Himself and was given certain purposes, laws and blessings by Him.

At the very beginning of the human race, when God created Adam and Eve, He instituted Marriage. We read in the book of Genesis: "And God created man to His own image; to the image of God He created him. Male and female He created them. And God blessed them, saying, 'Increase and multiply, and fill the earth, and subdue it, and rule over the fish of the sea, and the fowl of the air, and all living creatures that move upon the earth'" (Genesis 1:27-28).

God instituted Marriage for the procreation and education of children and for the mutual fulfillment of husband and wife.

Sacred Scripture

"Wherefore a man shall leave his father and mother, and shall cleave to his wife. And they shall be two in one flesh."

Genesis 2:24

Vatican Council II

"The intimate partnership of life and the love which constitutes the married state has been established by the creator and endowed by him with its own proper laws: it is rooted in the contract of its partners, that is, in their irrevocable personal consent. It is an institution confirmed by the divine law and receiving its stability, even in the eyes of society, from the human act by which the partners mutually surrender themselves to each other; for the good of the partners, of the children, and of society this sacred bond no longer depends on human decision alone." *Modern World, 48*

See Papally Promulgated
Catechism of the Catholic Church

Q. 226. See paragraphs: 1602-1605

Q. 227. Who raised Marriage to the dignity of a sacrament?

Jesus Christ raised Marriage of the baptized to the dignity of a sacrament. He made sacramental Marriage a lifelong, sacred union of husband and wife, by which they give themselves in complete surrender to each other and to Christ. Christ is the third partner in every sacramental Marriage.

Christian Marriage is the union of a man and woman who agree to totally share life, love, and Christian faith with one another and with God. It is a sacrament. The human relationship of Marriage is the sign through which God shows His love and communicates His life.

Vatican Council II

"Christ our Lord has abundantly blessed this love, which is rich in its various features, coming as it does from the spring of divine love and modeled on Christ's own union with the Church. Just as of old God encountered his people with a covenant of love and fidelity, so our Saviour, the spouse of the Church, now encounters Christian spouses through the sacrament of marriage." *Modern World, 48*

Q. 228. Who are the ministers of this sacrament?

The spouses, expressing their personal and lasting consent, are the ministers of the sacrament. The Sacrament of Marriage is begun in the mutual promises between husband and wife in the marriage ceremony; after that, it continues to be strengthened, as these promises are carried out in the years of married life. As the spouses selflessly share their lives in God, the husband is the minister of God's grace to his wife, and the wife is the minister of God's grace to her husband. A Bishop, priest or deacon officiates at the ceremony as the Church's witness to this act of grace.

Vatican Council II

"The intimate union of marriage, as a mutual giving of two persons, and the good of the children demand total fidelity

See Papally Promulgated
Catechism of the Catholic Church

Q. 227. See paragraph: 1601
Q. 228. See paragraphs: 1623, 1625-1630

from the spouses and require an unbreakable unity between them." *Modern World, 48*

Prayer

*H*eavenly Father, by this Sacrament of Matrimony, Your grace unites man and woman in an unbreakable bond of love and peace. You have designed the chaste love of husband and wife for the increase of both the human family and Your own family, which is born in Baptism.

*Y*ou are the loving Father of the world of nature; You are the loving Father of the new creation: nature's gift of children enriches the world as Your grace enriches Your Church.

*F*ather, You have made the bond of sacramental Marriage a holy mystery, a symbol of Christ's love for His Church. When You created mankind, You willed that man and wife should be one. By Your power, You have made everything out of nothing. In the beginning, You created the universe, and made mankind in Your own likeness. You gave man the constant help of woman so that man and woman should no longer be two, but one flesh; You teach us that what You have united may never be divided.

*B*y Your plan, man and woman are united. Married life has been established as the one blessing not forfeited by original sin or washed away in the flood.

*W*ith faith in You and in each other, those who are married have pledged their love. May their lives always bear witness to the reality of that love. Bind them in the loving union of Matrimony, and make their love fruitful, so that they may be living witnesses to Your divine love in the world. By Your divine providence, You have brought them together; now bless them all the days of their married life, through Jesus Christ our Lord and Savior. Amen.

The Sacrament of Matrimony - II

Q. 229. In what do we see the dignity of this sacrament?

We see the dignity of the sacrament in the fact that the spouses (1) *live together in Christ's grace;* (2) *imitate Christ's own love for His Church.*

1. *The spouses live together in Christ's grace.*

In the Sacrament of Matrimony, Christ comes to the man and wife to live with them, to give them His grace, and to help them fulfill their rights and duties to God, to each other, and to their children faithfully, until death.

Christian marriage is a sacrament because the Holy Spirit breathes God's own love into the love between husband and wife, so that each becomes a source of grace for the other. As a result, their many acts of self-giving not only strengthen their life together, but also cause them to grow in the life of God. He incorporates them as husband and wife in Christ, and gives them the means by which they can adjust to one another.

2. *The spouses imitate Christ's own love for His Church.*

The Sacrament of Matrimony shows God's love for man by showing how close Jesus is to His people. St. Paul tells us that marriage is a sign of the relationship between Jesus and His Church: "Husbands, love your wives, as Christ also loved the Church, and delivered Himself up for it ... This is a great mystery; but I speak in Christ and in the Church" (Ephesians 5:25; 32).

St. Paul calls the union between Christ and the Church a great mystery. He describes the Church as the Bride of Christ, decked out in splendor, and made beautiful by her Spouse. Christ has delivered Himself up for His Bride, that He might sanctify her and cleanse her of sin with His precious Blood. Marriage is the best human example of love, because in it, we see how deeply Jesus is committed to His followers.

Sacred Scripture

"Likewise, you husbands, dwelling with them according to knowledge, giving honor to the female as to the weaker vessel and as to the co-heirs of the grace of life; that your prayers may not be hindered." *1 Peter 3:7*

Vatican Council II

"He abides with them in order that by their mutual self-giving spouses will love each other with enduring fidelity, as He loved the Church and delivered himself for it. Authentic married love is caught up into divine love and is directed and enriched by the redemptive power of Christ and the salvific action of the Church, with the result that the spouses are effectively led to God and are helped and strengthened in their lofty role as fathers and mothers."*Modern World, 48*

> **Prayer:** *Heavenly Father, You created mankind in Your own image, and made man and woman to be joined as husband and wife in a union of bodies and hearts and so fulfill their mission in this world. To reveal the plan of Your love, You made the union of husband and wife an image of the covenant between You and Your people. In the fulfillment of this sacrament, the Marriage of Christian men and women is a sign of the marriage between Christ and the Church.*
>
> *Father, hear our prayers for those who have been united in Christian Marriage before Your altar. Give them Your blessing, and strengthen their love for each other. In Your fatherly love, watch over and protect those whom You have united in the Sacrament of Marriage. We ask this through Christ, our Lord. Amen.*

Q. 230. What do Christian spouses pledge themselves to do?

By this sacrament, Christian spouses are, as it were, consecrated to God (1) *to uphold the dignity of Matrimony* and (2) *to carry out its duties.*

1. *By this sacrament, Christian spouses are, as it were, consecrated to God to uphold the dignity of Matrimony.*

See Papally Promulgated
Catechism of the Catholic Church

Q. 229. See paragraph: 1617
Q. 230. See paragraphs: 1621, 1644-1648

The dignity of sacramental Marriage is seen in mutual fulfillment, through sacrificial love for one another, and in the procreation and creation of human life. Through their mutual love, the couple help each other, and their children, to fully become what God has created each to be. At the same time, through the sexual expression of their love, they become partners with God in the bringing forth of new life.

2. By this sacrament, Christian spouses are, as it were, consecrated to God to carry out its duties.

In this sacrament, the spouses are given special graces which enable them to carry out the duties of Matrimony, toward each other and towards their children. The sacrament confers an increase in sanctifying grace and in all the actual graces that are needed for the fulfillment of the vocation of parenthood. These graces bring about an ever deeper union of man and wife in soul and body, that they might live up to what they have promised in their marriage vows.

Vatican Council II

"Spouses, therefore, are fortified and, as it were, consecrated for the duties and dignity of their state by a special sacrament, fulfilling their conjugal and family role by virtue of this sacrament, spouses are penetrated with the spirit of Christ and their whole life is suffused by faith, hope, and charity; thus they increasingly further their own perfection and their mutual sanctification, and together they render glory to God." *Modern World, 48*

"Christian couples are, for each other, for their children and for their relatives, co-operators of grace and witnesses of the faith. They are the first to pass on the faith to their children and to educate them in it. By word and example they form them to a Christian and apostolic life; they offer them wise guidance in the choice of vocation, and if they discover in them a sacred vocation they encourage it with all care.

"To give clear proof in their own lives of the indissolubility and holiness of the marriage bond; to assert with vigor the right and duty of parents and guardians to give their children a Christian upbringing; to defend the dignity and legitimate autonomy of the family: this has always been the duty of married persons; today, however, it has become the most important aspect of their apostolate." *Lay People, 11*

Prayer

Heavenly Father, stretch out Your hand and bless those who have received the Sacrament of Marriage. May spouses share with each other the gifts of Your love, and become one in heart and mind, as a witness to Your presence in their marriage. Help them to create a home together, and give them children to be formed by the Gospel, and to have a place in Your family.

Give Your blessing to wives, so that they may be good wives and mothers, caring for the home, faithful in love for their husbands, generous, and kind. Give Your blessing to husbands, so that they may be faithful husbands and exemplary fathers.

Lord God, bless those You have joined together in Holy Matrimony. Keep them close to You always. May their love for each other proclaim to all the world their faith in You. Grant that as they come together to Your table on earth, they may one day also have the joy of sharing Your feast in Heaven.

God the Father, give them Your joy and bless them in their children. God the Son, have mercy on them and help them in good times and bad. God the Holy Spirit, always fill their hearts with Your love. Holy Trinity, One God, we praise You and adore You, now and forever. Amen.

The Sacrament of Matrimony - III

Q. 231. Why was marriage instituted?

Marriage was instituted (1) *to bring children into the world and to educate them,* and (2) *to promote and deepen the love of the spouses for each other.*

1. *Marriage was instituted to bring children into the world and to educate them.*

From married love comes children. Nature and Scripture teach us that begetting children is one of the purposes as well as a blessing of Marriage. God blessed Adam and Eve and said: "Increase and multiply, and fill the earth and subdue it" (Genesis 1:28). In His love for us, God gives us life and the care we need as children through our parents.

Vatican Council II

"Married couples should regard it as their proper mission to transmit human life and to educate their children; they should realize that they are thereby cooperating with the love of God the Creator and are, in a certain sense, its interpreters. This involves the fulfillment of their role with a sense of human and Christian responsibility and the formation of correct judgments through docile respect for God and common reflection and effort; it also involves a consideration of their own good and the good of their children already born or yet to come, an ability to read the signs of the times and of their own situation on the material and spiritual level, and, finally, an estimation of the good of the family, of society, and of the Church. It is the married couple themselves who must in the last analysis arrive at these judgments before God. Married people should realize that in their behavior they may not sim-

See Papally Promulgated
Catechism of the Catholic Church

Q. 231. See paragraphs: 1603-1605, 1643, 1652-1654

ply follow their own fancy but must be ruled by conscience —
and conscience ought to be conformed to the law of God in the
light of the teaching authority of the Church, which is the authentic interpreter of divine law.

"But marriage is not merely for the procreation of children:
its nature as an indissoluble compact between two people and
the good of the children demand that the mutual love of the
partners be properly shown, that it should grow and mature.
Even in cases where despite the intense desire of the spouses
there are no children, marriage still retains its character of
being a whole manner and communion of life and preserves
its value and indissolubility." *Modern World, 50*

"By its very nature the institution of marriage and married
love is ordered to the procreation and education of the offspring and it is in them that it finds its crowning glory. Thus
the man and woman, who 'are no longer two but one' (Mt. 19:6),
help and serve each other by their marriage partnership;
they become conscious of their unity and experience it more
deeply from day to day." *Modern World, 48*

2. *Marriage was instituted to promote and deepen the love
of the spouses for each other.*

God's holy purpose in marriage is clear. The Lord God said:
"It is not good for man to be alone; let us make him a help
mate like unto himself" (Genesis 2:18). The love between a husband and wife should be a source of great strength and comfort to them in the important task of taking care of their
children according to God's will.

Vatican Council II

"The Lord, wishing to bestow special gifts of grace and divine love on it [i.e., married love], has restored, perfected, and
elevated it. A love like that, bringing together the human and
the divine, leads the partners to a free and mutual giving of
self, experienced in tenderness and action, and permeates
their whole lives; besides, this love is actually developed and
increased by the exercise of it. This is a far cry from mere
erotic attraction which is pursued in selfishness and soon
fades away in wretchedness.

"Married love is uniquely expressed and perfected by the
exercise of the acts proper to marriage. Hence the acts in
marriage, by which the intimate and chaste union of the
spouses takes place, are noble and honorable; the truly human performance of these acts fosters the self-giving they sig-

nify and enriches the spouses in joy and gratitude. Endorsed by mutual fidelity and, above all, consecrated by Christ's sacrament, this love abides faithfully in mind and body in prosperity and adversity and hence excludes both adultery and divorce. The unity of marriage, distinctly recognized by our Lord, is made clear in the equal personal dignity which must be accorded to man and wife in mutual and unreserved affection." *Modern World, 49*

"God Himself said: 'It is not good for man to be alone; let us make him a help like unto himself' (Gen. 2:18), and 'from the beginning (he) made them male and female' (Mt. 19:4); wishing to associate them in a special way with his own creative work, God blessed man and woman with the words: 'Be fruitful and multiply' (Gen. 1:28)." *Modern World, 50*

> **Prayer:** *Heavenly Father, increase the faith of newly-weds in You and in each other, and, through them, bless Your Church with Christian children. You made man and woman one in the Sacrament of Marriage. May the mystery of Christ's unselfish love, which we celebrate in the Eucharist, increase their love for You and for each other. May the husband put his trust in his wife and recognize that she is his equal and heir with him to the life of grace. May he always honor her and love her as Christ loves His Bride, the Church. May wives always follow the example of the holy women whose praises are sung in the Scripture!*
>
> *God, Heavenly Father, Creator of the universe, Maker of man and woman in Your own likeness, source of blessing for married life, we humbly pray to You for those who are united in the Sacrament of Marriage. May Your fullest blessing come upon them, so that they may together rejoice in Your grace, be happy in their married love, and enrich Your Church. We ask this through Jesus Christ our Lord, to Whom with You and the Holy Spirit be all honor and glory. Amen.*

Q. 232. How long does the bond of sacramental marriage last?

See Papally Promulgated
Catechism of the Catholic Church

Q. 232. See paragraphs: 1601, 1614-1615

The bond of sacramental marriage lasts until the death of one of the spouses.

The marital bond is rooted in the conjugal covenant of personal consent, whereby spouses give themselves to each other and accept one another. A relationship arises which, by divine will, is a lasting one. This bond no longer depends on human decisions alone.

Marriage is for life. It lasts until the death of one of the parties. Marriage is permanent because Jesus taught that married people should belong completely to each other just as He belongs completely to His Church. This mutual giving and acceptance of one another is expressed in the personal consent which cements the marital bond.

In order to protect the holy state of sacramental Marriage, the people who enter into it, and their children, God revealed that a man may marry only one wife, unless his wife dies; and a wife only one husband, unless her husband dies.

Since Marriage is life-long, divorce is an evil. The love of a Christian husband and wife for each other must endure. Divorce should be unthinkable for Christians, just as it is unthinkable that Christ should separate Himself from His Bride, the Church. In extreme cases, civil divorce is permitted, but only for its civil effects. There may be no remarriage, for in civil divorce there is no real breaking of the marital bond created between a Christian husband and wife.

Jesus Christ forbade divorce and remarriage when He said: "What therefore God has joined together, let not man put asunder" (Mark 10:9). "And in the house again His disciples asked Him concerning the same thing. And He said to them, 'Whosoever shall put away his wife and marry another, commits adultery against her. And if the wife shall put away her husband, and be married to another, she commits adultery'" (Mark 10:11-12).

St. Paul says: "For the woman that has a husband, while her husband lives is bound by the law. But if her husband dies, she is loosed from the law of her husband" (Romans 7:2).

Not even the Pope can dissolve a valid Christian Marriage. Even after a divorce has been granted by a civil court, the husband and wife of a valid Christian Marriage remain husband and wife before God.

Prayer

Heavenly Father, keep married couples always true to Your commandments. Keep them faithful to one another, and let them be living examples of Christian life. Give them the strength which comes from the Gospel, so that they may be witnesses of Christ to others.

Bless them with children and help them to be good parents. May they live to see their children's children, and, after a happy old age, grant them fullness of life with the saints in the Kingdom of Heaven. We ask this in the Name of Christ our Lord. Amen.

Chapter One Hundred Five

The Sacrament of Matrimony - IV

Q. 233. What is the aim of conjugal love and family life?

The true practice of conjugal love, and the whole meaning of the family life which results from it, has this aim: that the couple be ready, with generous hearts, to cooperate with the love of the Creator and the Savior, Who through them, will enlarge and enrich His own family day by day.

The most complete expression of the unity of husband and wife is the sexual act, the fulfillment of the mutual love which Christ so desires for them. A man and woman united in Christian Marriage are a sign of the union between the risen Christ and His Church.

The married couple's responsibility for new life is this: Each couple must determine, in the light of all the circumstances of their married life, what the unique creative partnership that God invites them to share with Him is. They plan their family through a conscientious assessment of what they can do to further the good of their whole family and of society.

In this they are helped by the teaching of the Church, their own knowledge of themselves and their family situation, and the example of other faithful Christians. As in all of life's decisions, here, too, people must finally make their decisions according to well-informed Christian consciences.

Sacred Scripture

"And God blessed them and said, 'Increase and multiply, and fill the earth and subdue it.' " *Genesis 1:28*

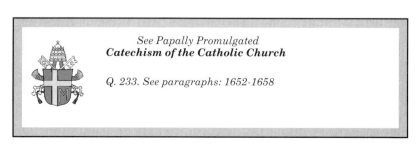

See Papally Promulgated
Catechism of the Catholic Church

Q. 233. See paragraphs: 1652-1658

473

Vatican Council II

"In virtue of the sacrament of Matrimony by which they signify and share (cf. Eph. 5:32) the mystery of the unity and faithful love between Christ and the Church, Christian married couples help one another to attain holiness in their married life and in the rearing of their children. Hence by reason of their state in life and of their position they have their own gifts in the People of God. (cf. 1 Cor. 7:7) From the marriage of Christians there comes the family in which new citizens of human society are born and, by the grace of the Holy Spirit in Baptism, those are made children of God so that the People of God may be perpetuated throughout the centuries."

The Church, 11

"As it is the parents who have given life to their children, on them lies the gravest obligation of educating their family. They must therefore be recognized as being primarily and principally responsible for their education. The role of parents in education is of such importance that it is almost impossible to provide an adequate substitute. It is therefore the duty of parents to create a family atmosphere inspired by love and devotion to God and their fellow-men which will promote an integrated, personal and social education of their children. The family is therefore the principal school of the social virtues which are necessary to every society. It is therefore above all in the Christian family, inspired by the grace and the responsibility of the sacrament of matrimony, that children should be taught to know and worship God and to love their neighbor, in accordance with the faith which they have received in earliest infancy and in the sacrament of Baptism. In it, also, they will have their first experience of a well-balanced human society and of the Church. Finally it is through the family that they are gradually initiated into association with their fellow-men in civil life and as members of the People of God. Parents should, therefore, appreciate how important a role the truly Christian family plays in the life and progress of the whole people of God." *Education, 3*

Prayer: *God of goodness and mercy, to Your fatherly protection we commend our family, our household, and all that belongs to us. We entrust all of them to Your love and keeping. Fill our home with Your blessings as You filled the Holy House of Nazareth with Your presence.*

Q. 234. What is the calling of every family?

The calling of every family is to share their lives together with deep love, according to God's Will. The family is the most sacred of all societies. In His love for us God gives us life and the care we need as children through our parents. Character, beliefs, thoughts, and virtues should be nurtured by good, loving parents. The members of the family form a community and share their lives together on a deep, personal level. Through a truly Christian Marriage, the family functions perfectly as a community. It is part of the family's vocation to become a community, one which is open to the Church and to the world. Problems and misunderstandings should be expected in sacramental Marriage, for it is a union of two sinful human beings. In this sacrament, however, Christ gives husband and wife the power to deal with these tensions, and the grace to destroy the sins which cause them.

Vatican Council II

"The family is the place where different generations come together and help one another to grow wiser and harmonize the rights of individuals with other demands of social life; as such it constitutes the basis of society. Everyone, therefore, who exercises an influence in the community and in social groups should devote himself effectively to the welfare of marriage and the family." *Modern World, 52*

See Papally Promulgated
Catechism of the Catholic Church

Q. 234. See paragraphs: 1646-1651, 2201-2206, 2214-2231, 2364-2365

Q. 235. How does the Christian family manifest the Savior's living presence in the world?

The Christian family manifests the Savior's living presence in the world by (1) *the mutual love of the spouses,* (2) *the spouses' generous fruitfulness,* (3) *their union and faithfulness,* and (4) *the loving way in which the members work together.*

1. *The Christian family manifests the Savior's living presence in the world by the mutual love of the spouses.*

Marriage is a life-long partnership of love. Since Christ elevated Matrimony to the dignity of a sacrament for the baptized, the husband and wife, living in Christ's grace, imitate and, in a certain way, represent the love of Christ Himself for His Church. By their love for each other, they manifest Christ's presence in the world.

2. *The Christian family manifests the Savior's living presence in the world by their generous fruitfulness.*

Children are a great blessing in the Sacrament of Marriage. One of the principal fruits of this sacramental union is children, who make the love of husbands and wives richer and so fulfill one of the purposes of Matrimony.

In the Sacrament of Matrimony, the Holy Spirit unites man and woman, and consecrates them so that they may bring Christ's three-fold mission of prophet, king and priest into family life. United in Christ, they build up the Church by

See Papally Promulgated
Catechism of the Catholic Church

Q. 235. See paragraphs: 1655-1658, 2204-2206

teaching, guiding, and sanctifying their children and one another. If husbands and wives are generous to God in working with Him, according to His will, and enlarging His own family on earth, He will bless them in this life and especially in Heaven. Their fruitfulness manifests Christ's presence in the world.

3. *The Christian family manifests the Savior's living presence in the world by the spouses' union and faithfulness.*

Christian Marriage teaches people self-giving and sacrifice. It creates a caring climate for the raising of children. It educates the young to cooperate with and have concern for others. This can be accomplished only with the help of Christ's grace.

If a couple is to carry on Christ's mission, it is essential that they present themselves to their family and to the world as one in Christ. With the generous actual graces of the Spirit, given in the Sacrament of Matrimony, they can grow ever closer together. The Spirit gives them power to dedicate themselves fully to each other and to do work on whatever might divide them: being indifferent to each other's needs, hurting each others feelings, and failing to understand.

4. *The Christian family manifests the Savior's living presence in the world by the loving way in which the members work together.*

Anything expressive of love is already a reaching out to God. God uses man's efforts at selflessness to draw him ever more deeply into His own life.

In making it a sacrament, Christ gave Matrimony a new beauty and a new power to sanctify. Sacramental Marriage is not merely the lawful union of man and wife; it is a source of holiness — a means of closer union of a man and woman with God, as well as with each other. The union of husband and wife is a life-giving union which imparts grace to their souls. As this grace reaches the children of a family, the Christian family can manifest Christ's presence in the world.

Vatican Council II

"The mission of being the primary vital cell of society has been given to the family by God himself. This mission will be accomplished if the family, by the mutual affection of its members and by family prayer, presents itself as a domestic sanctuary of the Church; if the whole family takes its part in the Church's liturgical worship; if finally, it offers active hospitality, and practices justice and other good works for the benefit of all its brothers suffering from want." *Lay People, 11*

"The Christian family springs from marriage, which is an image and a sharing in the partnership of love between Christ and the Church; it will show forth to all men Christ's living presence in the world and the authentic nature of the Church by the love and generous fruitfulness of the spouses, by their unity and fidelity, and by the loving way in which all members of the family cooperate with each other."

Modern World, 48

Prayer

Jesus, bless and protect our family. Mary, Mother of grace and mercy, defend us against the wicked spirits. Reconcile us with your Son, and entrust us to His keeping, that we may be made worthy of His promises.

Give all of us the grace to live in perfect harmony and charity toward our neighbors. Grant that every one of us may deserve, by a holy life, the comfort of the holy sacraments at the hour of death.

Saint Joseph, foster-father of our Savior, guardian of His holy Mother, head of the Holy Family, intercede for us, bless us, and defend our home at all times. Saint Michael, defend us against all evil that might threaten our souls. Saint Gabriel, make us understand the Holy Will of God. Saint Raphael, keep us free from all sickness, and from every danger to our lives. Our holy Guardian Angels, keep us safely on the path of salvation. Our holy Patrons, pray for us at the throne of God.

Bless our home, God the Father, Who created us, God the Son, Who suffered for us upon the Cross, and God the Holy Spirit, Who sanctified us in Baptism. May the one God in three divine Persons preserve our bodies, purify our minds, direct our hearts, and bring us all to everlasting life.

Lord, our God, we offer You our hearts, united in the strongest and most sincere love. We pray that Jesus in the Blessed Sacrament of the Altar may be the daily food of our souls and bodies, and that Jesus may be the center of our affections, just as He was for Mary and Joseph. Finally, Lord, let sin never disturb our union on earth. May we be eternally united in Heaven with You and all Your saints. Glory be to the Father, glory be to the Son, and glory be to the Holy Spirit! Amen.

The Sacraments - II

—

The Holy Eucharist and Prayer

The Holy Eucharist

Bloody sacrifice　　**Unbloody Sacrifice**

The Holy Eucharist
The Old Testament Sacrifices

Q. 236. What is a sacrifice to God?

A sacrifice to God consists in a lawful priest offering some befitting gift to God, as a victim in the name of the people, in order to acknowledge God's absolute sovereignty over creation.

In a sacrifice, man gives to God something of his own property; this surrender occurs through real or symbolic destruction, whereby the gift is removed from its usefulness to man. In this manner, man recognizes that God is the Lord of everything he has. This homage is worship or the act of adoration. A sacrifice may also express one's thanks to God for His blessings and of imploring Him to continue His goodness.

The sacrifices of the Old Testament are divided into bloody and unbloody offerings. The material of the bloody sacrifices was the animals of the herd, such as cattle, sheep, and goats. According to the reasons for offering, sacrifices were divided into holocausts, or burnt offerings, sin offerings, and peace offerings. Holocausts, or the burning and offering up of an entire victim to God, served to remind the ancient Hebrews of God's supreme dominion over His creatures and of the need for inner purity and complete self-surrender to His will. Sin offerings were made in atonement for sin. A peace offering was a thank or praise offering.

Just as the burnt offering and sin offering were types (or foreshadows) of Christ's sacrificial death on the Cross, so, too, the peace offering was a type (or foreshadow) of the Blessed Sacrament.

The Passover was one of the three major feasts of ancient Judaism that was celebrated every year, the others being the

See Papally Promulgated
Catechism of the Catholic Church

Q. 236. See paragraphs: 433, 696, 1032, 1334, 1539, 2581

feasts of Pentecost and Tabernacles. It was obligatory at the Passover for every male Israelite to appear before the sanctuary of the tabernacle (or Temple) at Jerusalem. Before sunset on the fourteenth day of the month of Nisan, an unblemished lamb was to be slaughtered in the court of the Temple, and after sunset, this lamb, which was roasted, was eaten with unleavened bread, bitter herbs, and wine. During the meal various psalms were recited or sung.

The Passover was a memorial commanded by God, in memory of, and in thanksgiving for the deliverance of the Israelites from the slavery of Egypt. At that time, the angel of the Passover "passed over" the homes of the Israelites which were marked with the blood of the lamb that had been sacrificed. But the angel put to death the first-born son of each Egyptian family as a punishment from God. It was the most terrible of the ten plagues which God sent to the Egyptians for refusing to release the Israelites from slavery.

The lamb sacrificed for the feast is taken by St. John and St. Paul as a type or figure of Jesus Christ as the Victim. Indeed, Jesus is called the Lamb; this term refers to His innocence.

Prayer: *Jesus our Savior, You redeemed us by Your death and Resurrection. You went up to Jerusalem to suffer and die on the Cross, and so enter Your glory only to bring Your Church to the Passover feast of Heaven.*

You were lifted high on the Cross, the tree of life; give its fruit to those who have been reborn in Baptism. On the Cross You forgave the repentant thief; forgive us our sins.

We thank You, Jesus, for bringing us life by Your death on the Cross, the supreme sacrifice offered to Your Father in atonement for our sins. The sacrifices of the Old Testament were only symbols of this one true sacrifice. By Your death, You raised us to life. You have shown us Your love and fidelity and have made us new creations by Your Passion. Keep us from falling again into sin. Help us to deny ourselves, yet not deny those in need.

You made Your Cross the tree of life; grant its fruit to those reborn in Baptism. Savior of mankind, through Your sacrifice of the Cross, offered again in each Holy Mass, bring us sinners into Your Kingdom. All power and glory be to the Father, Son, and Holy Spirit. Amen.

When John the Baptist caught sight of Jesus coming toward him, he exclaimed: "Behold the Lamb of God, behold Him who takes away the sin of the world" (John 1:29).

St. Paul told the Corinthians: "Purge out the old leaven, that you may be a new mass of dough, as you are unleavened. For Christ our Passover is sacrificed. Therefore let us feast, not with the old leaven, nor with the leaven of malice and wickedness; but with the unleavened bread of sincerity and truth" (1 Corinthians 5:7-8).

The Passover lamb was a real sacrifice, a combination of the sin and peace offerings; similarly, our Lord died for us as a sin offering on the Cross, and gives Himself to us as a peace offering in the Blessed Sacrament of the Altar.

It was during the Passover meal which Jesus ate with His Apostles that He instituted the Holy Eucharist. He is the true Lamb of God, sacrificed on the Cross and offered again in an unbloody manner at Mass; He is also the food of our souls in Holy Communion.

What is the most perfect and most pleasing sacrifice that we can offer to God?

Jesus Christ, the Lamb of God Who takes away the sins of the world is the most perfect and most pleasing sacrifice we can offer to God.

Indeed, any other sacrifice we offer is pleasing to God only when we, being in the state of grace, offer it in union with the supreme sacrifice of His Son.

How can we offer Jesus to God on our behalf?

When we worship God at Mass, we baptized Catholics, as sharers in Christ's priesthood, are privileged to participate in His eternal sacrifice of Himself to the Father on our behalf. As members of the priesthood of the faithful, we offer not only ourselves to the Father, along with our intentions, but especially that which is most precious and acceptable to Him, namely His Divine Son, the perfect Victim Who takes away the sins of the world.*

---

*[Editor's Note - See Vatican Council II document, "Dogmatic Constitution on the Church," section 10.]

Sacred Scripture

"And whereas indeed He was the Son of God, He learned obedience by the things which He suffered. And being consummated, He became, to all that obey Him, the cause of eternal salvation. Called by God a high priest according to the order of Melchisedech." *Hebrews 5:8-10*

"...Melchisedech the King of Salem bringing forth bread and wine, for he was the priest of the most high God."

Genesis 14:18

Vatican Council II

"The wonderful works of God among the people of the Old Testament were but a prelude to the work of Christ our Lord in redeeming mankind and giving perfect glory to God. He achieved his task principally by the paschal mystery of his blessed passion, resurrection from the dead, and glorious ascension, whereby 'dying, he destroyed our death, and rising, restored our life.' " *Sacred Liturgy, 5*

Prayer

Father, by the blood of Your own Son, You have set us free and saved us from death. Continue Your work of salvation within us, that by constantly celebrating the mystery of our salvation in the Holy Sacrifice of the Mass, we may reach the eternal life it promises. May the blood of our Savior be for us a fountain of water, springing up to eternal life.

Father, You have given us life on this earth, and have blessed us with the grace of redemption through the Eucharistic Sacrifice of Your beloved Son. Bestow Your greatest blessing on us, the fullness of eternal life with You.

God our Father, to show the way of salvation, You chose to put the standard of the Cross before us; You fulfilled the ancient prophecies in Christ's Passover from death to life. Do not let us rouse Your indignation by sin, but, rather, through the sacrifice of ourselves, with Him in the Holy Sacrifice of the Mass, may He give us everlasting life.

He promised: "I am the living bread which has come down from Heaven. Anyone who eats this bread will live forever; and the bread that I shall give is My flesh, for the life of the world" (John 6:51). May we come to possess His divine life completely in the Kingdom where He lives forever. Amen.

The Institution of The Eucharist

Q. 237. What is the Eucharist?

The Eucharist is the sacrament of the Body and Blood of Jesus Christ. Under the appearance of bread and wine, the Body, Blood, Soul, and Divinity of Christ are really, truly, and substantially present for the nourishment of souls, and as a sacrifice of the Church.

Vatican Council II

"[Christ] is present in the Sacrifice of the Mass not only in the person of his minister, 'the same now offering, through the ministry of priests, who formerly offered himself on the Cross,' but especially in the eucharistic species." *Sacred Liturgy, 7*

Q. 238. Why is the Eucharistic celebration carried out?

The Eucharistic celebration is carried out in obedience to the words of Jesus at the Last Supper: "Do this as a memorial of Me."

St. Luke writes of Jesus at the Last Supper, "And taking bread, He gave thanks, and broke it; and gave it to them, saying 'This is My Body, which is given for you. Do this for a commemoration of Me.' In like manner the chalice also, after He had supped, saying: 'This is the chalice, the New Testament in My Blood, which shall be shed for you.' " (Luke 22:19-20)

Jesus gave the Apostles both the command and the power to bring the Eucharist to us when He said, "Do this for a commemoration of Me" (Luke 22:19-20).

The Mass is the Church's way of doing what Jesus did at the Last Supper. St. Paul wrote, "For I have received of the Lord that which also I delivered unto you, that the Lord Jesus, the same night in which He was betrayed, took bread,

See Papally Promulgated
Catechism of the Catholic Church

Q. 237. See paragraphs: 1322-1332
Q. 238. See paragraphs: 1356-1358

and giving thanks, broke it, and said: 'Take and eat: this is My Body, which shall be delivered for you: do this for the commemoration of Me.' In like manner also the chalice, after He had supped, saying: 'This chalice is the New Testament in My Blood: do this, as often as you shall drink, for the commemoration of Me.' For as often as you shall eat this bread, and drink the chalice, you shall show the death of the Lord, until He comes" (1 Corinthians 11:23-26).

The Church does this to remember Jesus, and to be reunited with Him. At the Last Supper, Jesus gave the Apostles His own Body and Blood, under the appearance of bread and wine. He then asked them to remember Him always by doing this same thing among themselves.

Sacred Scripture

"And the disciples did as Jesus appointed to them, and they prepared the Passover. But when it was evening, He sat down with His twelve disciples." *Matthew 26:19-20*

Vatican Council II

"At the Last Supper, on the night he was betrayed, our Savior instituted the eucharistic sacrifice of his Body and Blood. This he did in order to perpetuate the sacrifice of the Cross throughout the ages until he should come again, and so to entrust to his beloved Spouse, the Church, a memorial of his death and resurrection: a sacrament of love, a sign of unity, a bond of charity, a paschal banquet in which Christ is consumed, the mind is filled with grace, and a pledge of future glory is given to us." *Sacred Liturgy, 47*

Prayer

Jesus, the Last Supper was the solemn opening of Your holy Passion; whereby You suffered death for the world's salvation. For the first time You pronounced the words of sublime mystery whereby You changed bread and wine into Your Sacred Body and Blood.

The Eucharist is a memorial of Your Passion and death. The flesh which You gave to Your Apostles to eat at the Last Supper was that of a sacrificial Victim: the blood was that blood which would be shed on the Altar of the Cross. Thus, the sacrifice of the Cross was offered beforehand in a spiritual manner.

You combined the institution of the Holy Eucharist with the celebration of the legal Passover, immediately before Your Passion. No Old Testament type (or prefigurement) symbolizes the Eucharist as sacrifice and sacrament so closely as does the paschal lamb, which is at once a sacrifice and a communion.

Jesus, You bequeathed to the Church its choicest treasure and chief riches — the Blessed Sacrament. It is its very heart, of which every Mass that is celebrated is a pulsation, sending its lifeblood — Your own Blood — into every member of its body, imparting life, growth, and well-being.

Jesus, Your last will is expressed in the words of St. Luke: "Take and eat... Do this in memorial of Me." You gave the Apostles and those who would follow them, the Bishops and priests of the Church, the power and the command to do, at Holy Mass, what You Yourself had done. Thus, You continue to keep Your promise to give Your Body and Blood. At the words of consecration spoken by the priest, "This is My Body...this is My Blood," what takes place can only be verified by faith. We believe that You, the Son of God, become present under the outward forms of bread and wine. You change them into Your Body and Blood through the agency of Your priests. Only the appearances of bread and wine remain.

Your last will is addressed not only to the Apostles who are to consecrate the Eucharist, but also to the faithful who are to receive It. Since the salvation of souls is the great desire of Your Sacred Heart, You certainly want people to use the means You have given to save their souls. May we always receive it with great love and devotion, for Your greater honor and glory, and for the salvation of souls. Amen.

Chapter One Hundred Eight

The Eucharist Made Present

Q. 239. What happens when a priest speaks the words of Eucharistic consecration?

When, in the Eucharistic Prayer, a priest pronounces the words of Eucharistic consecration, the bread and wine, by the power of the Holy Spirit, are changed into the Body and Blood of Christ, which were given for us in sacrifice.

Jesus' words and power made Him really and substantially present under the outward appearances of bread and wine which He gave the Apostles to eat; so, they actually received Jesus in that meal and were united with Him. This made the Apostles one with Jesus and all that He did. They shared in both His gift of Himself to His Father on the Cross and in the Father's gift of life to Jesus in the Resurrection. The Apostles then gave Christ to the People of God in the Eucharist.

The Church re-creates the Last Supper by bringing followers of Jesus together and by recalling, through readings and prayers, what God has done for His people. Then the priest repeats what Jesus said at the Last Supper, and himself offers the consecrated Bread (and, on some occasions, consecrated Wine) to the people.

Many Protestants object to the Catholic priesthood, claiming that it counters what is written in the New Testament Letter to the Hebrews. The passage referred to says: "We are sanctified through the offering of the Body of Christ once for all. And every [Old Testament high] priest stands daily ministering and offering oftentimes the same sacrifices, which can never take away sins. But this man [Jesus], after He had offered one sacrifice for sins for ever, sat down on the right hand of God" (Hebrews 10:10-13). How does the Catholic Church interpret these words?

See Papally Promulgated
Catechism of the Catholic Church

Q. 239. See paragraphs: 1373-1377

The Catholic Church teaches that the Holy Sacrifice of the Mass does not involve Christ's death for us anew. Rather, it is a participation in the one sacrifice of Christ on Calvary, in an unbloody manner, the benefits of which continue into eternity. Jesus continually lives to make intercession for us, offering to the Father, on our behalf, Himself, given for us on the Cross.

"[Christ] has an everlasting priesthood...always living to make intercession for us" (Hebrews 7:24-25).

Every ordained Catholic priest participates in the one priesthood of Christ, which alone can take away the sins of the world. When the priest pronounces the words of Eucharistic consecration, he is said to do so " in persona Christi," that is, in the person of Christ. It is really Christ speaking through the words of His priest, when the priest says, "This is My Body," and "This is My Blood." The Old Testament sacrifices could never take away sins, but the sacrifice of Jesus on the Cross can. We participate in this sacrifice when we participate in the Holy Sacrifice of the Mass over which an ordained priest presides.

Sacred Scripture

" 'I am the living Bread which came down from Heaven. If any man eats of this Bread, he shall live for ever; and the Bread that I will give, is My Flesh, for the life of the world.' The Jews therefore strove among themselves, saying, 'How can this man give us His Flesh to eat?' Then Jesus said to them, 'Amen, amen I say unto you, except you eat the Flesh of the Son of Man, and drink His Blood, you shall not have life in you.' " *John 6:51-53*

"The chalice of benediction, which we bless, is it not the communion of the Blood of Christ? And the bread, which we break, is it not the partaking of the Body of the Lord?"

1 Corinthians 10:16

Vatican Council II

"[Christ] is present in the Sacrifice of the Mass not only in the person of His minister, the same now offering, through the ministry of priests, Who formerly offered Himself on the cross, but especially in the eucharistic species." *Sacred Liturgy, 7*

Q. 240. How is Christ present in the Eucharist?

Christ Himself, true God and true man, is really and substantially present, in a mysterious way, under the appearances of bread and wine.

After the priest speaks the words of consecration, the appearances of bread and wine remain, meaning that bread and wine appear to be there but are not really there substantially. When our Lord gave the Apostles, at the Last Supper, His Body, the Body looked like bread and even tasted like bread, but it was not bread; it was His Body, for He said so. When our Lord gave the Apostles His Blood, the Blood appeared to be wine and even tasted like wine, but it was not wine; it was His Blood, for He said so.

This holy sacrament looks like bread and tastes like bread, but it is not bread; it is Jesus. To come to us, Jesus covers Himself with the appearances of bread and wine. We cannot understand this, but we take the word of God that it is so. We have such belief in God, Who is all-truthful, that we believe all that He said about the Holy Eucharist. Therefore, the Eucharist is called the Mystery of Faith.

All Catholic priests have the power to change bread and wine into Christ. In the Eucharist, it is Christ Himself Who consecrates through the priest as the words of consecration are said: "This is My Body... This cup is the New Covenant in My Blood."

Roman Curial Document

"For even in the reserved sacrament [Christ] is to be adored because he is substantially present there through the conversion of bread and wine which, as the Council of Trent tells us, is most aptly named transubstantiation."

Instruction on Worship of the Eucharistic Mystery,
Sacred Congregation of Rites, May 25, 1967, Introduction, 48

Prayer: *Father, Almighty God, You teach us, in both the Old and the New Testaments, to celebrate the Passover mystery of the Eucharist in*

See Papally Promulgated
Catechism of the Catholic Church

Q. 240. See paragraphs: 1373-1381

the Mass. Help us to understand Your great love for us. May the goodness You now show us confirm our hope in Your future mercy. May we celebrate the Eucharist with reverence and love, for when we proclaim the death of the Lord, You continue the work of His redemption. All glory and praise be to You, to Your divine Son, and to the Holy Spirit, now and forever. Amen.

Prayer

God our Father, at Mass we gather to share in the supper which Your only Son left to His Church to reveal His love. He gave it to us when He was about to die, and commanded us to celebrate it as the new and eternal Sacrifice of the Mass. He offered Himself as a Victim for our deliverance and taught us to make this offering in His memory. As we eat His Body which He gave for us, we grow in strength. As we drink His Blood which He poured out for us, we are washed clean.

At the Last Supper, as Jesus sat at table with His Apostles, He offered Himself to You; His heavenly Father, as the spotless Lamb, the acceptable gift that gives Him perfect praise. He has given us this memorial of His Passion to bring us its saving power until the end of time.

In this great sacrament Jesus feeds us, His people, and strengthens us in holiness, so that we, the family of mankind, may come to walk in the light of one Faith, in one communion of love.

We come then to this wonderful sacrament to be fed at Your table, Father, and to grow into Your likeness. Earth unites with Heaven to sing the new song of creation as we adore and praise You in this Sacrament of Divine Love. Amen.

The Sacrifice of the Mass - I
Remembrance and Sacrifice

Q. 241. What is the Sacrifice of the Mass?

The Sacrifice of the Mass is not only a ritual which reminds us of the sacrifice of Calvary, but through the ministry of ordained priests, Christ continues, till the end of time, the sacrifice of the Cross in an unbloody manner.

The Mass does more than remember Jesus, for He is more than a memory. Through His Resurrection, He is present and active among us in His Spirit. The Mass is a sacrifice in which the Church not only remembers Jesus, but really brings Him, His saving death, and His Resurrection into the present, so that His followers might become part of it. The Church can do this because Jesus is united to His Church in the Holy Spirit. When the Church celebrates the Eucharist, Jesus is really there, and it is He Who does once more what He did at the Last Supper.

At the Last Supper, our Savior instituted the Eucharistic Sacrifice of His Body and Blood, to continue for all time by the sacrifice of the Cross until He would come again. He gave His Church a remembrance of His death and Resurrection, the Mass, which is a true sacrifice. Through the hands of priests and in the name of the whole Church, the Sacrifice of Jesus is offered in the Eucharist in an unbloody and sacramental manner. The priest, by the sacred power he enjoys, acting in the Person of Christ, brings about the Eucharistic Sacrifice and offers it to God in the name of all the people.

The Mass is a prayer to the Father and a sacrifice which brings us the resurrected Christ.

The Mass is *a prayer to the Father,* in which His people give Him thanks and praise for the wonderful future He has given

See Papally Promulgated
Catechism of the Catholic Church

Q. 241. See paragraphs: 1362-1367

them in His Son, Jesus Christ. There are also times in the Mass when we ask forgiveness for our sins and beg the Father's blessing upon ourselves and our fellow men.

The Mass is a *sacrifice* because it brings into the present our Lord's own offering of Himself to His Father on the Cross. By participating in the Mass, in memory of Him, we enter into that offering and become a part of it.

The Mass *makes present to us Jesus' Resurrection* because His sacrifice establishes a common life of friendship and love between the Father and His children. Just as we share in Jesus' death at Mass, so we also share in the new life of the Spirit which was bestowed upon Jesus in His Resurrection.

The Mass is very important, because it brings together all of the gifts which the Father has given us in Jesus Christ. It brings into our lives the very presence of Jesus, His sacrifice on the Cross, and the new life of the Spirit which He opened to us by His Resurrection.

Prayer: *Lord our God, in the Eucharist, we proclaim the death and Resurrection of Christ. Make us partners in His suffering, and lead us to share His happiness and the glory of eternal life. May the power of this sacrament give us courage to proclaim His death and Resurrection also in our lives. May our obedient service bring us to the fullness of Your redemption.*

Lord God, in the blood of Christ, You have ratified a new and everlasting covenant with Your people, and have renewed it in the Sacrament of the Altar. We offer You the Sacrifice of the Mass by which Your Son reconciles mankind. Accept this pure sacrifice for the forgiveness of our sins. May this sacrifice, once offered on the Cross to take away the sins of the world, now free us from our sins.

Most Merciful Father, may the sacrifice of praise, the sacrifice of Your Son in the Mass, purify us in mind and heart, and make us always eager to serve You. You give us the Body and Blood of Your Son to renew Your life within us. In Your mercy, assure our redemption and bring us to the eternal life we celebrate in this Eucharist.

Heavenly Father, You gave us the Eucharist as the memorial of Your Son's suffering and death. May our worship of this sacrament of Jesus' Body and Blood help us to experience the salvation He won for us and the peace of Your Kingdom, now and forever. Amen.

Sacred Scripture

"For as often as you shall eat this Bread and drink the chalice, you shall show the death of the Lord until He comes."

1 Corinthians 11:26

Vatican Council II

"The liturgy is the summit toward which the activity of the Church is directed; it is also the fount from which all her power flows. For the goal of apostolic endeavor is that all who are made sons of God by faith and baptism should come together to praise God in the midst of his Church, to take part in the Sacrifice and to eat the Lord's Supper.

"The liturgy, in its turn, moves the faithful filled with 'the paschal sacraments' to be 'one in holiness'; it prays that 'they hold fast in their lives to what they have grasped by their faith.' The renewal in the Eucharist of the covenant between the Lord and man draws the faithful and sets them aflame with Christ's insistent love." *Sacred Liturgy, 10*

Prayer

Jesus, Victim for our sins, You trusted Your Father's protection and kept silent when You were tormented. Give us that same confidence, and we will gladly suffer with You and for You. We offer the Father our sacrifice of praise, and walk before Him in the light of Your truth and love.

At Mass, we place the offering of our lives before You. Send Your Holy Spirit to cleanse our hearts, so that our offering may be acceptable, in union with Yours, for the glory of the Father. May the gifts we offer in faith and love be continual sacrifices in Your honor, and thus truly become our Eucharist and our salvation.

Lord Jesus, with confidence in Your love, we come bringing the gift of ourselves, and all we have, and do, and suffer, as a sacrifice to Your Father; may our gifts be one with Your own sacrifice. Renew Your peace and love within us, that we may give Him perfect worship in Holy Mass. By the mystery of this Eucharist, purify us and renew Your life within us, and prepare us to celebrate Your coming in eternity. May You be praised and glorified now and forever. Amen.

The Sacrifice of the Mass - II

Q. 242. What is the liturgy?

The liturgy, is seen as an exercise of the priestly office of Jesus Christ. It involves the presentation of man's sanctification under the guise of signs which can be perceived by the senses, and its accomplishment in ways appropriate to each of these signs. In the liturgy, full public worship is performed by the Mystical Body of Jesus Christ, that is, by the Head and His members.

Sacred Scripture

"I was glad when they said unto me, 'We will go into the house of the Lord.' " *Psalm 122:1*

"O worship the Lord in the beauty of holiness. Let the whole earth stand in awe of Him." *Psalm 96:9*

Vatican Council II

"From this it follows that every liturgical celebration, because it is an action of Christ the Priest and of his Body, which is the Church, is a sacred action surpassing all others. No other action of the Church can equal its efficacy by the same title and to the same degree." *Sacred Liturgy, 7*

Q. 243. What is the most important form of all Christian liturgy?

The most important form of all Christian liturgy is the Mass. Within the setting of a Jewish Passover meal, the Lord instituted the Eucharistic sacrificial meal of the New Covenant. It was from this rite that the New Testament liturgy was born.

The Passover meal was a ritual. It called for certain foods, including bread and wine, as well as certain prayers and ex-

See Papally Promulgated
Catechism of the Catholic Church

Q. 242. See paragraphs: 1069-1070
Q. 243. See paragraphs: 1068, 1074, 1097, 1099, 1113, 1328-1330

planations. On the night before He died, Jesus took some of the unleavened bread, offered it to the Father, and said, "This is My Body." He gave His Body to the Apostles to eat. He took a cup of the Passover wine and said, "This is My Blood, the Blood of the New Testament." He gave His Blood to the Apostles to drink. He told them, "Do this in memory of Me."

Obedient to Christ, the Church does what Christ did, in memory of Him. The worship of the Church, and its whole inner life, have always centered on the Eucharistic sacrifice, the Mass.

> **Prayer:** *Our Father, at the Last Supper Your beloved Son, Jesus Christ, established the unending Sacrifice of the Mass, as He sat at table with His Apostles. As the true and eternal High Priest, He offered Himself as a Victim for our deliverance, and taught us to make this offering in His memory.*
>
> *He offered Himself to You as the spotless Lamb, the acceptable gift that gives You perfect praise.*
>
> *May our worship in spirit and truth bring us salvation. Help us to live the example of love we celebrate in the Eucharist, that we may come to its fulfillment in Your presence, through Jesus our Lord. Amen.*

Q. 244. What are the two principal parts of the Holy Sacrifice of the Mass?

The two principal parts of the Holy Sacrifice of the Mass are: (1) *the Liturgy of the Word,* i.e., the Scripture readings together with the homily, the Profession of Faith, and the Prayer of the Faithful, and (2) *the Liturgy of the Eucharist.*

The Liturgy of the Eucharist has three stages: (1) the *Offertory rite;* (2) the *Eucharistic prayer* and; (3) the *Communion rite.* In the *Offertory rite*, the gifts of bread and wine are brought to the altar and are offered to the Lord; in the *Eucha-*

See Papally Promulgated
Catechism of the Catholic Church

Q. 244. See paragraphs: 1349-1355

ristic Prayer, the saving mysteries of the Lord's Passion and Resurrection are recalled by a sacramental action which makes these mysteries present again in the midst of the people; in the *Communion rite*, the Body and Blood of Christ are received in a sacred meal, to gather in closest unity with Christ those who have received life through Him.

Vatican Council II

"The two parts which in a sense go to make up the Mass, viz. the liturgy of the word and the eucharistic liturgy, are so closely connected with each other that they form but one single act of worship." *Sacred Liturgy, 56*

Roman Curial Documents

"The Church has arranged the celebration of the Eucharist so that its several parts correspond with the words and actions of Christ.

"(a) In the Preparation of the Gifts there are brought to the altar, bread and wine with water, the very same elements which Christ took into his hands.

"(b) In the Eucharistic Prayer God is thanked for the whole work of redemption, and the gifts become the Body and Blood of Christ.

"(c) In the breaking of one bread the unity of the faithful is signified, and in Communion they receive the Body and Blood of the Lord as the apostles once did from the hands of Christ himself." *General Instruction on the Roman Missal, 48 (Sacred Congregation for Divine Worship, 1970)*

Prayer

Father, by the blood of Your own Son You have set all men free and have saved us from death. For Your glory and for our salvation You appointed Jesus Christ eternal High Priest. May the people He gained for You by His blood come to share in the power of His Cross and Resurrection by celebrating His memorial in the Eucharist.

Continue Your work of love within us, that by constantly celebrating the mystery of our salvation in the unbloody renewal of His sacrifice of the Cross at Mass, we may reach the eternal life it promises. May the Blood of our Savior be for us a fountain of water springing up to eternal life.

By sharing in this sacrifice which Your Son commanded us to offer as His memorial, may we become, with Him, an everlasting gift to you. We ask this through the same Christ our Lord. Amen.

Chapter One Hundred Eleven

The Sacrifice of the Mass - III

Q. 245. Why is the Holy Mass offered?

The Holy Mass is offered to give adoration and glory to God the Father; to give praise and thanks for Christ's immeasurable love for us; to intercede for those in need; and to obtain forgiveness of sins and the remission of the punishment for sins.

Sacred Scripture

"I am the Living Bread come down from Heaven. If any man shall eat of this Bread, he shall live forever. And the Bread that I will give is My Flesh, for the life of the world."

John 6:51

Roman Curial Document

"The celebration of the Mass, as an action of Christ and the people of God hierarchically ordered, is the center of the whole Christian life for the universal Church, the local Church and for each and every one of the faithful. For therein is the culminating action whereby God sanctifies the world in Christ and men worship the Father as they adore him through Christ the Son of God. The mysteries of man's redemption are in some way made present throughout the course of the year by the celebration of Mass. All other sacred celebrations and the activities of the Christian life are related to the Mass; they spring forth from it and culminate in it."

General Instruction on the Roman Missal, 1

Vatican Council II

"[Christ's] humanity united with the Person of the Word was the instrument of our salvation. Therefore, 'in Christ the perfect achievement of our reconciliation came forth and the fullness of divine worship was given to us.'" *Sacred Liturgy, 5*

See Papally Promulgated
Catechism of the Catholic Church

Q. 245. See paragraphs: 1323, 1356-1381

Q. 246. How do lay people participate in the Mass?

Lay people participate in the Mass not only by the reception of Holy Communion, but by fully exercising their status as members of the priesthood of the faithful. For example, they offer the Victim and themselves, not only through the hands of the priest, but also with him.

Vatican Council II

"Mother Church earnestly desires that all the faithful should be led to that full, conscious, and active participation in liturgical celebrations which is demanded by the very nature of the liturgy, and to which the Christian people, 'a chosen race, a royal priesthood, a holy nation, a redeemed people' (1 Pet. 2:9; 4-5), have a right and obligation by reason of their baptism." *Sacred Liturgy, 14*

"Christ, indeed, always associates the Church with himself in this great work in which God is perfectly glorified and men are sanctified. The Church is his beloved Bride who calls to

See Papally Promulgated
Catechism of the Catholic Church

Q. 246. See paragraphs: 901-903, 1348

her Lord, and through him offers worship to the eternal Father." *Sacred Liturgy, 7*

"Through the ministry of priests the spiritual sacrifice of the faithful is completed in union with the sacrifice of Christ the only mediator, which in the Eucharist is offered through the priests' hands in the name of the whole Church in an unbloody and sacramental manner until the Lord himself comes." *Priests, 2*

Roman Curial Document

"The celebration of Mass is the action of Christ and the People of God assembled to worship. It is of the greatest importance that the Mass be so arranged that the ministers and the faithful may take their own proper part in it and thus gain its fruits more fully. That is the reason why Christ instituted the Eucharistic sacrifice of His Body and Blood and entrusted it to His Bride, the Church, as a memorial of His Passion and Resurrection. This purpose will be accomplished if the celebration is planned to bring about conscious, active, and full participation of the people, motivated by faith, hope, and love. Such participation of mind and body is desired by the Church. It is the right and duty of Christians by reason of their baptism." *General Instruction on the Roman Missal, 62*

Prayer

Heavenly Father, we offer our prayers in the Name of Jesus Christ, Your Son and our Lord and God, in the Holy Sacrifice of the Mass. We have faith that we will receive whatever we ask for in His Name, for this is what He promised: "Whatever you ask for in my Name I will do, so that the Father may be glorified in the Son" (John 14:13).

May we, who honor Jesus in the Mass enjoy His friendship in this life and be filled with eternal joy in His heavenly Kingdom. May all people find salvation in the Name of Jesus. May He be praised and honored now and forever, especially in the Holy Eucharist. Amen.

The Sacrifice of the Mass - IV

Q. 247. Why is the Mass both a sacrifice and a sacred meal?

The Mass is both a sacrifice and a sacred meal. This is so because it is an unbloody representation of the sacrifice of the Cross; in application of its sacred power, the Lord is immolated in the Sacrifice of the Mass. When the words of consecration are said, this immolation or sacrifice of Christ becomes present in a sacramental form under the appearances of bread and wine and becomes the spiritual food of the faithful.

Sacred Scripture

"And Jesus said to them, 'I am the Bread of Life. He that comes to Me shall not hunger. And he that believes in Me shall never thirst.' " *John 6:35*

Vatican Council II

"The eucharistic celebration is the center of the assembly of the faithful over which the priest presides. Hence priests teach the faithful to offer up the divine victim to God the Father in the sacrifice of the Mass and with the victim to make an offering of their whole life.

"For in the most blessed Eucharist is contained the whole spiritual good of the Church, namely Christ himself our Pasch and the living bread which gives life to men through his flesh — that flesh which is given life and gives life through the Holy Spirit. Thus men are invited and led to offer themselves, their works and all creation with Christ." *Priests, 5*

Papal Documents

"In an unbloody representation of the sacrifice of the Cross and in application of its saving power, the Lord is immolated

See Papally Promulgated
Catechism of the Catholic Church

Q. 247. See paragraphs: 1356-1372, 1382-1390

in the Sacrifice of the Mass when, through the words of consecration, He becomes present in a sacramental form under the appearances of bread and wine to be the spiritual food of the faithful." *Paul VI, The Mystery of Faith, (Mysterium Fidei), 34*

Q. 248. Why is the Mass the one sacrifice of Christ?

The Mass is the one sacrifice of Christ because His one sacrifice on the Cross is made present to men in every celebration of Mass.

Vatican Council II

"[Christ] is present in the Sacrifice of the Mass not only in the person of his minister, 'the same now offering, through the ministry of priests, who formerly offered himself on the cross'; but especially in the eucharistic species" *Sacred Liturgy, 7*

Ecumenical Council of Trent (1545-1563)

"The bloody sacrifice which was once offered on the Cross is made present, its memory preserved to the end of the world, and its salvation-bringing power applied to the forgiveness of sins which are daily committed by us."

Council of Trent, Session 22

Q. 249. Who has been empowered to offer the Eucharistic Sacrifice?

Only ordained priests and Bishops are called to offer the Eucharistic Sacrifice to the Father, with Christ, in the Holy Spirit, for the living and the dead, and for the salvation of all.

Christ commanded His Apostles to celebrate this sacrifice when He said, "Do this for the commemoration of Me" (1 Corinthians 11:24). This is a sacred task: to act in the person of Christ, to be His minister, to speak words which make present the living Christ and which renew the Paschal mysteries. This can be done only by the will of Christ, by those whom He has empowered to act as His ministers, by calling them and sealing them in the Sacrament of Holy Orders.

See Papally Promulgated
Catechism of the Catholic Church

Q. 248. See paragraphs: 1362-1372
Q. 249. See paragraphs: 1555-1568

When, in the person of Christ, Bishops and priests pronounce the words of consecration, the Sacrifice of the New Covenant is made present to the faithful in such a way that they too can participate in it.

Vatican Council II

"God, who alone is the holy one and the sanctifier, has willed to take men as allies and helpers to become humble servants in the work of sanctification. The purpose then for which priests are consecrated by God through the ministry of the bishop is that they should be made sharers in a special way in Christ's priesthood and, by carrying out sacred functions, act as his ministers who through his Spirit continually exercises his priestly function for our benefit in the liturgy... and especially by the celebration of Mass they offer Christ's sacrifice sacramentally... For in the most blessed Eucharist is contained the whole spiritual good of the Church, namely Christ himself our Pasch and the living bread which is given life and gives life through the Holy Spirit." *Priests, 5*

Prayer

Our Father, Your Son gave us the Eucharist as the memorial of His suffering and death. May our worship of this sacrament of His Body and Blood help us to experience the salvation He won for us on the Cross and the peace of His Kingdom.

He gave His Body and Blood in the Eucharist as a sign that even now we share in His life. Whatever the changes and chances of this mortal life, may we always find strength in His unchanging love, for He is the Savior of the world and the joy of all mankind.

He promised that those who feed on His Flesh and drink His Blood will have eternal life, and will be raised up on the last day. May we come to possess His divine life completely in the Kingdom where He lives forever.

Father, You have brought to fulfillment the work of our redemption in the Easter mystery of Christ Your Son. May we, who faithfully proclaim His death and Resurrection in these sacramental signs, experience the constant growth of Your salvation in our lives. May our sharing at this Holy Table make us holy. By the Body and Blood of Christ, join all Your people in brotherly love. Amen.

Holy Communion - I

Q. 250. What is Holy Communion?

Holy Communion is the Eucharistic meal of the Body and Blood of Christ which: *(1) reminds us of the Last Supper, (2) celebrates our unity together in Christ,* and *(3) is a foretaste of the Messianic Banquet in the Kingdom of Heaven.*

1. *Holy Communion is the Eucharistic meal of the Body and Blood of Christ which reminds us of the Last Supper.*

In the Sacrifice of the Mass, Jesus Christ offers Himself together with us to His Father as He did on the Cross, by giving Himself, the Bread of Life, to us as nourishment for our souls. We are nourished with the Victim of the Sacrifice of the Cross, because at this sacrificial meal we recall what happened at the Last Supper, and actually partake of the Body and Blood of the Victim of our Redemption. Thus St. Paul reminds the people: "The chalice of benediction, which we bless, is it not the Communion of the Blood of Christ? And the Bread, which we break, is it not the partaking of the Body of the Lord?" (1 Corinthians 10:16).

2. *Holy Communion is the Eucharistic meal of the Body and Blood of Christ which celebrates our unity together in Christ.*

The whole Jesus is in Holy Communion. He, the God-man, is this Sacrificial Meal.

The Communion of the Mass is the meal of consecrated Bread which nourishes us with the life of God, and which unites us to Jesus and to one another. In drawing us to union with Jesus, our Father draws us closer to each other. The Eucharist is both an expression of the unity and love which binds us to each other and to Jesus, and an action through which the bonds are strengthened.

See Papally Promulgated
Catechism of the Catholic Church

Q. 250. See paragraphs: 1355, 1382-1401

3. *Holy Communion already gives us a part in the banquet of Christ in the Kingdom of Heaven* because we receive the same Son of God made man Who will be united with us in a union of joy forever in Heaven.

At the Last Supper, Jesus said, "And I say to you, I will not drink from henceforth of this fruit of the vine, until that day when I shall drink it with you anew in the Kingdom of My Father" (Matthew 26:29).

Jesus also promised that our bodies would some day enjoy His presence: "He that eats my Flesh, and drinks my Blood, has everlasting life: and I will raise him up in the last day" (John 6:54). In this way Jesus anticipates the Messianic Banquet of the Kingdom. The Eucharistic meal not only reminds us of the Church's heavenly reunion with Christ, but prepares us to take part in that heavenly communion with Christ and His Father.

Sacred Scripture

"He who eats My Flesh and drinks My Blood has everlasting life and I will raise him up on the last day. For My Flesh is meat indeed, and My Blood is drink indeed. He who eats My Flesh and drinks My Blood abides in Me, and I in Him."

John 6:55-56

Vatican Council II

"Really sharing in the body of the Lord in the breaking of the eucharistic bread, we are taken up into communion with him and with one another. 'Because the bread is one, we, though many, are one body, all of us who partake of the one bread' (1 Cor. 10:17). In this way all of us are made members of his body (cf. 1 Cor. 12:27), 'but severally members one of another' (Romans 12:4)." *The Church, 7*

"That more perfect form of participation in the Mass whereby the faithful, after the priest's communion, receive the Lord's Body from the same sacrifice, is warmly recommended." *Sacred Liturgy, 55*

Prayer

Jesus, after the miracle of the loaves, the people desired more material bread and expected You to work a miracle greater than that of the manna that fell from Heaven, in order to nourish them. But You declared instead that You Yourself are the true Bread of Life in the Holy Eucharist. You told the multitudes not "to labor for the food which perishes, but for that which endures unto everlasting life, which the Son of Man will give you" (John 6:27).

You revealed the whole mystery of the Holy Eucharist when You said, "I am the living Bread which came down from Heaven. If any man eats of this Bread, he shall live for ever; and the Bread that I will give, is My Flesh, for the life of the world" (John 6:51). "He that eats My Flesh, and drinks My Blood, has everlasting life: and I will raise him up on the last day. For My Flesh is meat indeed: and My Blood is drink indeed" (John 6:54-55).

We believe that the Holy Eucharist is Your Flesh, Blood, Divinity, and Humanity, under the appearances of bread and wine. You spoke of the Holy Eucharist as a sacrament and as a sacrifice, and You prescribed the eating of It as a condition for eternal life. Strengthen our faith in this divine mystery, which is the greatest gift of Your Sacred Heart to us.

Jesus, we believe in Your teaching that the Holy Eucharist really unites us to You, for You are present in this sacrament with your Body, Blood, Soul, and Divinity. You said, "He who eats My Flesh, and drinks My Blood, abides in Me, and I in him. As the living Father has sent Me, and I live by the Father, so he that eats Me, the same also shall live by Me" (John 6:56-57).

We believe that Holy Communion has the power to sustain the life of our souls, even as food sustains the life of our bodies. The greatest blessing that Holy Communion gives us is an increase of sanctifying grace, the very life of our souls. It makes us share in Your own divine life; but we also receive actual graces — helps from above — to preserve Your divine life in our souls. Through these helps which You give us at Holy Communion and in times of need, our minds receive the light to see, and our wills the strength to avoid what is wrong. Thus, Holy Communion is a divine medicine whereby our souls are preserved from infection by the deadly poison of sin, for It imparts to us strength to keep us free from sin and to withstand the force of temptation. We thank You for the abundance of grace which You impart to our souls in each Holy Communion.

Jesus, You are the true and eternal High Priest Who established the unending Sacrifice of the Mass. You offered Yourself as a Victim for our deliverance, and taught us to make this offering in Your memory. As we eat Your Body, which You gave for us, we grow in strength. As we drink Your Blood, which You poured out for us, we are washed clean. We thank You for the gift of the Eucharist, which You give to us at Mass in Holy Communion. May You be praised and glorified forever and ever. Amen.

Holy Communion - II

Q. 251. Why is the Eucharist a sacrament of unity?

The Eucharist is a sacrament of unity because it unites the faithful more closely with Christ and with one another.

By eating the Body of the Lord, we are taken up into a close union with Him and with one another. In this sacrament the unity of all those who believe in Jesus is not only shown but is also accomplished. This is what St. Paul meant when he wrote, "For we, being many, are one bread, one body, all that partake of one bread" (1 Corinthians 10:17).

As Christ grafts us onto Himself, He brings us closer to one another. As Israel's sacrificial meals united them as a nation, so the Eucharist unites us as God's family: it makes the Church one. Thus, the Eucharist, when eaten in faith and in the state of grace, brings about gradual changes within the hearts of Christ's faithful. It is a transforming food which continues to make us like Christ, Who dwells in us.

Since the Eucharist makes us one in Christ, it strengthens our charitable respect for one another. Having been nourished by the Lord Himself, the Christian should, with an active love, eliminate all prejudices and all barriers to brotherly cooperation with others. We eat It in order to be able to sacrifice ourselves for our neighbor's good. As the Eucharist inspires us with the memory of Christ's holy Passion and death, when He offered His Body and Blood for our salvation, so, when we eat this Bread of Life, we, too, will be able to practice charity.

Vatican Council II

"In the sacrament of the eucharistic bread, the unity of believers, who form one body in Christ (cf. 1 Cor. 10:17), is both ex-

See Papally Promulgated
Catechism of the Catholic Church

Q. 251. See paragraphs: 1331, 1391, 1396

pressed and brought about. All men are called to this union with Christ, Who is the light of the world, from Whom we go forth, through Whom we live, and towards Whom our whole life is directed." *The Church, 3*

"They [Bishops] should therefore see to it that the faithful know and live the paschal mystery more deeply through the Eucharist, forming one closely-knit body, united by the charity of Christ." *Bishops, 15*

Prayer: *Jesus, we believe that the Eucharist is a sacrament of unity because it unites us more closely with God and with one another. Through this holy sacrament, we are united most intimately to You, and, with the help of Your grace, we can love our neighbors.*

Almighty Father, You renew us at Your Table with the Bread of Life, that we may grow in unity within the Body of Your Son. May the bread and cup we offer bring Your Church the unity and peace they signify. You give us the Body and Blood of Your Son in the Eucharist as a sign that, even now, we share Your life. May we come to possess it completely in the Kingdom where You live for ever and ever. Amen.

Q. 252. What does Jesus do for properly prepared Catholics in the Eucharist?

In the Eucharist, Jesus nourishes properly prepared Catholics with Himself, the Bread of Life, so that they may become a people *(1) pleasing to God* and *(2) filled with greater love of God and neighbor.*

1. *In the Eucharist we become a people acceptable to God.*

In this great celebration of our common Faith, we, the followers of Jesus relive the experience of Him, and thank our Father for it. We remember what our Father has given us. At the same time, we receive the same gift of Jesus Christ and so

See Papally Promulgated
Catechism of the Catholic Church

Q. 252. See paragraphs: 1391-1401

enter more deeply into union with Him in the Holy Spirit. Mass is the place where the Catholic community both acts out its faith, and is renewed and strengthened in all its members. Especially in the Mass we become a people who are acceptable to God.

2. *In the Eucharist we become a people filled with greater love of God and neighbor.*

Holy Communion helps us to love God more, because divine grace is increased in our souls. This same grace helps us to love others for the love of God. Our Lord came into this world to redeem us and to keep us from sin; He comes into our souls for the same purpose. He strengthens us through actual or sacramental graces that we may overcome temptation and avoid sinning against God and our neighbor. Only by His help can we succeed in living a life of true charity, and thus fulfill His greatest commandment.

To receive the Eucharist worthily, the Catholic must be in the state of grace. St. Paul says, "Therefore whoever shall eat this Bread, or drink the Chalice of the Lord unworthily, shall be guilty of the Body and of the Blood of the Lord" (1 Corinthians 11:27). As long as we are in the state of grace, we are prepared to receive our Lord each time we are present at the Holy Sacrifice of the Mass, because His Body is the fruit of the Sacrifice, and, for us, is the way to Eternal Life.

The best way to prepare our souls for union with Jesus in Holy Communion is to offer Him, and ourselves with Him, reverently to God the Father in the Sacrifice of the Mass. Confession is not necessary before Holy Communion unless we have a serious sin to confess.

Prayer

Lord, through the Sacrament of the Eucharist, You make us one family in Christ Your Son, one in the sharing of His Body and Blood, and one in the Communion of His Spirit. Help us to grow in love for one another and to come to the full maturity of the Body of Christ.

Your Word of Life gives us a new birth. May we receive it with open hearts, live it with joy, and express it in love. Let the Eucharist we share fill us with Your life.

May the love of Christ, which we celebrate at the Holy Sacrifice of the Mass, touch our lives and lead us to You, so that His high priestly prayer to You may be fulfilled: "That they all may be one, as You, Father, in Me, and I in You; that they also may be one in Us; that the world may believe that You have sent Me" (John 17:21). We ask this through Jesus Christ our Lord. Amen.

The Effects of
Holy Communion - I

Q. 253. Does reception of the Holy Eucharist at Holy Communion increase the supernatural life of our soul?

Yes. One of the principal effects received from the Holy Eucharist at Holy Communion is the intensification and strengthening of supernatural life. Being a sign of nourishment, the Holy Eucharist is meant to do for the soul what material food does for the body, and that is to preserve life and to protect it. As material food enables us to continue living and tends to protect us from fatal disease, so Holy Communion preserves the spiritual life of our souls and protects us from the spiritual disease of mortal sin.

Jesus Himself is our food in Holy Communion. He, (His Body, Blood, Soul, and Divinity), is entirely ours as the food of our souls. He is united to us in order to make us like Himself. He said, "I am the living Bread which came down from Heaven. If any man eat of this Bread, he shall live for ever; and the Bread that I will give, is My Flesh, for the life of the world" (John 6:51). The sharing of divine life means that God lives in us and we in Him, and that as God the Son has by nature the same life as the Father in its infinite fullness, so do we share it by grace.

Our Lord compared the Most Holy Sacrament of the Altar with the manna given to the Jews, because the Holy Eucharist was intended to be the daily spiritual food of Christians, just as manna was the daily food of the Israelites in the desert.

It was in the midst of a meal, under the form of food, that Jesus chose to institute the Eucharist. He gave Himself to us as the nourishment of our souls: "For My Flesh is meat indeed: and My Blood is drink indeed" (John 6:55).

See Papally Promulgated
Catechism of the Catholic Church

Q. 253. See paragraphs: 1392-1395

Jesus Christ is not only glad to accept our invitation to come into our hearts, but He told us that we must receive Him as our Guest. "Amen, amen I say unto you: Except you eat the Flesh of the Son of man, and drink His Blood, you shall not have life in you" (John 6:53).

Sanctifying grace is that grace which gives our souls new life, that is, a sharing in the life of God Himself. Sanctifying grace makes our souls holy and pleasing to God, especially by increasing divine love in our hearts. Sanctifying grace makes us adopted children of God and temples of the Holy Spirit.

Just as our souls are the life of our bodies, so sanctifying grace is the life of our souls. We need sanctifying grace to save our souls. Mortal sin brings death to our souls, because it takes away sanctifying grace, and this means losing God Himself.

To understand why the Church incessantly stresses the advantages of receiving the sacraments frequently, particularly the Holy Eucharist, we have but to recall her doctrine concerning sanctifying grace.

The Holy Eucharist is the sacrament that produces in us, by means of Holy Communion, an increase of habitual or sanctifying grace. It not only preserves the life of our souls, but increases it, just as the body is not only supported by means of natural food, but also is strengthened.

Holy Communion also preserves and increases all the various virtues which have been bestowed upon our souls together with sanctifying grace. By increasing the theological virtues of faith, hope, and charity, Holy Communion enables us to enter into closer union with God. By strengthening the moral virtues of prudence, temperance, justice, and fortitude, Holy Communion enables us to regulate better our whole attitude toward God, our neighbor, and ourselves. Holy Communion also opens our understanding and wills to the inspirations and promptings of the Holy Spirit.

Vatican Council II

"In order that the liturgy may be able to produce its full effects, it is necessary that the faithful come to it with proper dispositions, that their minds be attuned to their voices, and that they cooperate with heavenly grace lest they receive it in vain (cf. 2 Cor. 6:1)." *Sacred Liturgy, 11*

519

Q. 254. Does Holy Communion unite our souls more closely to Jesus?

Yes, Holy Communion unites our souls to Jesus' divine and human natures.

It is an article of Faith that the Blessed Sacrament of the Altar is truly, really, and substantially the Body and Blood of Christ, together with His soul and divinity. Therefore, when we receive Holy Communion, we receive the real, physical Body and Blood of Christ, together with His soul and His divinity, veiled under the appearances of bread and wine.

Put another way, during Holy Communion, we receive the same Body of Jesus which He took from His most pure Virgin Mother, and which arose in glory from the tomb; His Precious Blood, with which He redeemed us — one drop of It would have been enough to redeem a thousand worlds! — and His most sacred soul, the abode of graces and virtues in absolute perfection.

We share in Christ's life as the Divine Word, and as the only Son of the Father. We receive the life the Father gives to the Son from all eternity. We can possess His divinity in our souls at all times by remaining in the state of grace; but it is only at the time of Holy Communion that we enjoy the great privilege of being intimately united with the human nature of our Lord.

The Three Divine Persons are already in us by grace, but at the moment of Communion they are present within us in a special manner. As we are then physically united to the Incarnate Word, the Three Divine Persons are also, through Him and by Him, united to us, and They love us as the Word Incarnate, Whose members we are. When we carry Jesus in our hearts, we also bear the Father, and the Holy Spirit with Him. Thus, Holy Communion is a foretaste of Heaven.

To receive our Lord in Holy Communion is the most wonderful thing that can happen to us, because it means having

See Papally Promulgated
Catechism of the Catholic Church

Q. 254. See paragraphs: 1391-1395

the God-man, Jesus, in our own hearts. The Holy Eucharist is the greatest and the holiest of the sacraments, because it is our Savior, Jesus Christ, Himself, God Who became man for our salvation.

Holy Communion also brings about a special union between us and the Three Divine Persons of the Holy Trinity. Jesus said, "If anyone loves Me, he will keep My word, and My Father will love him, and We will come to him, and will make Our abode with him" (John 14:23).

Roman Curial Document

"On those who receive the Body and Blood of Christ, the gift of the Spirit is poured out abundantly like living water, (cf. John 7:37-39) provided that this Body and Blood have been received sacramentally and spiritually, namely, by that faith which operates through charity."

Instruction on the Worship of the Eucharistic Mystery, 38

Prayer

Jesus, we believe that Holy Communion gives us an increase of sanctifying grace, the very life of our souls. It makes us sharers in Your own divine life. You said, "He who eats My Flesh and drinks My Blood lives in Me and I live in him" (John 6:57).

Just as the heavenly Father gives You His divinity, His power, His goodness, and His life, from all eternity, so do You, Jesus, give us Your divine life in Holy Communion. You said, "As I, Who am sent by the living Father, Myself draw life from the Father, so whoever eats Me will draw life from Me" (John 6:58).

Jesus, our Lord, just as the stem and the branches of a vine are the same being, nourished and acting together, producing the same fruits because they are fed by the same sap, so too You circulate our divine life of grace in our souls through Holy Communion in such a way that we live by Your life and really become like You. You said, "I am the vine, you are the branches. Whoever remains in Me, with Me in him, bears fruit in plenty; for cut off from Me you can do nothing" (John 15:5).

$\mathcal{M}$ost compassionate Christ, how marvelous is the fruit of sanctifying grace! It makes our souls holy, beautiful, and pleasing to God, sacred temples of the Holy Spirit. Sanctifying grace, which is increased in our souls in Holy Communion, not only makes us adopted children of God, but also helps us to act as other Christs. It gives us the right to enter Heaven, for without this grace, we can never see God.

$\mathcal{J}$esus, we believe You make us Christ-like, not only by giving us sanctifying grace at Holy Communion, but also by giving us actual graces — helps from above — to preserve Your divine life in our souls. Through these helps given us at Holy Communion, and in times of need, our minds receive the light to see, and our wills are imbued with the strength to do what is right and to avoid what is wrong. Through frequent Holy Communion, help us to think, desire, speak, and act like You.

$\mathcal{L}$ord Jesus, the Eucharist is the most wonderful work of Your love. Out of Your infinite love, You have given us not only what You have, but what You are. At Holy Communion, You give us Your Body, Your Blood, Your soul, Your divinity, Your merits, and Your graces. Nowhere do You bestow these graces more abundantly than in this sacrament. May such love awaken a return of love in our hearts!

$\mathcal{J}$esus, our Divine Love, we want to receive You in Holy Communion frequently, so that we may live in You, and You in us. You said, "He who eats My Flesh and drinks My Blood has everlasting life: and I will raise him up on the last day. For My Flesh is meat indeed: and My Blood is drink indeed" (John 6:54-55). "He that eats My Flesh, and drinks My Blood, abides in Me, and I in him" (John 6:56).

$\mathcal{L}$ord Jesus, no where is Your love for us greater than in this sacrament. Your gift of love to us is nothing less than Yourself, whole and entire: Your Body, Blood, soul, and divinity. You are generous, not for Your own sake, but for the sake of our salvation and happiness. Love for us, and for all mankind, urged You to leave us the treasure of Holy Communion as a parting testament on the night before You died. We can make no better return of love than to receive You often in this sacrament of love. Our unworthiness and sinfulness should not keep us away from Your Holy Table; rather, conscious of our shortcomings, we should come to You more frequently in order that our souls may be cleansed and sanctified. Only in this way shall we become more worthy to receive You. Give us the grace to overcome our carelessness and lack of faith.

Jesus, be our Companion throughout life by frequent Holy Communion; be our unfailing Companion during the last painful struggle of death. Come in that decisive hour to protect our souls, which You bought with Your own Precious Blood, and lead us safely into the home of Your Father and ours.

Change us more and more into Yourself, O Bread of Life. Let each Holy Communion fill our hearts with greater love for You and bind them so closely to Your own that we may always think as You do, desire what You desire, and do everything as You would, even as St. Paul said of himself, "With Christ I am nailed to the Cross. And I live, now not I; but Christ lives in me. And that I live now in the flesh: I live in the faith of the Son of God, Who loved me and delivered Himself for me" (Galatians 2:19-20). We do not want to think, will, or act in our own way, but in Your way. Our only desire is to live Your life, that we may resemble You, our Elder Brother.

Jesus, Bread of Life, in the Eucharist You touch our lives. Keep Your love alive in our hearts, that we may be worthy of You and pleasing to Your heavenly Father, now and forever. Amen.

The Effects of
Holy Communion - II

Q. 255. Does Holy Communion increase our love for God?

Yes, Holy Communion is a source of the theological virtue of charity.

The Holy Eucharist is the sacrament which most fittingly increases man's love for God, because it was begun and inspired by God's love for man. St. John pointed to that love when he wrote: "Jesus, knowing that His hour was come, that He should pass out of this world to the Father, having loved His own who were in the world, loved them unto the end" (John 13:1). Then the Evangelist tells us that the Savior gave us the Eucharist to show this love. The love of His Sacred Heart discovered the wonderful mystery of the union that could henceforth be effected unceasingly on the altar.

Jesus once said: "I am come to cast fire to the earth, and what do I desire, but that it be kindled?" (Luke 12:49) Through the Holy Eucharist, Jesus casts fire into men's hearts. He Himself is that flame of love.

Sanctifying grace, which we receive through Holy Communion, and which attaches itself to the very essence of our souls, brings with it supernatural powers which enable us to perform virtuous deeds. The most important of these deeds are acts of charity [sacrificial love] by which we love God above all things for His sake and our neighbor as ourselves for the love of God.

At Holy Communion, Jesus is within us, bringing His most pure and holy love. He longs for our love and asks us to give Him our whole hearts and all of our love. Jesus' love is a great gift, and it is in Communion that He gives it.

See Papally Promulgated
Catechism of the Catholic Church

Q. 255. See paragraphs: 1390, 1392, 1394, 1402

The only obstacle to this complete reign of Christ in us is our selfishness. We must die to our selfish lives in order to avail ourselves fully of the divine life. The Christ-life in us is a life of self-surrender and of love. Love yields our wills to Christ, and through them, our whole beings and all our energies. Christ gives Himself to us according to the measure of our love. If we give ourselves to Him unreservedly, with a pure heart, Jesus, in exchange, gives Himself to us as only God is able to do. St. John wrote, "And we have known, and have believed the love, which God has for us. God is love, and he that abides in love, abides in God, and God in him" (1 John 4:16).

If we yield to the workings of His grace, we will find our minds and wills more ready to do what Jesus will inspire us to do. If we do not put obstacles in the way of God's grace, and if our fervor in receiving Holy Communion continues, the life of Jesus will manifest itself more distinctly in us. Let our hearts, which love so little, be subjected to the transforming influence of the tremendous love of Jesus' Sacred Heart, that we may become one with Him in Holy Communion.

Vatican Council II

"The renewal in the Eucharist of the covenant between the Lord and man draws the faithful and sets them aflame with Christ's insistent love. From the liturgy, therefore, and especially from the Eucharist, grace is poured forth as from a fountain, and the sanctification of men in Christ and the glorification of God to which all other activities of the Church are directed, as toward their end, are achieved with maximum effectiveness." *Sacred Liturgy, 10*

Prayer

Jesus, we believe that, at Holy Communion, we drink at the very fountain of grace, holiness, and love. In It, You give us Your Sacred Heart, the source of all grace and love. Holy Communion unites us in divine love to You, most lovable God. True joy springs from divine love.

How earnestly You invite us to this banquet of Divine Love, which You prepared for our souls so that we might partake of Your own Body and Blood! "Come to me, all you that labor and are burdened, and I will refresh you" (Matthew 11:28). At Holy Communion, a world of life, light, and love, and a gracious outpouring of the treasures of Your Sacred Heart are opened for us.

Jesus, the moments of union with You in Holy Communion are the happiest of our lives. How much this union of love means to us! It is the climax of Your divine love for us, and it should therefore be the object of our fondest desires. You have made our hearts for Yourself. They yearn to be with You, and to possess You even here on earth, so that they may prepare for an eternal union with You in Heaven.

Holy Communion fills our hearts with love because It fills our souls with sanctifying grace, the source of true love. In our union with You through this sacrament, may we find the strength and courage to undertake anything You might ask of us, for Your glory and the welfare of our neighbors. Let Holy Communion be the foundation of our faith, the support of our hope, the nourishment of our love, for It inflames our hearts with Your love. To You, the Father and the Holy Spirit, be all honor and glory. Amen.

The Effects of Holy Communion - III

Q. 256. Does Holy Communion increase our love of neighbor?

Yes, since Holy Communion increases sanctifying grace in our souls, it also increases our love of neighbor.

In Holy Communion, we are united directly to Jesus Christ, and through Him, to the Father and to the Holy Spirit, Who are in Him. We also are united with Him, and through Him, to all His members, and especially to those who are perfectly united with Him in glory.

The Eucharist is the bond of love that unites all Christians as members of one spiritual body, the Church. St. Paul says, "The chalice of benediction, which we bless, is it not the Communion of the Blood of Christ? And the Bread, which we break, is it not the partaking of the Body of the Lord? For we, being many, are one bread, one body, all that partake of one bread" (I Corinthians 10:16-17). Jesus is that one Bread in Holy Communion.

Through frequent Holy Communion, Jesus will give us help to carry out His great commandment of love for our neighbors and to put away all unkindness. He will give us the grace to love our neighbors as ourselves for His sake; to respect and love them as God's image and likeness, as children of our heavenly Father, and as temples of the Holy Spirit. We must not be unkind to those whom Christ loves, and for whom He died on the Cross.

By frequent Holy Communion, we learn to overcome our selfishness; to resist feelings and reactions such as hatred and bitterness; to develop kindness and sympathy, forbearance, and forgiveness; to think kindly of everyone and to find

See Papally Promulgated
Catechism of the Catholic Church

Q. 256. See paragraphs: 1392-1395, 1397

our happiness in making others happy, and thus we will unite ourselves by love to Christ and to the members of His Mystical Body. By uniting all of the faithful to Jesus, Holy Communion unites us to each other in love.

Vatican Council II

"No Christian community is built up which does not grow from and hinge on the celebration of the most holy Eucharist. From this all education for community spirit must begin. (cf. Didascalia, II, 59, 1-3) This eucharistic celebration, to be full and sincere, ought to lead on the one hand to the various works of charity and mutual help, and on the other hand to missionary activity and the various forms of Christian witness." *Priests, 6*

"Really sharing in the body of the Lord in the breaking of the eucharistic bread, we are taken up into communion with him and with one another. 'Because the bread is one, we though many, are one body, all of us who partake of the one bread' (1 Cor. 10:17). In this way all of us are made members of his body (cf. 1 Cor. 12:27), 'but severally members one of another' (Rom. 12:5)." *The Church, 7*

> **Prayer:** *Jesus, through frequent Holy Communion, help us to carry out Your great commandment of love for our neighbors, and give us the grace to put away all unkindness. We want to love our neighbors as ourselves and for Your sake. Let us respect and love them as God's image and likeness, as children of our Heavenly Father, and as temples of the Holy Spirit. We ask this in Your most powerful and holy Name. Amen.*

Q. 257. Why is Holy Communion a pledge of future glory?

Holy Communion gives us a pledge of future glory because it establishes physical contact between Jesus Christ Who reigns in glory and ourselves on earth.

See Papally Promulgated
Catechism of the Catholic Church

Q. 257. See paragraphs: 1402-1404

The glory which is reserved for us in Heaven is twofold — the glory of the soul and the glory of the body. The glory of the soul consists in the Beatific Vision of God. God communicates to the soul a wondrous gift known as the light of glory, whereby His own splendor pervades the human mind and empowers it to see God as He sees Himself.

Secondly, there is the glory of the body, a supernatural gift whereby our frail bodies are made like the glorified body of our risen Savior. On the last day, the bodies of the just will be brilliant like the sun, endowed with the power of angelic swiftness, spiritualized, and made incapable of suffering.

The Blessed Sacrament is the pledge of, and the preparation for, the eternal glory of the soul and of the body. Our souls, being brought into such close contact with our Savior, share in His divine life. As we eat His Flesh and drink His Blood, we enjoy a pledge of the glory of everlasting life, for He said, "I am the living Bread which came down from Heaven. If any man eat of this Bread, he shall live for ever; and the Bread that I will give, is My Flesh, for the life of the world" (John 6:5).

Holy Communion establishes between Jesus Christ and us not merely spiritual contact, but physical contact as well, through the "species" or outward appearances of bread. The resurrection of the body can be traced to this physical contact with Christ. Holy Communion provides us with a promise of resurrection; our bodies will be more strikingly glorified; if we have frequently been in contact during life with the risen body of our Lord.

Though our bodies will die and be changed to the dust of the earth, they will be reunited to our souls on the last day and share their immortality. Jesus said, "I am the resurrection and the life: he that believes in Me, although he be dead, shall live: and every one that lives and believes in Me, shall not die for ever" (John 11:25-26).

The glorious resurrection of the body is an effect of Holy Communion. It confers on us the right to a glorious resurrection, which Christ promised to those who eat His Flesh and drink His Blood. "He that eats My Flesh, and drinks My Blood, has everlasting life: and I will raise him up on the last day" (John 6:54).

Sacred Scripture

"This is the Bread that came down from Heaven. Not as

your Fathers did eat manna in the desert and are dead. He who eats this Bread shall live forever." *John 6:58*

Vatican Council II

"The Church, therefore, earnestly desires that Christ's faithful, when present at this mystery of faith, should not be there as strangers or silent spectators. On the contrary, through a good understanding of the rites and prayers they should take part in the sacred action, conscious of what they are doing, with devotion and full collaboration. They should be instructed by God's word, and be nourished at the table of the Lord's Body. They should give thanks to God. Offering the immaculate victim, not only through the hands of the priest but also together with him, they should learn to offer themselves. Through Christ, the Mediator, (Cf. St. Cyril of Alexandria: "Commentary on the Gospel of St. John," Book 11, ch. 11-12) they should be drawn day by day into ever more perfect union with God and each other, so that finally God may be all in all."

Sacred Liturgy, 48

Prayer

Jesus, when You were about to depart from this world, You laid upon us Your last commendation: that we should love one another. "This is My commandment, that you love one another, as I have loved you. Greater love than this no man has, that a man lay down his life for his friends. You are My friends, if you do the things that I command you. These things I command you, that you love one another" (John 15: 12-14, 17). We must imitate Your example by loving our neighbors with a supernatural love and by being kind to them, for You said, "By this shall all men know that you are My disciples, if you have love for one another" (John 13:35).

Jesus, we believe that Holy Communion preserves and increases this love for our neighbors. It is a Banquet of Love which You have prepared for the children of God. Even the outward tokens of the Eucharist remind us of brotherly love and kindness. Many grains of wheat are ground and mingled together to make one Bread, and many grapes are crushed to fill the Eucharistic Chalice; similarly must we become one through love and Holy Communion. The Eucharist is the bond of love which animates the members of one spiritual Body, the Church, just as the soul gives life to each member of the human body.

Jesus, our Lord, You love our neighbors as You love us, and You give Yourself to them in Holy Communion as You give Yourself to us. How can we show disrespect to those whom You respect so highly? Through Holy Communion, help us to be kind to our neighbors as we would have them be kind to us; for You said, "All things therefore whatever you would that men should do to you, do you also to them. For this is the law and the prophets" (Matthew 7:12).We cannot receive You into our hearts if we refuse to forgive. Intimately united with Your loving Heart at Holy Communion, we can best learn the lesson of forgiving kindness and thus obtain the help we need to practice it.

Jesus, we believe that the richness of the Sacrament of the Eucharist is infinite since It contains You, the Son of God, God's greatest gift to us. All the fruits of the Redemption contained in the Eucharist become ours. You earnestly want to give us a share in them.

Give us great faith, firm confidence, and ardent love, that the fruits of each Holy Communion may be more abundant. We shall not thirst, for this fountain of grace will bring our souls to life everlasting. Therefore, help us to receive You with sincere preparation, that the Eucharist may add to our personal merits a rich bounty of grace. Sanctifying grace is the very life of our souls and it will enable us to live forever.

Jesus, may Your Eucharist be for us the heavenly manna which strengthens us weary pilgrims along the road of life. Through it, may we be united to You. Help us to receive You often, so that, from this intimate union, we may draw the divine light and moral strength necessary to fashion our lives according to the divine will. Thus, may we come to live with You, as You promised. Through this divine life, in which we share through Holy Communion, may we be protected from mortal sin, purified of venial sins and imperfections, and encouraged by divine love to reach true holiness.

We beg You, Eucharistic Savior, for the two-fold grace of true repentance and final perseverance. Through frequent Communion and its many graces, prepare our souls for that day when, casting aside the veil which now hides the glory and majesty of Your divine face, You will come to us in the splendor of Your Godhead, and we shall behold You face to face. Amen

The Real Presence - I

Q. 258. Why does Jesus become present in the Holy Eucharist?

Jesus becomes present in the Holy Eucharist to renew the sacrifice of Calvary in an unbloody manner on our altars, to nourish our souls in Holy Communion, and to remain bodily among us by His Real Presence in our tabernacles.

Faith teaches us that Jesus Christ is truly, really, and substantially present, Body and soul, divinity and humanity, under the veil of the sacramental species of bread and wine, so long as these species continue to exist. Under the appearances of bread our Lord's Blood and soul, as well as His Body, are present. Furthermore, under the appearances of wine, His Body and soul as well as His Blood are present, because in the Holy Eucharist the Body and Blood of the glorified Christ Who is in Heaven are present. In Heaven, the Body, Blood, and soul of Christ are inseparably united. The divinity of Christ is present under both the appearance of bread and the appearance of wine, because, from the time of the Incarnation, the divinity has been constantly and inseparably united to the entire human nature of Christ.

Jesus remains in the tabernacles in Catholic churches day and night, full of life and in continual action. First, He is always in loving adoration before His heavenly Father. Sublime is the honor which Jesus renders to Him in each tabernacle at all times. His adoration is of infinite value because it is offered by the very Son of God.

Secondly, Jesus occupies Himself at the same time with our dearest interests. He thanks God for us, prays continually for us, asks pardon for our sins, and makes reparation and amends for them. He continually offers Himself in sacrifice to

See Papally Promulgated
Catechism of the Catholic Church

Q. 258. See paragraphs: 1356-1401

God, and continually pours out His graces upon all of mankind as our Eucharistic Mediator.

The Holy Eucharist continues the life of Jesus among us. Every day He is "born again," so to speak, in a state that is similar to that of the Incarnation. At the words of consecration spoken by the priest, and under the appearance of bread and wine, He comes upon the altar as God and man.

He renews His public life by His presence everywhere in the world as Teacher, Healer, and Friend. How many miracles are worked in the souls of men through Holy Mass and Communion! How many souls are taught, blessed, comforted, and healed! Now He is everywhere, ready to assist us all as the Son of God, with all of His divine power and infinite love; to radiate His sacred influence upon our souls; and to be the source of all strength, life, and joy.

The mysteries of His Passion are contained in the Eucharist, for It is a remembrance of His death. Holy Mass is a representation of the Sacrifice of the Last Supper and of the Sacrifice of the Cross.

The glory of His risen life is renewed in the Eucharist. He is present there in His glorious, transfigured body, just as He appeared after His Resurrection. He makes Himself the friendly Companion of our pilgrimage; comforting, encouraging, and blessing our work. All of the mysteries of the life of Jesus are renewed in the Holy Eucharist for the benefit of our souls.

Sacred Scripture

"Teach them to observe all things whatsoever I have commanded you. And behold I am with you, even to the consummation of the world." *Matthew 28:20*

Roman Curial Document

"There should be no doubt in anyone's mind 'that all the faithful ought to show to this most holy sacrament the worship which is due to the true God, as has always been the custom of the Catholic Church. Nor is it to be adored any the less because it was instituted by Christ to be eaten.' For even in the Reserved Sacrament He is to be adored, because He is substantially present there through that conversion of bread and wine which, as the Council of Trent tells us, is most aptly named transubstantiation.

"The mystery of the Eucharist should therefore be considered in all its fullness, not only in the celebration of Mass but also in devotion to the sacred species which remain after Mass and are reserved to extend the grace of the sacrifice."

Worship of the Eucharistic Mystery, 3

Prayer

Jesus, You greatly desired to eat the Passover with Your Apostles before You suffered, because You were about to give us the greatest gift of love which Your Sacred Heart could offer.

We believe that it is especially in the Holy Sacrifice of the Mass that we can look upon You Who have been pierced by our sins, for Your sacrifice at Calvary is renewed in an unbloody manner at Holy Mass. You offer Yourself to Your heavenly Father in the same spirit of love and resignation to His Holy Will as You did on Calvary, because You are present in the Sacred Host as the Victim of Calvary. As the Sacred Host is raised after the consecration, we cry out with the faith of the centurion who pierced Your side, "You are truly the Son of God;" With St. Thomas we exclaim, "My Lord and my God!"

We unite ourselves with You as You offer Yourself again to Your Father, and we wish to become one sacrifice with You. Everything that You send us, or permit in our lives, whether favorable or unfavorable, sweet or bitter, is acceptable to us, for we have resolved to conform ourselves to the divine will in all things.

Jesus, we believe that Holy Communion opens the treasury of all of the graces which You merited for us by Your bloody death on the Cross. May its richest grace be for us a most intimate union with You. At Holy Communion, we drink at the very fountain of grace, holiness, and happiness, because, in It, You give us Your Sacred Heart, the source of all grace, holiness, and peace. You remain with us after Mass and Communion in the tabernacles of our churches. Before ascending into Heaven, You gave Your disciples the instruction, "Teach them to observe all things whatever I have commanded you: and behold I am with you all days, even to the consummation of the world" (Matthew 28:20).

*I*t is by adoration and visits to You, Lord Jesus, in the Blessed Sacrament that we can open our souls to Your transforming action. We want to share with You our joys and sorrows, our feelings and affections, and our plans and desires. May our whole life be a sharing with You, especially by our prayer before the tabernacle. You are close to us in the tabernacle, You are our best Friend and our Companion in exile, with a heart that is human like our own; a heart that can understand our sorrows and problems, since it has experienced all that we must bear. Your heart sympathizes with us and befriends us in our hour of need; You love us with the love that the best of friends share. Like a real furnace of fire, Your Heart burns for us with a love that knows no end, because It has Its source in the depths of the Godhead — It is for us, as if there were no other to share Its infinite warmth. The tender affection You pour out upon countless other souls never lessens Your love for us. Even when we forget You, You think of us; even when we offend or disappoint You, You sacrifice Yourself for us at Mass; when we have trials, You are ready to console and strengthen us.

*J*esus, we thank You for being our best Friend and for being present in the holy Sacrament of the Altar. Help us to declare our faith in Your Real Presence in the Eucharist, and to express our love for You with sincere devotion. We wish to answer Your invitation: "Come to Me, all you who labor, and are burdened, and I will refresh you" (Matthew 11:28). Lord, may we come to You, now and forever. Amen.

The Real Presence - II

Q. 259. Why is the Eucharist reserved in our churches?

The Eucharist is reserved in our churches in order to greatly enhance our adoration of Jesus and to increase our love for others. It is also reserved in the churches in order to be taken to the sick.

The Jewish Passover of the Old Covenant was a symbol of the Eucharist of the New Covenant. Jesus surpassed and fulfilled the Jewish Passover meal when He instituted the Eucharist at the Last Supper. As the first People of God, the Jews, ate manna in the desert; the new People of God, Christians, eat the Eucharist. As the Ark of the Covenant and the pillar of fire were a sign of God's special presence with His people during their long journey through the desert, so Jesus is present with us in the tabernacle to be our comfort in our journey through life; He is our Emmanuel — God with us.

Jesus keeps the promise He made before ascending into Heaven: "And know that I am with you always; yes, to the end of time" (Matthew 28:20).

Jesus is present at Mass in His words which are read to the people. He is present in the priest, and in the people through whom He acts, when they re-enact what He did at the Last Supper. He is most present in the bread and wine which becomes His Body and Blood after the consecration in the Mass. The Church extends this Presence of Jesus in the Eucharist by reserving the consecrated species of bread.

Reservation of the Blessed Sacrament means, that at the end of Communion, the remaining consecrated Hosts are placed in the tabernacle where they are reverently preserved. Thus, the Blessed Sacrament of the Eucharist is always available, both as a continuing sign of Jesus' Real Presence among His people and as spiritual food for the sick and dying.

See Papally Promulgated
Catechism of the Catholic Church

Q. 259. See paragraphs: 1378-1381

Q. 260. What do we owe to Christ, reserved in the Blessed Sacrament?

We owe gratitude, adoration, and devotion to the Real Presence of Christ, reserved in the Blessed Sacrament.

Our devotion is expressed in visits to the tabernacle in our churches, at Benediction, and in Eucharistic processions. Benediction is a brief ceremony in which the Blessed Sacrament is exposed to the people for reverence and adoration. It concludes with the priest's blessing of the people with the consecrated Host. It is our duty to thank Jesus for all of His blessings and to adore Him as our God and Savior. We must offer ourselves to His service with all the love in our hearts.

The Eucharist was the center of the early Christian community. It is still the center of all worship of God in the Church today, and will be so until the end of time.

Vatican Council II

"The house of prayer in which the most holy Eucharist is celebrated and reserved, where the faithful assemble, and where is worshiped the presence of the Son of God our Saviour, offered for us on the sacrificial altar for the help and consolation of the faithful— this house ought to be in good taste and a worthy place for prayer and sacred ceremonial (cf. St. Jerome, Epist., 114.2:)." *Priests, 5*

Prayer: *Jesus, our God, we firmly believe that You are really and bodily present in the Blessed Sacrament of the Altar. From the very depths of our hearts, we adore You and worship Your Sacred Presence with all possible humility. What a joy it is to have You always with us in the tabernacle and to be able to speak to You, heart to heart, with all confidence! May You be praised and adored forever. Amen.*

See Papally Promulgated
Catechism of the Catholic Church

Q. 260. See paragraphs: 1359, 1378-1381

Q. 261. Why is the Eucharist the center of all sacramental life?

The Eucharist is the center of all sacramental life because It unites and strengthens the Church.

Baptism begins the Christian life. It initiates man into the life of the Father, Son, and Holy Spirit; but the Christian must grow ever more alive in this divine life by praying, receiving the sacraments, hearing the word of God, and serving others with a Christ-like attitude.

Jesus Christ is present in the Holy Eucharist to be our Sacrifice; our Food; our Life; our Companion Who strengthens and nourishes us with His Flesh and Blood, and Who unites us to Himself, to the Father, to the Holy Spirit, and to all the members of the Church. Therefore, the Eucharist is the center of all sacramental life in the Church.

Sacred Scripture

"And all that believed were together and had all things in common... And continuing daily with one accord in the temple and breaking bread from house to house, they took their food with gladness and simplicity of heart." *Acts 2:44, 46*

"And on the first day of the week, when they were assembled together to break bread, Paul discoursed with them."
Acts 20:7

Vatican Council II

"The other sacraments, and indeed all ecclesiastical ministries and works of the apostolate are bound up with the Eucharist and are directed towards it. For in the most blessed Eucharist is contained the whole spiritual good of the Church, namely Christ himself our Pasch and the living bread which gives life to men through his flesh — that flesh which is given life and gives life through the Holy Spirit. Thus men are invited and led to offer themselves, their works

See Papally Promulgated
Catechism of the Catholic Church

Q. 261. See paragraphs: 1322-1327

and all creation with Christ. For this reason the Eucharist appears as the source and the summit of all preaching of the Gospel: catechumens are gradually led up to participation in the Eucharist, while the faithful who have already been consecrated in baptism and confirmation are fully incorporated in the Body of Christ by the reception of the Eucharist."

Priests, 5

Papal Document

"Indeed, the Eucharist is the ineffable sacrament! The essential commitment and, above all, the visible grace and source of supernatural strength for the Church as the People of God is to persevere and advance constantly in Eucharistic life and Eucharistic piety and to develop spiritually in the climate of the Eucharist. With all the greater reason, then, it is not permissible for us, in thought, life or action, to take away from this truly most holy sacrament its full magnitude and its essential meaning. It is *at one and the same time a sacrifice-sacrament*, a *communion-sacrament*, and a *presence-sacrament*." [Emphasis added]

Pope John Paul II Encyclical, The Redeemer of Man (Redemptor Hominis), 20

Prayer

*W*e thank *Y*ou, *D*ivine *R*edeemer, for coming upon the earth for our sakes, and for instituting the adorable *S*acrament of the *A*ltar in order to remain with us until the end of the world. *W*e thank *Y*ou for veiling *Y*ourself beneath the *E*ucharistic species, *Y*our infinite majesty and beauty, which *Y*our angels delight to behold, so that we might have the courage to approach the throne of *Y*our mercy.

*W*e thank *Y*ou, most loving *J*esus, for having made *Y*ourself our food for the nourishment and salvation of our souls in *H*oly *C*ommunion. *W*e thank *Y*ou for giving *Y*ourself to us in this *B*lessed *S*acrament, and for so enriching it with the treasures of *Y*our love that *Y*ou have no greater gift left to give us.

*W*e thank *Y*ou also for offering *Y*ourself as a continual sacrifice to *Y*our *E*ternal *F*ather for our salvation in *H*oly *M*ass. *W*e thank *Y*ou for offering *Y*ourself as a sacrifice daily upon our altars, in order to give worthy adoration and thanksgiving to God, and to make amends for our sins. We thank You for renewing, in this daily sacrifice, the actual sacrifice of the Cross that You offered on Calvary to satisfy divine justice for us poor sinners.

We thank You, dear Jesus, for having become the priceless Victim in order to merit for us the fullness of heavenly favors. Awaken in us great confidence in You, for You offered Yourself in thanksgiving to God to obtain for us all His benefits, spiritual and temporal

We thank You, dear Jesus, hidden beneath the sacramental veils. We adore You present in the tabernacle, our hidden God. You are the only Way. Make us always walk in the path of Your Commandments, following Your example, so that we may arrive at eternal salvation.

Lord, grant that, having adored Your divine Majesty here on earth in this wonderful sacrament, we may be able to adore It eternally in Heaven.

Our Jesus, may You be known, adored, loved, and thanked by all devoted Christians in the most holy and divine Sacrament of the Altar! Amen.

Prayer

What Prayer Is - I

Q. 262. What is prayer?

Prayer is the lifting of our minds and hearts to God.

We lift our minds and hearts to God to praise His goodness, to thank Him for His kindness, to acknowledge our sins, to plead for pardon, to ask His aid for our salvation, and to give glory to Him.

When we pray, both our minds and our hearts are active: our minds occupy themselves with thinking of God and our relationship with Him; our hearts perform acts of worship.

Prayer is conversation with God. Being aware of God, looking at Him with the eyes of our souls, we reach toward Him to converse with Him, to give Him what we have, to make our wills one with His. We adore, praise, and thank Him. We ask for His help and His pardon. We trust God in the simplest way, confiding to Him all that we have most at heart — our sorrows and joys, our hopes and fears, and our desires and plans. In return, we receive from Him help, consolation, and advice. We speak quite plainly with God of important matters, often without any feeling or emotion. All that matters, is that we speak honestly and earnestly. We pray well when we tell God what is in our hearts. Thus, prayer is communication of spirit with Spirit, of man with God.

Prayer is the simplest and most natural expression of worship. All intelligent creatures are bound to think about God and to converse with Him; in other words, to pray to Him. In order to pray, you need only understand Who God is and who you are; how great God's fatherly goodness is, and how deep is your own misery. Faith will teach you all that is necessary. Your prayer, in order to be true prayer, must be from the heart.

See Papally Promulgated
Catechism of the Catholic Church

Q. 262. See paragraphs: 2559-2565

You can pray to God at any time and in any place, for you are always in His presence. His love for you is always the same. Even when You are swamped with worldly cares and selfish interests, He is close to you; you will always find Him waiting to listen and ready to answer.

Prayer is the means by which we communicate with God. It is an indescribable grace and honor to have God listen to you and allow you to seek His presence. Nowhere else are you received so sincerely and so lovingly. Try to appreciate the great privilege of being able to talk with God.

Without prayer, you dare not face life. If you are out of touch with God, Our Lady, and the saints, you cannot properly do your work or carry your burdens or hope to reach eternal life.

Prayer is not necessarily a matter of words. It is, fundamentally, an active attitude of the soul. It is an attitude of eager longing for grace. It is a humble and trustful unfolding of your real needs before God, a pleading with Him to satisfy those needs, and a disposition to welcome gifts of God. Above all, a readiness to abandon yourself to God's will in all things.

Sacred Scripture

"Pray for one another, that you may be saved. For the continual prayer of a just man avails much." *James 5:16*

"Let him decline from evil and do good. Let him seek after good and pursue it. Because the eyes of the Lord are upon the just, and His ears unto their prayers." *1 Peter 3:11-12*

Vatican Council II

"The spiritual life, however, is not limited solely to participation in the liturgy. The Christian is indeed called to pray with others, but he must also enter into his bedroom to pray to his Father in secret; (cf. Mt. 6:6) furthermore, according to the teaching of the apostle [i.e., St. Paul], he must pray without ceasing (cf. 1 Th. 5:17). We also learn from the same apostle that we must always carry around in our bodies the dying of Jesus, so that the life also of Jesus may be made manifest in our mortal flesh (cf. 2 Cor. 4:10-11)." *Sacred Liturgy, 12*

Prayer: *Almighty and everlasting God, may our prayers rise like incense before You; our hands like the evening sacrifice. Hear our* prayers, and protect us both by night and day, that whatever the changes and chances of this mortal life, we may always find strength in Your unchanging love, through Christ our Lord. Amen.

Prayer

Eternal Father, from the rising of the sun to its setting, Your Name is worthy of all praise. With joy and gladness we cry out to You, and ask You to open our hearts, that we may sing Your praises and announce Your goodness and truth.

Be near to all who call upon You in truth, and increase the dedication of those who revere You. Hear their prayers and save them, that they may always love You and praise Your holy Name.

Lord God, You fill the hungry with good things and break sinners' chains. Hear Your people, who call to You in their need, and lead Your Church from the shadows of death. Gather us, from sunrise to sunset, that we may grow together in faith and love, and so give lasting thanks for Your kindness through our prayers.

Jesus, help us to understand the power there is in unity of prayer. You said, "Again I say to you, that if two of you shall consent upon earth, concerning any thing whatever they shall ask, it shall be done to them by My Father Who is in Heaven. For where there are two or three gathered together in My Name, there am I in the midst of them" (Matthew 18:19-20). Unite us all as children of the family of God, in which God is our common Father, and You, our Elder Brother. Look down upon our family when we are gathered in Your Name, and graciously pour out Your blessings upon us.

Lord our God, Whose power is beyond all words to describe, those glory is measureless, Whose mercy is without limits, and Whose love for mankind is beyond all telling, look down upon us, and in Your kindness, grant to us, and to all those praying with us, the riches of Your compassion and mercy. We ask this through Jesus our Lord, to Whom with You and the Holy Spirit be all honor and glory. Amen.

What Prayer Is - II

Q. 263. What is mental or interior prayer?

Mental or interior prayer (as distinct from vocal prayer, which normally is expressed by set formulas) begins with a serious consideration of the truths of the Faith, with a view to their practical application to our daily lives. During mental prayer, you grow in the knowledge of your Faith and acquire principles of right living by applying yourself to prolonged reflection on some doctrine of the Church or teaching of our Savior.

This reflection, however, is only a point of departure for spontaneous prayer. Such prayer is the principal part of every meditation. The subject of meditation provides incentives and matter for prayer. Prayer really begins at the moment when your will, set on fire with love, enters into direct communication with God, and yields lovingly to Him in order to please Him and to fulfill His commands and desires. Therefore, the essential element in mental prayer is contact with God, the source of all holiness.

It is in the heart that prayer essentially dwells. The Blessed Virgin Mary kept the words of Jesus "in her heart" (cf. Luke 2:51). When our Lord taught His Apostles to pray, He did not bid them apply themselves to reasoning, but to express the love of their hearts as simply as do little children. If meditation does not lead to conversation with God, then it is no longer an internal prayer, but a kind of study or examination of conscience, or a period of spiritual reading for information and enjoyment. The important point is not to think much, but to love much.

Successful meditation depends above all on prayer and a longing for perfection. Use a book only as a means of uniting your heart with God. If you can commune with God only

See Papally Promulgated
Catechism of the Catholic Church

Q. 263. See paragraphs: 2709-2719

through vocal prayer, then continue vocal prayer. The Holy Spirit has many ways of leading a soul nearer to God. If you are able to speak habitually and simply with God, and can gain much spiritual food from this communication, do not tie yourself down to any particular method. Once the best way is found, keep faithfully to it until the Holy Spirit draws you to another way. Be generously docile to His grace. Try to make at least a short meditation every day. You will find this practice an important means of growing in the love of God. You will gradually acquire the spirit of prayer, which, in other words, means the habit of having recourse to God more and more frequently.

The difference between vocal prayer and interior prayer is this: in vocal prayer we use a prepared form of words, either a standard prayer from a prayer book, or a prayer we have made up by ourselves, and we recite this prayer, aloud or silently, from the book or from memory. In interior prayer we do not use a prepared form of words at all, but merely raise our minds and hearts to God spontaneously, addressing Him with words of love, or in no words at all.

Vocal prayer also forms an essential prayer of the external worship of God. Vocal prayer, expressed in public worship, has special power with God and is very pleasing to Him, for Our Lord said, "Again I say to you, that if two of you shall consent upon earth, concerning any thing whatever they shall ask, it shall be done to them by My Father Who is in Heaven. For where there are two or three gathered together in My Name, there am I in the midst of them." (Matthew 18:19-20)

"Thus therefore you shall pray, 'Our Father Who art in Heaven, hallowed be Thy Name. Thy Kingdom come. Thy will be done...' " (Matthew 6:9-10).

There comes a point in the spiritual life when, after faithful practice of Christian virtue and prayer, the Holy Spirit acts and prays within us. As Scripture says, "We do not know how to pray as we ought. But the Holy Spirit, with unspeakable groanings, prays within us" (Romans 8:26).

Through the gifts of the Holy Spirit, we come to experience what is called infused prayer. Infused prayer means "poured into." "The love of God is poured forth in our hearts by the Holy Spirit Who is given to us" (Romans 5:5).

The grace of infused prayer does not require any extraordinary mystical graces or experiences. It is the development of the ordinary graces of Baptism.

Vatican Council II

"In the various seasons of the year and in keeping with her traditional discipline, the Church completes the formation of the faithful by means of pious practices of soul and body, by instruction, prayer, and works of penance and mercy."

Sacred Liturgy, 105

Prayer

Almighty and everlasting God, may our prayers rise like incense before You. As we contemplate Your presence in word and sacrament, and in the lives of our brothers and sisters, rekindle in us the fire of that love which Jesus Your Son brought on earth by His Passion, and which burns in our hearts by the Holy Spirit.

Author of undying light, quench our mortal thirst with the grace of the Spirit, that our lips may praise You, our lives may honor You, and our meditations may glorify You, as we seek to find You in prayer and to reflect upon Your truth and commandments.

Jesus, You pointed out Martha as an example of external activity, and Mary, as an example of union with God in prayer. I want to combine both: to be active, without thereby losing the spirit of prayer amid the pressure of the occupations of my calling, and, on the other hand, to devote myself to prayer, without allowing it to interfere with the duties of my state in life.

Like Mary, I am resolved to learn, at Your feet, the lessons of holiness and salvation, not only by meditation but also by my frequent Holy Communions and prayers before the tabernacle. Thus, my union with You in loving friendship will make my active life more fruitful, because my activity will be penetrated by Your Spirit and sanctified by Your blessing. May I praise You forever and ever. Amen.

Chapter One Hundred Twenty-Two

Why Prayer Is Necessary

Q. 264. Why is prayer necessary?

Prayer is necessary *(1) because God has commanded us to pray (since the very need for prayer is rooted in our nature); and (2) because it is the great unconditional means of obtaining grace. The need for prayer is rooted in man's very nature as a creature of God who receives gifts from His generosity.*

1. *Prayer is necessary because God has commanded us to pray.*

The First Commandment of God binds man to religion and worship of God: "I, the Lord, am Your God. You shall not have other gods besides Me" (Exodus 20:2; Deuteronomy 5:6). The First Commandment obliges us to offer to God alone the supreme worship that is due Him. Man must recognize and honor God as His Creator. Religion consists in giving God the recognition and honor He deserves

Prayer to God is an act of the virtue of religion, the highest of all the moral virtues which leads us to fulfill our duty to our Creator by showing Him respect and submission. Created by God and totally dependent upon Him at every instant, we must always be in a state of reverence toward Him. When we pray, our mind, our noblest faculty, recognizes Him as Creator and Lord, and expresses our need for Him.

Other virtues are involved in prayer, especially the theological virtues of faith, hope, and charity. Through faith, we know God and His merciful power to which we appeal. Charity governs our desires, and in so doing, brings order to our petitions. Hope gives us the confident expectation that these desires will be granted. The virtues of humility and penitence then cooperate with the virtue of religion to deepen our sentiments of reverence toward God.

See Papally Promulgated
Catechism of the Catholic Church

Q. 264. See paragraphs: 2566, 2725

God requires prayer not because of any need of His, for He has need of nothing, but because of His justice and holiness. He is our Lord, our Father, and the source of all our good. Hence, honor is due to Him, and He cannot deny Himself by allowing this honor to be given to another.

Prayer is the means ordained by God for His creatures to reach Him and remain with Him. We were created by God to know, love, praise, adore, and serve Him. Through prayer, we attain these ends, as far as we can do so on earth. In Heaven, there will be eternal prayer.

Our Lord often taught the necessity of prayer. He said, "Ask and it shall be given you: seek and you shall find: knock, and it shall be opened to you" (Matthew 7:7). "Watch, and pray, that you enter not into temptation" (Matthew 26:41). "Amen, amen I say to you: if you ask the Father anything in My name, He will give it to you" (John 16:23). Our Lord tells us that we should pray "always" (Luke 18:1). St. Paul says: "Never cease praying" (1 Thessalonians 5:17), which means that we should always be ready to pray at the proper times and that our prayers should constantly influence our other actions.

2. *Prayer is necessary because it is a great unconditional means of obtaining grace.*

The sacraments and prayer, together with good works, are the divinely instituted means of obtaining grace. Whatever fruits our good works produce in us must derive nourishment and strength from God, the source of all grace. We all need this important means of grace called prayer. Without it, it is impossible to lead a Christian life and to die a happy death.

Without God's grace, there is no salvation; without prayer, no grace can be expected in those who have reached the age of reason. Prayer, therefore, is a grace itself. Without the grace of God, we can do nothing in the supernatural order. We cannot overcome temptation, or gain spiritual merit for any good deed performed.

God knows all our wants and needs even before we express them to Him, and He is ever ready to help us; but He has established prayer as the condition for obtaining His grace and favors.

Moreover, since our minds have been darkened and our wills have been weakened by original sin, it is difficult to resist temptation or stay out of grave sin without the help of God's grace, which is given in answer to our prayers. Prayer, therefore, is the remedy for our human weakness. When we pray, God gives us the strength to do that which we cannot do by ourselves.

Sacred Scripture

"And the smoke of the incense of the prayers of the saints ascended up before God from the hand of the angel."

Revelation 8:4

Vatican Council II

"All the disciples of Christ, persevering in prayer and praising God (cf. Acts 2:42-47), should present themselves as a sacrifice, living, holy and pleasing to God (cf. Romans 12:1). They should everywhere on earth bear witness to Christ and give an answer to everyone who asks a reason for the hope of an eternal life which is theirs (cf. 1 Pet. 3:15)." *The Church, 10*

Prayer: *Heavenly Father, We believe that we are bound in conscience to pray — not simply in order to ask You for favors, but to adore You, thank You, and ask Your pardon for our sins. If we are careless with our prayers, we deprive our souls of many graces and blessings which You would give us in answer to our prayers. May Your Holy Spirit always help us to pray as we ought, through Christ our Lord. Amen.*

Prayer

*L*ord Jesus Christ, we believe that prayer is as necessary as grace, without which there is no salvation, simply because, in the ordinary course of things, no grace is obtained without prayer. Without prayer, our souls must lose what grace and union they possess. Neglect of prayer spells doom to our souls.

*W*e also believe that prayer is more than a duty. It is a great and holy privilege, second only to the surpassing privilege of receiving the sacraments. When we pray, we engage in the same great work in which You are now engaged eternally in Heaven, where You are always making intercession for us. We share in the great work of Mary and the saints; to their prayers, we join our own, that they may offer them to God for us. Help us to appreciate the privilege of prayer by praying as often as we possibly can.

*J*esus, help us to understand that nothing is more important or necessary for us than to be in close union with You, the Father, and the Holy Spirit, for all holiness consists in this union. Give us the grace to imitate Your example of living with God through prayer.

*O*ur lives are fruitless unless You bless our efforts with Your grace, for without You, Jesus, we can do nothing. Help us always to remain in You by divine love and prayer, but especially through frequent Holy Communion. If we are united with You, then as often as we perform actions with good intentions, and out of love for You, we shall be successful. All our actions, however unimportant they may seem, will be pleasing to You and will merit a reward. To You be all honor, glory, and praise, now and forever. Amen.

Chapter One Hundred Twenty-Three

The Four Purposes of Prayer

Q. 265. What are the four purposes of prayer?

The four purposes of prayer are: (1) *adoration,* (2) *thanksgiving,* (3) *repentance,* and (4) *petition*

1. *The first purpose of prayer is adoration.*

Our first and foremost duty is to acknowledge God's supreme dominion over us, as our Creator and Father; our absolute dependence on Him, as His creatures and children; and His supreme excellence. The worship of God, Father, Son, and Holy Spirit, is called the worship of adoration. The worship we give to the angels and saints is called veneration, to stress its difference from the adoration which is due to God and to God alone.

Adoration is due to God alone, because God alone is supreme. All other beings are creatures, being made by God and ruled by Him.

Adoration is the essential act of prayer, because it expresses the creature's awareness of the Creator. Consecration of ourselves to God is an ideal prayer of adoration.

"I will give praise to You, O Lord, with my whole heart. I will relate all Your wonders. I will be glad and rejoice in You. I will sing to Your Name, O You, Most High" (Psalm 9:1-2).

"Seven times a day I have given praise to You for the judgments of Your justice" (Psalm 119:164).

2. *The second purpose of prayer is thanksgiving.*

We pray, secondly, to thank God for His favors. God's purpose in creating the world was not only to give us material goods and security, but also to inspire in us grateful thoughts about Him, so that we might reach our sublime destiny. Our

See Papally Promulgated
Catechism of the Catholic Church

Q. 265. See paragraphs: 2626-2643

entire beings are God's free gifts of love. He has given us immortality so that we can know, love, and possess Him for all eternity. Through the Redemption, He has raised us to a supernatural plane; that is, He has made us His children, brothers and sisters of Jesus, and heirs of Heaven. By His providence, He watches over us day and night with unfailing care and bestows on us many blessings. When we wander away from God through sin, He forgives us through the saving grace of the Sacrament of Penance. When we become hungry and tired in soul, He nourishes us with His own Body and Blood. In our prayers, we can put our gratitude into words for these marvelous gifts.

"Hear, O Lord, my prayer: and let my cry come to You. Turn not away Your face from me. In the day when I am in trouble, incline Your ear to me" (Psalm 102:2-3).

"Be filled with the Holy Spirit, speaking to yourselves in psalms and hymns, and spiritual canticles, singing and making melody in your hearts to the Lord. Giving thanks always for all things, in the Name of our Lord Jesus Christ, to God the Father" (Ephesians 5:18-20).

For all this generosity we can make only one fitting return — the offering of Jesus Christ to God the Father in the Mass. We should unite ourselves to Jesus and offer ourselves, too, with all that we are and do, in thanksgiving for the limitless graces and blessings that have been bestowed upon us. Frequently during the day, as we go about our work, we should turn our thoughts and affections to God by offering Him prayers of gratitude.

> **Prayer:** *Heavenly Father, by Whose wisdom we are created and by Whose providence we are governed, give us the grace to offer You our thanks as best we can, for unless You direct us by Your Holy Spirit, we will not know how to address You as we ought in prayer. We ask this through Jesus Christ , our Lord and Savior. Amen.*

3. *The third purpose of prayer is repentance.*

We pray, thirdly, to obtain from God the pardon of our sins and the remission of their punishment. When we break God's law, we offend God. Sorrow for sin makes for fruitful conversation with God. The terrifying fact that you have actually offended the All-Good and All-Holy God should ever keep you in the attitude of the penitent sinner.

4. *The fourth purpose of prayer is petition.*

We pray to ask for graces and blessings for ourselves and others. We need God every moment of our lives in the natural order. We depend upon God for everything, and for that reason, we pray to Him for help. We may ask for temporal as well as spiritual favors.

Our need for God in the supernatural order is even greater. God is the limitless source of all good, and He longs to share this good with others. He has even assured us that our goal is to reign with Him in Heaven and to share His own happiness there forever. We should appeal to God in prayer frequently. Our Lord has urged us to make such appeals: "Ask, and it shall be given you: seek, and you shall find: knock, and it shall be opened to you" (Matthew 7:7).

Sacred Scripture

"I desire therefore, first of all, that supplications, prayers, intercessions, and thanksgivings be made for all men: for kings, and for all that are in high station: that we may lead a quiet and a peaceable life in all piety and chastity." *1 Timothy 2:1-2*

"Confess therefore your sins one to another, and pray one for another, that you may be saved. For the continual prayer of a just man avails much." *James 5:16*

"For if he had not hoped that they that were slain should rise again, it would have seemed superfluous and vain to pray for the dead, and because he [Judas Maccabees] considered that they who had fallen asleep with godliness, had great grace laid up for them. It is therefore a holy and wholesome thought to pray for the dead, that they may be loosed from sins." *2 Maccabees 12: 44-46*

Vatican Council II

"The practice of religion of its very nature consists primarily of those voluntary and free internal acts by which a man directs himself to God. Acts of this kind cannot be commanded, or forbidden by any merely human authority. But his own social nature requires that man give external expression to these internal acts of religion, that he communicate with others on religious matters, and profess his religion in community." *Liberty, 3*

Papal Document

"The discovery of intimacy with God, the necessity for adoration, the need for intercession — the experience of Christian holiness shows us the fruitfulness of prayer, in which God reveals himself to the spirit and heart of his servants. The Lord gives us this knowledge of himself in the fervor of love" *Pope Paul VI, Apostolic Exhortation on the Renewal of Religious Life, 43*

Prayer

Hear our prayers, Lord Jesus, and cover us with the wings of Your Cross, that whatever the changes and chances of this mortal life, we may always find strength in Your unchanging love, for You are the Savior of the world and the joy of mankind. You promised to be with those who pray in Your Name; help us to always pray with You to the Father, in the Holy Spirit.

Lord Jesus, Whose pierced hands were lifted toward Your holy Father and Whose life was rescued out of death, be the Shepherd of Your Chosen People; Lead us through the trials and tribulations of this present life and help us to sing hymns of praise to the Blessed Trinity.

Lord Jesus Christ, by Your death and Resurrection, You reconciled everything in Heaven and on earth; by the power of Your blessed Passion, set us apart so that we may sing the praise of God in union with the angels and saints in Heaven.

Watch over Your people who come to You in prayer, and strengthen the hearts of those who hope in You, that they may proclaim Your saving acts of kindness in the Heavenly City.

God of all compassion, Father of all goodness, to heal the wounds that our sins and selfishness bring upon us, You bid us turn to prayer and to sharing with our brothers. We acknowledge our sinfulness. Our guilt is ever before us. When our weakness causes discouragement, let Your compassion fill us with hope and lead us, through repentance, to the beauty of eternal joy.

May Your love never abandon us. Continue Your saving work among us as we endeavor to serve You well. May the saving Sacrifice of the Mass bring us Your forgiveness so that, freed from sin, we may always please You. May our sharing in the Bread of Life bring us Your protection, forgiveness, and life. Amen.

How We Should Pray

Q. 266. How should we pray?

We should pray with (1) *attention,* (2) *with a spirit of humility,* (3) *with a deep desire for the graces we beg of God,* (4) *with a loving trust in God's goodness,* (5) *with resignation to God's will,* and (6) *with perseverance.*

1. *We should pray with attention* by forming in our minds the intentions of praying well and of fixing our minds on God. It is only when our distractions are voluntary, coming from a careless lack of interest in what we are doing, that our prayer ceases to be a prayer. God asks only that we do our best. He does not hold us accountable for what we cannot help.

2. *We should pray with a spirit of humility,* with a consciousness of our complete dependence on God and our helplessness without Him.

3. *We should pray with a deep desire for the graces we need from God.* We should also seek His help in removing whatever may be hindering His grace from working in our souls.

4. *We should pray with a loving trust in God's goodness.* This means to pray with childlike confidence that God does hear us and that He will answer us.

5. *We should pray with resignation to God's will* because He knows what is best for us and because He loves us. Jesus taught us to say, "Thy will be done."

6. *We should pray with perseverance.* The man who never quits praying for grace and salvation is the one who is certain to go to Heaven. "Pray without ceasing. In all things give thanks; for this is the will of God in Christ Jesus concerning you all" (1 Thessalonians 5:17-18). We would not grow discouraged if we remembered that whatever God does, He does in

See Papally Promulgated
Catechism of the Catholic Church

Q. 266. See paragraphs: 2598-2622, 2729-2745

His own way and in His own best time. Our confidence should endure. Only in Heaven will we know how many blessings have come to us in response to prayer which, at the time, seemed to go unanswered.

Sacred Scripture

"Let us go, therefore, with confidence, to the throne of grace that we may obtain mercy and find grace with timely help." *Hebrews 4:16*

Papal Document

"The interior man is aware that times of silence are demanded by love of God. As a rule he needs a certain solitude so that he may hear God 'speaking to his heart' (Hosea 2:16) . . . The search for intimacy with God involves the truly vital need of a silence embracing the whole being, both for those who must find God in the midst of noise and confusion and for contemplatives."

Pope Paul VI, Apostolic Exhortation on the Renewal of Religious Life, 46

Prayer: *Lord Jesus, let us call, entreat, and continually ask You, the Father, and the Holy Spirit to grant our prayers. You always hear our prayers, even though You do not always answer them according to our will, since You know better than we what our real needs are. Sometimes You answer them by saying, "No," to our requests. Jesus, give us perseverance in prayer. We ask this through Your most Precious Blood. Amen.*

Prayer

Jesus, help us to pray with confidence. You speak of God as a Friend and a Father, to whom we may pray with childlike trust. "If you then, being evil, know how to give good gifts to your children, how much more will your Father from Heaven give the good Spirit to them that ask Him?" (Luke 11:13) People are normally kind to their children and friends, and certainly God is kinder than we can ever be. Your own words, Jesus, inspire confidence: "Ask, and it shall be given you: seek, and you shall find: knock, and it shall be opened to you. For every one that asks, receives, and he that seeks finds; and to him that knocks, it shall be opened" (Luke 11:9-10).

Jesus, we should not estimate the value of prayers by their length or by the number of prayers we say. It would be wrong to think that we must present our wants to God because He does not know them, or that we must or can influence Him by our prayers as people are influenced by reasoning. We do not dispose You in any way by our prayer, but we should dispose ourselves by removing the obstacles which may prevent You from granting our petitions. This is what we do by prayer: we beautifully confess our poverty, helplessness, and unworthiness, and on the other hand, we gloriously acknowledge Your power, goodness, and fidelity. In prayer, let us give You the poor gift of our lives — our bodies, our souls, our works, joys and sufferings. This we ask in Your most powerful and holy Name. Amen.

The Prayer Life of Jesus

Q. 267. Why is Jesus the Divine Model of prayer?

Jesus is the Divine Model of prayer because, by becoming man while remaining divine, He showed us by His example that we could draw close to God by prayer, since prayer played such an important part in His life.

During the thirty years of His hidden life, Jesus lived an ordinary, quiet, and prayerful life. Subject to Mary and Joseph, He labored as a carpenter; He also prayed.

Forty days of prayer and penance were the prelude to His three years as a missionary. He not only spoke often of prayer, encouraged, and taught people to pray, but He also practiced prayer Himself. Interiorly, He enjoyed the constant vision of God, and therefore He was always engaged in inward communion with His Father.

But Jesus also prayed outwardly. In His brief teaching career, He always found time for prayer, even prolonged prayer. He rose very early to pray before He began to teach, and He left the company of His followers in the evening to seek His Father in prayer.

"And rising up very early, going out, He went into a desert place, and there He prayed" (Mark 1:35).

"And it came to pass in those days that He went out to a mountain to pray. And He passed the whole night in the prayer of God" (Luke 6:12).

Jesus prayed publicly and vocally. He taught His disciples how to pray, especially by giving them the most beautiful prayer ever composed, the "Our Father." After the "Our Father," the most sublime prayer of Jesus was the high-priestly prayer He uttered at the Last Supper. He prayed that His Fa-

See Papally Promulgated
Catechism of the Catholic Church

Q. 267. See paragraphs: 2598-2616, 2620

ther might glorify Him. There He prayed for His disciples and for those who, through the teachings of the disciples, were to believe in Him; that all might be one, even as He and the Father are one. "That they all may be one, as You, Father, are in Me, and I in You; that they also may be one in Us; that the world may believe that You have sent Me" (John 17:21).

Jesus prayed at ordinary times in the synagogue, and elsewhere, on various occasions. He prayed before undertaking any important project. Before He chose His twelve Apostles, He prayed all night. Before the great miracle of the multiplication of the loaves, He prayed in thanksgiving. Before raising Lazarus to life, Jesus lifted His eyes and thanked His Father for the miracle He was about to perform.

Jesus closed His life with prayer. He prayed in the Garden of Gethsemane. He prayed on the Cross, asking not for justice, but for mercy and pardon to be granted those who were putting Him to death. When He yielded His soul up to God, He cried out, "Father, into your hands I commend My spirit" (Luke 23:46). The supreme act of His life was completed by a prayer of trustful love to His heavenly Father.

The glorified life of Jesus is entirely engulfed in prayer. In the Holy Eucharist, He always lovingly adores His heavenly Father, taking delight in contemplation of the infinite perfections of the Triune God and in glorification of Him by His prayer life in the tabernacle. In the Eucharist, Jesus also occupies Himself with the interests of mankind. He thanks God for us, continually prays for us, asks pardon for our sins, and makes constant reparation for those sins. He continually offers Himself to God and pours out His graces upon all mankind as our Eucharistic Mediator.

In Heaven, Jesus is the Representative and High Priest of all humanity. He honors His Father and implores heavenly help for us. The whole Church and all individuals are sustained by His prayer of mediation, as they are by His doctrine, by His labors, and by His sufferings.

Jesus prays in the Mass. Even now, though He has ascended into Heaven, He renews, throughout time, the perfect offering of Himself to God the Father by the Sacrifice of the Mass. Each Mass shows us His death, which was a sacrifice in blood upon the Cross. In each Mass, the same High Priest offers Himself to the Father, by the hands of His priests, in an unbloody manner; He perpetuates the Sacrifice of the Cross and applies the fruits of His Redemption to our souls.

Since the price that was paid is infinite, there is no grace for which we may not hope, if we beg for it through the Divine Mediator.

Vatican Council II

"Christ is always present in his Church, especially in her liturgical celebrations. He is present in the Sacrifice of the Mass not only in the person of his minister... but especially in the eucharistic species...every liturgical celebration, because it is an action of Christ the Priest and of his Body, which is the Church, is a sacred action surpassing all others." *Sacred Liturgy, 7*

Prayer: *Jesus, Your public life was spent not only in activity, but also in seclusion and prayer. Prayer played an important part in Your life, because God has willed that the salvation of mankind be accomplished not only by toil and suffering, but also by prayer — even prolonged prayer. Help us to understand that nothing is more important and necessary than being in close union with God, for all holiness consists in this union. Give us the grace that we will need to imitate Your example of living with God through prayer, through Your most holy Name. Amen.*

Prayer

Jesus, Your work on earth was the glory of God and the salvation of souls. Souls are saved by prayer and sacrifice. The destruction of the kingdom of satan in this world can only be brought about by the power of God Who is stronger than he. We join our prayers and sacrifices to Yours for this intention.

Jesus, You taught the disciples to present their petitions to the Eternal Father in Your Name. "If you ask the Father anything in My Name, He will give it to you" (John 16:23). "Ask, and you shall receive; that your joy may be full" (John 16:24).

You assured them that, by reason of the merits of Your Redemption, the power of such prayer would be irresistible.

But the greatness of our prayer's power will depend largely on our loyalty to and love for You. Since those who love You remain in You, prayer offered in Your Name is, as it were, Your own.

Jesus, faith in You and the power of Your Name is the greatest spiritual force in the world today. It is a source of joy and inspiration in our youth; of strength in our adulthood, when only Your holy Name and Your grace can enable us to overcome temptation. It is a source of hope, consolation, and confidence at the hour of our death, when more than ever before, we realize that the meaning of Jesus is "Lord, the Savior."

Lord Jesus, our Savior and our God, give us always the water of life to drink, the free gift of the Spirit which flows from Your Sacred Heart, for You are good and You love mankind. May we imitate Your example of prayer and glorify You, Your eternal Father, and Your life-giving Spirit, now and forever. Amen.

The "Our Father"

Q. 268. Why is the "Our Father" a prayer of perfect and unselfish love?

The "Our Father" (see Matthew 6:9-13) is a prayer of perfect and unselfish love because, in saying it, we offer ourselves entirely to God and ask Him for the best things, not only for ourselves, but also for our neighbor.

Our Father, Who art in Heaven... God is our last end. To possess Him on earth, and someday in Heaven, is our true happiness. To possess Him, we must have childlike trust and love.

Hallowed be Thy name. As loving children of our heavenly Father, we should try to be eager for His interests. May His honor be our primary concern.

Thy Kingdom come. Since love seeks intimate union, we ought to desire that God should rule more and more both our minds and hearts.

Thy will be done on earth as it is in Heaven. We will reach eternal happiness by fulfilling God's will daily. Let's ask Him to help us to do His holy will in all things, as His will is accomplished by the angels and saints in Heaven. This life in Heaven is a model of perfect union between Creator and creature.

Give us this day our daily bread. By living our human lives as we ought, let us try to conform ourselves to God's will. For a complete life we need good things for soul and body. Let us look to God to supply us with both.

Forgive us our trespasses as we forgive those who trespass against us, and lead us not into temptation. Sin imposes itself between our souls and God. Let's ask God to strengthen us in temptation, because it is a constant danger to the friendship between us, mere creatures, and God, our Creator.

See Papally Promulgated
Catechism of the Catholic Church

Q. 268. See paragraphs: 2759-2776

But deliver us from evil. Let us beg our heavenly Father not to permit us to give up, and so prove faithless under the heavy crosses of life; let us ask Him to preserve us from the greatest of all evils, mortal sin.

Papal Teaching

"We who now form the Church of Christ on earth... must meet in the dimension of truth of the kingdom of God: Christ came to reveal this kingdom and launch it on this earth, in every place of the earth, in men and among men.

"This kingdom of God is in our midst (cf. Luke 17:21), as it was in all the generations of your fathers and ancestors. But like them, we too still pray in the 'Our Father' every day: 'Thy kingdom come.' These words bear witness that the kingdom of God is still ahead of us, that we are moving towards it, advancing along the confused paths, and in fact sometimes even the wrong ones, of our earthly existence. We bear witness with these words that the kingdom of God is being continually realized and is approaching, even if we often lose sight of it and no longer see its form, described by the Gospel. It often seems that the one and only dimension of our existence is 'this world': the 'kingdom of this world' with its visible form, its breathtaking progress in science and technology, in culture and in economy... breathtaking and often also worrying! But if we kneel down to pray every day, or at least from time to time, we always utter, amid these circumstances of life, the same words: 'Thy kingdom come.' "

Homily by Pope John Paul II, November 15, 1980

Prayer

Jesus, give us the grace we need in order to understand the depth and beauty of the prayer You taught us. God is our Father, since You, the Son of God, became our Brother through the Incarnation. By our sacramental union with You, we are made members of Your Mystical Body, the Church.

May the Name of God be hallowed by all men. May we grow to know more and more about His infinite goodness, and learn to love Him and praise Him above all things.

May Your Kingdom come for us, the Kingdom promised us by the Father and purchased for us by Your holy Passion: the Kingdom of grace here, and the Kingdom of glory hereafter.

Help us, Jesus, to renounce our own wills so that we may do the will of God as it is done in Heaven, for such obedience is the heart and soul of all holiness. May neither sin nor carelessness ever prevent us from partaking of the daily Bread of Life in Holy Communion, that we may continually be with You and live for You.

Forgive us our guilt, and help us to be reconciled with our brethren.

Guard us, Lord, from such temptations as might prove too strong for us, and deliver us from the evil of sin, and all that leads to or results from it.

Jesus, give us the spirit of forgiveness which is expressed in Your prayer. We gladly pardon all who have, in any way, hurt us. We forgive them their offenses with all of our hearts, that we may deserve to be forgiven by Your heavenly Father, Whom we have grieved by our many sins more than anyone can grieve us. To You, to the Father, and to the Holy Spirit be all honor and glory now and forever. Amen.

The Ten Commandments

The Creed - V

Final Reunion with God

"...We look for the resurrection of the dead, and the life of the world to come. Amen."

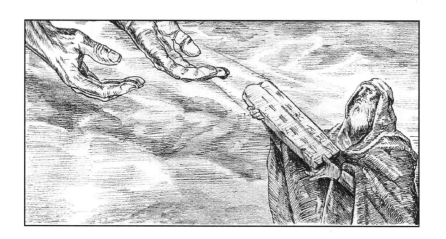

The Ten Commandments

The Moral Life of Christians - I

Q. 269. If we want to answer God's love with our love, what must we do?

If we want to answer God's love with our love, we must: (1) *observe everything that Jesus Christ has commanded (morals),* and (2) *believe all that He has revealed (faith).*

1. *If we want to answer God's love with our love, we must observe everything that Jesus Christ has commanded*

The teaching of the Church includes instructions on things which are to be done and to be avoided, that the followers of Jesus might live the Christian life according to His will. It is our duty as Christians to respond to God's love by faith and action. If we truly love God, we shall endeavor to do His holy will.

Sacred Scripture

"If you love Me, keep My commandments. He that does not love Me does not keep My word. And the word which you have heard is not Mine; but the Father's Who sent Me."

John 14:15, 24

Christ directed His Apostles to teach us this when He said: "Teach them to observe all things whatever I have commanded you. And behold I am with you all days, even to the consummation of the world" (Matthew 28:20). He told His Apostles to go forth and preach the Gospel of the New Covenant to every nation, for He intended His Kingdom, the Church, to encompass all people. The Apostles gathered those who believed into communities, uniting them to Christ and to one another through God's holy Word and the Mass.

2. *If we want to answer God's love with our love, we must believe all that He has revealed.*

See Papally Promulgated
Catechism of the Catholic Church

Q. 269. See paragraphs: 1950-1986, 2032-2055

The Church continues to teach what Jesus revealed and studies the changing conditions of human life in the light of the Gospel in order to help people know how best to apply His unchangeable teaching on a daily basis.

Vatican Council II

"The highest norm of human life is the divine law itself — eternal, objective and universal — by which God orders, directs and governs the whole world and the ways of the human community according to a plan conceived in his wisdom and love." *Liberty, 3*

Q. 270. What does Christian morality teach?

Christian morality teaches us a way of life that is worthy of human beings who are adopted sons of God. We must grow in the new life which God gave us through Jesus Christ.

The Catholic Church expresses her moral teaching by stating moral precepts, or commands, by making judgments about the morality of certain actions, and by making laws that concern the implementation of moral principles and precepts. The Church's teaching expresses the will of God that we become both sharers in Christ's risen life and children in His holy family. We are to live lives worthy of the members of a community of worshipers and believers who are destined for Heaven.

The moral laws which govern human conduct come from an unchanging God and apply to an unchanging human nature. Whatever might be said in favor of the theory of human evolution, once rational man, i.e. , *homo sapiens*, appeared on the earth, his nature has not changed one iota. The first rational humans were essentially the same as those who live today. Therefore, the laws that govern their moral conduct remain the same. Thus, it will always be sinful to lie, to cheat, to gossip, to commit adultery, to contracept, to abuse others, to torture, etc.

See Papally Promulgated
Catechism of the Catholic Church

Q. 270. See paragraphs: 1949-1986

Vatican Council II

"The Council proclaims that all must accept the absolute primacy of the objective moral order. It alone is superior to and is capable of harmonizing all forms of human activity, not excepting art, no matter how noble in themselves. Only the moral order touches man in the totality of his being as God's rational creature, called to a supernatural destiny. If the moral order is fully and faithfully observed, it leads man to full perfection and happiness." *Social Communications, 6*

"The good news of Christ continually renews the life and culture of fallen man; it combats and removes the error and evil which flow from the ever-present attraction of sin. It never ceases to purify and elevate the morality of peoples."
Modern World, 58

Q. 271. How is Christian morality supported and guided?

Christian morality is supported and guided by the grace and gifts of the Holy Spirit which help us in many ways. He persuades us to hold each other in high esteem. He gives us a common bond of friendship so that we may become a community of love, united in Christ because we share His life of grace.

Moreover, He causes us to have the desire and the power to do things which are pleasing to our heavenly Father through His actual graces. The Spirit makes clear what Jesus taught us in the Gospel, and He gives us the help we need to fight satan and to remain true to Jesus and the Catholic Church no matter what the situation. Without these helps, it would be impossible to do anything that could gain our own salvation or the salvation of others.

Vatican Council II

"The gifts of the Spirit are manifold: some men are called to testify openly to mankind's yearning for its heavenly home

See Papally Promulgated
Catechism of the Catholic Church

Q. 271. See paragraphs: 1960, 1966, 1972, 1983

and keep the awareness of it vividly before men's minds; others are called to dedicate themselves to the earthly service of men and in this way to prepare the way for the kingdom of heaven. But of all the Spirit makes free men, who are ready to put aside love of self and integrate earthly resources into human life, in order to reach out to that future day when mankind itself will become an offering accepted by God."

Modern World, 38

Prayer: *Life-giving Spirit, our Creator and Sanctifier, You have given us life and being, and have led us into Your holy Catholic Church, which is the ordinary means of salvation. You have adorned our souls with sanctifying grace, made them Your temples, enriched them with heavenly virtues, and sanctified them through the holy sacraments. All of these benefits have come to us through Your holy Catholic Church. We thank You for having created it. Make us faithful children of our holy Mother Church which is the pillar and foundation of truth. Help us to uphold her doctrines, to seek her interests, and to defend her rights. Help us to be ever obedient to the Holy See, Your infallible mouthpiece. All this we ask through Jesus Christ our Lord. Amen.*

Prayer

Merciful Comforter, to Your mercy we entrust the entire Catholic Church, all its undertakings, and the souls entrusted to her care. We pray for the Pope, the Bishops, priests, Religious, and consecrated singles. By Your supernatural power, confirm in them the desire to spend their lives in Your holy service for the salvation of souls. Divine Fire, enkindle in all those who share in Your apostolate the flames which transformed the disciples in the Upper Room on the first Christian Pentecost (cf. Acts 2). They will be no longer ordinary men, but men who live in order to transfuse the divine life to the souls of their fellow men. Enkindle in their wills an ardent desire for the inner life, for their apostolate will be successful only in the measure in which they themselves live that supernatural life, of which You are the sovereign Principle, and Jesus Christ, the Source.

Be merciful also to all the children of Your holy Catholic Church, that they may be faithful to her teaching and so save their souls. Finally, be merciful to unrepentant sinners and non-believers. Grant them the grace they need to recognize You, with the Father and the Son, as the only source of true happiness, and to love You with their whole heart. Look graciously upon the Poor Souls in Purgatory; comfort and refresh them with the graces which flow from Your merciful love. To You, the Father, and the Son, be all honor and glory, now and forever. Amen.

The Moral Life of Christians - II

Q. 272. What is conscience?

Conscience is a personal, reasoned, practical judgment that something is right or wrong; that is, whether it is in accordance with the will and law of God that is written within one's soul.

Conscience makes us aware of what God wants us to do at a given time. Furthermore, it helps us to know when we have sinned. Conscience tells us whether an action is right or wrong and whether it is a mortal or a venial sin. Our conscience is our mind's ability to judge moral matters. It is important to note, however, that, for most people, reason alone is not a sufficient guide in moral matters. The conscience must be instructed and formed. We must learn from Christ as He speaks to us in the hidden recesses of our souls, and as He teaches us through His Catholic Church.

Sacred Scripture

"He set His eye upon their hearts to show the greatness of His works... Moreover, He gave them instructions and the law of life for an inheritance." *Ecclesiasticus 17:7,9*

"For when the Gentiles, who do not have the law, do by nature those things that are of the law; these not having the law are a law unto themselves: who show the work of the law written on their hearts." *Romans 2:14-15*

Vatican Council II

"Deep within his conscience man discovers a law which he has not laid upon himself but which he must obey. Its voice, ever calling him to love and to do what is good and to avoid evil, tells him inwardly at the right moment: do this, shun that. For man has in his heart a law inscribed by God. His

See Papally Promulgated
Catechism of the Catholic Church

Q. 272. See paragraphs: 1776-1782

dignity lies in observing this law, and by it he will be judged. (cf. Rom. 2:15-16) His conscience is man's most secret core, and his sanctuary. There he is alone with God whose voice echoes in his depths. By conscience, in a wonderful way, that law is made known which is fulfilled in the love of God and of one's neighbor (cf. Mt. 22:37-40; Gal. 5:14)." *Modern World, 16*

Q. 273. Must each person have a right conscience?

Each person must have a right conscience and follow it. A Catholic must form a right conscience by learning and obeying the teaching authority, or Magisterium, of the Catholic Church.

Moreover, the moral life of Christians is guided by the grace and gifts of the Holy Spirit. We do not always know with certainty whether our consciences are right, but we can train them over a period of time to be evermore aware of the Truth, by listening to the Word of God in Scripture, in the Church's teaching, and by being attentive to the inspiration of the Holy Spirit within us.

Vatican Council II

"It is through his conscience that man sees and recognizes the demands of the divine law. He is bound to follow this conscience faithfully in all his activity so that he may come to God, who is his last end. Therefore he must not be forced to act contrary to his conscience. Nor must he be prevented from acting according to his conscience, especially in religious matters." *Liberty, 3*

"Through loyalty to conscience, Christians are joined to other men in the search for truth and for the right solution to so many moral problems which arise both in the life of individuals and from social relationships. Hence, the more a correct conscience prevails, the more do persons and groups turn aside from blind choice and try to be guided by the objective standards of moral conduct. Yet it often happens that con-

See Papally Promulgated
Catechism of the Catholic Church

Q. 273. See paragraphs: 1783-1785, 1790-1794

science goes astray through ignorance which it is unable to avoid, without thereby losing its dignity. This cannot be said of the man who takes little trouble to find out what is true and good, or when conscience is by degrees almost blinded through the habit of committing sin." *Modern World, 16*

> **Prayer:** *Father, let Your Spirit come upon us with power and fill us with His gifts. May He make our hearts pleasing to You and ready to do Your will. Let our spiritual sacrifice at Mass, in union with Christ's, make us an everlasting gift to You. Renew us by the mysteries we share in Holy Communion. Help us to know You and Your will, and prepare us for the gifts of the Spirit, that we may live truly Christian lives that are pleasing to You through Christ our Lord. Amen.*

Q. 274. How must a Catholic form a right conscience?

A Catholic must form a right conscience by studying and obeying the teaching authority of the Catholic Church.

It is the duty of the teaching authority of the Catholic Church, or Magisterium, to give guidance for applying the enduring norms and values of Christian morality to specific situations of everyday life.

Christian freedom needs to be ruled and directed by the specific circumstances of human life. Accordingly, the consciences of the faithful, even when informed by the virtue of prudence, must be subject to the teaching authority of the Church. It is the Church's duty to explain the whole moral law authoritatively, in order that it may rightly and correctly make known the objective moral order.

The conscience of the Catholic Christian must pay respectful and obedient attention to the teaching authority of the Catholic Church.

See Papally Promulgated
Catechism of the Catholic Church

Q. 274. See paragraphs: 1783-1794

"In availing of any freedom men must respect the moral principle of personal and social responsibility: in exercising their rights individual men and social groups are bound by the moral law to have regard for the rights of others, their own duties to others and the common good of all. All men must be treated with justice and humanity." *Liberty, 7*

"For the Catholic Church is by the will of Christ the teacher of truth. It is her duty to proclaim and teach with authority the principles of the moral order which spring from human nature itself." *Liberty, 14*

"Although the bishops, taken individually, do not enjoy the privilege of infallibility, they do, however, proclaim infallibly the doctrine of Christ on the following conditions: namely, when, even though dispersed throughout the world but preserving for all that amongst themselves and with Peter's successor, the bond of communion, in their authoritative teaching concerning matters of faith and morals, they are in agreement that a particular teaching is to be held definitively and absolutely. This is still more clearly the case when, assembled in an ecumenical council, they are, for the universal Church, teachers of and judges in matters of faith and morals, whose decisions must be adhered to with the loyal and obedient assent of faith." *The Church, 25*

"Bishops who teach in communion with the Roman Pontiff are to be revered by all as witnesses of divine and Catholic truth; the faithful for their part, are obliged to submit to their bishops' decision, made in the name of Christ, in matters of faith and morals, and to adhere to it with a ready and respectful allegiance of mind. This loyal submission of the will and intellect must be given, in a special way, to the authentic teaching authority of the Roman Pontiff, even when he does not speak *ex cathedra* in such wise, indeed, that his supreme teaching authority be acknowledged with respect, and that one sincerely adhere to decisions made by him, conformably with his manifest mind and intention, which is made known principally either by the frequency with which a certain doctrine is proposed, or by the manner in which the doctrine is formulated." *The Church, 25*

Q. 275. What does obedience to the Holy Spirit include?

Obedience to the Holy Spirit includes a faithful observance of the commandments of God, the laws and precepts of the Church, and just civil laws.

Without the assistance of the Holy Spirit, we can do nothing to obtain our salvation. The Spirit gives us the power to make a lasting commitment to Christ and also the help needed to keep that commitment.

We should let the Spirit have His way with us. He will bend our wills and touch our hearts if we let Him. We ought to pray each day for the strength to say yes to whatever the Spirit wants to accomplish in us.

Christian witness is especially powerful when it defends the values of God rather than those of the world. Our Lord called us "the salt of the earth," and "the light of the world." Therefore, the good Christian should take an interest in and participate in civic affairs. Only in this way can he expect to carry the principles of Christ into the world.

Vatican Council II

"Since this mission continues and, in the course of history, unfolds the mission of Christ, who was sent to evangelize the poor, then the Church, urged on by the Spirit of Christ, must walk the road Christ himself walked, a way of poverty and obedience, of service and self-sacrifice even to death, a death from which he emerged victorious by his resurrection."

Missionary Activity, 5

See Papally Promulgated
Catechism of the Catholic Church

Q. 275. See paragraphs: 1952, 2042-2043, 2052-2055, 2235, 2242

Prayer

God, our Father, You gave Your Holy Spirit to Your Church on Pentecost. Let the Spirit You sent to Your Church to begin the teaching of the Gospel continue to work in the world through the hearts of all those who believe.

Father of lights, from Whom every good gift comes, send Your Spirit into our lives with the power of a mighty wind, and, by the flame of Your wisdom, open the horizons of our minds. By the power of the Holy Spirit, loosen our tongues so that we may praise You properly. For without Your Spirit, man could never raise his voice in words of peace or announce the truth that Jesus is Lord.

On Pentecost, You enlightened the minds of the disciples by sending the Holy Spirit. May He bless us and give us His gifts. May that fire which hovered over the disciples as tongues of flame burn all evil from our hearts and make them glow with Your light. You enabled the Apostles to speak in different tongues so that they could proclaim the one Faith. May the Holy Spirit strengthen our faith and sustain our hope that we may someday see Him face to face.

By glorifying Christ and sending us Your Spirit, You open the way to eternal life. May our sharing in this gift of the most holy Godhead, increase our love and make our faith grow stronger. Unite Your Church in the Holy Spirit so that we may serve You with our whole heart and work together with unselfish love. Send Your Spirit to help the Church You love so that it may show Your salvation to all the world. This we ask in Jesus' Name. Amen.

Perfect Christian Love - I

Q. 276. What is the summary of all of the commandments?

The commandments, summed up, deal specifically with the love of God and the love of neighbor.

"And you shall love the Lord your God with your whole heart, and with your whole soul, and with your whole mind, and with your whole strength. This is the first commandment. And the second is like to it: 'You shall love your neighbor as yourself' " (Mark 12:30-31). Other words and examples of Jesus tell us how these two commandments are to be practiced.

Vatican Council II

"In his fatherly care for all of us, God desired that all men should form one family and deal with each other in a spirit of brotherhood. All, in fact, are destined to the very same end, namely God Himself, since they have been created in the likeness of God Who 'made from one every nation of men who live on all the face of the earth' (Acts 17:26). Love of God and one's neighbor, then, is the first and greatest commandment."

Modern World, 24

"The greatest commandment of the law is to love God with one's whole heart and one's neighbor as oneself (cf. Mt. 22:37-39). Christ has made this love of neighbor his personal commandment and has enriched it with a new meaning when he willed himself, along with his brothers, to be the object of this charity saying: 'When you showed it to one of the least of my brothers here, you showed it to me' (Mt. 25:40). In assuming human nature Christ has united all humanity to himself in a supernatural solidarity which makes us one family. He has made charity the distinguishing mark of his disciples, by His

See Papally Promulgated
Catechism of the Catholic Church

Q. 276. See paragraphs: 1814, 2196

words: 'By this will all men know you for my disciples, by the love you bear one another' (Jn. 13:35)." *Lay People, 8*

Q. 277. Why is love of God the soul of morality?

Love of God is the soul of morality because: (1) *God is love* and; (2) *in God's plan that love reaches out to men in Jesus Christ, so that men might be united by their love for God and for one another.*

1. *Love of God is the soul of morality because God is love.*

God loves us. He always has loved us and always will love us. He has loved us from the moment He thought of creating us, and He will love us for all eternity. St. John tells us of the depth of God's love for each individual. "For God so loved the world, as to give His only begotten Son; that whoever believes in Him, may not perish, but may have life everlasting" (John 3:16).

Because God loves every human being with an undying, deep love, St. John goes so far as to call God "love" or "charity." "Dearly beloved, let us love one another, for charity is of God. And every one that loves, is born of God, and knows God. He that loves not, knows not God: for God is charity" (1 John 4:7-8).

God watches over us every moment of our existence. Every beat of our hearts depends on Him. God gave us all of the good things in life which we have: our lives, our health, our families and our friends, and our possessions. God made us His children in Baptism, and promised to grant us eternal life with Him in Heaven, if we are faithful to Him.

He gives us the privilege of sharing His divine life by giving us sanctifying grace through the sacraments. He continues to grant us the blessings of the Catholic Church, especially through the sacraments and God's truth. Because of His immense love for us, He forgives our sins, if we are repentant. Jesus said, "For the Father Himself loves you, be-

See Papally Promulgated
Catechism of the Catholic Church

Q. 277. See paragraphs: 1822-1829

cause you have loved Me, and have believed that I came out from God" (John 16:27).

Whenever we think of God's great love for us, we ought to desire to love God in return. Our one aim in life should be union with God — through a love which expresses itself in faithful service. Our lives must be joyous since God is with us.

> **Prayer:** *Jesus, You teach us that the law of charity demands that we love God with our whole heart, soul, and mind, that is, with our whole being. Yet, our love for God need not be a love that we can feel, for, essentially, true love consists not in any sensible feeling, but in acts of the mind and will. Since You are truth and goodness themselves, and since You have loved us with an everlasting love, we ought to love You above all creatures and with our entire beings. May this always be so. Amen.*

2. Love of God is the soul of morality because in God's plan that love reaches out to men in Jesus Christ, so that men might be united by their love for God and for one another.

Jesus Christ, in His perfect love for us, died on the Cross to atone for, or make up for, our sins and to regain for us the life of grace and eternal life with God. Christ is our Mediator with God. God's love reaches us through Jesus Christ, the God-man.

Christ and His Father sent God the Holy Spirit into the hearts of the Apostles. The Spirit — Who is the love of God in the Trinity — is God's supreme gift to the Church. The great work of the Spirit is to unite men into a community of love.

The Holy Spirit's chief gift is His personal presence in those who believe in and follow Christ. By means of His personal presence and His gift of sanctifying grace, the Spirit makes us pleasing to God and set apart for Him. Through sanctifying grace, He makes us children in the family of God, and unites us in faith and charity to Christ and to each other. As a community of believers, we become heirs of God's Kingdom. This is God's plan for us, a plan that has its source in His love.

All of Christianity is based on love, i.e., charity, or unselfish love. Man is created to love, grows by loving, and finally, finds himself by loving. St. Paul said: "If I speak with the tongues of men, and of angels, and have not charity, I am become as sounding brass, or a tinkling cymbal" (1 Corinthians 13:1).

Sacred Scripture

"Owe no man anything, but to love one another. For he that loves his neighbor, has fulfilled the law. For you shall not commit adultery. You shall not kill. You shall not steal. You shall not bear false witness. You shall not covet. And if there be any other commandment, it is comprised in this word, you shall love your neighbor as yourself. The love of our neighbor works no evil. Love, therefore, is the fulfilling of the law."

Romans 13:8-10

Vatican Council II

"'God is love, and he who abides in love abides in God, and God abides in him' (1 Jn. 4:16). God has poured out His love in our hearts through the Holy Spirit who has been given to us (cf. Rm. 5:5); therefore the first and most necessary gift is charity, by which we love God above all things and our neighbor because of Him." *The Church, 42*

Prayer: *Our God, we wish to love You for Your own sake. Let our love for You not be selfish. May we not love You to advance our own interests, but rather let us love You with our whole heart in a free and generous gift of ourselves. If beauty, truth, goodness, and love attract and claim our admiration, love, and devotion, we should not find it difficult to love You, our God, in Whom all these qualities reside to the highest degree. May we love You above all things now and forever. Amen.*

Prayer

Lord, we want to love You perfectly by consecrating ourselves to Your service, with all our powers of body and soul, so that we may present our bodies in chastity as living sacrifices, holy and pleasing to God. May all the powers of our souls be turned towards You; may our minds think of You, our affections delight in You, and our wills conform themselves to Your will.

All is vanity, except loving You and serving You. If we love You with our whole heart, we shall fear neither death nor punishment, neither judgment nor hell, because perfect love will prepare our souls for a more intimate union with You.

Besides, You have been very kind to us. Love moved You to create us and to redeem us. Innumerable are the graces and blessings which You have given us in Your love. All that we see, hear, or feel which is good and beautiful is a gift from You. May all creatures be so many mirrors wherein we may behold You, and so many steps whereby we may ascend to You, the God of our love. Amen.

Perfect Christian Love - II

Q. 278. What is man's greatest responsibility?

Man's greatest responsibility in life is: (1) *to do God's will by living in His love,* and (2) *to practice the "new commandment" of love of neighbor.*

1. *Man's greatest responsibility is to do God's will by living in His love.*

Jesus said: "As the Father has loved Me, I also have loved you. Abide in My love. If you keep My commandments you shall abide in My love; as I also have kept My Father's commandments, and do abide in His love" (John 15: 9-10).

Man's greatest responsibility and the source of his greatest dignity is to live a life loving God first and foremost, and loving his fellow man.

The action of the Spirit of Christ is made clear when the distinctive characteristic of Christian moral teaching — love — is brought to light. All precepts and counsels of this moral teaching are summarized as faith working through love. Love (charity) is, as it were, faith's soul.

2. *Man's greatest responsibility is to practice the "new commandment" of sacrificial love of neighbor, that is, to love our neighbor as Jesus has loved us.*

Jesus taught about God's way of life, that is, that God's life is totally and completely sacrificial love. God is forever giving Himself. To belong to His Kingdom means to live by love, as well. Like Jesus, we must be willing to live for others.

Man, therefore, is called to embrace, in faith, a life of charity towards God and towards human beings; in this lies his greatest responsibility and his exalted moral dignity.

See Papally Promulgated
Catechism of the Catholic Church

Q. 278. See paragraphs: 1823, 1962, 1968, 1970

Sacred Scripture

"By this has the charity of God appeared towards us, because God has sent His only begotten Son into the world, that we may live by Him. In this is charity: not as though we had loved God, but because He has first loved us, and sent His Son to be a propitiation for our sins. My dearest ones, if God has so loved us; we also ought to love one another. No man has seen God at any time. If we love one another, God abides in us. In this we know that we abide in Him, and He in us, because He has given us of His Spirit. And we have seen, and do testify, that the Father has sent His Son to be the Savior of the world. Whoever shall confess that Jesus is the Son of God, God abides in him, and he in God. And we have known, and have believed the charity, which God has to us. God is charity: and he that abides in charity, abides in God, and God in him."

1 John 4:9-16

Vatican Council II

"But if charity is to grow and fructify in the soul like a good seed, each of the faithful must willingly hear the word of God and carry out his will with deeds, with the help of his grace; he must frequently partake of the sacraments, chiefly the Eucharist, and take part in the liturgy; he must constantly apply himself to prayer, self-denial, active brotherly service and the practice of all virtues." *The Church, 4*

"Love, as the bond of perfection and fullness of the law (cf. Col. 3:14; Rom. 13:10) governs, gives meaning to, and perfects all the means of sanctification. Hence the true disciple of Christ is marked by love both of God and of his neighbor." *The Church, 42*

"A life like this [in union with Christ] calls for a continuous exercise of faith, hope and charity." *Lay People, 4*

"If this exercise of charity is to be above all criticism, and seen to be so, one should see in one's neighbor the image of God to which he has been created, and Christ the Lord to whom is really offered all that is given to the needy. The liberty and dignity of the person helped must be respected with the greatest sensitivity. Purity of intention should not be stained by any self-seeking or desire to dominate. The demands of justice must first of all be satisfied; that which is already due in justice is not to be offered as a gift of charity. The cause of evils, and not merely their effects, ought to disappear. The aid contributed should be organized in such a way that beneficiaries are gradually freed from their dependence on others and become self-supporting." *Lay People, 8*

588

Q. 279. How does a person obtain holiness?

A person obtains holiness, whatever his state of life may be, by loving God above all else.

Jesus' humanity shows that God's life is holy because it is lived with love. Father, Son, and Holy Spirit are forever giving Themselves to each other. God asks us to be holy. To be holy means to be like God. He wants us to be as much like Him as possible. This means sharing more and more of our lives with Him by loving Him. In this way He can complete the good work that He began in us through His grace in Baptism — when we first received His divine life and became His children (cf. Philippians 1:6).

Sacred Scripture

"Wherefore having the loins of your mind girt up, being sober, trust perfectly in the grace which is offered you in the revelation of Jesus Christ, as children of obedience, not fashioned according to the former desires of your ignorances. But according to Him that has called you, Who is holy, be also in all manner of conversation holy, because it is written: 'You shall be holy, for I am holy.' " *1 Peter 1:13-16*

Vatican Council II

"The forms and tasks of life are many but holiness is one — that sanctity which is cultivated by all who act under God's Spirit and, obeying the Father's voice and adoring God the Father in spirit and in truth, follow Christ, poor, humble and cross-bearing, that they may deserve to be partakers of his glory. Each one, however, according to his own gifts and duties must steadfastly advance along the way of a living faith, which arouses hope and works through love." *The Church, 41*

"All Christians, in any state or walk of life, are called to the fullness of the Christian life and to the perfection of love, and by this holiness, a more human manner of life is fostered also in earthly society. In order to reach this perfection, the faith-

---

See Papally Promulgated
Catechism of the Catholic Church

Q. 279. See paragraphs: 375, 398, 773, 823-829

ful should use the strength dealt out to them by Christ's gift, so that, following in his footsteps and conformed to his image, doing the will of God in everything, they may wholeheartedly devote themselves to the glory of God and to the service of their neighbor." *The Church, 40*

Q. 280. Why do men and women accept Religious vocations?

Men and women accept Religious vocations to show, in a special and necessary way, their love of God by true service to mankind.

The Religious state is a special state to which our Lord God calls some people. Like all states of Christian life, the Religious life is a way to perfection. The seeds of this special vocation are found in the Gospels where Jesus speaks of poverty, chastity, and obedience. Those who enter the Religious life accept what are called the "evangelical counsels" of poverty, chastity, and obedience. They bind themselves to these counsels by public vows. Besides the profession of these three vows, the observance of a rule of common life is an essential aspect of the Religious life.

Perfect love of God is the aim and ideal of the Religious state. This state is a permanent condition of life, officially recognized as such by the Church, wherein a person binds him or herself to strive after perfection.

The perfection of Christian life essentially consists in love — first and foremost in the love of God, then in the love of neighbor. The whole life of a Religious is to be one continuous act of love, in the service of God and the Church. Hence, Religious vocations are important to humanity and to the Church.

Vatican Council II

"Jesus, the Son of God, showed his love by laying down his life for us. No one has greater love than he who lays down his

---

See Papally Promulgated
Catechism of the Catholic Church

Q. 280. See paragraphs: 915-916, 925-926

life for Christ and for his brethren (cf. 1 John 3:16; John 15:13)."

The Church, 42

"The teaching and example of Christ provide the foundation for the evangelical counsels of chaste self-dedication to God, of poverty and of obedience. The Apostles and Fathers of the Church commend them as an ideal of life, and so do her doctors and pastors. They therefore constitute a gift of God which the Church has received from her Lord and which by his grace she always safeguards." *The Church, 43*

"Guided by the Holy Spirit, Church authority has been at pains to give a right interpretation of the counsels, to regulate their practice and also to set up stable forms of living embodying them." *The Church, 43*

Prayer

Jesus, You said to Your followers, "You are the salt of the earth. But if the salt loses its savor, wherewith shall it be salted? It is good for nothing any more but to be cast out, and to be trodden on by men" (Matthew 5:13).

We are the salt of the earth in the measure that we are holy. Like true salt, we are to be real agents of preservation in a world filled with corruption. Help us to be the salt of the earth by leading holy lives through frequent Holy Communion and fervent prayer; for how can we influence others to be good, if we ourselves have lost Your Spirit? Never permit us to lose the desire for holiness by letting ourselves be infected by a worldly spirit, or by not living according to our holy Faith in self-denial and detachment.

Jesus, You said: "You are the light of the world. A city seated on a mountain cannot be hidden...so let your light shine before men, that they may see your good works, and glorify your Father who is in Heaven" (Matthew 5:14,16).

*M*ost Sacred Heart, as You are the Light of the world, by putting into practice Your holy doctrine and example, so too, in our lives may we be the light of the world, that the brightness of our good example, may scatter the darkness of the spirit of the world and radiate true and lasting happiness which comes from You alone.

*J*esus, purify our hearts with Your truth and guide us in the way of holiness, so that we may always do what is pleasing in Your sight. Help us always to do what is good, right, and true in Your sight. Jesus, our Light shining in the darkness, lead us to life and give our mortal nature the gift of holiness. May we spend our lives in praise of Your glory. Help us to seek You always with all the love of our hearts.

*G*ood Master, show us the way You have chosen for us in this life. May we walk in it, and so find fulfillment and happiness. Give us the grace we need to enter more deeply into the mystery of Your life, so that our lives may always reveal You more effectively.

*I*n Your mercy, Jesus, send the Holy Spirit to shine on us, so that our lives may radiate holiness, love, and faith. Healer of body and soul, cure the sickness of our spirits, so that we may grow in holiness through Your constant care. We ask this in Your most holy Name. Amen.

Chapter One Hundred Thirty-One

Our Duties Toward God - I

Q. 281. How do we know the duties which flow from love of God and man?

We know the duties that flow from the love of God and man by: (1) *the Ten Commandments of God;* (2) *the Sermon on the Mount, especially in the Beatitudes;* (3) *the spiritual and corporal works of mercy;* (4) *the cardinal virtues;* and (5) *the laws of the Church.*

1. *We know the duties that flow from the love of God and man by the Ten Commandments of God.*

The covenant between God and His people, which God delivered to Moses, included, as an essential part of the message of salvation, the Ten Commandments. Like the first People of God, we Christians make obedience to the commandments our response to God's love for us. By keeping the commandments, we surrender ourselves in obedience to God and unite ourselves to Him.

All of the commandments can be summarized in the two commandments of love of God and love of neighbor. Of the Ten Commandments, the first three show us how we must love God; and the last seven show us how to love others for the sake of God. The Ten Commandments of God are of special importance in teaching the specifics of morality. The Old Testament, the New Testament, and the long use which the Church has made of the Ten Commandments, testify to this importance.

2. *We know the duties that flow from the love of God and man by the Sermon on the Mount, especially in the Beatitudes.*

The Beatitudes express the high standards of Christ's Kingdom and the reward which is promised to those who live

See Papally Promulgated
Catechism of the Catholic Church

Q. 281. See paragraphs: 1716-1717, 1724, 1803-1845, 1866, 1965-1974, 2041-2043, 2052-2089, 2447

according to these standards. In the Sermon on the Mount, Christ tells us how to attain happiness in this life. The primary reward promised in each of these Beatitudes is Heaven, but if we live according to the plan of Christ, we shall have a foretaste of the happiness of Heaven in this life.

Christ tells us that we will be happy if we do, for His sake, the very things which many think will make them unhappy. He tells us that we must not set our hearts on money; that we must forgive our enemies and love them; that we must avoid all sin, and that we must be willing to suffer for His sake. Christ has not only told us how to live; He has shown us by His example. What is more, He gives us all the help we need to follow His example.

3. *We know the duties that flow from love of God and man by the spiritual and corporal works of mercy.*

Some of the most important works of mercy are: to help convert the sinners, to advise the doubtful, to instruct the ignorant, to comfort the sorrowful, to bear wrongs patiently, to pray for the living and the dead, to feed the hungry, to clothe the poor, to support the homeless, to visit the sick, and to bury the dead.

4. *We know the duties that flow from the love of God and man by the cardinal virtues.*

We would not be able to love God or one another as children of God, without a special gift from God — the gift of charity. It is one of the great powers which God bestows on us along with the gift of sanctifying grace. God also gives us the powers to believe in Him and to hope in Him. These three powers are the virtues of faith, hope, and charity, called the "theological virtues" because they refer to God.

The cardinal or principal moral virtues are: prudence, which inclines us to form right judgments about what we should or should not do; justice, which inclines us to give to all men whatever is due to them; temperance, which inclines us to control our appetites according to what is right and pleasing to God; and fortitude, which inclines us to do what God desires, even when it is disagreeable or difficult.

5. *We know the duties that flow from the love of God and man by the laws of the Church.*

From time to time, the Church has listed certain specific duties of Catholics. The duties which are expected of Catholic

Christians today are the laws of the Church. These laws are traditionally called the Precepts of the Church. Some of them are: 1) to participate in Mass every Sunday and holy day of obligation; 2) to receive Holy Communion frequently; 3) to receive the Sacrament of Penance frequently; 4) to observe the Church's marriage laws; and 5) to do penance.

Sacred Scripture

"And if a man loves justice, her labors have great virtues. For she teaches temperance and prudence and justice and fortitude, which are such things that as men can have nothing more profitable in life." *Wisdom 8:7*

Vatican Council II

"Let him be convinced that obedience is the special virtue of a minister of Christ who by his obedience redeemed the human race." *Missionary Activity, 24*

Prayer

Lord God, You proclaim victorious those whose lives are blameless. You give Your law to those who seek it. Make us seek Your righteous ways with our whole heart.

Father, You cut down the fruitless branch to burn it, and prune the fertile one to make it bear more fruit. Make us grow like laden vines in Your Kingdom, firmly rooted in the power of the mercy of Your Son. May You gather from our lives fruit worthy of eternal life. Help us to receive good things from Your bounty with a deep sense of gratitude, and to accept with patience the evil that comes to us. Teach us to be loving, not only in great and exceptional moments, but above all, in the ordinary events of daily life.

Eternal Father, You give us life despite our guilt, and even add days and years to our lives in order to bring us wisdom. Make us love and obey You, so that the works of our hands may always display what Your hands have done, until the day when we will gaze upon the beauty of Your face.

God our Father and Protector, without You, nothing is holy; nothing has value. Guide us to everlasting life by helping us to use wisely the blessings You have given us. Fill us with Your gifts and make us always eager to serve You in faith, hope, and love. Let the gift of Your life continue to grow in us, drawing us from death to faith, hope, and love. Keep us alive in Christ Jesus. Make us watchful in prayer and true to His teaching until Your glory is revealed in us.

Heavenly Father, may we love You in all things and above all things, and so reach the joy You have prepared for us which is beyond all our imagining. By offering ourselves, and all that You have given us in the Mass, may we receive the life of Christ Himself, the Bread of Life, in Holy Communion. By this sacrament, make us one with Christ. By becoming more like Him on earth, may we come to share His glory in Heaven. Amen.

Our Duties Toward God - II

Q. 282. What can be said in general about a Christian's duties towards God?

Towards God, the Christian has the lifelong obligations of love and service.

This means: (1) *the will of God must be put first on the list of his personal values, and must be kept there throughout life;* (2) *his attitude towards God must be that of a son towards an all-loving Father;* (3) *he must never think or live as if he were independent of God;* and (4) *he must, without hesitancy, give God genuine worship and true prayer, both liturgical and private.*

1. *The will of God must be put first on the list of his personal values, and must be kept there throughout life.*

Our Lord's first concern was to give honor to His Father in Heaven. Doing His Father's will, He said, was His food. We who are united to Christ and who share His divine life should also share in His devotion to the Father. Like our eldest brother, Christ, we should approach the Father with reverence and obedience. Our first aim in life should be to do His holy will in all things.

2. *His attitude towards God must be that of a son towards an all-loving Father.*

Adoration, or worship, is the high honor we owe to God. This is because God, in His high perfection, has willed to create us, to keep us in existence, to watch over us as a father watches over his children, to forgive our sins and even to make us like Himself through divine grace. Realizing God's infinite perfection and His love for us, we acknowledge our total dependence on Him. Our attitude toward Him should be one of a devoted son to an all-loving Father.

See Papally Promulgated
Catechism of the Catholic Church

Q. 282. See paragraphs: 901-903, 1807, 2083-2084, 2095-2096

3. *He must never think or live as if he were independent of God.*

The virtue of religion — the first of all moral virtues — enables us to render homage to God because it is due to Him. This virtue inclines us to acknowledge, by acts of worship, the rights of God, Who is the Beginning and the Last End of all things.

4. *He must gladly give to God genuine worship and true prayer, both liturgical and private.*

The offering of sacrifice is the supreme, visible, and social act of adoration. Sacrifice is an outward sign which expresses the intimate sentiments of the heart of man as he renders worship to God. When we perform acts of piety and recite vocal prayers, the words and gestures are intended to express the thought and intentions of the soul.

We worship God by fulfilling the duties of our state in life, by learning what God teaches, by praying and sacrificing, by believing in God, by hoping in Him, and by loving Him with our whole heart, by practicing acts of love toward those whom God also created — our neighbors, and by publicly adoring God at Mass.

But adoration must not be outward alone; it must be from the heart. This is true worship, as Jesus told the Samaritan woman: "But the hour comes, and now is, when the true adorers shall adore the Father in spirit and in truth. For the Father also seeks such to adore Him" (John 4:23). "Jesus also said to him, 'You shall love the Lord your God with your whole heart and with your whole soul and with your whole mind'" (Matthew 22:37).

Vatican Council II

"The dignity of man rests above all on the fact that he is called to communion with God. The invitation to converse with God is addressed to man as soon as he comes into being. For if man exists it is because God has created him through love, and through love continues to hold him into existence. He cannot live fully according to truth unless he freely acknowledges that love and entrusts himself to his creator."

Modern World, 19

"Wishing to come down to topics that are practical and of some urgency, the Council lays stress on respect for the human person: everyone should look upon his neighbor (without any exception) as another self, bearing in mind above all his life and the means necessary for living it in a dignified way lest he follow the example of the rich man who ignored Lazarus, the poor man.

"Today there is an inescapable duty to make ourselves the neighbor of every man, no matter who he is, and if we meet him, to come to his aid in a positive way, whether he is an aged person abandoned by all, a foreign worker despised without reason, a refugee, an illegitimate child wrongly suffering for a sin he did not commit, or a starving human being who awakens our conscience by calling to mind the words of Christ 'As you did it to one of the least of these my brethren, you did it to me' (Matthew 25:40)." *Modern World, 27*

Prayer: *Eternal Father, turn our hearts to You. By seeking Your Kingdom and loving one another, may we become a people who worships You in spirit and truth. May we be renewed by the Eucharist and become more like Christ Your Son. May the Eucharistic food we receive assure us of Your constant love.*

Father, accept us as sacrifices of praise, so that we may go through life unburdened by sin, walking in the way of salvation, and always giving thanks to You through Jesus Christ our Savior. Amen.

Prayer

Father, Creator of unfailing light, give that same light to those who call to You. May our lips praise You, our lives proclaim Your goodness, our work give You honor, and our voices celebrate You forever.

Lord, extolled in the heights by angelic powers, You are also praised by all earth's creatures, each in its own way. With all the splendor of heavenly worship that You receive, You still delight in such tokens of love as earth can offer. May Heaven and earth together acclaim You as King; may the praise that is sung in Heaven resound in the heart of every creature on earth.

God our Father, may all nations and peoples praise You. May Jesus, Who is called faithful and true, and Who lives with You eternally, possess our hearts forever.

Guide the Church and gather it together so that we may worship You in peace and tranquillity.

Praise, thanksgiving, glory, honor, and exaltation be to the Father Who created us, to the Son Who redeemed us, and to the Holy Spirit Who sanctifies us. Blessed be the holy and undivided Trinity, now and always. Amen.

Our Duties Toward God - III

Q. 283. How do we sin against the honor due to God?

We sin against the honor due to God: (1) *by putting anyone or anything in God's place;* (2) *by blaspheming God or perjuring ourselves;* (3) *by failing to show respect for persons, places, and things related especially to God;* (4) *by atheism, heresy, and schism;* and (5) *by missing Mass on Sundays and holy days of obligation.*

1. *We sin against the honor due to God by putting anyone or anything in God's place.*

The First Commandment states, "I, the Lord, am your God. You shall not have other gods besides Me" (Deuteronomy 5:6-7; cf. Exodus 20: 1-17). This commandment binds us to adoration. We honor God by praising Him, by serving Him, and by offering sacrifices to Him.

The First Commandment warns us against any action which would lead us away from the true adoration of the living God. This includes neglecting to learn the truths God has taught or refusing to believe these truths once we understand them; leaving God's Catholic Church, (when we have believed it is completely faithful in teaching all of God's truths which He has intended man to know for his salvation); and giving in to superstitious practices by which we show belief that certain persons or things have powers which only God has.

Sacred Scripture

"The Lord your God you shall adore, and Him only shall you serve." *Matthew 4:10*

Vatican Council II

"Many, however, of our contemporaries either do not at all perceive, or else explicitly reject, this intimate and vital bond

See Papally Promulgated
Catechism of the Catholic Church

Q. 283. See paragraphs: 1856, 2110-2114, 2123-2126, 2142-2155, 2180-2183

of man to God. Atheism must therefore be regarded as one of the most serious problems of our time, and one that deserves more thorough treatment." *Modern World, 19*

"Atheism must be countered both by presenting true teaching in a fitting manner and by the full and complete life of the Church and of her members. For it is the function of the Church to render God the Father and his incarnate Son present and as it were visible, while ceaselessly renewing and purifying herself under the guidance of the Holy Spirit."

Modern World, 21

2. We sin against the honor due to God by blaspheming God or perjuring ourselves.

The Second Commandment is: "You shall not take the Name of the Lord your God, in vain" (Deuteronomy 5:11; Exodus 20:7). This commandment tells us to have respect for God's Name and for everything connected with that Name. St. Peter, filled with the Holy Spirit, spoke to the leaders of the people of Israel: "This is the stone which was rejected by you, the builders, which is become the head of the corner. Neither is there salvation in any other. For there is no other Name under Heaven given to men, whereby we must be saved" (Acts 4:11-12).

We honor God's Name by invoking Him with reverence in our prayers. The Church praises the Name of God in her liturgical prayers, especially at Mass. We honor God when we call upon Him in an oath to witness the truth of our statement or when we make a vow to follow God more closely as in the Religious life.

To use the Name of God irreverently is to sin against this commandment. To use God's Name with insolence, hate, or abuse is a serious sin. We should have nothing to do with blasphemy, perjury, or any other irreverent treatment of God's name.

3. We sin against the honor due to God by failing to show respect for persons, places, and things related especially to God.

When we speak with reverence of the Holy Father, Bishops, priests, and Religious sisters and brothers dedicated to God, we honor God. It is sinful to speak irreverently about those dedicated to God. Holy things dedicated to God, such as the Bible, the altar, and rosaries, should be treated with respect.

4. *We sin against the honor due to God by atheism, heresy, and schism.*

Atheism, heresy, and schism are to be rejected as a failure to fulfill our duties toward God. The greatest way in which the faithful can help our atheistic and agnostic world to come to God is by living a life which agrees with the message of Christ's love. Our lives must manifest a living and mature faith which is made visible by works of justice and charity.

> **Prayer:** *Almighty God, how wonderful is Your Name. You have made every creature subject to You. Make us worthy to give You service. Give lasting happiness, Lord, to those who reverence Your Name, so that our lives and works may be such as to deserve Your approval. Bring us, laden with good fruit, to our everlasting home, through Christ our Lord. Amen.*

5. *We sin against the honor due to God by missing Mass on Sundays and on holy days of obligation.*

The Third Commandment is: "Remember to keep holy the Sabbath day." Scripture says: "For in six days the Lord made heaven and earth, and the sea, and all things that are in them, and rested on the seventh day: therefore the Lord blessed the seventh day, and sanctified it" (Deuteronomy 5:12; Exodus 20:11).

We are obliged to participate in the Holy Sacrifice of the Mass each Sunday (or Saturday evening) and all holy days of obligation. St. Luke says: "And on the first day of the week, when we were assembled to Break Bread, Paul discoursed with them" (Acts 20:7). Christ expects us to unite our hearts with His as He and the Church adore the Father. In each Mass, we praise the Father for His great glory, thank Him for His abundant goodness, and ask for His continued help. We also ask pardon for our sins.

The Mass is the highest form of worship. Sunday, especially Sunday Mass, is a weekly reminder of Christ's Easter victory and of the joy which God's people share with Christ. By resting from our usual work, we find it easier to join with family members and other Christians in making Sunday a day of celebration and thanksgiving for the triumph of Jesus Christ.

Vatican Council II

"The liturgical life of the parish and its relation to the bishop must be fostered in the spirit and practice of the laity and clergy. Efforts must also be made to encourage a sense of community within the parish, above all in the common celebration of the Sunday Mass." *Sacred Liturgy, 42*

"Although the sacred liturgy is principally the worship of the divine majesty it likewise contains much instruction for the faithful. For in the liturgy God speaks to his people, and Christ is still proclaiming his Gospel. And the people reply to God by song and prayer.

"Moreover the prayers addressed to God by the priest who, in the person of Christ, presides over the assembly, are said in the name of the entire holy people and of all present. And the visible signs which the sacred liturgy uses to signify invisible divine things have been chosen by Christ or by the Church. Thus not only when things are read 'which were written for our instruction' (Rom. 15:4), but also when the Church prays or sings or acts, the faith of those taking part is nourished, and their minds are raised to God so that they may offer him their spiritual homage and receive his grace more abundantly."

Sacred Liturgy, 33

"By a tradition handed down from the apostles, which took its origin from the very day of Christ's resurrection, the Church celebrates the paschal mystery every seventh day, which day is appropriately called the Lord's Day or Sunday. For on this day Christ's faithful are bound to come together into one place. They should listen to the word of God and take part in the Eucharist, thus calling to mind the passion, resurrection, and glory of the Lord Jesus, and giving thanks to God who has begotten them again, through the resurrection of Christ from the dead, unto a living hope' (1 Pet. 1:3). The Lord's Day is the original feast day, and it should be proposed to the faithful and taught to them so that it may become in fact a day of joy and freedom from work. Other celebrations, unless they be truly of the greatest importance, shall not have precedence over Sunday, which is the foundation and kernel of the whole liturgical year." *Sacred Liturgy, 106*

Prayer: *Lord Jesus, Word of God, in surrendering the brightness of Your glory, You became man so that we may be raised from the dust to* share Your very being. May there be innumerable children of the Church to offer homage to Your Name on the Lord's day — from the rising of the sun to its setting. This we ask in Your most holy and powerful Name. Amen.

Prayer

Lord God, may we who honor the holy Name of Jesus enjoy His friendship in this life and be filled with eternal joy in His Kingdom. We have faith that we will receive whatever we ask for in His Name, for this is what He promised. May we more and more honor our Lord Jesus Christ and His holy Name, for You wish all men to worship Him and to find salvation in His Name.

Almighty God, the saving work of Christ has made our peace with You. You have given us this memorial of His saving work as the perfect form of worship in the Holy Sacrifice of the Mass. Through the Mass, renew that peace within us and prepare us to celebrate the coming of our Savior in eternity.

During Mass, we celebrate the mystery of Christ's suffering and death. May we share in the eternal life He has won for us. The Eucharist proclaims the death of Your Son. Increase our faith in its saving power and strengthen our hope in the life it promises.

Son of the Father, our Master and our Brother, You have made us a kingdom of priests for our God. May we offer You our joyful sacrifice of praise, especially on Sundays, to commemorate Your glorious Resurrection.

Holy God, our heavenly Father, the angels sing Your glory, and all the powers of Heaven and earth fall down before You. Allow us, sinful as we are, to stand before Your holy altar on Sunday, the day You have set aside for Your worship, and to offer You the praise and worship You deserve. Pardon our sins, and sanctify us by the merits of Jesus Christ our Savior, Who lives and reigns with You and the Holy Spirit forever and ever. Amen.

Chapter One Hundred Thirty-Four

Our Duties Toward Our
Neighbor - I

Q. 284. What are our duties toward our fellow men?

Our duties toward our fellow men can be divided into four areas: (1) *human rights;* (2) *the justice and charity of Christ;* (3) *the standard of Christ;* and (4) *regard for all lawful authority.*

Like Christ, we must show our love for our fellow men. We do this when we: (1) are concerned about *our neighbor's rights;* his freedom, his housing, his food, his health, and his right to work; (2) *show to others the justice and charity of Christ* — that is, reaching out in the spirit of the Beatitudes to help others; to build up a better society in the local community, and to promote justice and peace throughout the world; (3) *speak and judge others by the standard of charity* — due to all sons of God; (4) *respect and obey all lawful authority* — in the home, in civil society, and in the Church.

The second great commandment of God, "You shall love your neighbor as yourself" (Luke 10:27), is like the first: "You shall love the Lord your God with all your heart" (Luke 10:27), because it springs from the same principle and motive — to love. The norm for the love of God is the totality of the very depths and powers of the soul: "with all your heart, with all your soul, with all your strength, with all your mind."

The norm for the love of neighbor is the proper love of self; to love our neighbor as ourselves. But our Lord raised that norm to the sphere of the divine when He commanded us to love our neighbor as He loves us. The Redeemer's love for us is without limit.

The commandment to love our neighbor is founded in the Old Testament. But it is carried over into the new dispensa-

See Papally Promulgated
Catechism of the Catholic Church

Q. 284. See paragraphs: 952, 954, 1789, 1807, 1822, 1844, 1889, 1931, 2052, 2196

tion, or the New Testament, where it is renewed. However, it takes on a new, special relationship to Christ, the God-man, for He declared that this commandment of fraternal love is His favorite commandment. It is His own commandment. "This is My commandment, that you love one another, as I have loved you" (John 13:34). This love is the sign by which His disciples will be clearly recognized.

Today we are challenged to live our lives in such a way that we will bear witness to God by serving the needs of man. As Christians, we can serve our fellow man by personally taking care of his spiritual, physical, and social needs. We can serve others personally through the ministries of medicine, nursing, teaching, social work, and many other activities which help others in one way or another. Perhaps we can, in some way, be of service to man and society in the fields of business, education, law, government, and public health. Since not every Christian can be a servant professionally, each should be a servant according to the gifts and talents he has received from God.

Sacred Scripture

St. Paul says: "Now there are diversities of graces, but the same Spirit; and there are diversities of ministries, but the same Lord; and there are diversities of operations, but the same God who works all in all. And the manifestation of the Spirit is given to every man unto profit." *1 Corinthians 12:4-7*

Vatican Council II

"The greatest commandment of the law is to love God with one's whole heart and one's neighbor as oneself (cf. Mt. 22:37-40). Christ has made this love of the neighbor His personal commandment and has enriched it with a new meaning when He willed Himself, along with His brothers, to be the object of this charity saying: 'When you showed it to one of the least of my brothers here, you showed it to me' (Mt. 25:40)." *Lay People, 8*

"The laity should learn to distinguish carefully between the rights and the duties which they have as belonging to the Church and those which fall to them as members of the human society. They will strive to unite the two harmoniously, remembering that in every temporal affair they are to be guided by a Christian conscience, since not even in temporal business may any human activity be withdrawn from God's dominion." *The Church, 36*

"The presence of Christians among these human groups should be one that is animated by that love with which we are loved by God, Who desires that we should love each other with that self-same love (cf. 1 John 4:11). Christian charity is extended to all without distinction of race, social condition, or religion, and seeks neither gain nor gratitude. Just as God loves us with a gratuitous love, so too the faithful, in their charity, should be concerned for mankind, loving it with that same love with which God sought man. As Christ went about all the towns and villages healing every sickness and infirmity, as a sign that the Kingdom of God had come (cf. Mt. 9:35 ff.; Acts 10:38), so the Church, through its children, joins itself with men of every condition, but especially with the poor and afflicted, and willingly spends herself for them (cf. 2 Cor. 12:15). It shares their joys and sorrows, it is familiar with the hopes and problems of life, it suffers with them in the anguish of death. It wishes to enter into fraternal dialogue with those who are working for peace, and to bring them the peace and light of the Gospel." *Missionary Activity, 12*

Prayer: *Lord Jesus, how highly You value charity towards our neighbor! You are the infinitely great God; man is unspeakably small, and yet, You declare that no one truly loves You who withholds his love from his fellow man.*

Jesus, help us to have compassion upon our neighbor, and to do whatever we can to lighten the burden of his misery. Make us generous enough to consider our enemies among our neighbors. This we ask in Your most holy Name. Amen.

Prayer

Jesus, You teach us the law of charity which demands that we love God with our entire heart, soul and mind, that is, with our whole being. Yet, our love of God need not be a love that we can feel. It is a love which is demonstrated by acts of the mind and will. Since You have loved us with an everlasting love, we must love You above all creatures and with our entire being.

You teach us the law of charity which demands that we also love our neighbors, because they, too, carry in their souls the image of God, and reflect His perfections, and like us, are created for eternal union with God.

Jesus, You have given us the parable of the Good Samaritan to teach us who our neighbor is. If we want to possess eternal life, we must imitate the Samaritan in his exercise of the law of charity, because he is an image of You. When we see our fellow men in pain or sorrow, let us do as the Samaritan did. Regardless of a man's creed, country, or social standing, we believe that the image of God is engraved upon his soul. Your blood was shed for his salvation; he is intended for eternal glory. A child of God and Your brother, he is also our brother.

We often meet bruised hearts. Sometimes through carelessness, sometimes through malice, through accident, these hearts have been wounded. Perhaps failure, ingratitude, poverty, sickness, ignorance, or sin, is the cause of suffering. Help us to be good Samaritans, and try to bind up the heart-wounds of those we meet. Let us pour in the oil of sympathy and the strengthening wine of cheerful words or deeds to give those in sorrow a spiritual uplift.

Give us the grace, through frequent Holy Communion and prayer, to overcome our selfishness; to resist our sinful temptations and reactions, such as hatred and bitterness; to develop kindness and sympathy, forbearance, and forgiveness; to think kindly of everyone, and to find happiness in making others happy. May we thus unite ourselves by love to You and to the members of Your Mystical Body, the Church, now and forever. Amen.

Our Duties Toward Our Neighbor - II

Q. 285. How can we show the justice and charity of Christ to others?

Like Christ, we must be just and show our love for our fellow men. We do this when we show to others the justice and charity of Christ — that is, reaching out in the spirit of the Beatitudes to help others, to build up a better society in the local community, and to promote justice and peace throughout the world.

We must show the justice and charity of Christ to others by letting our Catholic Faith, with its beautiful truths and attainable ideals, fill our lives with the spirit of the Gospel. If we really believe in Jesus Christ, we know that we must re-shape our lives so that they are living examples of the Gospel in the spirit of the Beatitudes. This is the Christian life.

Christ said: "Blessed are the merciful: for they shall obtain mercy. Blessed are the pure of heart: for they shall see God. Blessed are the peacemakers: for they shall be called the children of God. Blessed are they that suffer persecution for justice's sake: for theirs is the Kingdom of Heaven" (Matthew 5:7-10).

The Church urges us to serve God by serving our fellow-man, after the example of Jesus Christ. After He had washed the feet of His disciples, Jesus said to them: "Do you know what I have done to you? You call me Master, and Lord; and you speak well, for so I am. If then I being your Lord and Master, have washed your feet; you also ought to wash one another's feet. For I have given you an example, that as I have done to you, so do you, also" (John: 13:12-15).

See Papally Promulgated
Catechism of the Catholic Church

Q. 285. See paragraphs: 905, 2044, 2472

The Church calls upon Christians to live for others as Jesus lived and died for all. Such a life calls for sacrifice and earnest effort, and it will help to make our Christian Faith alive and real. The Church wishes us to make room in our hearts for all people, so that we might labor with all men to build up human society.

By friendship with all men, the People of God can become a sign and instrument of union with God and of the unity of all mankind. A life of service to others is the best way of letting people know that God is present in the world and that He loves all of them.

Vatican Council II

"In assuming human nature He has united to Himself all humanity in a supernatural solidarity which makes of it one single family. He has made charity the distinguishing mark of His disciples, in the word, 'By this will all men know you for My disciples, by the love you bear one another' (Jn. 13:35)."

Lay People, 8

"Charitable action today can and should reach all men and all needs." *Lay People, 8*

Prayer

Jesus, You are the Good Samaritan Who, journeying along the road of life, stops by the wayside to care for and assist fallen humanity who lies flat on the ground through sin, and who has been stripped of its garments of grace by satan. At the cost of Your own life, You exercise Your mission of mercy and love toward Your wounded neighbor; You restore him to divine favor and spiritual health, and so enable him to continue along the road to Heaven.

How often have our souls been beaten and robbed by the powers of evil! Our hearts overflow with love and gratitude to You, Good Samaritan, to Whom we are indebted for our rescue. You poured into our open wounds the strengthening wine of Your sacred doctrines; You dropped into them the holy oil of the graces Your sacraments impart. As the Good Shepherd, how often have You carried this straying sheep upon Your shoulder to the inn of peace and friendship of God. Help us to imitate Your love and compassion in our dealings with our neighbor.

Jesus, before the Last Supper, You gave us an example of Your deep humility and charity, and Your purity of heart. Though You are Master and Lord, You performed the lowest task, the one which was usually done by slaves: You washed the feet of Your Apostles. If we do not accept the lesson, whether in regard to purity of heart — which the washing signifies — or love, or humility, we will have no part with You — no part in Your Spirit, Your character, or Your life. We want to imitate Your loving humility and tender love in serving our neighbor, for it is the union of these two virtues which is the real spirit of the Church and of Christianity.

Jesus, teach us to be ready to do all things for our fellowman, and to consider no act of assistance beneath our dignity. Help us to make use of every opportunity which presents itself to us to perform acts of love toward our neighbor, in remembrance of the great example You have given us. May You be praised forever. Amen.

Our Duties Toward Our Neighbor - III

Q. 286. How are our judgments of others and our speech to be ruled?

Like Christ, we must show our love for our fellowman. We do this when we speak and judge others by the standard of charity — which is due to all those created in the image and likeness of God. Our judgment and speech are to be ruled by charity. God commands us to think kindly of others.

Jesus said: "Judge not, that you may not be judged. For with what judgment you judge, you shall be judged: and with what measure you mete, it shall be measured to you again. And why look at the mote that is in your brother's eye; and yet not see the beam that is in your own eye? Or, why say to your brother: 'Let me cast the mote out of your eye;' and behold a beam is in your own eye?" (Matthew 7:1-4).

Kindness is a very positive virtue. Its essence is the strength of a person's self-control and the conquest of his egoism, especially within the family. Its object is the giving of self to others. This interior disposition inclines a person to think kindly of others, to wish them well, and to do good.

The basis of every type of love is kind thinking. Kindness excludes malicious and suspicious thoughts — thoughts which ascribe evil intentions and vicious purposes to others, or thoughts which make evil interpretations of the gestures, actions, words and even silence of others.

When we speak about others, what we say must also be ruled by charity. The sin of uncharitable talk is a vicious destroyer of internal unity within any family. It violates

See Papally Promulgated
Catechism of the Catholic Church

Q. 286. See paragraphs: 2464-2492

truth, justice, and love. Our Lord's new law of love demands that we avoid not only bodily injury to our neighbor, but also angry, uncharitable words and feelings against him.

Sacred Scripture

"If I speak with the tongues of men, and of angels, and have not charity, I am become as sounding brass, or a tinkling cymbal. And if I should have prophecy and should know all mysteries and all knowledge, and if I should have all faith, so that I could move mountains, and have not charity, I am nothing. And if I should distribute all my goods to feed the poor, and if I should deliver my body to be burned, and have not charity, it profits me nothing. Charity is patient, is kind. Charity envies not, deals not perversely, is not puffed up, is not ambitious, seeks not its own, is not provoked to anger, thinks no evil, rejoices not in iniquity, but rejoices with the truth; bears all things, believes all things, hopes in all things, endures all things. Charity never falls away, whether prophecies shall be made void, or tongues shall cease, or knowledge shall be destroyed. For we know in part, and we prophesy in part. But when that which is perfect is come, that which is in part shall be done away.

"When I was a child, I spoke as a child, I understood as a child, I thought as a child. But, when I became a man, I put away the things of a child. We see now through a glass darkly, but then face to face. Now I know in part; but then I shall know as I am known. And now there remain faith, hope, and charity, these three: but the greatest of these is charity."

1 Corinthians 13:1-13

Vatican Council II

"If the exercise of charity is to be above all criticism, and seen to be so, one should see in one's neighbor the image of God to which he has been created, and Christ the Lord to Whom is really offered all that is given to the needy. The liberty and dignity of the person helped must be respected with the greatest sensitivity. Purity of intention should not be stained by any self-seeking or desire to dominate. The demands of justice must first of all be satisfied; that which is already due in justice is not to be offered as a gift of charity. The cause of evils, and not merely their effects, ought to disappear. The aid contributed should be organized in such a way that beneficiaries are gradually freed from their dependence on others and become self-supporting." *Lay People, 8*

Prayer: *Jesus, give us the grace we need in order to be kind in our judgments, for only a kind soul can judge and understand others fairly. Give us kind eyes that we may see beyond other peoples' weakness and failings, like a mother who looks on her child more kindly, but also more correctly, than a stranger. All this we ask in Your most holy Name. Amen.*

Prayer

Jesus, You forbid hasty judging, to which we may be led by uncharitableness or pride. Besides, we have no authority to judge. We have not been appointed by God as judge. By so acting, we commit a fault equal to, or even worse than that for which we condemn our neighbor. We are not as holy as we would like to think we are, and yet we condemn others. Pardon us for such uncharitableness.

Help us to be kind in our thoughts about our neighbors, that on the day of judgment we may also receive kindness and mercy. We wish to step out of the narrow circle of selfishness. Help us to try to find some excuse for what others do, not forcing ourselves to view things in the wrong light, but keeping our eyes open to the whole truth, lest hasty judgments and prejudices close them to a part of the truth.

No one ever saw human frailties more clearly than You saw them in Your Apostles: their dullness, their worldliness, and their faults. Yet You remained patient and untiring towards them because Your kindness was without limit. You looked on them with a kind eye and led them with a kind hand. Help us to imitate Your kindness.

Jesus, help us to be kind in speech. You never met a sad person without offering him a word of comfort; a fearful one without giving him a word of encouragement; a persecuted one without defending him; or a needy one without granting his request. Your words of comfort, recognition, and blessing were always perfectly simple and natural, because they were prompted by a sincere love for people.

Help us to realize that kind words make both us and other people happy. When a kind word proceeds from our lips, it blesses us first. Nearly always, the reward of a kind word is the experience of feeling God's presence. Let us always talk in such a way as to promote the other person's interests. Let us always try to bring happiness to others by our kind words. Each kind word costs us only a moment in this world, but will have an important bearing on the kind of eternity we spend, for You said, "For by your words you shall be justified, and by your words you shall be condemned" (Matthew 12:37). Lord, may Your will be done on earth as it is in Heaven. Amen.

Our Duties Toward Our Neighbor - IV

Q. 287. In obedience to lawful authority, how do we show our love for our neighbor?

We show our love for our neighbor when we obey all lawful authority, whether it be in the home, in civil society, or in the Church.

With respect to lawful authority in the home, the Fourth Commandment of God says: "Honor your father and your mother" (Deuteronomy 5:16; Exodus 20:12).

St. Paul wrote: "Children, obey your parents in the Lord for this is just. Honor your father and your mother, which is the first commandment with a promise: that it may be well with you, and that you may live long upon the earth" (Ephesians 6:1-3).

Even the authority of the civil government comes from God. St. Paul wrote: "Let every soul be subject to higher powers, for there is no power but from God. And those that are, are ordained of God. Therefore he that resists the power, resists the ordinance of God. And they that resist, purchase damnation for themselves" (Romans 13:1-2).

Authority comes from God in order to ensure the well-being of those who are subject to that authority, not for the honor or gain of those who exercise the right and duty of governing. Christians who possess authority should consider themselves the servants of those they govern.

Jesus said: "You know that the princes of the Gentiles lord it over them; and they that are the greater, exercise power upon them. It shall not be so among you. But whoever will be the greater among you, let him be your minister. And he that

See Papally Promulgated
Catechism of the Catholic Church

Q. 287. See paragraphs: 1897-1927, 2238-2243

will be first among you, shall be your servant" (Matthew 20:25-27).

Jesus was obedient to Mary and Joseph. He respected civil and temple authorities as well. He did not consider Himself immune to the duty of paying taxes. He obeyed the regulations which had been established for the good of the society in which He lived. In these matters, Christ was really showing respect for His Father in Heaven, for all authority stems from Him.

We who are members of the Mystical Body of Jesus are to imitate the reverence which He showed to those in authority. We are commanded to give our parents consideration and affection. As children, we owe them obedience.

Like our Brother Christ, we must also obey legitimate civil authorities. All just laws, whether they please us or not, are to be accepted as expressions of God's will. In a special way, the laws of the Catholic Church represent God's will. The risen Christ speaks to us through the Church. Therefore, we should look upon Church laws as commands from God Himself.

Christ exercised His authority over others with charity. The way in which He gave orders to His Apostles and sent them forth was always respectful and kind. He knew that the Father had entrusted the Apostles to Him and that it was His responsibility to lead them safely back to the Father. We, whom the Father has called to share the life of Jesus Christ, must use our authority over others in a responsible, kind way as Christ Himself did. Parents should understand that their children have been entrusted to them by our Father in Heaven. They should instruct their children about Christ and His Church, and should teach them to love their neighbors.

Parents who fail to exercise right authority over their children, children who fail to obey and honor their parents, citizens who offend the common good by violating laws — these are all, in some way, offending God.

Sacred Scripture

"My son, hear the instruction of your father, and forsake not the law of your mother." *Proverbs 1:8*

Vatican Council II

"Children as living members of the family contribute in their own way to the sanctification of their parents. With sen-

618

timents of gratitude, affection and trust, they will repay their parents for the benefits given to them and will come to their assistance as devoted children in times of hardship and in the loneliness of old age." *Modern World, 48*

Prayer: *Lord, we pray for those who serve us in public office. Guide their minds and hearts, so that all men may live in true peace and freedom. You know the longings of men's hearts, and You protect their rights. In Your goodness, watch over those in authority, so that people everywhere may enjoy religious freedom, security, and peace.*

Give those in authority a true concern for the brothers and sisters who have been entrusted to their care, and inspire the people to support their leaders according to their conscience, through Christ our Lord. Amen.

Prayer

Almighty and everlasting God, in the secret counsels of Your loving providence, You have called us into life by means of our parents, who thereby share in Your divine power and authority. Mercifully hear the prayer of childlike love which we offer to You for those who, in Your fatherly kindness, You have called to parenthood. Fill all parents with Your choicest blessings and enrich their souls with Your holy grace.

Grant that they may guard their holy union faithfully and constantly, since it is a sign of Your divine Son's spiritual union with the Church. Fill them with holy fear, which is the beginning of wisdom, and let them impart it to their children. Thus may they ever walk in the way of Your commandments; may their children be their joy during their earthly exile and their crown of glory in their heavenly home.

God, our Father, You gave us our fathers and mothers and made them an image of Your authority, love, and tender watchfulness. You commanded us to love, honor, and obey them. Give children the grace they need to love their parents sincerely, to honor them, to yield a ready obedience to their commands, to comply with their wishes, to accept their corrections with humility, and to bear their shortcomings with patience. Let them seek their parents' happiness in everything. Thus, make them worthy of the reward You promised to those who honor their father and their mother according to Your Fourth Commandment — that it will be well with them in this life and in the next.

Give Your grace to children, that they may grow in Your favor, and to young people, that they may reach their full stature by loving You and by keeping Your commandments. All this we ask through our Lord and Savior, Jesus Christ. Amen.

Chapter One Hundred Thirty-Eight

Sins Against Our Neighbor

Q. 288. How do we sin against our neighbor?

We sin against our neighbor in four general areas, namely, the areas of: (1) *justice;* (2) *God's gift of life;* (3) *speech;* and (4) *sexuality.*

1. In the area of *justice* it is sinful to be selfishly apathetic toward others in their needs, to violate the rights of others, to steal, to deliberately damage another's good name or property, to cheat, to not pay one's debts, to show anger or hatred, or to be racist or unjustly discriminatory.

The Seventh Commandment of God is, "You shall not steal" (Deuteronomy 5:19; Exodus 20:15).

The Tenth Commandment is, "You shall not covet anything that belongs to your neighbor" (Deuteronomy 5:21; Exodus 20:17).

All of the goods of this world come from the good God. He has put more than enough of them at the disposal of men. The material goods that God gives us are not for ourselves alone. He gave them to us not only for the benefit of ourselves and our families, but also that we may help others, especially those in need, to happiness here and hereafter. True happiness comes from doing God's will. But His will, in most instances, cannot be done without adequate material goods, such as food, clothing, and shelter.

"Do not be anxious for goods unjustly gotten; for they will not profit you in the day of calamity and revenge" (Ecclesiasticus 5:10).

In the Seventh and Tenth Commandments, God forbids taking something that belongs to another against his reasonable wish. Stealing; depriving another of his money or property by deceiving him — fraud; deliberately damaging property

See Papally Promulgated
Catechism of the Catholic Church

Q. 288. See paragraphs: 2196, 2258, 2351-2359, 2380-2391, 2401, 2464, 2475-2492, 2514-2516, 2534-2540

of another; not paying just debts; not making a reasonable effort to find the owner of an article we have found; depriving a laborer of a just wage; wasting the time, money, or property of an employer; and depriving one's family of needed money by gambling, drinking, or foolish spending are all violations of these two commandments. If the damage is not serious, the sin is venial.

Anytime that our wrong words or actions are such as to encourage sin in another, we become guilty of the sin of scandal, the sin of bad example. The sin is serious, if the possible harm we do is serious. It may cause the death of another person's soul if we lead it to mortal sin.

Sacred Scripture

"He that is partaker with a thief hates his own soul."

Proverbs 29:24

"But the children of men shall put their trust under the cover of your wings." *Psalms 36 (35):8*

"Place alms in the heart of the poor, and it shall obtain help for you against all evil." *Ecclesiasticus 29:15*

Vatican Council II

"Every man has the right to possess a sufficient amount of the earth's goods for himself and his family. This has been the opinion of the Fathers and Doctors of the Church, who taught that men are bound to come to the aid of the poor and to do so not merely out of their superfluous goods. When a person is in extreme necessity he has the right to supply himself with what he needs out of the riches of others." *Modern World, 69*

2. In the area of *God's gift of life,* the Christian must be respectful. Innocent lives, such as those of babies in the womb, infants, and the elderly, are to be protected from those who might rob them of their God-given right to life.

The Fifth Commandment of God is: "You shall not kill" (Deuteronomy 5:17, Exodus 20:13). This commandment directs us to care for our bodies and souls and to care for the bodies and souls of our neighbors. Our lives and our bodies are the means that God gives us to serve Him, to serve ourselves, and to serve our neighbors. We must take care of our bodies, our lives, and health. We must practice Christian self-discipline in the use of food, alcohol, and tobacco.

Christ came to give life, not to take it away. His followers, accordingly, should oppose whatever tends to destroy or

622

abuse human life: murder, suicide, abortion, mercy-killing (euthanasia), drug abuse, drunkenness, fighting, and anger.

Sacred Scripture

"For it is You, O Lord, that has power of life and death, and leads down to the gates of death, and brings back again: a man indeed kills through malice, and when the spirit is gone forth, it shall not return, neither shall he call back the soul that is received." *Wisdom 16:13-14*

"Whoever hates his brother is a murderer. And you know that no murderer has eternal life abiding in himself." *1 John 3:15*

"You have heard that it was said to them of old: You shall not kill. And whoever shall kill shall be in danger of the judgment. But I say to you, that whoever is angry with his brother, shall be in danger of the judgment. And whoever shall say to his brother, 'Raca,' shall be in danger of the council. And whoever shall say, 'You fool,' shall be in danger of hell fire." *Matthew 5:21-22*

Vatican Council II

"All these human activities, which are daily endangered by pride and inordinate self-love, must be purified and perfected by the cross and resurrection of Christ." *Modern World, 37*

"The teaching of Christ even demands that we forgive injury and the precept of love, which is the commandment of the New Law, includes all our enemies: 'You have heard that it was said, "You shall love your neighbor and hate your enemy." But I say to you, love your enemies, do good to them that hate you' (Mt. 5:43-44)." *Modern World, 28*

3. In the area of *speech,* sins of lying, detraction, and calumny are forbidden.

The Eighth Commandment of God is: "You shall not bear false witness against your neighbor" (Deuteronomy 5:20; Exodus 20:16). A good name consists in the esteem which people have for a person, and the mutual confidence resulting from it. Mutual confidence, based on mutual respect, is the foundation of all family life. Without this respect, doubt, mistrust, and suspicion make their appearance to disrupt a family, a community or a society.

Every unjustified violation of a person's good name is a sin. This occurs either when the uncharitable talk is based on truth, which is detraction, or when it is based on a lie, which is calumny. Calumny is the greater sin, because not only justice and love, but also truth, is violated.

"Devise not a lie against your brother: neither do the like against your friend" (Ecclesiasticus 7:13).

"Admonish them to be subject to princes and powers, to obey at a word, to be ready for every good work, to speak evil of no man, not to be litigious, but gentle: showing all mildness towards all men" (Titus 3:1-2).

Revealing a person's hidden faults, gossiping about a person's known faults, exaggerating his faults, and telling tales about him are ways of damaging a person's reputation. It is never permitted to tell a lie, because every lie is an abuse of the sacred power given to us by God. Lies can start quarrels and discord, and may even separate friends.

Sacred Scripture

"The whisperer and the double-tongued is accursed: for he has troubled many that were at peace." *Ecclesiasticus 28:13*

"Do not utter again a wicked and harsh word, and you won't fare the worse. Do not speak your mind to friend or foe: and if you have a sin, do not disclose it. For he will listen to you and will watch you, and as it were defending your sin he will hate you, and so will he be with you always. Have you heard a word against your neighbor? Let it die within you, knowing that you will not burst." *Ecclesiasticus 19:6-9*

Prayer: *Lord, all justice and all goodness come from You. You hate evil and abhor lies. Lead us, Your servants, in the path of Your justice, so that all who hope in You may rejoice with the Church and in Christ, now and forever. Amen.*

4. In the area of *sexuality,* the Christian should be modest in behavior and dress and should protect others from ideas, actions, and images which are opposed to the Church's teaching on sexuality.

The Sixth Commandment of God is: "You shall not commit adultery." The Ninth Commandment is: "You shall not covet your neighbor's wife" (Deuteronomy 5:18, 21; Exodus 20:17).

The virtue of Christian chastity helps a Christian to regulate the use of his sexual powers according to the law of God.

624

A Christian consecrates his soul and body to Jesus Christ. The procreative faculty, given to us by God as a sacred power, is something holy. It is something good in itself, and is important in God's plan of creation and providence. The misuse of it is evil.

The use of the sexual faculty is a right and privilege of those who are validly married. Therefore, adultery, fornication, masturbation, pornography, premarital sex, indecent entertainment of every description, other acts of impurity, and the fully deliberate desire to commit these acts are all seriously wrong. Though it is impossible to keep all evil thoughts and desires from our minds, we can, at least, refuse to give them a welcome. Unwelcome desires, no matter how wrong they seem, cannot defile our hearts.

Sacred Scripture

"But he that is an adulterer, for the folly of his heart shall destroy his own soul." *Proverbs 6:32*

"You have heard that it was said to them of old, 'You shall not commit adultery.' But I say to you, that whoever shall look on a woman to lust after her, has already committed adultery with her in his heart." *Matthew 5:27-28*

"Don't you know that the unjust shall not possess the Kingdom of God? Do not err: neither fornicators, nor idolaters, nor adulterers, nor the effeminate, nor sodomites, nor thieves, nor covetous, nor drunkards, nor railers, nor extortioners, shall possess the Kingdom of God." *1 Corinthians 6:9-10*

"Now the works of the flesh are manifest, which are fornication, uncleanness, immodesty, luxury, idolatry, witchcrafts, enmities, contentions, emulations, wraths, quarrels, dissensions, sects, envies, murders, drunkenness, revelings, and such like. Of the which I foretell you, as I have foretold to you, that they who do such things shall not obtain the Kingdom of God." *Galatians 5:19-21*

"But fornication, and all uncleanness, or covetousness, let it not so much as be named among you, as becomes saints."
Ephesians 5:3

Vatican Council II

"It is imperative to give suitable and timely instruction to young people, above all in the heart of their own families, about the dignity of married love, its role and its exercise; in this way they will be able to engage in honorable courtship and enter upon a marriage of their own." *Modern World, 49*

"Parents, on their part, should remember that it is their duty to see that entertainment and publications which might endanger faith and morals do not enter their houses and that their children are not exposed to them elsewhere."

Social Communications, 10

Prayer: *Lord God, King of Heaven and earth, direct and sanctify, rule and guide our hearts and bodies, our thoughts, our words, and deeds, so that we may follow Your law and keep Your commandments. If we are faithful to You everyday, we will be kept safe and free.*

Lord, we are citizens of this earth. We ask to be made citizens of Heaven by Your free gift. Help us to run in the way of Your commandments and to set our hearts on You alone. Send the fire of Your Holy Spirit deep within us, so that we can serve You with chaste bodies and please You with pure minds. We ask this through Jesus Christ our Savior and God. Amen.

Prayer

May our words in praise of Your commandments find favor with You, Lord. May our faith prove we are not slaves, but sons. We are not as much subjected to Your law as we are sharers in Your power.

All powerful Father, the refuge and strength of Your people, You protect in adversity and defend in prosperity those who put their trust in You. May we persevere in seeking Your will and find our way to You through obedience to Your commandments.

Strengthen our faith, hope, and love. May we do with loving hearts what You ask of us, and so come to share in the life You promise.

Praise be to You, God and Father of our Lord Jesus Christ. There is no power for good which does not come from Your covenant, and no promise which Your love has not offered. Strengthen our faith, that we may accept Your covenant; give us the love we need to carry out Your commandments, through Christ our Lord. Amen.

Our Duties Toward Self - I

Q. 289. What are our duties toward self?

Our duties toward self are: (1) *to be an example of Christian goodness;* (2) *to be humble and patient with ourselves;* (3) *to be simple in the use of the things of this world;* (4) *to be pure in words and actions;* and (5) *to avoid pride, laziness, envy, and intemperance in food and drink.*

1. *Our duties toward self include being an example of Christian goodness.*

No one has ever spent himself for others as much as Christ did when He dwelt among us. In his life in the world, the Christian should endeavor to personify the love of Christ in such a warm and attractive way that others will be induced to imitate it. The Christian should also communicate to others an impartial and selfless love which is as strong and as true as the love of Christ. His external conduct should be marked by the dignity worthy of a Christian. By his example, he can spread to others the faith that is in him, especially when he gives, through charitable assistance, to his neighbor.

2. *Our duties toward self include being humble and patient with ourselves.*

Self-denial imitates Jesus. Having come down from Heaven with the purpose of showing us the way to eternal life, Jesus followed no other way than that of the Cross. He suffered for us that we might walk in His footsteps. He said, "If any man will come after Me, let him deny himself, and take up his cross, and follow Me" (Matthew 16:24).

The true way to holiness is to love God and our neighbor for God's sake, and to sacrifice ourselves in order to better fulfill it. We sacrifice ourselves because we love, because we want to

See Papally Promulgated
Catechism of the Catholic Church

Q. 289. See paragraphs: 1706, 1711, 1713, 1715, 2281

love still more, and because God loves a cheerful giver. Our patience in the face of our own shortcomings, pleases God more than our zeal. Our sufferings, when borne for love of God, produce more fruit than our activity. Our failures, when accepted with renewed confidence in God, lead more souls to Him than our successes. All that matters is that God may be glorified and that souls may be saved, starting with our own.

3. *Our duties toward self include being simple in the use of the things of this world.*

Detachment from earthly possessions is one of the first sacrifices Christ asks of those whom He calls to share His mission. A Christian should have a spirit of simplicity and dependence upon God as Christ did; he should see poverty of spirit as a key to genuine freedom, and as a way to become Christ-like. Christ declared: "Blessed are the poor in spirit: for theirs is the Kingdom of Heaven" (Matthew 5:3).

In a world which feverishly seeks for earthly riches and material things, there is an urgent need for those who, by the example of their simplicity and detachment, bear witness to Christ's teaching that spiritual, supernatural and divine things have the highest value. The witness of Christ-like simplicity in Christians who are devoted to the glory of God and the salvation of souls can be an inspiration to other Christians who may be negligent in this area. This neglect often occurs because such Christians are overly concerned with providing material goods for their own family.

4. *Our duties toward self include being pure in words and actions.*

In these days, when sensual love and the pleasures of the flesh are emphasized and often depicted as ends in themselves, the example of chastity is particularly impressive. To this world, where the body and sensuality seem to count for so much, the true Christian, by a life of decency in word and action, demonstrates that purity is possible, fruitful, and liberating for both those who are single and those who are married.

5. *Our duties toward self include avoiding pride, laziness, envy, and intemperance in food and drink.*

Christians must guard against the capital sins of pride, with its many manifestations; spiritual, intellectual and physical sloth (laziness); envy of other people's success, and of their financial and material possessions; intemperance i.e., lack of self-control; and abuse of one's bodily health by overindulgence in food and alcohol, (and the abuse of all drugs).

Deliberate sin, whether mortal or venial, is preceded by an inducement to sin, which we call temptation. The sources of temptation are three: the world about us, the devil, and our own inclinations to sin. The principal temptations are those dealing with pride, covetousness, lust, anger, gluttony, envy, and sloth. If we pray, God will always give us the strength we need to overcome our temptations. In order to avoid sin, we must also avoid any person, place, or thing which in all probability will lead us to sin.

Sacred Scripture

"For what does it profit a man, if he gains the whole world, and suffers the loss of his own soul? Or what exchange shall a man give for his soul?" *Matthew 16:26*

Vatican Council II

"All these human activities, which are daily endangered by pride and inordinate self-love, must be purified and perfected by the cross and resurrection of Christ." *Modern World, 37*

"Man, though made of body and soul, is a unity. Through his very bodily condition he sums up in himself the elements of the material world. Through him they are thus brought to their highest perfection and can raise their voice in praise freely given to the Creator (cf. Dan. 3:57-90). For this reason, man may not despise his bodily life. Rather he is obliged to regard his body as good and hold it in honor since God has created it and will raise it up on the last day. Nevertheless man has been wounded by sin. He finds by experience that his body is in revolt. His very dignity therefore requires that he should glorify God in his body, (cf. 1 Cor. 6:13-20) and not allow it to serve the evil inclinations of his heart.

"When he is drawn to think about his real self he turns to those deep recesses of his being where God who probes the heart awaits him, and where he himself decides his own destiny in the sight of God. So when he recognizes in himself a spiritual and immortal soul, he is not being led astray by false imaginings that are due to merely physical or social causes. On the contrary, he grasps what is profoundly true in this matter." *Modern World, 14*

"The Church wishes to emphasize that there can be no conflict between the divine laws governing the transmission of life and the fostering of authentic married love.

"God, the Lord of life, has entrusted to men the noble mission of safeguarding life, and men must carry it out in a manner worthy of themselves. Life must be protected with the utmost care from the moment of conception: abortion and infanticide are abominable crimes. Man's sexuality and the faculty of reproduction wondrously surpass the endowments of lower forms of life; therefore the acts proper to married life are to be ordered according to authentic human dignity and must be honored with the greatest reverence." *Modern World, 51*

"Therefore all the faithful are invited and obliged to holiness and the perfection of their own state of life. Accordingly let all of them see that they direct their affections rightly, lest they be hindered in their pursuit of perfect love by the use of worldly things and by an adherence to riches which is contrary to the spirit of evangelical poverty." *The Church, 42*

Prayer: *Lord Jesus, gentle and humble of heart, You declared that whoever receives a little child In Your Name receives You, and You promised Your Kingdom to those who are like children. Never let pride reign in our hearts. May the Father's compassion reward and embrace all who willingly bear Your gentle yoke. May You be honored and praised now and forever. Amen.*

Prayer

Lord, You humbled Yourself by being obedient, even to accepting death — death on the Cross. Give all who serve You the gifts of obedience and patient endurance.

Jesus, meek and humble of heart, clothe us with compassion, kindness, and humility. Make us want to be patient with everyone. Teach us to be true neighbors to all who are in trouble and distress, so that we may imitate You, the Good Samaritan. Grant us the gift of Your mercy, forgive our sins, and remit their punishment. Look with love on those who suffer because of our indifference; come to their aid, and turn our uncaring hearts to works of justice and charity. Give Your strength to all those who are in distress, and help us to raise them up by our loving concern.

Loving Redeemer, through Your Passion, teach us self-denial, strengthen us against evil and adversity. Increase our faith, hope, and love, and make us ready for eternal life.

Heavenly Father, God of mercy and fidelity, You made a new and lasting pact with men, and sealed it in the blood of Your Son. Forgive the folly of our disloyalty and help us to keep Your commandments, so that, in Your New Covenant, we may be witnesses and heralds of Your faithfulness and love on earth, and sharers of Your glory in Heaven. Amen.

Chapter One Hundred Forty

Our Duties Toward Self - II

Q. 290. What does the thought of the duties and obligations which flow from the love of God and man help the Christian to do?

The thought of the duties and obligations which flow from the love of God and man helps the Christian: (1) *to form a right conscience,* (2) *to choose always what is right,* (3) *to avoid sin and the occasions of sins,* (4) *and to live in this world according to the Spirit of Christ, for the love of God.*

1. *The thought of the duties and obligations which flow from the love of God and man helps the Christian to form a right conscience.*

In order to sanctify our actions, we must see to it that they are inspired by supernatural love, or charity. This love must rule and guide us in all our actions, so that our whole life may be directed to God. Supernatural love comes to us from God. It is the splendid prerogative of the children of adoption. Following the advice of St. Paul, we should make charity "the root and foundation of our life" (Ephesians 3:17). "Let everything be done in charity" (1 Corinthians 16:14).

Our conscience tells us whether an action is right or wrong, and whether it is a mortal or venial sin. Conscience is our mind's judge on moral matters, but it must be instructed. We must learn from Christ, Who teaches us through His Church. Only with the guidance of the Holy Spirit can we consistently form a right conscience.

2. *The thought of the duties and obligations which flow from the love of God and man helps the Christian to choose always what is right.*

We need the light and strength of actual grace to always

See Papally Promulgated
Catechism of the Catholic Church

Q. 290. See paragraphs: 890, 1783-1785

choose what is right and then to do it. Hence, we should frequently pray to the Holy Spirit to guide and to help us.

3. *The thought of the duties and obligations which flow from the love of God and man helps the Christian to avoid sin and the occasions of sins.*

We need the help of the Holy Spirit, especially, in order to avoid sin and the occasions of sin. Since the world about us, the devil, and our own inclinations to sin are so powerful in the face of our human weaknesses, we must put our confidence in the even greater power of God's grace.

4. *The thought of the duties and obligations which flow from the love of God and man helps the Christian to live in this world according to the Spirit of Christ, for the love of God.*

The great commandment of love requires that we act toward God as His children and that we act toward our fellow men as our brothers, as children of the same Father. Our duties towards God and our neighbor are set forth especially in the Ten Commandments. If we love God, we will keep the first three commandments; they tell us about our duties towards God. If we love our neighbor, we will keep the other seven commandments; they tell us of our duties towards ourselves and our neighbors.

The Ten Commandments (reflecting the natural law written in our hearts), flow from our very nature as human beings (cf. Romans 1:35). Because we were created by God and depend on Him completely, we must, as intelligent responsible beings, acknowledge that dependence. We must praise God, love Him, believe and trust Him, and show reverence for His Name. Because each human being has certain rights which He receives from God, we must respect those rights.

In studying the commandments, we learn about the laws which tell us how we, as human beings, must behave toward God and toward our fellowman. More importantly, we, as children of God, learn about the laws which will help us to fulfill the great law of love. We will then live in this world according to the Spirit of Christ, for the love of God.

Sacred Scripture

"Wherefore, my dearly beloved, as you have always obeyed, not as in my presence only, but much more now in my absence, with fear and trembling work out your salvation."

Philippians 2:12

633

Vatican Council II

"Accordingly all Christians, in the conditions, duties and circumstances of their life and through all these, will sanctify themselves more and more if they receive all things with faith from the hand of the heavenly Father and cooperate with the divine will, thus showing forth in that temporal service the love with which God has loved the world." *The Church, 41*

Papal Document

"Following the Master, every Christian should deny himself, take up his own cross and share in the sufferings of Christ: transformed in this way into an image of Christ's death he becomes capable of meditating on the glory of the Resurrection. Since he is following the Master he should not live any more for himself but for Him who loved him and gave Himself for him, and should also live for his brothers, fulfilling 'in his flesh what is missing in the suffering of Christ...for the sake of His body which is the Church.' (Colossians 1:24)."

John Paul II, Penance and Reconciliation, 1

Prayer: Father, guide us, as You guide creation, according to Your law of love. May we love one another and come to perfection in the eternal life which You prepared for us.

The perfection of justice is found in Your love. All mankind needs Your law. May justice be attained by obedience to Your commandments., through Jesus Christ our Lord. Amen.

Prayer

*F*ather in Heaven, the loving plan of Your wisdom took flesh in Jesus Christ. The history of mankind was changed by Jesus' command of perfect love. May our fulfillment of His command reflect Your wisdom and so bring Your salvation to the ends of the earth. You have promised to remain forever with those who do what is just and right. Help us to live in Your presence. Lord, may we treasure Your commandments as the greatest of all riches; never let us fear that anything could be lacking while You are at our side.

*M*ake us so love Your law, Father, as to ponder it continually in our hearts. May it bear fruit in works acceptable to You.

*B*less Your people, Lord. You have given us the law that we may walk from strength to strength, and raise our minds to You in this valley of tears. May we receive the gifts You have gained for us. You are the crowning glory of all the saints. Give us, Your children, the gift of obedience, which is the beginning of wisdom, so that we may do what You command and be filled with Your grace. May we live to praise You and never forget Your commandments.

*L*ord, send the spirit of the Gospel into our hearts, that we may walk in the way of Your commandments. You gave the Law to Moses on Mount Sinai, and brought it to perfection in Your Anointed One, Jesus Christ. May all people recognize the moral law which is written in their hearts, and keep it faithfully as a covenant, so that they may reach eternal life with You.

*L*ord God, King of Heaven and earth, direct, sanctify, rule, and guide our hearts, our bodies, our thoughts, words, and deeds so that we may keep Your commandments. Your commandments are the light of the world; they teach us to accomplish what is right and holy. Bless Your people and sanctify Your inheritance. Fill us with reverence for Your holy Name. Enable us to praise You worthily, and thus reach our heavenly home, through Jesus Christ our Lord and Savior. Amen.

Final Reunion
with God

Soul in Grace

Death, Judgment, Hell, Purgatory, and Heaven - I

Q. 291. Why should we face death with courage and joy?

We have reason to face death with courage and joy because: (1) *Christ's Resurrection has conquered death;* (2) *in the risen Christ we live, die, and shall live again;* and (3) *we look ahead to our homecoming with God our loving Father.*

1. *We have reason to face death with courage and joy because the Lord's Resurrection has conquered death.*

Death is the separation of body and soul. It is the passage of the soul over the threshold between earthly life and the life beyond. Though the soul continues to exist, it is disturbed by the dissolution of the body, for the soul loses the instrument through which it has acted.

Christ gave death, which was introduced after Adam's fall, a new significance. He changed it into an event that brings salvation. By becoming man, and by taking death upon Himself, as mankind's representative, Jesus gave Himself as a perfect sacrifice to the heavenly Father. He expiated, or made satisfaction for, Adam's surrender to satan, the effects of which passed on to all mankind. From the time of the Crucifixion, man has been able to face death with the expectation of obtaining everlasting life in God's Kingdom.

Prayer: *Lord, may the thought of death be ever present to the eyes of our souls. May the remembrance of the final judgment and of the torment which the lost experience, be continually in our minds, that we may never deliberately commit sin. When You return from the*

See Papally Promulgated
Catechism of the Catholic Church

Q. 291. See paragraphs: 1010-1014

2. *We have reason both to live and to face death with courage and joy because in the risen Christ we live, die, and shall live again.*

The Resurrection of Christ is the most important testimony of Scripture to our future resurrection in the body. Through Christ's merits, God has set up a new order, according to which Christ is the beginning of our resurrection.

St. Paul said: "For by a man came death, and by a man the resurrection of the dead. And as in Adam all die, so also in Christ all shall be made alive. But every one in his own order: the first fruits Christ, then they that are of Christ, who have believed in His coming" (1 Corinthians 15:21-23). As the second Adam, Who gives new life to all things, Christ achieves His final victory over satan, the lord of the earth, who gained dominion over all mankind by the fall of the first Adam.

3. *We have reason both to live and to face death with courage and joy because we look ahead to our homecoming with God — our loving Father.*

We believe that the just, who have been made perfect through death and Purgatory, are now in Heaven, though they have not yet risen in the body, nor undergone the final judgment.

Heaven is the fullness of the Kingdom of God. It would be insufficient to consider Heaven only as the place or state of reward from the standpoint of individual happiness. In fact, it is primarily a place and form of the manifestation of God's glory. We are called to glorify God in Heaven in a perfect manner. The essential element in this adoration and honor is our love and self-surrender to Him.

God is the highest good Whom we not only shall know and love, but also live within, in a mysterious sharing of His life. This life is purest joy, everlasting rest, fullest attainment, and quiet happiness. We look forward to this state of perfection, the greatest experience of our whole lives. It surpasses any experience we may have on this earth. So, we should face death with courage and joy, looking ahead to our homecoming to God our loving Father.

Sacred Scripture

"Let your loins be girt and lamps burning in your hands. And you yourselves like to men who wait for their Lord, when He shall return from the wedding; that when He comes and knocks, they may open to Him immediately. Blessed are those servants whom the Lord, when He comes, shall find them watching. Truly I say to you, He will gird Himself and make them sit down to eat and passing will wait on them. And if He shall come in the second watch or come in the third watch and find them ready, blessed are those servants." *Luke 12:35-38*

Vatican Council II

"While the mind is at a loss before the mystery of death, the Church, taught by divine Revelation, declares that God has created man in view of a blessed destiny that lies beyond the limits of his sad state on earth. Moreover, the Christian faith teaches that bodily death, from which man would have been immune had he not sinned, will be overcome when that wholeness which he lost through his own fault will be given once again to him by the almighty and merciful Saviour. For God has called man, and still calls him, to cleave with all his being to him in sharing for ever a life that is divine and free from all decay." *Modern World, 18*

Prayer

Jesus, we want to prepare ourselves for Your coming by detaching our affections from earthly things. When we are called upon to meet You, we must not be hindered by attachments to the things of the earth. We want to lift high in the darkness of this mortal existence, "a burning lamp," to symbolize the flame of our devotion, which has been fed by meditation on the eternal truths, as a lamp is fed by oil, that You may see its bright light immediately upon our coming.

Help us to live as watchful servants of our heavenly Master, lives that are withdrawn, by self-sacrifice, from the interests of this passing world, and which tend toward the eternal and heavenly country by means of prayer, good works, and frequent reception of the sacraments.

Jesus, help us to die in the state of grace, so that the day of our death may be for us a day of redemption, a day that we may hail with gladness. But, best of all, may it be the day on which we shall see You, the Friend Whom we have loved and served all our lives. Even if You send us away from Your presence for a while, until we are cleansed from the remnants of venial sins which still stain our souls, we know that we shall soon be admitted to the beatific vision of Your glorious face forever and ever. Amen.

Death, Judgment, Hell, Purgatory, Heaven - II

Q. 292. What is the particular judgment?

At the very instant that the soul leaves the body, it is judged by Almighty God. This is the particular judgment.

If we die with no sins on our soul which require atonement or satisfaction, the immediate sight of God in Heaven will itself be our judgment.

Prayer: *Father, You weigh what is in our hearts. Free us from all evil, and, as we wait for Your day of judgment, set a firm guard on our thoughts, so that, as we return good for evil, we may praise your kind justice for ever and ever. Amen.*

Vatican Council II

"When the Lord will come in glory, and all his angels with him, (cf. Mt. 25:31) death will be no more and all things will be subject to him (cf. 1 Cor.15:26-27). But at the present time some of his disciples are pilgrims on earth. Others have died and are being purified, while still others are in glory, contemplating, 'in full light, God himself triune and one, exactly as he is.' [Ecumenical Council of Florence (1438-45), *Decree for the Greeks*]. All of us, however, in varying degrees and in different ways share in the same charity towards God and our neighbors, and we all sing the one hymn of glory to our God. All, indeed, who are of Christ and who have his Spirit form one Church and in Christ cleave together (Eph. 4:16). So it is that the union of the wayfarers with the brethren who sleep in the peace of Christ is in no way interrupted, but on the contrary, according to the

See Papally Promulgated
Catechism of the Catholic Church

Q. 292. See paragraphs: 1021-1022

constant faith of the Church, this union is reinforced by an exchange of spiritual goods." *The Church, 49*

Q. 293. What is hell?

Hell is the eternal separation from God.

The person who dies in the state of mortal sin has deliberately torn himself from God during life, and has died without that bond of union with God which we call sanctifying grace. He has no means by which to establish contact with God and has lost Him forever. He is in hell.

We know that in hell there is everlasting fire, because Jesus Himself said so. It is not the kind of fire we see on earth; earthly fire cannot afflict the soul, since it is a spirit. There is in hell a "pain of sense" of such a nature that it cannot be better described by any other word in our human language than by the word "fire." What matters most is the "pain of loss." The eternal separation from God constitutes the worst of hell's suffering. It will be extreme loneliness.

Sacred Scripture

"Then He shall say to them also that shall be on His left hand, 'Depart from Me, you cursed, into everlasting fire, which was prepared for the devil and his angels.' And these shall go into everlasting fire punishment, but the just into everlasting life." *Matthew 25:41,46*

"And they shall go out and see the carcasses of the men that have transgressed against Me. Their worm shall not die and their fire shall not be quenched. And they shall be loathsome sight to all flesh." *Isaiah 66:24*

"And whoever shall scandalize one of these little ones who believe in Me, it would be better for him that a millstone be hanged about his neck and he be cast into the sea." *Mark 9:42*

Vatican Council II

"Since we know neither the day nor the hour, we should fol-

See Papally Promulgated
Catechism of the Catholic Church

Q. 293. See paragraphs: 1033-1037

low the advice of the Lord and watch constantly so that, when the single course of our earthly life is completed (cf. Heb. 9:27), we may merit to enter with him into the marriage feast and be numbered among the blessed (cf. Mt. 25:31-46) and not, like the wicked and slothful servants, (cf. Mt. 25:26) be ordered to depart into the eternal fire, (cf. Mt. 25:41) into the outer darkness where 'men will weep and gnash their teeth' (Mt. 22:13 and 25:30)." *The Church, 48*

Q. 294. What is Purgatory?

Purgatory is a place of spiritual cleansing. Anyone who dies in the grace of God, but is not free from all temporal punishment due to sins, cannot go to Heaven at once. Those who still have to do penance for their sins go first to Purgatory.

"There shall not enter into it [Heaven] anything defiled or that works abomination or makes a lie. But those who are written in the book of life of the Lamb" (Revelation 21:27).

Purification is a matter of purging the soul and of preparing it for the full perfection of the supernatural life, which it already possesses. The soul must complete what was lacking in its fidelity and honor to God on earth. The soul's final turning to God happens through suffering. The real element which effects this cleansing and fulfillment of the soul in Purgatory is its living love of God, which it possessed on leaving this life.

The soul in Purgatory is animated by an ardent desire for absolute holiness, in order to please God. Purgatory will continue to exist until the whole world has been judged on the Last Day. After this final judgment, there will be nothing left but Heaven and hell.

Sacred Scripture

"Amen I say to you, you shall not leave from there until you have paid the last farthing." *Matthew 5:26*

Vatican Council II

"When the Lord will come in glory, and all his angels with him (cf. Mt. 25-31), death will be no more and all things will be subject to him (cf. 1 Cor. 15:26-27). But at the present time some of his disciples are pilgrims on earth. Others have died and are being purified, while still others are in glory, contemplating 'in full light, God himself triune and one, exactly as he is.' [Ecumenical Council of Florence, (1438-45) *Decree for the Greeks*]. All of us, however, in varying degrees and in different ways share in the same charity towards God and our neighbors, and we all sing the one hymn of glory to our God. All, indeed, who are in Christ and who have his Spirit form one Church and in Christ cleave together." *The Church, 49*

Q. 295. What is the Beatific Vision?

The Beatific Vision is an immediate vision of God.

We believe that the just who have been made perfect through death and Purgatory are now in Heaven, though they have neither risen in the body nor undergone the final judgment. We are called to glorify God in Heaven in a perfect manner by loving Him and surrendering ourselves to Him. God is the highest Good, Whom we shall not only know and love, but also live in, in a mysterious sharing of His life.

This face-to-face union with God is the happiness of Heaven. God will give the saved or predestined a full flowering of supernatural life in Heaven because He is infinitely merciful. They shall be with Him forever.

The Beatific Vision is a union with God. God possesses the soul and the soul possesses God in a unity which is so complete that it is infinitely beyond the happiness of any human love. This happiness is eternal; man was created for Heaven, the only place where he can truly be happy.

Sacred Scripture

"We now see through a glass in a dark manner, but then face to face. Now I know in part, but then I shall know even as I am known" *1 Corinthians 13:12*

"But as it is written, 'That eye has not seen, nor ear heard, neither has it entered into the heart of man, what things God has prepared for those who love Him.' " *1 Corinthians 2:9*

Vatican Council II

"Christ won this victory when he rose to life, for by his

See Papally Promulgated
Catechism of the Catholic Church

Q. 295. See paragraphs: 163, 1023, 1028, 1032, 1045

death he freed man from death. Faith, therefore, with its solidly based teaching, provides every thoughtful man with an answer to his anxious queries about his future lot. At the same time it makes him able to be united in Christ with his loved ones who have already died, and gives hope that they have found true life with God." *Modern World, 18*

"Animated and drawn together in his Spirit we press onwards on our journey towards the consummation of history which fully corresponds to the plan of his love: 'to unite all things in him, things in heaven and things on earth' (Eph. 1:10)." *Modern World, 45*

"The Lord himself said: 'Behold, I am coming soon, bringing my recompense, to repay every one for what he has done. I am the alpha and the omega, the first and the last, the beginning and the end' " (Apoc. 22:12-13). *Modern World, 45*

Prayer: Heavenly Father, You raise us up from our lowliness by giving us the hope of eternal life. May we always serve You in this our pilgrimage, and come to enjoy the happiness of our home with You, through Christ our Lord. Amen.

Prayer

O God, You search the hearts of all, both the good and the wicked. May those who are in danger because of their love for You, find security in You now, and, on the day of judgment, may they rejoice in seeing you face to face.

Lord, You are the fullness of life, of holiness, and of joy. Fill our days with the love of Your wisdom, that we may bear fruit in the beauty of holiness, like a tree watered by running streams. Help us to seek the values which will bring us lasting joy in this changing world. In our desire for what You promise, make us one in mind and heart, through Jesus Christ our Lord and Savior. Amen.

Resurrection of the Body

Q. 296. What do we mean when we say, "We believe in the resurrection of the body"?

When we say "We believe in the resurrection of the body," we mean that we believe that, at the end of the world, all the bodies of those who have lived on earth will be raised from the dead and will be united again with their souls.

If the whole man — body and soul — has loved and served God, even at the cost of pain and sacrifice, it is just that the whole man, body as well as soul, enjoys that eternal union with God which is the reward of such love.

If the whole man has rejected God by unrepented mortal sin, it is just that the body should share, with the soul, in the eternal separation from God which the whole man has chosen.

Our bodies will no longer need food or drink or rest, and will be in some sense "spiritualized." In addition, the bodies of those who are in Heaven will be "glorified;" they will possess a perfection and beauty which will be a sharing in the perfection and beauty of the soul that has been united to God.

Sacred Scripture

"Behold, I tell you a mystery. We shall all indeed rise again, but we shall not all be changed. In a moment, in the twinkling of an eye, at the last trumpet: for the trumpet shall sound, and the dead shall rise again incorruptible. And we shall be changed. For the corruptible must put on incorruption, and this mortal body must put on immortality." *1 Corinthians 15:51-53*

"And the sea gave up the dead that were in it. And death and hell gave up their dead that were in them. And they were judged, everyone according to their works." *Revelation 20:13-14*

See Papally Promulgated
Catechism of the Catholic Church

Q. 296. See paragraphs: 988-991, 1002-1004

"For I know that my Redeemer lives. And on the last day I shall rise up out of the earth. And I shall be clothed again with my skin, and in my flesh I shall see my God, Whom I myself shall behold and my eyes shall see, and not another."

Job 19:25-27

"And when this mortal nature has put on immortality, then shall come to pass the saying, 'Death is swallowed in victory. O death, where is your victory? O death, where is your sting?' Now the sting of death is sin, and the power of sin is the law. But thanks be to God Who has given us the victory through our Lord Jesus Christ." *1 Corinthians 15:54-57*

Vatican Council II

"We know neither the moment of the consummation of the earth and of man (cf. Acts 1:7) nor the way the universe will be transformed. The form of this world, distorted by sin, is passing away and we are taught that God is preparing a new dwelling and a new earth in which righteousness dwells, whose happiness will fill and surpass all the desires of peace arising in the hearts of men. Then, with death conquered, the sons of God will be raised in Christ and what was sown in weakness and dishonor will put on the imperishable: charity and its works will remain and all of creation, which God made for man, will be set free from its bondage to decay."

Modern World, 39

Prayer: *God of mercy and compassion, grant that we who are baptized into the death of Your beloved Son may die to all sin and selfishness, and eagerly await the dawning of our joyful resurrection, through the merits of the same Christ our Lord and Savior. Amen.*

Q. 297. What do we mean when we say, "We believe in life everlasting"?

We believe that those who die in the state of grace will live with God forever. "Now this is eternal life: that they might

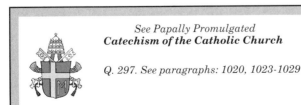

See Papally Promulgated
Catechism of the Catholic Church

Q. 297. See paragraphs: 1020, 1023-1029

know You, the only true God, and Jesus Christ, Whom You have sent" (John 17:3). In God alone can we find eternal happiness.

This life is a time of testing and trial. The eternal happiness of Heaven consists essentially in the fulfillment of love. Unless we depart this world with love for God in our hearts, we will be unable to experience the happiness of Heaven. Our life upon this earth is the time which God has given us to develop and to prove our love for Him. We must prove that our love for God is greater than any of His created gifts, such as pleasure, wealth, fame, or friendship. We must prove that our love can withstand the pressure of man-made evils, such as poverty, pain, humiliation, or injustice.

The thought of these final realities — death, judgment, Purgatory, Heaven, and hell — should fill us with Christian hope, but, at the same time, with an awareness of the responsibility we have to attain life everlasting.

Vatican Council II

"At the hour when Christ will appear, when the glorious resurrection of the dead will occur, the glory of God will light up the heavenly city, and the Lamb will be its lamp (cf. Apoc. 21:23)." *The Church, 51*

"In the earthly liturgy we take part in a foretaste of that heavenly liturgy which is celebrated in the Holy City of Jerusalem toward which we journey as pilgrims, where Christ is sitting at the right hand of God, Minister of the holies and of the true tabernacle. With all the warriors of the heavenly army we sing a hymn of glory to the Lord; venerating the memory of the saints, we hope for some part and fellowship with them; we eagerly await the Savior, our Lord Jesus Christ, until he our life shall appear and we too will appear with him in glory." *Sacred Liturgy, 8*

Prayer

Father, in Your plan of salvation, Your Son, Jesus Christ, accepted the Cross and thus freed us from the power of the enemy. May we come to share in the glory of His Resurrection. May we hold fast to the life of grace which You have given to us, and so come to the eternal gifts You promise. Watch over us, for we have been saved by Christ. May we, who are redeemed by His suffering and death, always rejoice in His Resurrection.

God our Father, may we look forward with hope to our resurrection, for You have made us Your sons and daughters and have restored the joy of our youth by giving us Your grace. Hear the prayers of Your newborn people and strengthen Your Church, that we may answer Your call. May we rise, and come forth into the light of day, to stand in Your presence until eternity dawns.

God of mercy, You have filled us with the hope of our resurrection by restoring man to His original dignity. May we who relive this mystery in the Mass come to share it in perpetual love. Grant that everything we do may be directed by the knowledge of Your truth. May the Eucharistic mysteries give us new purpose and bring us to a new life in You. May the Easter mystery we celebrate be effective throughout our life. You restored us to life by raising Christ from death. Strengthen us by this Easter sacrament; may we feel Its saving power in our daily lives. May It bring us to the glory of the resurrection and to eternal life with You. We ask this through Christ our Lord. Amen.

The Last Judgment - I

Q. 298. What is the last or general judgment?

The last or general judgment is the universal judgment of the human race at the resurrection of the dead at the end of the world.

"When the Son of Man shall come in His majesty, and all the angels with Him, then He shall sit upon the seat of His majesty. And all nations shall be gathered together before Him, and He shall separate them one from another, as the shepherd separates the sheep from the goats" (Matthew 25:31-32).

"Then I saw a great white throne and the One Who sat upon it, from Whose face the earth and heaven fled away. And there was no place found for them. And I saw the dead, great and small, standing in the presence of the throne. And the books were opened. And another book was opened, which was the book of life. And the dead were judged by those things which were written in the books, according to their works" (Revelation 20:11-12).

This last judgment will be a social judgment, because it will manifest to the world God's justice in condemning sinners and His mercy in those who are saved. It will also be a total judgment, since not only people's moral conduct but all the accumulated blessings or injuries which will have resulted from each person's good or evil deeds will be revealed.

The general judgment is called the last judgment, since it is not followed by another, and since its sentence endures forever. It takes place on the Last Day, and, along with the resurrection of the body and the renewal of the world, is an element in the coming of the Lord with power.

See Papally Promulgated
Catechism of the Catholic Church

Q. 298. See paragraphs: 1038-1040

The general judgment is more than the promulgation of the sentence already passed on so many at their particular judgments, for it concerns also those who are still living on that day. The whole human race will be judged. Judgment will be passed too on the angels — both good and bad; indeed on all of creation. Each individual person will once more be summoned to appear before the Lord as His Judge.

In this judgment each person will be given a view over his whole life and its significance. He will see it in the light of the Lord. The sentence which was passed upon us in our particular judgment will now be publicly confirmed. All of our sins — and all of our virtues, too — will be known.

Vatican Council II

"Already present in figure at the beginning of the world, this Church was prepared in marvellous fashion in the history of the people of Israel and in the old Alliance. Established in this last age of the world, and made manifest in the outpouring of the Spirit, it will be brought to glorious completion at the end of time. At that moment, as the Fathers put it, all the just from the time of Adam, 'from Abel, the just one, to the last of the elect' [See St. Gregory the Great, Homily, *In Evange.*19,1: PL 76; 1154B] will be gathered together with the Father in the universal Church." *The Church, 2*

Q. 299. What will happen on the day of the last judgment?

(1) *All of us will be revealed "before the judgment seat of Christ, that everyone may receive the proper things of the body, according as he has done, whether it be good or evil"* (2 Corinthians 5:10). Then (2) *"those who have done good shall come forth unto the resurrection of life, but those who have done evil, unto the resurrection of judgment"* (John 5:29).

1. *All of us will be revealed "before the judgment seat of Christ, that everyone may receive the proper things of the*

See Papally Promulgated
Catechism of the Catholic Church

Q. 299. See paragraphs: 1038-1041

body, according as he has done, whether it be good or evil" (2 Corinthians 5:10).

The office of judging all mankind at the end of the world is committed to our Lord Jesus Christ, not only as God, but also as Son of Man, or Messiah. Jesus Himself taught us that He would be the judge of mankind.

"For as the Father raises up the dead and gives life, so also the Son gives life to whom He wills. For neither does the Father judge any man, but has given all judgment to the Son that all men may honor the Son as they honor the Father" (John 5:21-23).

The divine reward of eternal life requires our faithfulness to God. Liberated from sin and made servants of God, Christians receive, as the fruit of their good works, an increase of personal sanctification and, in the end, eternal life, which is the greatest gift of God. St. Paul says: "But being made free from sin and become servants of God, you have your fruit unto sanctification, and the end, life everlasting. For the wages of sin is death, but the grace of God, life everlasting in Christ Jesus our Lord" (Romans 6:22-23).

2. Then *"those who have done good shall come forth unto the resurrection of life, but those who have done evil, unto the resurrection of judgment"* (John 5:29).

God will reward everyone according to his works on the day of the general judgment, and will give an eternal life of happiness to those who have persevered in good works to the end. He will punish unrepentant sinners. St. Paul says: "[God] will render to every man according to his works. To them indeed who, according to patience in good works, seek glory and honor and incorruption, eternal life" (Romans 2:6-7).

In Heaven the blessed shall be absorbed in possessing the infinitely perfect God, the greatest love that exists. The keenest human love is but a pale shadow of this love. They shall also see Christ, the God-man, in His glorified manhood. They shall live in community with the angels and the saints.

Happiness in this life is neither perfect nor complete. God, Who is infinitely good, would not place in human hearts the desire for perfect happiness if there were no way in which that desire could be satisfied. Union with God in Heaven will be more complete and joyous than we can ever imagine. St. Paul wrote about the wisdom that God has predestined to be our glory: "Eye has not seen, nor ear heard. Neither has it entered into the heart of man what things God has prepared for those who love Him" (1 Corinthians 2:9).

The blessed shall also know our loved ones in Heaven who will have died in the grace of God, and shall rejoice at their presence. In Heaven they shall find other relatives and friends.

Vatican Council II

"Before we reign with Christ in glory we must all appear 'before the judgment seat of Christ, so that each one may receive good or evil, according to what he has done in the body' (2 Cor. 5:10) and at the end of the world, 'they will come forth, those who have done good, to the resurrection of life, and those who have done evil, to the resurrection of judgment' (Jn. 5:29, Mt. 25:46)." *The Church, 48*

Prayer

Jesus, in the Incarnation You entered into the world, being clothed in the infirmities of man. You came to earth in order to set up in men's hearts the Kingdom of God, but You were rejected by the people of Your time. You died the death of a public criminal. Your mission, judged according to the opinion of the people, seemed a complete failure. This was part of the divine plan, however. Being an all-knowing and all-powerful God, You reserve Your triumph until the Last Day, when You will come in Your glory to complete triumphantly Your work upon earth, and to establish forever the New Jerusalem, the Kingdom of God in Heaven.

Your plan implies that we must be judged before being made citizens of the eternal Kingdom. Our entrance into the Kingdom will be based upon our acceptance of the divine will. The angels of God will gather together Your elect, and as the Founder of the Kingdom, You will judge all men.

We believe that the Last Judgment is universal. It will come unexpectedly and with extraordinary suddenness, like lightning.

*W*e believe that the dead will rise again. For the blessed, this resurrection will be glorious. Accompanied by angels, they will go in a glorious procession to the place of judgment. But the resurrection of the damned will be hideous, bearing, to their exceeding shame, the curse of their sins in their bodies. They will be driven by evil spirits to the place of judgment.

*T*hen You will come, glorious, majestic, and powerful. You will be publicly and solemnly acknowledged as Head, King, and Judge of nations and men. By the greatness of Your omnipotence, all consciences will suddenly be laid open and illuminated as one enormous picture — the great picture of the City of God and of hell below. The Last Judgment will be the grand finale of the whole history of the Church and of mankind. Lord, we believe in your words, which will not pass away.

*J*esus, a Heaven of goodness, love, and tenderness will beam upon the blessed as You turn to them with a kind and gentle glance, and say, "Come you whom My Father has blessed, take for your heritage the Kingdom prepared for you since the foundation of the world" (Matthew 25:34). You will give them the Kingdom in return for so little. You will assure them that their works, done out of faith and love for You, deserve this: for what they have done to the least of men, they have done to You. They will enter into life everlasting with You. May we be among them! Let us suffer in this world, in order to be glorified in the next. We despise the fallen world and its principles. May we possess You eternally.

*W*e believe that an irrevocable sentence of damnation must be pronounced upon the lost, because You cannot do otherwise than banish forever from Your presence those who hate You, and will hate you, forever.

*J*esus, You will be our Judge. At the moment of death, the opinions of other people will not concern us; we shall care only for what You think of us. While we are still in this life, help us to avail ourselves of all the gifts of Your love, to make use of Your sacraments, and to pray and perform works of mercy. Be not our Judge, but our Savior, when we appear before You at the Judgment. To You be all honor, praise, and glory, now and forever. Amen.

The Last Judgment - II

Q. 300. What will happen when Christ returns with power?

When Christ returns with power as Judge of the living and the dead, (1) *He will give His people to the Father;* and (2) *the Church will then reach perfection and enter into the fullness of God.*

1. *When Christ returns with power as Judge of the living and the dead, He will give His people to the Father.*

The great event of the Second Coming in power and glory will be, at the same time, the judgment and the raising of the dead in their bodies.

When Christ has subjected all things to Himself, He will deliver His dominion to the Father. "Afterwards [comes] the end when He shall have delivered up the Kingdom to God the Father. When He shall have brought to nothing every principality and power and virtue" (1 Corinthians 15:24). United to man through Christ, the whole creation shares in His continual sacrifice and perfect worship of the Father in the Holy Spirit. St. Paul says: "And when all things shall be subdued unto Him, then the Son also Himself shall also be subject to Him Who put all things under Him, so that God may be all in all" (1 Corinthians 15:28).

2. *When Christ returns with power as Judge of the living and the dead, the Church will then reach perfection and enter into the fullness of God.*

Death is the beginning of our resurrection. The particular judgment places the individual soul in its proper eternal setting. This placement is confirmed in the last or general judgment. Heaven and hell need, for their completion, the Coming

See Papally Promulgated
Catechism of the Catholic Church

Q. 300. See paragraphs: 1042-1050

of Christ. Christ, by raising up the bodies of mankind will restore to both the blessed and the lost, the human condition they once had, by giving them bodies which correspond to their state. The soul will demand its body. The new humanity requires fulfillment by the resurrection of the bodies of all mankind. Only then will the Church reach perfection and enter into the fullness of God.

> **Prayer:** *God our Father, as the Day of Christ Jesus draws near, bring to completion the good work which You have begun in us. Make us pure and blameless in Your sight, and prepare us for the Day of Christ. May we then attain the perfect goodness which He shall produce in the elect for Your glory and praise, forever and ever. Amen.*

Q. 301. When will each person fully reach his eternal destiny?

On the day of the Last Judgment, each person will fully reach his eternal destiny.

The primary happiness of Heaven consists in this: that we shall possess, in body and soul, the infinitely perfect God, and be possessed by Him. We shall be personally and consciously united to God Himself, Who is infinite Goodness, Truth and Beauty. God's love will fulfill every craving and desire of the human heart. We shall then experience a happiness which, once achieved, we will never lose. We shall fully reach this eternal destiny on the day of the Last Judgment.

At every moment on earth, we must be prepared for death. We must use the time allotted to us by the will of God, whether it be long or short, with this preparation in mind. We must live Christian lives which are deserving of a heavenly reward. Heaven; its happiness is worth this short life of sacrifice and pain.

See Papally Promulgated
Catechism of the Catholic Church

Q. 301. See paragraphs: 1038-1040

"The promised and hoped for restoration, therefore, has already begun in Christ. It is carried forward in the sending of the Holy Spirit and through him continues in the Church in which, through our faith, we learn the meaning of our earthly life, while we bring to term, with hope of future good, the task allotted to us in the world by the Father, and so work out our salvation (cf. Phil. 2:12)." *The Church, 48*

Prayer

*F*ather of glory, Who raised Jesus Christ from the dead and made Him sit at Your right hand, rescue us from our sins, bring us to a new life in Him, raise us up with Him on the Last Day, and give us a place with Him in Heaven.

*L*ord God Almighty, the Beginning and the End, the First and the Last, direct our hearts and bodies to the love of God and the patience of Christ. Bless us, defend us from all evil, and bring us safely to life everlasting.

*S*end Your abundant blessings to Your people who devoutly recall the death of Your Son in the sure hope of the resurrection of the dead. Grant us pardon; bring us comfort. May our faith grow stronger and our eternal salvation be assured.

*F*ather of love, watch over Your Church and bring us to the glory of the resurrection of the dead which is promised by the Paschal sacrament, the most holy Eucharist. We ask this through Christ our Lord. Amen.

Mary, Mother of God and of the Church - I

Q. 302. Why does Mary, after Christ, have the highest place in the Church?

Mary has the highest place in the Church after Christ (1) *because she is the Ever-Virgin Mother of Jesus Christ our Lord and God,* and (2) *because she is our spiritual mother.*

1. *Mary, after Christ, has the highest place in the Church because she is the Ever-Virgin Mother of Jesus Christ our Lord and God.*

The source of Mary's motherhood is the generous consent which she gave to the angel of the Annunciation, who had come to invite her to become the Mother of God; the Mother of God the Son. In the plan of God, the salvation of the world was made dependent on Mary's decision at that moment. She not only consented, but also willed, with a clear understanding of the meaning of the mission, that which was being confided to her.

2. *Mary has the highest place in the Church after Christ because she is our spiritual mother.*

The origin and foundation of the spiritual motherhood of Mary is intimately associated with the Incarnation. At the Incarnation, Mary gave Jesus to us. On Calvary, Jesus gave us His Mother, and He assigned to her a place near to Him, yet still of a secondary order, subordinated to Him. But this place, in relation to all mankind, is all-powerful, and unique. Christ, the Head Himself, has appointed her to be the mother of the Whole Christ, that is, of the Mystical Body of Christ, the Church.

See Papally Promulgated
Catechism of the Catholic Church

Q. 302. See paragraphs: 963-970

Sacred Scripture

"And the angel said to her, 'Fear not, Mary, for you have found favor with God. Behold you shall conceive in your womb and shall bring forth a son and you shall call His name, Jesus. He shall be great and shall be called the Son of the Most High. And the Lord God shall give Him the throne of His father, David. And He shall reign in the house of Jacob forever. And of His kingdom there shall be no end.' ... And Mary said, 'Behold the handmaid of the Lord. Be it done to me according to your word.' " *Luke 1:30-33,38*

"When Jesus had therefore seen His mother and the disciple standing whom He loved, He said to His mother. 'Woman, behold your son.' After that, He said to the disciple, 'Behold your mother.' " *John 19:26-27*

Vatican Council II

"Mary has by grace been exalted above all angels and men to a place second only to her Son, as the most holy mother of God who was involved in the mysteries of Christ: she is rightly honored by a special cult in the Church. From the earliest times the Blessed Virgin has been honored under the title of Mother of God, under whose protection the faithful take refuge together in prayer in all their perils and needs. Accordingly, following the Council of Ephesus, there was a remarkable growth in the cult of the People of God towards Mary, in veneration and love, in invocation and imitation, according to her own prophetic words: 'all generations shall call me blessed, because he that is mighty hath done great things to me' (Lk. 1:48-49).

"This cult, as it has always existed in the Church, for all its uniqueness, differs essentially from the cult of adoration, which is offered equally to the Incarnate Word and to the Father and the Holy Spirit, and it is most favorable to it. The various forms of piety towards the Mother of God, which the Church has approved within the limits of sound and orthodox doctrine, according to the dispositions and understanding of the faithful, ensure that while the mother is honored, the Son through whom all things have their being (cf. Col. 1:15-16), and in whom it has pleased the Father that all fullness should dwell (cf. Col. 1:19) is rightly known, loved and glorified and his commandments are observed." *The Church, 66*

"The Virgin Mary, who at the message of the angel received the Word of God in her heart and in her body and gave Life to the world, is acknowledged and honored as being truly the Mother of God and of the redeemer. Redeemed, in a more exalted fashion, by reason of the merits of her Son and united to him by a close and indissoluble tie, she is endowed with the high office and dignity of the Mother of the Son of God, and therefore she is also the beloved daughter of the Father and the temple of the Holy Spirit. Because of this gift of sublime grace she far surpasses all creatures, both in heaven and on earth. But, being of the race of Adam, she is at the same time also united to all those who are to be saved; indeed, 'she is clearly the mother of the members of Christ...since she has by her charity joined in bringing about the birth of believers in the Church, who are members of its head.' Wherefore she is hailed as pre-eminent and as a wholly unique member of the Church, and as its type and outstanding model in faith and charity. The Catholic Church taught by the Holy Spirit, honors her with the filial affection and devotion as a most beloved mother." *The Church, 53*

Prayer

Mary, Mother of God, how great is the honor which was given to you at the Annunciation! Within your humble home, in the little town of Nazareth, the Holy Spirit willed to perform a miracle which was the masterpiece of infinite power — the Incarnation of the Son of God.

With heavenly homage, the angelic messenger greeted you: 'Rejoice, O highly favored one! The Lord is with you" (Luke 1:28). In all humility, you attributed this holiness to God Who was working wondrously within you.

When the Triune God destined and elevated you, a mortal virgin, to the dignity of the Mother of the Redeemer, the Father had to endow you with a fullness of perfection which would be suitable to such a dignity. The Son, the Eternal Wisdom of God, in choosing you for His Mother, bestowed on you a certain fullness of grace so that, when you gave Christ His human nature, Christ, in a certain sense, brought you as close to God as a mere creature can come. The Holy Spirit, Who descended upon you in the Incarnation with all His fullness, conferred upon you such treasures of sanctity as would prepare you to receive the Son of God in your most pure womb.

Do not forsake us, Mother of Jesus and our Mother. If we confide our salvation to your loving care and faithfully imitate your virtues, we know you will keep us in your love, both now, and at the hour of our death. Amen.

Mary, Mother of God and of the Church - II

Q. 303. What are some of the special gifts Mary received from God?

Some of the special gifts which God gave to the Virgin Mary are: (1) *she became the Mother of God,* (2) *she was preserved from all stain of original sin,* and, (3) *she was assumed, body and soul, into Heaven, since she had such a special place in the history of salvation.*

1. *One of the special gifts which God gave to the Virgin Mary was that she became the Mother of God.*

The Blessed Virgin is the collaborator with the Divine Word and the Holy Spirit in the mighty work of the Incarnation. She occupies the same essential role in the work of sanctifying souls. Her dignity as the Mother of God and as the Mother of men, her function as Mediatrix of All Graces, as well as her own perfect holiness, obtain for her a place of great importance in the sublime work of imitating Christ.

2. *Another of the special gifts which God gave to the Virgin Mary was that she was preserved from all stain of original sin.*

In view of the merits of her Divine Son, Mary enjoyed the privilege of being preserved from all stain of original sin. From the moment of her Immaculate Conception, God willed that she should crush the head of the serpent, having decided from all eternity to make her the Mother of the Incarnate Word. Mary was never, even for an instant, subject to the evil spirit. She remained in the state of sanctifying grace forever.

3. *Yet, another of the special gifts which God gave to the Virgin Mary was that she was assumed, body and soul, into*

See Papally Promulgated
Catechism of the Catholic Church

Q. 303. See paragraphs: 411, 466, 490-511, 963-970

Heaven, since she had such a special place in the history of salvation.

After a most blessed death, Mary was triumphantly assumed into Heaven, with her soul and body, and was crowned Queen of Heaven by her own Son. The dogma of the Assumption — celebrated in one of the most ancient and solemn of Mary's feasts — was infallibly defined at Rome, on November 1, 1950, by Pope Pius XII.

Vatican Council II

"This motherhood of Mary in the order of grace continued uninterruptedly from the consent which she loyally gave at the Annunciation and which she sustained without wavering beneath the cross, until the eternal fulfillment of all the elect. Taken up to heaven she did not lay aside this saving office but by her manifold intercession continues to bring us gifts of eternal salvation. By her maternal charity, she cares for the brethren of her Son, who still journey on earth surrounded by dangers and difficulties, until they are led into their blessed home. Therefore, the Blessed Virgin is invoked in the Church under the titles of Advocate, Helper, Benefactress, and Mediatrix." *The Church, 62*

"Mary's function as mother of men in no way obscures or diminishes this unique mediation of Christ, but rather shows its power. But the Blessed Virgin's salutary influence on men originates not in any inner necessity but in the disposition of God. It flows forth from the superabundance of the merits of Christ, rests on his mediation, depends entirely on it and draws all its power from it. It does not hinder in any way the immediate union of the faithful with Christ but on the contrary fosters it." *The Church, 60*

"The Immaculate Virgin, preserved free from all stain of original sin, was taken up body and soul into heavenly glory, when her earthly life was over, and exalted by the Lord as Queen over all things, that she might be the more fully conformed to her Son, the Lord of lords, (cf. Apoc. 19:16) and conqueror of sin and death." *The Church, 59*

Q. 304. What is the wish of the Church concerning devotion to Mary?

The Church urges that special veneration be given to Mary. This honor is due to her as Mother of Christ, as Mother of the Church, and as our spiritual Mother. This veneration is to be shown to others by word and example.

Pope Paul VI solemnly brought the third session of Vatican Council II to a close on November 21, 1964, in the presence of the entire body of the Church's Bishops, with the words: "For the glory of the Virgin Mary and for our own consolation, we proclaim Mary the Mother of the Church, that is, of the whole People of God, of the faithful as well as of the pastors, and we wish that through this title the Mother of God should be still more honored and invoked by the entire Christian people."

In his homily in Washington, D.C., on October 6, 1979, Pope John Paul II said to the American people and to the world:

"Mary is not only the Mother of God, she is the Mother of the Church as well. In every stage of the march through history, the Church has benefited from the prayer and protection of the Virgin Mary. Holy Scripture and the experience of the faithful see the Mother of God as the one who, in a very special way, is united with the Church at the most difficult moments in its history, when attacks on the Church become most threatening. Precisely in periods when Christ, and therefore His Church, provokes premeditated contradiction, Mary appears particularly close to the Church, because for her the Church is always her beloved Christ.

"I, therefore, exhort you in Christ Jesus, to continue to look to Mary as the model of the Church, as the best example of the discipleship of Christ.

"Learn from her to be always faithful, to trust that God's word to you will be fulfilled, and that nothing is impossible with God.

"Turn to Mary frequently in your prayers 'for never was it known that anyone who fled to her protection, implored her help or sought her intercession was left unaided.'

"As a great sign that has appeared in the heavens, Mary guides and sustains us on our pilgrim way, urging us on to "the victory that overcomes the world, our faith" (cf. Revelation 12:1; 1 John 5:4).

See Papally Promulgated
Catechism of the Catholic Church

Q. 304. See paragraphs: 971, 1172

Key Sacred Scripture Passages about Mary

"And the angel came in, and said unto her, 'Hail, full of grace, the Lord is with thee. Blessed art thou among women.' " *Luke 1:28*

"And the angel said to her, 'Fear not, Mary, for thou hast found favor with God.' " *Luke 1:30*

"I will put enmity between you and the woman, and your seed and her seed. She* shall crush your head, and you shall lie in wait for her heel." *Genesis 3:15*

"And Mary said, 'Behold the handmaid of the Lord. May it be done unto me according to thy word.' " *Luke 1:38*

"When Elizabeth heard the salutation of Mary, the infant leaped in her womb. And Elizabeth was filled with the Holy Spirit. And she cried out with a loud voice and said, 'Blessed art thou among women and blessed is the fruit of thy womb.' " *Luke 1:41-42*

"And Mary said, 'My soul magnifies the Lord, and my spirit rejoices in God, my Savior. Because He has regarded the lowliness of his handmaid. For behold henceforth all generations shall call me blessed. Because He that is mighty has done great things for me, and holy is His Name.'" *Luke 1:46-49*

"And a great sign appeared in the heavens; a woman clothed with the sun, and the moon under her feet, and her head a crown of twelve stars." *Revelation 12:1* [*Revelation* is the last book in the Bible].

"And the dragon was angry against the woman, and went to make war with the rest of her seed, who keep the commandments of God and have the testimony of Jesus Christ." *Revelation 12:17*

---

* "The sacred writings of the Old and New Testaments, as well as venerable tradition, show the role of the Mother of the Saviour in the plan of salvation in an ever clearer light and call our attention to it. The books of the Old Testament describe the history of salvation, by which the coming of Christ into the world was slowly prepared. The earliest documents, *[as they are read in the Church and are understood in the light of a further and full revelation]*, bring the figure of a woman, [the] Mother of the Redeemer, into a gradually clearer light. Considered in this light, she is already prophetically foreshadowed in the promise of victory over the serpent which was given to our first parents after their fall into sin (cf. Gen. 3:15)." Chapter 8 of *The Dogmatic Constitution on the Church (Lumen Gentium)* [Consult also the *Catechism of the Catholic Church,* paragraph 411].

Vatican Council II

"And now, assumed into heaven, 'her motherly love keeps her attentive to her Son's brothers, still on pilgrimage amid the dangers and difficulties of life, until they arrive at the happiness of the fatherland.' Everyone should have a genuine devotion to her and entrust his life to her motherly care."

Lay People, 4

"In celebrating this annual cycle of the mysteries of Christ, Holy Church honors the Blessed Mary, Mother of God, with a special love. She is inseparably linked with her Son's saving work. In her the Church admires and exalts the most excellent fruit of redemption, and joyfully contemplates, as in a faultless image, that which she herself desires and hopes wholly to be." *Sacred Liturgy, 103*

Addendum on Our Lady

[The Second Vatican Council held Mary in great esteem. In fact, the entire eighth chapter of the Dogmatic Constitution on the Church (Lumen Gentium), included below, is devoted to her. It is the longest treatment of Our Lady contained in any of the Ecumenical Councils.]

Chapter VIII
Dogmatic Constitution on the Church

I. Introduction

52. Wishing in his supreme goodness and wisdom to effect the redemption of the world, "when the fullness of time came, God sent His Son, born of a woman...that we might receive the adoption of sons" (Gal. 4:4). "He, for us men, and for our salvation, came down from heaven, was incarnated by the Holy Spirit from the Virgin Mary."[1] This divine mystery of salvation is revealed to us and continued in the Church, which the Lord established as His body. Joined to Christ the head, and in communion with all His saints, the faithful must, in the first place, reverence the memory "of the glorious ever Virgin Mary, Mother of God and of our Lord Jesus Christ."[2]

53. The Virgin Mary, who at the message of the angel received the Word of God in her heart and in her body and gave Life to the world, is acknowledged and honored as being truly the Mother of God and of the Redeemer. Redeemed, in a more exalted fashion, by reason of the merits of her Son, and united

to Him by a close and indissoluble tie, she is endowed with the high office and dignity of the Mother of the Son of God, and therefore she is also the beloved daughter of the Father and the temple of the Holy Spirit. Because of this gift of sublime grace she far surpasses all creatures, both in heaven and on earth. But, being of the race of Adam, she is at the same time also united to all those who are to be saved; indeed, "she is clearly the mother of the members of Christ...since she has, by her charity, joined in bringing about the birth of believers in the Church, who are members of its head."[3] Wherefore she is hailed as pre-eminent and as a wholly unique member of the Church, and as its type and outstanding model in faith and charity. The Catholic Church, taught by the Holy Spirit, honors charity. The Catholic Church, taught by the Holy Spirit, honors her with filial affection and devotion as a most beloved mother.

54. Wherefore this sacred synod, while expounding the doctrine on the Church, in which the divine Redeemer brings about our salvation, intends to set forth painstakingly both the role of the Blessed Virgin in the mystery of the Incarnate Word and of the Mystical Body, and the duties of the redeemed towards the Mother of God, who is mother of Christ and mother of men, and most of all, of those who believe. It does not, however, intend to give a complete doctrine on Mary, nor does it wish to decide those questions which the work of theologians has not yet fully clarified. Those opinions therefore may be lawfully retained which are propounded in Catholic schools concerning her who occupies a place in the Church which is the highest after Christ and also closest to us.[4]

II. The Function of the Blessed Virgin in the Plan of Salvation

55. The sacred writings of the Old and New Testaments, as well as venerable tradition, show the role of the Mother of the Saviour in the plan of salvation in an ever clearer light and call our attention to it. The books of the Old Testament describe the history of salvation, by which the coming of Christ into the world was slowly prepared. The earliest documents, as they are read in the Church and are understood in the light of a further and full revelation, bring the figure of a woman, Mother of the Redeemer, into a gradually clearer light. Considered in this light, she is already prophetically foreshadowed in the promise of victory over the serpent which was given to our first parents after their fall into sin (cf. Gen. 3: 15). Likewise, she is the virgin who

shall conceive and bear a Son, whose name shall be called Emmanuel (cf. Is. 7:14; Mic. 5:2-3; Mt. 1:22-23). She stands out among the poor and humble of the Lord, who confidently hope for and receive salvation from Him. After a long period of waiting the times are fulfilled in her, the exalted Daughter of Sion, and the new plan of salvation is established, when the Son of God has taken human nature from her, that He might in the mysteries of His flesh free man from sin.

56. The Father of mercies willed that the Incarnation should be preceded by assent on the part of the predestined mother, so that just as a woman had a share in bringing about death, so also a woman should contribute to life. This is pre-eminently true of the Mother of Jesus, who gave to the world the Life that renews all things, and who was enriched by God with gifts appropriate to such a role. It is no wonder then that it was customary for the Fathers to refer to the Mother of God as all holy and free from every stain of sin, as though fashioned by the Holy Spirit and formed as a new creature.[5] Enriched from the first instant of her conception with the splendor of an entirely unique holiness, the Virgin of Nazareth is hailed by the heralding angel, by divine command, as "full of grace" (cf. Lk. 1:28), and to the heavenly messenger she replies: "Behold the handmaid of the Lord, be it done unto me according to thy word" (Lk. 1:38). Thus the daughter of Adam, Mary, consenting to the word of God, became the Mother of Jesus. Committing herself wholeheartedly and impeded by no sin to God's saving will, she devoted herself totally, as a handmaid of the Lord, to the person and work of her Son, under and with him, serving the mystery of redemption, by the grace of Almighty God. Rightly, therefore, the Fathers see Mary not merely as passively engaged by God, but as freely cooperating in the work of man's salvation through faith and obedience. For, as St. Irenaeus says, she "being obedient, became the cause of salvation for herself and for the whole human race."[6] Hence not a few of the early Fathers gladly assert with him in their preaching: "the knot of Eve's disobedience was untied by Mary's obedience: what the virgin Eve bound through her disbelief, Mary loosened by her faith."[7] Comparing Mary with Eve, they call her "Mother of the living,"[8] and frequently claim: "Death through Eve, life through Mary."[9]

57. This union of the mother with the Son in the work of salvation is made manifest from the time of Christ's virginal conception up to His death; first, when Mary, arising in haste to go to visit Elizabeth, is greeted by her as blessed because of

670

her belief in the promise of salvation and the precursor leaps with joy in the womb of his mother (cf. Lk. 1:41-5); then also at the birth of Our Lord, Who did not diminish His mother's virginal integrity but sanctified it,[10] the Mother of God joyfully showed her firstborn Son to the shepherds and the Magi: when she presented Him to the Lord in the temple, making the offering of the poor, she heard Simeon foretelling at the same time that her Son would be a sign of contradiction and that a sword would pierce the mother's soul, that out of many hearts thoughts might be revealed (cf. Lk. 2:34-35); when the Child Jesus was lost and they had sought Him sorrowing, His parents found Him in the temple, engaged in the things that were His Father's, and they did not understand the words of their Son. His mother, however, kept all these things to be pondered in her heart (cf. Lk. 2:41-51).

58. In the public life of Jesus, Mary appears prominently; at the very beginning, when at the marriage feast of Cana, moved with pity, she brought about by her intercession the beginning of miracles of Jesus the Messiah (cf. Jn. 2:1-11). In the course of her Son's preaching she received the words whereby, in extolling a kingdom beyond the concerns and ties of flesh and blood, He declared blessed those who heard and kept the word of God (cf. Mk. 3:35; par. Lk. 11:27-28), as she was faithfully doing (cf. Lk. 2:19; 51). Thus the Blessed Virgin advanced in her pilgrimage of faith, and faithfully persevered in her union with her Son unto the cross, where she stood, in keeping with the divine plan, enduring with her only begotten Son the intensity of His suffering, associated herself with His sacrifice in her mother's heart, and lovingly consenting to the immolation of this victim which was born of her. Finally, she was given by the same Christ Jesus, dying on the cross, as a mother to his disciple, with these words: "Woman, behold thy son" (Jn. 19:26-27).[11]

59. But since it had pleased God not to manifest solemnly the mystery of the salvation of the human race before he would pour forth the Spirit promised by Christ, we see the apostles, before the day of Pentecost, "persevering with one mind in prayer with the women and Mary the Mother of Jesus, and with His brethren" (Acts 1:14), and we also see Mary by her prayers imploring the gift of the Spirit, Who had already overshadowed her in the Annunciation. Finally the Immaculate Virgin, preserved free from all stain of original sin,[12] was taken up body and soul into heavenly glory[13] when her earthly life was over, and exalted by the Lord as Queen over all things, that she might be the more fully conformed to

671

her Son, the Lord of lords, (cf. Apoc. 19:16) and conqueror of sin and death.[14]

III. The Blessed Virgin and the Church

60. In the words of the apostle there is but one mediator, "for there is but one God and one mediator of God and men, the man Christ Jesus, Who gave Himself a redemption for all" (1 Tim. 2:5-6). But Mary's function as mother of men in no way obscures or diminishes this unique mediation of Christ, but rather shows its power. But the Blessed Virgin's salutary influence on men originates not in any inner necessity but in the disposition of God. It flows forth from the superabundance of the merits of Christ, rests on his mediation, depends entirely on it and draws all its power from it. It does not hinder in any way the immediate union of the faithful with Christ, but on the contrary fosters it.

61. The predestination of the Blessed Virgin as Mother of God was associated with the incarnation of the Divine Word: in the designs of Divine Providence, she was the gracious mother of the divine Redeemer here on earth, and above all others and in a singular way, the generous associate and humble handmaid of the Lord. She conceived, brought forth, and nourished Christ, she presented Him to the Father in the temple, shared her Son's sufferings as He died on the cross. Thus, in a wholly singular way, she cooperated by her obedience, faith, hope, and burning charity in the work of the Savior in restoring supernatural life to souls. For this reason, she is a mother to us in the order of grace.

62. This motherhood of Mary in the order of grace continues uninterruptedly from the consent which she loyally gave at the Annunciation, and which she sustained without wavering beneath the cross, until the eternal fulfillment of all the elect. Taken up to heaven, she did not lay aside this saving office but by her manifold intercession continues to bring us the gifts of eternal salvation.[15] By her maternal charity, she cares for the brethren of her Son, who still journey on earth, surrounded by dangers and difficulties, until they are led into their blessed home. Therefore the Blessed Virgin is invoked in the Church under the titles of Advocate, Helper, Benefactress, and Mediatrix.[16] This, however, is so understood that it neither takes away anything from nor adds anything to the dignity and efficacy of Christ, the one Mediator.[17] No creature could ever be counted along with the Incarnate Word and Redeemer; but just as the priesthood of Christ is shared in various ways both by his ministers and the faithful, and as the

one goodness of God is radiated in different ways among his creatures, so also the unique mediation of the Redeemer does not exclude but rather gives rise to a manifold cooperation, which is but a sharing in this one source. The Church does not hesitate to profess this subordinate role of Mary, which it constantly experiences and recommends to the heartfelt attention of the faithful, so that, encouraged by this maternal help, they may the more closely adhere to the Mediator and Redeemer.

63. By reason of the gift and role of her divine motherhood, by which she is united with her Son, the Redeemer, and with her unique graces and functions, the Blessed Virgin is also intimately united to the Church. As St. Ambrose taught, the Mother of God is a type of the Church in the order of faith, charity, and perfect union with Christ.[18] For in the mystery of the Church, which is itself rightly called mother and virgin, the Blessed Virgin stands out in eminent and singular fashion as exemplar both of virgin and mother.[19] Through her faith and obedience she gave birth on earth to the very Son of the Father, not through the knowledge of man but by the overshadowing of the Holy Spirit, in the manner of a new Eve who placed her faith, not in the serpent of old but in God's messenger without wavering in doubt. The Son whom she brought forth is He Whom God placed as the first born among many brethren (Rom. 8:29), that is, the faithful in whose generation and formation she cooperates with a mother's love.

64. The Church, indeed, contemplating her hidden sanctity, imitating her charity, and faithfully fulfilling the Father's will, by receiving the word of God in faith, becomes herself a mother. By preaching and baptism she brings forth sons, who are conceived of the Holy Spirit and born of God, to a new and immortal life. She herself is a virgin, who keeps, in its entirety and purity, the faith she pledged to her spouse. Imitating the mother of her Lord, and by the power of the Holy Spirit, she keeps intact faith, firm hope, and sincere charity.[20]

65. But while in the most Blessed Virgin the Church has already reached that perfection whereby she exists without spot or wrinkle (cf. Eph. 5:27), the faithful still strive to conquer sin and increase in holiness. And so they turn their eyes to Mary, who shines forth to the whole community of the elect as the model of virtues. Devoutly meditating on her, and contemplating her in the light of the Word made man, the Church reverently penetrates more deeply into the great mystery of the Incarnation and becomes more and more like

her spouse. Having entered deeply into the history of salvation, Mary, in a way, unites in her person and re-echoes the most important doctrines of the faith: and when she is the subject of preaching and worship, she prompts the faithful to come to her Son, to His sacrifice, and to the love of the Father. Seeking after the glory of Christ, the Church becomes more like her lofty type, and continually progresses in faith, hope, and charity, seeking and doing the will of God in all things. The Church, therefore, in her apostolic work, too, rightly looks to her who gave birth to Christ, Who was thus conceived of the Holy Spirit and born of a virgin, in order that, through the Church, He could be born and increased in the hearts of the faithful. In her life, the Virgin has been a model of that motherly love with which all who join in the Church's apostolic mission for the regeneration of mankind should be animated.

IV. The Cult of the Blessed Virgin in the Church

66. Mary has, by grace, been exalted above all angels and men to a place second only to her Son's, as the most holy Mother of God who was involved in the mysteries of Christ: she is rightly honored by a special cult in the Church. From the earliest times, the Blessed Virgin is honored under the title of Mother of God, in whose protection the faithful take refuge together in prayer, in all their perils and needs.[21] Accordingly, following the Council of Ephesus there was a remarkable growth in the cult of the People of God towards Mary, in veneration and love, and in invocation and imitation, according to her own prophetic words: "All generations shall call me blessed, because He Who is mighty hath done great things to me" (Luke 1:48). This cult, as it has always existed in the Church, for all its uniqueness, differs essentially from the cult of adoration, which is offered equally to the Incarnate Word and to the Father and the Holy Spirit, and it is most favorable to it. The various forms of piety towards the Mother of God, which the Church has approved within the limits of sound and orthodox doctrine, according to the dispositions and understanding of the faithful, ensure that while the mother is honored, the Son, through Whom all things have their being (cf. Col. 1:15-16) and in Whom it has pleased the Father that all fullness should dwell (cf. Col. 1:19), is rightly known, loved, and glorified, and his commandments are observed.

67. The sacred synod teaches this Catholic doctrine advisedly and, at the same time, admonishes all the sons of the

Church that the cult, especially the liturgical cult, of the Blessed Virgin, be generously fostered, and that the practices and exercises of devotion towards her, recommended by the teaching authority of the Church in the course of centuries, be highly esteemed, and that those decrees, which were given in the early days regarding the cult images of Christ, the Blessed Virgin, and the saints, be religiously observed.[22] But it strongly urges theologians and preachers of the word of God to be careful to refrain as much from all false exaggeration as from too summary an attitude in considering the special dignity of the Mother of God.[23] Following the study of Sacred Scripture, the Fathers, the Doctors, and the liturgy of the Church, and under the guidance of the Church's magisterium, let them rightly illustrate the duties and privileges of the Blessed Virgin which always refer to Christ, the source of all truth, sanctity, and devotion. Let them carefully refrain from whatever might by word or deed lead the separated brethren or any others whatsoever into error about the true doctrine of the Church. Let the faithful remember moreover that true devotion consists neither in sterile nor transitory affection, nor in a certain vain credulity, but proceeds from true faith, by which we are led to recognize the excellence of the Mother of God, and we are moved to a filial love towards our mother and to the imitation of her virtues.

V. Mary, Sign of True Hope and Comfort for the Pilgrim People of God

68. In the meantime, the Mother of Jesus, in the glory which she possesses in body and soul in heaven, is the image and beginning of the Church as it is to be perfected in the world to come. Likewise, she shines forth on earth, until the day of the Lord shall come (cf. 2 Pet. 3:10), a sign of certain hope and comfort to the pilgrim People of God.

69. It gives great joy and comfort to this sacred synod that among the separated brethren, too, there are those who give due honor to the Mother of Our Lord and Saviour, especially among the Easterns, who, with devout mind and fervent impulse, give honor to the Mother of God, ever virgin.[24] The entire body of the faithful pours forth urgent supplications to the Mother of God and of men that she, who aided the beginnings of the Church by her prayers, may now, exalted as she is above all the angels and saints, intercede before her Son in the fellowship of all the saints, until all families of people, whether they are honored with the title of Christian or

675

whether they still do not know the Saviour, may be happily gathered together in peace and harmony into one People of God, for the glory of the Most Holy and Undivided Trinity.

Endnotes

1. Creed of the Roman mass; Symbol of Constantinople: Mansi 3, 566. Cf. Council of Ephesus; ibid. 4, 1130 (*et ibid.* 2, 665 and 4, 1071); Council of Chalcedon, ibid. 7, 111-116, Council of Constantinople II. ibid. 9, 375-396.

2. Canon of the Roman Mass.

3. Cf. St. Augustine, *De S. Virginitate*, 6: *PL* 40, 399.

4. Cf. Paul VI, *Allocution to the Council*, 4 December 1963: *AAS* 56 (1964), p. 37.

5. Cf. Germanus of Constantinople, *Hom. in Annunt. Deiparae: PG* 98, 328A; *In Dorm.* 2, Col. 357. Anastasius of Antioch. *Serm. 2 de Annunt.* 2: *PG* 89, 1377 AB; *Serm. 3*.2: Col. 1388 C. St. Andrew of Crete, *Can. in B.V. Nat.* 4: PG 97, 1321 B. *In B.V. Nat.* 1: Col. 812 A. *Hom. in Dorm.* 1: Col. 1068C. St. Sophronius, *Or. 2 in Annunt.* 18: *PG* 87 (3), 3237 BD.

6. St. Irenaeus, *Adv. Haer.* III, 22, 4: *PG* 7, 959 A, Harvey, 2, 123.

7. St. Irenaeus, ibid.: Harvey 2, 124.

8. St. Epiphanius, *Haer.* 78, 18: *PG* 42, 728 CD-729 AB.

9. St. Jerome, *Epist.* 22, 21: *PL* 22, 408. Cf. St. Augustine, *Serm.* 51, 2, 3: PL 38, 335; *Serm.* 232, 2: Col. 1108. St. Cyril of Jerusalem, *Catech.* 12, 15: PG 33, 741 AB. St. John Chrysostom, *In Ps.* 44, 7: *PG* 55, 193. St. John Damascene, *Hom. 2 in dorm. B.M.V.*, 3: *PG* 96, 728.

10. Cf. Council of Lateran A.D. 649, Can. 3: Mansi 10, 1151. St. Leo the Great, *Epist. ad Flav.: PL* 54, 759. Council of Chalcedon: Mansi 7, 462. St. Ambrose, *De instit. virg.: PL* 16, 320.

11. Cf. Pius XII, Encycl. *Mystici Corporis*, 29 June 1943: *AAS* 35 (1943), pp. 247-248.

12. Cf. Pius IX, Bull *Ineffabilis*, 8 Dec. 1854: *Acta Pii IX*, 1, 1, p. 616 ; *Denz.* 1641 (2803).

13. Cf. Pius XII, Const. Apost. *Munificentissimus*, 1 Nov. 1950: *AAS* 42 (1950): *Denz.* 2333 (3903). Cf. St. John Damascene, *Enc. in dorm. Dei Genitricis, Hom.* 2 and 3: *PG* 96, 722-762, esp. Col. 728 B. St. Germanus of Constantinople, *In S. Dei gen. dorm. Serm.* 1: *PG* 78 (6), 340-348; Serm. 3: Col. 362. St. Modestus of Jerusalem, *In dorm. SS. Deiparae: PG* 86 (2), 3277-3312.

14. Cf. Pius XII, Encycl. *Ad coeli Reginam*, 11 Oct. 1954: *AAS* 46 (1954), pp. 633-636: *Denz.* 3914 ff. Cf. St. Andrew of Crete, *Hom. 3 in dorm. SS Deiparae: PG* 97, 1090-1109. St. John Damascene, *De fide orth.*, IV, 14: *PG* 94, 1153-1168.

15. Cf. Kleutgen, corrected text *De mysterio verbi incarnati*, ch. IV: Mansi 53, 290. Cf. St. Andrew of Crete, *In nat. Mariae, Serm.* 4: *PG* 97, 865 A. St. Germanus of Constantinople, *In ann. Deiparae: PG* 93, 322 BC. *In dorm. Deiparae* III: Col. 362 D. St. John Damascene, *In dorm. B.V.M., Hom.* 1, 8: *PG* 96, 712 BC-713 A.

16. Cf. Leo XIII, Encycl. *Adjutricem populi*, 5 Sept. 1895: AAS 15 (1895-1896), p. 303. St. Pius X, Encycl. *Ad diem illum*, 2 Feb. 1904: *Acta 1*, p. 154; *Denz.* 1978a (3370). Pius XI, Encycl. *Miserentissimus*, 8 May 1928; *AAS* 20 (1928), p. 178. Pius XII, Radio Message 13 May 1946: *AAS* 38 (1946), p. 268.

17. St. Ambrose, *Epist.* 63: *PL* 16,1218

18. Ambrose, *Expos. Lc. II.* 7: *PL* 15;1555.

19. Cf. Pseudo Peter Damien, *Serm.* 63: *PL* 144, 861 AB. Geoffrey (de Breteuil) of St. Victor, *In nat. b.m.*, MS. Paris, Mazarine, 1002, fol. 109. Gerhoch of Reichersberg, *De gloria et honore Filii hominis* 10: *PL* 194, 1105AB.

20. St. Ambrose 1.c., and *Expos. Lc. X*, 24-25: *PL* 15, 1810. St. Augustine, *In Io. Tr.* 13. 12: *PL* 35, 1499. Cf. *Serm.* 191, 2, 3: *PL* 38, 1010, etc. Cf. also Ven. Bede, *In Lc. Expo.*, 1, ch. II: 92, 330. Isaac of Stella, *Serm.* 31: PL 194, 1863 A. 21. *"Sub tuum praesidium."*

21. *"Sub tuum praesidium."*

22. Council of Nicea II. AD. 787: Mansi 13, 378-379; *Denz.* 302 (600-601). Council of Trent, Session 25: Mansi 33, 171-172.

23. Cf. Pius XII, radio message, 24 Oct. 1954: *AAS* 46 (1954), p. 679 Encycl. *Ad coeli Reginam*, 11 Oct. 1954. *AAS* 46 (1954), p. 637.

Prayer

Most Holy and Immaculate Virgin Mary, our loving Mother, the powerful Help of Christians, and Mother of the Church, we dedicate ourselves entirely to your love and to your devoted service. We consecrate to you our minds, with their thoughts; our hearts, with their affections; our bodies, with their senses and all their powers; and we promise always to work for the greater glory of God and the salvation of souls.

Most glorious Virgin, since you have always been the Help of Christians and Mother of the Church, pray for us and continue to show yourself a Mother to us, especially in these times. Humble the enemies of our religion, and make their wicked designs ineffective. Bless and protect our Holy Father, the Pope. Enlighten and strengthen the Bishops and priests, and keep them always united and obedient to the Pope, the infallible teacher. Preserve incautious youth from godlessness and vice. Promote holy vocations, and increase the number of priests so that, through them, the reign of Jesus Christ may be preserved among us and may extend throughout the earth.

We beg you, dearest Mother, look with eyes of pity upon youth who are exposed to so many dangers, and upon poor sinners and the dying.

Great Mother of God, Mother of the Church, we also pray for ourselves. Teach us to reproduce in ourselves your virtues — particularly your faith, hope, love and humility — so that in our behavior, by our words and example, though we live in the midst of the world, we may imitate as far as possible your divine Son, Jesus, and may make you known and loved. Grant that the remembrance of your love for your children may so strengthen us as to make us victorious over the enemies of our souls in life and death, so that we may be united with you forever in Heaven. Amen.

Appendix A

Catholic Essentials

Appendix B

Basic Prayers

680

Appendix A
Catholic Essentials

The Ten Commandmens of God

1. I am the Lord your God, Who brought you out of the land of Egypt, out of the house of bondage. You shall not have strange gods before Me. You shall not make to yourself a graven thing, nor the likeness of any thing that is in heaven above, or in the earth beneath, nor of those things that are in the waters under the earth. You shall not adore them, nor serve them.

2. You shall not take the name of the Lord your God in vain.

3. Remember to keep holy the sabbath day.

4. Honor your father and your mother.

5. You shall not kill.

6. You shall not commit adultery.

7. You shall not steal.

8. You shall not bear false witness against your neighbor.

9. You shall not covet your neighbor's wife.

10. You shall not covet your neighbor's goods.

The Beatitudes

1. Blessed are the poor in spirit, for theirs is the Kingdom of Heaven.

2. Blessed are the meek, for they shall possess the land.

3. Blessed are they that mourn, for they shall be comforted.

4. Blest are they that hunger and thirst after justice, for they shall be filled.

5. Blessed are the merciful, for they shall obtain mercy.

6. Blessed are the pure of heart, for they shall see God.

7. Blessed are the peacmakers: they shall be called the children of God.

8. Blessed are they that suffer persecution for rightiousness sake, for theirs is the Kingdom of Heaven.

Precepts (Commandments) of the Church

1. "On Sundays and other Holy Days of Obligation, the faithful are bound to participate in the Mass." (Canon 1247)

2. "After having attained the age of discretion, each of the faithful is bound by an obligation faithfully to confess serious sins at least once a year [in the Sacrament of Penance]." (Canon 989)

3. "All the faithful, after they have been initiated into the Most Holy Eucharist, are bound by the obligation of receiving Holy Communion at least once a year.

   "This precept must be fulfilled during the Easter season unless it is fulfilled for a just cause at some other time during the year." (Canon 920)

4. "All members of the Christian faithful in their own way are bound to do penance in virtue of divine law; in order that all may be joined in a common observance of penance, penitential days are prescribed in which the Christian faithful in a special way pray, exercise works of piety and charity, and deny themselves by fulfilling their responsibilities more faithfully and especially by observing fast and abstinence according to the norm of the following canons.

   "All Fridays through the year and the time of Lent are penitential days and times throughout the universal Church.

   "Abstinence from eating meat or another food according to the prescriptions of the conference of bishops is to be observed on Fridays throughout the year unless they are solemnities; abstinence and fast are to be observed on Ash Wednesday and on the Friday of the Passion and Death of our Lord Jesus Christ." (Canons 1249-1251)

5. "The Christian faithful are obliged to assist with the needs of the Church so that the Church has what is necessary for divine worship, for apostolic works and works of charity and for the decent sustenance of ministers.

   "They are also obliged to promote social justice and, mindful of the precept of the Lord, to assist the poor from their own resources." (Canon 222)

Basic Prayers

Sign of the Cross

In the Name of the Father, and of the Son, and of the Holy Spirit. Amen.

The Lord's Prayer

Our Father, Who art in Heaven, hallowed be Thy Name; Thy kingdom come; Thy will be done on earth as it is in Heaven.

Give us this day our daily bread; and forgive us our trespasses as we forgive those who trespass against us; and lead us not into temptation, but deliver us from evil. Amen.

Hail Mary

Hail Mary, full of grace! The Lord is with thee; blessed are you among women, and blessed is the fruit of thy womb, Jesus.

Holy Mary, Mother of God, pray for us sinners, now and at the hour of our death. Amen.

Doxology

Glory be to the Father, and to the Son, and to the Holy Spirit. As it was in the beginning, is now, and ever shall be, world without end. Amen.

The Apostle's Creed

I believe in God the Father Almighty, Creator of Heaven and earth; And in Jesus Christ, His only Son, our Lord; Who was conceived by the Holy Spirit, born of the Virgin Mary; suffered under Pontius Pilate, was crucified, died, and was buried; He descended into hell; on the third day He rose again from the dead; He ascended into Heaven, sits at the right hand of God the Father Almighty; from thence He shall come to judge the living and the dead. I believe in the Holy Spirit; the holy Catholic Church; the Communion of Saints; the forgiveness of sins; the resurrection of the body; and life everlasting. Amen.

Act of Contrition

O My God, I am heartily sorry for having offended Thee and I detest all my sins because I dread the loss of Heaven and the pains of hell, but most of all because they offend Thee, my God, who are all good and deserving of all my love. I firmly resolve, with the help of Thy grace, to confess my sins, to do penance and to amend my life. Amen.

Hail Holy Queen

Hail Holy Queen, Mother of mercy; our life, our sweetness, and our hope. To thee do we cry, poor banished children of Eve. To thee do we send up our sighs, mourning and weeping in this valley of tears.

Turn then, most gracious Advocate, thine eyes of mercy toward us. And after this our exile show unto us the blessed fruit of thy womb, Jesus. O clement, O loving, O sweet Virgin Mary.

Pray for us, O Holy Mother of God, that we may be made worthy of the promises of Christ. Amen.

The Blessing Before Meals

Bless us, O Lord, and these Thy gifts, which we are about to receive from Thy bounty, through Christ our Lord. Amen.

The Blessing After Meals

We give Thee thanks, almighty God, for all Thy benefits, which we have received from Thy bounty, through Christ our Lord. Amen.

The Stations of the Cross

1. Jesus is condemned to death
2. Jesus bears His Cross
3. Jesus falls the first time
4. Jesus meets His Mother
5. Jesus is helped by Simon
6. Veronica wipes the face of Jesus
7. Jesus falls a second time
8. Jesus speaks to the women
9. Jesus falls a third time
10. Jesus is stripped of His garments
11. Jesus is nailed to the Cross
12. Jesus dies on the Cross
13. Jesus is taken down from the Cross
14. Jesus is placed in the tomb

The Mysteries of the Rosary (Prayerbook #27)

The Joyful Mysteries

1. The Annunciation of the Archangel Gabriel to the Virgin Mary.
2. The Visitation of the Virgin Mary to the Parents of St. John the Baptist.
3. The Birth of Our Lord at Bethlehem.
4. The Presentation of Our Lord in the Temple.
5. The Finding of Our Lord in the Temple.

The Sorrowful Mysteries

1. The Agony of Our Lord in the Garden of Gethsemane.
2. The Scourging of Our Lord at the Pillar.
3. The Crowning of Our Lord with Thorns.
4. The Carrying of the Cross by Our Lord to Calvary.
5. The Crucifixion and Death of Our Lord.

The Glorious Mysteries

1. The Resurrection of Our Lord from the Dead.
2. The Ascension of Our Lord into Heaven.
3. The Descent of the Holy Spirit upon the Disciples.
4. The Assumption of Our Blessed Lady into Heaven.
5. The Coronation of Our Blessed Lady as Queen of Heaven and Earth.

Translations are from the traditional forms or from the "Enchiridion." (1969)

*The prayer Our Lady of Fatima requested to be said
after every decade of the Rosary.*

O My Jesus, forgive us our sins and save us from the fires of hell, lead all souls to Heaven, especially those who have most need of Thy Mercy.

The Memorare (Prayerbook #30)

Remember, O most gracious Virgin Mary, that never was it known that anyone who fled to your protection, implored your help or sought your intercession was left unaided. Inspired with this confidence, I fly to you, O Virgin of virgins, my Mother. To you I come, before you I stand sinful and sorrowful. O Mother of the Word Incarnate, despise not my petitions but in your mercy hear and answer me. Amen.

St. Joseph Prayer After the Rosary (Prayerbook #8)

*Please note that Pope Leo XIII recommended a prayer to St. Joseph be said
after the Rosary. This prayer is our response.*

Glorious St. Joseph, spouse of the Immaculate Virgin, obtain for me and all the members of my family and loved ones, a confident, sinless, generous, and patient heart, and perfect resignation to the Divine Will. Be our guide, father, and model throughout life, that we may merit a death like yours, in the arms of Jesus and Mary.

Help us, St. Joseph, in our earthly strife to fulfill our responsibilities and ever to lead a pure and blameless life.

Heavenly Father, please ask the Holy Spirit, Who resides in the innermost recesses of my soul, to help me to call to mind all of my sins and faults. Help me to detach myself from these faults and sins so that I can be a useful instrument in the hands of the Most Holy Family to achieve Your distinctive plan for my life. Let me now pause for a few moments to think of my sins, faults and omissions.

Other Popular Prayers

All of the prayers in this appendix should be said regularly and taught to our children. One good method is to say one of these prayers every day with the family, until it is completely memorized, and then move on to another. Periodically review these prayers so that all of them are committed to memory. Some families add one of these prayers after the Rosary every day and rotate them once the family has memorized them.

Fatima Prayer to The Holy Trinity (Prayerbook #21)

Most Holy Trinity, Father, Son and Holy Spirit, I adore You profoundly. I offer You the most precious Body and Blood, Soul and Divinity of Jesus Christ, present in all the tabernacles of the world, in reparation for the outrages, sacrileges, and indifferences by which He is offended. By the infinite merits of His Most Sacred Heart and through the Immaculate Heart of Mary, I beg conversion of poor sinners. Amen.

Fatima Prayer to Jesus

Most Sacred Heart of Jesus, I believe, I adore, I trust and I love You. I ask pardon for those who do not believe, do not adore, do not trust, and do not love You.

Fatima Prayer of Daily Offering (Prayerbook #29)

O My Jesus, I offer this for love of You, for the conversion of poor sinners, and in reparation for all sins committed against the Immaculate Heart of Mary.

Fatima Prayer approvals
Nihil Obstat: Canon Joseph Galamba de Oliveira, Leiria, April 26, 1968
† Imprimatur: John, Bishop of Leiria, Leiria, April 26, 1968

Appendix C

Papal and Vatican Council II Documents

687

Encyclical Letter

Of His Holiness

Pope Paul VI

Of Human Life

Humanae Vitae

Issued July 25, 1968

Table of Contents

Bishops of U.S. Ask Christian Response

The sacredness of Christian marriage makes it a special concern of the teaching mission of the Church. Its dignity must be carefully safeguarded and its responsibilities fulfilled. The recent encyclical of Pope Paul VI reflects this concern.

The Holy Father, speaking as the supreme teacher of the Church, has reaffirmed the principles to be followed in forming the Christian conscience of married persons in carrying out their reponsibilities.

Recognizing his unique role in the Universal Church, we, the bishops of the Church in the United States, unite with him in calling upon our priests and people to receive with sincerity what he has taught, to study it carefully, and to form their consciences in its light.

We are aware of the difficulties that this teaching lays upon so many of our conscientious married people. But we must face the reality that struggling to live out the will of God will often entail sacrifice.

In confident trust in the firmness of their faith, in their loyalty to the Holy Father and to his office, and their reliance on Divine help, we ask of them a true Christian response to this teaching.

United States Bishops' Statement, Issued July 31, 1968

Pope John Paul II:
To Participants
in a Study Conference

The Church's teaching on contraception is not a matter for free discussion among theologians

The Holy Father received in audience on Friday, 5 June the participants in a study conference on responsible procreation. The conference was sponsored by the "Centre for Studies and Research on the Natural Regulations of Fertility" of the Department of Medicine of the Catholic University of the Sacred Heart. The Pope spoke to the group as follows:

Dear Brothers and Sisters,

1. I greet you most warmly and thank you for your presence, while I congratulate the "Centre for Studies and Research on the Natural Regulation of Fertility" of the Department of Medicine of the Catholic University of the Sacred Heart for having promoted again this year a conference for study and updating with regard to responsible procreation.

Your commitment enters into and participates in the mission of the Church, due to a pastoral concern which is among the most urgent and important. It is a question of helping spouses to live their marriage in a holy way. You have resolved to assist them in their journey towards holiness, so that they might completely fulfil their conjugal vocation.

It is well known that often one of the main anxieties that spouses encounter is constituted by the difficulty of realizing the ethical value of responsible procreation in their conjugal life, as the Second Vatican Council pointed out (cf. *Gaudium et Spes*, 51,1). The Council itself places at the foundation of a just solution to this problem the truth that there cannot be a real contradiction between the divine law regarding the transmission of human life and authentic married love (cf. ibid., 2). To speak of a "conflict of values or goods" and of the consequent need to "weigh" them, choosing one and rejecting the other, is not morally correct, and generates only confusion in the consciences of spouses. Christ's grace gives married couples the real capacity to fulfil the entire "truth" of their conjugal love. You wish concretely to witness this possibility, and thus to provide married couples with a precious form of help: that of fully living their conjugal communion. Notwithstanding the difficulties you may encounter, it is necessary to continue with generous dedication.

2. The difficulties you encounter are various kinds. The first, and in a certain sense the most serious, is that even within the Christian community voices have been heard, and are still being heard, which cast doubt upon *the very truth* of the Church's teaching. This teaching has been vigorously expressed by Vatican II, by the Encyclical *Humanae Vitae*, by the Apostolic Exhortation *Familiaris Consortio*

691

and by the recent Instruction "The Gift of Life." A grave responsibility derives from this: those who place themselves in open conflict with the law of God, authentically taught by the Church, guide spouses along a false path. The Church's teaching on contraception does not belong to the category of matter open to free discussion among theologians. Teaching the contrary amounts to leading the moral consciences of spouses into error.

The second difficulty is constituted by the fact that many think that the Christian teaching, though true, is yet impracticable, at least in some circumstances. As the Tradition of the Church has constantly taught, God does not command the impossible, but every commandment also carries with it a gift of grace which assists human freedom in fulfilling it. However, there is need for constant prayer, frequent recourse to the sacraments and the exercise of conjugal chastity. Your efforts must not be limited, then, to the mere teaching of a method for monitoring human fertility. This information must be inserted into the context of a *complete* educational proposal which addresses the *person* of the spouses, considered as a whole. Without this anthropological context, your proposal runs the risk of being misunderstood. You are well convinced of this, because you have always made a proper anthropological and ethical reflection the basis for your courses.

Today more than in the recent past, man is once again beginning to feel within himself the need for truth and for right reason in his daily experience. Be always ready to speak, without ambiguity, the truth concerning the good and the evil of the individual and of the family.

With these sentiments I wish to encourage the important apostolate that you propose to realize in the dioceses and in centres for family formation. In educating towards responsible procreation, know how to encourage married couples to follow the moral principles intrinsic to the natural law and innate in healthy Christian consciences. Teach men and women to seek and to love the will of God. Encourage them to respect and to fulfil the sublime vocation of married love and of the gift of life.

I gladly bless all of you, your loved ones and your initiatives in the apostolate.

Encyclical Letter of His Holiness Pope Paul VI On the Regulation of Birth

To the venerable Patriarchs, Archbishops and Bishops and other local ordinaries in peace and communion with the Apostolic See, to priests, the faithful and to everyone of good will.

Venerable brothers and beloved sons and daughters:

The Transmission of Life

1. The most serious duty of transmitting human life, for which married persons are the free and responsible collaborators of God

692

the Creator, has always been a source of great joys to them, even if sometimes accompanied by not a few difficulties and by distress.

At all times the fulfillment of this duty has posed grave problems to the conscience of married persons, but, with the recent evolution of society, changes have taken place that give rise to new questions which the Church could not ignore, having to do with a matter which so closely touches upon the life and happiness of humanity.

I. New Aspects of the Problem and Competency of the Magisterium

New Formulation of the Problem

2. The changes which have taken place are in fact noteworthy and of varied kinds. In the first place, there is the rapid demographic development. Fear is shown by many that world population is growing more rapidly than the available resources, with growing distress to many families and developing countries, so that the temptation for authorities to counter this danger with radical measures is great. Moreover, working and lodging conditions, as well as increased exigencies both in the economic field and in that of education, often make the proper education of a large number of children difficult today. A change is also seen both in the manner of considering the person of woman and her place in society, and in the value to be attributed to conjugal love in marriage, and also in the appreciation to be made of the meaning of conjugal acts in relation to that love.

Finally and above all, man has made stupendous progress in the domination and rational organization of the forces of nature, such that he tends to extend this domination to his own total being: to the body, to psychical life, to social life and even to the laws which regulate the transmission of life.

3. This new state of things gives rise to new questions. Granted the conditions of life today, and granted the meaning which conjugal relations have with respect to the harmony between husband and wife and to their mutual fidelity, would not a revision of the ethical norms, in force up to now, seem to be advisable, especially when it is considered that they cannot be observed without sacrifices, sometimes heroic sacrifices?

And again: by extending to this field the application of the so-called "principle of totality," could it not be admitted that the intention of a less abundant but more rationalized fecundity might transform a materially sterilizing intervention into a licit and wise control of birth? Could it not be admitted, that is, that the finality of procreation pertains to the totality of conjugal life, rather than to its single acts? It is also asked whether, in view of the increased sense of responsibility of modern people, the moment has not come for them to entrust to their reason and their will, rather than to the biological rhythms of their own bodies, the task of regulating birth.

Competency of the Magisterium

4. Such questions required from the teaching authority of the

Church a new and deeper reflection upon the principles of the moral teaching on marriage: a teaching founded on the natural law, illuminated and enriched by divine revelation.

No believer will wish to deny that the teaching authority of the Church is competent to interpret even the natural moral law. It is, in fact, indisputable, as our predecessors have many times declared,[1] that Jesus Christ, when communicating to Peter and to the Apostles His divine authority and sending them to teach all nations His commandments,[2] constituted them as guardians and authentic interpreters of all the moral law, not only, that is, of the law of the Gospel, but also of the natural law, which is also an expression of the will of God, the faithful fulfillment of which is equally necessary for salvation.[3]

Conformably to this mission of hers, the Church has always provided — and even more amply in recent times — a coherent teaching concerning both the nature of marriage and the correct use of conjugal rights and the duties of husband and wife.[4]

Special Studies

5. The consciousness of that same mission induced us to confirm and enlarge the study commission which our predecessor Pope John XXIII of happy memory had instituted in March, 1963. That commission which included, besides several experts in the various pertinent disciplines, also married couples, had as its scope the gathering of opinions on the new questions regarding conjugal life, and in particular on the regulation of births, and of furnishing opportune elements of information so that the magisterium could give an adequate reply to the expectation not only of the faithful, but also of world opinion.[5]

The work of these experts, as well as the successive judgments and counsels spontaneously forwarded by or expressly requested from a good number of our brothers in the episcopate, have permitted us to measure more exactly all the aspects of this complex matter. Hence with all our heart we express to each of them our lively gratitude.

Reply of the Magisterium

6. The conclusions at which the commission arrived could not, nevertheless, be considered by us as definitive, nor dispense us from a personal examination of this serious question; and this also because, within the commission itself, no full concordance of judgments concerning the moral norms to be proposed had been reached, and above all because certain criteria of solutions had emerged which depart from the moral teaching on marriage proposed with constant firmness by the teaching authority of the Church.

Therefore, having attentively sifted the documentation laid before us, after mature reflection and assiduous prayers, we now intend, by virtue of the mandate entrusted to us by Christ, to give our reply to these grave questions.

II. Doctrinal Principles
A Total Vision of Man

7. The question of birth, like every other problem regarding human life, is to be considered, beyond partial perspectives — whether of the biological or psychological, demographic or sociological orders — in the light of an integral vision of man and of his vocation, not only his natural and earthly, but also his supernatural and eternal vocation. And since, in the attempt to justify artificial methods of birth control, many have appealed to the demands both of conjugal love and of "responsible parenthood," it is good to state very precisely the true concept of these two great realities of married life, referring principally to what was recently set forth in this regard, and in a highly authoritative form, by the Second Vatican Council in its pastoral constitution *Gaudium et Spes (Constitution on the Church in the Modern World)*.

8. Conjugal love reveals its true nature and nobility when it is considered in its supreme origin, God, Who is love,[6] "the Father, from whom every family in heaven and on earth is named."[7]

Marriage is not, then, the effect of chance or the product of evolution of unconscious natural forces; it is the wise institution of the Creator to realize in mankind His design of love. By means of the reciprocal personal gift of self, proper and exclusive to them, husband and wife tend towards the communions of their beings in view of mutual personal perfection, to collaborate with God in the generation and education of new lives.

For baptized persons, moreover, marriage invests the dignity of a sacramental sign of grace, inasmuch as it represents the union of Christ and of the Church.

Its Characteristics

9. Under this light, there clearly appear the characteristic marks and demands of conjugal love, and it is of supreme importance to have an exact idea of these.

This love is first of all fully human, that is to say, of the senses and of the spirit at the same time. It is not, then, a simple transport of instinct and sentiment, but also, and principally, an act of the free will, intended to endure and to grow by means of the joys and sorrows of daily life, in such a way that husband and wife become one only heart and one only soul, and together attain their human perfection.

Then, this love is total, that is to say, it is a very special form of personal friendship, in which husband and wife generously share everything, without undue reservations or selfish calculations. Whoever truly loves his marriage partner loves not only for what he receives, but for the partner's self, rejoicing that he can enrich his partner with the gift of himself.

Again, this love is faithful and exclusive until death. Thus in fact do bride and groom conceive it to be on the day when they freely and in full awareness assume the duty of the marriage bond. A fidelity, this, which can sometimes be difficult, but is always possible, always noble and meritorious, as no one can deny. The example of so many married persons down through the centuries shows, not only that fidelity is according to the nature of marriage, but also that it is a source of profound and lasting happiness and finally, this love is fecund for it is not exhausted by the communions between husband and wife, but is destined to continue, raising up new lives. "Marriage and conjugal love are by their nature ordained toward the begetting and educating of children. Children are really the supreme gift of marriage and contribute very substantially to the welfare of their parents."[8]

Responsible Parenthood

10. Hence conjugal love requires in husband and wife an awareness of their mission of "responsible parenthood," which today is rightly much insisted upon, and which also must be exactly understood. Consequently it is to be considered under different aspects which are legitimate and connected with one another.

In relation to the biological processes, responsible parenthood means the knowledge and respect of their functions; human intellect discovers in the power of giving life biological laws which are part of the human person.[9]

In relation to the tendencies of instinct or passion, responsible parenthood means that necessary dominion which reason and will must exercise over them.

In relation to physical, economic, psychological and social conditions, responsible parenthood is exercised, either by the deliberate and generous decision to raise a numerous family, or by the decision, made for grave motives and with due respect for the moral law, to avoid for the time being, or even for an indeterminate period, a new birth.

Responsible parenthood also and above all implies a more profound relationship to the objective moral order established by God, of which a right conscience is the faithful interpreter. The responsible exercise of parenthood implies, therefore, that husband and wife recognize fully their own duties towards God, towards themselves, towards the family and towards society, in a correct hierarchy of values.

In the task of transmitting life, therefore, they are not free to proceed completely at will, as if they could determine in a wholly autonomous way the honest path to follow; but they must conform their activity to the creative intention of God, expressed in the very nature of marriage and of its acts, and manifested by the constant teaching of the Church.[10]

Respect for the Nature and Purpose of the Marriage Act

11. These acts, by which husband and wife are united in chaste intimacy, and by means of which human life is transmitted, are, as

696

the council recalled, "noble and worthy,"[11] and they do not cease to be lawful if, for causes independent of the will of husband and wife, they are foreseen to be infecund, since they always remain ordained towards expressing and consolidating their union. In fact, as experience bears witness, not every conjugal act is followed by a new life. God has wisely disposed natural laws and rhythms of fecundity which, of themselves, cause a separation in the succession of births. Nonetheless the Church, calling men back to the observance of the norms of the natural law, as interpreted by its constant doctrine, teaches that each and every marriage act *(quilibet matrimonii usus)* must remain open to the transmission of life.[12]

Two Inseparable Aspects: Union and Procreation

12. That teaching, often set forth by the magisterium, is founded upon the inseparable connection, willed by God and unable to be broken by man on his own initiative, between the two meanings of the conjugal act: the unitive meaning and the procreative meaning. Indeed, by its intimate structure, the conjugal act, while most closely uniting husband and wife, capacitates them for the generation of new lives, according to laws inscribed in the very being of man and of woman. By safeguarding both these essential aspects, the unitive and the procreative, the conjugal act preserves in its fullness the sense of true mutual love and its ordination towards man's most high calling to parenthood. We believe that people of our day are particularly capable of seizing the deeply reasonable and human character of this fundamental principle.

Faithfulness to God's Design

13. It is in fact justly observed that a conjugal act imposed upon one's partner without regard for his or her condition and lawful desires is not a true act of love, and therefore denies an exigency of right moral order in the relationships between husband and wife. Hence, one who reflects well must also recognize that a reciprocal act of love, which jeopardizes the responsibility to transmit life which God the Creator, according to particular laws, inserted therein, is in contradiction with the design constitutive of marriage, and with the will of the Author of life. To use this divine gift destroying, even if only partially, its meaning and its purpose is to contradict the nature both of man and of woman and of their most intimate relationship, and therefore it is to contradict also the plan of God and His will. On the other hand, to make use of the gift of conjugal love while respecting the laws of the generative process means to acknowledge oneself not to be the arbiter of the sources of human life, but rather the minister of the design established by the Creator. In fact, just as a person does not have unlimited dominion over his body in general, so also, with particular reason, he has no such dominion over his generative faculties as such, because of their intrinsic ordination towards raising up life, of which God is the principle. "Human life is sacred," Pope John XXIII recalled; "from its very inception it reveals the creating hand of God."[13]

Illicit Ways of Regulating Birth

14. In conformity with these landmarks in the human and Christian vision of marriage, we must once again declare that the direct interruption of the generative process already begun, and, above all, directly willed and procured abortion, even if for therapeutic reasons, are to be absolutely excluded as licit means of regulating birth.[14]

Equally to be excluded, as the teaching authority of the Church has frequently declared, is direct sterilization, whether perpetual or temporary, whether of the man or of the woman.[15] Similarly excluded is every action which, either in anticipation of the conjugal act, or in its accomplishment, or in the development of its natural consequences, proposes, whether as an end or as a means, to render procreation impossible.[16]

To justify conjugal acts made intentionally infertile, one cannot invoke as valid reasons the lesser evil, or the fact that such acts would constitute a whole together with the fertile acts already performed or to follow later, and hence would share in one and the same moral goodness. In truth, if it is sometimes licit to tolerate a lesser evil in order to avoid a greater evil or to promote a greater good,[17] it is not licit, even for the gravest reasons, to do evil so that good may follow therefrom[18] that is, to make into the object of a positive act of the will something which is intrinsically disorder, and hence unworthy of the human person, even when the intention is to safeguard or promote individual, family or social well-being. Consequently it is an error to think that a conjugal act which is deliberately contraceptive and so is intrinsically wrong could be made honest and right by the totality of a fruitful conjugal life.

Licitness of Therapeutic Means

15. The Church, on the contrary, does not at all consider illicit the use of those therapeutic means truly necessary to cure diseases of the organism, even if an impediment to procreation, which may be foreseen, should result therefrom, provided such impediment is not, for whatever motive, directly willed.[19]

Licitness of Recourse to Infertile Periods

16. To this teaching of the Church on conjugal morals, the objection is made today, as we observed earlier (no. 3), that it is the prerogative of the human intellect to dominate the energies offered by irrational nature and to direct them towards an end conformable to the good of man. Now, some may ask: in the present case, is it not reasonable in many circumstances to have recourse to artificial birth control if, thereby, we secure the harmony and peace of the family, and better conditions for the education of the children already born? To this question it is necessary to reply with clarity: the Church is the first to praise and recommend the intervention of intelligence in a function which so closely associates the rational creature with his

Creator; but she affirms that this must be done with respect for the order established by God.

If, then, there are serious motives to space out births, which derive from the physical or psychological conditions of husband and wife, or from external conditions, the Church teaches that it is then licit to take into account the natural rhythms immanent in the generative functions, for the use of marriage in the infertile periods only, and in this way to regulate birth without offending the moral principles which have been recalled earlier.[20]

The Church is consistent with herself when she considers recourse to the infertile periods to be licit, while at the same time condemning, as being always illicit, the use of means directly contrary to fertilization, even if such use is inspired by reasons which may appear honest and serious. In reality, there are essential differences between the two cases; in the former, the married couple make legitimate use of a natural disposition; in the latter, they impede the development of natural processes. It is true that, in the one and the other case, the married couple concur in the positive will of avoiding children for plausible reasons, seeking the certainty that offspring will not arrive; but it is also true that only in the former case are they able to renounce the use of marriage in the fertile periods when, for just motives, procreation is not desirable, while making use of it during infertile periods to manifest their affection and to safeguard their mutual fidelity. By so doing, they give proof of a truly and integrally honest love.

Grave Consequences of Methods of Artificial Birth Control

17. Upright people can even better convince themselves of the solid grounds on which the teaching of the Church in this field is based, if they care to reflect upon the consequences of methods of artificial birth control. Let them consider, first of all, how wide and easy a road would thus be opened up towards conjugal infidelity and the general lowering of morality. Not much experience is needed in order to know human weakness, and to understand that people — especially the young, who are so vulnerable on this point — have need of encouragement to be faithful to the moral law, so that they must not be offered some easy means of eluding its observance. It is also to be feared that the man, growing used to the employment of contraceptive practices, may finally lose respect for the woman and, no longer caring for her physical and psychological equilibrium, may come to the point of considering her as a mere instrument of selfish enjoyment, and no longer as his respected and beloved companion.

Let it be considered also that a dangerous weapon would thus be placed in the hands of those public authorities who take no heed of moral requirements. Who could blame a government for applying to the solution of the problems of the community those means acknowledged to be licit for married couples in the solution of a family problem? Who will stop rulers from favoring, from even imposing upon their peoples, if they were to consider it necessary, the method of contraception which they judge to be most effective? In such a way people, wishing to avoid individual, family, or social difficulties encountered in the observance of the divine law, would reach the point of placing at the mercy of the intervention of public authorities the most personal and most reserved sector of conjugal intimacy.

Consequently, if the mission of generating life is not to be exposed to the arbitrary will of people, one must necessarily recognize insurmountable limits to the possibility of man's domination over his own body and its functions; limits which no person, whether a private individual or one invested with authority, may licitly surpass. And such limits cannot be determined otherwise than by the respect due to the integrity of the human organism and its functions, according to the principles recalled earlier, and also according to the correct understanding of the "principle of totality" illustrated by our predecessor Pope Pius XII.[21]

The Church, Guarantor of True Human Values

18. It can be foreseen that this teaching will perhaps not be easily received by all: Too numerous are those voices — amplified by the modern means of propaganda — which are contrary to the voice of the Church. To tell the truth, the Church is not surprised to be made, like her divine Founder, a "sign of contradiction,"[22] yet she does not because of this cease to proclaim with humble firmness the entire moral law, both natural and evangelical. Of such laws the Church was not the author, nor consequently can she be their arbiter; she is only their depository and their interpreter, without ever being able to declare to be licit that which is not so by reason of its intimate and unchangeable opposition to the true good of mankind.

In defending conjugal morals in their integral wholeness, the Church knows that she contributes towards the establishment of a truly human civilization; she engages everyone not to abdicate from their own responsibility in order to rely on technical means; by that very fact she defends the dignity of man and wife. Faithful to both the teaching and the example of the Savior, she shows herself to be the sincere and disinterested friend of everyone, whom she wishes to help, even during their earthly sojourn, "to share as sons and daughters in the life of the living God, the Father of all mankind."[23]

III. Pastoral Directives
The Church,
Mater et Magistra

19. Our words would not be an adequate expression of the thought and solicitude of the Church, mother and teacher of all peoples, if, after having recalled everyone to the observance and respect of the divine law regarding matrimony, we did not strengthen them in the path of honest regulation of birth, even amid the difficult conditions which today afflict families and peoples. The Church, in fact, cannot have a different conduct towards people than that of the Redeemer.

700

She knows their weaknesses, has compassion on the crowd, receives sinners; but she cannot renounce the teaching of the law which is, in reality, that law proper to a human life restored to its original truth and conducted by the spirit of God.[24]

Possibility of Observing the Divine Law

20. The teaching of the Church on the regulation of birth, which promulgates the divine law, will easily appear to many to be difficult or even impossible of actuation. And indeed, like all great beneficent realities, it demands serious engagement and much effort, individual, family and social effort. More than that, it would not be practicable without the help of God, who upholds and strengthens the good will of all people. Yet, to anyone who reflects well, it cannot but be clear that such efforts ennoble man and are beneficial to the human community.

Mastery of Self

21. The honest practice of regulation of birth demands first of all that husband and wife acquire and possess solid convictions concerning the true values of life and of the family, and that they tend towards securing perfect self-mastery. To dominate instinct by means of one's reason and free will undoubtedly requires ascetical practices, so that the affective manifestations of conjugal life may observe the correct order, in particular with regard to the observance of periodic continence. Yet this discipline which is proper to the purity of married couples, far from harming conjugal love, rather confers on it a higher human value. It demands continual effort yet, thanks to its beneficent influence, husband and wife fully develop their personalities, being enriched with spiritual values. Such discipline bestows upon family life fruits of serenity and peace, and facilitates the solution of other problems; it favors attention for one's partner, helps both parties to drive out selfishness, the enemy of true love; and deepens their sense of responsibility. By its means, parents acquire the capacity of having a deeper and more efficacious influence in the education of their offspring; little children and youths grow up with a just appraisal of human values, and in the serene and harmonious development of their spiritual and sensitive faculties.

Creating an Atmosphere Favorable to Chastity

22. On this occasion, we wish to draw the attention of educators, and of all who perform duties of responsibility in regard to the common good of human society, to the need of creating an atmosphere favorable to education in chastity, that is, to the triumph of healthy liberty over license by means of respect for the moral order.

Everything in the modern media of social communications which leads to sense excitation and unbridled customs, as well as every form of pornography and licentious performances, must arouse the frank and unanimous reaction of all those who are solicitous for the progress of civilization and the defense of the common good of the human spirit. Vainly would one seek to justify such depravation with the pretext of artistic or scientific needs,[25] or to deduce an argument from the freedom allowed in this sector by the public authorities.

Appeal to Public Authorities

23. To rulers, who are those principally responsible for the common good, and who can do so much to safeguard moral customs, we say: Do not allow the morality of your peoples to be degraded; do not permit that by legal means practices contrary to the natural and divine law be introduced into that fundamental cell, the family. Quite other is the way in which public authorities can and must contribute to the solution of the demographic problem: namely, the way of a provident policy for the family, of a wise education of peoples in respect of moral law and the liberty of citizens.

We are well aware of the serious difficulties experienced by public authorities in this regard, especially in the developing countries. To their legitimate preoccupations we devoted our encyclical letter *Populorum Progressio* (The Development of Peoples). But with our predecessor Pope John XXIII, we repeat: no solution to these difficulties is acceptable "which does violence to man's essential dignity" and is based only on an utterly materialistic conception of man himself and of his life. The only possible solution to this question is one which envisages the social and economic progress both of individuals and of the whole of human society, and which respects and promotes true human values.[26] Neither can one, without grave injustice, consider divine providence to be responsible for what depends, instead, on a lack of wisdom in government, on an insufficient sense of social justice, on selfish monopolization, or again on blame-worthy neglect in confronting the efforts and the sacrifices necessary to ensure the raising of living standards of a people and of all its children.[27]

May all responsible public authorities—as some are already doing so laudably—generously revive their efforts. And may mutual aid between all the members of the great human family never cease to grow: This is an almost limitless field which thus opens up to the activity of the great international organizations.

To Men of Science

24. We wish now to express our encouragement to men of science, who "can considerably advance the welfare of marriage and the family, along with peace of conscience, if by pooling their efforts they labor to explain more thoroughly the various conditions favoring a proper regulation of births."[28] It is particularly desirable that, according to the wish already expressed by Pope Pius XII, medical science succeed in providing a sufficiently secure basis for a regulation of birth, founded on the observance of natural rhythms.[29] In this way, scientists and especially Catholic scientists will contribute to demonstrate in actual fact that, as the Church teaches, "a true contradiction cannot exist between the divine laws pertaining to the transmission of life and those pertaining to the fostering of authentic conjugal love."[30]

To Christian Husbands and Wives

25. And now our words more directly address our own children, particularly those whom God calls to serve Him in marriage. The Church, while teaching that the demands of the divine law may not be broken, announces the tidings of salvation, and by means of the sacraments opens up the paths of grace, which makes man a new creature, capable of corresponding with love and true freedom to the design of his Creator and Savior, and of finding the yoke of Christ to be sweet.[31]

Christian married couples, then, docile to her voice must remember that their Christian vocation, which began at Baptism, is further specified and reinforced by the Sacrament of Matrimony. By it husband and wife are strengthened and as it were consecrated for the faithful accomplishment of their proper duties, for the carrying out of their proper vocation even to perfection, and the Christian witness which is proper to them before the whole world.[32] To them the Lord entrusts the task of making visible to men the holiness and sweetness of the law which unites the mutual love of husband and wife with their cooperation with the love of God the Author of human life.

We do not at all intend to hide the sometimes serious difficulties in-herent in the life of Christian married persons; for them as for everyone else, "the gate is narrow and the way is hard, that leads to life."[33] But the hope of that life must illuminate their way, as with courage they strive to live with wisdom, justice and piety in this present time,[34] knowing that the figure of this world passes away.[35]

Let married couples, then, face up to the efforts needed, supported by the faith and hope which "do not disappoint...because God's love has been poured into our hearts through the Holy Spirit, who has been given to us."[36] Let them implore divine assistance by persevering prayer; above all, let them draw from the source of grace and charity in the Eucharist. And if sin should still keep its hold over them, let them not be discouraged, but rather have recourse with humble perseverance to the mercy of God, which is poured forth in the Sacrament of Penance. In this way they will be enabled to achieve the fullness of conjugal life described by the Apostle: "husbands, love your wives, as Christ loved the Church...husbands should love their wives as their own bodies. He who loves his wife loves himself. For no man ever hates his own flesh, but nourishes and cherishes it, as Christ does the Church...this is a great mystery, and I mean in reference to Christ and the Church. However, let each one of you love his wife as himself, and let the wife see that she respects her husband."[37]

Apostolate in Homes

26. Among the fruits which ripen forth from a generous effort of fidelity to the divine law, one of the most precious is that married couples themselves not infrequently feel the desire to communicate their experience to others. Thus there comes to be included in the vast pattern of the vocation of the laity a new and most noteworthy form of the apostolate of like to like; it is married couples themselves who become apostles and guides to other married couples. This is assuredly, among so many forms of apostolate, one of those which seem most opportune today.[38]

To Doctors and Medical Personnel

27. We hold those physicians and medical personnel in the highest esteem who, in the exercise of their profession, value above every human interest the superior demands of their Christian vocation. Let them persevere, therefore, in promoting on every occasion the discovery of solutions inspired by faith and right reason, let them strive to arouse this conviction and this respect in their associates. Let them also consider as their proper professional duty the task of acquiring all the knowledge needed in this delicate sector, so as to be able to give to those married persons who consult them wise counsel and healthy direction, such as they have a right to expect.

To Priests

28. Beloved priest sons, by vocation you are the counselors and spiritual guides of individual persons and of families. We now turn to you with confidence. Your first task— especially in the case of those who teach moral theology—is to expound the Church's teaching on marriage without ambiguity. Be the first to give, in the exercise of your ministry, the example of loyal internal and external obedience to the teaching authority of the Church. That obedience, as you know well, obliges not only because of the reasons adduced, but rather because of the light of the Holy Spirit, which is given in a particular way to the pastors of the Church in order that they may illustrate the truth.[39] You know, too, that it is of the utmost importance, for peace of consciences and for the unity of the Christian people, that in the field of morals as well as in that of dogma, all should attend to the magisterium of the Church, and all should speak the same language. Hence, with all our heart we renew to you the heartfelt plea of the great Apostle Paul: "I appeal to you, brethren, by the name of Our Lord Jesus Christ, that all of you agree and that there be no dissensions among you, but that you be united in the same mind and the same judgment."[40]

29. To diminish in no way the saving teaching of Christ constitutes an eminent form of charity for souls. But this must ever be accompanied by patience and goodness, such as the Lord Himself gave example of in dealing with people. Having come not to condemn but to save,[41] He was uncompromising with evil, but merciful toward individuals.

In their difficulties, may married couples always find, in the words and in the heart of a priest, the echo of the voice and the love of the Redeemer.

And then speak with confidence, beloved sons, fully convinced that the spirit of God, while He assists the magisterium in proposing doctrine, illumines internally the hearts of the faithful inviting them to give their assent. Teach married couples the indispensable way of prayer; prepare them to have recourse often and with faith to the sacraments of the Eucharist and of Penance, without ever allowing themselves to be discouraged by their own weakness.

To Bishops

30. Beloved and venerable brothers in the episcopate, with whom we most intimately share the solicitude of the spiritual good of the people of God, at the conclusion of this encyclical our reverent and affectionate thought turn to you. To all of you we extend an urgent invitation. At the head of the priests, your collaborators, and of your faithful, work ardently and incessantly for the safeguarding and the holiness of marriage, so that it may always be lived in its entire human and Christian fullness. Consider this mission as one of your most urgent responsibilities at the present time.

As you know, it implies concerted pastoral action in all the fields of human activity, economic, cultural and social; for, in fact, only a simultaneous improvement in these various sectors will make it possible to render the life of parents and of children within their families not only tolerable, but easier and more joyous, to render the living together in human society more fraternal and peaceful, in faithfulness to God's design for the world.

Final Appeal

31. Venerable brothers, most beloved sons, and everyone of good will, great indeed is the work of education, of progress and of love to which we call you, upon the foundation of the Church's teaching, of which the successor of Peter is, together with his brothers in the episcopate, the depositary and interpreter. Truly a great work, as we are deeply convinced, both for the world and for the Church, since the human person cannot find true happiness—towards which he aspires with all his being— other than in respect of the laws written by God in his very nature, laws which he must observe with intelligence and love. Upon this work, and upon all of you, and especially upon married couples, we invoke the abundant graces of the God of holiness and mercy, and in pledge thereof we impart to you all our apostolic blessing.

Given at Rome, from St. Peter's, this 25th day of July, feast of St. James the Apostle, in the year 1968, the sixth of our pontificate.

PAULUS PP. VI.

Footnotes

1. Cf. Pius IX, encyclical *Qui Pluribus*, Nov. 9, 1846; in PII IX P.M. Acta, I, pp. 9-10; St. Pius X, encyc. *Singulari Quadam*, Sept. 24, 1912; in AAS IV (1912), p. 658; Pius XI, encyc. *Casti Connubii*, Dec. 31, 1930; in AAS XXII (1930), pp. 579-581; Pius XII, allocution *Magnificate Dominum* to the episcopate of the Catholic world, Nov. 2, 1954; in AAS XLVI (1954), pp. 671-672; John XXIII, encyc. *Mater et Magistra*, May 15, 1961; in AAS LIII (1961), p. 457.

2. Cf. Matt. 28:18-19.

3. Cf. Matt. 7:21.

4. Cf. *Catechismus Romanus Concilii Tridentini*, part II, ch. VIII; Leo XIII, encyc. *Arcanum*, Feb. 19, 1880; in *Acta Leonis* XIII, II (1881), pp. 26-29; Pius XI, encyc. *Divini Illius Magistri*, Dec. 31, 1929, in AAS XXII (1930), pp. 58-61; encyc. *Casti Connubii*, in AAS XXII (1930), pp. 545-546; Pius XII, alloc. to the Italian medico-biological union of St. Luke, Nov. 12, 1944, in *Discorsi e Radiomessaggi*, VI, pp. 191-192; to the Italian Catholic union of midwives, Oct. 29, 1951, in AAS XLIII (1951), pp. 857-859; to the seventh Congress of the International Society of Haematology, Sept. 12, 1958, in AAS L (1958), pp. 734-735; John XXIII, encyc. *Mater et Magistra*, in AAS LIII (1961), pp. 446-447; *Codex Iuris Canonici*, Canon 1067; Can. 1968, S 1; Can. 1066, S 1-2; Second Vatican Council, pastoral constitution *Gaudium et Spes*, nos. 47-52.

5. Cf. Paul VI, allocution to the Sacred College, June 23, 1964, in AAS LVI (1964), p. 588; to the Commission for Study of Problems of Population, Family, and Birth, March 27, 1965, in AAS LVII (1965), p. 388, to the National Congress of the Italian Society of Obstetrics and Gynaecology, Oct. 29, 1966, in AAS LVIII (1966), p. 1168.

6. Cf. 1 John 4:8.

7. Cf. Eph. 3:15.

8. Cf. Second Vatican Council, pastoral constitution *Gaudium et Spes*, no. 50.

9. Cf. St. Thomas, *Summa Theologica*, I-II, q. 94, art. 2.

10. Cf. pastoral constitution *Gaudium et Spes*, nos. 50, 51.

11. Ibid., no. 49.

12. Cf. Pius XI, encyc. *Casti Connubii*, in AAS XXII (1930), p. 560; Pius XII, in AAS XLIII (1951), p. 843.

13. Cf. John XXIII, encyc. *Mater et Magistra*, in AAS LIII (1961), p. 447.

14. Cf. *Catechismus Romanus Concilii Tridentini*, part. II, Ch. VIII; Pius XI, encyc. *Casti Connubii*, in AAS XXII (1930), pp. 562-564; Pius XII, *Discorsi e Radiomessaggi*, CI (1944), pp. 191-192; AAS XLIII (1951), pp. 842-843; pp. 857-859; John XXIII, encyc. *Pacem in Terris*, Apr. 11, 1963, in AAS LV (1963), pp. 259-260; *Gaudium et Spes*, no. 51.

15. Cf. Pius XI, encyc. *Casti Connubii*, in AAS XXII (1930) p. 565; decree of the Holy Office, Feb. 22, 1940, in AAS L (1958), pp. 734-735.

16. Cf. *Catechismus Romanus Concilii Tridentini*, part. II, Ch. VIII; Pius XI, encyc. *Casti Connubii*, in AAS XXII (1930), pp. 559-561; Pius XII, AAS XLIII (1951), p. 843; AAS L. (1958), pp. 734-735; John XXIII, encyc. *Mater et Magistra*, in AAS LIII (1961), p. 447.

17. Cf. Pius XII, alloc. to the National Congress of the Union of Catholic Jurists, Dec. 6, 1953, in AAS XLV (1953), pp. 798-799.

18. Cf. Rom. 3:8.

19. Cf. Pius XII, alloc. to Congress of the Italian Association of Urology, Oct. 8, 1953, in AAS XLV (1953), pp. 674-675; AAS L (1958), pp. 734-735.

20. Cf. Pius XII, AAS XLIII (1951), p. 846.

706

21. Cf. AAS XLV (1953), pp. 674-675; AAS XLVIII (1956), pp. 461-462.

22. Cf. Luke 2:34.

23. Cf. Paul VI, encyc. *Populorum Progressio*, March 26, 1967, no. 21.

24. Cf. Rom. 8.

25. Cf. Second Vatican Council, decree *Inter Mirifica* on the Media of Social Communication, nos. 6-7.

26. Cf. encyc. *Mater et Magistra*, in AAS LIII (1961), p. 447

27. Cf. encyc. *Populorum Progressio*, nos. 48-55.

28. Cf. pastoral constitution *Gaudium et Spes*, no. 52.

29. Cf. Matt. 11:30.

30. Cf. pastoral constitution *Gaudium et Spes*, no. 51.

31. Cf. Matt. 11:30.

32. Cf. pastoral constitution *Gaudium et Spes*, no. 48; Second Vatican Council, dogmatic constitution *Lumen Gentium*, no. 35.

33. Matt. 7:14; cf. Heb. 11:12.

34. Cf. Tit. 2:12.

35. Cf. 1 Cor. 7:31.

36. Cf. Rom. 5:5.

37. Eph. 5:25, 28-29, 32-33.

38. Cf. dogmatic constitution *Lumen Gentium*, nos. 35 and 41; pastoral constitution *Gaudium et Spes*, nos. 48-49; Second Vatican Council, decree *Apostolicam Actuositatem*, no. 11.

39. Cf. dogmatic constitution *Lumen Gentium*, no. 25.

40. Cf. 1 Cor. 1:10.

41. Cf. John 3:17.

APOSTOLIC EXHORTATION

THE ROLE OF
THE CHRISTIAN FAMILY
IN THE MODERN WORLD

Familiaris Consortio

Addressed by His Holiness

POPE JOHN PAUL II
TO THE EPISCOPATE
TO THE CLERGY
AND TO THE FAITHFUL
OF THE WHOLE CATHOLIC CHURCH

CONTENTS

INTRODUCTION

The Church at the Service of the Family

1. The family in the modern world, as much as and perhaps more than any other institution, has been beset by the many profound and rapid changes that have affected society and culture. Many families are living this situation in fidelity to those values that constitute the foundation of the institution of the family. Others have become uncertain and bewildered over their role or even doubtful and almost unaware of the ultimate meaning and truth of conjugal and family life. Finally, there are others who are hindered by various situations of injustice in the realization of their fundamental rights.

Knowing that marriage and the family constitute one of the most precious of human values, the Church wishes to speak and offer her help to those who are already aware of the value of marriage and the family and seek to live it faithfully, to those who are uncertain and anxious and searching for the truth, and to those who are unjustly impeded from living freely their family lives. Supporting the first, illuminating the second and assisting the others, the Church offers her services to every person who wonders about the destiny of marriage and the family.[1]

In a particular way the Church addresses the young, who are beginning their journey towards marriage and family life, for the purpose of presenting them with new horizons, helping them to discover the beauty and grandeur of the vocation to love and the service of life.

The Synod of 1980 in Continuity with Preceding Synods

2. A sign of this profound interest of the Church in the family was the last Synod of Bishops, held in Rome from September 26 to October 25, 1980. This was a natural continuation of the two preceding Synods:[2] the Christian family, in fact, is the first community called to announce the Gospel to the human person during growth and to bring him or her, through a progressive education and catechesis, to full human and Christian maturity.

Furthermore, the recent Synod is logically connected in some way as well with that on the ministerial priesthood and on justice in the modern world. In fact, as an educating community, the family must help man to discern his own vocation and to accept responsibility in the search for greater justice, educating him from the beginning in interpersonal relationships, rich in justice and in love.

At the close of their assembly, the Synod Fathers presented me with a long list of proposals in which they had gathered the fruits of their reflections, which had matured over intense days of work, and they asked me unanimously to be a spokesman before humanity of the Church's lively care for the family and to give suitable indications for renewed pastoral effort in this fundamental sector of the life of man and of the Church.

As I fulfill that mission with this Exhortation thus actuating in a particular matter the apostolic ministry with which I am entrusted, I wish to thank all the members of the Synod for the very valuable contribution of teaching and experience that they made, especially through the *Propositiones*, the text of which I am entrusting to the Pontifical Council for the Family with instructions to study it so as to bring out every aspect of its rich content.

The Precious Value of Marriage and of the Family

3. Illuminated by the faith that gives her an understanding of all the truth concerning the great value of marriage and the family and their deepest meaning, the Church once again feels the pressing need to proclaim the Gospel, that is the "good news," to all people without exception, in particular to all those who are called to marriage and are preparing for it, to all married couples and parents in the world.

The Church is deeply convinced that only by the acceptance of the Gospel are the hopes that man legitimately places in marriage and in the family capable of being fulfilled.

Willed by God in the very act of creation,[3] marriage and the family are interiorly ordained to fulfillment in Christ[4] and have need of His graces in order to be healed from the wounds of sin[5] and restored to their "beginning,"[6] that is, to full understanding and the full realization of God's plan.

At a moment of history in which the family is the object of numerous forces that seek to destroy it or in some way to deform it, and aware that the well being of society and her own good are intimately tied to the good of the family,[7] the Church perceives in a more urgent and compelling way her mission of proclaiming to all people the plan of God for marriage and the family, ensuring their full vitality and human and Christian development, and thus contributing to the renewal of society and of the People of God.

PART ONE

BRIGHT SPOTS AND SHADOWS FOR THE FAMILY TODAY

The Need To Understand the Situation

4. Since God's plan for marriage and the family touches men and women in the concreteness of their daily existence in specific social and cultural situations, the Church ought to apply herself to understanding the situations within which marriage and the family are lived today, in order to fulfill her task of serving.[8]

This understanding is, therefore, an inescapable requirement of the work of evangelization. It is, in fact, to the families of our times that the Church must bring the unchangeable and ever new Gospel of Jesus Christ, just as it is the families involved in the present conditions of the world that are called to accept and to live the plan of God that pertains to them. Moreover, the call and demands of the Spirit resound in the very events of history, and so the Church can also be guided to a more profound understanding of the inexhaustible mystery of marriage and the family by the circumstances, the

713

questions and the anxieties and hopes of the young people, married couples and parents of today.[9]

To this ought to be added a further reflection of particular importance at the present time. Not infrequently ideas and solutions which are very appealing, but which obscure in varying degrees the truth and the dignity of the human person, are offered to the men and women of today, in their sincere and deep search for a response to the important daily problems that affect their married and family life. These views are often supported by the powerful and pervasive organization of the means of social communication, which subtly endanger freedom and the capacity for objective judgment.

Many are already aware of this danger to the human person and are working for the truth. The Church, with her evangelical discernment, joins with them, offering her own service to the truth, to freedom and to the dignity of every man and every woman.

Evangelical Discernment

5. The discernment effected by the Church becomes the offering of an orientation in order that the entire truth and the full dignity of marriage and the family may be preserved and realized.

This discernment is accomplished through the sense of faith,[10] which is a gift that the Spirit gives to all the faithful,[11] and is therefore the work of the whole Church according to the diversity of the various gifts and charisms that, together with and according to the responsibility proper to each one, work together for a more profound understanding and activation of the word of God. The Church, therefore, does not accomplish this discernment only through the Pastors, who teach in the name and with the power of Christ, but also through the laity: Christ "made them His witnesses and gave them understanding of the faith and the grace of speech (cf. Acts 2:17-18; Rv. 19:10), so that the power of the Gospel might shine forth in their daily social and family life."[12] The laity, moreover, by reason of their particular vocation have the specific role of interpreting the history of the world in the light of Christ, in as much as they are called to illuminate and organize temporal realities according to the plan of God, Creator and Redeemer.

The "supernatural sense of faith"[13] however does not consist solely or necessarily in the consensus of the faithful. Following Christ, the Church seeks the truth, which is not always the same as the majority opinion. She listens to conscience and not to power, and in this way she defends the poor and the downtrodden. The Church values sociological and statistical research, when it proves helpful in understanding the historical context in which pastoral action has to be developed and when it leads to a better understanding of the truth. Such research alone, however, is not to be considered in itself an expression of the sense of faith.

Because it is the task of the apostolic ministry to ensure that the Church remains in the truth of Christ and to lead her ever more deeply into that truth, the Pastors must promote the sense of the faith in all the faithful, examine and authoritatively judge the genuineness of its expressions, and educate the faithful in an ever more mature evangelical discernment.[14]

Christian spouses and parents can and should offer their unique and irreplaceable contribution to the elaboration of an authentic evangelical discernment in the various situations and cultures in which men and women live their marriage and their family life. They are qualified for this role by their charism or specific gift, the gift of the sacrament of matrimony.[15]

The Situation of the Family in the World Today

6. The situation in which the family finds itself presents positive and negative aspects: the first are a sign of the salvation of Christ operating in the world; the second, a sign of the refusal that man gives to the love of God.

On the one hand, in fact, there is a more lively awareness of personal freedom and greater attention to the quality of interpersonal relationships in marriage, to promoting the dignity of women, to responsible procreation, to the education of children. There is also an awareness of the need for the development of interfamily relationships, for reciprocal spiritual and material assistance, the rediscovery of the ecclesial mission proper to the family and its responsibility for the building of a more just society. On the other hand, however, signs are not lacking of a disturbing degradation of some fundamental values: a mistaken theoretical and practical concept of the independence of the spouses in relation to each other; serious misconceptions regarding the relationship of authority between parents and children; the concrete difficulties that the family itself experiences in the transmission of values; the growing number of divorces; the scourge of abortion; the ever more frequent recourse to sterilization; the appearance of a truly contraceptive mentality.

At the root of these negative phenomena there frequently lies a corruption of the idea and the experience of freedom, conceived not as a capacity for realizing the truth of God's plan for marriage and the family, but as an autonomous power of self-affirmation, often against others, for one's own selfish well-being.

Worthy of our attention also is the fact that, in the countries of the so-called Third World, families often lack both the means necessary for survival, such as food, work, housing and medicine, and the most elementary freedoms. In the richer countries, on the contrary, excessive prosperity and the consumer mentality, paradoxically joined to a certain anguish and uncertainty about the future, deprive married couples of the generosity and courage needed for raising up new human life: thus life is often perceived not as a blessing, but as a danger from which to defend oneself.

The historical situation in which the family lives therefore appears as an interplay of light and darkness.

This shows that history is not simply a fixed progression towards what is better, but rather an event of freedom, and even a struggle between freedoms that are in mutual conflict, that is, according to the well-known expression of St. Augustine, a conflict between two loves: the love of God to the point of disregarding self, and the love of self to the point of disregarding God.[16]

It follows that only an education for love rooted in faith can lead to the capacity of interpreting "the signs of the times," which are the historical expression of this two-fold love.

The Influence of Circumstances on the Consciences of the Faithful

7. Living in such a world, under the pressures coming above all from the mass media, the faithful do not always remain immune from the obscuring of certain fundamental values, nor set themselves up as the critical conscience of family culture and as active agents in the building of an authentic family humanism.

Among the more troubling signs of this phenomenon, the Synod Fathers stressed the following, in particular: the spread of divorce and of recourse to a new union, even on the part of the faithful; the acceptance of purely civil marriage in contradiction to the vocation of the baptized to "be married in the Lord;" the celebration of the marriage sacrament without living faith, but for other motives; the rejection of the moral norms that guide and promote the human and Christian exercise of sexuality in marriage.

Our Age Needs Wisdom

8. The whole Church is obliged to a deep reflection and commitment, so that the new culture now emerging may be evangelized in depth, true values acknowledged, the rights of men and women defended, and justice promoted in the very structures of society. In this way the "new humanism" will not distract people from their relationship with God, but will lead them to it more fully.

Science and its technical applications offer new and immense possibilities in the construction of such a humanism. Still, as a consequence of political choices that decide the direction of research and its applications, science is often used against its original purpose, which is the advancement of the human person.

It becomes necessary, therefore, on the part of all, to recover an awareness of the primacy of moral values, which are the values of the human person as such. The great task that has to be faced today for the renewal of society is that of recapturing the ultimate meaning of life and its fundamental values. Only an awareness of the primacy of these values enables man to use the immense possibilities given him by science in such a way as to bring about the true advancement of the human person in his or her whole truth, in his or her freedom and dignity. Science is called to ally itself with wisdom.

The following words of the Second Vatican Council can therefore be applied to the problems of the family: "Our era needs such wisdom more than bygone ages if the discoveries made by man are to be further humanized. For the future of the world stands in peril unless wiser people are forthcoming."[17]

The education of the moral conscience, which makes every human being capable of judging and of discerning the proper ways to achieve self-realization according to his or her original truth, thus becomes a pressing requirement that cannot be renounced.

Modern culture must be led to a more profoundly restored covenant with divine Wisdom. Every man is given a share of such Wisdom through the creating action of God. And it is only in faithfulness to this covenant that the families of today will be in a position to influence positively the building of a more just and fraternal world.

Gradualness and Conversion

9. To the injustice originating from sin—which has profoundly penetrated the structures of today's world—and often hindering the family's full realization of itself and of its fundamental rights, we must all set ourselves in opposition through a conversion of mind and heart, following Christ Crucified by denying our own selfishness: such a conversion cannot fail to have a beneficial and renewing influence even on the structures of society.

What is needed is a continuous, permanent conversion which, while requiring an interior detachment from every evil and an adherence to good in its fullness, is brought about concretely in steps which lead us ever forward. Thus a dynamic process develops, one which advances gradually with the progressive integration of the gifts of God and the demands of His definitive and absolute love in the entire personal and social life of man. Therefore an educational growth process is necessary, in order that individual believers, families and peoples, even civilization itself, by beginning from what they have already received of the mystery of Christ, may patiently be led forward, arriving at a richer understanding and a fuller integration of this mystery in their lives.

Inculturation

10. In conformity with her constant tradition the Church receives from the various cultures everything that is able to express better the unsearchable riches of Christ.[18] Only with the help of all the cultures will it be possible for these riches to be manifested ever more clearly, and for the Church to progress towards a daily more complete and profound awareness of the truth, which has already been given to her in its entirety by the Lord.

Holding fast to the two principles of the compatibility with the Gospel of the various cultures to be taken up, and of communion with the universal Church, there must be further study, particularly by the Episcopal Conferences and the appropriate departments of the Roman Curia, and greater pastoral diligence so that this "inculturation" of the Christian faith may come about ever more extensively, in the context of marriage and the family as well as in other fields .

It is by means of "inculturation" that one proceeds towards the full restoration of the covenant with the Wisdom of God, which is Christ Himself. The whole Church will be enriched also by the cultures which, though lacking technology, abound in human wisdom and are enlivened by profound moral values.

So that the goal of this journey might be clear and consequently the way plainly indicated, the Synod was right to begin by considering in depth the original design of God for marriage and the family: it "went back to the beginning," in deference to the teaching of Christ.[19]

PART TWO
THE PLAN OF GOD FOR MARRIAGE AND THE FAMILY

Man, the Image of the God Who Is Love

11. God created man in His own image and likeness:[20] calling him to existence *through love*, He called him at the same time *for love*.

God is love[21] and in Himself He lives a mystery of personal loving communion. Creating the human race in His own image and continually keeping it in being, God inscribed in the humanity of man and woman the vocation, and thus the capacity and responsibility, of love and communion.[22] Love is therefore the fundamental and innate vocation of every human being.

As an incarnate spirit, that is a soul which expresses itself in a body and a body informed by an immortal spirit, man is called to love in his unified totality. Love includes the human body, and the body is made a sharer in spiritual love.

Christian revelation recognizes two specific ways of realizing the vocation of the human person, in its entirety, to love: marriage and virginity or celibacy. Either one is, in its own proper form, an actuation of the most profound truth of man, of his being "created in the image of God."

Consequently, sexuality, by means of which man and woman give themselves to one another through the acts which are proper and exclusive to spouses, is by no means something purely biological, but concerns the innermost being of the human person as such. It is realized in a truly human way only if it is an integral part of the love by which a man and a woman commit themselves totally to one another until death. The total physical self-giving would be a lie if it were not the sign and fruit of a total personal self-giving, in which the whole person, including the temporal dimension, is present: if the person were to withhold something or reserve the possibility of deciding otherwise in the future, by this very fact he or she would not be giving totally.

This totality which is required by conjugal love also corresponds to the demands of responsible fertility. This fertility is directed to the generation of a human being, and so by its nature it surpasses the purely biological order and involves a whole series of personal values. For the harmonious growth of these values a persevering and unified contribution by both parents is necessary.

The only "place" in which this self-giving in its whole truth is made possible is marriage, the covenant of conjugal love freely and consciously chosen, whereby man and woman accept the intimate community of life and love willed by God Himself,[23] which only in this light manifests its true meaning. The institution of marriage is not an undue interference by society or authority, nor the extrinsic imposition of a form. Rather it is an interior requirement of the covenant of conjugal love which is publicly affirmed as unique and exclusive, in order to live in complete fidelity to the plan of God, the Creator. A person's freedom, far from being restricted by this fidelity, is secured against every form of subjectivism or relativism and is made a sharer in creative Wisdom.

Marriage and Communion Between God and People

12. The communion of love between God and people, a fundamental part of the Revelation and faith experience of Israel, finds a meaningful expression in the marriage covenant which is established between a man and a woman.

For this reason the central word of Revelation, "God loves His people," is likewise proclaimed through the living and concrete word whereby a man and a woman express their conjugal love. Their bond of love becomes the image and the symbol of the covenant which unites God and His people.[24] And the same sin which can harm the conjugal covenant becomes an image of the infidelity of the people to their God: idolatry is prostitution,[25] infidelity is adultery, disobedience to the law is abandonment of the spousal love of the Lord. But the infidelity of Israel does not destroy the eternal fidelity of the Lord, and therefore the ever faithful love of God is put forward as the model of the relations of faithful love which should exist between spouses.[26]

Jesus Christ, Bridegroom of the Church, and the Sacrament of Matrimony

13. The communion between God and His people finds its definitive fulfillment in Jesus Christ, the Bridegroom who loves and gives Himself as the Savior of humanity, uniting it to Himself as His body.

He reveals the original truth of marriage, the truth of the "beginning,"[27] and, freeing man from his hardness of heart, He makes man capable of realizing this truth in its entirety.

This revelation reaches its definitive fullness in the gift of love which the Word of God makes to humanity in assuming a human nature, and in the sacrifice which Jesus Christ makes of Himself on the Cross for His bride, the Church. In this sacrifice there is entirely revealed that plan which God has imprinted on the humanity of man and woman since their creation[28]; the marriage of baptized persons thus becomes a real symbol of that new and eternal covenant sanctioned in the blood of Christ. The Spirit which the Lord pours forth gives a new heart, and renders man and woman capable of loving one another as Christ has loved us. Conjugal love reaches that fullness to which it is interiorly ordained, conjugal charity, which is the proper and specific way in which the spouses participate in and are called to live the very charity of Christ who gave Himself on the Cross.

In a deservedly famous page, Tertullian has well expressed the greatness of this conjugal life in Christ and its beauty: "How can I ever express the happiness of the marriage that is joined together by the Church, strengthened by an offering, sealed by a blessing, announced by angels and ratified by the Father? ...How wonderful the bond between two believers with a single hope, a single desire, a single observance, a single service! They are both brethren and both fellow-servants; there is no separation between them in spirit or flesh; in fact they are truly two in one flesh and where the flesh is one, one is the spirit."[29]

Receiving and meditating faithfully on the word of God, the Church has solemnly taught and continues to teach that the marriage of the baptized is one of the seven sacraments of the New Covenant.[30]

Indeed, by means of baptism, man and woman are definitively placed within the new and eternal covenant, in the spousal covenant of Christ with the Church. And it is because of this indestructible insertion that the intimate community of conjugal life and love, founded by the Creator,[31] is elevated and assumed into the spousal charity of Christ, sustained and enriched by His redeeming power.

By virtue of the sacramentality of their marriage, spouses are bound to one another in the most profoundly indissoluble manner. Their belonging to each other is the real representation, by means of the sacramental sign, of the very relationship of Christ with the Church.

Spouses are therefore the permanent reminder to the Church of what happened on the Cross; they are for one another and for the children witnesses to the salvation in which the sacrament makes them sharers. Of this salvation event marriage, like every sacrament, is a memorial, actuation and prophecy: "As a memorial, the sacrament gives them the grace and duty of commemorating the great works of God and of bearing witness to them before their children. As actuation, it gives them the grace and duty of putting into practice in the present, towards each other and their children, the demands of a love which forgives and redeems. As prophecy, it gives them the grace and duty of living and bearing witness to the hope of the future encounter with Christ."[32]

Like each of the seven sacraments, so also marriage is a real symbol of the event of salvation, but in its own way. "The spouses participate in it as spouses, together, as a couple, so that the first and immediate effect of marriage (res et sacramentum) is not supernatural grace itself, but the Christian conjugal bond, a typically Christian communion of two persons because it represents the mystery of Christ's incarnation and the mystery of His covenant. The content of participation in Christ's life is also specific: conjugal love involves a totality, in which all the elements of the person enter—appeal of the body and instinct, power of feeling and affectivity, aspiration of the spirit and of will. It aims at a deeply personal unity, the unity that, beyond union in one flesh, leads to forming one heart and soul; it demands indissolubility and faithfulness in definitive mutual giving; and it is open to fertility (cf. *Humanae vitae*, 9). In a word it is a question of the normal characteristics of all natural conjugal love, but with a new significance which not only purifies and strengthens them, but raises them to the extent of making them the expression of specifically Christian values."[33]

Children, the Precious Gift of Marriage

14. According to the plan of God, marriage is the foundation of the wider community of the family, since the very institution of marriage and conjugal love are ordained to the procreation and education of children, in whom they find their crowning.[34]

In its most profound reality, love is essentially a gift; and conjugal love, while leading the spouses to the reciprocal "knowledge" which makes them "one flesh,"[35] does not end with the couple, because it makes them capable of the greatest possible gift, the gift by which they become cooperators with God for giving life to a new human person. Thus the couple, while giving themselves to one another, give not just themselves but also the reality of children, who are a living reflection of their love, a permanent sign of conjugal unity and a living and inseparable synthesis of their being a father and a mother.

When they become parents, spouses receive from God the gift of a new responsibility. Their parental love is called to become for the children the visible sign of the very love of God, "from whom every family in heaven and on earth is named."[36]

It must not be forgotten however that, even when procreation is not possible, conjugal life does not for this reason lose its value. Physical sterility in fact can be for spouses the occasion for other important services to the life of the human person, for example, adoption, various forms of educational work, and assistance to other families and to poor or handicapped children.

The Family, a Communion of Persons

15. In matrimony and in the family a complex of interpersonal relationships is set up—married life, fatherhood and motherhood, filiation and fraternity—through which each human person is introduced into the "human family" and into the "family of God," which is the Church.

Christian marriage and the Christian family build up the Church: for in the family the human person is not only brought into being and progressively introduced by means of education into the human community, but by means of the rebirth of baptism and education in the faith the child is also introduced into God's family, which is the Church.

The human family, disunited by sin, is reconstituted in its unity by the redemptive power of the death and Resurrection of Christ.[37]

Christian marriage, by participating in the salvific efficacy of this event, constitutes the natural setting in which the human person is introduced into the great family of the Church.

The commandment to grow and multiply, given to man and woman in the beginning, in this way reaches its whole truth and full realization.

The Church thus finds in the family, born from the sacrament, the cradle and the setting in which she can enter the human generations, and where these in their turn can enter the Church.

Marriage and Virginity or Celibacy

16. Virginity or celibacy for the sake of the Kingdom of God not only does not contradict the dignity of marriage but presupposes it and confirms it. Marriage and virginity or celibacy are two ways of expressing and living the one mystery of the covenant of God with His people. When marriage is not esteemed, neither can consecrated virginity or celibacy exist; when human sexuality is not regarded as a great value given by the Creator, the renunciation of it for the sake of the Kingdom of Heaven loses its meaning.

Rightly indeed does St. John Chrysostom say: "Whoever denigrates marriage also diminishes the glory of virginity. Whoever praises it makes virginity more admirable and resplendent. What appears good only in comparison with evil would not be particularly good. It is something better than what is admitted to be good that is the most excellent good."[39]

In virginity or celibacy, the human being is awaiting, also in a bodily way, the eschatological marriage of Christ with the Church, giving himself or herself completely to the Church in the hope that Christ may give Himself to the Church in the full truth of eternal life. The celibate person thus anticipates in his or her flesh the new world of the future resurrection.[39]

By virtue of this witness, virginity or celibacy keeps alive in the Church a consciousness of the mystery of marriage and defends it from any reduction and impoverishment.

Virginity or celibacy, by liberating the human heart in a unique way,[40] "so as to make it burn with greater love for God and all humanity,"[41] bears witness that the Kingdom of God and His justice is that pearl of great price which is preferred to every other value no matter how great, and hence must be sought as the only definitive value. It is for this reason that the Church, throughout her history, has always defended the superiority of this charism to that of marriage, by reason of the wholly singular link which it has with the Kingdom of God.[42]

In spite of having renounced physical fecundity, the celibate person becomes spiritually fruitful, the father and mother of many, co-operating in the realization of the family according to God's plan.

Christian couples therefore have the right to expect from celibate persons a good example and a witness of fidelity to their vocation until death. Just as fidelity at times becomes difficult for married people and requires sacrifice, mortification and self-denial, the same can happen to celibate persons, and their fidelity, even in the trials that may occur, should strengthen the fidelity of married couples.[43]

These reflections on virginity or celibacy can enlighten and help those who, for reasons independent of their own will, have been unable to marry and have then accepted their situation in a spirit of service.

PART THREE
THE ROLE OF THE CHRISTIAN FAMILY

Family, Become What You Are

17. The family finds in the plan of God the Creator and Redeemer not only its *identity*, what it is, but also its *mission*, what it can and should do. The role that God calls the family to perform in history derives from what the family is; its role represents the dynamic and existential development of what it is. Each family finds within itself a summons that cannot be ignored, and that specifies both its dignity and its responsibility: family, *become* what you *are*.

Accordingly, the family must go back to the "beginning" of God's creative act, if it is to attain self-knowledge and self-realization in accordance with the inner truth not only of what it is but also of what it does in history. And since in God's plan it has been established as an "intimate community of life and love,"[44] the family has the mission to become more and more what it is, that is to say, a community of life and love, in an effort that will find fulfillment, as will everything created and redeemed, in the Kingdom of God. Looking at it in such a way as to reach its very roots, we must say that the essence and role of the family are in the final analysis specified by love. Hence the family has the *mission to guard, reveal and communicate love*, and this is a living reflection of and a real sharing in God's love for humanity and the love of Christ the Lord for the Church His bride.

Every particular task of the family is an expression and concrete actuation of that fundamental mission. We must therefore go deeper into the unique riches of the family's mission and probe its contents, which are both manifold and unified.

Thus, with love as its point of departure and making constant reference to it, the recent Synod emphasized four general tasks for the family:

1) forming a community of persons;
2) serving life;
3) participating in the development of society;
4) sharing in the life and mission of the Church.

I — FORMING A COMMUNITY OF PERSONS

Love as the Principle and Power of Communion

18. The family, which is founded and given life by love, is a community of persons: of husband and wife, of parents and children, of

relatives. Its first task is to live with fidelity the reality of communion in a constant effort to develop an authentic community of persons.

The inner principle of that task, its permanent power and its final goal is love: without love the family is not a community of persons and, in the same way, *without love the family cannot live, grow and perfect itself as a community of persons*. What I wrote in the Encyclical *Redemptor hominis* applies primarily and especially within the family as such: "Man cannot live without love. He remains a being that is incomprehensible for himself, his life is senseless, if love is not revealed to him, if he does not encounter love, if he does not experience it and make it his own, if he does not participate intimately in it."[45]

The love between husband and wife and, in a derivatory and broader way, the love between members of the same family—between parents and children, brothers and sisters and relatives and members of the household—is given life and sustenance by an unceasing inner dynamism leading the family to ever deeper and more intense communion, which is the foundation and soul of the community of marriage and the family.

The Indivisible Unity of Conjugal Communion

19. The first communion is the one which is established and which develops between husband and wife: by virtue of the covenant of married life, the man and woman "are no longer two but one flesh"[45] and they are called to grow continually in their communion through day-to-day fidelity to their marriage promise of total mutual self-giving.

This conjugal communion sinks its roots in the natural complementarity that exists between man and woman, and is nurtured through the personal willingness of the spouses to share their entire life-project, what they have and what they are: for this reason such communion is the fruit and the sign of a profoundly human need. But in the Lord Christ, God takes up this human need, confirms it, purifies it and elevates it, leading it to perfection through the sacrament of matrimony: the Holy Spirit who is poured out in the sacramental celebration offers Christian couples the gift of a new communion of love that is the living and real image of that unique unity which makes of the Church the indivisible Mystical Body of the Lord Jesus.

The gift of the Spirit is a commandment of life for Christian spouses and at the same time a stimulating impulse so that every day they may progress towards an ever richer union with each other on all levels—of the body, of the character, of the heart, of the intelligence and will, of the soul[47]—revealing in this way to the Church and to the world the new communion of love, given by the grace of Christ.

Such a communion is radically contradicted by polygamy: this, in fact, directly negates the plan of God which was revealed from the beginning, because it is contrary to the equal personal dignity of

724

men and women who in matrimony give themselves with a love that is total and therefore unique and exclusive. As the Second Vatican Council writes: "Firmly established by the Lord, the unity of marriage will radiate from the equal personal dignity of husband and wife, a dignity acknowledged by mutual and total love."[48]

An Indissoluble Communion

20. Conjugal communion is characterized not only by its unity but also by its indissolubility: "As a mutual gift of two persons, this intimate union, as well as the good of children, imposes total fidelity on the spouses and argues for an unbreakable oneness between them."[49]

It is a fundamental duty of the Church to reaffirm strongly, as the Synod Fathers did, the doctrine of the indissolubility of marriage. To all those who, in our times, consider it too difficult, or indeed impossible, to be bound to one person for the whole of life, and to those caught up in a culture that rejects the indissolubility of marriage and openly mocks the commitment of spouses to fidelity, it is necessary to reconfirm the good news of the definitive nature of that conjugal love that has in Christ its foundation and strength.[50]

Being rooted in the personal and total self-giving of the couple, and being required by the good of the children, the indissolubility of marriage finds its ultimate truth in the plan that God has manifested in His revelation: He wills and He communicates the indissolubility of marriage as a fruit, a sign and a requirement of the absolutely faithful love that God has for man and that the Lord Jesus has for the Church.

Christ renews the first plan that the Creator inscribed in the hearts of man and woman, and in the celebration of the sacrament of matrimony offers a "new heart": thus the couples are not only able to overcome "hardness of heart,"[51] but also and above all they are able to share the full and definitive love of Christ, the new and eternal Covenant made flesh. Just as the Lord Jesus is the "faithful witness,"[52] the "yes" of the promises of God[53] and thus the supreme realization of the unconditional faithfulness with which God loves His people, so Christian couples are called to participate truly in the irrevocable indissolubility that binds Christ to the Church His bride, loved by Him to the end.[54]

The gift of the sacrament is at the same time a vocation and commandment for the Christian spouses, that they may remain faithful to each other forever, beyond every trial and difficulty, in generous obedience to the holy will of the Lord: "What therefore God has joined together, let not man put asunder."[55]

To bear witness to the inestimable value of the indissolubility and fidelity of marriage is one of the most precious and most urgent tasks of Christian couples in our time. So, with all my Brothers who participated in the Synod of Bishops, I praise and encourage those numerous couples who, though encountering no small difficulty, preserve and develop the value of indissolubility: thus, in a humble and courageous manner, they perform the role committed to them

of being in the world a "sign"—a small and precious sign, sometimes also subjected to temptation, but always renewed—of the unfailing fidelity with which God and Jesus Christ love each and
every human being. But it is also proper to recognize the value of
the witness of those spouses who, even when abandoned by their
partner, with the strength of faith and of Christian hope have not
entered a new union: these spouses too give an authentic witness to
fidelity, of which the world today has a great need. For this reason
they must be encouraged and helped by the pastors and the faithful
of the Church.

The Broader Communion of the Family

21. Conjugal communion constitutes the foundation on which is
built the broader communion of the family, of parents and children,
of brothers and sisters with each other, of relatives and other members of the household.

This communion is rooted in the natural bonds of flesh and
blood, and grows to its specifically human perfection with the establishment and maturing of the still deeper and richer bonds of
the spirit: the love that animates the interpersonal relationships of
the different members of the family constitutes the interior
strength that shapes and animates the family communion and
community.

The Christian family is also called to experience a new and original communion which confirms and perfects natural and human
communion. In fact the grace of Jesus Christ, "the first-born among
many brethren,"[56] is by its nature and interior dynamism "a grace
of brotherhood," as St. Thomas Aquinas calls it.[57] The Holy Spirit,
who is poured forth in the celebration of the sacraments, is the living source and inexhaustible sustenance of the supernatural communion that gathers believers and links them with Christ and with
each other in the unity of the Church of God. The Christian family
constitutes a specific revelation and realization of ecclesial communion, and for this reason too it can and should be called "the domestic Church."[58]

All members of the family, each according to his or her own gift,
have the grace and responsibility of building, day by day, the communion of persons, making the family "a school of deeper
humanity:"[59] this happens where there is care and love for the little
ones, the sick, the aged; where there is mutual service every day;
when there is a sharing of goods, of joys and of sorrows.

A fundamental opportunity for building such a communion is
constituted by the educational exchange between parents and
children,[60] in which each gives and receives. By means of love, respect and obedience towards their parents, children offer their specific and irreplaceable contribution to the construction of an
authentically human and Christian family.[61] They will be aided in
this if parents exercise their unrenounceable authority as a true
and proper "ministry," that is, as a service to the human and Christian well-being of their children, and in particular as a service

726

aimed at helping them acquire a truly responsible freedom, and if parents maintain a living awareness of the "gift" they continually receive from their children.

Family communion can only be preserved and perfected through a great spirit of sacrifice. It requires, in fact, a ready and generous openness of each and all to understanding, to forbearance, to pardon, to reconciliation. There is no family that does not know how selfishness, discord, tension, and conflict violently attack and at times mortally wound its own communion: hence there arise the many and varied forms of division in family life. But, at the same time, every family is called by the God of peace to have the joyous and renewing experience of "reconciliation," that is, communion re-established, unity restored. In particular, participation in the sacrament of Reconciliation and in the banquet of the one Body of Christ offers to the Christian family the grace and the responsibility of overcoming every division and of moving towards the fullness of communion willed by God, responding in this way to the ardent desire of the Lord: "that they may be one."[62]

The Rights and Role of Women

22. In that it is, and ought always to become, a communion and community of persons, the family finds in love the source and the constant impetus for welcoming, respecting and promoting each one of its members in his or her lofty dignity as a person, that is, as a living image of God. As the Synod Fathers rightly stated, the moral criterion for the authenticity of conjugal and family relationships consists in fostering the dignity and vocation of the individual persons, who achieve their fullness by sincere self-giving.[63]

In this perspective the Synod devoted special attention to women, to their rights and role within the family and society. In the same perspective are also to be considered men as husbands and fathers, and likewise children and the elderly.

Above all it is important to underline the equal dignity and responsibility of women with men. This equality is realized in a unique manner in that reciprocal self-giving by each one to the other and by both to the children which is proper to marriage and the family. What human reason intuitively perceives and acknowledges is fully revealed by the word of God: the history of salvation, in fact, is a continuous and luminous testimony of the dignity of women.

In creating the human race "male and female,"[64] God gives man and woman an equal personal dignity, endowing them with the inalienable rights and responsibilities proper to the human person. God then manifests the dignity of women in the highest form possible, by assuming human flesh from the Virgin Mary, whom the Church honors as the Mother of God, calling her the new Eve and presenting her as the model of redeemed woman. The sensitive respect of Jesus towards the women that He called to His following and His friendship, His appearing on Easter morning to a woman before the other disciples, the mission entrusted to women to carry the good news of the Resurrection to the apostles—these are all signs that confirm the special esteem of the Lord Jesus for women. The Apostle Paul will say: "In Christ Jesus you are all children of God through faith.... There is neither Jew nor Greek, there is neither slave nor free, there is neither male nor female; for you are all one in Christ Jesus."[65]

Women and Society

23. Without intending to deal with all the various aspects of the vast and complex theme of the relationships between women and society, and limiting these remarks to a few essential points, one cannot but observe that in the specific area of family life a widespread social and cultural tradition has considered women's role to be exclusively that of wife and mother, without adequate access to public functions, which have generally been reserved for men.

There is no doubt that the equal dignity and responsibility of men and women fully justifies women's access to public functions. On the other hand the true advancement of women requires that clear recognition be given to the value of their maternal and family role, by comparison with all other public roles and all other professions. Furthermore, these roles and professions should be harmoniously combined, if we wish the evolution of society and culture to be truly and fully human.

This will come about more easily if, in accordance with the wishes expressed by the Synod, a renewed "theology of work" can shed light upon and study in depth the meaning of work in the Christian life and determine the fundamental bond between work and the family, and therefore the original and irreplaceable meaning of work in the home and in rearing children.[66] Therefore the Church can and should help modern society by tirelessly insisting that the work of women in the home be recognized and respected by all in its irreplaceable value. This is of particular importance in education: for possible discrimination between the different types of work and professions is eliminated at its very root once it is clear that all people, in every area, are working with equal rights and equal responsibilities. The image of God in man and in woman will thus be seen with added luster.

While it must be recognized that women have the same right as men to perform various public functions, society must be structured in such a way that wives and mothers are *not in practice compelled* to work outside the home, and that their families can live and prosper in a dignified way even when they themselves devote their full time to their own family.

Furthermore, the mentality which honors women more for their work outside the home than for their work within the family must be overcome. This requires that men should truly esteem and love women with total respect for their personal dignity, and that society should create and develop conditions favoring work in the home.

With due respect to the different vocations of men and women, the Church must in her own life promote as far as possible their

728

equality of rights and dignity: and this for the good of all, the family, the Church and society.

But clearly all of this does not mean for women a renunciation of their femininity or an imitation of the male role, but the fullness of true feminine humanity which should be expressed in their activity, whether in the family or outside of it, without disregarding the differences of customs and cultures in this sphere.

Offenses Against Women's Dignity

24. Unfortunately the Christian message about the dignity of women is contradicted by that persistent mentality which considers the human being not as a person but as a thing, as an object of trade, at the service of selfish interest and mere pleasure: the first victims of this mentality are women.

This mentality produces very bitter fruits, such as contempt for men and for women, slavery, oppression of the weak, pornography, prostitution—especially in an organized form—and all those various forms of discrimination that exist in the fields of education, employment, wages, etc.

Besides, many forms of degrading discrimination still persist today in a great part of our society that affect and seriously harm particular categories of women, as for example childless wives, widows, separated or divorced women, and unmarried mothers.

The Synod Fathers deplored these and other forms of discrimination as strongly as possible. I therefore ask that vigorous and incisive pastoral action be taken by all to overcome them definitively so that the image of God that shines in all human beings without exception may be fully respected.

Men as Husbands and Fathers

25. Within the conjugal and family communion-community, the man is called upon to live his gift and role as husband and father.

In his wife he sees the fulfillment of God's intention: "It is not good that the man should be alone; I will make him a helper fit for him,"[67] and he makes his own the cry of Adam, the first husband: "This at last is bone of my bones and flesh of my flesh."[68]

Authentic conjugal love presupposes and requires that a man have a profound respect for the equal dignity of his wife: "You are not her master," writes St. Ambrose, "but her husband; she was not given to you to be your slave, but your wife.... Reciprocate her attentiveness to you and be grateful to her for her love."[69] With his wife a man should live "a very special form of personal friendship."[70] As for the Christian, he is called upon to develop a new attitude of love, manifesting towards his wife a charity that is both gentle and strong like that which Christ has for the Church.[71]

Love for his wife as mother of their children and love for the children themselves are for the man the natural way of understanding and fulfilling his own fatherhood. Above all where social and cultural conditions so easily encourage a father to be less concerned with his family or at any rate less involved in the work of education, efforts must be made to restore socially the conviction that the place and task of the father in and for the family is of unique and irreplaceable importance.[72] As experience teaches, the absence of a father causes psychological and moral imbalance and notable difficulties in family relationships, as does, in contrary circumstances, the oppressive presence of a father, especially where there still prevails the phenomenon of "machismo," or a wrong superiority of male prerogatives which humiliates women and inhibits the development of healthy family relationships.

In revealing and in reliving on earth the very fatherhood of God,[73] a man is called upon to ensure the harmonious and united development of all the members of the family: he will perform this task by exercising generous responsibility for the life conceived under the heart of the mother, by a more solicitous commitment to education, a task he shares with his wife,[74] by work which is never a cause of division in the family but promotes its unity and stability, and by means of the witness he gives of an adult Christian life which effectively introduces the children into the living experience of Christ and the Church.

The Rights of Children

26. In the family, which is a community of persons, special attention must be devoted to the children by developing a profound esteem for their personal dignity, and a great respect and generous concern for their rights. This is true for every child, but it becomes all the more urgent the smaller the child is and the more it is in need of everything, when it is sick, suffering, or handicapped.

By fostering and exercising a tender and strong concern for every child that comes into this world, the Church fulfills a fundamental mission: for she is called upon to reveal and put forward anew in history the example and the commandment of Christ the Lord, who placed the child at the heart of the Kingdom of God: "Let the children come to me, and do not hinder them; for to such belongs the kingdom of heaven."[75]

I repeat once again what I said to the General Assembly of the United Nations on October 2, 1979: "I wish to express the joy that we all find in children, the springtime of life, the anticipation of the future history of each of our present earthly homelands. No country on earth, no political system can think of its own future otherwise than through the image of these new generations that will receive from their parents the manifold heritage of values, duties and aspirations of the nation to which they belong and of the whole human family. Concern for the child, even before birth, from the first moment of conception and then throughout the years of infancy and youth, is the primary and fundamental test of the relationship of one human being to another. And so, what better wish can I express for every nation and for the whole of mankind, and for all the children of the world than a better future in which respect for human rights will become a complete reality throughout the third millennium, which is drawing near?"[76]

Acceptance, love, esteem, many-sided and united material, emotional, educational and spiritual concern for every child that comes into this world should always constitute a distinctive, essential characteristic of all Christians, in particular of the Christian family: thus children, while they are able to grow "in wisdom and in stature, and in favor with God and man,"[77] offer their own precious contribution to building up the family community and even to the sanctification of their parents.[78]

The Elderly in the Family

27. There are cultures which manifest a unique veneration and great love for the elderly: far from being outcasts from the family or merely tolerated as a useless burden, they continue to be present and to take an active and responsible part in family life, though having to respect the autonomy of the new family; above all they carry out the important mission of being a witness to the past and a source of wisdom for the young and for the future.

Other cultures, however, especially in the wake of disordered industrial and urban development, have both in the past and in the present set the elderly aside in unacceptable ways. This causes acute suffering to them and spiritually impoverishes many families.

The pastoral activity of the Church must help everyone to discover and to make good use of the role of the elderly within the civil and ecclesial community, in particular within the family. In fact, "the life of the aging helps to clarify a scale of human values; it shows the continuity of generations and marvelously demonstrates the interdependence of God's people. The elderly often have the charism to bridge generation gaps before they are made: how many children have found understanding and love in the eyes and words and caresses of the aging! And how many old people have willingly subscribed to the inspired word that the 'crown of the aged is their children's children' (Prv. 17:6)!"[79]

II — SERVING LIFE

1. *The Transmission of Life*

Cooperators in the Love of God the Creator

28. With the creation of man and woman in His own image and likeness, God crowns and brings to perfection the work of His hands: He calls them to a special sharing in His love and in His power as Creator and Father, through their free and responsible cooperation in transmitting the gift of human life: "God blessed them, and God said to them, 'Be fruitful and multiply, and fill the earth and subdue it.' "[80]

Thus the fundamental task of the family is to serve life, to actualize in history the original blessing of the Creator—that of transmitting by procreation the divine image from person to person.[81]

Fecundity is the fruit and the sign of conjugal love, the living testimony of the full reciprocal self-giving of the spouses: "While not making the other purposes of matrimony of less account, the true practice of conjugal love, and the whole meaning of the family life which results from it, have this aim: that the couple be ready with stout hearts to cooperate with the love of the Creator and the Savior, who through them will enlarge and enrich His own family day by day."[82]

However, the fruitfulness of conjugal love is not restricted solely to the procreation of children, even understood in its specifically human dimension: it is enlarged and enriched by all those fruits of moral, spiritual and supernatural life which the father and mother are called to hand on to their children, and through the children to the Church and to the world.

The Church's Teaching and Norm, Always Old Yet Always New

29. Precisely because the love of husband and wife is a unique participation in the mystery of life and of the love of God Himself, the Church knows that she has received the special mission of guarding and protecting the lofty dignity of marriage and the most serious responsibility of the transmission of human life.

Thus, in continuity with the living tradition of the ecclesial community throughout history, the recent Second Vatican Council and the magisterium of my predecessor Paul VI, expressed above all in the Encyclical *Humanae vitae*, have handed on to our times a truly prophetic proclamation, which reaffirms and reproposes with clarity the Church's teaching and norm, always old yet always new, regarding marriage and regarding the transmission of human life.

For this reason the Synod Fathers made the following declaration at their last assembly: "This Sacred Synod, gathered together with the Successor of Peter in the unity of faith, firmly holds what has been set forth in the Second Vatican Council (cf. *Gaudium et spes*, 50) and afterwards in the Encyclical *Humanae vitae*, particularly that love between husband and wife must be fully human, exclusive and open to new life (*Humanae vitae*, 11; cf. 9, 12)."[83]

The Church Stands for Life

30. The teaching of the Church in our day is placed in a social and cultural context which renders it more difficult to understand and yet more urgent and irreplaceable for promoting the true good of men and women .

Scientific and technical progress, which contemporary man is continually expanding in his dominion over nature, not only offers the hope of creating a new and better humanity, but also causes ever greater anxiety regarding the future. Some ask themselves if it is a good thing to be alive or if it would be better never to have been born; they doubt therefore if it is right to bring others into life when perhaps they will curse their existence in a cruel world with unforeseeable terrors. Others consider themselves to be the only ones for whom the advantages of technology are intended and they exclude others by imposing on them contraceptives or even worse means. Still others, imprisoned in a consumer mentality and whose sole concern is to bring about a continual growth of material goods, finish by ceasing to understand, and thus by refusing, the spiritual riches of a new human life. The ultimate reason for these mentalities is the absence in people's hearts of God, whose love alone is stronger than all the world's fears and can conquer them.

Thus an anti-life mentality is born, as can be seen in many current issues: one thinks, for example, of a certain panic deriving from the studies of ecologists and futurologists on population growth, which sometimes exaggerate the danger of demographic increase to the quality of life.

But the Church firmly believes that human life, even if weak and suffering, is always a splendid gift of God's goodness. Against the pessimism and selfishness which cast a shadow over the world, the Church stands for life: in each human life she sees the splendor of that "Yes," that "Amen," who is Christ Himself.[84] To the "No" which assails and afflicts the world, she replies with this living "Yes," thus defending the human person and the world from all who plot against and harm life.

The Church is called upon to manifest anew to everyone, with clear and stronger conviction, her will to promote human life by every means and to defend it against all attacks, in whatever condition or state of development it is found.

Thus the Church condemns as a grave offense against human dignity and justice all those activities of governments or other public authorities which attempt to limit in any way the freedom of couples in deciding about children. Consequently, any violence applied by such authorities in favor of contraception or, still worse, of sterilization and procured abortion, must be altogether condemned and forcefully rejected. Likewise to be denounced as gravely unjust are cases where, in international relations, economic help given for the advancement of peoples is made conditional on programs of contraception, sterilization and procured abortion.[85]

That God's Design May Be Ever More Completely Fulfilled

31. The Church is certainly aware of the many complex problems which couples in many countries face today in their task of transmitting life in a responsible way. She also recognizes the serious problem of population growth in the form it has taken in many parts of the world and its moral implications.

However, she holds that consideration in depth of all the aspects of these problems offers a new and stronger confirmation of the importance of the authentic teaching on birth regulation reproposed in the Second Vatican Council and in the Encyclical *Humanae vitae*.

For this reason, together with the Synod Fathers I feel it is my duty to extend a pressing invitation to theologians, asking them to unite their efforts in order to collaborate with the hierarchical Magisterium and to commit themselves to the task of illustrating ever more clearly the biblical foundations, the ethical grounds and the personalistic reasons behind this doctrine. Thus it will be possible, in the context of an organic exposition, to render the teaching of the Church on this fundamental question truly accessible to all people of good will, fostering a daily more enlightened and profound understanding of it: in this way God's plan will be ever more completely fulfilled for the salvation of humanity and for the glory of the Creator.

A united effort by theologians in this regard, inspired by a convinced adherence to the Magisterium, which is the one authentic guide for the People of God is particularly urgent for reasons that include the close link between Catholic teaching on this matter and the view of the human person that the Church proposes: doubt or error in the field of marriage or the family involves obscuring to a serious extent the integral truth about the human person, in a cultural situation that is already so often confused and contradictory. In fulfillment of their specific role, theologians are called upon to provide enlightenment and a deeper understanding, and their contribution is of incomparable value and represents a unique and highly meritorious service to the family and humanity.

In an Integral Vision of the Human Person and of His or Her Vocation

32. In the context of a culture which seriously distorts or entirely misinterprets the true meaning of human sexuality, because it separates it from its essential reference to the person, the Church more urgently feels how irreplaceable is her mission of presenting sexuality as a value and task of the whole person, created male and female in the image of God.

In this perspective the Second Vatican Council clearly affirmed that "when there is a question of harmonizing conjugal love with the responsible transmission of life, the moral aspect of any procedure does not depend solely on sincere intentions or on an evaluation of motives. It must be determined by *objective standards*. These, *based on the nature of the human person and his or her acts*, preserve the full sense of mutual self-giving and human procreation in the context of true love. Such a goal cannot be achieved unless the virtue of conjugal chastity is sincerely practiced."[86]

It is precisely by moving from "an integral vision of man and of his vocation, not only his natural and earthly, but also his supernatural and eternal vocation,"[87] that Paul VI affirmed that the teaching of the Church "is founded upon the inseparable connection, willed by God and unable to be broken by man on his own initiative, between the two meanings of the conjugal act: the unitive meaning and the procreative meaning."[88] And he concluded by re-emphasizing that there must be excluded as intrinsically immoral "every action which, either in anticipation of the conjugal act, or in its accomplishment, or in the development of its natural consequences, proposes, whether as an end or as a means, to render procreation impossible."[89]

When couples, by means of recourse to contraception, separate these two meanings that God the Creator has inscribed in the being of man and woman and in the dynamism of their sexual communion, they act as "arbiters" of the divine plan and they "manipulate" and degrade human sexuality—and with it themselves and their married partner—by altering its value of "total" self-giving. Thus the innate language that expresses the total reciprocal self-giving of husband and wife is overlaid, through contraception, by an objectively contradictory language, namely, that of not giving oneself totally to the other. This leads not only to a positive refusal to be open to life but also to a falsification of the inner truth of conjugal love, which is called upon to give itself in personal totality.

When, instead, by means of recourse to periods of infertility, the couple respect the inseparable connection between the unitive and procreative meanings of human sexuality, they are acting as "ministers" of God's plan and they "benefit from" their sexuality according to the original dynamism of "total" self-giving, without manipulation or alteration.[90]

In the light of the experience of many couples and of the data provided by the different human sciences, theological reflection is able to perceive and is called to study further *the difference, both anthropological and moral,* between contraception and recourse to the rhythm of the cycle: it is a difference which is much wider and deeper than is usually thought, one which involves in the final analysis two irreconcilable concepts of the human person and of human sexuality. The choice of the natural rhythms involves accepting the cycle of the person, that is the woman, and thereby accepting dialogue, reciprocal respect, shared responsibility and self-control. To accept the cycle and to enter into dialogue means to recognize both the spiritual and corporal character of conjugal communion, and to live personal love with its requirement of fidelity. In this context the couple comes to experience how conjugal communion is enriched with those values of tenderness and affection which constitute the inner soul of human sexuality in its physical dimension also. In this way sexuality is respected and promoted in its truly and fully human dimension, and is never "used" as an "object" that, by breaking the personal unity of soul and body, strikes at God's creation itself at the level of the deepest interaction of nature and person.

The Church as Teacher and Mother for Couples in Difficulty

33. In the field of conjugal morality the Church is Teacher and Mother and acts as such.

As Teacher, she never tires of proclaiming the moral norm that must guide the responsible transmission of life. The Church is in no way the author or the arbiter of this norm. In obedience to the truth which is Christ, whose image is reflected in the nature and dignity of the human person, the Church interprets the moral norm and proposes it to all people of good will, without concealing its demands of radicalness and perfection.

As Mother, the Church is close to the many married couples who find themselves in difficulty over this important point of the moral life: she knows well their situation, which is often very arduous and at times truly tormented by difficulties of every kind, not only individual difficulties but social ones as well; she knows that many couples encounter difficulties not only in the concrete fulfillment of the moral norm but even in understanding its inherent values.

But it is one and the same Church that is both Teacher and Mother. And so the Church never ceases to exhort and encourage all to resolve whatever conjugal difficulties may arise without ever falsifying or compromising the truth: she is convinced that there can be no true contradiction between the divine law on transmitting life and that on fostering authentic married love.[91] Accordingly, the concrete pedagogy of the Church must always remain linked with her doctrine and never be separated from it. With the same conviction as my predecessor, I therefore repeat: "To diminish in no way the saving teaching of Christ constitutes an eminent form of charity for souls."[92]

On the other hand, authentic ecclesial pedagogy displays its realism and wisdom only by making a tenacious and courageous effort to create and uphold all the human conditions—psychological, moral and spiritual—indispensable for understanding and living the moral value and norm.

There is no doubt that these conditions must include persistence and patience, humility and strength of mind, filial trust in God and in His grace, and frequent recourse to prayer and to the sacraments of the Eucharist and of Reconciliation.[93] Thus strengthened, Christian husbands and wives will be able to keep alive their awareness of the unique influence that the grace of the sacrament of marriage has on every aspect of married life, including therefore their sexuality: the gift of the Spirit, accepted and responded to by husband and wife, helps them to live their human sexuality in accordance with God's plan and as a sign of the unitive and fruitful love of Christ for His Church.

But the necessary conditions also include knowledge of the bodily aspect and the body's rhythms of fertility. Accordingly, every effort must be made to render such knowledge accessible to all married people and also to young adults before marriage, through clear, timely, and serious instruction and education given by married couples, doctors, and experts. Knowledge must then lead to education in self-control: hence the absolute necessity for the virtue of chastity and for permanent education in it. In the Christian view, chastity by no means signifies rejection of human sexuality or lack of esteem for it: rather it signifies spiritual energy capable of defending love from the perils of selfishness and aggressiveness, and able to advance it towards its full realization.

With deeply wise and loving intuition, Paul VI was only voicing the experience of many married couples when he wrote in his Encyclical: "To dominate instinct by means of one's reason and free will undoubtedly requires ascetical practices, so that the affective manifestations of conjugal life may observe the correct order, in particular with regard to the observance of periodic continence. Yet this discipline which is proper to the purity of married couples, far from harming conjugal love, rather confers on it a higher human value. It demands continual effort, yet, thanks to its beneficent influence, husband and wife fully develop their personalities, being enriched with spiritual values. Such discipline bestows upon family life fruits of serenity and peace, and facilitates the solution of other problems; it favors attention for one's partner, helps both parties to drive out selfishness, the enemy of true love, and deepens their sense of responsibility. By its means, parents acquire the capacity of having a deeper and more efficacious influence in the education of their offspring."[94]

The Moral Progress of Married People

34. It is always very important to have a right notion of the moral order, its values and its norms, and the importance is all the greater when the difficulties in the way of respecting them become more numerous and serious.

Since the moral order reveals and sets forth the plan of God the Creator, for this very reason it cannot be something that harms man, something impersonal. On the contrary, by responding to the deepest demands of the human being created by God, it places itself at the service of that person's full humanity with the delicate and binding love whereby God Himself inspires, sustains and guides every creature towards its happiness.

But man, who has been called to live God's wise and loving design in a responsible manner, is an historical being who day by day builds himself up through his many free decisions; and so he knows, loves and accomplishes moral good by stages of growth.

Married people too are called upon to progress unceasingly in their moral life, with the support of a sincere and active desire to gain ever better knowledge of the values enshrined in and fostered by the law of God. They must also be supported by an upright and generous willingness to embody these values in their concrete decisions. They cannot however look on the law as merely an ideal to be achieved in the future: they must consider it as a command of Christ the Lord to overcome difficulties with constancy. "And so what is known as 'the law of gradualness' or step-by-step advance cannot be identified with 'gradualness of the law,' as if there were different degrees or forms of precept in God's law for different individuals and situations. In God's plan, all husbands and wives are called in marriage to holiness, and this lofty vocation is fulfilled to the extent that the human person is able to respond to God's command with serene confidence in God's grace and in his or her own will."[95] On the same lines, it is part of the Church's pedagogy that husbands and wives should first of all recognize clearly the teaching of *Humanae vitae* as indicating the norm for the exercise of their sexuality, and that they should endeavor to establish the conditions necessary for observing that norm.

As the Synod noted, this pedagogy embraces the whole of married life. Accordingly, the function of transmitting life must be integrated into the overall mission of Christian life as a whole, which without the Cross cannot reach the Resurrection. In such a context it is understandable that sacrifice cannot be removed from family life, but must in fact be wholeheartedly accepted if the love between husband and wife is to be deepened and become a source of intimate joy.

This shared progress demands reflection, instruction and suitable education on the part of the priests, religious, and lay people engaged in family pastoral work: they will all be able to assist married people in their human and spiritual progress, a progress that demands awareness of sin, a sincere commitment to observe the moral law, and the ministry of reconciliation. It must also be kept in mind that conjugal intimacy involves the wills of two persons, who are however called to harmonize their mentality and behavior: this requires much patience, understanding, and time. Uniquely important in this field is unity of moral and pastoral judgment by priests, a unity that must be carefully sought and ensured, in order that the faithful may not have to suffer anxiety of conscience.[96]

It will be easier for married people to make progress if, with respect for the Church's teaching and with trust in the grace of Christ, and with the help and support of the pastors of souls and the entire ecclesial community, they are able to discover and experience the liberating and inspiring value of the authentic love that is offered by the Gospel and set before us by the Lord's commandment.

Instilling Conviction and Offering Practical Help

35. With regard to the question of lawful birth regulation, the ecclesial community at the present time must take on the task of instilling conviction and offering practical help to those who wish to live out their parenthood in a truly responsible way.

In this matter, while the Church notes with satisfaction the results achieved by scientific research aimed at a more precise knowledge of the rhythms of women's fertility, and while it encourages a more decisive and wide-ranging extension of that research, it cannot fail to call with renewed vigor on the responsibility of all—doctors, experts, marriage counselors, teachers and married couples—who can actually help married people to live their love with respect for the structure and finalities of the conjugal act which expresses that love. This implies a broader, more decisive and more systematic effort to make the natural methods of regulating fertility known, respected and applied.[97]

A very valuable witness can and should be given by those husbands and wives who through the joint exercise of periodic continence have reached a more mature personal responsibility with regard to love and life. As Paul VI wrote: "To them the Lord entrusts the task of making visible to people the holiness and sweetness of the law which unites the mutual love of husband and wife with their cooperation with the love of God, the author of human life."[98]

2. Education

The Right and Duty of Parents Regarding Education

36. The task of giving education is rooted in the primary vocation of married couples to participate in God's creative activity: by begetting in love and for love a new person who has within himself or herself the vocation to growth and development, parents by that very fact take on the task of helping that person effectively to live a fully human life. As the Second Vatican Council recalled, "since parents have conferred life on their children, they have a most solemn obligation to educate their offspring. Hence, parents must be acknowledged as the first and foremost educators of their children. Their role as educators is so decisive that scarcely anything can compensate for their failure in it. For it devolves on parents to create a family atmosphere so animated with love and reverence for God and others that a well-rounded personal and social development will be fostered among the children. Hence, the family is the first school of those social virtues which every society needs."[99]

The right and duty of parents to give education is essential, since it is connected with the transmission of human life; it is *original and primary* with regard to the educational role of others, on account of the uniqueness of the loving relationship between parents and children; and it is *irreplaceable and inalienable*, and therefore incapable of being entirely delegated to others or usurped by others.

In addition to these characteristics, it cannot be forgotten that the most basic element, so basic that it qualifies the educational role of parents, is *parental love*, which finds fulfillment in the task of education as it completes and perfects its service of life: as well as being a *source*, the parents' love is also the *animating principle* and therefore the *norm* inspiring and guiding all concrete educational activity, enriching it with the values of kindness, constancy, goodness, service, disinterestedness and self-sacrifice that are the most precious fruit of love.

Educating in the Essential Values of Human Life

37. Even amid the difficulties of the work of education, difficulties which are often greater today, parents must trustingly and courageously train their children in the essential values of human life. Children must grow up with a correct attitude of freedom with regard to material goods, by adopting a simple and austere life style and being fully convinced that "man is more precious for what he is than for what he has."[100]

In a society shaken and split by tensions and conflicts caused by the violent clash of various kinds of individualism and selfishness, children must be enriched not only with a sense of true justice, which alone leads to respect for the personal dignity of each individual, but also and more powerfully by a sense of true love, understood as sincere solicitude and disinterested service with regard to others, especially the poorest and those in most need. The family is the first and fundamental school of social living: as a community of love, it finds in self-giving the law that guides it and makes it grow. The self-giving that inspires the love of husband and wife for each other is the model and norm for the self-giving that must be practiced in the relationships between brothers and sisters and the different generations living together in the family. And the communion and sharing that are part of everyday life in the home at times of joy and at times of difficulty are the most concrete and effective pedagogy for the active, responsible and fruitful inclusion of the children in the wider horizon of society.

Education in love as self-giving is also the indispensable premise for parents called to give their children a clear and delicate *sex education*. Faced with a culture that largely reduces human sexuality to the level of something commonplace, since it interprets and lives it in a reductive and impoverished way by linking it solely with the body and with selfish pleasure, the educational service of parents must aim firmly at a training in the area of sex that is truly and fully personal: for sexuality is an enrichment of the whole person—body, emotions, and soul—and it manifests its inmost meaning in leading the person to the gift of self in love.

Sex education, which is a basic right and duty of parents, must always be carried out under their attentive guidance, whether at home or in educational centers chosen and controlled by them. In this regard, the Church reaffirms the law of subsidiarity, which the school is bound to observe when it cooperates in sex education, by entering into the same spirit that animates the parents.

In this context *education for chastity* is absolutely essential, for it is a virtue that develops a person's authentic maturity and makes him or her capable of respecting and fostering the "nuptial meaning" of the body. Indeed Christian parents, discerning the signs of God's call, will devote special attention and care to education in virginity or celibacy as the supreme form of that self-giving that constitutes the very meaning of human sexuality.

In view of the close links between the sexual dimension of the person and his or her ethical values, education must bring the children to a knowledge of and respect for the moral norms as the necessary and highly valuable guarantee for responsible personal growth in human sexuality.

For this reason the Church is firmly opposed to an often widespread form of imparting sex information dissociated from moral principles. That would merely be an introduction to the experience of pleasure and a stimulus leading to the loss of serenity—while still in the years of innocence—by opening the way to vice.

The Mission To Educate and the Sacrament of Marriage

38. For Christian parents the mission to educate, a mission rooted, as we have said, in their participation in God's creating activity, has a new specific source in the sacrament of marriage, which consecrates them for the strictly Christian education of their children:

that is to say, it calls upon them to share in the very authority and love of God the Father and Christ the Shepherd, and in the motherly love of the Church, and it enriches them with wisdom, counsel, fortitude and all the other gifts of the Holy Spirit in order to help the children in their growth as human beings and as Christians.

The sacrament of marriage gives to the educational role the dignity and vocation of being really and truly a "ministry" of the Church at the service of the building up of her members. So great and splendid is the educational ministry of Christian parents that Saint Thomas has no hesitation in comparing it with the ministry of priests: "Some only propagate and guard spiritual life by a spiritual ministry: this is the role of the sacrament of Orders; others do this for both corporal and spiritual life, and this is brought about by the sacrament of marriage, by which a man and a woman join in order to beget offspring and bring them up to worship God."[101]

A vivid and attentive awareness of the mission that they have received with the sacrament of marriage will help Christian parents to place themselves at the service of their children's education with great serenity and trustfulness, and also with a sense of responsibility before God, who calls them and gives them the mission of building up the Church in their children. Thus in the case of baptized people, the family, called together by word and sacrament as the Church of the home, is both teacher and mother, the same as the worldwide Church.

First Experience of the Church

39. The mission to educate demands that Christian parents should present to their children all the topics that are necessary for the gradual maturing of their personality from a Christian and ecclesial point of view. They will therefore follow the educational lines mentioned above, taking care to show their children the depths of significance to which the faith and love of Jesus Christ can lead. Furthermore, their awareness that the Lord is entrusting to them the growth of a child of God, a brother or sister of Christ, a temple of the Holy Spirit, a member of the Church, will support Christian parents in their task of strengthening the gift of divine grace in their children's souls.

The Second Vatican Council describes the content of Christian education as follows: "Such an education does not merely strive to foster maturity... in the human person. Rather, its principal aims are these: that as baptized persons are gradually introduced into a knowledge of the mystery of salvation, they may daily grow more conscious of the gift of faith which they have received; that they may learn to adore God the Father in spirit and in truth (cf. Jn. 4:23), especially through liturgical worship; that they may be trained to conduct their personal life in true righteousness and holiness, according to their new nature (Eph. 4:22-24), and thus grow to maturity, to the stature of the fullness of Christ (cf. Eph. 4:13), and devote themselves to the upbuilding of the Mystical Body. Moreover, aware of their calling, they should grow accustomed to giving witness to the hope that is in them (cf. 1 Pt. 3:15), and to promoting the Christian transformation of the world."[102]

The Synod too, taking up and developing the indications of the Council, presented the educational mission of the Christian family as a true ministry through which the Gospel is transmitted and radiated so that family life itself becomes an itinerary of faith and in some way a Christian initiation and a school of following Christ. Within a family that is aware of this gift, as Paul VI wrote, "all the members evangelize and are evangelized."[103]

By virtue of their ministry of educating, parents are, through the witness of their lives, the first heralds of the Gospel for their children. Furthermore, by praying with their children, by reading the word of God with them and by introducing them deeply through Christian initiation into the Body of Christ—both the Eucharistic and the ecclesial Body—they become fully parents, in that they are begetters not only of bodily life but also of the life that through the Spirit's renewal flows from the Cross and Resurrection of Christ.

In order that Christian parents may worthily carry out their ministry of educating, the Synod Fathers expressed the hope that a suitable *catechism for families* would be prepared, one that would be clear, brief and easily assimilated by all. The Episcopal Conferences were warmly invited to contribute to producing this catechism.

Relations with Other Educating Agents

40. The family is the primary but not the only and exclusive educating community. Man's community aspect itself—both civil and ecclesial—demands and leads to a broader and more articulated activity resulting from well-ordered collaboration between the various agents of education. All these agents are necessary, even though each can and should play its part in accordance with the special competence and contribution proper to itself.[104]

The educational role of the Christian family therefore has a very important place in organic pastoral work. This involves a new form of cooperation between parents and Christian communities, and between the various educational groups and pastors. In this sense, the renewal of the Catholic school must give special attention both to the parents of the pupils and to the formation of a perfect educating community.

The right of parents to choose an education in conformity with their religious faith must be absolutely guaranteed.

The State and the Church have the obligation to give families all possible aid to enable them to perform their educational role properly. Therefore both the Church and the State must create and foster the institutions and activities that families justly demand, and the aid must be in proportion to the families' needs. However, those in society who are in charge of schools must never forget that the parents have been appointed by God Himself as the first and principal educators of their children and that their right is completely inalienable.

But corresponding to their right, parents have a serious duty to commit themselves totally to a cordial and active relationship with the teachers and the school authorities.

If ideologies opposed to the Christian faith are taught in the schools, the family must join with other families, if possible through family associations, and with all its strength and with wisdom help the young not to depart from the faith. In this case the family needs special assistance from pastors of souls, who must never forget that parents have the inviolable right to entrust their children to the ecclesial community.

Manifold Service to Life

41. Fruitful married love expresses itself in serving life in many ways. Of these ways, begetting and educating children are the most immediate, specific and irreplaceable. In fact, every act of true love towards a human being bears witness to and perfects the spiritual fecundity of the family, since it is an act of obedience to the deep inner dynamism of love as self-giving to others.

For everyone this perspective is full of value and commitment, and it can be an inspiration in particular for couples who experience physical sterility.

Christian families, recognizing with faith all human beings as children of the same heavenly Father, will respond generously to the children of other families, giving them support and love not as outsiders but as members of the one family of God's children. Christian parents will thus be able to spread their love beyond the bonds of flesh and blood, nourishing the links that are rooted in the spirit and that develop through concrete service to the children of other families, who are often without even the barest necessities.

Christian families will be able to show greater readiness to adopt and foster children who have lost their parents or have been abandoned by them. Rediscovering the warmth of affection of a family, these children will be able to experience God's loving and provident fatherhood witnessed to by Christian parents, and they will thus be able to grow up with serenity and confidence in life. At the same time the whole family will be enriched with the spiritual values of a wider fraternity.

Family fecundity must have an unceasing "creativity," a marvelous fruit of the Spirit of God, who opens the eyes of the heart to discover the new needs and sufferings of our society and gives courage for accepting them and responding to them. A vast field of activity lies open to families: today, even more preoccupying than child abandonment is the phenomenon of social and cultural exclusion, which seriously affects the elderly, the sick, the disabled, drug addicts, ex-prisoners, etc.

This broadens enormously the horizons of the parenthood of Christian families: these and many other urgent needs of our time are a challenge to their spiritually fruitful love. With families and through them, the Lord Jesus continues to "have compassion" on the multitudes.

III — PARTICIPATING IN THE DEVELOPMENT OF SOCIETY

The Family as the First and Vital Cell of Society

42. "Since the Creator of all things has established the conjugal partnership as the beginning and basis of human society," the family is "the first and vital cell of society."[105]

The family has vital and organic links with society, since it is its foundation and nourishes it continually through its role of service to life: it is from the family that citizens come to birth and it is within the family that they find the first school of the social virtues that are the animating principle of the existence and development of society itself.

Thus, far from being closed in on itself, the family is by nature and vocation open to other families and to society, and undertakes its social role.

Family Life as an Experience of Communion and Sharing

43. The very experience of communion and sharing that should characterize the family's daily life represents its first and fundamental contribution to society.

The relationships between the members of the family community are inspired and guided by the law of "free giving." By respecting and fostering personal dignity in each and every one as the only basis for value, this free giving takes the form of heartfelt acceptance, encounter and dialogue, disinterested availability, generous service and deep solidarity.

Thus the fostering of authentic and mature communion between persons within the family is the first and irreplaceable school of social life, and example and stimulus for the broader community relationships marked by respect, justice, dialogue and love.

The family is thus, as the Synod Fathers recalled, the place of origin and the most effective means for humanizing and personalizing society: it makes an original contribution in depth to building up the world, by making possible a life that is properly speaking human, in particular by guarding and transmitting virtues and "values." As the Second Vatican Council states, in the family "the various generations come together and help one another to grow wiser and to harmonize personal rights with the other requirements of social living."[106]

Consequently, faced with a society that is running the risk of becoming more and more depersonalized and standardized and therefore inhuman and dehumanizing, with the negative results of many forms of escapism—such as alcoholism, drugs and even terrorism—the family possesses and continues still to release formidable energies capable of taking man out of his anonymity, keeping him conscious of his personal dignity, enriching him with deep humanity and actively placing him, in his uniqueness and unrepeatability, within the fabric of society.

44. The social role of the family certainly cannot stop short at procreation and education, even if this constitutes its primary and irreplaceable form of expression.

Families therefore, either singly or in association, can and should devote themselves to manifold social service activities, especially in favor of the poor, or at any rate for the benefit of all people and situations that cannot be reached by the public authorities' welfare organization.

The social contribution of the family has an original character of its own, one that should be given greater recognition and more decisive encouragement, especially as the children grow up, and actually involving all its members as much as possible.[107]

In particular, note must be taken of the ever greater importance in our society of hospitality in all its forms, from opening the door of one's home and still more of one's heart to the pleas of one's brothers and sisters, to concrete efforts to ensure that every family has its own home, as the natural environment that preserves it and makes it grow. In a special way the Christian family is called upon to listen to the Apostle's recommendation: "Practice hospitality,"[108] and therefore, imitating Christ's example and sharing in His love, to welcome the brother or sister in need: "Whoever gives to one of these little ones even a cup of cold water because he is a disciple, truly, I say to you, he shall not lose his reward."[109]

The social role of families is called upon to find expression also in the form of *political intervention*: families should be the first to take steps to see that the laws and institutions of the State not only do not offend but support and positively defend the rights and duties of the family. Along these lines, families should grow in awareness of being "protagonists" of what is known as "family politics" and assume responsibility for transforming society; otherwise families will be the first victims of the evils that they have done no more than note with indifference. The Second Vatican Council's appeal to go beyond an individualistic ethic therefore also holds good for the family as such.[110]

Society at the Service of the Family

45. Just as the intimate connection between the family and society demands that the family be open to and participate in society and its development, so also it requires that society should never fail in its fundamental task of respecting and fostering the family.

The family and society have complementary functions in defending and fostering the good of each and every human being. But society—more specifically the State—must recognize that "the family is a society in its own original right"[111] and so society is under a grave obligation in its relations with the family to adhere to the principle of subsidiarity.

By virtue of this principle, the State cannot and must not take away from families the functions that they can just as well perform

745

on their own or in free associations; instead it must positively favor and encourage as far as possible responsible initiative by families. In the conviction that the good of the family is an indispensable and essential value of the civil community, the public authorities must do everything possible to ensure that families have all those aids—economic, social, educational, political and cultural assistance—that they need in order to face all their responsibilities in a human way.

The Charter of Family Rights

46. The ideal of mutual support and development between the family and society is often very seriously in conflict with the reality of their separation and even opposition.

In fact, as was repeatedly denounced by the Synod, the situation experienced by many families in various countries is highly problematical, if not entirely negative: institutions and laws unjustly ignore the inviolable rights of the family and of the human person; and society, far from putting itself at the service of the family, attacks it violently in its values and fundamental requirements. Thus the family, which in God's plan is the basic cell of society and a subject of rights and duties before the State or any other community, finds itself the victim of society, of the delays and slowness with which it acts, and even of its blatant injustice.

For this reason, the Church openly and strongly defends the rights of the family against the intolerable usurpations of society and the State. In particular, the Synod Fathers mentioned the following rights of the family:

—the right to exist and progress as a family, that is to say, the right of every human being, even if he or she is poor, to found a family and to have adequate means to support it;

—the right to exercise its responsibility regarding the transmission of life and to educate children;

—the right to the intimacy of conjugal and family life;

—the right to the stability of the bond and of the institution of marriage;

—the right to believe in and profess one's faith and to propagate it;

—the right to bring up children in accordance with the family's own traditions, and religious and cultural values, with the necessary instruments, means and institutions;

—the right, especially of the poor and the sick, to obtain physical, social, political, and economic security;

—the right to housing suitable for living family life in a proper way;

—the right to expression and to representation, either directly or through associations, before the economic, social and cultural public authorities and lower authorities;

—the right to form associations with other families and institutions, in order to fulfill the family's role suitably and expeditiously;

—the right to protect minors by adequate institutions and legislation from harmful drugs, pornography, alcoholism, etc.;

—the right to wholesome recreation of a kind that also fosters family values;

—the right of the elderly to a worthy life and a worthy death;

—the right to emigrate as a family in search of a better life.[112]

Acceding to the Synod's explicit request, the Holy See will give prompt attention to studying these suggestions in depth and to the preparation of a Charter of Rights of the Family, to be presented to the quarters and authorities concerned.

The Christian Family's Grace and Responsibility

47. The social role that belongs to every family pertains by a new and original right to the Christian family, which is based on the sacrament of marriage. By taking up the human reality of the love between husband and wife in all its implications, the sacrament gives to Christian couples and parents a power and a commitment to live their vocation as lay people and therefore to "seek the kingdom of God by engaging in temporal affairs and by ordering them according to the plan of God."[113]

The social and political role is included in the kingly mission of service in which Christian couples share by virtue of the sacrament of marriage, and they receive both a command which they cannot ignore and a grace which sustains and stimulates them.

The Christian family is thus called upon to offer everyone a witness of generous and disinterested dedication to social matters, through a "preferential option" for the poor and disadvantaged. Therefore, advancing in its following of the Lord by special love for all the poor, it must have special concern for the hungry, the poor, the old, the sick, drug victims and those who have no family.

For a New International Order

48. In view of the worldwide dimension of various social questions nowadays, the family has seen its role with regard to the development of society extended in a completely new way: it now also involves cooperating for a new international order, since it is only in worldwide solidarity that the enormous and dramatic issues of world justice, the freedom of peoples and the peace of humanity can be dealt with and solved.

The spiritual communion between Christian families, rooted in a common faith and hope and given life by love, constitutes an inner energy that generates, spreads and develops justice, reconciliation, fraternity and peace among human beings. Insofar as it is a "small-scale Church," the Christian family is called upon, like the "large-scale Church," to be a sign of unity for the world and in this way to exercise its prophetic role by bearing witness to the Kingdom and peace of Christ, towards which the whole world is journeying .

Christian families can do this through their educational activity—that is to say by presenting to their children a model of life based on the values of truth, freedom, justice and love—both through active and responsible involvement in the authentically human growth of society and its institutions, and by supporting in various ways the associations specifically devoted to international issues.

IV — SHARING IN THE LIFE AND MISSION OF THE CHURCH

The Family, Within the Mystery of the Church

49. Among the fundamental tasks of the Christian family is its ecclesial task: the family is placed at the service of the building up of the Kingdom of God in history by participating in the life and mission of the Church.

In order to understand better the foundations, the contents and the characteristics of this participation, we must examine the many profound bonds linking the Church and the Christian family and establishing the family as a "Church in miniature" *(Ecclesia domestica)*,[114] in such a way that in its own way the family is a living image and historical representation of the mystery of the Church.

It is, above all, the Church as Mother that gives birth to, educates and builds up the Christian family, by putting into effect in its regard the saving mission which she has received from her Lord. By proclaiming the word of God, the Church reveals to the Christian family its true identity, what it is and should be according to the Lord's plan; by celebrating the sacraments, the Church enriches and strengthens the Christian family with the grace of Christ for its sanctification to the glory of the Father; by the continuous proclamation of the new commandment of love, the Church encourages and guides the Christian family to the service of love, so that it may imitate and relive the same self-giving and sacrificial love that the Lord Jesus has for the entire human race.

In turn, the Christian family is grafted into the mystery of the Church to such a degree as to become a sharer, in its own way, in the saving mission proper to the Church: by virtue of the sacrament, Christian married couples and parents "in their state and way of life have their own special gift among the People of God."[115] For this reason they not only *receive* the love of Christ and become a *saved* community, but they are also called upon to *communicate* Christ's love to their brethren, thus becoming a *saving* community. In this way, while the Christian family is a fruit and sign of the supernatural fecundity of the Church, it stands also as a symbol, witness and participant of the Church's motherhood."[118]

A Specific and Original Ecclesial Role

50. The Christian family is called upon to take part actively and responsibly in the mission of the Church in a way that is original and specific, by placing itself, in what it is and what it does as an "intimate community of life and love," at the service of the Church and of society.

Since the Christian family is a community in which the relationships are renewed by Christ through faith and the sacraments, the family's sharing in the Church's mission should follow a *community pattern*: the spouses together *as a couple*, the parents and children *as a family*, must live their service to the Church and to the world. They must be "of one heart and soul"[117] in faith, through the shared apostolic zeal that animates them, and through their shared commitment to works of service to the ecclesial and civil communities.

The Christian family also builds up the Kingdom of God in history through the everyday realities that concern and distinguish *its state of life*. It is thus in *the love between husband and wife and between the members of the family*—a love lived out in all its extraordinary richness of values and demands: totality, oneness, fidelity and fruitfulness[118]—that the Christian family's participation in the prophetic, priestly and kingly mission of Jesus Christ and of His Church finds expression and realization. Therefore, love and life constitute the nucleus of the saving mission of the Christian family in the Church and for the Church.

The Second Vatican Council recalls this fact when it writes: "Families will share their spiritual riches generously with other families too. Thus the Christian family, which springs from marriage as a reflection of the loving covenant uniting Christ with the Church, and as a participation in that covenant will manifest to all people the Savior's living presence in the world, and the genuine nature of the Church. This the family will do by the mutual love of the spouses, by their generous fruitfulness, their solidarity and faithfulness, and by the loving way in which all the members of the family work together."[119]

Having laid the *foundation* of the participation of the Christian family in the Church's mission, it is now time to illustrate its *substance in reference to Jesus Christ as Prophet, Priest and King*—three aspects of a single reality—by presenting the Christian family as 1) a believing and evangelizing community, 2) a community in dialogue with God, and 3) a community at the service of man.

1. The Christian Family as a Believing and Evangelizing Community

Faith as the Discovery and Admiring Awareness of God's Plan for the Family

51. As a sharer in the life and mission of the Church, which listens to the word of God with reverence and proclaims it confidently,[120] *the Christian family fulfills its prophetic role by welcoming and announcing the word of God*: it thus becomes more and more each day a believing and evangelizing community.

Christian spouses and parents are required to offer "the obedience of faith."[121] They are called upon to welcome the word of the Lord which reveals to them the marvelous news—the Good News—of their conjugal and family life sanctified and made a source of sanctity by Christ Himself. Only in faith can they discover and admire with joyful gratitude the dignity to which God has deigned to raise marriage and the family, making them a sign and meeting place of the loving covenant between God and man, between Jesus Christ and His bride, the Church.

The very preparation for Christian marriage is itself a journey of faith. It is a special opportunity for the engaged to rediscover and deepen the faith received in Baptism and nourished by their Christian upbringing. In this way they come to recognize and freely accept their vocation to follow Christ and to serve the Kingdom of God in the married state.

The celebration of the sacrament of marriage is the basic moment of the faith of the couple. This sacrament, in essence, is the proclamation in the Church of the Good News concerning married love. It is the word of God that "reveals" and "fulfills" the wise and loving plan of God for the married couple, giving them a mysterious and real share in the very love with which God Himself loves humanity. Since the sacramental celebration of marriage is itself a proclamation of the word of God, it must also be a "profession of faith" within and with the Church, as a community of believers, on the part of all those who in different ways participate in its celebration.

This profession of faith demands that it be prolonged in the life of the married couple and of the family. God, who called the couple *to* marriage, continues to call them *in* marriage.[122] In and through the events, problems, difficulties and circumstances of everyday life, God comes to them, revealing and presenting the concrete "demands" of their sharing in the love of Christ for His Church in the particular family, social and ecclesial situation in which they find themselves.

The discovery of and obedience to the plan of God on the part of the conjugal and family community must take place in "togetherness," through the human experience of love between husband and wife, between parents and children, lived in the Spirit of Christ.

Thus the little domestic Church, like the greater Church, needs to be constantly and intensely evangelized: hence its duty regarding permanent education in the faith.

The Christian Family's Ministry of Evangelization

52. To the extent in which the Christian family accepts the Gospel and matures in faith, it becomes an evangelizing community. Let us listen again to Paul VI: "The family, like the Church, ought to be a place where the Gospel is transmitted and from which the Gospel radiates. In a family which is conscious of this mission, all the members evangelize and are evangelized. The parents not only communicate the Gospel to their children, but from their children they can themselves receive the same Gospel as deeply lived by them. And such a family becomes the evangelizer of many other families, and of the neighborhood of which it forms part."[123]

As the Synod repeated, taking up the appeal which I launched at Puebla, the future of evangelization depends in great part on the

Church of the home.[124] This apostolic mission of the family is rooted in Baptism and receives from the grace of the sacrament of marriage new strength to transmit the faith, to sanctify and transform our present society according to God's plan.

Particularly today, the Christian family has a special vocation to witness to the paschal covenant of Christ by constantly radiating the joy of love and the certainty of the hope for which it must give an account: "The Christian family loudly proclaims both the present virtues of the Kingdom of God and the hope of a blessed life to come."[125]

The absolute need for family catechesis emerges with particular force in certain situations that the Church unfortunately experiences in some places: "In places where anti-religious legislation endeavors even to prevent education in the faith, and in places where widespread unbelief or invasive secularism makes real religious growth practically impossible, 'the Church of the home' remains the one place where children and young people can receive an authentic catechesis."[126]

Ecclesial Service

53. The ministry of evangelization carried out by Christian parents is original and irreplaceable. It assumes the characteristics typical of family life itself, which should be interwoven with love, simplicity, practicality and daily witness.[127]

The family must educate the children for life in such a way that each one may fully perform his or her role according to the vocation received from God. Indeed, the family that is open to transcendent values, that serves its brothers and sisters with joy, that fulfills its duties with generous fidelity, and is aware of its daily sharing in the mystery of the glorious Cross of Christ, becomes the primary and most excellent seedbed of vocations to a life of consecration to the Kingdom of God.

The parents' ministry of evangelization and catechesis ought to play a part in their children's lives also during adolescence and youth, when the children, as often happens, challenge or even reject the Christian faith received in earlier years. Just as in the Church the work of evangelization can never be separated from the sufferings of the apostle, so in the Christian family parents must face with courage and great interior serenity the difficulties that their ministry of evangelization sometimes encounters in their own children.

It should not be forgotten that the service rendered by Christian spouses and parents to the Gospel is essentially an ecclesial service. It has its place within the context of the whole Church as an evangelized and evangelizing community. In so far as the ministry of evangelization and catechesis of the Church of the home is rooted in and derives from the one mission of the Church and is ordained to the upbuilding of the one Body of Christ,[128] it must remain in intimate communion and collaborate responsibly with all the other evangelizing and catechetical activities present and at work in the ecclesial community at the diocesan and parochial levels.

To Preach the Gospel to the Whole Creation

54. Evangelization, urged on within by irrepressible missionary zeal, is characterized by a universality without boundaries. It is the response to Christ's explicit and unequivocal command: "Go into all the world and preach the Gospel to the whole creation."[129]

The Christian family's faith and evangelizing mission also possesses this catholic missionary inspiration. The sacrament of marriage takes up and reproposes the task of defending and spreading the faith, a task that has its roots in Baptism and Confirmation,[130] and makes Christian married couples and parents witnesses of Christ "to the end of the earth,"[131] missionaries, in the true and proper sense, of love and life.

A form of missionary activity can be exercised even within the family. This happens when some member of the family does not have the faith or does not practice it with consistency. In such a case the other members must give him or her a living witness of their own faith in order to encourage and support him or her along the path towards full acceptance of Christ the Savior.[132]

Animated in its own inner life by missionary zeal the Church of the home is also called to be a luminous sign of the presence of Christ and of His love for those who are "far away," for families who do not yet believe, and for those Christian families who no longer live in accordance with the faith that they once received. The Christian family is called to enlighten "by its example and its witness...those who seek the truth."[133]

Just as at the dawn of Christianity Aquila and Priscilla were presented as a missionary couple,[134] so today the Church shows forth her perennial newness and fruitfulness by the presence of Christian couples and families who dedicate at least a part of their lives to working in missionary territories, proclaiming the Gospel and doing service to their fellowman in the love of Jesus Christ.

Christian families offer a special contribution to the missionary cause of the Church by fostering missionary vocations among their sons and daughters [135] and, more generally, "by training their children from childhood to recognize God's love for all people."[136]

2. The Christian Family as a Community in Dialogue with God

The Church's Sanctuary in the Home

55. The proclamation of the Gospel and its acceptance in faith reach their fullness in the celebration of the sacraments. The Church which is a believing and evangelizing community is also a priestly people invested with the dignity and sharing in the power of Christ the High Priest of the New and Eternal Covenant.[137]

The Christian family too is part of this priestly people which is the Church. By means of the sacrament of marriage, in which it is rooted and from which it draws its nourishment, the Christian family is continuously vivified by the Lord Jesus and called and engaged by Him in a dialogue with God through the sacraments, through the offering of one's life, and through prayer.

This is the *priestly role* which the Christian family can and ought to exercise in intimate communion with the whole Church, through the daily realities of married and family life. In this way the Christian family *is called to be sanctified and to sanctify the ecclesial community and the world.*

Marriage as a Sacrament of Mutual Sanctification and an Act of Worship

56. The sacrament of marriage is the specific source and original means of sanctification for Christian married couples and families. It takes up again and makes specific the sanctifying grace of Baptism. By virtue of the mystery of the death and Resurrection of Christ, of which the spouses are made part in a new way by marriage, conjugal love is purified and made holy: "This love the Lord has judged worthy of special gifts, healing, perfecting and exalting gifts of grace and of charity."[138]

The gift of Jesus Christ is not exhausted in the actual celebration of the sacrament of marriage, but rather accompanies the married couple throughout their lives. This fact is explicitly recalled by the Second Vatican Council when it says that Jesus Christ "abides with them so that, just as He loved the Church and handed Himself over on her behalf, the spouses may love each other with perpetual fidelity through mutual self-bestowal.... For this reason, Christian spouses have a special sacrament by which they are fortified and receive a kind of consecration in the duties and dignity of their state. By virtue of this sacrament, as spouses fulfill their conjugal and family obligations, they are penetrated with the Spirit of Christ, who fills their whole lives with faith, hope, and charity. Thus they increasingly advance towards their own perfection, as well as towards their mutual sanctification, and hence contribute jointly to the glory of God."[139]

Christian spouses and parents are included in the universal call to sanctity. For them this call is specified by the sacrament they have celebrated and is carried out concretely in the realities proper to their conjugal and family life.[140] This gives rise to the grace and requirement of an authentic and profound *conjugal and family spirituality* that draws its inspiration from the themes of creation, covenant, cross, resurrection, and sign, which were stressed more than once by the Synod.

Christian marriage, like the other sacraments, "whose purpose is to sanctify people, to build up the body of Christ, and finally, to give worship to God,"[141] is in itself a liturgical action glorifying God in Jesus Christ and in the Church. By celebrating it, Christian spouses profess their gratitude to God for the sublime gift bestowed on them of being able to live in their married and family lives the very love of God for people and that of the Lord Jesus for the Church, His bride.

Just as husbands and wives receive from the sacrament the gift and responsibility of translating into daily living the sanctification bestowed on them, so the same sacrament confers on them the grace and moral obligation of transforming their whole lives into a "spiritual sacrifice."[142] What the Council says of the laity applies also to Christian spouses and parents, especially with regard to the earthly and temporal realities that characterize their lives: "As worshippers leading holy lives in every place, the laity consecrate the world itself to God."[143]

Marriage and the Eucharist

57. The Christian family's sanctifying role is grounded in Baptism and has its highest expression in the Eucharist, to which Christian marriage is intimately connected. The Second Vatican Council drew attention to the unique relationship between the Eucharist and marriage by requesting that "marriage normally be celebrated within the Mass."[144] To understand better and live more intensely the graces and responsibilities of Christian marriage and family life, it is altogether necessary to rediscover and strengthen this relationship.

The Eucharist is the very source of Christian marriage. The Eucharistic Sacrifice, in fact, represents Christ's covenant of love with the Church, sealed with His blood on the Cross.[145] In this sacrifice of the New and Eternal Covenant, Christian spouses encounter the source from which their own marriage covenant flows, is interiorly structured and continuously renewed. As a re-presentation of Christ's sacrifice of love for the Church, the Eucharist is a fountain of charity. In the Eucharistic gift of charity the Christian family finds the foundation and soul of its "communion" and its "mission": by partaking in the Eucharistic bread, the different members of the Christian family become one body, which reveals and shares in the wider unity of the Church. Their sharing in the Body of Christ that is "given up" and in His Blood that is "shed" becomes a never-ending source of missionary and apostolic dynamism for the Christian family .

The Sacrament of Conversion and Reconciliation

58. An essential and permanent part of the Christian family's sanctifying role consists in accepting the call to conversion that the Gospel addresses to all Christians, who do not always remain faithful to the "newness" of the Baptism that constitutes them "saints." The Christian family too is sometimes unfaithful to the law of baptismal grace and holiness proclaimed anew in the sacrament of marriage.

Repentance and mutual pardon within the bosom of the Christian family, so much a part of daily life, receive their specific sacramental expression in Christian Penance. In the Encyclical *Humanae vltae*, Paul VI wrote of married couples: "And if sin should still keep its hold over them, let them not be discouraged, but rather have recourse with humble perseverance to the mercy of God, which is abundantly poured forth in the sacrament of Penance." [146]

The celebration of this sacrament acquires special significance for family life. While they discover in faith that sin contradicts not only the covenant with God, but also the covenant between husband and wife and the communion of the family, the married couple and the other members of the family are led to an encounter with God, who is "rich in mercy,"[147] who bestows on them His love which is more powerful than sin,[148] and who reconstructs and brings to perfection the marriage covenant and the family communion.

Family Prayer

59. The Church prays for the Christian family and educates the family to live in generous accord with the priestly gift and role received from Christ the High Priest. In effect, the baptismal priesthood of the faithful, exercised in the sacrament of marriage, constitutes the basis of a priestly vocation and mission for the spouses and family by which their daily lives are transformed into "spiritual sacrifices acceptable to God through Jesus Christ."[149] This transformation is achieved not only by celebrating the Eucharist and the other sacraments and through offering themselves to the glory of God, but also through a life of prayer, through prayerful dialogue with the Father, through Jesus Christ, in the Holy Spirit.

Family prayer has its own characteristic qualities. It is prayer offered *in common*, husband and wife together, parents and children together. Communion in prayer is both a consequence of and a requirement for the communion bestowed by the sacraments of Baptism and Matrimony. The words with which the Lord Jesus promises His presence can be applied to the members of the Christian family in a special way: "Again I say to you, if two of you agree on earth about anything they ask, it will be done for them by my Father in heaven. For where two or three are gathered in my name, there am I in the midst of them."[150]

Family prayer has for its very own object *family life itself*, which in all its varying circumstances is seen as a call from God and lived as a filial response to His call. Joys and sorrows, hopes and disappointments, births and birthday celebrations, wedding anniversaries of the parents, departures, separations and homecomings, important and far-reaching decisions, the death of those who are dear, etc.—all of these mark God's loving intervention in the family's history. They should be seen as suitable moments for thanksgiving, for petition, for trusting abandonment of the family into the hands of their common Father in heaven. The dignity and responsibility of the Christian family as the domestic Church can be achieved only with God's unceasing aid, which will surely be granted if it is humbly and trustingly petitioned in prayer.

Educators in Prayer

60. By reason of their dignity and mission, Christian parents have the specific responsibility of educating their children in prayer, introducing them to gradual discovery of the mystery of God

755

and to personal dialogue with Him: "It is particularly in the Christian family, enriched by the grace and the office of the sacrament of Matrimony, that from the earliest years children should be taught, according to the faith received in Baptism, to have a knowledge of God, to worship Him and to love their neighbor."[151]

The concrete example and living witness of parents is fundamental and irreplaceable in educating their children to pray. Only by praying together with their children can a father and mother—exercising their royal priesthood—penetrate the innermost depths of their children's hearts and leave an impression that the future events in their lives will not be able to efface. Let us again listen to the appeal made by Paul VI to parents: "Mothers, do you teach your children the Christian prayers? Do you prepare them, in conjunction with the priests, for the sacraments that they receive when they are young: Confession, Communion and Confirmation? Do you encourage them when they are sick to think of Christ suffering, to invoke the aid of the Blessed Virgin and the saints? Do you say the family rosary together? And you, fathers, do you pray with your children, with the whole domestic community, at least sometimes? Your example of honesty in thought and action, joined to some common prayer, is a lesson for life, an act of worship of singular value. In this way you bring peace to your homes: *Pax huic domui*. Remember, it is thus that you build up the Church."[152]

Liturgical Prayer and Private Prayer

61. There exists a deep and vital bond between the prayer of the Church and the prayer of the individual faithful, as has been clearly reaffirmed by the Second Vatican Council.[153] An important purpose of the prayer of the domestic Church is to serve as the natural introduction for the children to the liturgical prayer of the whole Church, both in the sense of preparing for it and of extending it into personal, family and social life. Hence the need for gradual participation by all the members of the Christian family in the celebration of the Eucharist, especially on Sundays and feast days, and of the other sacraments, particularly the sacraments of Christian initiation of the children. The directives of the Council opened up a new possibility for the Christian family when it listed the family among those groups to whom it recommends the recitation of the Divine Office in common.[154] Likewise, the Christian family will strive to celebrate at home, and in a way suited to the members, the times and feasts of the liturgical year.

As preparation for the worship celebrated in church, and as its prolongation in the home, the Christian family makes use of private prayer, which presents a great variety of forms. While this variety testifies to the extraordinary richness with which the Spirit vivifies Christian prayer, it serves also to meet the various needs and life situations of those who turn to the Lord in prayer. Apart from morning and evening prayers, certain forms of prayer are to be expressly encouraged, following the indications of the Synod Fathers, such as reading and meditating on the word of God, preparation for the reception of the sacraments, devotion and consecration to the Sacred Heart of Jesus, the various forms of veneration of the Blessed Virgin Mary, grace before and after meals, and observance of popular devotions. While respecting the freedom of the children of God, the Church has always proposed certain practices of piety to the faithful with particular solicitude and insistence. Among these should be mentioned the recitation of the rosary: "We now desire, as a continuation of the thought of our predecessors, to recommend strongly the recitation of the family rosary.... There is no doubt that...the rosary should be considered as one of the best and most efficacious prayers in common that the Christian family is invited to recite. We like to think, and sincerely hope, that when the family gathering becomes a time of prayer the rosary is a frequent and favored manner of praying."[155] In this way authentic devotion to Mary which finds expression in sincere love and generous imitation of the Blessed Virgin's interior spiritual attitude, constitutes a special instrument for nourishing loving communion in the family and for developing conjugal and family spirituality. For she who is the Mother of Christ and of the Church is in a special way the Mother of Christian families, of domestic Churches.

Prayer and Life

62. It should never be forgotten that prayer constitutes an essential part of Christian life, understood in its fullness and centrality. Indeed, prayer is an important part of our very humanity: it is "the first expression of man's inner truth, the first condition for authentic freedom of spirit."[156] Far from being a form of escapism from everyday commitments, prayer constitutes the strongest incentive for the Christian family to assume and comply fully with all its responsibilities as the primary and fundamental cell of human society. Thus the Christian family's actual participation in the Church's life and mission is in direct proportion to the fidelity and intensity of the prayer with which it is united with the fruitful vine that is Christ the Lord.[157] The fruitfulness of the Christian family in its specific service to human advancement, which of itself cannot but lead to the transformation of the world, derives from its living union with Christ, nourished by the Liturgy, by self-oblation and by prayer.[158]

3. *The Christian Family*

The New Commandment of Love

63. The Church, a prophetic, priestly and kingly people, is endowed with the mission of bringing all human beings to accept the word of God in faith, to celebrate and profess it in the sacraments and in prayer, and to give expression to it in the concrete realities of life in accordance with the gift and new commandment of love.

The law of Christian life is to be found not in a written code, but in the personal action of the Holy Spirit who inspires and guides the Christian. It is the "law of the Spirit of life in Christ Jesus".[159]

"God's love has been poured into our hearts through the Holy Spirit who has been given to us."[160]

This is true also for the Christian couple and family. Their guide and rule of life is the Spirit of Jesus poured into their hearts in the celebration of the sacrament of Matrimony. In continuity with Baptism in water and the Spirit, marriage sets forth anew the evangelical law of love, and with the gift of the Spirit engraves it more profoundly on the hearts of Christian husbands and wives. Their love, purified and saved, is a fruit of the Spirit acting in the hearts of believers and constituting, at the same time, the fundamental commandment of their moral life to be lived in responsible freedom.

Thus, the Christian family is inspired and guided by the new law of the Spirit and, in intimate communion with the Church, the kingly people, it is called to exercise its "service" of love towards God and towards its fellow human beings. Just as Christ exercises His royal power by serving us,[161] so also the Christian finds the authentic meaning of his participation in the kingship of his Lord in sharing His spirit and practice of service to man. "Christ has communicated this power to his disciples that they might be established in royal freedom and that by self-denial and a holy life they might conquer the reign of sin in themselves (cf. Rom. 6:12). Further, He has shared this power so that by serving Him in their fellow human beings they might through humility and patience lead their brothers and sisters to that King whom to serve is to reign. For the Lord wishes to spread His kingdom by means of the laity also, a kingdom of truth and life, a kingdom of holiness and grace, a kingdom of justice, love and peace. In this kingdom, creation itself will be delivered out of its slavery to corruption and into the freedom of the glory of the children of God (cf. Rom. 8:21)."[162]

To Discover the Image of God in Each Brother and Sister

64. Inspired and sustained by the new commandment of love, the Christian family welcomes, respects and serves every human being, considering each one in his or her dignity as a person and as a child of God.

It should be so especially between husband and wife and within the family, through a daily effort to promote a truly personal community, initiated and fostered by an inner communion of love. This way of life should then be extended to the wider circle of the ecclesial community of which the Christian family is a part. Thanks to love within the family, the Church can and ought to take on a more homelike or family dimension, developing a more human and fraternal style of relationships.

Love, too, goes beyond our brothers and sisters of the same faith since "everybody is my brother or sister." In each individual, especially in the poor, the weak, and those who suffer or are unjustly treated love knows how to discover the face of Christ, and discover a fellow human being to be loved and served.

In order that the family may serve man in a truly evangelical way, the instructions of the Second Vatican Council must be carefully put into practice: "That the exercise of such charity may rise above any deficiencies in fact and even in appearance, certain fundamentals must be observed. Thus, attention is to be paid to the image of God in which our neighbor has been created, and also to Christ the Lord to whom is really offered whatever is given to a needy person."[163]

While building up the Church in love, the Christian family places itself at the service of the human person and the world, really bringing about the "human advancement" whose substance was given in summary form in the Synod's Message to families: "Another task for the family is to form persons in love and also to practice love in all its relationships, so that it does not live closed in on itself, but remains open to the community, moved by a sense of justice and concern for others, as well as by a consciousness of its responsibility towards the whole of society."[164]

PART FOUR
PASTORAL CARE OF THE FAMILY: STAGES, STRUCTURES, AGENTS AND SITUATIONS
I — STAGES OF PASTORAL CARE OF THE FAMILY

The Church Accompanies the Christian Family on Its Journey Through Life

65. Like every other living reality, the family too is called upon to develop and grow. After the preparation of engagement and the sacramental celebration of marriage, the couple begin their daily journey towards the progressive actuation of the values and duties of marriage itself.

In the light of faith and by virtue of hope, the Christian family too shares, in communion with the Church, in the experience of the earthly pilgrimage towards the full revelation and manifestation of the Kingdom of God.

Therefore, it must be emphasized once more that the pastoral intervention of the Church in support of the family is a matter of urgency. Every effort should be made to strengthen and develop pastoral care for the family, which should be treated as a real matter of priority, in the certainty that future evangelization depends largely on the domestic Church.[165]

The Church's pastoral concern will not be limited only to the Christian families closest at hand; it will extend its horizons in harmony with the Heart of Christ, and will show itself to be even more lively for families in general and for those families in particular which are in difficult or irregular situations. For all of them the Church will have a word of truth, goodness, understanding, hope and deep sympathy with their sometimes tragic difficulties. To all of them she will offer her disinterested help so that they can come closer to that model of a family which the Creator intended from "the beginning" and which Christ has renewed with His redeeming grace.

The Church's pastoral action must be progressive, also in the sense that it must follow the family, accompanying it step by step in the different stages of its formation and development.

Preparation for Marriage

66. More than ever necessary in our times is preparation of young people for marriage and family life. In some countries it is still the families themselves that, according to ancient customs, ensure the passing on to young people of the values concerning married and family life, and they do this through a gradual process of education or initiation. But the changes that have taken place within almost all modern societies demand that not only the family but also society and the Church should be involved in the effort of properly preparing young people for their future responsibilities. Many negative phenomena which are today noted with regret in family life derive from the fact that, in the new situations, young people not only lose sight of the correct hierarchy of values but, since they no longer have certain criteria of behavior, they do not know how to face and deal with the new difficulties. But experience teaches that young people who have been well prepared for family life generally succeed better than others.

This is even more applicable to Christian marriage, which influences the holiness of large numbers of men and women. The Church must therefore promote better and more intensive programs of marriage preparation, in order to eliminate as far as possible the difficulties that many married couples find themselves in, and even more in order to favor positively the establishing and maturing of successful marriages.

Marriage preparation has to be seen and put into practice as a gradual and continuous process. It includes three main stages: remote, proximate and immediate preparation.

Remote preparation begins in early childhood, in that wise family training which leads children to discover themselves as being endowed with a rich and complex psychology and with a particular personality with its own strengths and weaknesses. It is the period when esteem for all authentic human values is instilled, both in interpersonal and in social relationships, with all that this signifies for the formation of character, for the control and right use of one's inclinations, for the manner of regarding and meeting people of the opposite sex, and so on. Also necessary, especially for Christians, is solid spiritual and catechetical formation that will show that marriage is a true vocation and mission, without excluding the possibility of the total gift of self to God in the vocation to the priestly or religious life.

Upon this basis there will subsequently and gradually be built up the *proximate preparation*, which—from the suitable age and with adequate catechesis, as in a catechumenal process—involves a more specific preparation for the sacraments, as it were, a rediscovery of them. This renewed catechesis of young people and others preparing for Christian marriage is absolutely necessary in order that the sacrament may be celebrated and lived with the right moral and spiritual dispositions. The religious formation of young people should be integrated, at the right moment and in accordance with the various concrete requirements, with a preparation for life as a couple. This preparation will present marriage as an interpersonal relationship of a man and a woman that has to be continually developed, and it will encourage those concerned to study the nature of conjugal sexuality and responsible parenthood, with the essential medical and biological knowledge connected with it. It will also acquaint those concerned with correct methods for the education of children, and will assist them in gaining the basic requisites for well-ordered family life, such as stable work, sufficient financial resources, sensible administration, notions of housekeeping.

Finally, one must not overlook preparation for the family apostolate, for fraternal solidarity and collaboration with other families, for active membership in groups, associations, movements and undertakings set up for the human and Christian benefit of the family.

The *immediate preparation* for the celebration of the sacrament of Matrimony should take place in the months and weeks immediately preceding the wedding, so as to give a new meaning, content and form to the so-called premarital enquiry required by Canon Law. This preparation is not only necessary in every case, but is also more urgently needed for engaged couples that still manifest shortcomings or difficulties in Christian doctrine and practice.

Among the elements to be instilled in this journey of faith, which is similar to the catechumenate, there must also be a deeper knowledge of the mystery of Christ and the Church, of the meaning of grace and of the responsibility of Christian marriage, as well as preparation for taking an active and conscious part in the rites of the marriage liturgy.

The Christian family and the whole of the ecclesial community should feel involved in the different phases of the preparation for marriage, which have been described only in their broad outlines. It is to be hoped that the Episcopal Conferences, just as they are concerned with appropriate initiatives to help engaged couples to be more aware of the seriousness of their choice and also to help pastors of souls to make sure of the couples' proper dispositions, so they will also take steps to see that there is issued a *Directory for the Pastoral Care of the Family*. In this they should lay down, in the first place, the minimum content, duration and method of the "Preparation Courses," balancing the different aspects—doctrinal, pedagogical, legal and medical—concerning marriage, and structuring them in such a way that those preparing for marriage will not only receive an intellectual training but will also feel a desire to enter actively into the ecclesial community.

Although one must not underestimate the necessity and obligation of the immediate preparation for marriage—which would happen if dispensations from it were easily given—nevertheless such preparation must always be set forth and put into practice in such a way that omitting it is not an impediment to the celebration of marriage.

67. Christian marriage normally requires a liturgical celebration expressing in social and community form the essentially ecclesial and sacramental nature of the conjugal covenant between baptized persons.

Inasmuch as it is a *sacramental action of sanctification*, the celebration of marriage—inserted into the liturgy, which is the summit of the Church's action and the source of her sanctifying power[166] must be *per se* valid, worthy and fruitful. This opens a wide field for pastoral solicitude, in order that the needs deriving from the nature of the conjugal covenant, elevated into a sacrament, may be fully met, and also in order that the Church's discipline regarding free consent, impediments, the canonical form and the actual rite of the celebration may be faithfully observed. The celebration should be simple and dignified, according to the norms of the competent authorities of the Church. It is also for them—in accordance with concrete circumstances of time and place and in conformity with the norms issued by the Apostolic See[167]—to include in the liturgical celebration such elements proper to each culture which serve to express more clearly the profound human and religious significance of the marriage contract, provided that such elements contain nothing that is not in harmony with Christian faith and morality.

Inasmuch as it is a *sign*, the liturgical celebration should be conducted in such a way as to constitute, also in its external reality, a proclamation of the word of God and a profession of faith on the part of the community of believers. Pastoral commitment will be expressed here through the intelligent and careful preparation of the Liturgy of the Word and through the education to faith of those participating in the celebration and in the first place the couple being married.

Inasmuch as it is a *sacramental action of the Church*, the liturgical celebration of marriage should involve the Christian community, with the full, active and responsible participation of all those present, according to the place and task of each individual: the bride and bridegroom, the priest, the witnesses, the relatives, the friends, the other members of the faithful, all of them members of an assembly that manifests and lives the mystery of Christ and His Church. For the celebration of Christian marriage in the sphere of ancestral cultures or traditions, the principles laid down above should be followed.

Celebration of Marriage and Evangelization of Non-believing Baptized Persons

68. Precisely because in the celebration of the sacrament very special attention must be devoted to the moral and spiritual dispositions of those being married, in particular to their faith, we must here deal with a not infrequent difficulty in which the pastors of the Church can find themselves in the context of our secularized society.

In fact, the faith of the person asking the Church for marriage can exist in different degrees, and it is the primary duty of pastors to bring about a rediscovery of this faith and to nourish it and bring it to maturity. But pastors must also understand the reasons that lead the Church also to admit to the celebration of marriage those who are imperfectly disposed.

The sacrament of Matrimony has this specific element that distinguishes it from all the other sacraments: it is the sacrament of something that was part of the very economy of creation; it is the very conjugal covenant instituted by the Creator "in the beginning." Therefore the decision of a man and a woman to marry in accordance with this divine plan, that is to say, the decision to commit by their irrevocable conjugal consent their whole lives in indissoluble love and unconditional fidelity, really involves, even if not in a fully conscious way, an attitude of profound obedience to the will of God, an attitude which cannot exist without God's grace. They have thus already begun what is in a true and proper sense a journey towards salvation, a journey which the celebration of the sacrament and the immediate preparation for it can complement and bring to completion, given the uprightness of their intention.

On the other hand it is true that in some places engaged couples ask to be married in church for motives which are social rather than genuinely religious. This is not surprising. Marriage, in fact, is not an event that concerns only the persons actually getting married. By its very nature it is also a social matter, committing the couple being married in the eyes of society. And its celebration has always been an occasion of rejoicing that brings together families and friends. It therefore goes without saying that social as well as personal motives enter into the request to be married in church.

Nevertheless, it must not be forgotten that these engaged couples, by virtue of their Baptism, are already really sharers in Christ's marriage Covenant with the Church, and that, by their right intention, they have accepted God's plan regarding marriage and therefore at least implicitly consent to what the Church intends to do when she celebrates marriage. Thus, the fact that motives of a social nature also enter into the request is not enough to justify refusal on the part of pastors. Moreover, as the Second Vatican Council teaches, the sacraments by words and ritual elements nourish and strengthen faith[168]: that faith towards which the married couple are already journeying by reason of the uprightness of their intention, which Christ's grace certainly does not fail to favor and support.

As for wishing to lay down further criteria for admission to the ecclesial celebration of marriage, criteria that would concern the level of faith of those to be married, this would above all involve grave risks. In the first place, the risk of making unfounded and discriminatory judgments; secondly, the risk of causing doubts about the validity of marriages already celebrated, with grave harm to Christian communities, and new and unjustified anxieties to the consciences of married couples; one would also fall into the danger of calling into question the sacramental nature of many

763

marriages of brethren separated from full communion with the Catholic Church, thus contradicting ecclesial tradition.

However, when in spite of all efforts, engaged couples show that they reject explicitly and formally what the Church intends to do when the marriage of baptized persons is celebrated, the pastor of souls cannot admit them to the celebration of marriage. In spite of his reluctance to do so, he has the duty to take note of the situation and to make it clear to those concerned that, in these circumstances, it is not the Church that is placing an obstacle in the way of the celebration that they are asking for, but themselves.

Once more there appears in all its urgency the need for evangelization and catechesis before and after marriage, effected by the whole Christian community, so that every man and woman that gets married celebrates the sacrament of Matrimony not only validly but also fruitfully.

Pastoral Care After Marriage

69. The pastoral care of the regularly established family signifies, in practice, the commitment of all the members of the local ecclesial community to helping the couple to discover and live their new vocation and mission. In order that the family may be ever more a true community of love, it is necessary that all its members should be helped and trained in their responsibilities as they face the new problems that arise, in mutual service, and in active sharing in family life.

This holds true especially for young families, which, finding themselves in a context of new values and responsibilities, are more vulnerable, especially in the first years of marriage, to possible difficulties, such as those created by adaptation to life together or by the birth of children. Young married couples should learn to accept willingly, and make good use of, the discreet, tactful and generous help offered by other couples that already have more experience of married and family life. Thus, within the ecclesial community—the great family made up of Christian families—there will take place a mutual exchange of presence and help among all the families, each one putting at the service of others its own experience of life, as well as the gifts of faith and grace. Animated by a true apostolic spirit, this assistance from family to family will constitute one of the simplest, most effective and most accessible means for transmitting from one to another those Christian values which are both the starting point and goal of all pastoral care. Thus young families will not limit themselves merely to receiving, but in their turn, having been helped in this way, will become a source of enrichment for other longer established families, through their witness of life and practical contribution.

In her pastoral care of young families, the Church must also pay special attention to helping them to live married love responsibly in relationship with its demands of communion and service to life. She must likewise help them to harmonize the intimacy of home life with the generous shared work of building up the Church and society. When children are born and the married couple becomes a family in the full and specific sense, the Church will still remain close to the parents in order that they may accept their children and love them as a gift received from the Lord of life, and joyfully accept the task of serving them in their human and Christian growth.

II — STRUCTURES OF FAMILY PASTORAL CARE

Pastoral activity is always the dynamic expression of the reality of the Church, committed to her mission of salvation. Family pastoral care too—which is a particular and specific form of pastoral activity—has as its operative principle and responsible agent the Church herself, through her structures and workers.

The Ecclesial Community and in Particular the Parish

70. The Church, which is at the same time a saved and a saving community, has to be considered here under two aspects: as universal and particular. The second aspect is expressed and actuated in the diocesan community, which is pastorally divided up into lesser communities, of which the parish is of special importance.

Communion with the universal Church does not hinder but rather guarantees and promotes the substance and originality of the various particular Churches. These latter remain the more immediate and more effective subjects of operation for putting the pastoral care of the family into practice. In this sense every local Church and, in more particular terms, every parochial community, must become more vividly aware of the grace and responsibility that it receives from the Lord in order that it may promote the pastoral care of the family. No plan for organized pastoral work, at any level, must ever fail to take into consideration the pastoral care of the family.

Also to be seen in the light of this responsibility is the importance of the proper preparation of all those who will be more specifically engaged in this kind of apostolate. Priests and men and women religious, from the time of their formation, should be oriented and trained progressively and thoroughly for the various tasks. Among the various initiatives I am pleased to emphasize the recent establishment in Rome, at the Pontifical Lateran University, of a Higher Institute for the study of the problems of the family. Institutes of this kind have also been set up in some dioceses. Bishops should see to it that as many priests as possible attend specialized courses there before taking on parish responsibilities. Elsewhere formation courses are periodically held at Higher Institutes of theological and pastoral studies. Such initiatives should be encouraged, sustained, increased in number, and of course are also open to lay people who intend to use their professional skills (medical, legal, psychological, social or educational) to help the family.

The Family

71. But it is especially necessary to recognize the unique place that, in this field, belongs to the mission of married couples and

Christian families, by virtue of the grace received in the sacrament. This mission must be placed at the service of the building up of the Church, the establishing of the Kingdom of God in history. This is demanded as an act of docile obedience to Christ the Lord. For it is He who, by virtue of the fact that marriage of baptized persons has been raised to a sacrament, confers upon Christian married couples a special mission as apostles, sending them as workers into His vineyard, and, in a very special way, into this field of the family.

In this activity, married couples act in communion and collaboration with the other members of the Church, who also work for the family, contributing their own gifts and ministries. This apostolate will be exercised in the first place within the families of those concerned, through the witness of a life lived in conformity with the divine law in all its aspects, through the Christian formation of the children, through helping them to mature in faith, through education to chastity, through preparation for life, through vigilance in protecting them from the ideological and moral dangers with which they are often threatened, through their gradual and responsible inclusion in the ecclesial community and the civil community, through help and advice in choosing a vocation, through mutual help among family members for human and Christian growth together, and so on. The apostolate of the family will also become wider through works of spiritual and material charity towards other families, especially those most in need of help and support; towards the poor, the sick, the old, the handicapped, orphans, widows, spouses that have been abandoned, unmarried mothers and mothers-to-be in difficult situations who are tempted to have recourse to abortion, and so on.

Associations of Families for Families

72. Still within the Church, which is the subject responsible for the pastoral care of the family, mention should be made of the various groupings of members of the faithful in which the mystery of Christ's Church is in some measure manifested and lived. One should therefore recognize and make good use of—each one in relationship to its own characteristics, purposes, effectiveness and methods—the different ecclesial communities, the various groups and the numerous movements engaged in various ways, for different reasons and at different levels, in the pastoral care of the family.

For this reason the Synod expressly recognized the useful contribution made by such associations of spirituality, formation and apostolate. It will be their task to foster among the faithful a lively sense of solidarity, to favor a manner of living inspired by the Gospel and by the faith of the Church, to form consciences according to Christian values and not according to the standards of public opinion; to stimulate people to perform works of charity for one another and for others with a spirit of openness which will make Christian families into a true source of light and a wholesome leaven for other families.

It is similarly desirable that, with a lively sense of the common good, Christian families should become actively engaged, at every level, in other non-ecclesial associations as well. Some of these associations work for the preservation, transmission and protection of the wholesome ethical and cultural values of each people, the development of the human person, the medical, juridical and social protection of mothers and young children, the just advancement of women and the struggle against all that is detrimental to their dignity, the increase of mutual solidarity, knowledge of the problems connected with the responsible regulation of fertility in accordance with natural methods that are in conformity with human dignity and the teaching of the Church. Other associations work for the building of a more just and human world; for the promotion of just laws favoring the right social order with full respect for the dignity and every legitimate freedom of the individual and the family, on both the national and international level; for collaboration with the school and with the other institutions that complete the education of children, and so forth.

III — AGENTS OF THE PASTORAL CARE OF THE FAMILY

As well as the family, which is the object but above all the subject of pastoral care of the family, one must also mention the other main agents in this particular sector.

Bishops and Priests

73. The person principally responsible in the diocese for the pastoral care of the family is the Bishop. As father and pastor, he must exercise particular solicitude in this clearly priority sector of pastoral care. He must devote to it personal interest, care, time, personnel and resources, but above all personal support for the families and for all those who, in the various diocesan structures, assist him in the pastoral care of the family. It will be his particular care to make the diocese ever more truly a "diocesan family," a model and source of hope for the many families that belong to it. The setting up of the Pontifical Council for the Family is to be seen in this light: to be a sign of the importance that I attribute to pastoral care for the family in the world, and at the same time to be an effective instrument for aiding and promoting it at every level.

The Bishops avail themselves especially of the priests, whose task—as the Synod expressly emphasized—constitutes an essential part of the Church's ministry regarding marriage and the family. The same is true of deacons to whose care this sector of pastoral work may be entrusted.

Their responsibility extends not only to moral and liturgical matters but to personal and social matters as well. They must support the family in its difficulties and sufferings, caring for its members and helping them to see their lives in the light of the Gospel. It is not superfluous to note that from this mission, if it is exercised with due discernment and with a truly apostolic spirit, the minister of the Church draws fresh encouragement and spiritual energy for his own vocation too and for the exercise of his ministry.

Priests and deacons, when they have received timely and serious preparation for this apostolate, must unceasingly act towards families as fathers, brothers, pastors and teachers, assisting them with the means of grace and enlightening them with the light of truth. Their teaching and advice must therefore always be in full harmony with the authentic Magisterium of the Church, in such a way as to help the People of God to gain a correct sense of the faith, to be subsequently applied to practical life. Such fidelity to the Magisterium will also enable priests to make every effort to be united in their judgments, in order to avoid troubling the consciences of the faithful.

In the Church, the pastors and the laity share in the prophetic mission of Christ: the laity do so by witnessing to the faith by their words and by their Christian lives; the pastors do so by distinguishing in that witness what is the expression of genuine faith from what is less in harmony with the light of faith; the family, as a Christian community, does so through its special sharing and witness of faith. Thus there begins a dialogue also between pastors and families. Theologians and experts in family matters can be of great help in this dialogue, by explaining exactly the content of the Church's Magisterium and the content of the experience of family life. In this way the teaching of the Magisterium becomes better understood and the way is opened to its progressive development. But it is useful to recall that the proximate and obligatory norm in the teaching of the faith—also concerning family matters—belongs to the hierarchical Magisterium. Clearly defined relationships between theologians, experts in family matters and the Magisterium are of no little assistance for the correct understanding of the faith and for promoting—within the boundaries of the faith—legitimate pluralism.

Men and Women Religious

74. The contribution that can be made to the apostolate of the family by men and women religious and consecrated persons in general finds its primary, fundamental and original expression precisely in their consecration to God. By reason of this consecration, "for all Christ's faithful religious recall that wonderful marriage made by God, which will be fully manifested in the future age, and in which the Church has Christ for her only spouse,"[169] and they are witnesses to that universal charity which, through chastity embraced for the Kingdom of heaven, makes them ever more available to dedicate themselves generously to the service of God and to the works of the apostolate.

Hence the possibility for men and women religious, and members of Secular Institutes and other institutes of perfection, either individually or in groups, to develop their service to families, with particular solicitude for children, especially if they are abandoned, unwanted, orphaned, poor or handicapped. They can also visit families and look after the sick, they can foster relationships of respect

768

and charity towards one-parent families or families that are in difficulties or are separated; they can offer their own work of teaching and counseling in the preparation of young people for marriage, and in helping couples towards truly responsible parenthood; they can open their own houses for simple and cordial hospitality, so that families can find there the sense of God's presence and gain a taste for prayer and recollection, and see the practical examples of lives lived in charity and fraternal joy as members of the larger family of God.

I would like to add a most pressing exhortation to the heads of institutes of consecrated life to consider—always with substantial respect for the proper and original charism of each one—the apostolate of the family as one of the priority tasks, rendered even more urgent by the present state of the world.

Lay Specialists

75. Considerable help can be given to families by lay specialists (doctors, lawyers, psychologists, social workers, consultants, etc.) who either as individuals or as members of various associations and undertakings offer their contribution of enlightenment, advice, orientation and support. To these people one can well apply the exhortations that I had the occasion to address to the Confederation of Family Advisory Bureaus of Christian Inspiration: "Yours is a commitment that well deserves the title of mission, so noble are the aims that it pursues, and so determining, for the good of society and the Christian community itself, are the results that derive from it.... All that you succeed in doing to support the family is destined to have an effectiveness that goes beyond its own sphere and reaches other people too and has an effect on society. The future of the world and of the Church passes through the family."[170]

Recipients and Agents of Social Communications

76. This very important category in modern life deserves a word of its own. It is well known that the means of social communication "affect, and often profoundly, the minds of those who use them, under the affective and intellectual aspect and also under the moral and religious aspect," especially in the case of young people.[171] They can thus exercise a beneficial influence on the life and habits of the family and on the education of children, but at the same time they also conceal "snares and dangers that cannot be ignored."[172] They could also become a vehicle—sometimes cleverly and systematically manipulated, as unfortunately happens in various countries of the world—for divisive ideologies and distorted ways of looking at life, the family, religion and morality, attitudes that lack respect for man's true dignity and destiny.

This danger is all the more real inasmuch as "the modern life style—especially in the more industrialized nations—all too often causes families to abandon their responsibility to educate their children. Evasion of this duty is made easy for them by the presence of television and certain publications in the home, and in this way they keep their children's time and energies occupied."[173] Hence "the duty. . .to protect the young from the forms of aggression they are subjected to by the mass media," and to ensure that the use of the media in the family is carefully regulated. Families should also take care to seek for their children other forms of entertainment that are more wholesome, useful and physically, morally and spiritually formative, "to develop and use to advantage the free time of the young and direct their energies."[174]

Furthermore, because the means of social communication, like the school and the environment, often have a notable influence on the formation of children, parents as recipients must actively ensure the moderate, critical, watchful and prudent use of the media, by discovering what effect they have on their children and by controlling the use of the media in such a way as to "train the conscience of their children to express calm and objective judgments, which will then guide them in the choice or rejection of programs available."[175]

With equal commitment parents will endeavor to influence the selection and the preparation of the programs themselves, by keeping in contact—through suitable initiatives—with those in charge of the various phases of production and transmission. In this way they will ensure that the fundamental human values that form part of the true good of society are not ignored or deliberately attacked. Rather they will ensure the broadcasting of programs that present in the right light family problems and their proper solution. In this regard my venerated predecessor Paul VI wrote: "Producers must know and respect the needs of the family, and this sometimes presupposes in them true courage, and always a high sense of responsibility. In fact they are expected to avoid anything that could harm the family in its existence, its stability, its balance and its happiness. Every attack on the fundamental value of the family —meaning eroticism or violence, the defense of divorce or of antisocial attitudes among young people—is an attack on the true good of man."[176]

I myself, on a similar occasion, pointed out that families "to a considerable extent need to be able to count on the good will, integrity and sense of responsibility of the media professionals —publishers, writers, producers, directors, playwrights, newsmen, commentators and actors."[177] It is therefore also the duty of the Church to continue to devote every care to these categories, at the same time encouraging and supporting Catholics who feel the call and have the necessary talents, to take up this sensitive type of work.

IV — PASTORAL CARE OF THE FAMILY IN DIFFICULT CASES

Particular Circumstances

77. An even more generous, intelligent and prudent pastoral commitment, modelled on the Good Shepherd, is called for in the case of families which, often independently of their own wishes and through pressures of various other kinds, find themselves faced by situations which are objectively difficult.

In this regard it is necessary to call special attention to certain particular groups which are more in need not only of assistance but also of more incisive action upon public opinion and especially upon cultural, economic and juridical structures, in order that the profound causes of their needs may be eliminated as far as possible.

Such for example are the families of migrant workers; the families of those obliged to be away for long periods, such as members of the armed forces, sailors and all kinds of itinerant people; the families of those in prison, of refugees and exiles; the families in big cities living practically speaking as outcasts; families with no home; incomplete or single-parent families; families with children that are handicapped or addicted to drugs; the families of alcoholics families that have been uprooted from their cultural and social environment or are in danger of losing it; families discriminated against for political or other reasons; families that are ideologically divided; families that are unable to make ready contact with the parish; families experiencing violence or unjust treatment because of their faith; teenage married couples; the elderly, who are often obliged to live alone with inadequate means of subsistence.

The families of migrants, especially in the case of manual workers and farm workers, should be able to find a homeland everywhere in the Church. This is a task stemming from the nature of the Church, as being the sign of unity in diversity. As far as possible these people should be looked after by priests of their own rite, culture and language. It is also the Church's task to appeal to the public conscience and to all those in authority in social, economic and political life, in order that workers may find employment in their own regions and homelands, that they may receive just wages, that their families may be reunited as soon as possible, be respected in their cultural identity and treated on an equal footing with others, and that their children may be given the chance to learn a trade and exercise it, as also the chance to own the land needed for working and living.

A difficult problem is that of the family which is *ideologically divided*. In these cases particular pastoral care is needed. In the first place it is necessary to maintain tactful personal contact with such families. The believing members must be strengthened in their faith and supported in their Christian lives. Although the party faithful to Catholicism cannot give way, dialogue with the other party must always be kept alive. Love and respect must be freely shown, in the firm hope that unity will be maintained. Much also

771

depends on the relationship between parents and children. Moreover, ideologies which are alien to the faith can stimulate the believing members of the family to grow in faith and in the witness of love.

Other difficult circumstances in which the family needs the help of the ecclesial community and its pastors are: the children's adolescence, which can be disturbed, rebellious and sometimes stormy; the children's marriage, which takes them away from their family; lack of understanding or lack of love on the part of those held most dear; abandonment by one of the spouses, or his or her death, which brings the painful experience of widowhood, or the death of a family member, which breaks up and deeply transforms the original family nucleus.

Similarly, the Church cannot ignore the time of old age, with all its positive and negative aspects. In old age married love, which has been increasingly purified and ennobled by long and unbroken fidelity, can be deepened. There is the opportunity of offering to others, in a new form, the kindness and the wisdom gathered over the years, and what energies remain. But there is also the burden of loneliness, more often psychological and emotional rather than physical, which results from abandonment or neglect on the part of children and relations. There is also suffering caused by ill-health, by the gradual loss of strength, by the humiliation of having to depend on others, by the sorrow of feeling that one is perhaps a burden to one's loved ones, and by the approach of the end of life. These are the circumstances in which, as the Synod Fathers suggested, it is easier to help people understand and live the lofty aspects of the spirituality of marriage and the family, aspects which take their inspiration from the value of Christ's Cross and Resurrection, the source of sanctification and profound happiness in daily life, in the light of the great eschatological realities of eternal life.

In all these different situations let prayer, the source of light and strength and the nourishment of Christian hope, never be neglected.

Mixed Marriages

78. The growing number of mixed marriages between Catholics and other baptized persons also calls for special pastoral attention in the light of the directives and norms contained in the most recent documents of the Holy See and in those drawn up by the Episcopal Conferences, in order to permit their practical application to the various situations.

Couples living in a mixed marriage have special needs, which can be put under three main headings.

In the first place, attention must be paid to the obligations that faith imposes on the Catholic party with regard to the free exercise of the faith and the consequent obligation to ensure, as far as is possible, the Baptism and upbringing of the children in the Catholic faith.[178]

There must be borne in mind the particular difficulties inherent in the relationships between husband and wife with regard to respect for religious freedom: this freedom could be violated either by undue pressure to make the partner change his or her beliefs, or by placing obstacles in the way of the free manifestation of these beliefs by religious practice.

With regard to the liturgical and canonical form of marriage, Ordinaries can make wide use of their faculties to meet various necessities.

In dealing with these special needs, the following points should be kept in mind:

—In the appropriate preparation for this type of marriage, every reasonable effort must be made to ensure a proper understanding of Catholic teaching on the qualities and obligations of marriage, and also to ensure that the pressures and obstacles mentioned above will not occur.

—It is of the greatest importance that, through the support of the community, the Catholic party should be strengthened in faith and positively helped to mature in understanding and practicing that faith, so as to become a credible witness within the family through his or her own life and through the quality of love shown to the other spouse and the children.

Marriages between Catholics and other baptized persons have their own particular nature, but they contain numerous elements that could well be made good use of and developed, both for their intrinsic value and for the contribution that they can make to the ecumenical movement. This is particularly true when both parties are faithful to their religious duties. Their common Baptism and the dynamism of grace provide the spouses in these marriages with the basis and motivation for expressing their unity in the sphere of moral and spiritual values.

For this purpose, and also in order to highlight the ecumenical importance of mixed marriages which are fully lived in the faith of the two Christian spouses, an effort should be made to establish cordial cooperation between the Catholic and the non-Catholic ministers from the time that preparations begin for the marriage and the wedding ceremony, even though this does not always prove easy.

With regard to the sharing of the non-Catholic party in Eucharistic Communion, the norms issued by the Secretariat for Promoting Christian Unity should be followed.[179]

Today in many parts of the world marriages between Catholics and non-baptized persons are growing in numbers. In many such marriages the non-baptized partner professes another religion, and his beliefs are to be treated with respect, in accordance with the principles set out in the Second Vatican Council's Declaration *Nostra aetate* on relations with non-Christian religions. But in many other such marriages, particularly in secularized societies, the non-baptized person professes no religion at all. In these marriages there is a need for Episcopal Conferences and for individual Bishops to ensure that there are proper pastoral safeguards for the faith of the Catholic partner and for the free exercise of his faith, above all in regard to his duty to do all in his power to ensure the Catholic baptism and education of the children of the marriage. Likewise the Catholic must be assisted in every possible way to offer within his family a genuine witness to the Catholic faith and to Catholic life.

Pastoral Action in Certain Irregular Situations

79. In its solicitude to protect the family in all its dimensions, not only the religious one, the Synod of Bishops did not fail to take into careful consideration certain situations which are irregular in a religious sense and often in the civil sense too. Such situations, as a result of today's rapid cultural changes, are unfortunately becoming widespread also among Catholics, with no little damage to the very institution of the family and to society, of which the family constitutes the basic cell.

a) *Trial Marriages*

80. A first example of an irregular situation is provided by what are called "trial marriages," which many people today would like to justify by attributing a certain value to them. But human reason leads one to see that they are unacceptable, by showing the unconvincing nature of carrying out an "experiment" with human beings, whose dignity demands that they should be always and solely the term of a self-giving love without limitations of time or of any other circumstance.

The Church, for her part, cannot admit such a kind of union, for further and original reasons which derive from faith. For, in the first place, the gift of the body in the sexual relationship is a real symbol of the giving of the whole person: such a giving, moreover, in the present state of things cannot take place with full truth without the concourse of the love of charity given by Christ. In the second place, marriage between two baptized persons is a real symbol of the union of Christ and the Church, which is not a temporary or "trial" union but one which is eternally faithful. Therefore between two baptized persons there can exist only an indissoluble marriage.

Such a situation cannot usually be overcome unless the human person, from childhood, with the help of Christ's grace and without fear, has been trained to dominate concupiscence from the beginning and to establish relationships of genuine love with other people. This cannot be secured without a true education in genuine love and in the right use of sexuality, such as to introduce the human person in every aspect, and therefore the bodily aspect too, into the fullness of the mystery of Christ.

It will be very useful to investigate the causes of this phenomenon, including its psychological and sociological aspect, in order to find the proper remedy.

b) *De Facto Free Unions*

81. This means unions without any publicly recognized institutional bond, either civil or religious. This phenomenon, which is becoming ever more frequent, cannot fail to concern pastors of souls,

also because it may be based on widely varying factors, the consequences of which may perhaps be containable by suitable action.

Some people consider themselves almost forced into a free union by difficult economic, cultural or religious situations, on the grounds that, if they contracted a regular marriage, they would be exposed to some form of harm, would lose economic advantages, would be discriminated against, etc. In other cases, however, one encounters people who scorn, rebel against or reject society, the institution of the family and the social and political order, or who are solely seeking pleasure. Then there are those who are driven to such situations by extreme ignorance or poverty, sometimes by a conditioning due to situations of real injustice, or by a certain psychological immaturity that makes them uncertain or afraid to enter into a stable and definitive union. In some countries, traditional customs presume that the true and proper marriage will take place only after a period of cohabitation and the birth of the first child.

Each of these elements presents the Church with arduous pastoral problems, by reason of the serious consequences deriving from them, both religious and moral (the loss of the religious sense of marriage seen in the light of the Covenant of God with His people; deprivation of the grace of the sacrament; grave scandal), and also social consequences (the destruction of the concept of the family; the weakening of the sense of fidelity, also towards society; possible psychological damage to the children; the strengthening of selfishness).

The pastors and the ecclesial community should take care to become acquainted with such situations and their actual causes, case by case. They should make tactful and respectful contact with the couples concerned, and enlighten them patiently, correct them charitably and show them the witness of Christian family life, in such a way as to smooth the path for them to regularize their situation. But above all there must be a campaign of prevention, by fostering the sense of fidelity in the whole moral and religious training of the young, instructing them concerning the conditions and structures that favor such fidelity, without which there is no true freedom; they must be helped to reach spiritual maturity and enabled to understand the rich human and supernatural reality of marriage as a sacrament.

The People of God should also make approaches to the public authorities, in order that the latter may resist these tendencies which divide society and are harmful to the dignity, security and welfare of the citizens as individuals, and they must try to ensure that public opinion is not led to undervalue the institutional importance of marriage and the family. And since in many regions young people are unable to get married properly because of extreme poverty deriving from unjust or inadequate social and economic structures, society and the public authorities should favor legitimate marriage by means of a series of social and political actions which will guarantee a family wage, by issuing directives ensuring housing fitting for family life and by creating opportunities for work and life.

c) *Catholics in Civil Marriages*

82. There are increasing cases of Catholics who, for ideological or practical reasons, prefer to contract a merely civil marriage, and who reject or at least defer religious marriage. Their situation cannot of course be likened to that of people simply living together without any bond at all, because in the present case there is at least a certain commitment to a properly-defined and probably stable state of life, even though the possibility of a future divorce is often present in the minds of those entering a civil marriage. By seeking public recognition of their bond on the part of the State, such couples show that they are ready to accept not only its advantages but also its obligations. Nevertheless, not even this situation is acceptable to the Church.

The aim of pastoral action will be to make these people understand the need for consistency between their choice of life and the faith that they profess, and to try to do everything possible to induce them to regularize their situation in the light of Christian principles. While treating them with great charity and bringing them into the life of the respective communities, the pastors of the Church will regrettably not be able to admit them to the sacraments.

d) *Separated or Divorced Persons Who Have Not Remarried*

83. Various reasons can unfortunately lead to the often irreparable breakdown of valid marriages. These include mutual lack of understanding and the inability to enter into interpersonal relationships. Obviously, separation must be considered as a last resort, after all other reasonable attempts at reconciliation have proved vain.

Loneliness and other difficulties are often the lot of separated spouses, especially when they are the innocent parties. The ecclesial community must support such people more than ever. It must give them much respect, solidarity, understanding and practical help, so that they can preserve their fidelity even in their difficult situation; and it must help them to cultivate the need to forgive which is inherent in Christian love, and to be ready perhaps to return to their former married life.

The situation is similar for people who have undergone divorce, but, being well aware that the valid marriage bond is indissoluble, refrain from becoming involved in a new union and devote themselves solely to carrying out their family duties and the responsibilities of Christian life. In such cases their example of fidelity and Christian consistency takes on particular value as a witness before the world and the Church. Here it is even more necessary for the Church to offer continual love and assistance, without there being any obstacle to admission to the sacraments.

e) *Divorced Persons Who Have Remarried*

84. Daily experience unfortunately shows that people who have obtained a divorce usually intend to enter into a new union, obviously not with a Catholic religious ceremony. Since this is an evil

that, like the others, is affecting more and more Catholics as well, the problem must be faced with resolution and without delay. The Synod Fathers studied it expressly. The Church, which was set up to lead to salvation all people and especially the baptized, cannot abandon to their own devices those who have been previously bound by sacramental marriage and who have attempted a second marriage. The Church will therefore make untiring efforts to put at their disposal her means of salvation.

Pastors must know that, for the sake of truth, they are obliged to exercise careful discernment of situations. There is in fact a difference between those who have sincerely tried to save their first marriage and have been unjustly abandoned, and those who through their own grave fault have destroyed a canonically valid marriage. Finally, there are those who have entered into a second union for the sake of the children's upbringing, and who are sometimes subjectively certain in conscience that their previous and irreparably destroyed marriage had never been valid.

Together with the Synod, I earnestly call upon pastors and the whole community of the faithful to help the divorced, and with solicitous care to make sure that they do not consider themselves as separated from the Church, for as baptized persons they can, and indeed must, share in her life. They should be encouraged to listen to the word of God, to attend the Sacrifice of the Mass, to persevere in prayer, to contribute to works of charity and to community efforts in favor of justice, to bring up their children in the Christian faith, to cultivate the spirit and practice of penance and thus implore, day by day, God's grace. Let the Church pray for them, encourage them and show herself a merciful mother, and thus sustain them in faith and hope.

However, the Church reaffirms her practice, which is based upon Sacred Scripture, of not admitting to Eucharistic Communion divorced persons who have remarried. They are unable to be admitted thereto from the fact that their state and condition of life objectively contradict that union of love between Christ and the Church which is signified and effected by the Eucharist. Besides this, there is another special pastoral reason: if these people were admitted to the Eucharist, the faithful would be led into error and confusion regarding the Church's teaching about the indissolubility of marriage.

Reconciliation in the sacrament of Penance, which would open the way to the Eucharist, can only be granted to those who, repenting of having broken the sign of the Covenant and of fidelity to Christ, are sincerely ready to undertake a way of life that is no longer in contradiction to the indissolubility of marriage. This means, in practice, that when, for serious reasons, such as for example the children's upbringing, a man and a woman cannot satisfy the obligation to separate, they "take on themselves the duty to live in complete continence, that is, by abstinence from the acts proper to married couples."[180]

Similarly, the respect due to the sacrament of Matrimony, to the

777

couples themselves and their families, and also to the community of the faithful forbids any pastor, for whatever reason or pretext even of a pastoral nature, to perform ceremonies of any kind for divorced people who remarry. Such ceremonies would give the impression of the celebration of a new sacramentally valid marriage, and would thus lead people into error concerning the indissolubility of a validly contracted marriage.

By acting in this way, the Church professes her own fidelity to Christ and to His truth. At the same time she shows motherly concern for these children of hers, especially those who, through no fault of their own, have been abandoned by their legitimate partner.

With firm confidence she believes that those who have rejected the Lord's command and are still living in this state will be able to obtain from God the grace of conversion and salvation, provided that they have persevered in prayer, penance and charity.

Those Without a Family

85. I wish to add a further word for a category of people whom, as a result of the actual circumstances in which they are living, and this often not through their own deliberate wish, I consider particularly close to the Heart of Christ and deserving of the affection and active solicitude of the Church and of pastors.

There exist in the world countless people who unfortunately cannot in any sense claim membership of what could be called in the proper sense a family. Large sections of humanity live in conditions of extreme poverty, in which promiscuity, lack of housing, the irregular nature and instability of relationships and the extreme lack of education make it impossible in practice to speak of a true family. There are others who, for various reasons, have been left alone in the world. And yet for all of these people there exists a "good news of the family."

On behalf of those living in extreme poverty, I have already spoken of the urgent need to work courageously in order to find solutions, also at the political level, which will make it possible to help them and to overcome this inhuman condition of degradation.

It is a task that faces the whole of society but in a special way the authorities, by reason of their position and the responsibilities flowing therefrom, and also families, which must show great understanding and willingness to help.

For those who have no natural family the doors of the great family which is the Church—the Church which finds concrete expression in the diocesan and the parish family, in ecclesial basic communities and in movements of the apostolate—must be opened even wider. No one is without a family in this world: the Church is a home and family for everyone, especially those who "labor and are heavy laden."[181]

CONCLUSION

86. At the end of this Apostolic Exhortation my thoughts turn

778

with earnest solicitude:

to you, married couples, to you, fathers and mothers of families;

to you, young men and women, the future and the hope of the Church and the world, destined to be the dynamic central nucleus of the family in the approaching third millennium;

to you, venerable and dear Brothers in the Episcopate and in the priesthood, beloved sons and daughters in the religious life, souls consecrated to the Lord, who bear witness before married couples to the ultimate reality of the love of God;

to you, upright men and women, who for any reason whatever give thought to the fate of the family.

The future of humanity passes by way of the family.

It is therefore indispensable and urgent that every person of good will should endeavor to save and foster the values and requirements of the family.

I feel that I must ask for a particular effort in this field from the sons and daughters of the Church. Faith gives them full knowledge of God's wonderful plan: they therefore have an extra reason for caring for the reality that is the family in this time of trial and of grace .

They must *show the family special love*. This is an injunction that calls for concrete action.

Loving the family means being able to appreciate its values and capabilities, fostering them always. Loving the family means identifying the dangers and the evils that menace it, in order to overcome them. Loving the family means endeavoring to create for it an environment favorable for its development. The modern Christian family is often tempted to be discouraged and is distressed at the growth of its difficulties; it is an eminent form of love to give it back its reasons for confidence in itself, in the riches that it possesses by nature and grace, and in the mission that God has entrusted to it. "Yes indeed, the families of today must be called back to their original position. They must follow Christ."[182]

Christians also have the mission of *proclaiming with joy and conviction the Good News about the family*, for the family absolutely needs to hear ever anew and to understand ever more deeply the authentic words that reveal its identity, its inner resources and the importance of its mission in the City of God and in that of man.

The Church knows the path by which the family can reach the heart of the deepest truth about itself. The Church has learned this path at the school of Christ and the school of history interpreted in the light of the Spirit. She does not impose it but she feels an urgent need to propose it to everyone without fear and indeed with great confidence and hope, although she knows that the Good News includes the subject of the Cross. But it is through the Cross that the family can attain the fullness of its being and the perfection of its love.

Finally, I wish to call on all Christians to *collaborate cordially and courageously* with all people of good will who are serving the family in accordance with their responsibilities. The individuals and groups, movements and associations in the Church which devote themselves to the family's welfare, acting in the Church's name and under her inspiration, often find themselves side by side with other individuals and institutions working for the same ideal. With faithfulness to the values of the Gospel and of the human person and with respect for lawful pluralism in initiatives this collaboration can favor a more rapid and integral advancement of the family.

And now, at the end of my pastoral message, which is intended to draw everyone's attention to the demanding yet fascinating roles of the Christian family, I wish to invoke the protection of the Holy Family of Nazareth.

Through God's mysterious design, it was in that family that the Son of God spent long years of a hidden life. It is therefore the prototype and example for all Christian families. It was unique in the world. Its life was passed in anonymity and silence in a little town in Palestine. It underwent trials of poverty, persecution and exile. It glorified God in an incomparably exalted and pure way. And it will not fail to help Christian families—indeed, all the families in the world—to be faithful to their day-to-day duties, to bear the cares and tribulations of life, to be open and generous to the needs of others, and to fulfill with joy the plan of God in their regard.

St. Joseph was "a just man," a tireless worker, the upright guardian of those entrusted to his care. May he always guard, protect and enlighten families.

May the Virgin Mary, who is the Mother of the Church, also be the Mother of "the Church of the home." Thanks to her motherly aid, may each Christian family really become a "little Church" in which the mystery of the Church of Christ is mirrored and given new life. May she, the Handmaid of the Lord, be an example of humble and generous acceptance of the will of God. May she, the Sorrowful Mother at the foot of the Cross, comfort the sufferings and dry the tears of those in distress because of the difficulties of their families.

May Christ the Lord, the Universal King, the King of Families, be present in every Christian home as He was at Cana, bestowing light, joy, serenity and strength. On the solemn day dedicated to His Kingship I beg of Him that every family may generously make its own contribution to the coming of His Kingdom in the world—"a kingdom of truth and life, a kingdom of holiness and grace, a kingdom of justice, love, and peace,"[183] towards which history is journeying.

I entrust each family to Him, to Mary, and to Joseph. To their hands and their hearts I offer this Exhortation: may it be they who present it to you, venerable Brothers and beloved sons and daughters, and may it be they who open your hearts to the light that the Gospel sheds on every family.

I assure you all of my constant prayers and I cordially impart the apostolic blessing to each and every one of you, in the name of the Father, and of the Son, and of the Holy Spirit.

780

Given in Rome, at St. Peter's, on the twenty-second day of November, the Solemnity of our Lord Jesus Christ, Universal King, in the year 1981, the fourth of the Pontificate.

Joannes Paulus PP II

FOOTNOTES

1. Cf. Second Vatican Ecumenical Council, Pastoral Constitution on the Church in the Modern World, *Gaudium et spes*, no. 52.

2. Cf. John Paul 11, Homily for the Opening of the Sixth Synod of Bishops (September 26,1980), 2: AAS 72 (1980), 1008.

3. Cf. Cn. 1-2.

4. Cf. Eph. 5.

5. Cf. Second Vatican Ecumenical Council, Pastoral Constitution on the Church in the Modern World, *Gaudium et spes*, no. 47; Pope John Paul 1I, Letter *Appropinquat lam* (August 15, 1980), 1: AAS 72 (1980), 791.

6. Cf. Mt. 19:4.

7. Cf. Second Vatican Ecumenical Council, Pastoral Constitution on the Church in the Modern World, *Gaudium et spes*, no. 47.

8. Cf. John Paul 11, Address to the Council of the General Secretariat of the Synod of Bishops (February 23, 1980): *Insegnamenti di Giovanni Paolo 11*, 111, 1 (1980), 472-476.

9. Cf. Second Vatican Ecumenical Council, Pastoral Constitution on the Church in the Modern World, *Gaudium et spes*, no. 4.

10. Cf. Second Vatican Ecumenical Council, Dogmatic Constitution on the Church, *Lumen gentium*, no. 12.

11. Cf. 1 Jn. 2:20.

12. Second Vatican Ecumenical Council, Dogmatic Constitution on the Church, *Lumen gentium*, no. 35.

13. Cf. Second Vatican Ecumenical Council, Dogmatic Constitution on the Church, *Lumen gentium*, no. 12; Sacred Congregation for the Doctrine of the Faith, Declaration *Mysterium Ecclesiae*, no. 2: AAS 65 (1973), 398-400.

14. Cf. Second Vatican Ecumenical Council, Dogmatic Constitution on the Church, *Lumen gentium*, no. 12; Dogmatic Constitution on Divine Revelation, *Dei Verbum*, no. 10.

15. Cf. John Paul II, Homily for the opening of the Sixth Synod of Bishops (September 26, 1980), 3: AAS 72 (1980), 1008.

16. Cf. St. Augustine, *De Civitate Dei*, XIV, 28: CSEL 40,11, 56-57.

17. Pastoral Constitution on the Church in the Modern World, *Gaudium et spes*, no. 15.

18. Cf. Eph. 3:8; Second Vatican Ecumenical Council, *Gaudium et spes*, no. 44; Decree on the Church's Missionary Activity, *Ad gentes*, nos. 15, 22.

19. Cf. Mt. 19:4-6.

20. Cf. Gn. 1:26-27.

21. 1 Jn. 4:8.

22. Cf. Second Vatican Ecumenical Council, Pastoral Constitution on the Church in the Modern World, *Gaudium et spes*, no. 12.

23. Cf. *ibid.*, no. 48.

24. Cf., e.g., Hos. 2:21; Jer. 3:6-13;1s. 54.

25. Cf. Ez. 16:25.

26. Cf. Hos. 3.

27. Cf. Gn. 2:24; Mt. 19:5.

28. Cf. Eph. 5:32-33.

29. Tertullian, *Ad Uxorem*, II, VIII, 6-8: CCL, I, 393.

30. Cf. Ecumenical Council of Trent, Session XXIV, canon 1: I. D. Mansi, *Sacrorum Conciliorum Nova et Amplissima Collectio*, 33, 149-150.

31. Cf. Second Vatican Ecumenical Council, Pastoral Constitution on the Church in the Modern World, *Gaudium et spes*, no. 48.

32. John Paul II, Address to the Delegates of the Centre de Liaison des Equipes de Recherche (November 3, 1979), 3: *Insegnamenti di Giovanni Paolo 11*, Il, 2 (1979), 1038.

33. Ibid., 4: loc. cit., 1032.

34. Cf. Second Vatican Ecumenical Council, Pastoral Constitution on the Church in the Modern World, *Gaudium et spes*, no. 50.

35. Cf. Gn. 2:24.

36. Eph. 3:15.

37. Cf. Second Vatican Ecumenical Council, Pastoral Constitution on the Church in the Modern World, *Gaudium et spes*, no. 78.

38. St. John Chrysostom, *Virginity*, X: PG 48:540.

39. Cf. Mt. 22:30.

40. Cf. 1 Cor. 7:32-35.

41. Second Vatican Ecumenical Council, Decree on Renewal of Religious Life, *Perfectae caritatis*, no. 12.

42. Cf. Pius XII, Encyclical *Sacra Virginitas*, II: AAS 46 (1954), 174ff.

43. Cf. John Paul Il, Letter *Novo Incipiente* (April 8, 1979), 9: AAS 71 (1979), 410-411.

44. Second Vatican Ecumenical Council, Pastoral Constitution on the Church in the Modern World, *Gaudium et spes*, no. 48.

45. Encyclical *Redemptor hominis*, 10: AAS 71 (1979), 274.

46. Mt. 19:6; cf. Gn. 2:24.

47. Cf. John Paul II, Address to Married People at Kinshasa (May 3,1980), 4: AAS 72 (1980), 426-427.

48. Pastoral Constitution on the Church in the Modern World, *Gaudium et spes*, no. 49; cf. John Paul II, Address to Married People at Kinshasa (May 3, 1980), 4: *loc. cit.*

49. Second Vatican Ecumenical Council, Pastoral Constitution on the Church in the Modern World, *Gaudium et spes*, no. 48.

50. Eph. 5:25.

51. Mt. 19:8.

52. Rv. 3:14.

53. Cf. 2 Cor. 1:20.

54. Jn. 13:1.

55. Mt. 19:6.

56. Rom. 8:29.

57 . St. Thomas Aquinas, *Summa Theologiae*, II-II, q. 14, art. 2, ad 4.

58. Second Vatican Ecumenical Council, Dogmatic Constitution on the Church, *Lumen gentium*, no. 11; cf. Decree on the Apostolate of the Laity, *Apostolicam Actuositatem*, no. 11.

59. Second Vatican Ecumenical Council, Pastoral Constitution on the Church in the Modern World, *Gaudium et spes*, no. 52.

60. Cf. Eph. 6:1-4; Col. 3:20-21.

61. Cf. Second Vatican Ecumenical Council, Pastoral Constitution on the Church in the Modern World, *Gaudium et spes*, no. 48.

62. Jn. 17:21.

63. Cf. Second Vatican Ecumenical Council, Pastoral Constitution on the Church in the Modern World, *Gaudium et spes*, no. 24.

64. Gn. 1:27.

65. Gal. 3:26, 28.

66. Cf. John Paul II, Encyclical *Laborem exercens*, no. 19: AAS 73 (1981), 625.

67. Gn. 2:18.

68. Gn. 2:23.

69. St. Ambrose, *Exameron*, V 7, 19: CSEL 32, I 154.

70. Paul VI, Encyclical *Humanae vitae*, no. 9: AAS 60 (1968), 486.

71. Cf. Eph. 5:25.

72. Cf. John Paul II, Homily to the faithful of Terni (March 19, 1981), 3-5: AAS 73 (1981), 268-271.

73. Cf. Eph. 3:15.

74. Cf. Second Vatican Ecumenical Council, Pastoral Constitution on the Church in the Modern World, *Gaudium et spes*, no. 52.

75. Lk. 18:16; cf. Mt. 19:14 Mk. 18:16.

76. John Paul II, Address to the General Assembly of the United Nations (October 2, 1979), 21: AAS 71 (1979), 1159.

77. Lk. 2:52.

78. Cf. Second Vatican Ecumenical Council, Pastoral Constitution on the Church in the Modern World, *Gaudium et spes*, no. 48.

79. John Paul II, Address to the participants in the International Forum on Active Aging (September 5, 1980), 5: *Insegnamenti di Giovanni Paolo 11*, III, 2 (1980), 539.

80. Gn. 1:28.

81. Cf. Gn. 5:1-3.

82. Second Vatican Ecumenical Council, Pastoral Constitution on the Church in the Modern World, *Gaudium et spes*, no. 50.

83. *Propositio* 21. Section 11 of the Encyclical *Humanae vitae* ends with the statement: "The Church, calling people back to the observance of the norms of the natural law, as interpreted by her constant doctrine, teaches that each and every marriage act must remain open to the transmission of life *(ut quilibet matrimonii usus ad vitam humanam procreandam per se destinatus permaneat)*": AAS 60 (1968), 488.

84. Cf. 2 Cor. 1:19; Rv. 3:14.

85. Cf. the Sixth Synod of Bishops' Message to Christian Families in the Modern World (October 24, 1980), 5.

86. Pastoral Constitution on the Church in the Modern World, *Gaudium et spes*, no. 51.

87. Encyclical *Humanae vitae*, no. 7: AAS 60 (1968), 485.

88. *Ibid.*, 12: *loc cit.*, 488-489.

89. *Ibid.*, 14: *loc. cit.*, 490.

90. *Ibid.*, 13: *loc. cit.*, 489.

91. Cf. Second Vatican Ecumenical Council, Pastoral Constitution on the Church in the Modern World, *Gaudium et spes*, no. 51.

92. Encyclical Humanae vitae, no. 29: AAS 60 (1968), 501.

93. Cf. *ibid..* 25: *loc. cit.*, 498-499.

94. *Ibid.*, 21: *loc. cit.*, 496.

95. John Paul II, Homily at the close of the Sixth Synod of Bishops (October 25, 1980), 8: AAS 72 (1980), 1083.

96. Cf. Paul Vl, Encyclical *Humanae vitae*, 28: AAS 60 (1968), 501.

97. Cf. John Paul 11, Address to the Delegates of the Centre de Liaison des Equipes de Recherche (November 3, 1979), 9: *Insegnamenti di Giovanni Paolo 11*, Il, 2 (1979), 1035; and cf. Address to the participants in the First Congress for the Family of Africa and Europe (January 15, 1981): *L'Osservatore Romano*, January 16, 1981.

98. Encyclical *Humanae vitae*, 25: AAS 60 (1968), 499.

99. Declaration on Christian Education, *Gravissimum educationis*, no. 3.

100. Second Vatican Ecumenical Council, Pastoral Constitution on the Church in the Modern World, *Gaudium et spes*, no. 35.

101. St. Thomas Aquinas, *Summa contra Gentiles*, IV, 58.

102. Declaration on Christian Education, *Gravissimum educationis*, no. 2.

103. Apostolic Exhortation *Evangelii nuntiandi*, no. 71: AAS 68 (1976), 60-61.

104. Cf. Second Vatican Ecumenical Council, Declaration on Christian Education, *Gravissimum educationis*, no. 3.

105. Second Vatican Ecumenical Council, Decree on the Apostolate of the Laity, *Apostolicam actuositatem*, no. 11.

106. Second Vatican Ecumenical Council, Pastoral Constitution on the Church in the Modern World, *Gaudium et spes*, no. 52.

107. Cf. Second Vatican Ecumenical Council, Decree on the Apostolate of the Laity, *Apostolicam actuositatem*, no. 11.

108. Rom. 12:13.

109. Mt. 10:42.

110. Cf. Second Vatican Ecumenical Council, Pastoral Constitution on the Church in the Modern World, *Gaudium et spes*, no. 30.

111. Second Vatican Ecumenical Council, Declaration on Religious Freedom, *Dignitatis humanae*, no. 5.

112. Cf. *Propositio* 42.

113. Second Vatican Ecumenical Council, Dogmatic Constitution on the Church, *Lumen gentium*, no. 31.

114. Cf. Second Vatican Ecumenical Council, Dogmatic Constitution on the Church, *Lumen gentium*, no. 11; Decree on the Apostolate of the Laity, *Apostolicam actuositatem*, 11; Pope John Paul II, Homily for the opening of the Sixth Synod of Bishops (September 26,1980), 3: AAS 72 (1980), 1008.

115. Second Vatican Ecumenical Council, Dogmatic Constitution on the Church, *Lumen gentium*, no. 11.

116. Cf. *ibid.*, no. 41.

117. Acts 4:32.

118. Cf. Paul VI, Encyclical *Humanae vitae*, no. 9: AAS 60 (1968), 486-487.

119. Second Vatican Ecumenical Council, Pastoral Constitution on the Church in the Modem World, *Gaudium et spes*, no. 48.

120. Cf. Second Vatican Ecumenical Council, Dogmatic Constitution on Divine Revelation, *Dei Verbum*, no. 1.

121. Rom. 16:26.

122. Cf. Paul Vl, Encyclical *Humanae vitae*, no. 25: AAS 60 11968), 498.

123. Apostolic Exhortation *Evangelii nuntiandi*, no. 71: AAS 68 (1976), 60-61.

124. Cf. Address to the Third General Assembly Of the Bishops Of Latin America (January 28 1979), IV a: AAS 71(1979), 204.

125. Second Vatican Ecumenical Council, Dogmatic Constitution on the Church, *Lumen gentium*, no. 35.

126. John Paul II, Apostolic Exhortation *Catechesi tradendae*, 68: AAS 71 (1979), 1334.

127. Cf. *ibid.*, 36: IQC. cit. 1308.

128. Cf. 1 Cor. 12:4-6; Eph. 4:12-13.

129. Mk. 16:15.

130. Cf. Second Vatican Ecumenical Council, Dogmatic Constitution on the Church, *Lumen gentium*, no. 11.

131. Acts 1:8.

132. Cf. 1 Pt. 3:1-2.

133. Second Vatican Ecumenical Council, Dogmatic Constitution on the Church *Lumen gentium*, no. 35; cf. Decree on the Apostolate of the Laity, *Apostolicam actuositatem*, no. 11.

134. Cf. Acts 18; Rom. 16:3-4.

135. Cf. Second Vatican Ecumenical Council, Decree on the Church's Missionary Activity, *Ad gentes*, no. 39.

136. Second Vatican Ecumenical Council, Decree on the Apostolate of the Laity, *Apostolicam actuositatem*, no. 30.

137. Cf. Second Vatican Ecumenical Council, Dogmatic Constitution on the Church, *Lumen genitum*, no. 10.

138. Second Vatican Ecumenical Council, Pastoral Constitution on the Church in the Modern World, *Gaudium et spes*, no. 49.

139. Ibid., no. 48.

140. Cf. Second Vatican Ecumenical Council, Dogmatic Constitution on the Church, *Lumen gentium*, no. 41.

141. Second Vatican Ecumenical Council, Constitution on the Sacred Liturgy, *Sacrosanctum concilium*, no. 59.

142. Cf. 1 Pt. 2:5; Second Vatican Ecumenical Council, Dogmatic Constitution on the Church, *Lumen gentium*, no. 34.

143. Second Vatican Ecumenical Council, Dogmatic Constitution on the Church, *Lumen gentium*, no. 34.

144. Constitution on the Sacred Liturgy, *Sacrosanctum concilium*, no. 78.

145. Cf. Jn. 19:34.

146. Section 25: AAS 60 (1968), 499.

147. Eph. 2:4.

148. Cf. John Paul II, Encyclical *Dives in misericordia*, no. 13: AAS 72 (1980), 1218-1219.

149. 1 Pt. 2:5.

150. Mt. 18:19-20.

151. Second Vatican Ecumenical Council, Declaration on Christian Education, *Gravissimum educationis*, no. 3; cf. Pope John Paul II, Apostolic Exhortation *Catechesi tradendae*, no. 36: AAS 71 (1979), 1308.

152. General Audience Address, August 11, 1976: *Insegnamenti di Paolo VI*, XIV (1976), 640.

153. Cf. Constitution on the Sacred Liturgy, *Sacrosanctum concilium*, no. 12.

154. Cf. *Institutio Generalis de Liturgia Horarum*, no. 27.

155. Paul VI, Apostolic Exhortation *Marialis Cultus* nos. 52, 54: AAS 66 (1974), 160-161.

156. John Paul II, Address at the Mentorella Shrine (October 29, 1978): *Insegnamenti di Giovanni Paolo II*, I (1978), 78-79.

157. Cf. Second Vatican Ecumenical Council, Decree on the Apostolate of the Laity, *Apostolicam actuositatem*, no. 4.

158. Cf. John Paul I, Address to the Bishops of the Twelfth Pastoral Region of the United States of America (September 21, 1978): AAS 70 (1978), 21, 1978): AAS 70 (1978), 767.

159. Rom. 8:2.

160. Rom. 5:5.

161. Cf. Mk. 10:45.

162. Second Vatican Ecumenical Council, Dogmatic Constitution on the Church, *Lumen gentium*, no. 36.

163. Decree on the Apostolate of the Laity, *Apostolicam actuositatem*, no. 8.

164. Cf. the Sixth Synod of Bishops' Message to Christian Families in the Modern World (October 24, 1980), 12.

165. Cf. John Paul 11, Address to the Third General Assembly of the Bishops of Latin America (January 28, 1979), IV a: AAS 71 (1979), 204.

166. Cf. Second Vatican Ecumenical Council, Constitution on the Sacred Liturgy, *Sacrosanctum concilium*, no. 10.

167. Cf. *Ordo Celebrandi Matrimonium*, no. 17.

168. Cf. Second Vatican Ecumenical Council, Constitution on the Sacred Liturgy, *Sacrosanctum concilium*, no. 59.

169. Second Vatican Ecumenical Council, Decree on Renewal of Religious Life, *Perfectae caritatis*, no. 12.

170. John Paul 11, Address to the Confederation of Family Advisory Bureaus of Christian Inspiration (November 29, 1980), 3-4: *Insegnamenti di Giovanni Paolo 11*, III, 2 (1980), 1453-1454.

171. Paul VI, Message for the Third Social Communications Day (April 7, l969): AAS 61 (1969), 455

172. John Paul II, Message for the 1980 World Social Communications Day (May 1,1980): *Insegnamenti di Giovanni Paolo ll*, III, 1 (1980), 1042.

173. John Paul II, Message for the 1981 World Social Communications Day (May 10, 1981), 5: *L'Osservatore Romano*, May 22, 1981.

174. *Ibid.*

175. Paul VI, Message for the Third Social Communications Day: AAS 61(1969), 456.

176. *Ibid.*

177. John Paul II, Message for the 1980 World Social Communications Day: *Insegnamenti di Giovanni Paolo 11*, III, 1 (1980), 1044.

178. Cf. Paul Vl, Motu Proprio *Matrimonia mixta*, nos. 4-5: AAS 62 (1970), 257-259; John Paul 11, Address to the participants in the plenary meeting of the Secretariat for Promoting Christian Unity (November 13, 1981): *L'Osservatore Romano*, November 14, 1981.

179. Instruction *In quibus rerum circumstantiis* (June 15, 1972): AAS 64 (1972), 518-525; Note of October 17, 1973: AAS 65 (1973), 616-619.

180. John Paul 11, Homily at the close of the Sixth Synod of Bishops, (October 25, 1980), 7: AAS 72 (1980), 1082.

181. Mt. 11:28.

182. John Paul 11, Letter *Appropinquat lam* (August 15, 1980), 1: AAS 72 (1980), 791.

183. The Roman Missal, Preface of Christ the King.

Decree on
The Apostolate of Lay People[a]
Apostolicam Actuositatem
Vatican Council II
18 November, 1965

Introduction

INTRODUCTION

1. In its desire to intensify the apostolic activity of the People of God,[1] the Council now earnestly turns its thoughts to the Christian laity. Mention has already been made in other documents of the laity's special and indispensable role in the mission of the Church.[2] Indeed, the Church can never be without the lay apostolate; it is something that derives from the layman's very vocation as a Christian. Scripture clearly shows how spontaneous and fruitful was this activity in the Church's early days (cf. Acts 11:19-21; 18:26; Rom. 16:1-16; Phil. 4:3).

No less fervent a zeal on the part of lay people is called for today; present circumstances, in fact, demand from them an apostolate infinitely broader and more intense. For the constant increase in population, the progress in science and technology, the shrinking of the gaps that have kept men apart, have immensely enlarged the field of the lay apostolate, a field that is in great part open to the laity alone; they have in addition given rise to new problems which require from the laity an intelligent attention and examination. All the more urgent has this apostolate become, now that autonomy—as is only right—has been reached in numerous sectors of human life, sometimes with a certain relinquishing of moral and religious values, seriously jeopardizing the Christian life. Besides, in many regions where priests are very scarce or (as is sometimes the case) deprived of the freedom they need for their ministry, it is hard to see how the Church could make her presence and action felt without the help of the laity.

The need for this urgent and many-sided apostolate is shown by the manifest action of the Holy Spirit moving laymen today to a deeper and deeper awareness of their responsibility and urging them on everywhere to the service of Christ and the Church.[3]

The Council will explain in this Decree the nature of the lay apostolate, its character and the variety of its forms; it will state fundamental principles and give pastoral directives for its more effective exercise. These are all to serve as norms in the revision of Canon Law concerned with the lay apostolate.

CHAPTER I

THE VOCATION OF LAY PEOPLE TO THE APOSTOLATE

PARTICIPATION OF LAITY IN THE CHURCH'S MISSION

2. The Church was founded to spread the kingdom of Christ over all the earth for the glory of God the Father, to make all men partakers in redemption and salvation,[4] and through them to establish the right relationship of the entire world to Christ. Every activity of the Mystical Body with this in view goes by the name of "apostolate;" the Church exercises it through all its members, though in various ways. In fact, the Christian vocation is, of its nature, a voca-

tion to the apostolate as well. In the organism of a living body no member plays a purely passive part; sharing in the life of the body it shares at the same time in its activity. The same is true for the Body of Christ, the Church: "the whole Body achieves full growth in dependence on the full functioning of each part" (Eph. 4:16). Between the members of this body there exists, further, such a unity and solidarity (cf. Eph. 4:16) that a member who does not work at the growth of the body to the extent of his possibilities must be considered useless both to the Church and to himself.

In the Church there is diversity of ministry but unity of mission. To the apostles and their successors Christ has entrusted the office of teaching, sanctifying, and governing in his name and by his power. But the laity are made to share in the priestly, prophetical, and kingly office of Christ; they have therefore, in the Church and in the world, their own assignment in the mission of the whole People of God.[5] In the concrete, their apostolate is exercised when they work at the evangelization and sanctification of men; it is exercised too when they endeavor to have the Gospel spirit permeate and improve the temporal order, going about it in a way that bears clear witness to Christ and helps forward the salvation of men. The characteristic of the lay state being a life led in the midst of the world and of secular affairs, laymen are called by God to make of their apostolate, through the vigor of their Christian spirit, a leaven in the world.

FOUNDATIONS OF THE LAY APOSTOLATE

3. From the fact of their union with Christ the Head flows the laymen's right and duty to be apostles. Inserted as they are in the Mystical Body of Christ by baptism, and strengthened by the power of the Holy Spirit in confirmation, it is by the Lord himself that they are assigned to the apostolate. If they are consecrated a kingly priesthood and a holy nation (cf. 1 Pet. 2:4-10), it is in order that they may in all their actions offer spiritual sacrifices and bear witness to Christ all the world over. Charity, which is, as it were, the soul of the whole apostolate, is given to them and nourished in them by the sacraments, the Eucharist above all.[6]

The apostolate is lived in faith, hope, and charity poured out by the Holy Spirit into the hearts of all the members of the Church. And the precept of charity, which is the Lord's greatest commandment, urges all Christians to work for the glory of God through the coming of his kingdom and for the communication of eternal life to all men, that they may know the only true God and Jesus Christ Whom He has sent (cf. Jn. 17:3).

On all Christians, accordingly, rests the noble obligation of working to bring all men throughout the whole world to hear and accept the divine message of salvation.

The Holy Spirit sanctifies the People of God through the minis-

789

try and the sacraments. However, for the exercise of the apostolate he gives the faithful special gifts besides (cf. 1 Cor. 12:7), "allotting them to each one as he wills" (1 Cor. 12:11), so that each and all. putting at the service of others the grace received may be "as good stewards of God's varied gifts" (1 Pet. 4-10), for the building up of the whole body in charity (cf. Eph. 4:16). From the reception of these charisms, even the most ordinary ones, there arises for each of the faithful the right and duty of exercising them in the Church and in the world for the good of men and the development of the Church, of exercising them in the freedom of the Holy Spirit who "breathes where he wills" (Jn. 3:8), and at the same time in communion with his brothers in Christ, and with his pastors especially. It is for the pastors to pass judgment on the authenticity and good use of these gifts, not certainly with a view to quenching the Spirit but to testing everything and keeping what is good (cf. 1 Th. 5:12, 19, 21).[7]

THE SPIRITUALITY OF LAY PEOPLE

4. Christ, sent by the Father, is the source of the Church's whole apostolate. Clearly then, the fruitfulness of the apostolate of lay people depends on their living union with Christ; as the Lord said himself: "Whoever dwells in me and I in him bears much fruit, for separated from me you can do nothing" (Jn. 15:5). This life of intimate union with Christ in the Church is maintained by the spiritual helps common to all the faithful, chiefly by active participation in the liturgy.[8] Laymen should make such a use of these helps that, while meeting their human obligations in the ordinary conditions of life, they do not separate their union with Christ from their ordinary life; but through the very performance of their tasks, which are God's will for them, actually promote the growth of their union with him. This is the path along which laymen must advance, fervently, joyfully, overcoming difficulties with prudent patient efforts.[9] Family cares should not be foreign to their spirituality, nor any other temporal interest; in the words of the apostle: "Whatever you are doing, whether speaking or acting, do everything in the name of the Lord Jesus Christ, giving thanks to God the Father through him" (Col. 3 :17).

A life like this calls for a continuous exercise of faith, hope, and charity.

Only the light of faith and meditation on the Word of God can enable us to find everywhere and always the God "in Whom we live and exist" (Acts 17:28); only thus can we seek his will in everything, see Christ in all men, acquaintance or stranger, make sound judgments on the true meaning and value of temporal realities both in themselves and in relation to man's end.

Those with such a faith live in the hope of the revelation of the sons of God, keeping in mind the cross and resurrection of the Lord.

On life's pilgrimage they are hidden with Christ in God, are free from the slavery of riches, are in search of the goods that last for ever. Generously they exert all their energies in extending God's kingdom, in making the Christian spirit a vital energizing force in the temporal sphere. In life's trials they draw courage from hope, "convinced that present sufferings are no measure of the future glory to be revealed in us" (Rom. 8:18).

With the love that comes from God prompting them, they do good to all, especially to their brothers in the faith (cf. Gal. 6:10), putting aside "all ill will and deceit, all hypocrisy, envy and slander" (1 Pet. 2:1), in this way attracting men to Christ. Divine love, "poured into our hearts by the Holy Spirit Who has been given to us" (Rom. 5:5), enables lay people to express concretely in their lives the spirit of the Beatitudes. Following in His poverty Jesus, they feel no depression in want, no pride in plenty: imitating the humble Christ, they are not greedy for vain show (cf. Gal. 5:26). They strive instead to please God rather than men, always ready to abandon everything for Christ (cf. Lk. 14:26) and to endure persecution in the cause of right (cf. Mt. 5:10), having in mind the Lord's saying: "If any man wants to come my way, let him renounce self, take up his cross and follow me" (Mt. 16:24). Preserving a Christian friendship with one another, they afford mutual support in all needs.

This lay spirituality will take its particular character from the circumstances of one's state in life (married and family life, celibacy, widowhood), from one's state of health, and from one's professional and social activity. Whatever the circumstances, each one has received suitable talents; and these should be cultivated, as should also the personal gifts he has from the Holy Spirit.

Similarly laymen who have followed their particular vocation and become members of any of the associations or institutions approved by the Church aim sincerely at making their own the forms of spirituality proper to these bodies.

They should also hold in high esteem professional competence, family and civic sense, and the virtues related to social behavior such as honesty, sense of justice, sincerity, courtesy, and moral courage; without them there is no true Christian life.

Perfect model of this apostolic spiritual life is the Blessed Virgin Mary, Queen of Apostles. While on earth her life was like that of any other, filled with labors and the cares of the home; always, however, she remained intimately united to her Son and cooperated in an entirely unique way in the Saviour's work. And now, assumed into heaven, "her motherly love keeps her attentive to her Son's brothers, still on pilgrimage amid the dangers and difficulties of life, until they arrive at the happiness of the fatherland."[10] Everyone should have a genuine devotion to her and entrust his life to her motherly care.

CHAPTER II

OBJECTIVES

5. The work of Christ's redemption concerns essentially the salvation of men; it takes in also, however, the renewal of the whole temporal order. The mission of the Church, consequently, is not only to bring men the message and grace of Christ but also to permeate and improve the whole range of the temporal. The laity, carrying out this mission of the Church, exercise their apostolate therefore in the world as well as in the Church, in the temporal order well as in the spiritual. These orders are distinct; they are nevertheless so closely linked that God's plan is, in Christ, to take the whole world up again and make of it a new creation, in an initial way here on earth, in full realization at the end of time. The layman, at one and the same time a believer and a citizen of the world, has only a single con science, a Christian conscience; it is by this that he must be guided continually in both domains.

THE APOSTOLATE OF EVANGELIZATION AND SANCTIFICATION

6. The Church's mission is concerned with the salvation of men; and men win salvation through the grace of Christ and faith in him. The apostolate of the Church therefore, and of each of its members, aims primarily at announcing to the world by word and action the message of Christ and at communicating to it the grace of Christ. The principal means of bringing this about is the ministry of the word and of the sacraments. Committed in a special way to the clergy, it leaves room however for a highly important part for the laity, the part namely of "helping on the cause of truth" (3 Jn. 8). It is in this sphere most of all that the lay apostolate and the pastoral ministry complete each other.

Laymen have countless opportunities for exercising the apostolate of evangelization and sanctification. The very witness of a Christian life, and good works done in a supernatural spirit, are effective in drawing men to the faith and to God; and that is what the Lord has said: "Your light must shine so brightly before men that they can see your good works and glorify your Father Who is in heaven" (Mt. 5:16).

This witness of life, however, is not the sole element in the apostolate; the true apostle is on the lookout for occasions of announcing Christ by word, either to unbelievers to draw them towards the faith, or to the faithful to instruct them, strengthen them, incite them to a more fervent life, "for Christ's love urges us on" (2 Cor. 5:14); and in the hearts of all should the Apostle's words find echo: "Woe to me if I do not preach the Gospel" (1 Cor. 9:16).[11]

At a time when new questions are being put and when grave errors aiming at undermining religion, the moral order, and human society itself are rampant, the Council earnestly exhorts the laity to take a more active part, each according to his talents and knowledge, and in fidelity to the mind of the Church, in the explanation and defense of Christian principles and in the correct application of them to the problems of our times

THE RENEWAL OF THE TEMPORAL ORDER

7. That men, working in harmony, should renew the temporal order and make it increasingly more perfect: such is God's design for the world.

All that goes to make up the temporal order: personal and family values, culture, economic interests, the trades and professions, institutions of the political community, international relations, and so on, as well as their gradual development: all these are not merely helps to man's last end; they possess a value of their own, placed in them by God, whether considered individually or as parts of the integral temporal structure: "And God saw all that He had made and found it very good" (Gen. 1:31). This natural goodness of theirs receives an added dignity from their relation with the human person, for Whose use they have been created. And then, too, God has willed to gather together all that was natural, all that was supernatural, into a single whole in Christ, "so that in everything He would have the primacy" (Col. 1:18). Far from depriving the temporal order of its autonomy, of its specific ends, of its own laws and resources, or its importance for human well-being, this design, on the contrary, increases its energy and excellence, raising it at the same time to the level of man's integral vocation here below.

In the course of history the use of temporal things has been tarnished by serious defects. Under the influence of original sin, men have often fallen into very many errors about the true God, human nature, and the principles of morality. As a consequence human conduct and institutions became corrupted, the human person itself held in contempt. Again in our own days, not a few, putting an immoderate trust in the conquests of science and technology, turn to a kind of idolatry of the temporal; they become the slaves of it rather than the masters.

It is the work of the entire Church to fashion men able to establish the proper scale of values on the temporal order and to direct it towards God through Christ. Pastors have the duty to set forth clearly the principles concerning the purpose of creation and the use to be made of the world, and to provide moral and spiritual helps for the renewal of the temporal order in Christ.

Laymen ought to take on themselves as their distinctive task this renewal of the temporal order. Guided by the light of the Gospel and the mind of the Church, prompted by Christian love, they should act in this domain in a direct way and in their own specific manner. As citizens among citizens they must bring to their cooperation with others their own special competence, and act on their own responsibility; everywhere and always they have to seek the justice of the kingdom of God. The temporal order is to be renewed in such a way that, while its own principles are fully respected, it is harmonized with the principles of the Christian life and adapted to the various conditions of times, places, and peoples. Among the tasks of this apostolate, Christian social action is pre-eminent. The Council desires to see it extended today to every sector of life, not forgetting the cultural sphere.[12]

CHARITABLE WORKS AND SOCIAL AID

8. While every activity of the apostolate should find in charity its origin and driving force, certain works are of their nature a most eloquent expression of this charity; and Christ has willed that these should be signs of His messianic mission (cf. Mt. 11:4-5).

The greatest commandment of the law is to love God with one's whole heart and one's neighbor as oneself (cf. Mt. 22:37-40). Christ has made this love of the neighbor His personal commandment and has enriched it with a new meaning when He willed himself, along with His brothers, to be the object of this charity saying: "When you showed it to one of the least of My brothers here, you showed it to Me" (Mt. 25:40). In assuming human nature, He has united to Himself all humanity in a supernatural solidarity which makes of it one single family. He has made charity the distinguishing mark of His disciples, in the words: "By this will all men know you for My disciples, by the love you bear one another" (Jn. 13:35).

In the early days the Church linked the "agape" to the eucharistic supper, and by so doing showed itself as one body around Christ united by the bond of charity. So, too, in all ages, love is its characteristic mark. While rejoicing at initiatives taken elsewhere, it claims charitable works as its own mission and right. That is why mercy to the poor and the sick, and charitable works and works of mutual aid for the alleviation of all kinds of human needs, are held in special honor in the Church.[13]

Today these activities and works of charity have become much more urgent and worldwide; now that means of communication are more rapid, distance between men has been more or less conquered, people in every part of the globe have become as members of a single family. Charitable action today can and should reach all men and all needs.

Wherever men are to be found who are in want of food and drink, of clothing, housing, medicine, work, education, the means necessary for leading a truly human life, wherever there are men racked by misfortune or illness, men suffering exile or imprisonment, Christian charity should go in search of them and find them out, comfort them with devoted care and give them the helps that will relieve their needs. This obligation binds first and foremost the more affluent individuals and nations.[14]

If this exercise of charity is to be above all criticism, and seen to be so, one should see in one's neighbor the image of God to which he has been created, and Christ the Lord to Whom is really offered all that is given to the needy. The liberty and dignity of the person helped must be respected with the greatest sensitivity. Purity of intention should not be stained by any self-seeking or desire to dominate.[15] The demands of justice must first of all be satisfied; that which is already due in justice is not to be offered as a gift of charity. The cause of evils, and not merely their effects, ought to disappear. The aid contributed should be organized in such a way that beneficiaries are gradually freed from their dependence on others and become self-supporting.

The laity should therefore highly esteem, and support as far as they can, private or public works of charity and social assistance movements, including international schemes. By these channels effective help is brought to individuals and nations in need. They should collaborate in this with all men of good will.[16]

CHAPTER III

THE VARIOUS FIELDS OF THE APOSTOLATE

9. The lay apostolate, in all its many aspects, is exercised both in the Church and in the world. In either case different fields of apostolic action are open to the laity. We propose to mention here the chief among them: Church communities, the family, the young, the social environment, national and international spheres. Since in our days women are taking an increasingly active share in the whole life of society, it is very important that their participation in the various sectors of the Church's apostolate should likewise develop.

CHURCH COMMUNITIES

10. Participators in the junction of Christ, priest, prophet, and king, the laity have an active part of their own in the life and action of the Church. Their action within the Church communities is so necessary that without it the apostolate of the pastors will frequently be unable to obtain its full effect. Following in the footsteps of the men and women who assisted Paul in the proclamation of the Gospel (cf. Acts 18:18-26; Rom. 16:3), lay persons of a genuinely apostolic spirit supply the needs of their brothers and are a source of consolation no less to the pastors than to the rest of the faithful (cf. 1 Cor. 16:17-18). Nourished by their active participation in the liturgical life of their community, they engage zealously in its apostolic works; they draw men towards the Church who had been perhaps very far away from it; they ardently cooperate in the spread of the Word of God, particularly by catechetical instruction; by their expert assistance they increase the efficacy of the care of souls as well as of the administration of the goods of the Church.

The parish offers an outstanding example of community apostolate, for it gathers into a unity all the human diversities that are found there and inserts them into the universality of the Church.[17] The laity should develop the habit of working in the parish in close union with their priests,[18] of bringing before the ecclesial community their own problems, world problems, and questions regarding man's salvation, to examine them together and solve them be general discussion. According to their abilities the laity ought to operate in all the apostolic and missionary enterprises of their ecclesial family.

The laity will continuously cultivate the "feeling for the diocese," of which the parish is a kind of cell; they will be always ready on the invitation of their bishop to make their own contribution to diocesan undertakings. Indeed, they will not confine their cooperation within the limits of the parish or diocese, but will endeavor, in response to the needs of the towns and rural districts,19 to extend it to inter-parochial, inter-diocesan, national and international spheres. This widening of horizons is all the more necessary in the present situation, in which the increasing frequency of population shifts, the development of active solidarity and the ease of communications no longer allow any one part of society to live in isolation. The laity will therefore have concern for the needs of the People of God scattered throughout the world. Especially will they make missionary works their own by providing them with material means and even with personal service. It is for Christians a duty and an honor to give God back a portion of the goods they have received from him.

THE FAMILY

11. The Creator of all made the married state the beginning and foundation of human society: by His grace He has made of it, too, a great mystery in Christ and in the Church (cf. Eph. 5:32); and so the apostolate of married persons and of families has a special importance for both Church and civil society.

Christian couples are, for each other, for their children, and for their relatives, cooperators of grace and witnesses of the faith. They are the first to pass on the faith to their children and to educate them in it. By word and example they form them to a Christian and apostolic life; they offer them wise guidance in the choice of vocation; and if they discover in them a sacred vocation, they encourage it with all care.

To give clear proof in their own lives of the indissolubility and holiness of the marriage bond; to assert with vigor the right and duty of parents and guardians to give their children a Christian upbringing; to defend the dignity and legitimate autonomy of the family: this has always been the duty of married persons; today, however, it has become the most important aspect of their apostolate. They and all the faithful, therefore, should collaborate with men of good will in seeing that these rights are perfectly safeguarded in civil legislation; that in social administration, consideration is given to the requirements of families in the matter of housing, education of children, working conditions, social security, and taxes; and that in emigration regulations, family life is perfectly safeguarded.[20]

The mission of being the primary vital cell of society has been given to the family by God Himself. This mission will be accomplished if the family, by the mutual affection of its members and by family prayer, presents itself as a domestic sanctuary of the Church; if the whole family takes its part in the Church's liturgical worship; if, finally, it offers active hospitality, and practises justice and other good works for the benefit of all its brothers suffering from want. Among the various works of the family apostolate the following may be listed: adopting abandoned children, showing a loving welcome to strangers, helping with the running of schools, supporting adolescents with advice and help, assisting engaged couples to make a better preparation for marriage, taking a share in catechism-teaching, supporting married people and families in a material or moral crisis, and in the case of the aged not only providing them with what is indispensable but also procuring for them a fair share of the fruits of economic progress.

Everywhere and always, but especially in regions where the first seeds of the Gospel are just being sown, or where the Church is still in its infancy or finds itself in a critical situation, Christian families bear a very valuable witness to Christ before the world when all their life they remain attached to the Gospel and hold up the example of Christian marriage.[21]

To attain the ends of their apostolate more easily it can be of advantage for families to organize themselves into groups.[22]

YOUNG PEOPLE

12. Young people exert a very important influence in modern society:[23] The circumstances of their life, their habits of thought, their relations with their families, have been completely transformed. Often they enter too rapidly a new social and economic environment. While their social and even political importance is on the increase day by day, they seem unequal to the weight of these new responsibilities.

The growth of their social importance demands from them a corresponding apostolic activity; and indeed their natural character inclines them in this direction. Carried along by their natural ardor and exuberant energy, when awareness of their own personality ripens in them they shoulder responsibilities that are theirs and are eager to take their place in social and cultural life. If this enthusiasm is penetrated with the spirit of Christ, animated by a sense of obedience and love towards the pastors of the Church, a very rich harvest can be expected from it. The young should become the first apostles of the young, in direct contact with them, exercising the apostolate by themselves among themselves, taking account of their social environment.[24]

Adults should be anxious to enter into friendly dialogue with the young, where, despite the difference in age, they could get to know one another and share with one another their own personal aches. It is by example first of all and, on occasion, by sound advice and practical help that adults should persuade the young to undertake the apostolate. The young, on their side, will treat their elders with respect and confidence; and though by nature inclined to favor what is new, they will have due esteem for praiseworthy traditions.

Children too have an apostolate of their own. In their own measure they are true living witnesses of Christ among their companions.

APOSTOLATE OF LIKE TOWARDS LIKE

13. The apostolate in one's social environment endeavors to infuse the Christian spirit into the mentality and behavior, laws, and structures of the community in which one lives. To such a degree is it the special work and responsibility of lay people, that no one else can ever properly supply for them. In this area laymen can conduct the apostolate of like towards like. There the witness of their life is completed by the witness of their word.[25] It is amid the surroundings of their work that they are best qualified to be of help to their brothers, in the surroundings of their profession, of their study, residence, leisure or local group.

The laity accomplish the Church's mission in the world principally by that blending of conduct and faith which makes them the light of the world; by that uprightness in all their dealings which is for every man such an incentive to love the true and the good and which is capable of inducing him at last to go to Christ and the Church: by that fraternal charity that makes them share the living conditions and labors, the sufferings and yearnings of their brothers, and thereby prepare all hearts, gently, imperceptibly, for the action of saving grace; by that full awareness of their personal responsibility in the development of society, which drives them on to perform their family, social, and professional duties with Christian generosity. In this way their conduct makes itself gradually felt in the surroundings where they live and work.

This apostolate should reach out to every single person in that environment; and it must not exclude any good, spiritual or temporal, that can be done for them. Genuine apostles are not content, however, with just this; they are earnest also about revealing Christ by word to those around them. It is a fact that many men cannot hear the Gospel and come to acknowledge Christ except through the laymen they associate with.

THE NATIONAL AND INTERNATIONAL LEVELS

14. On the national and international planes, the field of the apostolate is vast; and it is there that the laity more than others are the channels of Christian wisdom. In their patriotism and in their fidelity to their civic duties Catholics will feel themselves bound to promote the true common good; they will make the weight of their convictions so influential that, as a result, civil authority will be justly exercised and laws will accord with the moral precepts and the common good. Catholics versed in politics and, as should be the case, firm in the faith and Christian teaching, should not decline to enter public life; for by a worthy discharge of their functions, they can work for the common good and at the same time prepare the way for the Gospel.

Catholics are to be keen on collaborating with all men of good will in the promotion of all that is true, just, holy: all that is worthy of love (cf. Phil. 4:8). They are to enter into dialogue with them, approaching them with understanding and courtesy; and are to search for means of improving social and public institutions along the lines of the Gospel.

Among the signs of our times, particularly worthy of note is the ever growing and inescapable sense of the solidarity of all peoples. It is the task of the lay apostolate to take pains in developing this sense and transforming it into a really sincere desire for brotherly union. The laity should have an awareness also of the international sector, of the doctrinal and practical problems and solutions that are brought forward there, in particular those concerned with newly developing nations.[26]

Everyone who works in foreign nations or brings them aid must remember that relations among peoples should be a real fraternal interchange in which both parties give and at the same time receive. Those who travel abroad, for international activities, on business or on holiday, should keep in mind that no matter where they may be, they are the travelling messengers of Christ, and should bear themselves really as such.

CHAPTER IV

THE DIFFERENT FORMS OF THE APOSTOLATE

15. The laity can exercise their apostolic activity either singly or grouped in various communities or associations.

INDIVIDUAL APOSTOLATE

16. The apostolate to be exercised by the individual—which flows abundantly from a truly Christian life (cf. Jn. 4:11)— is the starting point and condition of all types of lay apostolate, including the organized apostolate; nothing can replace it.

The individual apostolate is everywhere and always in place; in certain circumstances it is the only one appropriate, the only one possible. Every lay person, whatever his condition, is called to it, is obliged to it, even if he has not the opportunity or possibility of collaborating in associations.

The apostolate, through which the laity build up the Church, sanctify the world, and get it to live in Christ, can take on many forms.

A special form of the individual apostolate is the witness of a whole lay life issuing from faith, hope, and charity; it is a sign very much in keeping with our times, and a manifestation of Christ living in his faithful. Then, by the apostolate of the word, which in certain circumstances is absolutely necessary, the laity proclaim Christ, explain and spread his teachings, each one according to his condition and competence, and profess those teachings with fidelity.

Moreover, cooperating as citizens of this world in all that has to do with the constructing and conducting of the temporal order, the laity should, by the light of faith, try to find the higher motives that should govern their behavior in the home and in professional, cultural, and social life; they should, too, given the opportunity, let these motives be seen by others, conscious that by so doing they become cooperators with God the creator, redeemer, and sanctifier, and give Him glory.

Finally, the laity should vitalize their lives with charity and, to the extent of the capability of each, give concrete expression to it in works.

All should remember that by public worship and by prayer, by penance and the willing acceptance of the toil and hardships of life by which they resemble the suffering Christ (cf. 2 Cor. 4:10; Col. 1:24), they can reach all men and contribute to the salvation of the entire world.

INDIVIDUAL APOSTOLATE IN CERTAIN CIRCUMSTANCES

17. There is an imperative need for the individual apostolate in those areas where the Church's freedom is seriously hampered. In such difficult circumstances the laity take over as far as possible the work of priests, jeopardizing their own freedom and sometimes their lives; they teach Christian doctrine to those around them, train them in a religious way of life and in Catholic attitudes, encourage them to receive the sacraments frequently and to cultivate piety, especially eucharistic piety.[27] The Council renders God most heartfelt thanks that even in our own times He is still raising up laymen with heroic courage in the midst of persecutions; the Council embraces them with gratitude and fatherly affection.

The individual apostolate has a special field in regions where Catholics are few and scattered. In such circumstances the laity who exercise only the personal apostolate—whether from the reasons mentioned above or from particular motives arising, among other things, from their professional activity—can gather for discussion into small groups with no rigid form of rules or organization. This is particularly appropriate in the present instance, for it ensures the continual presence before the eyes of others of a sign of the Church's community, a sign that will be seen as a genuine witness of love. Thus, by affording mutual spiritual aid by friendship and the exchange of personal experiences, they get the courage to surmount the difficulties of too isolated a life and activity and can increase the yield of their apostolate.

GROUP APOSTOLATE

18. The faithful are called as individuals to exercise an apostolate in the various conditions of their life. They must, however, remember that man is social by nature and that it has been God's pleasure to assemble those who believe in Christ and make of them the People of God (cf. 1 Pet. 2:5-10), a single body (cf. 1 Cor. 12:12). The group apostolate is in happy harmony, therefore, with a fundamental need in the faithful, a need that is both human and Christian. At the same time it offers a sign of the communion and unity of the Church in Christ, Who said: "Where two or three are gathered together in My name, I am there in the midst of them" (Mt. 18:20).

For that reason, Christians will exercise their apostolate in a spirit of concord.[28] They will be apostles both in their families and in the parishes and dioceses, which already are themselves expressions of the community character of the apostolate; apostles, too, in the free associations they will have decided to form among themselves.

The group apostolate is very important also for another reason: often, either in ecclesial communities or in various other environments, the apostolate calls for concerted action. Organizations created for group apostolate afford support to their members, train them for the apostolate, carefully assign and direct their apostolic activities; and as a result a much richer harvest can be hoped for from them than if each one were to act on his own.

In present circumstances it is supremely necessary that, wherever the laity are at work, the apostolate under its collective and organized form should be strengthened. In actual fact only a well-knit combination of efforts can completely attain all the aims of the modern apostolate and give its fruits good protection.[29] From this point of view it is particularly important for the apostolate to establish contact with the group attitudes and social conditions of the persons who are its object; otherwise these will often be incapable of withstanding the pressure of public opinion or of social institutions.

VARIOUS TYPES OF GROUP APOSTOLATE

19. Great variety is to be found in apostolic associations.[30] Some look to the general apostolic end of the Church; others aim specifically at evangelization and sanctification; others work for the permeation of the temporal order by the Christian spirit; and others engage in works of mercy and of charity as their special way of bearing witness to Christ.

First among these associations to be given consideration should be those which favor and promote a more intimate unity between the faith of the members and their everyday life. Associations are not ends in themselves; they are meant to be of service to the Church's mission to the world. Their apostolic value depends on their conformity with the Church's aims, as well as on the Christian witness and evangelical spirit of each of their members and of the association as a whole.

As a consequence of the progress of institutions and the rapid evolution of modern society, the universal nature of the Church's mission requires that the apostolic initiatives of Catholics should more and more perfect the various types of international organizations. Catholic international organizations will the more surely gain their object, the more intimately the groups that compose them, as well as their members, are united to them.

While preserving intact the necessary link with ecclesiastical authority,[31] the laity have the right to establish and direct associations,[32] and to join existing ones. Dissipation of forces must, however, be avoided; this would happen if new associations and works were created without sufficient reason, if old ones now grown useless were held on to, if out-of-date methods continued to be employed. It will not always be a wise procedure, either, to transfer indiscriminately into some particular country forms that have arisen in another.[33]

CATHOLIC ACTION

20. Several decades ago lay people, dedicating themselves increasingly to the apostolate, in many countries formed themselves into various kinds of movements and societies which, in closer union with the hierarchy, have pursued and continue to pursue ends properly apostolic. Among these institutions, as indeed among other similar older ones, special mention must be made of those which, though using differing methods, have yielded abundant fruit for the kingdom of Christ. Deservedly praised and promoted by the popes and numerous bishops, they have received from them the name of Catholic Action, and have most often been described by them as a collaboration of the laity in the hierarchical apostolate.[34]

These types of apostolate, whether or not they go by the name of Catholic Action, are today doing a work of much value. They are constituted by the combination of all the following characteristics:

(a) The immediate end of organizations of this class is the apostolic end of the Church; in other words: the evangelization and sanctification of men and the Christian formation of their conscience, so as to enable them to imbue with the Gospel spirit the various social groups and environments.

(b) The laity, cooperating in their own particular way with the hierarchy, contribute their experience and assume responsibility in the direction of these organizations, in the investigation of the conditions in which the Church's pastoral work is to be carried on, in the elaboration and execution of their plan of action.

(c) The laity act in unison after the manner of an organic body, to display more strikingly the community aspect of the Church and to render the apostolate more productive.

(d) The laity, whether coming of their own accord or in response to an invitation to action and direct cooperation with the hierarchical apostolate, act under the superior direction of the hierarchy, which can authorize this cooperation, besides, with an explicit mandate.

Organizations which, in the judgment of the hierarchy, combine all these elements should be regarded as Catholic Action, even if they have forms and names that vary according to the requirements of localities and peoples.

The Council most earnestly commends those institutions which certainly meet the requirements of the Church's apostolate in many countries; it invites the priests and laity working in them to develop more and more the characteristics mentioned above, and always to give brotherly cooperation in the Church to all other forms of the apostolate.

SPECIAL COMMENDATION

21. Proper esteem is to be shown to all associations of the apostolate; those, however, which the hierarchy has praised, commended, or decided to found as more urgent to meet the needs of times and places, should be valued most by priests, religious and lay people, and developed each in its own way. And among these organizations today especially must be numbered the international associations or societies of Catholics.

22. Worthy of special respect and praise in the Church are the laity, single or married, who, in a definitive way or for a period, put their person and their professional competence at the service of institutions and their activities. It is a great joy to the Church to see growing day by day the number of lay people who are offering their personal service to associations and works of the apostolate, whether within the confines of their own country, or in the international

803

field, or, above all, in the Catholic communities of the missions and of the young Churches.

Pastors are to welcome these lay persons with joy and gratitude. They will see to it that their conditions of life satisfy as perfectly as possible the requirements of justice, equity, and charity, chiefly in the matter of resources necessary for the maintenance of themselves and their families. They should, too, be provided with the necessary training and with spiritual comfort and encouragement.

CHAPTER V

THE ORDER TO BE OBSERVED

23. The lay apostolate, individual or collective, must be set in its true place within the apostolate of the whole Church. Union with those whom the Holy Spirit has appointed to rule the Church of God (cf. Acts 20:28) is an essential element of the Christian apostolate. Not less necessary is collaboration among the different undertakings of the apostolate; it is the hierarchy's place to put proper system into this collaboration.

Mutual esteem for all forms of the Church's apostolate, and good coordination, preserving nevertheless the character special to each, are, in fact, absolutely necessary for promoting that spirit of unity which will cause fraternal charity to shine out in the Church's whole apostolate, common aims to be reached, and ruinous rivalries avoided.[35]

This is appropriate most of all when some particular action in the Church calls for the agreement and apostolic cooperation of both classes of the clergy, of religious, and of the laity.

RELATIONS WITH THE HIERARCHY

24. The hierarchy's duty is to favor the lay apostolate, furnish it with principles and spiritual assistance, direct the exercise of the apostolate to the common good of the Church, and see to it that doctrine and order are safeguarded.

Yet the lay apostolate allows of different kinds of relations with the hierarchy, depending on the various forms and objects of this apostolate.

In the Church are to be found, in fact, very many apostolic enterprises owing their origin to the free choice of the laity and run at their own discretion. Such enterprises enable the Church, in certain circumstances, to fulfill her mission more effectively; not seldom, therefore, are they raised and commended by the hierarchy.[36] But no enterprise must lay claim to the name "Catholic" if it has not the approval of legitimate ecclesiastical authority.

Certain types of the lay apostolate are explicitly recognized by the hierarchy though in different ways.

Ecclesiastical authority, looking to the needs of the common good of the Church, may also, from among apostolic associations and undertakings aiming immediately at a spiritual goal, pick out some which it will foster in a particular way; in these it assumes a special responsibility. And so, organizing the apostolate differently according to circumstances, the hierarchy brings into closer conjunction with its own apostolic functions such-and-such a form of apostolate, without, however, changing the specific nature of either or the distinction between the two, and consequently without depriving the laity of their rightful freedom to act on their own initiative. This act of the hierarchy has received the name of "mandate" in various ecclesiastical documents.

Finally, the hierarchy entrusts the laity with certain charges more closely connected with the duties of pastor in the teaching of Christian doctrine, for example, in certain liturgical actions, in the care of souls. In virtue of this mission, the laity are fully subject to superior ecclesiastical control in regard to the exercise of these charges.

As for works and institutions of the temporal order, the duty of the ecclesiastical hierarchy is the teaching and authentic interpretation of the moral principles to be followed in this domain. It is also in its province to judge, after mature reflection and with the help of qualified persons, of the conformity of such works or institutions with moral principles, and to pronounce in their regard concerning what is required for the safeguard and promotion of the values of; the supernatural order.

RELATIONS WITH THE CLERGY AND WITH RELIGIOUS

25. Bishops, parish priests, and other priests of the secular and regular clergy will remember that the right and duty of exercising the apostolate are common to all the faithful, whether clerics or lay; and that in the building up of the Church the laity, too, have parts of their own to play.[37] For this reason they will work as brothers with the laity in the Church and for the Church, and will have a special concern for the laity in their apostolic activities.[38]

A careful choice will be made of priests with the ability and appropriate training for helping special forms of the lay apostolate.[39] Those who take part in this ministry in virtue of a mission received from the hierarchy represent the hierarchy in this pastoral action of theirs. Ever faithfully attached to the spirit and teaching of the Church, they will promote good relations between laity and hierarchy, they will devote their energies to fostering the spiritual life and the apostolic sense of the Catholic associations confided to them; their wise advice will be there to help these along in their apostolic labors; their encouragement will be given to their enterprises. In constant dialogue with the laity, they will make painstaking search for methods capable of making apostolic action more fruitful; they will develop the spirit of unity within the association, and between it and others.

Lastly, religious Brothers and Sisters will hold lay apostolic works in high regard; and will gladly help in promoting them in accordance with the spirit and rules of their institute;[40] they will strive to support, assist, and complete the ministrations of the priest.

SPECIAL COUNCILS

26. In dioceses, as far as possible, councils should be set up to assist the Church's apostolic work, whether in the field of evangelization and sanctification or in the fields of charity, social relations, and the rest; the clergy and religious working with the laity in whatever way proves satisfactory. These councils can take care of the mutual coordinating of the various lay associations and undertakings, the autonomy and particular nature of each remaining untouched.[41]

Such councils should be found too, if possible, at parochial, inter-parochial, inter-diocesan level, and also on the national and international plane.[42]

In addition, a special secretariat should be established at the Holy See for the service and promotion of the lay apostolate. This secretariat will act as a center which, with the proper equipment, will supply information about the different apostolic initiatives of the laity. It will undertake research on the problems arising today in this domain; and with its advice will assist the hierarchy and laity in the field of apostolic activities. The various apostolic movements and institutes of the lay apostolate all the world over should be represented in this secretariat. Clerics and religious should also be there to collaborate with the laity.

COOPERATION WITH OTHER CHRISTIANS
AND NON-CHRISTIANS

27. The common patrimony of the Gospel and the common duty resulting from it of bearing a Christian witness make it desirable, and often imperative, that Catholics cooperate with other Christians, either in activities or in societies; this collaboration is carried on by individuals and by ecclesial communities, and at national or international levels.[43]

Not seldom also do human values common to all mankind require of Christians working for apostolic ends that they collaborate with those who do not profess Christianity but acknowledge these values.

Through this dynamic, yet prudent, cooperation,[44] which is of great importance in temporal activities, the laity bears witness to Christ the Saviour of the world, and to the unity of the human family.

CHAPTER VI

TRAINING FOR THE APOSTOLATE

THE NEED FOR TRAINING

28. A training, at once many-sided and complete, is indispensable if the apostolate is to attain full efficacy. This is required, not only by the continuous spiritual and doctrinal progress of the layman himself, but also by the variety of circumstances, persons, and duties to which he should adapt his activity. This education to the apostolate must rest on those foundations which the Council has in other places set down and expounded Not a few types of apostolate require, besides the education common to all Christians, a specific and individual training, by reason of the diversity of persons and circumstances.

PRINCIPLES OF TRAINING

29. Since the laity participate in the Church's mission in a way that is their own, their apostolic training acquires a special character precisely from the secularity proper to the lay state and from its particular type of spirituality.

Education for the apostolate presupposes an integral human education suited to each one's abilities and conditions. For the layman ought to be, through an intimate knowledge of the contemporary world, a member well integrated into his own society and its culture.

But in the first place he should learn to accomplish the mission of Christ and the Church, living by faith in the divine mystery of creation and redemption, moved by the Holy Spirit Who gives life to the People of God and urges all men to love God the Father, and in Him to love the world of men. This education must be considered the foundation and condition of any fruitful apostolate.

Besides spiritual formation, solid grounding in doctrine is required: in theology, ethics, and philosophy, at least, proportioned to the age, condition, and abilities of each one. The importance, too, of a general culture linked with a practical and technical training is something which should by no means be overlooked.

If good human relations are to be cultivated, then it is necessary for genuine human values to stand at a premium, especially the art of living and working on friendly terms with others and entering into dialogue with them.

Training for the apostolate cannot consist in theoretical teaching alone; on that account there is need, right from the start of training, to learn gradually and prudently to see all things in the light of faith, to judge and act always in its light, to improve and perfect oneself by working with others, and in this manner to enter actively into the service of the Church.[46] Inasmuch as the human person is

807

continuously developing and new problems are forever arising, this education should be steadily perfected; it requires an ever more thorough knowledge and a continual adaptation of action. While meeting all its demands, concern for the unity and integrity of the human person must be kept always in the foreground, in order to preserve and intensify its harmony and equilibrium.

In this way the layman actively inserts himself deep into the very reality of the temporal order and takes his part competently in the work of the world. At the same time, as a living member and witness of the Church, he brings its presence and its action into the heart of the temporal sphere.[47]

THOSE WHO TRAIN OTHERS FOR THE APOSTOLATE

30. Training for the apostolate should begin from the very start of a child's education. But it is more particularly adolescents and youth who should be initiated into the apostolate and imbued with its spirit. This training should be continued all through life, to fit them to meet the demands of fresh duties. It is clear, then, that those with responsibility for Christian education have also the duty of attending to this apostolic education.

It rests with parents to prepare their children from an early age, within the family circle, to discern God's love for all men; they will teach them little by little—and above all by their example—to have concern for their neighbors' needs, material and spiritual. The whole family, accordingly, and its community life should become a kind of apprenticeship the apostolate.

Children must be trained besides, to go beyond the confines of the family and to take an interest in both ecclesial and temporal communities. Their integration into the local parish community should succeed in bringing them to the awareness of being living, active members of the People of God. Priests, for their part, should not lose sight of this question of training for the apostolate when catechizing, preaching, and directing souls, and in other functions of the pastoral ministry.

Schools and colleges and other Catholic educational institutions should foster in the young a Catholic outlook and apostolic action. If the young do not get this type of education, either because they do not attend these schools, or for some other reason, all the greater is the responsibility for it that devolves upon parents, pastoral and apostolic bodies. As for teachers and educators, who by their calling and position practice an outstanding form of lay apostolate, adequate learning and a thorough grasp of pedagogy is a prerequisite to any success in this branch of education.

The various lay groups and associations dedicated to the apostolate or to any other supernatural end should look after this education to the apostolate with care and constancy, in ways consistent with their objectives and limits.[48] Frequently they are the ordinary channel of adequate apostolic training: doctrinal, spiritual, and practical. The members, gathered in small groups with their companions or friends, evaluate the methods and results of their apostolic action, and measure their everyday behavior by the Gospel.

The training should be pursued in such a way as to take account of the entire range of the lay apostolate, an apostolate that is to be exercised in all circumstances and in every sector of life—in the professional and social sectors especially—and not confined within the precincts of the associations. In point of fact, every single lay person should himself actively undertake his own preparation for the apostolate. Especially for adults does this hold true: for as the years pass, self-awareness expands and so allows each one to get a clearer view of the talents with which God has enriched his life and to bring in better results from the exercise of the charisms given him by the Holy Spirit for the good of his brothers.

FIELDS CALLING FOR SPECIALIZED TRAINING

31. Different types of apostolate require their own appropriate method of training:

(a) The apostolate of evangelization and sanctification: the laity are to be specially trained for engaging in dialogue with others, believers or non-believers, their aim being to set the message of Christ before the eyes of all.[49] But as materialism under various guises is today spreading far and wide, even among Catholics, the laity should not only make a careful study of Catholic doctrine, especially points that are called into question, but should confront materialism of every type with the witness of evangelical life.

(b) The Christian renewal of the temporal order: the laity are to be instructed in the true meaning and value of temporal goods, both in themselves and in their relation to all the aims of the human person. The laity should gain experience in the right use of goods and in the organization of institutions, paying heed always to the common good in the light of the principles of the Church's moral and social teaching. They should acquire such a knowledge of social teaching, especially its principles and conclusions, as will fit them for contributing to the best of their ability to the progress of that teaching, and for making correct application of these same principles and conclusions in individual cases.[50]

(c) Works of charity and mercy bear a most striking testimony to Christian life; therefore, an apostolic training which has as its object the performance of these works should enable the faithful to learn from very childhood how to sympathize with their brothers, and help them generously when in need.[51]

AIDS TO TRAINING

32. Many aids are now at the disposal of the laity who devote themselves to the apostolate: namely, sessions, congresses, recollections, retreats, frequent meetings, conferences, books, and periodicals; all these enable them to deepen their knowledge of holy scripture and Catholic doctrine, nourish the spiritual life, and become acquainted also with world conditions and discover and adopt suitable methods.[52]

These educational aids take into account the various types of apostolate exercised in this or that particular area. With this end in view, higher centers or institutes have been created; these have already given excellent results.

The Council rejoices at initiatives of this kind now flourishing in certain regions; it desires to see them take root in other places, too, wherever the need for them makes itself felt.

Moreover, centers of documentation and research should be established, not only in theology but also in anthropology, psychology, sociology, and methodology, for the benefit of all fields of the apostolate. The purpose of such centers is to create a more favorable atmosphere for developing the aptitudes of the laity, men and women, young and old.

EXHORTATION

33. The Council, then, makes to all the laity an earnest appeal in the Lord to give a willing, noble, and enthusiastic response to the voice of Christ, Who at this hour is summoning them more pressingly, and to the urging of the Holy Spirit. The younger generation should feel this call to be addressed in a special way to themselves; they should welcome it eagerly and generously. It is the Lord Himself, by this Council, Who is once more inviting all the laity to unite themselves to Him ever more intimately, to consider His interests as their own (cf. Phil. 2:5), and to join in His mission as Savior: It is the Lord Who is again sending them into every town and every place where He Himself is to come (cf. Lk. 10:1). He sends them on the Church's apostolate, an apostolate that is one yet has different forms and methods, an apostolate that must all the time be adapting itself to the needs of the moment; He sends them on an apostolate where they are to show themselves His cooperators, doing their full share continually in the work of the Lord, knowing that in the Lord their labor cannot be lost (cf. Cor. 15:58).

FOOTNOTES

a. Translated by Father Finnian, O.S.C.O.

1. Cf. John XXIII, Apostolic Constitution *Humanae Salutis*, 25 Dec. 1961: *AAS* 54 (1962) p. 7-10.

2. Cf. Dogmatic Constitution *De Ecclesia*, ch. IV, no. 33 ff.: *AAS* 57 (1965) p. 39 ff.; cf. Constitution *De Sacra Liturgia*, nos. 26-40: *AAS* 56 (1964) pp. 107-111; cf. Decree *De instrumentis communicationis socialis*: *AAS* 56 (1964) pp. 143-153; cf. Decree *De Oecumenismo*: *AAS* 57 (1965) pp. 90-107; cf. Decree *De pastorali Episcoporum munere in Ecclesia*, nos. 16, 17, 18; cf. Declaration *De educatione Christiana*, nos. 3, 5, 7.

3. Cf. Pius XII, *Alloc. ad Cardinales*, 18 Feb. 1946: *AAS* 38 (1946) pp. 101-102; *idem., Sermo ad Iuvenes Operarios Catholicos*, 25 Aug. 1957: *AAS* 49 (1957) p. 843.

4. Cf. Pius XI, Encyclical Letter *Rerum Ecclesiae*: *AAS* 18 (1926) p. 65.

5. Cf. Dogmatic Constitution *De Ecclesia*, chap. IV, no. 33: *AAS* 57 (1965) p. 37.

6. Cf. Dogmatic Constitution *De Ecclesia*, chap. IV, no. 33: *AAS* 57 (1965) p. 39. Cf. also no. 10, ibid., p. 14.

7. Cf. ibid., no. 12: *AAS* 57 (1965) p. 16.

8. Cf. Constitution *De Sacra Liturgia*, chap. I, no. 11: *AAS* 56 (1964) pp. 102-103.

9. Cf. Dogmatic Constitution *De Ecclesia*, chap. IV, no. 32: *AAS* 57 (1965) p. 38. Cf. also chap. V, nos. 40-41, ibid.,pp. 45-47.

10. Cf. ibid., chap. VIII, no. 62: *AAS* 57 (1965) p. 63. Cf. also no. 65, ibid., pp. 64-65.

11. Cf. Pius XI, Encyclical Letter *Ubi arcano*, 23 Dec. 1922: *AAS* 14 (1922) p. 659; Pius XII, Encyclical Letter *Summi Pontificatus*, 20 Oct. 1939: *AAS* 31 (1939) pp. 442-443.

12. Cf. Leo XIII, Encyclical Letter *Rerum Novarum*: *AAS* 23 (1890-1891) p. 647; Pius XI, Encyclical Letter *Quadragesimo Anno*: *AAS* 23 (1931) p. 190; Pius XII, *Nuntius Radiophonicus*, 1 June 1941: *AAS* 33 (1941) p. 207.

13. Cf. John XXIII, Encyclical Letter *Mater et Magistra*: *AAS* 53 (1961) p. 402.

14. Cf. ibid., pp. 440-441.

15. Cf. ibid., pp. 442-443.

16. Cf. Pius XII, *Alloc. ad Pax Romana M.I.I.C.*, 25 April 1957: *AAS* 49 (1957) pp. 298-299; and especially John XXIII, *Conventum*

Consilii 'Food and Agriculture Organization' (F.A.O.), 10 Nov. 1959: *AAS* 51 (1959) pp. 856, 866.

17. Cf. Pius X, Apostolic Letter *Creationis duarum novarum paroeciarum*, 1 June 1905: *AAS* 3 (1905) pp. 65-67; Pius II, *Alloc. ad fideles Paroeciae S. Saba*, 11 Jan. 1953. *Discorsi e Radiomessaggi di S.S. Pio XII*, 14 (1952-1953) pp. 449-454; John XXIII, *Alloc. Clero et christifidelibus e diocesi suburbicaria Albanensi, ad Arcem Gandulfi habita*, 16 Aug. 1962: *AAS* 54 (1962) pp. 656-660.

18. Cf. Leo XIII, *Alloc.*, 28 Jan. 1894: Acts 14 (1894) pp. 424-425.

19. Cf. Pius XII, *Alloc. ad Parochos, etc.*, 6 Feb. 1951: *Discorsi e Radiomessaggi di S.S. Pio XII*, 12 (1950-1951) pp.437-443; 8 March 1952: ibid., 14 (1952-1953) pp. 5-10; 27 March 1953: ibid., 15 (1953-1954) pp. 27-35; 28 Feb. 1954: ibid., pp. 585-590.

20. Pius XI, Encyclical Letter *Casti Connubii*: *AAS* 22 (1930) p. 554; Pius XII, *Nuntius Radiophonicus*, 1 June 1941: *AAS* 33 (1941) p. 203; *idem., Delegatis ad Conventum Unionis Internationalis sodalitatum ad iura familiae tuenda*, 20 Sept. 1949: *AAS* 41 (1949) p. 552; *idem., AD patresfamilias e Gallia Roman peregrinantes*, 18 Sept. 1951, p. 731: *AAS* 45 (1953) p. 41; *idem., Nuntius Radiophonicus in Natali Domini*, 1952: *AAS* 45 (1953) p. 41; John XXIII, Encyclical Letter *Mater et Magistra*, 15 May 1961: *AAS* 53 (1961) pp.429, 439.

21. Cf. Pius XII, Encyclical Letter *Evangelii Praecones*, 2 June 1951: *AAS* 43 (1951) p. 514.

22. Cf. Pius XII, *Delegatis ad Conventum Unionis Internationalis sodalitatum ad iura familiae tuenda*, 20 Sept. 1949: *AAS* 41 (1949) p. 552.

23. Cf. Pius X, *Alloc. ad catholicam Associationem Iuventutis Gallicae de pietate, scientia, et actione*, 25 Sept. 1904: *AAS* 37 (1904-1905) pp. 296-300.

24. Cf. Pius XII, *Ad Conventum J.O.C. Montreal*, 24 May 1947; *AAS* 39 (1974) p. 257; *Nuntius Radiophonicus ad J.O.C. Bruxelles*, 3 Sept. 1950: *AAS* 42 (1950) pp. 640-641.

25. Cf. Pius XI, Encyclical Letter *Quadragesimo Anno*, 15 May 1931: *AAS* 23 (1931) pp. 225-226.

26. Cf. John XIII, Encyclical Letter *Mater et Magistra*, 15 May 1961: *AAS* 53 (1961) pp. 448-450.

27. Cf. Pius XII, *Alloc. ad I Conventum ex Omnibus Gentibus Laicorum Apostolatui provehendo*, 15 Oct. 1951: *AAS* 43 (1951) p. 788.

28. Cf. Pius XII, *Alloc. ad I Conventum ex Omnibus Gentibus Laicorum Apostolatui provehendo*, 15 Oct. 1951: *AAS* 43 (1951) pp. 787-788.

29. Cf. Pius XII, Encyclical Letter *Le pélegrinage de Lourdes*, 2

July 1957: *AAS* 49 (1957) p. 615.

30. Cf. Pius XII, *Alloc. ad Consilium Foederationis internationalis virorum catholicorum*, 8 Dec. 1956: *AAS* 49 (1957) pp. 26-27.

31. Cf. below, chap. V, no. 24.

32. Cf. Decree of the Sacred Congregation of the Council, *Corrienten.*, 13 Nov. 1920: *AAS* 13 (1921) p. 139.

33. Cf. John XXIII, Encyclical Letter *Princeps Pastorum*, 10 Dec. 1959. *AAS* 51 (1959) p. 836.

34. Pius XI, Letter *Quae nobis*, to Cardinal Bertram, 13 Nov. 1928: *AAS* 20 (1928) p. 385. Cf. also Pius XII, *Alloc. ad A.C. Italicam*, 4 Sept. 1940: *AAS* 32 (1940) p. 362.

35. Cf. Pius XI Encyclical Letter *Quamvis Nostra*, 30 April 1936: *AAS* 28 (1936) pp. 160-161.

36. Cf. Sacred Congregation of the Council, Resolution *Corrienten.*, 13 Nov. 1920: *AAS* 13 (1921) pp. 137-140.

37. Cf. Pius XII, *Ad II Conventum ex Omnibus Gentibus Laicorum Apostolatui provehendo*, 5 Oct. 1957: *AAS* 49 (1957) p. 927.

38. Cf. Dogmatic Constition *De Ecclesia*, chap. IV, no. 37: *AAS* 57 (1965) pp. 42-43.

39. Cf. Pius XII Apostolic Exhortation *Menti Nostrae*, 23 Sept. 1950: *AAS* 42 (1950) p. 660.

40. Cf. Decree *De Accomodata renovatione vitae religiosae*, no. 8.

41. Cf. Benedict XIV, *De Synodo Dioecesana*, book III, chap. IX, no.VII.

42. Cf. Pius XI, Encyclical Letter *Quamvis Nostra*, 30 April 1936; *AAS* 28 (1936) pp. 160-161.

43. Cf. John XXIII, Encyclical Letter *Mater et Magistra*, 15 May 1961: *AAS* 53 (1961) pp. 456-457; cf. Decree *De Oecumenismo*, chap. II, no. 12: *AAS* 57 (1965) pp. 99-100.

44. Cf. Decree *De Oecumenismo*, chap. II, no. 12: *AAS* 57 (1965) p. 100; cf. also Dogmatic Constitution *De Ecclesia*, chap. II, no. 15: *AAS* 57 (1965) pp. 19-20.

45. Cf. Dogmatic Constitution *De Ecclesia*, chaps. II, IV, V: *AAS* 57 (1965) pp. 12-21, 37-49; cf. also Decree *De Oecumenismo*, nos. 4, 6, 7,12: *AAS* 57 (1965) pp. 94, 96, 97, 99, 100; cf. also above, no. 4.

46. Cf. Pius XII, *Ad I Conferentiam internationalem 'boy-scouts,'* 6 June 1952: *AAS* 44 (1952) pp. 579-580; John XXIII, Encyclical Letter *Mater et Magistra*, 15 May 1961: *AAS* 53 (1961) p. 456.

47. Cf. Dogmatic Constitution *De Ecclesia*, chap. IV, no. 33: *AAS* 57 (1965) p. 39.

48. Cf. John XXIII, Encyclical Letter *Mater et Magistra*, 15 May 1961: *AAS* 53 (1961) p. 455.

49. Cf. Pius XII, Encyclical Letter *Sertum laetitiae*, 1 Nov. 1939: *AAS* 31 (1939) pp. 635- 644; cf. *idem., Ad 'Laureati' Act. Cath. It.*, 24 May 1953.

50. Cf. Pius XII, *Ad congressum Universalem Foederationis Juventutis Femininae Catholicae*, 18 April 1952: *AAS* 44 (1952) pp. 414-419; cf. *idem., Ad Associationem Christianam Operariorum Italiae* (A.C.L.I.), 1 May 1955: *AAS* 47 (1955) pp. 403-404.

51. Cf. Pius XII, *Ad Delegatos Conventus Sodalitatum Caritas*, 27 April 1952 *AAS*, pp. 470-471.

52. Cf. John XXIII, Encyclical Letter *Mater et Magistra*, 15 May 1961: *AAS* 53 (1961) p.454.

Appendix D

The Apostolate's Focus
on the Marian and
Family-centered Spirituality
of Pope John Paul II

Totus Tuus
Totally Yours

Families for Christ and His Gospel

Keynote speech by Roman Curia
Cardinal Francis Arinze at the
Commemoration of the 15th Anniversary of the
Apostolate for Family Consecration and the official
opening of the Apostolate's 800-acre John Paul II Holy
Family Center in Bloomingdale, Ohio,
Diocese of Steubenville

August 5, 1990
The Feast of the Dedication of St. Mary Major

INTRODUCTION

The commemoration of the 15th anniversary of the Apostolate for Family Consecration is an occasion for gratitude to Almighty God for all He has accomplished through this dynamic association. It is a time to congratulate Mr. and Mrs. Jerome Coniker and all their co-workers for the huge amount of work done. It is also a suitable period to reflect on what this apostolate stands for, to plan ahead, and to make resolutions. The Apostolate for Family Consecration regards as particularly important its Marian Era of Evangelization Campaign. I therefore wish to propose reflections to you on three aspects of this campaign, namely, True Devotion to the Most Blessed Virgin Mary, The Apostolate's Family Catechism, and The John Paul II Holy Family Center.

I. TRUE DEVOTION
TO THE MOST BLESSED VIRGIN MARY

The Apostolate for Family Consecration is particularly devoted to Pope John Paul II and wishes always to follow his teachings and directives. We should therefore begin our reflection with a thought on the Holy Father's Marian spirituality and on his teaching on the role of Mary in our preparation for the year 2000.

1. The Pope's Marian Spirituality

Pope John Paul II is deeply devoted to Mary Immaculate, Mother of God and Mother of the Church. His coat of arms displays a large "M" under the Cross. His motto from his ordination as Bishop is "Totus Tuus:" All Yours. The Holy Father is proclaiming that he has put himself under Mary's protection, that he belongs entirely to her.

Pope John Paul II has given homilies and made addresses on the Blessed Virgin Mary on an impressive number of occasions. His March 25, 1987, encyclical letter on *Mother of the Redeemer* (*Redemptoris Mater* in Latin) beautifully sums up his teaching on the Holy Mother of God. The Pope, moreover, promoted devotion to Mary in a magnificent way through the 1987-1988 Marian year. His visits or apostolic pilgrimages to dioceses of Italy, and to more than eight dozen countries in all the continents, are generally never completed without a pilgrimage to a Marian shrine. Many of his homilies end with a commendation to the Mother of God. His "Angelus" and "Regina Coeli" weekly addresses are familiar.

This year, 1990, a writer in Madrid, Alberto Garcia Ruiz, has produced a book, *Oraciones de Juan Pablo II a la Virgen*, on prayers pronounced publicly by Pope John Paul II to Mary. The prayers, excluding short invocations, number 150. They are heavily charged with Scripture and theology. In them we see the Pope carrying with him the weight of his ministry as visible head of the universal Church, prophet, teacher, and interpreter of the needs of the men and women of our time. Problems such as the following surface in these prayers: peace, justice, hunger, violence, oppression, freedom, and solidarity. The Pope entrusts all to Mary. Indeed, no Pope has made as many public prayers to Our Lady

Apostolate's 15th Anniversary speakers at the Franciscan University from left to right: Fr. Peter Lappin, prominent Salesian author who recently completed a book on The Apostolate entitled "Challenge and the Change"; Bishop Albert Ottenweller of the Diocese of Steubenville welcoming The Apostolate into his diocese and speaking on the origins of the Vianney Center which is now the Apostolate's John Paul II Holy Family Center; Francis Cardinal Arinze, prominent member of the Roman Curia and keynote speaker; Gwen Coniker, co-founder of the Apostolate and mother of 13 (one with the Lord), speaking from a mother's point of view; Fr. Michael Scanlan, President of the Franciscan University of Steubenville, speaking about the University's association with the Apostolate for Family Consecration (he is one of the Apostolate's primary spiritual advisors) and Jerome Coniker, founder of the Family Apostolate.

as Pope John Paul II. Devotion to Mary is one of the dominant notes in his life and ministry (cf. "Quando il 'Totus Tuus' del Papa diventa invocazione filiale," in *L'Osservatore Romano*, 8 June 1990, p.5).

Pope John Paul II urges all the faithful to pay special attention to the special presence of the Mother of God in the mystery of Christ and His Church. He recalls the insistence of the Second Vatican Council on true devotion to the Most Blessed Virgin Mary, or true Marian spirituality (cf. *Lumen Gentium* 66-67). He extols the teaching and example of St. Louis Marie Grignion de Montfort on true devotion to Mary. "St. Grignion de Montfort," says the Pope, "proposes consecration to Christ through the hands of Mary as an effective means for Christians to live faithfully their baptismal commitments" (*Redemptoris Mater*, 48). The Pope is happy to note that this spirituality and this devotion flourish in our time.

2. The Role of Mary in our Preparation for the Year 2000

The Holy Father in these past years has often drawn our attention to the approach of the end of this millennium and to the necessity of our preparation for it under the leadership of Mary. The year 2000, now drawing near, being the Bimillennial Jubilee of the birth of Jesus Christ, at the same time directs our gaze towards the Mother of Christ. The Pope calls Mary the "Morning Star" in the "night" of the Advent expectation. The Morning Star precedes the Rising Sun (Christ) Who has come from on high to visit us (cf. Lk 1:78).

For these reasons the Pope urges intensified Marian spirituality in this last decade of the second millennium. He says: "We Christians who know that the providential plan of the Most Holy Trinity is the central reality of Revelation and of faith feel the need to emphasize the unique presence of the Mother of Christ in history, especially during these last years leading up to the year 2000" (*Redemptoris Mater*, 3). Mary is very much a part of God's providential plan for our redemption through Jesus Christ, the Son of God made man for us. The necessity of more fervent recourse to Mary becomes even more evident when we consider the effects of one person's sin or holiness on society.

3. Effects of Sin

Sin is a violation of the universal order set up by God. Sin does harm to the sinner. But it also does harm to every other man and woman because of human solidarity. Many times in the Old Testament we see how the sin of one person brought suffering to many others. Examples are Abimelech's ambition to be king which brought disaster to the people of Shechem (cf. Jg 9); the sins of Heli's children and their father's neglect which caused the defeat of the Israelites in battle and the capture of the Ark of God (cf. Sm 2,3,4); David's sin with Bathsheba which brought on a chain of woes (cf. II Sm 11 and following chapters); David's vanity in conducting a census which had as chastisement a pestilence that killed 70,000 people (cf. II Sm 24:25); and Solomon's sins against chastity and worship of the true God which had as punishment the secession of the greater part of his father's kingdom (cf. I King 11:11). These examples show the biblical understanding of sin—the effects of sin being carried on, and defeats and other calamities being consequences of sin.

Francis Cardinal Arinze in the Apostolate's St. John Vianney Chapel giving a homily on personal prayer.

The prophet Ezekiel, however, underlines individual responsibility. Pope Paul VI in his 1967 *Apostolic Constitution on the Revision of Indulgences*, n. 4, says that "By the hidden and kindly mystery of God's will a supernatural solidarity reigns among men. A consequence of this is that the sin of one person harms other people just as one person's holiness helps others."

Pope John Paul II returns to the same theme in his Apostolic Exhortation following the 1983 Synod on Reconciliation and Penance. He spells it out in great detail: "To speak of social sin means in the first place to recognize that, by virtue of a human solidarity which is as mysterious and intangible as it is real and concrete, each individual's sin in some way affects others. This is the other aspect of that solidarity which on the religious level is developed in the profound and magnificent mystery of the Communion of Saints, thanks to which it has been possible to say that 'every soul that rises above itself, raises up the world'. To this law of ascent there unfortunately corresponds the law of descent. Consequently one can speak of a communion of sin, whereby a soul that lowers itself through sin drags down with itself the Church and, in some way, the whole world" (*Reconciliatio et Paenitentiae*, 16).

The same Holy Father also spoke of the effects of sin in earlier encyclical letters. In his letter on Divine Mercy, *Dives in Misericordia*, 11, he lists various sources of uneasiness in today's world such as the prospect of war because of atomic stock piles, the consequences of abuse of power by individuals or societies, the fear that inner freedom may be crushed and access to the truth impeded, the inequalities existing between individuals in society and between nations— in short, a world in which there is so much evil, both physical and moral. In his encyclical letter on human suffering, *Salvifici Doloris*, 8, the Pope mentions the consequences of the last two world wars and the threat of a nuclear war with its potential of self-destruction for humanity. Since one person's sin drags along with it negative results which affect us, we need to do penance, and we need to cry to Heaven for help.

4. One Person's Holiness Affects Others

Just as one person's sin affects other people, so also one person's holiness can offset or at least lessen the effects of another's sin and bring blessings to many. The heroic faith and obedience of Abraham were rewarded by God in generations that followed that great patriarch (cf. Gn 22: 15-18). Joseph's chastity and charity in Egypt were used by God to prepare a place for Jacob and all his children during the years of famine (cf. Gn 39:7-20; 41:37-40).

The righteousness of Moses and his prayers held off God's anger from the sinful people of Israel.

Pope Paul VI, in the *Apostolic Constitution on the Revision of Indulgences* already referred to, stressed this truth of spiritual solidarity: "Following in Christ's steps, those who believe in Him have always tried to help one another along the path which leads to the heavenly Father, through prayer, the exchange of spiritual goods and penitential expiation. The more they have been immersed in the fervor of love, the more they have imitated Christ in His sufferings. They have carried their crosses to make expiation for their own sins and the sins of others. They were convinced that they could help their brothers to obtain salvation from God, Who is the Father of

Mercies. This is the very ancient dogma called the Communion of Saints" (*Indulgentiarum Doctrina*, 5).

Within this Communion of Saints, Mary has a very special place. The Message of Fatima can serve as a reminder. Our Blessed Mother asks for devotion and consecration to her Immaculate Heart, for the rosary and penance, and for the Communion of reparation on the First Saturdays.

5. We Need Mary's Help

Our own penance, reparation, and prayers are, however, not enough. There is still much evil in the world, such as abortion, assassinations, injustices, wars, torture, deprivation of religious and civil freedom, religious indifference, etc. We need the help of Mary, Mother of Mercy. If we go to her and consecrate ourselves to her, with all our little efforts, initiatives and merits, she will know how to go to her Son and get our six pots of Cana water turned into six pots of excellent wine. **She will know how to associate our little merits with her own incalculable merits and set in motion positive spiritual forces of reparation due for the many sins committed against God's goodness.**

You can therefore see that the Apostolate for Family Consecration is on the right track when it stresses the practice of true devotion to the Blessed Virgin Mary, and especially the total consecration of ourselves and the offering of our merits to her. I recommend a prayerful study of the treatise of St. Louis Marie Grignion de Montfort on *True Devotion to the Blessed Virgin Mary*, and the encyclical letter of Pope John Paul II, *Redemptoris Mater*.

II. THE APOSTOLATE'S FAMILY CATECHISM

A second aspect of the "Marian Era of Evangelization Campaign" of the Apostolate for Family Consecration on which I would like now to direct our thoughts is *The Apostolate's Family Catechism*. The 1980 World Synod had "expressed the hope that a suitable catechism for families would be prepared, one that would be clear, brief and easily assimilated by all" (*Familiaris Consortio*, 39). The Apostolate for Family Consecration has led the way in producing one.

1. Characteristics of the Catechism

The *Apostolate's Family Catechism* is designed to help parents to teach all their children the Faith. The unabridged edition is divided into seven volumes, with 21 chapters in each volume. Each daily lesson has two or three short questions and answers. Parents are supplied further information with references to about seven more detailed adult catechisms. When the universal catechism for the whole Church is published, each question will be duly cross-referenced. [Editor's note:— This has been done.]

Other attractions of the *Family Catechism* are the following. Each day's lesson is enriched with references to Scripture and to the teachings of Vatican II. I understand that the Apostolate plans to add references to papal documents, and keep these up to date. A daily prayer summarizes the lesson for each day. Moreover, each weekly lesson is backed up with two half-hour video programs which feature Sister John Vianney answering children's questions. [*Since Cardinal Arinze's speech, The Family Apostolate has produced a complete audio and video series with Cardinal Arinze (each series contains 22 one-hour tapes) on the Apostolate's Family Catechism. See pages 843-846 for more details.*] These are questions such as parents would be reviewing with their children throughout the week. The videos are to be viewed each week in a neighborhood setting (see page 846 and 866) by both parents and children (also see page 849). They should not conflict with anything the children learn in school but should rather supplement it. And if any error has crept into what the children are learning in school, this would be a suitable time for such discrepancy to surface, so that the parents can discover it and correct it. After all, the parents are "the first and principal educators of their children" (*Familiaris Consortio*, 40).

2. Highly Commended

The *Apostolate's Family Catechism* has received many high recommendations. Silvio Cardinal Oddi, the former Prefect of the Congregation for the Clergy which oversees the Church's catechetical work, wrote Mr. Coniker on November 13, 1984: "We are happy to notice that the *Apostolate's Family Catechism* gives the parents a complete tool to fulfill their obligations as being the primary teachers of the Faith to their children, and at the same time, gives the parents a good refresher course in their Faith." Luigi Cardinal Ciappi, O.P., at that time Official Theologian of the Supreme Pontiff, wrote Mr. Coniker on September 12, 1984, in praise of the *Family Catechism*: "This is an excellent response to Pope John Paul II's Apostolic Exhortations *Catechesi Tradendae* and *Familiaris Consortio*, along with the revised Code of Canon Law, and the Holy See's *Charter of the Rights of the Family*, issued on October 22, 1983."

On November 15, 1984, the Pro-President of the Pontifical Council for the Family, Archbishop Edouard Gagnon, P.S.S., now Cardinal, wrote in praise of the Catechism: "I particularly encourage the use of the *Apostolate's Family Catechism* by parents as a helpful means for fulfilling their solemn duty to impart adequate knowledge of the Faith to their children and to prepare them properly for receiving the sacraments."

Mother Teresa of Calcutta wrote: "The *Apostolate's Family Catechism* will now enable parents to fulfill their primary obligation in teaching their children. I pray that every parent will join the Apostolate for Family Consecration and use the Apostolate's catechetical program in their neighborhood."

3. In Line with Church Documents

The Apostolate's Family Catechism has the merit of being in line with Church documents and directives. Let me mention a few recent documents.

"The family's catechetical activity has a special character, which is in a sense irreplaceable... The parents themselves profit from the effort that this demands of them, for in a catechetical dialogue of this sort each individual both receives and gives... Thus there cannot be too great an effort on the part of Christian parents to prepare for this ministry of being their own children's catechists and to carry it out with tireless zeal... Encouragement must also be given to the individuals or institutions that, through person-to-person contacts, through meetings, and through all kinds of pedagogical means, help parents to perform their task: The service they are doing to catechesis is beyond price" (*Catechesi Tradendae*, 68).

Cardinal Arinze and Dr. Burns Seeley, Staff Theologian, preparing for another television production

"The Christian family, in fact, is the first community called to announce the Gospel to the human person during growth and to bring him or her, through a progressive education and catechesis, to full human and Christian maturity" (*Familiaris Consortio*, 2).

"As the Second Vatican Council recalled, 'Since parents have conferred life on their children, they have a most solemn obligation to educate their offspring. Their role as educators is so decisive that scarcely anything can compensate for their failure in it" (FC, 36).

"To the extent in which the Christian family accepts the Gospel and matures in faith, it becomes an evangelizing community. Let us listen again to Paul VI: 'The parents not only communicate the Gospel to their children, but from their children they can themselves receive the same Gospel as deeply lived by them. And such a family becomes the evangelizer of many other families and of the neighborhood of which it forms a part" (FC, 52).

"Every family has the right to live freely its own domestic religious life under the guidance of the parents, as well as right to profess publicly and to propagate the faith" (Holy See, October 22, 1983, *Charter of the Rights of the Family*, Article 7).

"Catholic parents have also the duty and the right to choose means and institutes which, in their local circumstances, can best promote the Catholic education of their children" (Canon 793, the revised Code of Canon Law).

When parents have followed all these directives in the religious education of their children, they can then with quiet conscience read the prophet Ezekiel: "If someone hears the sound of the horn, but pays no attention, the sword will overtake him and destroy him: he will have been responsible for his own death. He has heard the sound of the horn and paid no attention: his death will be his own responsibility. But the life of someone who pays attention to the warning will be secure" (Ezek. 33:4-5).

III. THE JOHN PAUL II HOLY FAMILY CENTER

As our gathering this evening is the first official function focusing in on the John Paul II Holy Family Center of the Apostolate for Family Consecration, I wish to take this opportunity to congratulate The Apostolate and the Diocese of

Steubenville for making this complex possible. I understand that this center will be used to communicate Pope John Paul's Marian and family-centered spirituality through the use of thousands of videotapes. It will also serve for conducting retreats and evangelization programs for families and for clerics. The St. Kolbe television studio is under continual expansion and The Apostolate desires to equip it with the best that modern television technology can offer so that the Gospel can be brought to an ever-wider public, especially in the dynamic way in which the Holy Father presents it.

The purposes of this center are very praiseworthy. I want to highlight in particular the plan of the Apostolate for Family Consecration to bring entire families together to this center for a full week for Holy Family Fests. The aim would be to send them home with a determined and clear vision for evangelizing their neighborhood, in order to create God-centered communities of both adults and children.

CONCLUSION

These programs of the Apostolate for Family Consecration in its Marian Era of Evangelization deserve praise, support, encouragement, and meaningful participation, according to each person's possibilities. Mother Teresa of Calcutta writing the Founders of the Apostolate, Jerome and Gwen Coniker, on May 20, 1989, said: "Your videotaped presentations are excellent; they hold the interest of the entire family." The highest encouragement and commendation for the Marian Era of Evangelization Campaign came in the November 18, 1989, letter of the Secretariat of State of the Holy Father:

> "His Holiness hopes that as a result of the Committee's activities many Catholics will be led to a deeper appreciation of their Faith and to a renewed commitment to Christ and his Church. The wise use of the communications media in the service of teaching and pastoral guidance creates new possibilities for evangelization. By focusing on family life in the home, neighborhood and parish, the Committee's efforts strengthen the very foundations of Christian living for the benefit of the Church and all of society.
>
> As the Apostolate for Family Consecration works for a spiritual and moral transformation of society, the Holy Father commends all of you to God's loving care. In particular, he joins you in asking the intercession of the Blessed Virgin Mary so that all you do may be inspired by her

shining example of faith and trust. With confidence in her powerful protection, he willingly imparts the requested Apostolic Blessing."

After this papal commendation, it only remains for me to say "Amen," and to wish all you God's abundant blessing.

Francis Cardinal Arinze

Francis Cardinal Arinze, speaking at The Apostolate's Holy Family Fest. Cardinal Arinze usually comes every year to The Family Apostolate's week-long Holy Family Fest for extensive work in TV and video production and videotaped talks to the Fest participants.

Pope John Paul II on the Meaning of Consecration

On the Cross, Christ said, "Woman, behold your son!" With these words, He opened His Mother's heart in a new way. A little later, the Roman soldier's spear pierced the side of the Crucified One. That pierced Heart became a sign of the redemption, achieved through the death of the Lamb of God.

The Immaculate Heart of Mary, opened with the words, "Woman, behold your son!" is spiritually united with the Heart of her Son opened by the soldier's spear. Mary's heart was opened by the same love for man and for the world with which Christ loved man and the world, offering Himself for them on the Cross, until the soldier's spear struck that blow.

Consecrating the world to the Immaculate Heart of Mary means drawing near, through the Mother's intercession, to the very Fountain of life that sprang from Golgotha. This Fountain unceasingly pours forth redemption and grace. In it, reparation is continually made for the sins of the world. It is a ceaseless source of new life and holiness.

Consecrating the world to the Immaculate Heart of the Mother means returning beneath the Cross of the Son. It means consecrating this world to the pierced Heart of the Savior, bringing it back to the very source of its redemption. Redemption is always greater than man's sin and the "sin of the world." The power of the redemption is infinitely superior to the whole range of evil in man and the world.

The heart of the Mother is aware of this, more than any other heart in the whole universe, visible and invisible.

And so she calls us.

She not only calls us to be converted, she calls us to accept her motherly help to return to the source of redemption.

Pope John Paul delivered this homily at the shrine of Our Lady of Fatima on May 13, 1982, the 65th anniversary of the first apparitions at Fatima. His Holiness went to Fatima to consecrate the world to the Immaculate Heart of Mary, and to thank Our Lady for her intercessory help in the saving of his life exactly one year earlier, when an attempt was made on the his life in St. Peter's Square, Vatican City.

The Family Apostolate's Papally Blessed

MARIAN ERA
OF EVANGELIZATION CAMPAIGN
IN PREPARATION
FOR THE YEAR 2000

1. The family focus of the parish church as the Eucharistic Center:

   a) The "Be Not Afraid" Weekly Holy Hours (54 on videotape);

   b) The First Saturday "Light of the World Cenacle" programs for churches (40 on videotape).

2. The Vatican-approved *Apostolate's Family Catechism* by Fr. Lawrence Lovasik:

   a) 304 questions-and-answers and commentaries by Francis Cardinal Arinze of the Roman Curia (44 half-hour programs on videotape);

   b) 304 questions-and-answers and commentaries by Sister John Vianney, S.S.N.D., a gifted children's catechist (56 half-hour programs on videotape);

   c) The new 7-volume full color *Apostolate Family Catechism*, also a one-volume abridged edition.

3. The Family Apostolate's International Television and Radio Ministry (over 300 teachers, on over 6000 shows):

   a) Daily "Family Covenant" series;

   b) Weekly "Be Not Afraid Holy Hours";

   c) Weekly "Healing Our Families" series, with Fr. Michael Scanlan, T.O.R.;

   d) Monthly "First Saturday Light of the World Cenacle" series, featuring Pope John Paul II, Mother Teresa of Calcutta, one other speaker each month.

4. The Family Apostolate's Eastern European Television and Videotape Programs (A major effort is now under way to find translators to prepare our programs in various languages for television and videocassette).

5. The Family Apstolate's Neighborhood "Peace of Heart Forums" (using videotapes for weekly prayer meetings and gatherings — and for the general public).

6. Four annual "Holy Family Fests," at the Family Apostolate's 850-acre John Paul II Holy Family Center: here families experience authentic, joyful Catholic community for an entire week. They learn the Pope's formula for victory by the Year 2000.

7. The Apostolate's Family Life Retreat and Parish Evangelization and Catechetical Training Programs, held at the John Paul II Holy Family Center throughout the year for groups of 20 or more.

8. The Apostolate's Neighborhood Chapter Ministry of developing a prayer life, learning our Faith — then reaching out to those who are hurting and in need in our own parishes and neighborhoods. Parishes are free to establish their own structure or affiliate with The Family Apostolate's neighborhood chapter structure.

Jerome F. Coniker, President
Apostolate for Family Consecration
Route 2, Box 700
Bloomingdale, OH 43910

Dear Mr. Coniker:

Please allow me to take this opportunity to encourage and endorse the eight integrated programs listed on the reverse side of this letter which describe your papally blessed "Marian Era of Evangelization Campaign" for the year 2000. I am pleased to see that Mother Teresa of Calcutta has been the primary inspiration for the "Be Not Afraid" Eucharistic Holy Hours in churches on video.

Your "Be Not Afraid" Holy Hours and First Saturday video programs for churches enable the Holy Father and other leaders in the Church to communicate the truths to help families live consecrated lives in the modern world.

Cardinal Ciappi's statement that consecration is not just an act or a devotion, but a commitment to a way of life that must be nourished through continuous formation is very realistic. Mother Teresa's idea of presenting the truth on video in the Eucharistic Presence of Our Lord in churches truly will establish the parish as the Eucharistic Center and also the center for truth.

We believe that *The Apostolate's Family Catechism*, with which the Catechism for the Universal Church will be cross-referenced, will truly be a breakthrough for family formation and for parents, who indeed are the primary educators of their children. This integrated program of teaching the catechism in the home and then gathering together once a week with other families to hear Cardinal Arinze and others teach on your "Be Not Afraid" Holy Hours in churches can be very effective in rebuilding both the domestic church and the parish community.

Your entire "Marian Era of Evangelization Campaign" certainly does fulfill the Holy Father's vision for family renewal, catechetics and evangelization which are so vital to the life of the Church.

May God bless you, your family, and the entire work of the Apostolate for Family Consecration.

Yours in the Hearts of Jesus and Mary,

*Cardinal William Baum 6-15-92	Bishop Joseph J. Madera 10-21-92
*Cardinal Francis Arinze 7-24-92	Bishop Gilbert I. Sheldon 12-10-92
*Cardinal Paul Augustin Mayer 6-12-92	Msgr. John G. Woolsey 12-16-92
Archbishop J. Francis Stafford 10-20-92	*Rev. Robert J. Dempsey 12-16-92
*Archbishop Giovanni Cheli 6-11-92	Cardinal Anthony Bevilacqua 2-12-93

* = member of Roman Curia

Office of the Archbishop
Philadelphia, PA

September 25, 1989

Most Rev. Pio Laghi
Apostolic Pro-Nuncio

Washington, DC

RE: Apostolic Blessing for the "Marian Era of Evangelization Committee" (#3213/89/7)

Your Excellency:

Jerry Coniker, President of the Apostolate for Family Consecration, has asked me to write this formal request for an Apostolic Blessing on its "Marian Era of Evangelization Committee." As co-chairman of this Committee, I sincerely believe that this systematic approach to supporting the vision of Pope John Paul II will bear abundant fruit in preparation for the third millennium. Our committee will be promoting the following:

1) Reparation Programs in the Eucharistic Presence of Our Lord in churches throughout the world, with the Sacrament of Penance being made available to participants.

These Reparation Programs focus on family unity and the pro-life movement. They fall into two broad categories:

a) First Saturday "Light of the World Cenacles" including all of the components of the First Saturday formula given by Our Lady of Fatima. These Cenacles are also broadcast over Mother Angelica's EWTN network via satellite throughout North America.

b) Weekly Eucharistic Holy Hours for families in churches, issued in sets of nine, to make up a nine-week long Novena focused on topics such as the Immaculate Conception, Saint Joseph, the Mercy of God, etc. The Apostolate plans to produce a continuing flow of these Novenas. In my opinion, they can truly bring parish life back to the Eucharist and the Sacrament of Penance.

2) "Family Catechism Chapters", which will provide parents with solid catechetical materials to use with their children in homes, using The Apostolate's video programs to complement the teachings on the Faith that the children receive if they attend parochial schools. This will enable the parents to also participate in a dynamic refresher course as they teach their children the Faith with materials that will prevent misunderstandings.

3) Neighborhood chapters of the Apostolate for Family Consecration, which focus on the reinforcement of family life through the systematic transformation of neighborhoods into God-centered communities in the spirit of Pope John Paul II. Again, The Apostolate is drawing from its vast resource of over 4,000 one-half hour video programs that enable laymen and women to to fulfill their obligation to evangelize without falling into teaching errors, since all of the programs, including the printed materials, are reviewed and edited, where necessary, to reflect the Church's authentic magisterium presided over by the Holy Father.

4) International television apostolate. The Apostolate presently produces three weekly television series aired on Mother Angelica's EWTN network collectively ten times a week. Its programs are also aired on other networks throughout the United States and Canada and eventually will air in the Philippines.

I serve as one of the Apostolate for Family Consecration's Primary Theological and Spiritual Advisors. Others include Father Michael Scanlan, T.O.R, President of the Franciscan University of Steubenville, and Francis Cardinal Arinze. As someone associated with The Apostolate in this capacity, I want to stress that the "Marian Era of Evangelization Committee' is not just a "paper committee". It has the resources to effectively communicate Pope John Paul's message in a contemporary format to many of our people who hunger for this type of spiritual nourishment.

We would greatly appreciate an Apostolic Blessing for the goals and activities of this Committee.

I thank you for your continued support for the work of the Apostolate for Family Consecration.

Sincerely yours in Christ,

Anthony J. Bevilacqua
Archbishop of Philadelphia/
Co-chairman, the "Marian Era
of Evangelization Campaign" Committee

cc: Mr. Jerome F. Coniker

Please note: This Apostolic Blessing was given personally by Pope John Paul II to Jerry Coniker on Nov. 15, 1989, and confirmed in writing by the Vatican Secretariat of State on Nov. 18, 1989 (see page 834).

This Apostolate Family Catechism *and other Vatican-approved multi-media catechetical tools are an integral part of the Marian Era Evangelization Campaign.*

Letter from Pope John Paul II through his Secretary of State's Office

SECRETARIAT OF STATE

FIRST SECTION   ·   GENERAL AFFAIRS   FROM THE VATICAN, November 18, 1989

No. 250.418

Dear Mr. Coniker,

The Holy Father was pleased to learn about the "Marian Era of Evangelization Committee" of the Apostolate for Family Consecration, and he wishes me to convey his cordial greetings and good wishes to you and to all those associated in this worthy initiative.

His Holiness hopes that as a result of the Committee's activities many Catholics will be led to a deeper appreciation of their faith and to a renewed commitment to Christ and his Church. The wise use of the communications media in the service of teaching and pastoral guidance creates new possibilities for evangelization. By focusing on family life in the home, neighborhood and parish, the Committee's efforts strengthen the very foundations of Christian living for the benefit of the Church and all of society.

As the Apostolate for Family Consecration works for a spiritual and moral transformation of society, the Holy Father commends all of you to God's loving care. In particular, he joins you in asking the intercession of the Blessed Virgin Mary so that all you do may be inspired by her shining example of faith and trust. With confidence in her powerful protection, he willingly imparts the requested Apostolic Blessing.

With every good wish, I am

Sincerely yours,

+ E. Cassidy
Under Secretary of State

834

Appendix E

Multi-media Resources
For a New Evangelization

JESUS, I TRUST IN YOU

L'OSSERVATORE ROMANO

New media can serve the "new evangelization"

The Holy Father's Message for the 27th World Communications Day

Producers and consumers of media have important moral responsibilities in their regard, the Holy Father reminds us in his annual Message for World Communications Day, which will be celebrated on 23 May, but the Message was published on the Feast of St. Francis de Sales, patron of the Catholic press. The following is the English original of the message based on this year's theme, "Video Cassettes and Audiocassettes in the Formation of Culture and Conscience."

Dear Brothers and Sisters, more than a year after the publication of the Pastoral Instruction *Aetatis novae* on the communications media, I once again invite all of you to reflect on the vision of the modern world which the Instruction presented and on the practical implications of the situations it described. The Church cannot ignore the many unprecedented changes brought about by progress in this important and ubiquitous aspect of modern living. Each of us should ask for the wisdom necessary to appreciate the opportunities which developments in modern communications technology offer for serving God and his people, while at the same time recognizing the challenges such progress inevitably poses.

As the Pastoral Instruction *Aetatis novae* reminds us, "a vast expansion of human communications is profoundly influencing culture everywhere" (n. 1). Indeed we may speak of a "new culture" created by modern communications, which affects everyone, particularly the younger generation, and is itself largely the result of technological advances which have created "new ways of communicating, with new languages, new techniques and a new psychology" (cf. *Redemptoris missio*, n. 37). Today, as the Church strives to carry out her perennial mission of proclaiming the Word of God, she faces the immense challenge of evangelizing this new culture and expressing the unchanging truth of the Gospel in its language. Because all believers are affected by these developments, each of us is called to adapt to changing situations and to discover effective and responsible ways to use the communications media for God's glory and for the service of his creation.

In my message for World Communications Day last year, I mentioned

that among the realities we celebrate on this annual occasion are the God-given gifts of speech, of hearing and of sight which make communication possible between us. This year the theme of the Day focuses on two specific "new" media which serve these very senses in a remarkable way, namely, *audiocassettes and videocassettes.*

The audiocassette and the videocassette have made it possible for us to have at hand and easily transport unlimited numbers of programmes in voice and vision, whether for instruction or entertainment, for a more complete understanding of news and information or for the appreciation of beauty and artistry. These new resources should be recognized as instruments which God, by means of human intelligence and ingenuity, has put at our disposal. Like all of God's gifts, they are meant to be used for a good purpose and to assist individuals and communities to grow in knowledge and appreciation of the truth, as well as in sensitivity to the dignity and needs of others. Audiocassettes and videocassettes therefore have a powerful potential for helping individuals to develop culturally, socially, and in the religious sphere. They can be of great service in transmitting the faith, even though they can never replace the personal witness which is essential to the proclamation of the full truth and value of the Christian message.

It is my hope that those engaged professionally in the production of audio or video programmes in cassette or other forms, will reflect on the need for the Christian message to find expression, explicitly or implicitly, in the new culture created by modern communications (cf. *Aetatis novae*, n. 11). This should not only be expected to happen as a natural consequence of "the Church's active, sympathetic presence within the world of communications" (ibid.), but also as the result of a precise commitment on the part of communicators.

The professionals who rate at their true value the impact and influence of the media productions they create will take particular care to make them of such high moral quality that their effect upon the formation of culture will invariably be a positive one. They will resist the ever-present lure of easy profit and will firmly refuse to take part in any production which exploits human weakness, offends consciences, or affronts human dignity.

It is likewise important that those who make use of media such as the audiocassette or videocassette should not see themselves as mere consumers. Each individual, simply by making his or her reactions to media offerings known to those who produce and market them, can have a definite effect on the subject matter and moral tone of future offerings. The family in particular, as the basic unit of society, is deeply affected by the media environment in which it lives. Parents therefore have a grave duty to educate the family in a critical use of the means of social communication. The importance of this task needs to be explained especially to young married couples. Nor should catechetical programmes overlook the need to teach children and adolescents a proper and responsible use of the media.

On this World Communications Day, I extend my cordial best wishes to all the professional men and women striving to serve the human family through the communications media, to all the members of the international Catholic media organizations active throughout the world, and to the vast body of media consumers who are their audience and towards whom they bear a very weighty responsibility. May Almighty God pour forth his gifts upon you all.

From the Vatican, 24 January 1993, Feast of Saint Francis de Sales, Patron of the Press.

L'Osservatore Romano
N. 5 (1276) — 3 February 1993

The new *Catechism of the Catholic Church* promulgated by Pope John Paul II himself

The first "universal" catechism issued by the Holy See since the Council of Trent, over 400 years ago.

The new *Catechism of the Catholic Church* — divided into a logical, four part structure:

- Profession of Faith — what the Catholic Church believes
- Celebration of the Christian mysteries — the Seven Sacraments
- Life in Christ — morality and the Ten Commandments

The new *Catechism of the Catholic Church* draws abundant riches from the following sources:

Sacred Scripture, Sacred Tradition: especially the Church Fathers (both Eastern and Western), liturgy, the magisterium, the Code of Canon Law, and the lives and

839

At Fatima, Our Blessed Mother told us that we will have peace only if enough of us live our consecrations.

In John 17, Our Lord told us how to be consecrated when He said: "Consecrate them in truth."

The new *Catechism of the Catholic Church* also includes "In brief" sections:

Simple and concise summations are placed at the end of each section of the Catechism of the Catholic Church.

These "in brief" summaries condense the previous paragraphs into a few short sentences; they foster a clear Catholic identity and a common language of the Faith. They bridge the interval between doctrine and catechesis.

The "in brief" summaries also endeavor to facilitate memorization for children and adults.

On December 6, 1992, Pope John Paul II said:

*This new text [of the **Catechism of the Catholic Church**] represents a privileged tool and a pressing invitation to an appropriate Gospel formation in order to begin the new evangelization with firm conviction and apostolic foresight.*

Hence the urgent need for catechesis, called to break the bread of God's word, thus fostering an ever deeper understanding of it in regard to the challenges of our time.

This catechesis is certainly not exhausted in merely transmitting ideas. Its task is "to advance in fullness and to nourish day by day the Christian life of the faithful, young and old," so that the believer may be "impregnated" by the mystery of Christ, and thus learn ever better "to think like him, to judge like him, to act in conformity with his commandments, to hope as he invites us to" (Catechesi Tradendae, n. 20).

The new "catechism," a reference point for the catechesis of the Christian communities spread throughout the world, will provide a sure path in this direction.

Let us pray to the Blessed Virgin to give the whole Church a new impetus in the task of spreading the Good News of salvation. **(*L'Osservatore Romano* - December 9, 1992 issue)**

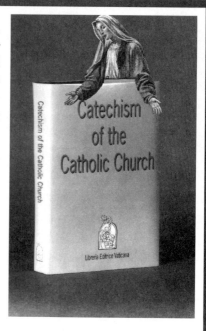

The Apostolate's Family Catechism on Tape™

"The Hour Has Come" (John 17:1) for the truth to set our families free — free to use the new papally-issued catechism; free to implement family catechetics; free to imitate the Holy Father by living the St. Louis de Montfort consecration; and free to start a new evangelization with video and other multimedia tools. These are main focal points that Cardinal Francis Arinze will review at The Family Apostolate's annual Totus Tuus "Consecrate Them in Truth" Conference which will always be focused on the Pope's priorities.

Cardinal Arinze is a leader who understands the spiritual attack on the family, the importance of the parish, the potential of the laity, and the art of evangelization. He is a member of the Roman Curia, the Holy Father's direct staff.

His Eminence is the President of the Pontifical Council for Inter-Religious Dialogue, and is a member of the Executive Committee of the Pontifical Council for the Laity.

When he was ordained to the episcopate (August 29, 1965), he was the youngest bishop in the world.

Cardinal Francis Arinze

He was on the cutting edge of the evangelization movement in Nigeria. After their civil war from 1967-1970, Cardinal Arinze, while he was Archbishop of Onitsha and later President of the Nigeria Council of Bishops, contributed to the mobilization of the native clergy, religious and laity, and doubled the number of Catholics in less than 14 years.

At the time he was called to Rome by the Holy Father in April of 1984, 65.6% of the population of the Onitsha Archdiocese was Catholic, while the national average of Catholics was only 11.2% of a population of 89 million.

This year the Archdiocese of Onitsha has 320 major seminarians, and over 1,100 in two Archdiocesan minor seminaries. Cardinal Arinze is also the founder of a religious community of men............."By their fruits you will know them."

His Eminence is a leading television personality in the United States, Puerto Rico, Canada, the Philippines, and parts of Mexico. He is televised on The Apostolate's "Family Covenant" and "Be Not Afraid Holy Hour" series on Mother Angelica's Eternal Word Television Network. But most important of all, Cardinal Arinze is a man of God, a man on fire for the Church and for the conversion of souls — a person for others!

One of the greatest communicators in the Church today.
Imagine . . . A Roman Curia Cardinal teaching catechism!

844

845

"Mother Teresa's Inspiration"
for

- Stopping Abortion!
- Healing Families!
- Building Parish Community Life!
- Focusing on our Eucharistic Lord, Mary, and the Papacy!

A new evangelization program of 54 weekly

Be Not Afraid Family Hours™

on video tape

Don't the forces that affect family life and stability seem to be almost out of control today?

Didn't Our Lady promise at Fatima an "era of peace" for the world if we consecrate ourselves to Jesus through Her Immaculate Heart? In reality, didn't she promise a transforming miracle even greater than the one she performed in 1531 in Tepeyac, outside of Mexico City, when an entire nation immersed in a death culture was converted?

If she did, then isn't Mary the precise instrument to transform divided and broken families into the image of Her Eucharistic Son? And isn't Jesus the key to bring the mercy of His Father, through Mary, to all mankind, and to perform a miracle of healing for our broken families that are so fragmented today?

Our Blessed Lord in the Holy Eucharist is the Alpha and the Omega, the beginning and the end — the very source of our Faith and the solution for all of our problems.

How can the members of a family (the domestic church) ask for a miracle of healing from God if they don't know Him, or don't even pray to Him?

Doesn't the Sacrament of Penance prepare our families for:
•a more fervent participation in the Holy Sacrifice of the Mass?
•a more worthy reception of Our Lord in Holy Communion?
•a more loving adoration of Our Lord?
•going forth to serve Our Lord in our own family members and neighbors?

850

And finally... how can our families be well disposed for the Sacrament of Penance if they do not know the Faith? We must know God before we can love Him; we must love Him before we can serve Him in others.

The Be Not Afraid Family Hours™
when shown to families every week will:

- prepare them to receive the Sacrament of Penance.

- enable them to live their baptismal consecrations with confidence and willl prepare them to receive the healing Eucharistic graces that mend broken hearts and relationships, thus preparing the way for that era of peace which was promised at Fatima.

- systematically teach the Faith like never before, and draw from the new papally-promulgated *Catechism of the Catholic Church.*

- reach our youth— those most effected by our "media culture— because the Eucharistic Family Hours are on videotape and they bring some of the best personalities in the Church right into parish churches and homes every week.

- be a new evangelization program to present to families and their neighbors — including fallen-away Catholics and non-Catholics.

- lift up our priests, many of whom have been very discouraged by the many cold or lukewarm people whom they seek to serve.

Missionaries of Charity
Calcutta, India

Dear Jerome and Gwen,

I want to encourage you in your efforts to bring families to church every week for a Holy Hour.

Your "Be Not Afraid Novena" weekly Eucharistic family Holy Hours will bring down many graces for the Church and expecially for our families.

Prayer is essential if we wish the scourge of abortion to be lifted, and families to be renewed. Eucharistic devotion is the most powerful form of prayer we can participate in, outside of the Holy Sacrifice of the Mass.

Drawing families once a week into the Eucharistic Presence of Our Lord, where the Sacrament of Penance and Reconciliation is being offered while your "Be Not Afraid Novena" videotape is presented, is a great grace for families.

I encourage all families to participate in this powerful devotion, which is calling down the Mercy of God upon all of us. Be assured of my continued prayers for the success of your work.

Give my love to your family and co-workers in the Apostolate for Family Consecration.

God bless you,

God bless you
M. Teresa m.c

M. Teresa, M.C.

851

- assure the bishop and pastors of a theologically sound program that conforms to the teachings of both the magisterium of the Church and Vatican Council II.
- build a parish community that is focused on the Eucharist and the Truth.
- teach the deep meaning behind our traditional devotions.
- lead the family to prayer, particularly, to the family Rosary and Eucharistic devotion.

The Be Not Afraid Family Hours are presented in a series of six 9-week programs (54 in all), with more being developed, so that a parish can continue to run them on a weekly basis.

The themes and devotions for the six series of 9-week programs:

1. St. Joseph — A Model for Husbands, Fathers, and Workers

2. The Immaculate Conception — Our Lady of Guadalupe — Total Consecration

3. The Living Eucharist

4. Our Mission is Mercy

5. The Holy Rosary

6. Healing Through Consecration according to St. Louis de Montfort

852

Besides one of 36 prominent teachers on each series, every one of the Be Not Afraid Family Hours features:

1. The Holy Rosary with vibrant pictures for each "Hail Mary," and with one Mystery depicted in movie format.

2. Pope John Paul II, speaking in English.

3. Francis Cardinal Arinze— a member of the Roman Curia— truly one of the greatest teachers and evangelists in the Church today.

4. Mother Teresa of Calcutta, who originated the idea of weekly Eucharistic Family Hours and who has continually encouraged the Family Apostolate to develop the Be Not Afraid Family Hours on video and to use them in churches.

The Be Not Afraid Family Hours video faculty also includes:

Anthony Cardinal Bevilacqua,** Archbishop of Philadelphia

Mario Luigi Cardinal Ciappi, O.P. * ** Roman Curia member and former papal theologian; the Family Apostolate's primary theological advisor

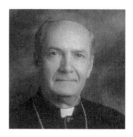

Edouard Cardinal Gagnon,* ** Former President of the Pontifical Council for the Family

Bernard Cardinal Law, ** Archbishop of Boston

Archbishop Agostino Cacciavillan, Apostolic Pro-Nuncio—official ambassador of the Holy See to the United States

Fr. Patrick Peyton, who coined the phrase, "The family that prays together stays together."

Pio Cardinal Laghi,* Prefect of the Vatican's Congregation for Catholic Education, including seminarians.

John Cardinal O'Connor,** Archbishop of New York *(where the Apostolate's Canonical Global center is located.)*

Jose Cardinal Sanchez,* Prefect of the Vatican's Congregation for the Clergy, who is directly responsible for catechetics throughout the world

Other video faculty members featured in our Family Hours are:

Archbishop John Foley * **
Bishop John Magee **
Bishop Juan F. Torres **
Bishop Peter Van Lierde * **
Msgr. Peter Elliott * **
Msgr. John McCarthy * **
Fr. John Bertolucci
Fr. Harold Cohen, S.J. **
Fr. Richard Drabik, M.I.C. **
Fr. Gregory Finn, O.S.J. **
Fr. Bernard Geiger, OFM, Conv.**
Fr. Brian Harrison, S.T.L. **
Fr. George Kosicki, C.S.B. **

Fr. M. Albert Krapiec, O.P.**
Fr. S. Michalenko, M.I.C. **
Fr. Michael Scanlan, T.O.R. **
Fr. Andrej Szostek M.I.C.**
Mother Immaculata**
Dr. Richard Dumont **
Helen Hayes
Dr. Alice von Hildebrand
Dr. Anthony Paruta **
Dr. Burns Seeley **
Carolyn Stegmann **
Loretta Young
Jerry and Gwen Coniker**

* = Roman Curia, ** = Co-chairman of the Apostolate's Marian Era Campaign and/or Advisory Council Member.

Vatican Encouragement to Use Videotapes in Churches With Our Lord Reserved in the Tabernacle

Cardinal Augustin Mayer, while Prefect of the Sacred Congregation for the Sacraments and Divine Worship in the Vatican, wrote the following to the Family Apostolate on November 15, 1987:

Dear Mr. Coniker:

I have known about the Apostolate for Family Consecration's "Be Not Afraid" Weekly Eucharistic Holy Hours and First Saturday "Light of the World Cenacle" video programs for showing in the Eucharistic Presence of Our Lord in churches throughout the world.

Pope John Paul II used television in a very powerful way to open up the Marian Year. I believe your videos, which are produced with such taste and tenderness for the Eucharist, can be a very powerful instrument to draw families to His Eucharistic Presence within parish communities. Here they can also be formed in the truth which will make them free and be motivated to go to confession, a sacrament so vital to the spiritual life.

I am happy to give my deepest encouragement for this type of formation and evangelization in the Eucharistic Presence of Our Lord. Properly produced videotape programs offer an entirely new dimension for the Church to communicate the truth.

Yours in the Hearts of Jesus and Mary,

Paul Augustin Card, Mayer

The Be Not Afraid Family Hours feature Roman Curia Cardinal Arinze, teaching from *The Apostolate's Family Catechism* which has been cross-referenced with the new papally-promulgated *Catechism of the Catholic Church.*

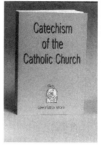

Cardinal William Baum, one of the three Roman Curia Cardinals on the Commission for the new papally-promulgated *Catechism of the Catholic Church,* wrote:

"We believe that The Apostolate's Family Catechism, *with which the Catechism for the Universal Church will be cross-referenced, will truly be a break through for family formation and for parents, who indeed are the primary educators of their children. This integrated program of teaching the catechism in the home, and then gathering together once a week with other families to hear Cardinal Arinze and others teach on your 'Be Not Afraid' Family Hours in churches, can be very effective in rebuilding both the domestic church and the parish community."*

Mother Teresa knows the best way to stop the holocaust of abortion and save family life: through weekly "Be Not Afraid Family Hours."

MISSIONARIES OF CHARITY

J.M.J.   22/3/92

Dear Jerry and Gwen Coniker,

Thank you for your kind letter and prayers for me. I am well thank God. It will be a real gift of God if the adoration of the Bl. Sacrament could fully penetrate family life. The holy hour as family prayer in our society has been the greatest gift of God. "Be Not Afraid" Our Lord will always be with you.

Bring prayer as much as possible into the family life. Consecration to the Sacred Heart and Rosary family - Very pleasing to the Heart of Jesus. Keep praying for our society, our Poor & me.   God bless you
                                                 M Teresa mc

Once families know Who our Eucharistic Lord is, the best fruits of the "Be Not Afraid Family Hours" will be:

1. Perpetual adoration by families, not just by individuals.

2. Weekly formation, confession, Adoration and Benediction of the Blessed Sacrament offered to families on a continual basis.

3. Parish solidarity—a spirit of helping those in need.

Knights of Columbus members are often honor guards for the "Be Not Afraid Family Hours."

Many parishes open every novena of Family Hours with a procession led by the Pilgrim Virgin Statue or another image of Our Lady, and pictures of the Pope and the local bishop. These images are all symbols of unity.

The Holy See has requested that the Blessed Sacrament be reserved in the tabernacle during the video presentation of the Family Hour. However, after the Family Hour video presentation, many parishes conclude the program with a short period of Eucharistic Adoration and Benediction, some with an entire hour of adoration.

Be Not Afraid Family Hour Preview Tapes for Sunday Masses

Each set of Family Hours includes a tenth tape which consists of nine 4-5-minute previews of each Family Hour program in that set. These 4-5 minute segments are designed to be shown after the homily or before the final blessing at all of the Sunday Masses each week.

In order to enjoy success in re-evangelizing the parish with the Be Not Afraid Family Hours, it is extremely important to enthusiastically promote them at every Sunday Mass by:
- showing the 4-5-minute preview
- having the pastor speak about them from the pulpit
- including inserts about them in the bulletin on a regular basis
- recruiting young people and others to put up posters, pass out flyers, and call neighbors.

If it is not possible to immediately promote and conduct the "Be Not Afraid Family Hours" in your church, then you can conduct them in your home, the "domestic church," every week. Ask your pastor to hear confessions in your home. Pray specifically that the "Be Not Afraid Family Hours" can soon be held in your parish church, where the Body, Blood, Soul, and Divinity of Our Eucharistic Lord dwells in the tabernacle. Both the members of the parish and of the family will be renewed and will experience that peace we all long for and the healing of family life and relationships.

While in Denver in 1993 for World Youth Day, the Holy Father challenged the youth to:

- defend life
- participate in a new evangelization
- carry their crosses

The "Be Not Afraid Family Hours" give the youth a complete program to follow and support the Holy Father. Young people can:

- use their creative energies to promote the Family Hours

- greet parishioners before and after every Mass with flyers about the Family Hours

- deliver press releases to your local newspapers and radio and TV news shows

- record testimonials from Family Hour participants which can be broadcast locally and nationally on T.V. and radio

- offer transportation to the handicapped or elderly of the area who cannot get to the Family Hour by themselves. Be available to babysit or conduct a child care program during the Family Hour programs. (However, we encourage children 5 years and older to participate in the actual Family Hour.)

- learn their Faith while attending the Family Hours, and ,as a consequence, be eager to evangelize and to draw new people into the Family Hours.

The Initial 54 "Be Not Afraid Family Hours"™
On Videotape

Designed for continuous presentation every week in churches or homes. The key is never to stop — when you complete one, nine-week novena series, immediately start the next one. Even after you have gone through the 54 weeks and do not wish to immediately acquire a new series, you can easily repeat the one-year cycle since these programs are so rich.

Each one-hour videotape of the series of 54 (6 sets of 9 programs focused on a specific theme) includes:

1. an opening with one of the 36 video faculty teachers listed on pages 853-855.

2. a theme prayer and moving hymns with beautiful picture overlays.

3. Roman Curia Cardinal Francis Arinze clearly and systematically teaching the *Family Catechism*. He is truly one of the greatest teachers in the world. Please note that each series covers questions and answers from this Vatican-approved *Apostolate's Family Catechism* in chronological order and without duplication. As you can see, this *Family Catechism* is methodically cross-referenced with the new papally promulgated *Catechism of the Catholic Church* (see pages xxx and 839 to 842). A sampling of the 304 questions and answers from The *Apostolate's Family Catechism* are covered on each program, beginning with the "St. Joseph" series and continuing all the way through the "Healing Through Consecration" series.

   When the catechism questions start over again, such as in the middle of the "Living Eucharist" and "Holy Rosary" series, different questions are reviewed.

4. a meditative Rosary with at least one mystery dramatized in a movie format. The beautiful pictures for each "Hail Mary" truly make the Rosary come to life.

5. Pope John Paul II himself, speaking in English.

6. a closing segment with Mother Teresa of Calcutta, who inspired the Family Apostolate to produce the "Be Not Afraid Family Hours" for families and churches.

Each set of the "Be Not Afraid Family Hour" also includes the following:

1. 9 one-hour programs on videotape (for 9 weeks).

2. one Sunday Mass preview tape (containing nine 4-5-minute preview segments to be shown after the homily or before the final blessing at all of the Sunday Masses over a 9-week period).

3. packets of spiritual bouquet cards for the Holy Father. His Holiness truly appreciates your prayers and sacrifices.

Be Not Afraid Family Hours   (in recomended order)

1. St. Joseph Set   *133-363VK includes:*

- 9 one-hour programs on videotape (for 9 weeks).

- 1 Sunday Mass Preview Tape which contains nine 4-5-minute Family Hour previews.

Cardinal Arinze reviews subjects relating to catechism questions #1-137.

This series also features: Fr. Gregory Finn (Oblates of St. Joseph) and Jerry Coniker. Topics covered include the virtues of St. Joseph, the joys and sorrows of St. Joseph, St. Joseph the Worker, the humility and obedience of St. Joseph, the trust of St. Joseph, and the silence of St. Joseph. St. Joseph is truly the model for husbands and fathers, while he presents a fatherly role model to families that have no father at home.

2. Our Lady of Guadalupe — the Immaculate Conception and Consecration Set   *133-361VK includes:*

- 9 one-hour programs on videotape (for 9 weeks).

- 1 Sunday Mass Preview Tape which contains nine 4-5-minute Family Hour previews.

Cardinal Arinze reviews subjects relating to catechism questions #138-268.

This series also features: Cardinal Edouard Gagnon, Cardinal Pio Laghi, Cardinal Bernard Law, Cardinal Anthony Bevilacqua, Cardinal John O'Connor, Fr. George Kosicki, Fr. Harold Cohen, Fr. Patrick Peyton, Loretta Young, Carolyn Stegmann, and Jerry Coniker. Topics includes Mary, Seat of Wisdom; the Marian Multiplier; Mary reveals Her name; Mary's purity; John Paul II's Marian devotion; and consecration to Mary.

3. The Living Eucharist Set   *133-390VK includes:*

- 9 one-hour programs on videotape (for 9 weeks).

- 1 Sunday Mass Preview Tape which contains nine 4-5-minute Family Hour previews.

Cardinal Arinze reviews subjects relating to catechism questions #269-304 and presents entirely new explanations for subjects related to questions #1-113. Week 4 starts a new cycle of different catechetical teachings.

This series also features: Cardinal Jose Sanchez, Cardinal Bernard Law, Bishop John Magee, Bishop Fremiot Torres, Fr. Brian Harrison, Fr. Michael Scanlan, Fr. George Kosicki, Carolyn Stegmann, and Jerry Coniker. Topics covered include reverence for the Eucharist, the Eucharistic Heart of Jesus, the Eucharist and John Paul II, and the Eucharist and the Family.

<u>Be Not Afraid Family Hours   (in recomended order)</u>

4. Our Mission is Mercy Set   *133-410VK includes:*

- 9 one-hour programs on videotape (for 9 weeks).

- 1 Sunday Mass Preview Tape which contains nine 4-5-minute Family Hour previews.

Each of the one-hour programs includes both the Holy Rosary and the Chaplet of Divine Mercy. Cardinal Arinze reviews different subjects taken from questions #114-235.

This series also features: Bishop John Magee, Msgr. John McCarthy, Fr. John Bertolucci, Fr. Brian Harrison, Fr. George Kosicki, Fr. S. Michalenko, Fr. Michael Scanlan, and Jerry and Gwen Coniker. Topics include Misery and Mercy, Three Levels of Mercy, the Chaplet of Divine Mercy, the Feast of Divine Mercy, Mercy and the Youth, and Mary, Mother of Mercy.

5. The Holy Rosary Set   *133-430VK includes:*

- 9 one-hour programs on videotape (for 9 weeks).

- 1 Sunday Mass Preview tape which contains nine 4-5-minute Family Hour previews.

Cardinal Arinze reviews entirely new material from catechism questions #236-304, and week 7 starts a new cycle of different catechetical discussions #1-71.

These Family Hours also include Cardinal Mario Luigi Ciappi, Cardinal Anthony Bevilacqua, Msgr. Peter Elliott, Fr. Bernard Geiger, Fr. Patrick Peyton, Mother Immaculata, Carolyn Stegmann, and Jerry Coniker. Topics include Fatima and the Rosary, the Joyful Mysteries, the Agony in the Garden, the meaning of suffering, the Cross & crucifixion, the Rosary & meditation, and Mary's triumph.

6. Healing Through Consecration Set   *133-450VK*
This kit, available after November 30, 1993, includes:

- 9 one-hour programs on videotape (for 9 weeks).

- 1 Sunday Mass Preview tape which contains nine 4-5-minute Family Hour previews.

Cardinal Arinze reviews entirely new material starting with questions 72 and 189.

These Family Hours also include Cardinal Pio Laghi; Archbishop John Foley; Fr. Roger Charest, S.M.M. (de Montfort missionary); Fr. Bernard Geiger, O.F.M., Conv. (an expert on St. Maximilian Koble); Mother Immaculata, H.M.C.; Loretta Young; and Jerry Coniker.

This series is to be used with St. Louis de Montfort's 33-day *Preparation for Total Consecration to Jesus through Mary*. It focuses on the Marian spiritualities of St. Louis de Montfort, St. Maximilian Kolbe, and Pope John Paul II. This series will show how, by living consecrated lives, and by grounding ourselves in the truths of our Faith, we will be better disposed to receive the graces to repair broken relationships and heal our families.

TEN DAY DIVINE MERCY NOVENA ON VIDEO

Divine Mercy Novena Set — for Good Friday through Mercy Sunday (first Sunday after Easter) *133-310VK includes:*

• 10 one-hour programs on videotape (for 10 days).

• 2 Sunday Preview Tapes which include Family Hour previews to be shown at the Sunday Masses before Good Friday and at all of the daily Masses and services during Holy Week, and at all of the weekday Masses and events following Easter Sunday. These also make ideal cable T.V. ads. There are ten 7-8-minute previews on both tapes.

This series does not include the Rosary, but it does contain the Chaplet of Divine Mercy.

The Divine Mercy Novena also features: Cardinal Edouard Gagnon, Cardinal Pio Laghi, Cardinal Anthony Bevilacqua, Archbishop John Foley, Bishop Peter Van Lierde, Bishop John Magee, Fr. John Bertolucci, Fr. Richard Drabik, Fr. Albert Krapiec, Fr. George Kosicki, Fr. Seraphim Michalenko, Fr. Patrick Peyton, Fr. Michael Scanlan, Fr. Andrej Szostek, Richard Dumont, Ph.D., Helen Hayes, Rabbi Harold Kushner, Anthony Paruta, Ph.D., Burns K. Seeley, Ph.D., and Jerry Coniker.

SUGGESTED VIDEOTAPES AND SACRAMENTALS TO PRECEDE AND FOLLOW FAMILY HOURS

Pre-Family Hour Music Video: "Reflection of the Hearts of Jesus and Mary" *198-250V*

May be played before the Family Hour to help create a prayerful atmosphere.

Pre-Family Hour Rosary Organ Concert videotapes *133-221VK*

Rosary video with organ concert and pictorial meditations, which may be played/prayed before the Family Hour. Set of three half-hour tapes includes the Joyful, Sorrowful, and Glorious Mysteries. The "Hail Mary's" are prayed silently by participants.

Soul of the Rosary videotapes *133-158VK*

Rosary video with pictorial meditations which may be played/prayed before the Family Hours. The "Hail Mary's" are recited audibly on the video. Set of 3 (Joyful, Sorrowful, and Glorious Mysteries) one-hour videotapes with 2 versions of the Rosary on each tape (shorter family version and longer First Saturday meditation version).

Soul of the Rosary audiotapes   *133-158AK*

Set of 3 one-hour tapes (same as above)

Family Consecration Prayer Book   *305-14*

Contains all the prayers used in the Family Hours. This is a spiritual classic that not only includes prayers but also papal documents, hymns, and spiritual standards for living a consecrated life.

Brilliant full-color 16" X 20" picture of the Holy Family featuring the Sacred Heart and the Immaculate Heart.

Perfect for the enthronement of the Sacred Heart in the home. Standard frame size. Packed in reusable mail tubes. *361-18*

Full-color pictures of the Holy Family, the Immaculate Conception, and Pope John Paul II   *361-13*

Includes three 8" X 10" pictures per set.

Spiritual Bouquet Cards   *312-498 (in lots of 100)*

Beautiful Pilgrim Virgin Statue with Crown   *505-29*

- 36" high.
- Ideal for Family Hour processions and for home visitations.

Sacred Heart Family Consecration video   *133-281*

- One-hour video featuring Mother Teresa of Calcutta.

Designed to be used in a program which includes the visitation of the Pilgrim Virgin Statue and the enthronement of the Holy Family-Sacred Heart picture, as well as the *Soul of the Rosary* tapes, *The Apostolate's Family Catechism* on tape with Cardinal Arinze (#115-93 audios or 115-93VK videos), and the *Family Consecration Prayer Book* (305-14), which are all dropped off by the "evangelizing family" for another family to use for a week. On the following Saturday the evangelizing family will return for the Enthronement of the Sacred Heart picture ceremony, which is presented on the videotape, and then go on to bring our Lady's statue and sacramental materials to another family.

Vatican-approved "Apostolate's Family Catechism" 22 audiocassettes   *115-93AK (see page 845)*

With Cardinal Francis Arinze.

Vatican-approved "Apostolate's Family Catechism" 22 videocassettes   *115-93VK (see page 846)*

Vatican-approved "Apostolate's Family Catechism"
850 page one-volume edition   *380-18 (see page xvii and xxx)*

AFTER FAMILY HOUR TAPES & SACRAMENTALS

Miraculous Medal Investiture Videotape   *133-212V*

For Miraculous Medals, call (314) 547-2508 or 1-800-264-6279

Brown Scapular Enrollment Videotape   *(133-216V)*

For Brown Scapulars, call (908) 689-1700 or (708) 969-5050

HOLY HOUR PROMOTIONAL & TRAINING TAPES & MATERIALS

"Mother Teresa's Inspiration" Videotape Set   *120-202VK*

A presentation tape, explaining the "Be Not Afraid Family Hours." Tape includes Pope John Paul II, Cardinal Pio Laghi, Cardinal Francis Arinze, Cardinal Anthony Bevilacqua, Archbishop J. Francis Stafford, Loretta Young, and Jerry Coniker. Contains a 60-second Family Hour T.V. commercial sample, excerpts of interviews with Mother Teresa, sample of one of the 54 Sunday Mass preview tapes and segments from one of the "Be Not Afraid Family Hours." This set includes a one-hour video and audiotape.

Promotional & Planning Meeting Videotape Set *133-376VK*

• Part I: Same material as is in the broadcast quality ¾" promo tape for T.V. stations (see below), which includes three 30-second commercials, two 60-second commercials, and one entire 28½ minute promotional T.V. show. (See *133-375SMD* below)

• Part II: A planning meeting presentation for parish team members who will promote and implement the "Be Not Afraid Family Hours." Includes testimonials from priests and a short explanation of the job descriptions for each team member.

• Set also includes "Face the Challenge Action Form for Volunteers" *(375-53)* along with "Activity Summary Form" *(375-61)* and our *Family Consecration Prayer Book (305-14)*, poster *(317-43)*, a news release, a newspaper ad artwork sheet and a spiritual bouquet card that can be copied.

Broadcast quality ¾" Video Promo Tape   *133-375SMD*

• For promotion of the Family Hours on T.V. Includes three 30-second and two 60-second commercials (so that you can have your local T.V. station list the time and place with their character generators) and a full 28½ minute T.V. show which promotes the Family Hours. (See *133-376VK* above for ½" video of this promotional tape.)

"Be Not Afraid Family Hours" posters — 11" x 17"   *317-53*

Peace of Heart Forums™
on audio & video tape

- A unique system for on-going spiritual formation: 331 hours of solid formation in an easy-to-understand discussion format. **Unless preceded by an asterisk (*), all audio and video sets are 4 hours in length.**

- Featuring some of the most profound teachers in the Church, from Roman Curia Cardinals to authors, who discuss their own books.

- Ideal for prayer groups, parish study clubs and various spiritual organizations.

- All Forums are tied into a book, with recommended readings for each day.

- We recommend that you set aside 15 to 30 minutes a day for praying your books. You are not asked to read all of the material; rather, allow the Holy Spirit to guide you in your reflections. Keep a spiritual diary, and at the end of your reflective reading time, write a note to God and Our Lady on the lights you have received from your spiritual appointment with Them. We suggest that you meet with other participants for 1½ to 2 hours a week for a ½-hour video program and for discussion on the insights underlined in your book or recorded in your diary and/or what you have learned from the videotape. After the discussion and a short break, you could then view another ½-hour video program, which previews the next week's readings so that you remain motivated to keep your daily appointments with God.

Some of the benefits:
- helps you to develop the habit of spiritual reading
- teaches you to "pray" a book
- gently guides you into fruitful meditation
- disposes you for contemplation
- fosters the development of relationships with others on a spiritual level
- develops a deeper community life focused on the truth.

Subjects include:
1. Papal Documents & Pope John Paul II (pp. 867 to 871)
2. Sacred Scriptures (pp. 871 to 874)
3. Mary & Consecration (pp. 874 to 875)
4. Saints & Youth (pp. 875 to 876)
5. Marriage & Family (pp. 876 to 877)
6. Liturgy & Purgatory (pp. 877 to 878)
7. Theology, Prayer & Philosophy (pp. 878 to 880)
8. Suffering (pp. 880)
9. Catechetics (p. 881 and 839 to 846)

1. PAPAL DOCUMENTS

Lay Members of Christ's Faithful People I
(*Christifideles Laici*) by Pope John Paul II
Video set: *126-3381VK*   Audio tape set: *126-3381AK*

Faculty: Francis Cardinal Arinze (Roman Curia), Bishop William D'Mello, Bishop John the Baptist Kakubi, Bishop Albert Ottenweller, Fr. Michael Scanlan, T.O.R., Fr. George Kosicki, C.S.B., Dr. Keith Fournier and Jerry Coniker.

Reference Book: *Lay Members of Christ's Faithful People* by Pope John Paul II. *503-EPO702.*

Lay Members of Christ's Faithful People II
(*Christifideles Laici*) by Pope John Paul II
Video set: *126-3397VK*   Audio tape set: *126-3397AK*

Faculty: Cardinal Anthony Bevilacqua, Bishop J.B. Kakubi, Fr. Michael Scanlan, T.O.R., Charles Presberg, Dr. Burns Seeley and Jerry Coniker.

Reference Book: *Lay Members of Christ's Faithful People*
by Pope John Paul II. *503-EPO702*

On Evangelization in the Modern World I
(*Evangelii Nuntiandi*) by Pope Paul VI
Video set: *126-1703VK*   Audio tape set: *126-1703AK*

Faculty: Fr. Michael Scanlan, T.O.R., Jerry Coniker and the
staff of the Franciscan University of Steubenville (Ohio).

Reference Book: *Evangelization in the Modern World*
by Pope Paul VI. *503-EPO850*

On Evangelization in the Modern World II
(*Evangelii Nuntiandi*) by Pope Paul VI
Video set: *126-1906VK*   Audio tape set: *126-1906AK*

Faculty: Bishop John Magee (former papal secretary), Msgr.
John McCarthy, Dr. Burns Seeley and Jerry Coniker.

Reference Book:*Evangelization in the Modern World*
by Pope Paul VI. *503-EPO850*.

To the Youth of the World I
by Pope John Paul II
Video set: *126-1541VK*   Audio tape set: *126-1541AK*

Faculty: Fr. Peter Elliott (Pontifical Council for the Family),
Dr. Burns Seeley and Jerry Coniker

Reference Book: *To the Youth of the World*
by Pope John Paul II. *503-EP1075*

To the Youth of the World II
by Pope John Paul II
Video set: *126-1667VK*   Audio tape set: *126-1667AK*

Faculty: Pope John Paul II, Bishop John Donoghue, Msgr.
John Woolsey, Dr. Burns Seeley and Jerry Coniker.

Reference Book: *To the Youth of the World*
by Pope John Paul II. *503-EP1075*

To the Youth of the World III
by Pope John Paul II
Video set: *126-1970VK*   Audio tape set: *126-1970AK*

Faculty: Pope John Paul II, Bishop John Magee (former Papal
Secretary), Dr. Burns Seeley and Jerry Coniker.

Reference Book: *To the Youth of the World*
by Pope John Paul II. *503-EP1075*

On Reconciliation and Penance I
(*Reconciliatio et Paenitentia*)
by Pope John Paul II
Video set: *126-1014VK*   Audio tape set: *126-1014AK*

Faculty: Fr. Alfred Kunz, Dr. Burns Seeley and Jerry Coniker.

Reference Book: *On Reconciliation and Penance*
by Pope John Paul II. *503-EPO894*

On Reconciliation and Penance II
(Reconciliatio et Paenitentia) by Pope John Paul II
Video set: *126-1839VK*   Audio tape set: *126-1839AK*

Faculty: Pope John Paul II, Fr. Timothy Byerley, Dr. Burns
Seeley and Jerry Coniker.

Reference Book: *On Reconciliation and Penance*
by Pope John Paul II. *503-EPO894*

On Reconciliation and Penance III
(Reconciliatio et Paenitentia) by Pope John Paul II
Video set: *126-3576VK*   Audio tape set: *126-3576AK*

Faculty: Charles Presberg, Dr. Damian Fedoryka, Dr. Burns
Seeley and Jerry Coniker.

Reference Book: *On Reconciliation and Penance*
by Pope John Paul II. *503-EPO894*

On Reconciliation and Penance IV
(Reconciliatio et Paenitentia) by Pope John Paul II
Video set: *126-3678VK*   Audio tape set: *126-3678AK*

Faculty: Cardinal Francis Arinze, Dr. Burns Seeley and
Jerry Coniker.

Reference Book: *On Reconciliation and Penance*
by Pope John Paul II. *503-EPO894*

On Reconciliation and Penance V
(Reconciliatio et Paenitentia) by Pope John Paul II
Video set: *126-3694VK*   Audio tape set: *126-3694AK*

Faculty: Fr. Michael Scanlan, T.O.R., Dr. Burns Seeley and
Jerry Coniker.

Reference Book: *On Reconciliation and Penance*
by Pope John Paul II. *503-EPO894*

On the Christian Meaning of Human Suffering
(Salvifici Doloris) by Pope John Paul II
Video set: *126-1305VK*   Audio tape set: *126-1305AK*

Faculty: Sr. John Vianney, S.S.N.D. (suffered for over 40 years
in bed), Dr. Burns Seeley and Jerry Coniker.

Reference Book: *On the Christian Meaning of Human
Suffering* by Pope John Paul II. *503-EPO145*

The Role of the Christian Family in the Modern World I
(Familiaris Consortio) by Pope John Paul II
Video set: *126-960VK*   Audio tape set: *126-960AK*

Faculty: Msgr. Diarmuid Martin (Pontifical Council for the
Family), Fr. John Hardon, S.J., Fr. Richard Talaska, Dr. Burns
Seeley and Jerry Coniker.

Reference Book: *The Role of the Christian Family in the Modern World* by Pope John Paul II. *503-EPO973*

The Role of the Christian Family in the Modern World II
(*Familiaris Consortio*) by Pope John Paul II
Video set: *126-1111VK*   Audio tape set: *126-1111AK*

Faculty: Msgr. Diarmuid Martin (Pontifical Council for the Family), Fr. Alfred Kunz, Sr. John Vianney, S.S.N.D., Fr. Stanley Smolenski, Mother Teresa, Sandy Redmond, Dr. Burns Seeley and Jerry Coniker.

Reference Book: *The Role of the Christian Family in the Modern World* by Pope John Paul II. *503-EPO973*

The Role of the Christian Family in the Modern World III
(*Familiaris Consortio*) by Pope John Paul II
Video set: *126-1466VK*   Audio tape set: *126-1466AK*

Faculty: Msgr. John Woolsey, Fr. James Genovesi, Dr. Richard Dumont, Dr. Burns Seeley and Jerry Coniker.

Reference Book: *The Role of the Christian Family in the Modern World* by Pope John Paul II. *503-EPO973*

The Role of the Christian Family in the Modern World IV
(*Familiaris Consortio*) by Pope John Paul II
Video set: *126-1482VK*   Audio tape set: *126-1482AK*

Faculty: Cardinal Edouard Gagnon (when he was President of the Pontifical Council for the Family), Msgr. John Woolsey, Fr. Peter Elliott, Dr. Richard Dumont, Dr. Burns Seeley and Jerry Coniker.

Reference Book: *The Role of the Christian Family in the Modern World* by Pope John Paul II. *503-EPO973*

Reflections on Humanae Vitae I
by Pope John Paul II
Video set: *126-1080VK*   Audio tape set: *126-1080AK*

Faculty: Fr. John Hardon, S.J. and Jerry Coniker.

Reference Book: *Reflections on Humanae Vitae* by Pope John Paul II. *503-EPO972*

Reflections on Humanae Vitae II
by Pope John Paul II
Video set: *126-1726VK*   Audio tape set: *126-1726AK*

Faculty: Pope John Paul II, Cardinal John Krol, Fr. Andrej Szostek, M.I.C. (Lublin University, Poland), Fred Martinez, Dr. Richard Dumont, Dr. Burns Seeley and Jerry Coniker.

Reference Book: *Reflections on Humanae Vitae* by Pope John Paul II. *503-EPO972*

Mercy of God II
(*Dives et Misericordia*) by Pope John Paul II
Video set: *126-3607VK*   Audio tape set: *126-3607AK*

Faculty: Fr. George Kosicki, C.S.B. and Jerry Coniker.

Reference Book: *On the Mercy of God*
by Pope John Paul II. *503-EPO863*

Vatican II - Decree on the Apostolate of the Laity
(*Apostolicam Actuositatem*)
Video set: *126-3710VK*   Audio tape set: *126-3710AK*

Faculty: Cardinal Francis Arinze, Dr. Burns Seeley and
Jerry Coniker.

Reference Book: *Decree on the Apostolate of the Laity*,
promulgated by Pope Paul VI. *503-EP0360*

Be Not Afraid I: on the interview of Pope John Paul II
by André Frossard
Video set: *126-1434VK*   Audio tape set: *126-1434AK*

Faculty: Fr. Albert Krapiec and Fr. Andrej Szostek (both from
Lublin University, Poland, where Pope John Paul II formally
studied and taught); Dr. Richard Dumont; Dr. Burns Seeley,
and Jerry Coniker.

Reference Book: No book is currently available for this series

2. SACRED SCRIPTURE

St. Matthew

Meditations on St. Matthew I
Video set: *126-114VK*   Audio tape set: *126-114AK*

Faculty: Bishop William D'Mello, Bishop Thomas Welsh,
Fr. Lawrence Lovasik, S.V.D., Mother Angelica, Mother
Immaculata, H.M.C., Fr. Michael Scanlan, T.O.R., Mother
Teresa, Admiral Jeremiah Denton, Charles Presberg, Peter
Mergen, Dr. Burns Seeley and Jerry Coniker.

Reference Book: *Meditations on St. Matthew*
by Dr. Burns K. Seeley. *323-76*

Meditations on St. Matthew II
Video set: *126-589VK*   Audio tape set: *126-589AK*

Faculty: Cardinal Anthony Bevilacqua, Charles Presberg,
Dr. Burns Seeley and Jerry Coniker.

Reference Book: *Meditations on St. Matthew*
by Dr. Burns K. Seeley. *323-76*

Meditations on St. Matthew III
Video set: *126-884VK*   Audio tape set: *126-884AK*

Faculty: Msgr. John McCarthy, Fr. John Hardon, S.J.,
Dr. Burns Seeley and Jerry Coniker.

Reference Book: *Meditations on St. Matthew*
by Dr. Burns K. Seeley. *323-76*

St. Mark

Meditations on St. Mark I

Video set: *126-459VK*   Audio tape set: *126-459AK*

Faculty: Fr. John Hardon, S.J., Dr. Burns Seeley and Jerry Coniker.

Reference Book: *The Navarre Bible - St. Mark*; Revised Standard Version and *New Vulgate* with commentary by the members of the Faculty of Theology of the University of Navarre. *511-43.*

St. Luke

•Meditations on St. Luke I

Video set: *126-477VK*   Audio tape set: *126-477A*K

Faculty: Fr. John Hardon, S.J., Dr. Burns Seeley and Jerry Coniker.

Reference Book: *The Navarre Bible - St. Luke*; Revised Standard Version and *New Vulgate* with commentary by the members of the Faculty of Theology of the University of Navarre. *511-44.*

Acts of the Apostles

Video set: *126-3493VK*   Audio tape set: *126-3493AK*

Faculty: Fr. Tom Forrest, C.SS.R., Dr. Burns Seeley and Jerry Coniker.

Reference Book: *The Navarre Bible - Acts of the Apostles*; Revised Standard Version and *New Vulgate* with commentary by the members of the Faculty of Theology of the University of Navarre. *511-60*

St. John

Meditations on St. John I

Video set: *126-102VK*   Audio tape set: *126-102AK*

Faculty: Msgr. Alphonse Popek, Fr. William Dorney, Mother Angelica, John Hand, Dr. Richard DeGraff, Laurie Coniker, Dr. Burns Seeley and Jerry Coniker.

Reference Book: *Meditations on St. John* by Dr. Burns K. Seeley. *323-75*

Meditations on St. John II

Video set: *126-561VK*   Audio tape set: *126-561AK*

Faculty: Fr. Ralph Skonieczny, Fr. Frederick Heuser, Fr. John Hardon, S.J., Dr. Burns Seeley and Jerry Coniker.

Reference Book: *Meditations on St. John* by Dr. Burns K. Seeley. *323-75*

The Book of Revelation

Video set: *126-3839VK*   Audio tape set: *126-3839AK*

Faculty: Fr. Randall Paine, O.R.C., Dr. Burns Seeley and Jerry Coniker.

Reference Book: *The Navarre Bible - the Book of Revelation*; Revised Standard Version and *New Vulgate* with commentary by the members of the Faculty of Theology of the University of Navarre. *511-59*

St. Paul

Meditations on St. Paul I
1 Corinthians, 2 Corinthians, Galatians, Ephesians, & Philippians
Video set: *126-126VK*   Audio tape set: *126-126AK*

Faculty: Fr. John Hardon, S.J., Mother Angelica, Dr. Richard DeGraff, Dr. Burns Seeley, Laurie Coniker and Jerry Coniker.

Reference Book: *Meditations on St. Paul* by Dr. Burns K. Seeley. *323-77*

Meditations on St. Paul II
(same Epistles as above)
Video set: *126-605VK*   Audio tape set: *126-605AK*

Faculty: Fr. Alfred Boeddeker, O.F.M., Fr. Bernard Geiger, O.F.M. Conv., Mother Immaculata, H.M.C., Dr. Burns Seeley and Jerry Coniker.

Reference Book: *Meditations on St. Paul* by Dr. Burns K. Seeley. *323-77*

Meditations on St. Paul III
(same Epistles as above)
Video set: *126-2123VK*   Audio tape set: *126-2123AK*

Faculty: Cardinal Mario Luigi Ciappi O.P. (Papal theologian), Fr. Peter Elliott, Fr. Michael Scanlan, T.O.R., Mother Angelica, Dr. Keith Fournier, Tim Croes, Peter Mergen, Dr. Burns Seeley and Jerry Coniker.

Reference Book: *Meditations on St. Paul* by Dr. Burns K. Seeley. *323-77*

Meditations on St. Paul IV
(same Epistles as above)
Video set: *126-2139VK*   Audio tape set: *126-2139AK*

Faculty: Fr. Michael Scanlan, T.O.R., Fr. Randall Paine, O.R.C., Mother Teresa, Robert and Rita Feduccia, Janie and Kerry Casserly, Tim Croes, Dr. Burns Seeley and Jerry Coniker.

Reference Book: *Meditations on St. Paul* by Dr. Burns K. Seeley. *323-77*

Reflections on St. Paul I
Colossians, 1 Thessalonians, 2 Thessalonians, 1 Timothy, 2 Timothy, Titus, Philemon, & Hebrews

Video set: *126-137VK*   Audio tape set: *126-137AK*

Faculty: Msgr. Alphonse Popek, Fr. William Dorney, John Hand, Dr. Burns Seeley and Jerry Coniker.

Reference Book: *Reflections on St. Paul* by Dr. Burns K. Seeley. *323-78*

Reflections on St. Paul II
(same Epistles as above)
Video set: *126-626VK*   Audio tape set: *126-626AK*

Faculty: Bishop John Joseph (from Pakistan), Fr. John Hardon, S.J., Dr. Burns Seeley and Jerry Coniker.

Reference Book: *Reflections on St. Paul* by Dr. Burns K. Seeley. *323-78*

Reflections on St. Paul IV
(same Epistles as above)
Video set: *126-1160VK*   Audio tape set: *126-1160AK*

Faculty: Fr. Seraphim Michalenko, M.I.C., Sr. John Vianney, S.S.N.D., Dr. Burns Seeley and Jerry Coniker.

Reference Book: *Reflections on St. Paul* by Dr. Burns K. Seeley. *323-78*

3. MARY AND CONSECRATION

Immaculate Conception
Video set: *126-1191VK*   Audio tape set: *126-1191AK*

Faculty: Cardinal Mario Luigi Ciappi, O.P., Cardinal Bernard Law, Cardinal Silvio Oddi, Bishop John Van Lierde O.S.A., Fr. Bernard Geiger, O.F.M. Conv., Mother Immaculata, H.M.C., Dr. Burns Seeley and Jerry Coniker.

Reference Book: *The Wonder of Guadalupe* by Francis Johnston. *510-085*

* Total Consecration I
by St. Louis de Montfort
* Video set (6 hours): *126-998VK*   * Audio set (6 hours): *126-998AK*

Faculty: Cardinal Francis Arinze, Fr. Dominic De Domenico, O.P., Fr. Bernard Geiger, O.F.M. Conv., Fr. Michael Scanlan, T.O.R., Dr. Burns Seeley and Jerry Coniker.

Reference Books: *True Devotion to the Blessed Virgin* by St. Louis de Montfort, *520-25*. *Preparation For Total Consecration according to St. Louis de Montfort*. *520-26*

Immaculate Conception and the Holy Spirit
Video set: *126-1557VK*   Audio tape set: *126-1557AK*

Faculty: Cardinal Mario Luigi Ciappi, O.P., Fr. Peter Elliott, Fr. Brian Harrison O.S., Dr. Burns Seeley and Jerry Coniker.

Reference Book: *Immaculate Conception and the Holy Spirit* by Fr. H.M. Manteau-Bonamy, O.P. *513-101-20*

874

Consecration in the Spirit of St. Vincent Pallotti

Video set: *126-927VK*   Audio tape set: *126-927AK*

Faculty: Fr. Joseph Mungari, S.A.C., Fr. John Hardon, S.J., Dr. Burns Seeley and Jerry Coniker.

Reference Book: *Yearning of a Soul*
by Fr. Flavin Bonifazi, S.A.C. *503-SPO830*

Immaculate Heart of Mary: True Devotion

by Fr. Robert Fox
Video set: *126-1638VK*   Audio tape set: *126-1638AK*

Faculty: Fr. Robert Fox, Dr. Burns Seeley and Jerry Coniker.

Reference Book: *Immaculate Heart of Mary: True Devotion*
by Fr. Robert J. Fox. *502-32*

First Lady of the World

by Fr. Peter Lappin, S.D.B.
Video set: *126-2034VK*   Audio tape set: *126-2034AK*

Faculty: Cardinal Pio Laghi, Fr. Peter Lappin, S.D.B., Melissa Pierce, Dr. Burns Seeley and Jerry Coniker.

Reference Book: *First Lady of the World*
by Fr. Peter Lappin, S.D.B. *527-091-6*

The Spirit and the Bride Say, "Come!"

by Fr. George Kosicki
Video set: *126-3544VK*   Audio tape set: *126-3544AK*

Faculty: Fr. George Kosicki, C.S.B. Fr. Harold Cohen, S.J. and Jerry Coniker.

Reference Book: *The Spirit and the Bride Say, "Come!"* by Fr. Gerald J. Farrell, M.M. and Fr. George Kosicki, C.S.B. *545-1*

4. SAINTS AND YOUTH

Give Me Souls — St. John Bosco

by Fr. Peter Lappin, S.D.B.
Video set: *126-2002VK*   Audio tape set: *126-2002AK*

Faculty: Fr. Peter Lappin, S.D.B., Sandy Redmond, Dr. Burns Seeley and Jerry Coniker.

Reference Book: *Give Me Souls!*
by Fr. Peter Lappin, S.D.B. *527-25*

* Bury Me Deep [About Zepherin Namuncurá]

by Fr. Peter Lappin, S.D.B.
*Video set (3 hours): *126-2060VK* *Audio set (3 hours): *126-2060AK*

Faculty: Fr. Peter Lappin, S.D.B., Monica Heithaus, Dr. Burns Seeley and Jerry Coniker

Reference Book: No book is currently available for this series

Blessed Kateri Tekakwitha

by Fr. Henri Bechard, S.J.
Video set: *126-1605VK*   Audio tape set: *126-1605AK*

875

Faculty: Msgr. Paul Lenz, Fr. Henri Bechard, S.J., Fr. Thomas Egan, S.J. and Jerry Coniker.

Reference Book: *Kateri Tekakwitha*
by Fr. F.X. Weiser, S.J. *569-25*

* **The Falcon and the Dove—Blessed Laura Vicuña**
by Fr. Peter Lappin, S.D.B.
*Video set (3 hours): *126-2047VK* *Audio set (3 hours): *126-2047AK*

Faculty: Fr. Peter Lappin, S.D.B., Monica Heithaus, Dr. Burns Seeley and Jerry Coniker.

Reference Book: No book is currently available for this series

Jerome Le Royer de la Dauversiere: His Friends and Enemies [Founder of Montreal]
by Henri Bechard, S.J.
Video set: *126-1621VK*   Audio tape set: *126-1621AK*

Faculty: Fr. Henri Bechard, S.J., Fr. Thomas Egan, S.J. and Jerry Coniker.

Reference Book: *Jerome Le Royer de la Dauversiere: His Friends and Enemies* by Fr. Henri Bechard, S.J. *323-92-S*

* **Dominic Savio, Teenage Saint**
by Fr. Peter Lappin, S.D.B.
*Video set (2 hours): *126-2069VK* *Audio set (2 hours): *126-2069AK*

Faculty: Fr. Peter Lappin, S.D.B., Sandy Redmond, Dr. Burns Seeley and Jerry Coniker.

Reference Book: *Dominic Savio, Teenage Saint*
by Fr. Peter Lappin, S.D.B. *527-055*

Special Urgency of Mercy, "Why Sr. Faustina?"
by Fr. George Kosicki
Video set: *126-3528VK*   Audio tape set: *126-3528AK*

Faculty: Fr. George Kosicki, C.S.B. and Jerry Coniker.

Reference Book: *Special Urgency of Mercy, "Why Sr. Faustina?"* by Fr. George Kosicki, C.S.B. *591-UP136*

5. MARRIAGE & FAMILY

Today's Parents
by Dr. Nino Camardese
Video set: *126-1938VK*   Audio tape set: *126-1938AK*

Faculty: Dr. Nino Camardese, Fr. Mauro Ventura, Jerry and Gwen Coniker.

Reference Book: *Today's Parents*
by Dr. Nino Camardese. *526-25*.

* **Love and Life Chastity Program**
*Video set (10 hours): *126-3427VK* *Audio set (10 hours): 126-3427AK

Faculty: Pope John Paul II, the Foxhoven Family, the "Foundation for the Family" (presenting "The Springtime of Your Life"), Sr. John Vianney, S.S.N.D., Dr. Burns Seeley, Jerry and Gwen Coniker.

Reference Books: *Love and Life Chastity Program Student Textbook/workbook* by Coleen Kelly Mast *582-106-6*. *Parents' Guide*, *582-107-4*. *Teacher's Manual*, *582-108-2* Complete set of 3 books and 10 videos: *126-3429VK*

St. Joseph, Blessed among Husbands, Blessed among Fathers
Video set: *126-2185VK*   Audio tape set: *126-2185AK*

Faculty: Fr. Stanley Smolenski, Fr. Francis Filas, S.J., Mother Teresa, Mother Immaculata, H.M.C., Frank Milligan, Pat Spenser, Dr. Burns Seeley and Jerry Coniker.

Reference Book: *Life With Joseph* by Fr. Paul J. Gorman. *552-26*

Marriage; the Mystery of Faithful Love
by Dr. Dietrich von Hildebrand
Video set: *126-3790VK*   Audio tape set: *126-3790AK*

Faculty: Dr. Alice von Hildebrand, Dr. Burns Seeley, Jerry and Gwen Coniker.

Reference Books: *Marriage; the Mystery of Faithful Love* by Dietrich von Hildebrand. *528-5*
By Love Refined; Letters to a Young Bride by Alice von Hildebrand. *528-2*

Religious Liberty and Contraception
by Fr. Brian Harrison, O.S.
Video set: *126-1922VK*   Audio tape set: *126-1922AK*

Faculty: Fr. Brian Harrison O.S., Dr. Burns Seeley and Jerry Coniker.

Reference Book: *Religious Liberty and Contraception* by Fr. Brian Harrison, O.S. *525-25*

6. LITURGY & PURGATORY

* Understanding the Mass
by Fr. Maynard Kolodziej, O.F.M.
*Video set (5 hours): *126-1858VK* *Audio set (5 hours): *126-1858AK*

Faculty: Pope John Paul II, Bishop John Magee, Fr. Maynard Kolodziej, O.F.M., Fr. Joseph Mungari, S.A.C., Dr. Burns Seeley and Jerry Coniker.

Reference Book: *Understanding the Mass* by Fr. Maynard Kolodziej, O.F.M. *567-25*

Purgatory
by Fr. F.X. Schouppe, S.J.
Video set: *126-1823*VK   Audio tape set: *126-1823AK*

Faculty: Bishop Thomas Welsh, Fr. Randall Paine, O.R.C., Dr. Burns Seeley and Jerry Coniker.

Reference Book: *Purgatory*
by Fr. F.X. Schouppe, S.J. *510-143*

7. THEOLOGY, PRAYER & PHILOSOPHY

Orthodoxy I - A Defense of Truth Against Modern Error
by G.K. Chesterton.
Video set: *126-1807VK*   Audio tape set: *126-1807AK*

Faculty: Fr. Randall Paine, O.R.C., Dr. Burns Seeley and Jerry Coniker.

Reference Book: *Orthodoxy - The Romance of Faith*
by G.K. Chesterton. *501-01536-4*

Spiritual Life in the Modern World I
by Fr. John Hardon, S.J.
Video set: *126-975VK*   Audio tape set: *126-975AK*

Faculty: Fr. John Hardon, S.J., Dr. Burns Seeley and Jerry Coniker.

Reference Book: *Spiritual Life in the Modern World*
by Fr. John Hardon, S.J. *503-SPO708.*

Theology of Prayer
by Fr. John Hardon, S.J.
Video set: *126-1402VK*   Audio tape set: *126-1402AK*

Faculty: Fr. John Hardon, S.J., Dr. Burns Seeley and Jerry Coniker.

Reference Book: *Theology of Prayer*
by Fr. John Hardon, S.J. *503-SPO745*

* Rejoice in the Lord
by Fr. George Kosicki
*Video set (3 hours): *126-3590VK* *Audio set (3 hours): *126-3590AK*

Faculty: Fr. George Kosicki, C.S.B. and Jerry Coniker.

Reference Book: No book is currently available for this series

The 12 Steps to Holiness and Salvation
by St. Alphonsus Liguori.
Video set: *126-3632VK*   Audio tape set: *126-3632AK*

Faculty: Fr. Francis Novak, C.SS.R., Sandy Redmond, Dr. Burns Seeley and Jerry Coniker.

Reference Book: *The 12 Steps to Holiness and Salvation*
by St. Alphonsus Liguori. *510-037*

Transformation in Christ I
by Dr. Dietrich von Hildebrand
Video set: *126-3726VK*   Audio tape set: *126-3726AK*

Faculty: Dr. Alice von Hildebrand, Dr. Burns Seeley and Jerry Coniker.

Reference Book: *Transformation in Christ* by Dietrich von Hildebrand. *528-3*

Transformation in Christ II
by Dr. Dietrich von Hildebrand
Video set: *126-3822VK*   Audio tape set: *126-3822AK*

Faculty: Dr. Alice von Hildebrand, Dr. Burns Seeley and Jerry Coniker.

Reference Book: *Transformation in Christ* by Dietrich von Hildebrand. *528-3*

* PHILOSOPHY COURSE
38 half-hour shows on 16 one-hour tapes. *163-490K*

With Father M. Alfred Krapiec, O.P., Ph.D., D.D., Father Andrej Szostek, M.I.C., Ph.D., Father Andrej Woznicki, M.A., Ph.D., M.S.L., Dr. Piotr Jaroszynski, Ph.D., Richard Dumont, Ph.D., and Burns K. Seeley, Ph.D.

Top-level scholars from the Catholic University of Lublin, Poland, (where Pope John Paul II held the Chair of Ethics) use *The Acting Person* by Pope John Paul II; *I, Man* by Father Krapiec; and *Introduction to St. Thomas Aquinas* as basic texts for this complete college level philosophy course.

Father Krapiec served for 13 years as rector of the Catholic University of Lublin, Poland, and at the time that this series was filmed, was the head of the Chair of Metaphysics there. He has known Pope John Paul II for over 40 years.

Father Szostek worked very closely with Cardinal Wojtyla as the assistant to the Chair of Ethics at the Catholic University of Lublin, Poland, before Cardinal Wojtyla became Pope John Paul II.

In this series, these colleagues of John Paul II discuss his teachings about the human person. Recommended for the serious scholar.

* THE SYNOPTIC GOSPELS
With Monsignor John F. McCarthy, J.C.D., S.T.D

70 half-hour programs on 35 one-hour tapes   *163-345K*

A challenging introduction to the Synoptic Gospels, presented in 70 half-hour programs by Monsignor John F. McCarthy, Vatican official and Director of the Society of the Oblates of Wisdom and of *Sedes Sapientiae* Study Center in Rome.

The principal aim of this college level theology course is to present the neo-Patristic method of interpreting Sacred Scripture, and to apply this method in particular to the interpretation of the Synoptic Gospels of Matthew, Mark and Luke. Monsignor McCarthy presents a new and highly scientific framework for the exegesis of the Sacred Text, taking the basic approach of the Fathers of the Church and other great Catholic exegetes of the past and systematizing it in a way and to a degree that has never been done before. The first fruit of this course is a new awareness of the levels of meaning enshrined in the text of the Gospels.

By means of a clear distinction between the literal and the mystical senses of the Inspired Word, a thorough refutation of form-criticism is given, the historical inerrancy of the Gospel text is fully demonstrated, and the validity of the mystical sense is defended.

This course is enlightening since it explains the levels of meaning in Scripture, and useful for applying the neo-Patristic method to one's personal study of Scripture. The method presented provides a basis for refutation of unfounded attacks upon the historical truth and mystical meanings of Holy Scripture and gives the viewer a solid introduction to contemporary Biblical interpretation from the viewpoint of Catholic Biblical tradition and of true historical science.

8. SUFFERING

* The Good News of Suffering
by Fr. George Kosicki
*Video set (2 hours): *126-3617VK* *Audio set (2 hours): *126-3617AK*

Faculty: Fr. George Kosicki, C.S.B. and Jerry Coniker.

Reference Book: No book is currently available for this series

On the Christian Meaning of Human Suffering II
(*Salvifici Doloris*) by Pope John Paul II
Video set: *126-1305VK*   Audio tape set: *126-1305AK*

Faculty: Sr. John Vianney, S.S.N.D. (has suffered for over 40 years in bed), Dr. Burns Seeley and Jerry Coniker.

Reference Book: *On the Christian Meaning of Human Suffering* by Pope John Paul II. *503-EPO145*

9. CATECHETICS

* The Apostolate's Family Catechism on Tape™
*Video set (22 hours): *115-93VK (see page 844 and 846)*
*Audio set (22 hours): *115-93AK (see page 844 and 845)*

Faculty: Roman Curia Cardinal Francis Arinze, interviewed by Jerry Coniker.

Reference Book: *The Apostolate's Family Catechism*, over 850 pages - soft cover *380-18*

Faith For Today
by Fr. Richard Hogan & Fr. John LeVoir
Video set: *126-2091VK*   Audio tape set: *126-2091AK*

Faculty: Fr. Richard Hogan, Fr. John LeVoir, Dr. Burns Seeley and Jerry Coniker.

Reference Book: *Faith For Today*
by Fr. Richard Hogan and Fr. John LeVoir. *582-12*

Please keep in mind that we are a non-profit ministry which offers many services to the people of God. Due to the lack of funds and the fact that we have one of the world's largest video libraries, we are only able to keep minimum quantities of video taped programs in stock of any one series. Please allow up to 6-12 weeks for us to duplicate and ship your order. We will try to ship your orders earlier, but we ask for your prayers as we pray for you. Thank you and God bless you.

First Saturday Cenacles on Video

Pio Cardinal Laghi, Vatican Prefect of the Congregation for Catholic Education, being interviewed by Jerry Coniker when the former was the Pro-Nuncio to the United States. This interview was featured on the initial First Saturday "Cenacle" video. This series of one-hour programs includes Pope John Paul II, Mother Teresa of Calcutta, one other guest speaker, and a meditative Rosary with a picture for each Hail Mary.

On July 1, 1940, Sr. Lucia, one of the Fatima seers, wrote Pope Pius XII a letter that included the following:

"In 1917, in the portion of the apparitions that we have designated 'the secret,' the Blessed Virgin revealed the end of the war that was then afflicting Europe, and predicted another forthcoming, saying that to prevent it, she would come and ask for the consecration of Russia to her Immaculate Heart as well as the Communion of Reparation on the First Saturday.

"She promised peace and the conversion of the nation if her request is attended to. She announced that otherwise the nation (Russia) would spread her errors throughout the world, and there would be wars, persecutions of the Church, martyrdom of many Christians, several persecutions and suffering reserved for your Holiness, and the annihilation of several nations."

Many people have become distraught, thinking that the Holy Father has not consecrated Russia properly, but according to Sr. Lucia of Fatima and Bishop John Magee, former Papal Secretary, this has been accomplished. There yet remains, though, as requested by Our Lady, the conversion of Russia. This in part can be accomplished by Communions of Reparation on the First Saturdays. We are asking our members and friends to focus on this devotion to bring about the reparation necessary for peace in our age.

Therefore, the First Saturday Communion of Reparation formula is not something peripheral. It is central for the conversion of Russia and for lasting peace in the world.

Our First Saturday program is designed to draw people together in churches in the Eucharistic Presence of Our Lord, in reparation for the sins that offend the Immaculate Heart of Mary.

Our Lady specifically asked that we do the following:
- receive Our Lord in Holy Communion,
- recite the Rosary while meditating on its mysteries for fifteen minutes,
- go to Confession within a reasonable period of time,
- offer all the above in reparation for the sins that offend the Immaculate Heart of Mary.

Our Blessed Mother told Sister Lucia that she promises to assist the souls who practice this devotion for five consecutive First Saturdays with all the necessary graces for their salvation at the hour of their death.

Sister Lucia's spiritual director asked her why Our Lady had asked for five First Saturday rather than seven (for the Seven Sorrows) or nine (like the Nine First Fridays devotion). She replied that Our Lord had appeared to her on the night of May 29th and 30th, 1930. At that time He said with reference to this devotion, *"My daughter, the motive is simple: There are five ways in which people offend, and*

Father Patrick Peyton being interviewed by Jerry and Gwen Coniker for the First Saturday "Light of the World Cenacle." People are gathering in churches throughout the world on the First Saturday of each month to participate in this program. Pope John Paul II leads the First Saturday Rosary regularly.

blaspheme against the Immaculate Heart of Mary." They are as follows:

1. The blasphemies against Her Immaculate Conception,

2. Blasphemies against Her Virginity,

3. Blasphemies against Her Divine Maternity, refusing at the same time to accept Her as the Mother of all mankind,

4. The sin of those who try to publicly implant in children's hearts indifference, contempt, and even hate against the Immaculate Mother of God,

5. The offense of those who insult Her directly by desecrating Her pcitures and statues.

Many of us don't realize that the Communion of Reparation is not for ALL sins, but specifically for the abovementioned sins that pertain to the Immaculate Heart of Mary. This is God's way of telling us that Our Lady is so important that He has literally placed the destiny of the world in Her hands.

Our Lady promises peace if we will only follow the simple plan She has outlined for us at Fatima.

We ask our friends to do all they can to fill the churches on the First Saturday of each month using the following videotapes.

OUR LADY'S FIRST SATURDAY REQUEST IS BEING FULFILLED

in the spirit of Pope John Paul II
First Saturday "Light of the World Cenacle"

Our one-hour First Saturday videotapes are designed to draw people together in churches to fulfill Our Lady's requests while learning and growing in their faith as a community.

Each videotape features insights from Pope John Paul II and Mother Teresa, as well as the meditative Rosary. Each month you'll also hear from one of today's foremost spiritual personalities, such as...

Cardinal Anthony Bevilacqua   Cardinal John O'Connor
Cardinal Luigi Ciappi   Cardinal Pio Laghi
Cardinal Bernard Law   Father Patrick Peyton

First Saturday Cenacle Videos

Each one-hour tape will give you new insights into living your consecration.

First Saturday Cenacle *157-45V* — Latest production

1st Set of 6 First Saturday Cenacle videotapes *157-1VK*

Each tape includes messages from Pope John Paul II and Mother Teresa, and a meditative Rosary, that follows the formula Our Lady gave to Sr. Lucia. The following six (6) videos are included in this set:

Video devotion 1 - Fr. Sebastian, M.C. *157-61V*
The head of Mother Teresa's order of priests talks about the Holy Family of Nazareth — a school of love.
Joyful Mysteries of the Rosary

Video devotion 2 - Fr. Bernard Geiger, O.F.M. Conv., and Mother Immaculata, H.M.C. *157-74V*
Both talk about Our Lady and the Brown Scapular of Mt. Carmel.
Sorrowful Mysteries of the Rosary

Video devotion 3 - Msgr. Anthony LeFemina *157-67V*
This member of the Vatican's Pontifical Council of the Family discusses the Pontifical document on drugs and addiction, and how Mary can put order into our broken relationships. Gives profound insights into The Holy Eucharist, Mary, and the Sacrament of Matrimony.
Glorious Mysteries of the Rosary

Video devotion 4 - Bishop Joseph Madera *157-70V*
He speaks about Our Lady of Guadalupe. Bishop Madera is on fire for Our Lady; he expands on the virtues of the Mexican people.
Joyful Mysteries of the Rosary

Video devotion 5 - Fr. John Galea *157-75V*
Fr. Galea gives one of the most moving descriptions of the Passion that you will ever hear (based on the Sacred Shroud of Turin). He also answers some of the false reports concerning the carbon testing of the Shroud.
Sorrowful Mysteries of the Rosary

Video devotion 6 - Fr. Randall Paine *157-76V*
Fr. Paine gives a stirring talk about commitment and Our Lady.
Glorious Mysteries of the Rosary

2nd Set of 6 First Saturday videotapes *157-2VK*
Each tape includes messages from Pope John Paul II and Mother Teresa, and a meditative Rosary, that follows the formula Our Lady gave to Sr. Lucia. The following six (6) videos are included in this set:

Video devotion 7 - Archbishop J. Francis Stafford
157-69V — The Archbishop of Denver who hosted the Holy Father's 1993 World Youth Day discusses the Pope's devotion to Mary.
Joyful Mysteries of the Rosary

Video devotion 8 - Bishop Juan Fremont Torres Oliver
157-68V — His Excellency, the Bishop of Ponce and the President of the Council of Bishops for Puerto Rico, discusses the fifth sin against the Immaculate Heart of Mary, and talks about Our Lady of Divine Providence.
Sorrowful Mysteries of the Rosary

Video devotion 9 - Fr. George Kosicki *157-66V*
Father Kosicki is one of the leading experts in the world on the Divine Mercy devotion. He discusses the Holy Father's encyclical on Divine Mercy.
Glorious Mysteries of the Rosary

Video devotion 10 - Fr. Michael Scanlan, T.O.R. *157-71V*
The President of the Franciscan University of Steubenville talks about the Church and Mary.
Joyful Mysteries of the Rosary

Video devotion 11 - Francis Cardinal Arinze *157-78V*
His Eminence talks about Mary, Mother of God and the Mother of the Church, as taught in St. Louis de Montfort's consecration.
Sorrowful Mysteries of the Rosary

Video devotion 12 - Fr. Gregory Finn, O.S.J. *157-58V*
This young, holy priest talks about St. Joseph, commitment, and the conditions for following our Lord as they were given to the rich young man in Mark 10:17-22 and Luke 18:18-23.
Glorious Mysteries of the Rosary

"Healing Our Families™" Video Series

The Family Apostolate's T.V. Series featuring Fr. Michael Scanlan, being interviewed by Jerry Coniker. Available on 60-minute audiotape or videotape.

Side 1: Mary, Our Spiritual Leader *172-134V*
Side 2: Overview: The Truth About Trouble

Side 1: Fidelity in the Family *172-135V*
Side 2: Confidence Through the Fog of Faith

Side 1: Freedom *172-136V*
Side 2: The Love of the Merciful Father

Side 1: Home Ministry of Reconciliation *172-137V*
Side 2: Uneven Match & Peer Pressure

Side 1: The Story of Babel & the Journey Back *172-138V*
Side 2: The Confessor & Penitent & Examination of Conscience

Side 1: The Importance of an Appointment with God   *172-139V*
Side 2: Getting into the Appointment with God

Side 1: Revelation and Listening 172-140V
Side 2: Intercessory Prayer

Side 1: Closing the Appointment *172-141V*
Side 2: Deliverance from the Evil Spirits

Side 1: The Joy of Repentance *172-142V*
Side 2: Suffering of the Cross

Side 1: Inner Healing *172-143V*
Side 2: Three Levels of Repentance

Side 1: Faith and Trials *172-144V*
Side 2: Consecration & Victory

Side 1: Mary, Our Mother *172-145V*
Side 2: Fear of the Lord

Side 1: Faithful Love *172-146V*
Side 2: Glory of the Cross

Side 1: The Family Cross *172-147V*
Side 2: Praying Always

Side 1: Rejoice Always *172-148V*
Side 2: Healing Principles

Side 1: Cross and Perseverance *172-149V*
Side 2: Healing Sacraments

The Apostolate's Catholic Corps
A Lifetime Call To Serve

Handmaid of the Lord

For Carolyn Stegmann, of House Springs, Missouri, becoming the Lord's "handmaid" means responding as generously as possible to the "responsibility of the present moment." Carolyn first responded to the Lord's invitation to give herself wholly and completely "to Jesus, through Mary," during a retreat she experienced, which was sponsored by the Apostolate for Family Consecration. The retreatants were meditating on Pope John Paul II's *Letter to the Youth of the World*. It was because of this powerful message that Carolyn realized that Christ

Carolyn Stegmann

was inspiring her to give to Him the "treasure" of her youth when she was only 19 years old.

Each day provides ample opportunities for Carolyn to give the gift of her youth to Jesus, her Spouse, through the work and mission of The Family Apostolate. Through responding to each grace with the help of Mary, her Mother and true model, Carolyn grows in the understanding of what it means to be a "handmaid of the Lord." Carolyn oversees the bookkeeping department of the The Family Apostolate and is also House Coordinator for the Women's Catholic Corps Community. All those who share apostolic work and community life with Carolyn are aware of her generous and humble response to the challenges she faces each day.

Harvester of Souls

Tim Croes could be likened to a modern-day "Barnabas", who, in the Acts of the Apostles, is known for having sold his farm after joining the Apostles in the early Christian community, following the Ascension of Jesus. Later, Sacred Scripture describes the hardships and joys of Barnabas and Paul during their wondrous missionary journeys amongst the Gentiles.

Tim Croes

After many years of successful farming on a New Richmond, Wisconsin family dairy farm (of which he shared ownership with his brother), Tim received a call in his heart to leave everything behind and follow Christ. He heard this call after attending a retreat sponsored by the Apostolate for Family Consecration. After a period of discernment, at the age of 28, Tim followed through with the desire of his heart to become a "harvester of souls."

Since becoming a member of the Family Apostolate's Catholic Corps Men's Community, and later becoming its House Coordinator, and accepting many other challenging responsibilities of coordinating the Evangelization Leadership Training Department and later becoming the Facilities Management Coordinator for the 850 acres of the John Paul II Holy Family Center (which also includes farming), Tim can truly witness to the fact that whenever one gives everything to Jesus, through Mary, in union with St. Joseph, all is returned in abundance. To his fellow community members, and to all who meet him, he truly is a "harvester of souls".

You Can Be an Apostle!

If you are ...
- *18-30 years of age*
- *interested in joining a team that uses modern communications to evangelize our media culture*
- *attracted to a life of fervent prayer, apostolic work and loyalty to the Pope*
- *able to make a commitment as a single person for a specified time while testing your vocation*
  ... write or call: The Apostolate's Catholic Corps
                Route 2, Box 700, Bloomingdale, OH 43910
                (614) 765-4301

889

The Family Apostolate's
  John Paul II Holy Family Center
    850 acres set apart for you to ...

- Come and learn how to use the papally promulgated *Catechism of the Catholic Church* and related catechetical resources to evangelize your family, your neighborhood, and your parish.

- Come and learn about Mother Teresa's inspiration for stopping abortion and strengthening family and parish life through our "Be Not Afraid Family Hours" and First Saturday Cenacles on video.

- Come and experience our Marriage and Family Life retreats.

- Come with your youth for a weekend of formation and "new evangelization" training.

- Come to our vocation discernment retreats.

- Come to one of the four "Holy Family Fests" and experience authentic Catholic community with your family for 7 days.

- Organize a group of 20 or more for a retreat on any of the above.

With heartfelt gratitude to the Holy Family, we give our thanks and praise and we warmly welcome you and your family to come and share with us at the Family Apostolate's John Paul II Holy Family Center.

We want to imitate the love and fidelity of the Holy Family and follow the example of our beloved Holy Father, Pope John Paul II, and share his Marian spirituality of total consecration to Jesus through Mary ...

Totus Tuus.

Jerry and Gwen Coniker, Founders

We invite you to join us with our consecrated staff to renew and enrich your family life and the family life of your parish and diocese.

The Coniker Family - 13 children and 18 grandchildren.

- Call for our evangelization training and retreat schedule.

- Arrange a group of 20 or more for your own retreat.

- Help us promote parish and family renewal through the Marian and family-centered spirit of Pope John Paul II.

- Please note that this center is a branch of St. Louis de Montfort's Confraternity of Mary, Queen of All Hearts. Please also note that Pope John Paul II's personal spirituality is that of St. Louis de Montfort. *Totus Tuus.*

Index

Creeds Q. 132

Cross Q. 74, 83, 84, 86, 89, 93, 94, 137, 139, 142, 176, 221, 225, 236, 241, 247, 277 289, 289

Crucifixion Q. 94-96

D

Damnation Q. 41, 287

Deacons Q. 150, 181, 218, 218, 221

Death Q. 23, 45, 49, 53, 59, 87, 98, 106, 107, 126

Desire for God Q. 21

Devil Q. 40, 41, 58, 71, 87, 131, 289, 290

Diocese Q. 172

Disciples Q. 31, 50, 83, 128, 150, 158, 181, 182

Disobedience Q. 57, 86

Divine Word Q. 33, 73, 75, 254, 302

Divinity of Christ Q. 76, 157, 250

Divorce Q. 231, 232

Duty Q. 88, 137, 140, 146, 153, 162, 165, 170, 186, 204, 217, 230, 233, 260, 264, 265, 274, 282, 287, 288

E

Easter proclamation Q. 101

Envy Q. 68, 69, 129, 289

Episcopal consecration Q. 205, 2183

Eternal life Q. 24, 48, 78, 91

Eucharist Q. 85, 194, 197, 204, 236, 240, 241, 243-251, 254, 255, 258, 258, 259, 260, 267, 283

Real Presence Q. 258

Eucharistic Sacrifice Q. 249

Evangelical counsels Q. 280

Evangelization Q. 164, 178

Evil Q. 71, 74, 187, 197, 232, 297

Existence Q. 19, 36, 80, 277, 282

Lay Faithful Q. 155, 156, 158, 163, 166, 168, 170, 176, 182, 196, 204, 209, 241, 246, 251, 256, 257, 258, 278, 283, 284, 289, 302, 304

F

Fall Q. 24, 38, 53, 291

Family Q. 201, 233,234, 235, 287

Father Q. 2, 16, 22, 23, 29, 31, 72, 80 84, 104, 107, 113, 115, 117, 123, 126, 127, 132, 161, 177, 189, 193, 226, 239, 254, 263, 264, 265, 282, 290, 298

Forgiveness Q. 65, 67, 189, 205, 206, 207, 241, 245

Fornication Q. 152, 288

Fortitude Q. 135

Free will Q. 5, 38, 43, 49

G

Gluttony Q. 69, 129, 130, 289

God Q. 1, 2

All-holy Q. 13

All-just Q. 15

All-merciful Q. 14

All-powerful Q. 24, 49

All-wise Q. 26

Almighty Q. 10

Eternal Q. 8, 22

Good Q. 7

Goodness of Q. 17

Present everywhere (omnipresent)

God the Son Q. 33

Gospel

Good News Q. 48, 138, 139, 160

H

Heaven Q. 15, 39, 149, 186, 187, 250, 253, 250, 264, 266, 266, 268, 291, 294, 299, 300

Hell Q. 293

Heresy Q. 283

History of salvation Q. 22, 303

Holiness Q. 49, 53, 71, 122, 131, 159, 177, 193, 206, 233, 235, 279, 289, 394, 303

Holy Communion Q. 236, 250, 252, 254, 255, 261

Holy Orders Q. 181, 204

Holy Scripture Q. 141

Holy Spirit Q. 30, 31, 34, 55, 72, 73, 101, 106, 107, 112, 114, 115, 116, 119, 120, 121, 123 Hope 133

Human nature Q. 54, 140

Humility Q. 105, 113, 136, 264, 266

I

Idolatry Q. 288

Image and likeness Q. 42

Image and likeness of God Q. 43, 150

Immaculate Conception Q. 56

Immodesty Q. 288

Immortality Q. 257, 265

Incarnation Q. 72, 73, 79, 87

Indissolubility [of marriage] Q. 230, 231

Indulgences Q. 185, 216, 217

Indwelling Holy Spirit Q. 71, 129

Infallibility Q. 153, 176

Infinite Q. 5

Infinitely good Q. 7

Intercession Q. 188, 198, 212, 265, 303

J

Jesus Q. 16, 27, 28, 29 47, 48, 50, 51, 65, 72, 74, 75, 77, 78, 79, 80, 81, 82, 83, 84, 85, 86, 87, 88, 90, 92, 94, 97, 100, 102, 103, 104, 106, 113, 116, 126, 262

Agony Q. 88, 94

Center of our Catholic Faith Q. 77

Center of all God's saving works Q. 113

Center of the history of salvation Q. 118

Glorified body Q. 257

Son of God Q. 82

True God Q. 75

True Man Q. 82

True Mediator between God and man Q. 74

Joseph Q. 82, 267

Joy Q. 17, 109, 250, 291

Judgment Q. 15, 288, 291, 294, 299, 300

Justice Q. 15, 135, 136, 281

Justification Q. 132

K

Kill Q. 277, 288,

L

Laity Q. 158, 158, 170, 193, 204

Laymen Q. 161

Last Judgment Q. 298, 299, 301

Liturgy Q. 244

Lucifer Q. 39

Lust Q. 69

Lying Q. 288

M

Man Q. 44, 170 195, 231, 232

Made of body and soul Q. 43

Mankind Q. 87, 110, 144, 159, 271, 291

Marks of the Church Q. 172

Martyrs Q. 195

Masturbation Q. 288

Matrimony Q. 195, 226, 229, 230, 233, 235

Meditation Q. 263

Mental prayer Q. 263

Mercy-killing (euthanasia) Q. 298

Mind Q. 42

Miracle Q. 267

Modesty Q. 129

Mortal sin Q. 58, 59, 62

Murder Q. 288

Mystical Body of Christ Q. 139, 158, 302

N

Nativity Q. 102

New Testament Q. 55, 145

O

Obedience Q. 17, 46, 87, 136, 155, 275, 280, 281, 302

Old Testament Q. 12, 30, 73, 129

Orders Q. 205, 221, 240

Original sin Q. 53, 56, 87, 189, 201, 264

P

Paraclete Q. 26, 31

Parents Q. 195, 233, 287

Passion Q. 74, 78, 86, 87

Patience Q. 24, 129, 224, 289

Penance [sacrament] Q. 66, 67, 188, 189, 195, 196, 197, 205, 206, 2207 209, 221

Pentecost Q. 31, 115, 117, 119, 139, 169

Perfect contrition Q. 189, 208

Perfections Q. 1

Persecution Q. 205

Perseverance Q. 266

Personal God Q. 24

Personal Sin Q. 53, 57, 68

Personal sins Q. 189, 201

Peter Q. 104, 140, 143, 150, 151, 152, 153, 166, 175, 180, 181. 189

Pope Q. 120, 137, 151, 152, 153, 154, 155, 158, 171, 175, 232

Poverty Q. 54, 74, 188, 258,

275, 280, 289, 297

Prayer Q. 16, 41, 129, 130, 134, 158, 182, 221, 241, 243, 259, 260, 262, 263, 264, 265, 266, 281, 282, 302, 304, 182, 224

Precepts Q. 113, 270, 275, 278, 281

Precepts of the Church Q. 275, 281

Pride Q. 69

Priesthood Q. 144, 152, 150, 195, 210, 219, 221

Priesthood of the laity Q. 150

Priests Q. 18, 143, 150, 155, 150, 176, 181, 194, 206, 207, 218, 221, 224, 239, 246, 258, 283

Prudence Q. 135

Punishment Q. 58, 98, 208, 210, 212, 216, 236, 265, 293, 294

Purgatory Q. 182, 185, 186, 211, 291, 294, 297

Purposes of Prayer Q. 265

R

Reason Q. 37, 64, 132, 272

Reconciliation Q. 37, 86, 205, 206, 222, 243

Redeemer Q. 65, 82, 87

Redemption Q. 24, 48, 82, 67, 92, 97, 155, 194, 212, 225, 244, 265, 267, 302, 304

Reformation Q. 177

Reparation Q. 87, 208, 250, 267

Repentance Q. 83, 205, 206, 207, 265

Resurrection Q. 51, 87, 98, 106, 102, 104, 106

Revelation Q. 23, 24

S

Sacrament of Orders Q. 152

Sacramentals Q. 190

Sacraments Q. 128, 140, 142,

189, 190, 192, 193, 194, 195, 196

Actions of Christ Q. 190, 194

Sacred Heart Q. 255

Sacred Scripture Q. 141

Sacred Tradition Q. 141

Sacrifice Q. 18, 150, 176, 217, 218, 235, 236, 237, 238, 241, 246, 248, 282, 285, 289, 296, 301

Sacrifices Q. 87, 239

Salvation Q. 38, 65, 81, 86, 106, 133 162, 192, 264

Sanctification Q. 150, 158, 164, 170, 192, 193, 195, 221, 230, 287, 303

Sanctifying grace Q. 45, 55, 124, 125, 128, 129, 131, 132, 139, 189

Sanctity Q. 131, 149, 160, 279, 304

Savior Q. 35, 48, 65, 81, 84, 85, 93, 138

Scandal Q. 288

Scientists Q. 4

Second Coming Q. 300

Self-sacrifice Q. 275

Seven last words Q. 95

Sexuality Q. 288, 289

Signs Q. 26, 128, 141, 148, 154, 166, 191, 191, 193, 195, 196, 242

Sin Q. 23, 45, 46, 56, 58, 59, 69, 61, 183, 197, 209, 252, 272, 288, 296

Sinner Q. 58, 65, 66, 96, 177, 189, 205, 206, 207, 221, 265, 281, 298

Slavery Q. 49, 85, 112, 133, 157

Sloth Q. 68, 69

Son of God Q. 28, 31, 72, 73, 74

Soul Q. 5, 42, 44

Soul of the Church Q. 121

Stealing Q. 69, 288

Successor of Peter Q. 167

Successors of the Apostles Q. 154

Suffering Q. 16, 45, 89, 129, 133, 135, 156, 163, 185, 221, 224, 241, 289, 293, 302

Suicide Q. 288

Supreme Being Q. 1

T

Temperance Q. 135

Temptation Q. 70

Temptations Q. 41

Ten Commandments Q. 16, 269, 290

Thanksgiving Q. 195, 265, 267

Theological Virtues Q. 131

Tradition Q. 141

Transubstantiation Q. 240

Trinity Q. 22, 25, 27, 33, 34, 48, 124, 130, 300, 304

Truth Q. 14, 26, 27, 77, 82, 101, 112, 119, 131, 141, 148, 177, 173, 26, 273, 288

Truths Q. 131

U

Universe Q. 36, 77, 79

V

Venial Sin Q. 57

Virgin Mary Q. 36, 120, 320, 322

Virginity Q. 177, 180

Vocal prayer Q. 202, 263, 282

Vocation Q. 150, 159, 170, 195, 280

W

Will Q. 5, 42

Woman Q. 44, 170, 231, 230

Word of God Q. 75, 79, 111, 302

Worship Q. 16, 17, 176, 192, 195, 242, 260, 262, 264, 266, 282, 283, 300